D1495839

Sociology of the Family

Investigating Family Issues

■ **Lee D. Millar Bidwell**
Longwood College

■ **Brenda J. Vander Mey**
Clemson University

Allyn and Bacon

Boston ■ London ■ Toronto ■ Sydney ■ Tokyo ■ Singapore

Editor-in-Chief, Social Sciences: Karen Hanson
Editor: Jeff Lasser
Editorial Assistant: Susan Hutchinson
Developmental Editor: Mary Ellen Lepionka
Editorial-Production Administrator: Deborah Brown
Editorial-Production Service: Susan Freese, Communicàto, Ltd.
Text Design/Electronic Composition: Denise Hoffman
Photo Researcher: Laurie Frankenthaler
Composition Buyer: Linda Cox
Manufacturing Buyer: Megan Cochran
Cover Administrator: Linda Knowles

Copyright © 2000 by Allyn & Bacon
A Pearson Education Company
160 Gould Street
Needham Heights, MA 02494
Internet: www.abacon.com

Between the time website information is gathered and then published, it is not unusual for some sites to have closed. Also, the transcription of URLs can result in unintended typographical errors. The publisher would appreciate being notified of any problems with URLs so that they may be corrected in subsequent editions.

Library of Congress Cataloging-in-Publication Data

Bidwell, Lee D. Millar.
    Sociology of the family : investigating family issues / Lee D. Millar Bidwell, Brenda J. Vander Mey
        p.   cm.
    Includes bibliographical references and index.
    ISBN 0–02–309672–1 (alk. paper)
    1. Family—United States.   2. Marriage—United States.   3. Interpersonal relations—United States.   4. Work and family—United States.
    5. Multiculturalism—United States.   6. Family violence—United States.
    I. Vander Mey, Brenda J.   II. Title.
    HQ535.B49 2000
    306.85'0973—dc21

                                                            99–051525

Printed in the United States of America
10 9 8 7 6 5 4 3 2 1   04 03 02 01 00 99

The photo credits appear on page 540, which constitutes a continuation of the copyright page.

Brief Contents

Contents

Part III   *Intimate Relationships: Issues in the Family Life Cycle*

Chapter 8   *Love and Partner Selection*   227

Chapter 9 *Sexual Attitudes, Behaviors, and Relationships*   265

Chapter 10   *Marital Relationships and Domestic Partnerships*   297

Chapter 11   *Fertility Patterns and Challenges of Parenthood*   341

Chapter 13   *Divorce and Remarriage*   423

Preface

Several years ago, I was sitting in my office trying to decide which textbook I should adopt for the undergraduate Sociology of Family class I would be teaching the next semester, when a textbook representative came by to offer his product. I had been teaching the course every semester for several years, so I had collected copies of almost all the textbooks on the market. I told this sales representative that although every textbook had its merits, certain key features were lacking in all of them. None of the textbooks gave a thorough explanation of the theoretical perspectives that are so useful in interpreting family issues, and even fewer applied theories to topics. Furthermore, the research methods used to uncover data about the family were generally ignored, and often the findings of research studies were reported without any mention of how the information was obtained. Finally, in many texts, there was little integration among chapters; once a topic had been discussed, it was never mentioned again, leaving students with the incorrect perception that family issues are entirely unrelated to each other.

After patiently listening to me rant about the defects I saw in the textbooks then on the market, the textbook representative quietly asked, "Then why don't you write your own textbook?" So I did.

How This Book Is Different

Sociology of the Family: Investigating Family Issues is designed to teach students how to understand and analyze family structure and dynamics sociologically. This textbook is different from other sociology of the family books in several ways. First, embedded within it is a collection of readings. Each chapter ends with a reading linked to the chapter topic—Readings for In-Depth Focus—along with a series of questions to encourage critical thinking about the material. These excerpts from articles and books in the contemporary literature bring sociological theory and method to bear on current family issues. The combination of expository text with primary source readings is intended to provide a structure for teaching the course and actively involving students.

This book also contains a more balanced coverage of theoretical perspectives and research methods than is found in most family texts. Although chapters may be assigned in a different order than appears in the text, the theme of evaluating theory and research preserves unity. In addition to theoretical perspectives and research methods, the perennial sociological variables of race, social class, and gender are applied in every chapter. Furthermore, information about family dynamics in other cultures is integrated throughout, enabling students to view the family as a global social institution uniquely shaped by the norms, values, and circumstances of society. Family diversity in U.S. society is a special focus of this text.

How This Book Is Organized

This textbook is divided into three sections. Part I, Sociology of the Family: The Foundations, gives students the basic knowledge necessary to understand and analyze family issues. Families are examined from a historical perspective in Chapter 1, showing how the present organization of families cannot be understood without knowing how family structures and dynamics have changed over time.

Chapters 2 and 3 are unique features of this book. Unlike other textbooks, in which theoretical perspectives and research methods are covered in a few pages, if at all, *Sociology of the Family: Investigating Family Issues* devotes separate chapters to each of these topics. In Chapter 2, students learn how scholarly research on the family is conducted as well as some of the problems researchers encounter when gathering and evaluating data on families. The basic theoretical orientations and concepts of sociology useful for analyzing family issues are discussed in Chapter 3. In Chapter 4, students are introduced to the cultural foundations of family studies and the diverse nature of families across the globe. Discussions of methodological issues, theoretical perspectives, and cross-cultural comparisons are continued in all subsequent chapters.

Sociologists who study the family continually examine the impact of three key variables—gender, socioeconomic status, and race and ethnicity—on all types of family issues. Each of these topics is examined in depth in Part II, Family Studies: The Perennial Sociological Variables (Chapters 5–7). The relevancies of gender, class, and race are then explored in each of the seven chapters of Part III, Intimate Relationships: Issues in the Family Life Cycle. These chapters (8–14) focus on family concerns at each stage of the life cycle, from partner selection, through marriage, parenthood, and into older adulthood. A separate chapter is devoted to sexual attitudes, behaviors, and relationships. Although family violence and divorce are not natural parts of the family life cycle, they are addressed in separate chapters, as well. Finally, the chapter on singlehood is presented last because this status can pertain to different stages of the life cycle. Each chapter in Part III examines impacts of sociological variables on the individual's experience of the life stage or conditions in intimate relationships. For example, Chapter 14 examines the impact of age on the experience of being single. The ways in which age and life stages relate to marital satisfaction, parenting, and divorce are addressed in Chapters 10, 11, and 13, respectively. Care has been taken to provide a truly comprehensive text that also engages and encourages students.

Supplements for Instructors

This book comes with an array of supplements that will assist instructors in using it and enriching students' learning experiences:

- *Instructor's Manual and Test Bank:* An Instructor's Manual and Test Bank is included with the book. The manual includes teaching tips, classroom exercises, learning objectives, and Internet exercises. The test bank, which is bound with the manual, contains multiple-choice, true/false, fill-in, and essay questions.

- *Computerized Testing:* Allyn and Bacon Test Manager is an integrated suite of testing and assessment tools for Windows and Macintosh. You can use Test Manager to create professional-looking exams in minutes by building tests from the existing database of questions, editing questions, or writing your own. Course management features include a class roster, gradebook, and item analysis. Test Manager also has everything you need to create and administer online tests. For first-time users, there is a guided tour of the entire Test Manager system and screen wizards to walk you through each area.

- *PowerPoint® Presentation Software:* The Allyn and Bacon Marriage and Family PowerPoint Presentation consists of a combination of graphic images and text on 13 standard topics. A PowerPoint® viewer is included, which allows you to access the slides. If you have PowerPoint® software, you can easily create customized presentations by rearranging the order of the slides, editing them, or adding new slides. Versions are available for both Windows and Macintosh.

Acknowledgments

This book has been a long time in the making and would not have been possible without the efforts and contributions of many wonderful people. The editorial staff at Allyn and Bacon, including Karen Hanson and Sarah Kelbaugh, provided support and encouragement in countless ways. I especially want to acknowledge the help of our developmental editor, Mary Ellen Lepionka. She is an extraordinary editor with a special gift for reworking others' writing as well as providing ideas and reassurance to discouraged, harried authors.

I also have had an extraordinary amount of help and encouragement from colleagues and students at Longwood College. I thank the members of the Department of Sociology and Anthropology for having faith that I would finish this project and offering advice and encouragement along the way. No longer will any of you need to ask, "So, how's the book coming?" Denise James offered tremendous help at the beginning of this project. Toward the end, Stephanie Meadows and Stacie Marable were godsends who patiently did anything I asked them to do, no matter how difficult or mundane.

I cannot thank my coauthor, Brenda Vander Mey, enough. She came into this project with great enthusiasm, even though she was up against tight deadlines and many other work and family responsibilities. I could not have completed this book on my own, and I am truly grateful that she agreed to work with me. Brenda's cross-cultural perspective and mastery of the family literature are invaluable contributions to this work.

I am blessed to be surrounded by loving, supportive friends and family, without whom I never would have had the confidence needed to tackle such a big project. My sons, Daniel and Samuel, have been sources of inspiration and were able to make me laugh even in the most stressful times. My husband, Larry, gave me the push I needed to start the book and was there every step of the way. I'm not sure he knew what he was getting into when he said, "Opportunity only knocks once, so go for it." He listened to me rant and cry and test out ideas; he took care of the children, cooked the meals, did the laundry, and anything else humanly possible to help me complete this book. Thank you, Larry, and I love you.

Lee D. Millar Bidwell

With all my heart and with what little energy I have left after writing at warp speed, I thank and thank again my husband, Gerald Vander Mey, and our son, Ian, for all their many sacrifices and sustained encouragement. I also thank Mary Ellen Lepionka, editor and cheerleader extraordinaire. My colleagues at Clemson University have my deepest thanks and appreciation. They shared their libraries with me, brought other books and articles to my attention, and helped me be the "Little Engine That Could." It is my hope that all sociologists are as blessed with colleagues as wonderful as mine. I also would like to acknowledge USAID's Bean/ Cowpea CRSP Program for giving me opportunities to gain firsthand knowledge of other countries and cultures.

Not least of all, I thank my coauthor, Lee Bidwell. We have worked together in an almost seamless fashion, like two sisters who know when the other needs support. To that end, I thank Mary Ellen Lepionka and Sarah Kelbaugh for having the good sense to bring the two of us together.

Brenda J. Vander Mey

We would both like to thank those individuals who reviewed earlier versions of this text and provided useful suggestions: Carol Chenault, Calhoun Community College; Robin Franck, Southwestern College; Kristi L. Hoffman, Roanoke College; Charles B. Hennon, Miami University; and David McConnell, College of Wooster.

Part I

Sociology of the Family
The Foundations

1 *American Families in Historical Perspective*

*T*wo weeks after I left for college, my parents filed for divorce. I probably should not have been surprised, since they had never been blissfully happy that I could remember, but I had just assumed they would always be together. I thought couples married for 20 years never got divorced. My father remarried within a year; my mother waited about a decade before remarrying.

Although my parents' divorce did not have an impact on my daily activities of going to class, going to work, or socializing, I somehow felt that ours was no longer a *real* family. In my mind, real families spent holidays together, joyfully sharing meals and stories; in my family, I had to decide which holiday would be spent with which parent. In real families, people always got along with each other; in my family, people argued a lot. In real families, everyone was loved; in my family, some people did not love each other any more. I was ashamed that my family was in such shambles compared to so-called normal families.

After studying sociology, I came to understand that I had been comparing my family situation to the cultural ideal of the perfect family. The cultural image of the happy, loving, close, forgiving, accepting family is constantly conveyed through movies, magazines, television, music, books, greeting cards, advertising, and numerous other media. Although in reality very few families today, or in the past, conform to the cultural image of the family, many people tend to use that image as a benchmark of their own family's success. Individuals often feel inadequate and ashamed if they come from a family that differs from the cultural ideal.

Cultural notions of the ideal family are influenced by contemporary perceptions of how the family used to be. However, perceptions of past family life often are based on nostalgia, rather than reality, and therefore are inaccurate. In this chapter, several myths about the family will be discussed and then dispelled by examining historical shifts in family structure and roles.

Myths Surrounding Families

The family of the past is often romanticized as flawless and perpetually harmonious. Contemporary families are viewed by some as deficient, declining, or disintegrating compared to an idealized vision of the way families used to be. The inaccurate, romanticized view of the family of the past often is based on a number of myths about how families used to function and be structured. Four of the most widely held myths about past families are (1) women were homemakers and men were breadwinners; (2) families were extended, with many kin living in the same household; (3) changes in family structure signal the disintegration of the family; and (4) white, middle-class families are the norm.

Homemaker/Breadwinner Myth

When I ask students to tell me what they know about families of the past, invariably they report that the husband was the breadwinner and the wife was the homemaker. When asked how long this sex-typed division of labor has characterized families in the United States, most students state with certainty, "That's how it's always been."

Not so. Prior to the Industrial Revolution, which began in the United States in the early nineteenth century, the family as a whole was "the primary unit of economic production and exchange" (Demos 1974: 424). In the largely agricultural economy, families either owned farms or small businesses, and the family was an interdependent economic unit in which both sexes were expected to work. Although sex distinctions were made, there were few differences in the type and amount of work done by men and women (Demos 1974). Generally, men did most of the physical farm work while women were responsible for doing or supervising the cooking, cleaning, spinning, weaving, and clothing production (Gordon 1978).

Men and women often worked together, especially during particularly busy times such as harvest seasons. Many women who were married to merchants were in business with their husbands (Flexner 1975). Even though men's work was accorded higher status, women's work was indispensable. Hence, "it was taken for granted that women provided for the family along with men" (Bernard 1989: 224). In other words, neither the husband nor the wife was considered the breadwinner. The homemaker/breadwinner distinction does not appear in families until approximately the mid-1800s, with the spread of the factory system.

Three-Generation Families Myth

Families of the past often are believed to have been very large, with several generations living under one roof. Households were larger during the preindustrial and early industrial era than they are today, but few families included extended kin. In 1790, the first year of the U.S. Census, the average household size at the time of the survey was 5.8 (U.S. Bureau of the Census 1975). Measures of household size in early censuses included members of the household who were not relatives, such as apprentices, hired laborers, orphaned children, and boarders (Carlson 1990). It was quite uncommon for the family to have extended kin living in the household, especially grandparents. Because of the high mortality rate, which prevailed until the twentieth century, few parents lived to see their grandchildren, much less live with them (Hareven 1992) (see Table 1.1). According to social historians, "There has never been in American society an era when three generations were coresiding in the same household" (Hareven 1992: 42).

Table 1.1   Life Expectancy by Race/Ethnicity and Sex, 1900–1970

	Total			White			People of Color		
Year	Both Sexes	Male	Female	Both Sexes	Male	Female	Both Sexes	Male	Female
1900	47.3	46.3	48.3	47.6	46.6	48.7	33.0	32.5	33.5
1910	50.0	48.4	51.8	50.3	48.6	52.0	35.6	33.8	37.5
1920	54.1	53.6	54.6	54.9	54.4	55.6	45.3	45.5	45.2
1930	59.7	58.1	61.6	61.4	59.7	63.5	48.1	47.3	49.2
1940	62.9	60.8	65.2	64.2	62.1	66.6	53.1	51.5	54.9
1950	68.2	65.6	71.1	69.1	66.5	72.2	60.8	59.1	62.9
1960	69.7	66.6	73.1	70.6	67.4	74.1	63.6	61.1	66.3
1970	70.9	67.1	74.7	71.7	68.0	75.6	65.3	61.3	69.4
1980	73.7	70.0	77.4	74.4	70.7	78.1	69.5	65.3	73.6
1990	75.4	71.8	78.8	76.1	72.7	79.4	71.2	67.0	75.2

Sources: Adapted from *Historical Statistics of the United States, Colonial Times to 1970, Bicentennial Edition, Part 1*, U.S. Bureau of the Census, 1975, Washington, DC: U.S. Government Printing Office; and *Statistical Abstract of the United States 1996* (116th edition), 1996, Washington, DC: U.S. Department of Commerce.

Family Disintegration Myth

Many demographers, historians, and politicians believe that changes in family structure foreshadow the disintegration of the family. Rising divorce rates and increases in out-of-wedlock births and single-parent households are often cited as indicators of family demise. Concern about the health and stability of the family is not new. Nineteenth-century social critics feared that the changing gender roles, declining birth rates, and increased immigration precipitated by the Industrial Revolution would lead to the demise of the family as a social institution.

The ongoing societal concern about the "stability and continuity of the family . . . points to the critical place that the family holds in American culture" (Hareven 1992: 40). Sociologists point out that, like other social institutions, the family both responds to and creates social change. Rather than signaling its demise, the fact that the family has withstood and adapted to major social changes can demonstrate how resilient it is. As a social system and as a social institution, the family remains a fundamental part of American culture.

Homogeneity Myth

By referring to *the family* in the singular form, it is implied that there is only one family structure in American culture. Yet, no society can boast that all families are **homogeneous**, or the same, especially pluralistic societies such as the United

States. American culture is comprised of families from all over the globe. Some families are first-generation immigrants; others have assimilated into mainstream society. The ethnic and racial diversity of American families is not found in other societies, such as Japan, which is more homogeneous. Diversity has characterized families in the United States. All over the world, some families are rich and some are poor; some families are large and some are small. Basic economic and demographic differences affect family structure, norms, and interactions.

Despite heterogeneity, one cannot ignore the fact that the "mainstream [white] middle-class family has defined the norms of family life in America" (Skolnick 1991: xix). Beginning with industrialization, the typical middle-class family structure became the ideal people were supposed to aspire to (Segalen 1996). Advertisers, politicians, and the media profile, cater to, and target middle-class families, and as such they have "played a style-setting role" in American culture (Demos 1979: 45).

Defining the Family

It seems only appropriate in the first chapter of a marriage and family textbook to provide a working definition of the term *family*. However, as you will see, defining what constitutes a family can be both difficult and controversial. The U.S. Bureau of the Census (1996: 6) defines *family* as "a group of two or more persons related by birth, marriage, or adoption and residing together in a household." That definition is constructed for purposes of counting units of people and is not intended to describe families in all cultures. For years, sociologists have struggled to construct a definition of family that is designed to be culturally universal. Several of the best known sociological definitions of family are presented in Figure 1.1. Take a moment to examine these definitions and note their similarities and differences. Which definition do you find most appealing and why?

Murdock's (1949) definition of the family was widely accepted by sociologists and anthropologists for a long time as an accurate description of families across the globe. Although Murdock's cataloging and analysis of hundreds of societies of the world, as reflected in the *World Ethnographic Atlas* (1957) and analyses derived from it, have yielded valuable information and a body of terms to help direct inquiry (Murdock 1949, 1957), his definition fails to consider some key features of family that sociologists deem important today. For instance, not all family members live in one household, nor do all married or cohabiting couples have children. Furthermore, Murdock's definition does not pay attention to power differentials among the different status holders in a family. No recognition is given to patriarchy or to adults' power over and responsibility for children that is normatively expected all over the world. Gendered roles for husbands and wives, fathers and mothers, are not addressed. Furthermore, Murdock's presumption that families must be formed through heterosexual marriage and include two parents and children is found objectionable by some people today.

Figure 1.1

Some Definitions of *Family*

> *"The family is a social group characterized by common residence, economic cooperation and reproduction, including adults of both sexes, at least one of whom maintain a socially approved sexual relationship, and one or more children, own or adopted, of the sexually cohabiting adults."*
>
> —George Peter Murdock (1949: 1)

> *"A relationship of indeterminate duration existing between parent(s) and children."*
>
> —M. F. Nimkoff and William F. Ogburn (1934: 6)

> *"The family institution is a small kinship-structured group with the key function of nurturant socialization of the newborn."*
>
> —Ira L. Reiss (1980: 29)

> *"The family is a basic societal structure centered about the basic societal function of replacement. The core relationships are husband-wife, parent-child, and sibling-sibling."*
>
> —Robert L. Winch (1971: 12)

> *"The family is . . . a group of persons united by ties of marriage, blood, or adoption; constituting a household; interacting and communicating with each other in their respective social roles of husband and wife, mother and father, son and daughter, brother and sister, and creating and maintaining a common culture."*
>
> —Ernest W. Burgess et al. (1971: 7)

> *"A family is any group of persons united by the ties of marriage, blood, or adoption, or any sexually expressive relationship, in which (1) the people are committed to one another in an intimate, interpersonal relationship, (2) the members see their identity as importantly attached to the group, and (3) the group has an identity of its own."*
>
> —E. Phillip Rice (1990: 4)

> *"Our definition of families is a broad one. It includes cohabiting groups of some duration composed of persons in intimate relationships based on biology, law, custom, or choice and usually economically interdependent."*
>
> —Joan Aldous and Wilfried Dumon (1990: 1137)

> *"Family can be defined as a relatively permanent group of people related to one another by ancestry, marriage, or adoption, who live together and whose adult members assume responsibility for the young."*
>
> —Brenda J. Vander Mey (early 1980s)

In reviewing the other definitions for family that are presented in Figure 1.1 (p. 8), note that the definitions provided by Nimkoff and Ogburn, Reiss, and Winch focus on children. The definition by Rice almost captures the essence of family as an institution in that it highlights belongingness and commitment, but it fails to capture roles—that is, social organization. The definition by Aldous and Dumon includes the important dimension of economic interdependence of members and a time factor. The definition transcribed from a lecture given when Dr. Vander Mey was a graduate student is strong on the time factor and more specific about how family members might be related to each other, but then limits family to household.

Burgess's definition was based on the assumption that "the family lives as long as interaction is taking place and only dies when it ceases" (Burgess in Burgess, Locke, and Thomas, 1971: 4). Burgess recognized that family has a structure to it. He also recognized that larger social forces—for example, urbanization, trends in birth rates, and elements of culture such as norms and customs—had an influence on family and could bring about changes within it. At the same time, he recognized that family was a dynamic entity which, through interaction, constructed and altered roles and provided children with sense of self as a social being (Burgess et al. 1971). However, the definition for family that Burgess and his colleagues provided (see in Figure 1.1) was limited to a single household and implied married heterosexual couples only.

Since the family is an institution, any definition of family should address the elements of an institution. Such a definition of family can be useful when you work through, for instance, Chapter 6 on social class and answer the question: What are the differences and similarities among family systems by social class in the United States? You then can look at such factors as the roles that parents assume in the different social classes, or the gender roles expected in the different social classes. Across the social classes, a similarity that can be discerned is that adults in all classes are supposed to take some kind of responsibility for the young. What will vary, especially by degree, is the nature and type of responsibility based on parental status and sex of parent. Likewise, when housework and child care are discussed in Chapters 10 and 11, you may return to this definition to further explain why certain patterns of behavior are evident.

The definition of family as an institution should reflect the fact that at this level of analysis the focus is on the family as a building block of society. Therefore, we suggest that a sufficient definition for family as an institution is the following: *Family refers to a collection of people, related to each other by marriage, ancestry, adoption, or affinity, who have a commitment to each other and a unique identity with each other. This collection forms an economic unit. The adults in the collection have varying degrees of responsibility for young members that might be a part of the collection.*

This definition, you will note, does not mandate children, but it does give recognition that all over the world, if children are present, the social norms of a group or society will identify who has what responsibility toward them. The definition also does not mandate that there be a heterosexual cohabiting couple in the collection, nor does it restrict family to a household. At the same time, the definition does speak to the family as an economic unit, which it is world-wide. That is, all over the world, families have some type of division of labor so that all needs are met. This can include child care, housecleaning, and working outside the home to bring home money to secure needed goods and services. This economic unit also provides intangible services for one another, such as social and psychological support, companionship, and guidance during intellectual development.

Families in Historical Perspective

"When schoolchildren return from vacation and are asked to list the good things and the bad things about their summer, their lists tend to be equally long" (Coontz 1992: 1). When the assignment is repeated throughout the year, the lists of bad things about their summer grow shorter, while the lists of good things grow longer "until by the end of the year the children are describing not actual vacations, but idealized images of Vacation" (Coontz 1992: 1). Families are idealized in much the same way schoolchildren idealize vacations. The result is an "ahistorical nostalgia," which can be corrected only by a thorough understanding of the family in historical context; "history is the best antidote to nostalgia" (Skolnick 1991: xvii).

Skolnick (1991: 47) suggests that to understand families in different historical eras, it may be useful to think of them "as if they were different cultures." Families, like cultures, must be examined in relation to the many forces that shape them, including the economy, demographics, social norms, and class structure. At the same time, the family is not a passive institution being mercilessly tossed about by the forces of history; families help shape the course of history, as well. Families respond to the economy, demographics, social norms, and class structures as they simultaneously help shape them.

Western European and Non-Western Traditions

Every era in U.S. history attests to family diversity. Spanish, French, Portuguese, and Dutch mariners and colonists predated the English colonists in the Western Hemisphere and were the first Europeans to come into contact with Native American peoples. The Europeans brought with them diverse expressions of the Western family tradition of the fifteenth and sixteenth centuries. This tradition was kinship and religion based. Marriage was a union of families and family interests. Familial role expectations were defined in terms of Catholic or Protestant Judeo-Christian values and elaborated both by civil law and by custom.

Native American family forms were even more diverse but declined through the catastrophic stress of contact with the Europeans. Similar influences weakened the family systems of the Europeans' African slaves. Among the Europeans, it was the English colonists who led the war of American independence, founded the national government, and developed industrial capitalism. As a consequence, the prosperous or middle-class *White Anglo-Saxon Protestant* family became enshrined in core American values as the cultural ideal.

Between then and now, every generation has brought fresh masses of immigrants reflecting other European and non-European family traditions. Only now, in the face of greatest diversity, is the traditional family ideal being challenged. The image persists, however—just as young children will draw ideal houses with features they have never actually seen.

Colonial Families

The colonial, preindustrial, or settlement phase of U.S. history runs from the founding of the English colonies to independence, but colonial influences persisted into the early 1800s (Demos 1979). During the colonial era, families were perceived as an extension of the community, rather than as a private social institution (Demos 1974). As such, the community took great interest in family matters. It was not unusual, for example, for outside officials such as magistrates to "compel a married couple 'to live more peaceably together' or to alter and upgrade the 'governance' of their children" (Demos 1979: 48–49). Today, such behavior would be unthinkable, except in extreme instances of family violence. Conversely, colonial families would be horrified at the lack of community control in contemporary families.

During the preindustrial period, the economy of the United States was largely agricultural. The family was a "community of work" in which all able-bodied members worked together to produce goods for the entire family unit (Demos 1979). Men and women, elders and children, all had economic responsibilities in families. The family and work were inseparable, creating an economic arrangement with a profound impact on family relationships. Marriage was expected and was strongly encouraged through social norms and legal policies. Women still single at age 25 were described as "ancient maids" and a "dismal spectacle," and single men were taxed at a higher rate than married men (Queen, Habenstein, and Quadagno 1985: 196). The typical couple in colonial New England got married in their early to mid-twenties and had a child within a year of their marriage (Queen, Habenstein, and Quadagno 1985).

As in marriages today, spouses "were dependent on each other both materially and emotionally" (Cancian 1987: 15), but the cultural ideal of a good marriage was quite different from the modern image of mutual love and expressed affection. Instead, husbands and wives "were likely to share a more formal and wordless kind of love, based on duty, working together, mutual help, and sex" (Cancian 1987: 17). The modern image of spouses as friends, confidants, helpmates, and lovers did not emerge until the twentieth century.

Marriages were expected to last "until death us do part." Nevertheless, marriages were short-lived. Because of the high mortality rate, especially for women in childbearing years, marriages lasted an average of only 10 years (Skolnick 1991). One-third to one-half of all children in colonial families lost at least one parent to death before they turned age 21 (Coontz 1992).

Role expectations of women and men, elders and children are also influenced by the economy, demographics, and social norms. In an argricultural economy, women's work and men's work are interdependent. Men generally had responsibility for tending to crops and bringing in the raw materials such as wheat, cotton, vegetables, and so on. Women had responsibility for turning the raw materials into finished goods such as food, clothes, soap, candles, and medicine (Carlson 1990). Some contemporary scholars have suggested that women in the colonial era may have had more autonomy and power in the family than women do today because their work was so critical to the survival of the family. However, although men may have been more aware of the contributions women made to the family, spousal relationships were far from egalitarian. As Carlson (1990: 18) states, "Despite the central contributions women made to the home economy . . . the preindustrial world was patriarchal."

Patriarchal Society

In **patriarchal society,** men are considered superior to women physically, intellectually, and morally, and men have far more power in the family and in society than women. Under English common law, which prevailed in the English colonies, "Women had many duties, but few rights" (Flexner 1975: 7). When women married, they suffered *civil death,* which meant that they were no longer considered a separate person apart from their husbands. Married women could not own property (even if they had inherited it before marrying), sign contracts, or get custody of their children following a legal separation (Flexner 1975).

Notions of women's intellectual and moral inferiority were shaped by interpretations of religious doctrine. In the Puritan colonial culture, women were considered morally inferior because of the belief that Eve, a woman, was responsible for original sin by eating the forbidden fruit from the tree of knowledge. Further assumptions about sex differences that are derived from this biblical story include the following:

1. Eve's actions revealed women's moral weakness.

2. Adam's own weakness in accepting the fruit showed that women are dangerous temptresses who must be controlled if men are to be morally strong.

3. God ordained that there must be a division of labor by which women bear children (in sorrow and pain) and men produce the means of existence (by the sweat of their brow).

4. Men shall rule over women. (Sapiro 1999: 48)

These beliefs about women influenced family roles and responsibilities. Mothers were responsible for bearing children and raising them from infancy until about age 3, when fathers assumed many parenting responsibilities (Rotundo 1985). The responsibility for teaching values and religious doctrines to children fell upon men because of the belief that women were more prone to temptation (Rotundo 1985).

Colonial Parenthood

In an agricultural society, the education of children largely occurs in the home. Thus, in the colonial era, fathers were given the responsibility of educating their children because of men's "superior endowment of 'reason'" (Demos 1982: 427). Women's "rational powers were so weak" (Demos 1982: 427) they certainly could not be assigned the responsibility of educating children.

Given modern parenting standards, women's power and responsibilities as mothers were quite limited, compared to men's. Fathers had considerable power and authority through owning property to bequeath to sons. Additionally, in this agricultural economy, the "domestic and productive life overlapped so substantially" that fathers were "a visible presence, year after year, day after day" (Demos 1982: 429). "Fathering was thus an extension, if not a part, of much routine activity" (Demos 1982: 429). Some parenting responsibilities were divided according to the sex of the parent and the sex of the child. Colonial parents considered "a boy as his father's child and a girl as her mother's" (Rotundo 1985: 9). Moth-

By what standards were these parents good mothers and fathers? How did parent and child roles and relationships change between colonial times and the Victorian era? What patterns in family life persisted from colonial to Victorian times and beyond?

ers instructed daughters in household tasks, and fathers trained sons in their trades (Rotundo 1985).

It has long been believed that children in the colonial era were perceived as miniature adults and were expected to behave and work as such. Historians have described colonial parents as emotionally distant from their children (Corsaro 1997). It has been speculated that the apparent emotional distance between parents and children during this period was a product of high infant and child mortality rates. Parents were said to be cautious about becoming too attached to children who might die young, so emotional distance was used as a protection from heartache.

However, some contemporary historical research suggests that parent-child relationships in the Puritan colonial era were not as formal, detached, and one sided as once believed. In her book *Forgotten Children*, Linda Pollack argues that "nearly all children were wanted, such developmental stages as weaning and teething aroused interest and concern, and parents revealed anxiety and distress at the illness or death of their children" (1983: 268).

In 1790, approximately 750,000 Africans were held as slaves in the United States (Carlson 1990). Marriages between slaves were not legally recognized, although many couples established long-lasting relationships and lived in nuclear families (Carlson 1990). Mortality rates were higher for African slaves than for their owners, and African families had to live with the constant fear and uncertainty that at any time a child or spouse could be sold away from the family unit. Role expectations of family members reflected the dangers of commitment and the slaveholder's status as the master of one's fate.

Victorian Families

After 1820, as the process of industrialization accelerated, home and work became separated. Families became units of consumption rather than production. No longer did husbands and wives, elders and children work together to produce the family's livelihood. Increasingly, at least one person left the family to seek work in a factory. Ideally, the worker was the "head of the household"—the husband.

Such drastic economic changes had a profound effect on the family. Perceptions of home and family changed dramatically. The family was transformed from an "integral part of the community"—a public place—to a "place of refuge"—a private, intimate place (Demos 1979):

> Home—and the word itself became highly sentimentalized—was pictured as a bastion of peace, of repose, of orderliness, of unwavering devotion to people and principles beyond the self. Here the woman of the family, and the children would pass most of their hours and days—safe from the grinding pressures and dark temptations of the world at large; here, too, the man of the family would retreat periodically for refreshment, renewal, and inner fortification against the dangers he encountered elsewhere. (Demos 1979: 51)

The knowledge and technology that are a part of industrialization helped prolong life. Infant and adult mortality declined, and throughout the Victorian era, birth rates also gradually declined. In 1800, the birth rate was 7.04 children per family; by 1900, the birth rate had declined to 3.56 children per family (Hareven 1992). These demographic changes had an impact on marriage. Couples were waiting longer to have children and spending fewer years in childrearing; thus, more emphasis was placed on marriage.

During the Victorian era marriage came to be perceived as a formal, contrived partnership, rather than a natural one (Demos 1974). The emotional requirements for husbands and wives also changed. The ability to love became defined as a feminine quality (Cancian 1987). Women were believed to have a "superior ability to love," which enabled them to "comfort and care for their children and husbands" (Cancian 23: 1987). Wives still were perceived as property, responsible for instrumental tasks (household chores) as well as expressive duties (sexual gratification and emotional support). Men were not obligated to express more than minimal affection for their wives (Scanzoni 1982).

The Industrial Revolution also produced "the most thoroughgoing system of sex-role differentiation ever seen in American history" (Demos 1974: 436). The home was the "woman's sphere," and the "world of affairs" belonged to men (Demos 1974). Women became perceived as pious, pure, submissive, and domestic—a set of expectations Welter (1966) labels the Cult of True Womanhood.

The Cult of True Womanhood

The data of social historians include recorded and oral life histories as well as primary source documents about people and events in the life of a community, such as diaries, newspapers, and court records. Sociologists and other social scientists can interpret historical data to explain how the social constructions of womanhood and motherhood changed so dramatically during the nineteenth century. These changes stemmed from transformations of roles and statuses caused by the shift from an agrarian to an industrial economy.

Welter describes the role expectations of nineteenth-century women—the Cult of True Womanhood—as follows:

> *The attributes of True Womanhood, by which a woman judged herself and was judged by her husband, her neighbors and society could be divided into four cardinal virtues—piety, purity, submissiveness and domesticity. Put them all together and they spelled mother, daughter, sister, wife—woman. Without them, no matter whether there was fame, achievement or wealth, all was ashes. With them she was promised happiness and power.* (1966: 152)

It may seem odd that Victorian women were extolled for their virtues when only a few decades earlier they were perceived as morally inferior. The explanation for the change is, again, rooted in the economic shift. Ideally, women during the Victorian era stayed home while men had to leave the confines of the home to work in the city. As such, men were believed to be exposed daily to sin, degradation, and other harsh realities of the world (Demos 1974). Women, however, remained pure and untainted because they were sheltered in the home, and thus they gained the responsibility of keeping men from being corrupted by the outside world. Demos, quoting from an unidentified sermon, illustrates the perception of women as moral caretakers:

> [It is the woman] who, like a guardian angel, watches over [her husband's] interests, warns him against dangers, comforts him under trial; and by her pious, assiduous, and attractive deportment, constantly endeavours to render him more virtuous, more useful, more honourable, and more happy. (1974: 433)

The Good Mother

Middle-class families in the nineteenth century were centered around the children (Lasch 1977). Childhood was conceptualized as an important, vulnerable phase of life, and parents were responsible for isolating children from "corrupting influences" (Lasch 1977: 5). Children were now considered delicate, impressionable beings who needed constant supervision and nurturing. Childrearing became more demanding, and emotional ties between parents and children intensified. Although childhood was supposed to be a time of innocence and freedom, such leisure was available only in middle-class Caucasian families. Poor children and slave children continued to work in demanding labor (Coontz 1992).

Women, described as "angels of consolation" (Lasch 1977), were believed to be "especially qualified for motherhood" (Demos 1982: 431). With industrialization came the mass production of childrearing books and women's magazines that emphasized the importance of mothers' influence over their children's development. Ministers declared that "mothers were more important than fathers in forming the 'tastes, sentiments, and habits of children,' and more effective in instructing them" (Cott 1977: 86). Women became solely responsible for the physical and emotional well-being of their children. "The outcome . . . was a deep intensification of the parent-child bond—or, to be more precise, of the mother-child bond" (Demos 1974: 441).

Mothers were expected to breastfeed for the mental, emotional, and physical health of their children (Badinter 1981). They also were expected to ask doctors for advice and help in childrearing to avoid making mistakes. Good mothers devoted all of their attention and devotion to their children through countless sacrifices.

The Good Father

The idealized and repressive view of women known as the Cult of True Womanhood had its counterpart in the male role (Demos 1974). The breadwinner or good-provider role (Bernard 1989) required men to be occupational successes.

Not only was the man the breadwinner but "he was also [the family's] sole representative in the world at large. His 'success' or 'failure'—terms which had now obtained a highly personal significance—would reflect directly on other members of the household. And this was a grievously heavy burden to carry" (Demos 1979: 53). To be an occupational success required "strength, cunning, inventiveness, endurance—a whole range of traits henceforth defined as exclusively 'masculine'" (Demos 1974: 436). Emotional expressiveness was not included in the masculine role, for women were to be the sole suppliers of nurturing and support in the family (Bernard 1989). Emotional expressiveness was associated with femininity and therefore was a sign of weakness. It was believed that expression of feeling would make a man more vulnerable in his harsh world of work.

The changes associated with industrialization are directly responsible for the changing role of men in the family. In an industrialized economy, work is a place away from home. The time men have for interaction and intimacy with their family is reduced (Bernard 1989). According to Rotundo, industrialized, "middle-class fathers were away from the house far too often to participate effectively in the everyday give-and-take" that fosters intimacy in families (1985: 12).

Not only did the changing economy undermine a man's opportunity for interaction with his wife and children, but much of a father's authority also was eroded with industrialization. Sons no longer needed fathers to teach them the family trade (Rotundo 1985). Young men had a world of work opportunities before them that required skills fathers could not teach sons. However, fathers remained the disciplinarians of the family and became responsible for teaching their sons how to survive in the competitive business world, even if they could not directly teach them the skills of the job.

The Rise of Domesticity

The changes brought about by industrialization varied by social class (Hareven 1992). The concept of the domestic "true woman" is rooted in the experience of "Yankee middle-class women" but was applied to all women (Cott 1977). Ironically, just at the time when rural and immigrant women were afforded more job opportunities than ever before—especially in the new textile factories—domesticity arose as the norm for middle-class women (Hareven 1992). Eventually, the norm of domesticity became the ideal to which all women aspired, even if they could not afford the luxury of not working. Hareven describes how the middle-class ideal for women became a part of womanhood regardless of social class:

> *The ideology of domesticity . . . began to influence working-class and immigrant families during the early part of the 20th century. As immigrants became "Americanized," particularly in the second generation, they internalized the values of domesticity and began to view women's work outside the home as demeaning, as having low status, or as compromising for the husband and dangerous for the children. Consequently married women entered the labor force only when driven by economic necessity.* (1992: 48)

Many poorer families preferred to send children to work rather than mothers (Skolnick 1991); a married employed woman signified to society that the husband was a failure as a breadwinner and the wife was a failure as a woman. By the end of the nineteenth century, only 2 to 3 percent of married women were employed (Hareven 1992; Skolnick 1991).

Families in the Twentieth Century

From the turn of the century until World War II, family structure and role expectations remained stable (Chafe 1972). The majority of married women continued to avoid employment, if possible. However, the work available to women who were employed did change. In 1870, most women who worked were employed in agriculture or domestic service; by 1910, women worked in factories, offices, stores, and telephone exchanges (Greenwald 1980). The women most likely to be working in these jobs were single Caucasians and immigrants.

World War I temporarily improved working conditions for married women who had to work—most particularly African American women. The demand for workers in wartime industries was so great that African American women were hired but only after single Caucasian American women had rejected the jobs (Greenwald 1980). Few women joined the labor force during World War I who were not employed prior to the conflict (Greenwald 1980).

During the Roaring Twenties, women gained the right to vote and there was a "momentous break with Victorian sexual norms" (Skolnick 1991: 41), but neither of these changes noticeably affected family structure. Single, college-educated women increasingly were able to support themselves in occupations such as teaching and nursing. Young men and women gained the independence of dating away from parents' view, and "necking and petting became part of a new code of premarital sexual behavior that staked out a middle ground between erotic yearning and the no-sex-at-all Victorian standard" (Skolnick 1991: 45). Such behavior, increasingly encouraged by new-founded privacy in the family automobile, was shocking to the older generation but did not dramatically alter family structure.

The Great Depression was a trying time for most families. Many formerly middle-class families slipped into poverty, and the homemaker/breadwinner role distinctions were difficult to maintain. Many men lost their jobs, which led to a sense of failure. Married women desperately looked for work, but employers tried to reserve the few available jobs for men (Chafe 1972). Degler notes that during the Depression, "the most common experience of married women who worked was to be fired or denied jobs if they had working husbands." In fact, "several states and many municipalities simply barred married women from any job, on the . . . ground that during a period of widespread unemployment men needed work more than married women" (1980: 413).

The World War II Transformation

World War II created the most dramatic, lasting changes in family and gender roles in American culture since the Industrial Revolution. After 1942, when the United States was fighting the war on the German and Japanese fronts, there was a strong, government-led effort to get white, working-class and middle-class women out of the home and into war industries. Fifteen million men and women who formerly were in the civilian work force were recruited into the armed services (Degler 1980). Workers were desperately needed to produce the ships, airplanes, tanks, and ammunition needed to fight the war.

A full-scale media campaign, now dubbed the *Rosie the Riveter campaign*, was used to convince women to leave the safety of the home to work in the war industries as a patriotic duty. Posters appeared on buses and in shops, familiarizing women with the idea of working in munitions factories. Women's committees in neighborhoods went door to door, recruiting women workers (Field 1987). A newsreel showing a woman wearing welding goggles proclaimed that "instead of cutting out dresses, this woman is cutting out patterns for airplane parts." Women were told "a lathe will hold no more terrors . . . than an electric washing machine" (Field 1987).

The rhetoric of the Rosie the Riveter campaign made it quite clear that women were working only as a patriotic duty to the country—a small sacrifce compared to the sacrifice of life and limb that the men in uniform were making. Propaganda also suggested that women's war work could benefit their family directly; they could be building the bombs that save their husbands' lives.

Also clear in the propaganda was the message that women's employment was to be temporary; they were expected to quit their jobs when the war ended. Employers preferred to hire middle-class, Caucasian, married women because these workers would readily give up their jobs after the war (Anderson 1981). No infrastructure was built to help women manage work and children. Day-care centers were rare and expensive. Women were informed explicitly and implicitly that they were not expected to combine work and family indefinitely.

The media campaign was tremendously successful in getting women into the work force. Between 1941 and 1944, 6.5 million women joined the labor force, over half of whom previously had been homemakers (Degler 1980). The aircraft industry is a good example of how quickly women workers were mobilized. In April 1941, only 143 women worked in seven aircraft factories; by October 1943, "these same factories had hired 65,000 women—an increase of over 450-fold" (Weiner 1985: 95).

World War II created a transition in the female labor force from one dominated by young single women to one dominated by older married women (Anderson 1981). Those most likely to join the labor force during the war were married women, over age 35, with no children under 14 years old (Anderson 1981). These same women, those with fewer household and child-care responsibilities, remained in the work force after the war.

Families in the 1950s

The 1950s was a time of rapid social change. Economic, demographic, and social changes had dramatic effects on family structure. The postwar years were a time of unprecedented economic growth. By the mid-1950s, 60 percent of Americans were middle class, and such prosperity, "after fifteen years of Depression and war . . . set off a mood of celebration and hope" (Skolnick 1991). Middle-class couples could afford to have four or five children and still enjoy the luxuries of postwar technology, such as washing machines, vacuum cleaners, and televisions. Returning soldiers could attend college on the G.I. Bill, and new homes in newly developed suburbs were affordable with low-interest mortgages. Most importantly, middle-class families could have all of this on one income.

In contrast to the Rosie the Riveter image cultivated during the war, women of the 1950s women were glorified as wives and mothers. The gender-role expectations that emerged during this era were much like the Victorian Cult of True Womanhood ideals. Parenting books and magazine articles of the 1950s and early 1960s focused on the primary importance of the mother-child relationship (Rapoport, Rapoport, and Strelitz 1980). Women were supposed to joyfully devote all their time to raising children with patience and love:

> *A child needs to feel he is an object of pleasure and pride to his mother; a mother needs to feel an expansion of her own personality in the personality of their child; each needs to feel closely identified with the other. . . . The provision of mothering cannot be considered in terms of hours per day, but only in terms of the enjoyment of each other's company which mother and child obtain.* (cited in Rapoport, Rapoport, and Strelitz 1980: 38)

Women were expected to live through their children; their entire identities were tied to motherhood (Skolnick 1991).

Women were not to consider combining work and motherhood, for it was believed that children would suffer psychological trauma from separation. Men were expected to be the sole economic providers for their families. As in Victorian times, their duty as husbands and fathers was primarily to earn a good living. However, men also were expected to offer emotional support to their wives and protect their families from harm. The relationship between fathers and children was virtually ignored in the parenting literature. One writer described the father's role as follows:

> *[The father] can provide a space in which the mother has elbow-room. Properly protected by her man, the mother is saved from having to turn outward to deal with her surroundings at the time she is wanting so much to turn inward. . . . The mother's bond with the baby is very powerful at the beginning, and we must do all we can to enable her to be preoccupied with her baby at this, the natural time.* (cited in Rapoport, Rapoport, and Strelitz 1980: 39)

How did conditions before, during, and after World War II affect the status of women in the United States? What conditions gave rise to the women's movement and feminist perspectives on marriage and the family?

Advertisements, television shows, movies, and music all reinforced these strict gender norms, and people responded. For the first time in over a century, the age of marriage and motherhood declined and birth rates rose (Coontz 1992). The family was portrayed as the place where all one's needs could be met.

What accounts for the rapid shift from Rosie the Riveter to June Cleaver on *Leave It to Beaver* or Harriet in *Ozzie and Harriett?* Skolnick (1991: 65) suggests that several factors explain the "embrace of marriage and parenthood" in the postwar years. The most obvious explanation is that Americans were ready to return to the security of home after the trauma of the Great Depression and World War II. The threat of the atomic bomb and the Cold War also "encouraged the retreat into the home in search for security in a dangerous new world" (Skolnick 1991: 68). Additionally, the expansive economy made it possible for young couples to afford children as soon as they married, and there was a concerted governmental effort to get women out of the work force so jobs would be available to returning soldiers. However, millions of women entered the labor force in the 1950s; as during the war, most were older with few child-care responsibilities.

African American, poor, and immigrant women continued to work, regardless of their marital or parental status. Approximately 40 percent of African American women with small children were employed (Coontz 1992). It is important to remember that not all families in the 1950s were middle-class suburbanites enjoying new appliances purchased with discretionary income. Some 25 percent of Americans were poor (Coontz 1992). Two-parent African American families had a poverty rate of more than 50 percent (Coontz 1992). But family diversity was ignored in the ideal American culture, and the image of the so-called perfect 1950s family persisted.

Contemporary Families: The 1960s to the Present

The 1960s marked a time of social revolution. The civil rights movement, which began in the 1950s; the women's movement, which evolved in the 1800s; the antiwar movement of the Vietnam War era; the sexual revolution; and the environmental conservation movement all occurred during this time. These social movements and the factors that fostered them help explain the changes that developed in the family.

The most common explanation for the revolutionary changes advanced during the 1960s is the vast number of young people in the culture. The first wave of children born during the postwar "baby boom" reached college age. Between 1960 and 1970, the number of youth between 18 to 24 years old grew by over 53 percent (Skolnick 1991), and many of these young adults attended college. By 1970, one-half of 18- to 21-year-olds were enrolled in college (Skolnick 1991).

Some historians have suggested that young people tend to lead social revolutions because they are old enough to understand economic and social injustice but young enough not to have the responsibilities of work and family. Baby boomers were on college campuses where they were learning about poverty and prejudice for the first time. Additionally, these young people, raised in the 1950s by attentive mothers, had been taught to be independent. Childrearing advice of the time encouraged parents to allow their children to express themselves and think independently, rather than to blindly obey. Young adults on college campuses during the 1960s had been raised to question authority and established social customs, although their parents probably did not consciously instill such values.

The women's movement, which gained momentum in the 1960s, challenged many of the gender norms promoted during the 1950s. No longer were women supposed to enter college with the main goal of finding a handsome, successful husband. Rather, women were encouraged to use their education in a career. As these women entered the work force, they encountered obstacles to success based on sexism. Policies that banned women from occupations simply on the basis of sex were challenged, and women fought for the right to receive pay equal to that of men for the same work.

The sexual revolution also changed family structure. Away at college, young people had the freedom to experiment with sexual relationships. The birth control pill, available in the early 1960s, meant that couples could engage in sexual intercourse with less threat of unwanted pregnancy. Sex no longer had to be postponed until marriage.

A variety of family forms were experimented with during the 1960s and early 1970s. Some couples lived together without being married (cohabited); others tried communal living. Some married couples tried "safe forms of infidelity," such as "mate swapping" and "open marriage" (Skolnick 1991). Most of these arrangements were quickly abandoned, although cohabitation became an accepted form of courtship in American culture. As young people began having sex at earlier ages and postponing marriage, teenage pregnancy and illegitimate birth rates rose. Divorce became an alternative for many women in unhappy marriages, as they became able to support themselves economically.

Trends: Does History Repeat Itself?

Families today contain vestiges of the past and reflect the economic and social realities of contemporary society. The image of the home as a refuge, which emerged during the Industrial Revolution, is still apparent today. However, a new image, what Demos (1979) calls "the home as encounter group," also has emerged. The family is perceived not only as a place for safety and comfort but also as a place for personal growth.

As in previous eras, the upwardly mobile family remains the ideal family, except that today, these families represent dual-income households. Cultural expectations of men and women reflect the needs of these families. Men still are expected to be the primary breadwinners and women the primary caregivers of children, but increasingly women are expected to share economic responsibilities and men are expected to share in child care. As divorce, single parenthood, and blended families become more common, they become more acceptable in society.

What kind of patterns can be discerned in over three centuries of American family life? Family structure and functions have shifted over time. Prior to industrialization, families were perceived as miniature churches, schools, and social reform agencies and the churches and courts were seen as large families (Demos 1974). With industrialization, the family became privatized and many of the functions formerly allocated to the family were institutionalized. The care of people with mental disturbances as well as the education of children were no longer the sole responsibility of families. However, the family also assumed new functions. Social and emotional support have become more important in today's fast-paced industrialized society. Families have come to provide comfort and security in an otherwise hectic and unpredictable world—a function formerly never considered necessary.

Summary

The family of the past is often romanticized as harmonious and happy. The inaccurate, nostalgic view of the family is based on a number of myths, however. Four of the most widely held myths about past families are (1) women were homemakers and men were breadwinners; (2) families were extended, with many kin living in the same household; (3) changes in family structure signal the disintegration of the family; and (4) white, middle-class families are the norm.

Family life is organized a variety of ways across the globe, making it difficult to construct a universally applicable definition of the family. Sociologists and anthropologists prefer to describe families according to patterns of marriage and kinship, residence, and descent.

Family life is influenced by historical, demographic, and economic factors. The earliest settlers from Europe to the United States depended largely on agricultural products for economic survival. All family members performed labor for the family farm or the small family business. Marriage was not expected to be openly affectionate. Division of labor in families was assigned based on gender. Women were perceived as morally and intellectually inferior, and therefore their contributions to the family were generally not recognized or respected. Fathers were expected to educate the children and teach sons their trade, whereas mothers were to instruct daughters in household tasks.

With industrialization, home and work became separated. Ideally, the husband was expected to be the primary economic provider, and the wife was expected to raise children and perform household chores. Strong sex-role distinctions were drawn, with women being expected to live up to the ideals of what has been labeled the Cult of True Womanhood.

Next to industrialization, World War II probably had the most significant impact on family roles than any other historical event. Women were called out of the home and into the war industries to supply soldiers with necessary military weaponry. Rosie the Riveter became the cultural symbol of women's patriotic duty to work in the factories and shipyards. After the war, women were expected to return to homemaking, but many older married women remained in the labor force. Furthermore, after the war, manufacturing declined and a more technologically based service economy emerged, ultimately providing more job opportunities for women.

In the decade following the war, the homemaker/breadwinner distinction was revived with a vengeance. Marriage and birth rates soared. Women were expected to bear and raise children and maintain the household while men provided for the family financially.

The social and political movements of the 1960s, combined with economic shifts led to significant changes in family roles and dynamics. Marriage rates dropped, divorce rates rose, couples waited longer to have children, and birth rates dropped. More women joined the labor force, even those with young children, and single-parent families became more common. Increasingly, the home-maker/breadwinner roles, which initially evolved with industrialization, have been challenged in families.

Readings for In-Depth Focus

Real versus Ideal Families

Americans have worried about the implications of family changes at least since the beginning of the Industrial Revolution. Social change, a constant unavoidable force in all cultures, inevitably has an impact on families. Changes in society, and ultimately in the family, are both positive and negative. As Stephanie Coontz points out in the reading that follows, families throughout history have had strengths and weaknesses. Rather than fretting over whether families are better or worse than before, people would do better to examine how and why change has occurred and to discover how contemporary families can be strengthened.

As you read, identify Coontz's thesis and compare the myths regarding families of the past that she identifies to the ones discussed at the beginning of the chapter. What evidence does Coontz provide to dispel these myths? According to Coontz, why is it difficult to assess whether the family as a social institution is improving or disintegrating?

■ ■ ■

The Way We Wish We Were
Defining the Family Crisis

Stephanie Coontz

When I begin teaching a course on family history, I often ask my students to write down ideas that spring to mind when they think of the "traditional family." Their lists always include several images. One is of extended families in which all members worked together, grandpar-ents were an integral part of family life, children learned responsibility and the work ethic from their elders, and there were clear lines of authority based on respect for age. Another is of nuclear families in which nurturing mothers sheltered children from premature exposure to sex, financial worries, or other adult concerns, while fathers taught adolescents not to sacrifice their education by going to work too early. Still another image gives pride of place to the couple relationship. In traditional families, my students write—half derisively, half wistfully—men and women remained chaste until marriage, at which time they extricated themselves from competing obligations to kin and neighbors and committed themselves wholly to the marital relationship, experiencing an all-encompassing intimacy that our more crowded modern life seems to preclude. As one freshman wrote: "They truly respected the marriage vowels"; I assume she meant *I-O-U*.

Such visions of past family life exert a powerful emotional pull on most Americans, and with good reason, given the fragility of many modern commitments. The problem is not only that these visions bear a suspicious resemblance to reruns of old television series, but also that the scripts of different shows have been mixed up: June Cleaver suddenly has a Grandpa Walton dispensing advice in her kitchen; Donna Stone, vacuuming the living room in her inevitable pearls and high heels, is no longer married to a busy modern pediatrician but to a small-town sheriff who, like Andy Taylor of "The Andy Griffith Show," solves community problems through informal, old-fashioned common sense.

Like most visions of a "golden age," the traditional family my students describe evaporates on closer examination. It is an ahistorical amalgam of structures, values, and behaviors that never coexisted in the same time and place. The notion that traditional families fostered intense intimacy between husbands and wives while creating mothers who were totally available to their children, for example, is an idea that combines some characteristics of the white, middle-class family in the mid-nineteenth century and some of a rival family ideal first articulated in the 1920s. The first family revolved emotionally around the mother-child axis, leaving the hus-

band-wife relationship stilted and formal. The second focused on an eroticized couple relationship, demanding that mothers curb emotional "overinvestment" in their children. The hybrid idea that a woman can be fully absorbed with her youngsters while simultaneously maintaining passionate sexual excitement with her husband was a 1950s invention that drove thousands of women to therapists, tranquilizers, or alcohol when they actually tried to live up to it.

Similarly, an extended family in which all members work together under the top-down authority of the household elder operates very differently from a nuclear family in which husband and wife are envisioned as friends who patiently devise ways to let the children learn by trial and error. Children who worked in family enterprises seldom had time for the extracurricular activities that Wally and the Beaver recounted to their parents over the dinner table; often, they did not even go to school full-time. Mothers who did home production generally relegated child care to older children or servants; they did not suspend work to savor a baby's first steps or discuss with their husband how to facilitate a grade-schooler's "self-esteem." Such families emphasized formality, obedience to authority, and "the way its always been" in their childrearing.

Nuclear families, by contrast, have tended to pride themselves on the "modernity" of parent-child relations, diluting the authority of grandparents, denigrating "old-fashioned" ideas about childraising, and resisting the "interference" of relatives. It is difficult to imagine the Cleavers or the college-educated title figure of "Father Knows Best" letting grandparents, maiden aunts, or in-laws have a major voice in childrearing decisions. . . .

THE ELUSIVE TRADITIONAL FAMILY

Whenever people propose that we go back to the traditional family, I always suggest that they pick a ballpark date for the family they have in mind. Once pinned down, they are invariably unwilling to accept the package deal that comes with their chosen model. Some people, for example, admire the discipline of colonial families, which were certainly not much troubled by divorce or fragmenting individualism. But colonial families were hardly stable: High mortality rates meant that the average length of marriage was less than a dozen years. One-third to one-half of all children lost at least one parent before the age of twenty-one; in the South, more than half of all children aged thirteen or under had lost at least one parent.[1]

While there are a few modern Americans who would like to return to the strict patriarchal authority of colonial days, in which disobedience by women and children was considered a small form of treason, these individuals would doubtless be horrified by other aspects of colonial families, such as their failure to protect children from knowledge of sexuality. Eighteenth-century spelling and grammar books routinely used *fornication* as an example of a four-syllable word, and preachers detailed sexual offenses in astonishingly explicit terms. Sexual conversations between men and women, even in front of children, were remarkably frank. It is worth contrasting this colonial candor to the climate in 1991, when the Department of Health and Human Services was forced to cancel a proposed survey of teenagers' sexual practices after some groups charged that such knowledge might "inadvertently" encourage more sex.[2]

Other people searching for an ideal traditional family might pick the more sentimental and gentle Victorian family, which arose in the 1830s and 1840s as household production gave way to wage work and professional occupations outside the home. A new division of labor by age and sex emerged among the middle class. Women's roles were redefined in terms of domesticity rather than production, men were labeled "breadwinners" (a masculine identity unheard of in colonial days), children were said to need time to play, and gentle maternal guidance

supplanted the patriarchal authoritarianism of the past.

But the middle-class Victorian family depended for its existence on the multiplication of other families who were too poor and powerless to retreat into their own little oases and who therefore had to provision the oases of others. Childhood was prolonged for the nineteenth-century middle class only because it was drastically foreshortened for other sectors of the population. The spread of textile mills, for example, freed middle-class women from the most time-consuming of their former chores, making cloth. But the raw materials for these mills were produced by slave labor. Slave children were not exempt from field labor unless they were infants, and even then their mothers were not allowed time off to nurture them. Frederick Douglass could not remember seeing his mother until he was seven.[3]

Domesticity was also not an option for the white families who worked twelve hours a day in Northern factories and workshops transforming slave-picked cotton into ready-made clothing. By 1820, "half the workers in many factories were boys and girls who had not reached their eleventh birthday." Rhode Island investigators found "little half-clothed children" making their way to the textile mills before dawn in 1845, shoemaking families and makers of artificial flowers worked fifteen to eighteen hours a day, according to the New York *Daily Tribune.*[4]

Within the home, prior to the diffusion of household technology at the end of the century, house cleaning and food preparation remained mammoth tasks. Middle-class women were able to shift more time into childrearing in this period only by hiring domestic help. Between 1800 and 1850, the proportion of servants to white households doubled, to about one in nine. Some servants were poverty-stricken mothers who had to board or bind out their own children. Employers found such workers tended to be "distracted," however; they usually preferred young girls. In his study of Buffalo,

New York, in the 1850s, historian Lawrence Glasco found that Irish and German girls often went into service at the age of eleven or twelve.[5]

For every nineteenth-century middle-class family that protected its wife and child within the family circle, then, there was an Irish or a German girl scrubbing floors in that middle-class home, a Welsh boy mining coal to keep the home-baked goodies warm, a black girl doing the family laundry, a black mother and child picking cotton to be made into clothes for the family, and a Jewish or an Italian daughter in a sweatshop making "ladies" dresses or artificial flowers for the family to purchase.

Furthermore, people who lived in these periods were seldom as enamored of their family arrangements as modern nostalgia might suggest. Colonial Americans lamented "the great neglect in many parents and masters in training up their children" and expressed the "greatest trouble and grief about the rising generation." No sooner did Victorian middle-class families begin to withdraw their children from the work world than observers began to worry that children were becoming *too* sheltered. By 1851, the Reverend Horace Bushnell spoke for many in bemoaning the passing of the traditional days of household production when the whole family was "harnessed, all together, into the producing process, young and old, male and female, from the boy who rode the plough-horse to the grandmother knitting under her spectacles."[6]

The late nineteenth century saw a modest but significant growth of extended families and a substantial increase in the number of families who were "harnessed" together in household production. Extended families have never been the norm in America; the highest figure for extended-family households ever recorded in American history is 20 percent. Contrary to the popular myth that industrialization destroyed "traditional" extended families, this high point occurred between 1850 and 1885, during the most intensive period of early industrialization. Many of these extended families, and most "pro-

ducing" families of the time, depended on the labor of children; they were held together by dire necessity and sometimes by brute force.[7]

▪ ▪ ▪

By the end of the nineteenth century, shocked by the conditions in urban tenements and by the sight of young children working full-time at home or earning money out on the streets, middle-class reformers put aside nostalgia for "harnessed" family production and elevated the antebellum model once more, blaming immigrants for introducing such "un-American" family values as child labor. Reformers advocated adoption of a "true American" family—a restricted, exclusive nuclear unit in which women and children were divorced from the world of work.

In the late 1920s and early 1930s, however, the wheel turned yet again, as social theorists noted the independence and isolation of the nuclear family with renewed anxiety. The influential Chicago School of sociology believed that immigration and urbanization had weakened the traditional family by destroying kinship and community networks. Although sociologists welcomed the increased democracy of "companionate marriage," they worried about the rootlessness of nuclear families and the breakdown of older solidarities. By the time of the Great Depression, some observers even saw a silver lining in economic hardship, since it revived the economic functions and social importance of kin and family ties. With housing starts down by more than 90 percent, approximately one-sixth of urban families had to "double up" in apartments. The incidence of three-generation households increased, while recreational interactions outside the home were cut back or confined to the kinship network. One newspaper opined: "many a family that has lost its car has found its soul."[8]

Depression families evoke nostalgia in some contemporary observers, because they tended to create "dependability and domestic inclination" among girls and "maturity in the management of money" among boys. But, in many cases, responsibility was inseparable from "a corrosive and disabling poverty that shattered the hopes and dreams of . . . young parents and twisted the lives of those who were 'stuck together' in it." Men withdrew from family life or turned violent; women exhausted themselves trying to "take up the slack" both financially and emotionally, or they belittled their husbands as failures; and children gave up their dreams of education to work at dead-end jobs.[9]

From the hardships of the Great Depression and the Second World War and the euphoria of the postwar economic recovery came a new kind of family ideal that still enters our homes in "Leave It to Beaver" and "Donna Reed" reruns. . . .

THE COMPLEXITIES OF ASSESSING FAMILY TRENDS

If it is hard to find a satisfactory model of the traditional family, it is also hard to make global judgments about how families have changed and whether they are getting better or worse. Some generalizations about the past are pure myth. Whatever the merit of recurring complaints about the "rootlessness" of modern life, for instance, families are *not* more mobile and transient than they used to be. In most nineteenth-century cities, both large and small, more than 50 percent—and often up to 75 percent— of the residents in any given year were no longer there ten years later. People born in the twentieth century are much more likely to live near their birthplace than were people born in the nineteenth century.[10]

■ ■ ■

A related myth is that modern Americans have lost touch with extended-kinship networks or have let parent-child bonds lapse. In fact, more Americans than ever before have grandparents alive, and there is good evidence that ties between grandparents and grandchildren have become stronger over the past fifty years. In the late 1970s, researchers returned to the "Middletown" studied by sociologists Robert and Helen Lynd in the 1920s and found that most people there maintained closer extended-family networks than in earlier times. There had been some decline in the family's control over the daily lives of youth, especially females, but "the expressive/emotional function of the family" was "more important for Middletown students of 1977 than it was in 1924." More recent research shows that visits with relatives did *not* decline between the 1950s and the late 1980s.[11]

Today 54 percent of adults see a parent, and 68 percent talk on the phone with a parent, at least once a week. Fully 90 percent of Americans describe their relationship with their mother as close, and 78 percent say their relationship with their grandparents is close. And for all the family disruption of divorce, most modern children live with at least *one* parent. As late as 1940, 10 percent of American children did not live with either parent, compared to only one in twenty-five today.[12]

What about the supposed eclipse of marriage? Neither the rising age of those who marry nor the frequency of divorce necessarily means that marriage is becoming a less prominent institution than it was in earlier days. Ninety percent of men and women eventually marry, more than 70 percent of divorced men and women remarry, and fewer people remain single for their entire lives today than at the turn of the century. One author even suggests that the availability of divorce in the second half of the twentieth century has allowed some women to try marriage who would formerly have remained single all their lives. Others argue that the rate of hidden marital separation in the late nineteenth century was not much less than the rate of visible separation today.[13]

Studies of marital satisfaction reveal that more couples reported their marriages to be happy in the late 1970s than did so in 1957, while couples in their second marriages believe them to be much happier than their first ones. Some commentators conclude that marriage is becoming less permanent but more satisfying. Others wonder, however, whether there is a vicious circle in our country, where no one even tries to sustain a relationship. Between the late 1970s and late 1980s, moreover, reported marital happiness did decline slightly in the United States. Some authors see this as reflecting our decreasing appreciation of marriage, although others suggest that it reflects unrealistically high expectations of love in a culture that denies people safe, culturally approved ways of getting used to marriage or cultivating other relationships to meet some of the needs that we currently load onto the couple alone.[14]

Part of the problem in making simple generalizations about what is happening to marriage is that there has been a polarization of experiences. Marriages are much more likely to be ended by divorce today, but marriages that do last are described by their participants as happier than those in the past and are far more likely to confer such happiness over many years. It is important to remember that the 50 percent divorce rate estimates are calculated in terms of a forty-year period and that many marriages in the past were terminated well before that date by the death of one partner. Historian Lawrence Stone suggests that divorce has become "a functional substitute for death" in the modern world. At the end of the 1970s, the rise in divorce rates seemed to overtake the fall in death rates, but the slight decline in divorce rates since then means that "a couple marrying today is more likely to celebrate a fortieth wedding anniversary than were couples around the turn of the century."[15]

A similar polarization allows some observers to argue that fathers are deserting their children while others celebrate the new commitment of fathers to childrearing. Both viewpoints are right. Sociologist Frank Furstenberg comments on the emergence of a "good dad–bad dad complex": Many fathers spend more time with their children than ever before and feel more free to be affectionate with them; others, however, feel more free simply to walk out on their families. According to 1981 statistics, 42 percent of the children whose father had left the marriage had not seen him in the past year. Yet studies show steadily increasing involvement of fathers with their children as long as they are in the home.[16]

These kinds of ambiguities should make us leery of hard-and-fast pronouncements about what's happening to the American family. In many cases, we simply don't know precisely what our figures actually mean. For example, the proportion of youngsters receiving psychological assistance rose by 80 percent between 1981 and 1988. Does that mean they are getting more sick or receiving more help, or is it some complex combination of the two? Child abuse reports increased by 225 percent between 1976 and 1987. Does this represent an actual increase in rates of abuse or a heightened consciousness about the problem? During the same period, parents' self-reports about very severe violence toward their children declined 47 percent. Does this represent a real improvement in their behavior or a decreasing willingness to admit to such acts?[17]

Assessing the direction of family change is further complicated because many contemporary trends represent a reversal of developments that were themselves rather recent. The expectation that the family should be the main source of personal fulfillment, for example, was not traditional in the eighteenth and nineteenth centuries. . . . Prior to the 1900s, the family festivities that now fill us with such nostalgia for "the good old days" (and cause such heartbreak when they go poorly) were "relatively undeveloped." Civic festivals and Fourth of July parades were more important occasions for celebration and strong emotion than family holidays, such as Thanksgiving. Christmas "seems to have been more a time for attending parties and dances than for celebrating family solidarity." Only in the twentieth century did the family come to be the center of festive attention and emotional intensity.[18]

Today, such emotional investment in the family may be waning again. This could be interpreted as a reestablishment of balance between family life and other social ties; on the other hand, such a trend may have different results today than in earlier times, because in many cases the extrafamilial institutions and customs that used to socialize individuals and provide them with a range of emotional alternatives to family life no longer exist.

In other cases, close analysis of statistics showing a deterioration in family well-being supposedly caused by abandonment of tradition suggests a more complicated train of events. Children's health, for example, improved dramatically in the 1960s and 1970s, a period of extensive family transformation. It ceased to improve, and even slid backward, in the 1980s, when innovative social programs designed to relieve families of some "traditional responsibilities" were repealed. While infant mortality rates fell by 4.7 percent a year during the 1970s, the rate of decline decreased in the 1980s, and in both 1988 and 1989, infant mortality rates did not show a statistically significant decline. Similarly, the proportion of low-birth-weight babies fell during the 1970s but stayed steady during the 1980s and had even increased slightly as of 1988. Child poverty is lower today than it was in the "traditional" 1950s but much higher than it was in the nontraditional late 1960s.[19]

WILD CLAIMS AND PHONY FORECASTS

Lack of perspective on where families have come from and how their evolution connects to other social trends tends to encourage contradictory claims and wild exaggerations about where families are going. One category of generalizations seems to be a product of wishful thinking. As of 1988, nearly half of all families with children had both parents in the work force. The two-parent family in which only the father worked for wages represented just 25 percent of all families with children, down from 44 percent in 1975. For people overwhelmed by the difficulties of adjusting work and schools to the realities of working moms, it has been tempting to discern a "return to tradition" and hope the problems will go away. Thus in 1991, we saw a flurry of media reports that the number of women in the work force was headed down: "More Choose to Stay Home with Children" proclaimed the headlines; "More Women Opting for Chance to Watch Their Children Grow."[20]

The cause of all this commotion? The percentage of women aged twenty-five to thirty-four who were employed dropped from 74 percent to 72.8 percent between January 1990 and January 1991. However, there was an exactly equal decline in the percentage of men in the work force during the same period, and for both genders the explanation was the same. "The dip is the recession," explained Judy Waldrop, research editor at *American Demographics* magazine, to anyone who bothered to listen. In fact, the proportion of *mothers* who worked increased slightly during the same period.[21]

This is not to say that parents, especially mothers, are happy with the pressures of balancing work and family life. Poll after poll reveals that both men and women feel starved for time. The percentage of women who say they would prefer to stay home with their children if they could afford to do so rose from 33 percent in 1986 to 56 percent in 1990. Other polls show that even larger majorities of women would trade a day's pay for an extra day off. But, above all, what these polls reveal is women's growing dissatisfaction with the failure of employers, schools, and government to pioneer arrangements that make it possible to combine work and family life. They do not suggest that women are actually going to stop working, or that this would be women's preferred solution to their stresses. The polls did not ask, for example, how *long* women would like to take off work, and failed to take account of the large majority of mothers who report that they would miss their work if they did manage to take time off. Working mothers are here to stay, and we will not meet the challenge this poses for family life by inventing an imaginary trend to define the problem out of existence.

At another extreme is the kind of generalization that taps into our worst fears. One example of this is found in the almost daily reporting of cases of child molestation or kidnapping by sexual predators. The highlighting of such cases, drawn from every corner of the country, helps disguise how rare these cases actually are when compared to crimes committed within the family.

A well-publicized instance of the cataclysmic predictions that get made when family trends are taken out of historical context is the famous *Newsweek* contention that a single woman of forty has a better chance of being killed by a terrorist than of finding a husband. It is true that the proportion of never-married women under age forty has increased substantially since the 1950s, but it is also true that the proportion has *decreased* dramatically among women over that age. A woman over thirty-five has a *better* chance to marry today than she did in the 1950s. In the past twelve years, first-time marriages have increased almost 40 percent for women aged thirty-five to thirty-nine. A single woman aged forty to forty-four still has a 24 percent probability of marriage, while 15 percent of women in their late forties will marry. These figures would undoubtedly be higher if many women over forty did not simply pass up opportunities that a more desperate generation might have snatched.[22]

Yet another example of the exaggeration that pervades many analyses of modern families is the widely quoted contention that "parents today spend 40 percent less time with their children than did parents in 1965." Again, of course,

part of the problem is where researchers are measuring from. A comparative study of Muncie, Indiana, for example, found that parents spent much more time with their children in the mid-1970s than did parents in the mid-1920s. But another problem is keeping the categories consistent. Trying to track down the source of the 40 percent decline figure, I called demographer John P. Robinson, whose studies on time formed the basis of this claim. Robinson's data, however, show that parents today spend about the same amount of time caring for children as they did in 1965. If the total amount of time devoted to children is less, he suggested, I might want to check how many fewer children there are today. In 1970, the average family had 1.34 children under the age of eighteen; in 1990, the average family had only .96 children under age eighteen—a decrease of 28.4 percent. In other words, most of the decline in the total amount of time parents spend with children is because of the decline in the number of children they have to spend time with![23]

Now I am not trying to say that the residual amount of decrease is not serious, or that it may not become worse, given the trends in women's employment. Robinson's data show that working mothers spend substantially less time in primary child-care activities than do nonemployed mothers (though they also tend to have fewer children); more than 40 percent of working mothers report feeling "trapped" by their daily routines; many routinely sacrifice sleep in order to meet the demands of work and family. Even so, a majority believe they are *not* giving enough time to their children. It is also true that children may benefit merely from having their parents available, even though the parents may not be spending time with them.

But there is no reason to assume the worst. Americans have actually gained free time since 1965, despite an increase in work hours, largely as a result of a decline in housework and an increasing tendency to fit some personal requirements and errands into the work day. And according to a recent Gallop poll, most modern mothers think they are doing a better job of communicating with their children (though a worse job of house cleaning) than did their own mothers and that they put a higher value on spending time with their family than did their mothers.[24]

NEGOTIATING THROUGH THE EXTREMES

Most people react to these conflicting claims and contradictory trends with understandable confusion. They know that family ties remain central to their own lives, but they are constantly hearing about people who seem to have *no* family feeling. Thus, at the same time as Americans report high levels of satisfaction with their *own* families, they express a pervasive fear that other peoples families are falling apart. In a typical recent poll, for example, 71 percent of respondents said they were "very satisfied" with their own family life, but more than half rated the overall quality of family life as negative: "I'm okay; you're not."[25]

■ ■ ■

Americans understand that along with welcome changes have come difficult new problems; uneasy with simplistic answers, they are willing to consider more nuanced analyses of family gains and losses during the past few decades. Indeed, argues political reporter E. J. Dionne, they are *desperate* to engage in such analyses.[26] Few Americans are satisfied with liberal and feminist accounts that blame all modern family dilemmas on structural inequalities, ignoring the moral crisis of commitment and obligation in our society. Yet neither are they convinced that "in the final analysis," as David Blankenhorn of the Institute for American Values puts it, "the problem is not the system. The problem is us."[27]

Despite humane intentions, an overemphasis on personal responsibility for strengthening family values encourages a way of thinking that leads to moralizing rather than mobilizing for concrete reforms. While values are important to Americans, most do not support the sort of scapegoating that occurs when all family problems are blamed on "bad values." Most of us are painfully aware that there is no clear way of separating "family values" from "the system." Our values may make a difference in the way we respond to the challenges posed by economic and political institutions, but those institutions also reinforce certain values and extinguish others. The problem is not to berate people for abandoning past family values, nor to exhort them to adopt better values in the future—the problem is to build the institutions and social support networks that allow people to act on their best values rather than on their worst ones. We need to get past abstract nostalgia for traditional family values and develop a clearer sense of how past families actually worked and what the different consequences of various family behaviors and values have been. Good history and responsible social policy should help people incorporate the full complexity and the tradeoffs of family change into their analyses and thus into action. Mythmaking does not accomplish this end.

ENDNOTES

1. Philip Greven, *Four Generations: Population, Land, and Family in Colonial Andover, Massachusetts* (Ithaca, N.Y.: Cornell University Press, 1970); Vivian Fox and Martin Quit, *Loving, Parenting, and Dying: The Family Cycle in England and America, Past and Present* (New York: Psychohistory Press, 1980), p. 401.

2. John Demos, *A Little Commonwealth: Family Life in Plymouth Colony* (New York: Oxford University Press, 1970), p. 108; Mary Ryan, *Cradle of the Middle Class: The Family in Oneida County, New York, 1790–1865* (New York: Cambridge University Press, 1981), pp. 33, 38–39; Carroll Smith-Rosenberg, *Disorderly Conduct: Visions of Gender in Victorian America* (New York: Oxford University Press, 1985), p. 24.

3. Frederick Douglass, *My Bondage and My Freedom* (New York: Dover, 1968), p. 48.

4. David Roediger and Philip Foner, *Our Own Time: A History of American Labor and the Working Day* (London: Greenwood, 1989), p. 9; Norman Ware, *The Industrial Worker, 1840–1860* (New York: Quadrangle, 1964), p. 5; Barbara Wertheimer, *We Were There: The Story of Working Women in America* (New York: Pantheon, 1977), p. 91; Sean Wilentz, *Chants Democratic: New York City and the Rise of the Working Class, 1788–1850* (New York: Oxford University Press, 1984), p. 126.

5. Faye Dudden, *Serving Women: Household Service in Nineteenth-Century America* (Middletown, Conn.: Wesleyan University Press, 1983), p. 206; Susan Strasser, *Never Done: A History of American Housework* (New York: Pantheon, 1982); Lawrence Glasco, "The Life Cycles and Household Structure of American Ethnic Groups," in *A Heritage of Her Own: Toward a New Social History of American Women*, ed. Nancy Cott and Elizabeth Pleck (New York: Simon & Schuster, 1979), pp. 281, 285.

6. Robert Bremner et al., eds., *Children and Youth in America: A Documentary History* (Cambridge: Harvard University Press, 1970), vol. 1, p. 39; Barbara Cross, *Horace Bushnell: Minister to a Changing America* (Chicago: University of Chicago Press, 1958); Ann Douglas, *The Feminization of American Culture* (New York: Knopf, 1977), p. 52.

7. Peter Laslett, "Characteristics of the Western Family Over Time," in *Family Life and Illicit Love in Earlier Generations*, ed. Peter Laslett (New York: Cambridge University Press, 1977); William Goode, *World Revolution and Family Patterns* (New York: Free Press, 1963); Michael Anderson, *Family Structure in Nineteenth-Century Lancashire* (Cambridge, England: Cambridge University Press, 1971); Tamara Hareven, ed., *Transitions: The Family and the Life Course in Historical Perspective* (New York: Academic Press, 1978); Tamara Hareven, "The Dynamics of Kin in an Industrial Community," in *Turning Points: Historical and Sociological Essays on the Family*, ed. John Demos and S. S. Boocock (Chicago: University of Chicago Press, 1978); Linda Gordon, *Heroes of Their Own Lives: The Politics and History of Family Violence, 1880–1960* (New York, Viking, 1988).

8. For examples of the analysis of the Chicago School, see Ernest Burgess and Harvey Locke, *The Family: From Institution to Companionship* (New York: American Book Company, 1945); Ernest Mowrer, *The Family: Its Organization and Disorganization* (Chicago: University of Chicago Press, 1932); W. I. Thomas and F. Znaniecki, *The Polish Peasant in Europe and America*, 5 vols. (Boston: Dover Publications, 1918–20). On families in the Depression, see Steven Mintz and Susan Kellogg, *Domestic Revolutions: A Social History of American Family Life* (New York: Free Press, 1988), pp. 133–49, quote on p. 136.

9. Glen Elder, Jr., *Children of the Great Depression: Social Change in Life Experience* (Chicago: University of Chicago Press, 1974), pp. 64–82; Lillian Rubin, *Worlds of Pain: Life in the Working-Class Family* (New York: Basic Books, 1976), p. 23; Edward Robb Ellis, *A Nation in Torment: The Great American Depression, 1929–1939* (New York: Coward McCann, 1970); Ruth Milkman, "Women's Work and the Economic Crisis," in *A Heritage of Her Own: Toward a New Social History of American Women*, ed. Nancy Cott and Elizabeth Pleck (New York: Simon & Schuster, 1979), pp. 507–41.

10. Rudy Ray Seward, *The American Family: A Demographic History* (Beverly Hills: Sage, 1978); Kenneth Winkle, *The Politics of Community: Migration and Politics in Antebellum Ohio* (New York: Cambridge University Press, 1988); Michael Weber, *Social Change in an Industrial Town: Patterns of Progress in Warren, Pennsylvania, from the Civil War to World War I* (University Park: Pennsylvania State University Press, 1976), pp. 138–48; Stephen Thernstrom, *Poverty and Progress* (Cambridge: Harvard University Press 1964).

11. Edward Kain, *The Myth of Family Decline: Understanding Families in a World of Rapid Social Change* (Lexington, Mass.: D. C. Heath, 1990), pp. 10, 37; Theodore Caplow, "The Sociological Myth of Family Decline," *The Tocqueville Review* 3 (1981): 366; Howard Bahr, "Changes in Family Life in Middletown, 1924–77," *Public Opinion Quarterly* 44 (1980): 51.

12. *American Demographics*, February 1990; Dennis Orthner, "The Family in Transition," in *Rebuilding the Nest: A New Commitment to the American Family*, ed. David Blankenhorn, Steven Bayme, and Jean Bethke Elshtain (Milwaukee: Family Service America, 1990), pp. 95–97; Sar Levitan and Richard Belous, *What's Happening to the American Family?* (Baltimore: Johns Hopkins University Press, 1981), p. 63.

13. Daniel Kallgren, "Women Out of Marriage: Work and Residence Patterns of Never Married American Women, 1900–1980" (Paper presented at Social Science History Association Conference, Minneapolis, Minn., October 1990), p. 8; Richard Sennett, *Families Against the City: Middle Class Homes in Industrial Chicago, 1872–1890* (Cambridge: Harvard University Press, 1984), pp. 114–15.

14. Mary Jo Bane, *Here to Stay: American Families in the Twentieth Century* (New York: Basic Books, 1976); Stephen Nock, *Sociology of the Family* (Englewood Cliffs, NJ.: Prentice Hall, 1987); Kain, *Myth of Family Decline*, pp. 71, 74–75; Joseph Veroff, Elizabeth Douvan, and Richard Kulka, *The Inner American: A Self Portrait from 1957 to 1976* (New York: Basic Books, 1981); Norval Glenn, "The Recent Trend in Marital Success in the United States," *Journal of Marriage and the Family* 53 (1991); Tracy Cabot, *Marrying Later, Marrying Smarter*

(New York: McGraw-Hill, 1990); Judith Brown, *Sanctions and Sanctuary: Cultural Perspectives on the Beating of Wives* (Boulder, Colo.: Westview Press, 1991); Maxine Baca Zinn and Stanley Eitzen, *Diversity in American Families* (New York: Harper & Row, 1987).

15. Dorian Apple Sweetser, "Broken Homes: Stable Risk, Changing Reason, Changing Forms," *Journal of Marriage and the Family* (August 1985). Lawrence Stone, "The Road to Polygamy," *New York Review of Books*, 2 March 1989, p. 13; Arlene Skolnick, *Embattled Paradise: The American Family in an Age of Uncertainty* (New York: Basic Books, 1991), p. 156.

16. Frank Furstenberg, Jr., "Good Dads-Bad Dads: Two Faces of Fatherhood," in *The Changing American Family and Public Policy*, ed Andrew Cherlin (Washington, D.C.: Urban Institute Press, 1988); Joseph Pleck, "The Contemporary Man," in *Handbook of Counseling and Psychotherapy*, ed. Murray Scher et al. (Beverly Hills: Sage, 1987).

17. National Commission on Children, *Beyond Rhetoric: A New Agenda for Children and Families* (Washington, D.C.: GPO, 1991), p. 34; Richard Gelles and Jon Conte, "Domestic Violence and Sexual Abuse of Children," in *Contemporary Families: Looking Forward, Looking Back*, ed. Alan Booth (Minneapolis: National Council on Family Relations, 1991), p. 328.

18. Arlene Skolnick, "The American Family: The Paradox of Perfection," *The Wilson Quarterly* (Summer 1980); Barbara Laslett, "Family Membership: Past and Present," *Social Problems* 25 (1978); Theodore Caplow et al., *Middletown Families: Fifty Years of Change and Continuity* (Minneapolis: University of Minnesota Press, 1982), p. 225.

19. *The State of America's Children, 1991* (Washington, D.C.: Children's Defense Fund, 1991), pp. 55–63; *Seattle Post-Intelligencer*, 19 April 1991; National Commission on Children, *Beyond Rhetoric*, p. 32; *Washington Post National Weekly Edition*, 13–19 May 1991; James Wetzel, *American Youth: A Statistical Snapshot* (Washington, D.C.: William T. Grant Foundation, August 1989), pp. 12–14.

20. *USA Today*, 12 May 1991, p. 1A; Richard Morin, "Myth of the Drop Out Mom," *Washington Post*, 14 July 1991; Christine Reinhardt, "Trend Check," *Working Woman*, October 1991, p. 34; Howard Hayghe, "Family Members in the Work Force," *Monthly Labor Review* 113 (1990).

21. Morin, "Myth of the Drop Out Mom"; Reinhardt, "Trend Check," p. 34.

22. "Too Late for Prince Charming," *Newsweek*, 2 June 1986, p. 55; John Modell, *Into One's Own: From Youth to Adulthood in the United States, 1920–1975* (Berkeley: University of California Press, 1989), p. 249; Barbara Lovenheim, *Beating the Marriage Odds: When You Are Smart, Single, and Over 35* (New York: William Morrow, 1990), pp. 26–27; *U.S. News & World Report*, 29 January 1990, p. 50; *New York Times*, 7 June 1991.

23. William Mattox, Jr., "The Parent Trap," *Policy Review* (Winter 1991): 6, 8; Sylvia Ann Hewlett, "Running Hard Just to Keep Up," *Time* (Fall 1990), and *When the Bough Breaks: The Cost of Neglecting Our Children* (New York: Basic Books, 1991), p. 73; Richard Whitmore, "Education Decline Linked with Erosion of Family," *The Olympian*, 1 October 1991; John Robinson, "Caring for Kids," *American Demographics*, July 1989, p. 52; "Household and Family Characteristics: March 1990 and 1989," *Current Population Reports*, series P-20, no. 447, table A:1. I am indebted to George Hough, Executive Policy Analyst, Office of Financial Management, Washington State, for finding these figures and helping me with the calculations.

24. John Robinson, "Time for Work," *American Demographics*, April 1989, p. 68, and "Time's Up," *American Demographics*, July 1989, p. 34; Trish Hall, "Time on Your Hands? You May Have More Than You Think," *New York Times*, 3 July 1991, pp. C1, C7; Gannett News Service Wire Report, 27 August 1991.

25. *New York Times*, 10 October 1989, p. A18.

26. Dionne, *Why Americans Hate Politics*.

27. David Blankenhorn, "Does Grandmother Know Best?" *Family Affairs* 3 (1990): 13,16.

Critical Thinking Questions

1. How does the *ahistorical* nostalgic view of families contrast with the realities and hardships families faced in each historical period from the preindustrial era through the 1950s?

2. How do technology and the media influence cultural perceptions of the health of American families and of characteristics of the ideal family?

3. Evaluate the strengths and weaknesses of Coontz's arguments.

4. What changes in family structure and function might you predict for the twenty-first century? What social and demographic and economic changes would lead to the changes you predict.

2 Gathering and Evaluating Data about Families

"*H*ow is this information relevant or useful to me?" This is a question I am frequently asked by students. I can honestly tell you that the information contained in this chapter and the remainder of the book will make reading the newspaper and watching television more engaging and can even make movie punch lines funnier. Here's why.

Today, reports of what researchers have discovered or concluded are broadcast daily in the media. Newspapers, magazines, morning and afternoon talk shows, and evening news programs contain reports of or references to the conclusions of scientific studies on marriage and family issues. Headlines from *USA Today* proclaim: "Nasty arguing may damage newlyweds' health" and "Taking spouse out to ball game may boost bond." Those who read past these interesting, somewhat sensationalistic headlines learn that researchers have found that negative behaviors during marital quarrels can lead to health problems (September 9, 1993: 1A) and that baseball might promote romance (April 12, 1993: 1D). Such conclusions are not very meaningful without knowing how scientific research should be conducted and how these particular studies were conducted. After learning more about research methods in this chapter, you will find watching television reports and reading newspaper and magazine accounts of scientific studies more interesting.

One cannot go to the movie theatre these days without finding references to family studies. A comic theme running through *Sleepless in Seattle* is reference to a study in which researchers allegedly conclude that single women over age 40 have a better chance of being killed by a terrorist than getting married. The male characters in the movie assert these research findings as "fact," whereas the female characters maintain that the study is not true—even though it "feels true." Familiarity with the study the characters are arguing over (which is discussed in Chapter 14, Singlehood in Perspective) makes the scene a lot more funny.

So, although it may not be apparent at the moment, learning to evaluate scholarly research will certainly come in handy time after time. Whether data are presented in the college classroom, on *The Oprah Winfrey Show*, or in a Hollywood production, the ability to critique research studies, assessing their strengths and weaknesses, is a valuable skill. This chapter presents the principles, process, and criteria by which family research should be conducted and evaluated.

Studying Families through Empirical Research

"Absence makes the heart grow fonder." "Out of sight, out of mind." "Opposites attract." "They go together like two peas in a pod." What other clichés in American culture describe intimate relationships? Separately, each expression makes intuitive sense, but taken together, these sayings reveal how people have drawn completely contradictory conclusions about intimate relationships. Which is correct? Do relationships become stronger or weaker when couples are apart? Do people seek out partners who are different from or similar to themselves?

Reliable answers to these questions can be obtained only through **empirical research**—research that has been gathered systematically and without bias. Information based on what one casually notices in a few families is considered **anecdotal data,** and can be used as the basis for a research question but it is not scientifically precise. Empirical studies are guided by a set of common principles and a common procedure known as the **scientific method.**

Process of Empirical Investigation: Using the Scientific Method

What steps or procedures must researchers follow when conducting an empirical study? The first step in the scientific method is to **identify the topic** or question to be studied. This step is not as easy as it appears, for the researcher must identify a topic or question narrow enough to manage yet broad enough to make a significant contribution to his or her knowledge and skills.

After identifying a topic or question, the researcher must then **review the literature** to see what information on the subject is currently available. When I ask students in class discussion to outline the research process, invariably they skip this crucial second step. Reviewing the literature is essential to conducting sound empirical research because investigators must know (1) what other researchers have found when studying the topic, (2) the methods other researchers have used to investigate the topic, and (3) the theoretical explanations that have been offered for the previous findings.

Although a thorough review of the literature is time consuming, in the long run it saves a tremendous amount of work. Researchers might discover studies on the topic they could reproduce, without having to design the research from scratch. Additionally, researchers might uncover instruments used by other investigators to measure the variables in question, freeing them from the tedious, time-consuming task of constructing a new instrument.

Previous research also reveals theoretical frameworks for investigating the topic, a valuable aid to the third step in the research process: **formulating a hypothesis.** After reviewing what other researchers have discovered regarding various aspects of the topic and the theoretical explanations offered, investigators should formulate a specific research question and hypothesize what the outcome should be. A **hypothesis** explicitly states the expected relationship between variables. The remaining steps in the process of scientific investigation are designed to verify or reject research hypotheses.

After formulating a hypothesis, the researcher then must decide the best way to **collect and analyze the data.** The decision about which research strategy to use for a study should be based on the research question. A variety of research strategies are available to researchers, such as surveys, interviews, observational studies, experiments, content analysis, and secondary data analysis. However, the nature of the research question very often eliminates several strategies, leaving the investigator with very few choices.

For example, consider a researcher who decided to study single women involved in sexual relationships with married men (Richardson 1985). She was interested in discovering why women entered into such relationships, how they became involved with the men, what the relationship was like, and if, how, and why the relationship ended. Given her research questions and her intimate and sensitive topic, the choice of research strategies immediately narrowed. Experimental and observational research would not be ethical, practical, or helpful in answering her research questions. Similarly, content analysis and secondary data analysis were eliminated as possible research techniques because they do not involve studying people directly and therefore would not yield the kind of data Richardson needed. Through the process of elimination, Richardson was left with the option of doing a self-report study, either a survey or personal interviews. Because she wanted to understand in depth the women she studied and to probe into their motivations and feelings, she decided that interviewing would be the most appropriate research strategy.

In classes in which a research project is assigned, students often say they want to conduct a survey but cannot decide on a topic. This approach is contrary to the logical process of the scientific method. Research strategies should not dictate topics; rather, topics should suggest research strategies.

The final step in the scientific method is to **disseminate the results** so others have access to the research. Studies that are conducted but never published or presented to others have little scientific value.

Principles of Scientific Investigation

Scientists, regardless of their discipline, must strive to produce research that is **objective, replicable, reliable,** and **valid** (Williamson, Karp, Dalphin, and Gray 1982). In other words, researchers must guarantee that (1) they took precautions to prevent results from being biased, (2) other researchers could repeat the study if they so desired, (3) the findings are not idiosyncratic or skewed, and (4) they accurately measured the constructs and variables they purport to study.

On the surface, these principles seem simple and easy to follow. Closer examination reveals that these principles prove difficult to preserve throughout the research process. The principles of objectivity, replicability, reliability, and validity are ideals that researchers strive to attain but rarely do with complete certainty.

Objectivity

Researchers should not let their personal beliefs bias a study in any way. Objectivity may be particularly difficult to maintain in family studies because all people, including researchers, have been raised in some type of family. As Adams

(1988: 12) suggests, "Everyone is an expert on one or two families, namely, their own, and furthermore, they have values about families." One of the problems inherent in family research is the difficulty researchers have in being value free (or objective), because the subject matter is extremely value laden (Adams 1988).

Clearly, objectivity is an ideal, and an elusive one at that. Social scientists are not robots; they cannot completely separate their values and their experiences from their research. Even the selection of a research topic may reveal some particular interest the investigator has. For example, people who have experienced divorce may be interested in studying the effects of divorce on children. People who have experienced the death of a child may be interested in studying the impact of this tragedy on marriages. Additionally, researchers usually begin projects with some idea of what they think they will find, because making hypotheses is an important part of the scientific method. However some researchers conducting studies might be swayed to draw conclusions that will influence public policy in a desired direction in which case objectivity is compromised.

Being objective does not require that researchers must be completely detached from the topic. However, the principle of objectivity does require researchers to construct, conduct, and interpret research without regard to their particular interest in the subject or the hypothesis they hope to confirm. Everyone has ideas about what should and should not occur in families, what is acceptable and unacceptable; yet these attitudes should not bias or prejudice the empirical study. The process of scientific investigation is designed to maximize the objectivity of research.

Replication

Research should be conducted and reported so that the study could be repeated (or replicated) by others (Williamson et al. 1982). In practical terms, this means that researchers must explain in detail the methods they used to conduct the study. Information about how the research was conducted, who was studied, and how people were selected for the study must be reported in minute detail. For example, a report of an experiment or survey should include *verbatim* the instructions given to the participants. A brief perusal of a scholarly journal illustrates just how meticulous researchers must be in reporting the method by which they collected data.

Detailed information about how a study is conducted allows other social scientists to repeat the study. Researchers may desire to repeat a study to corroborate it or to find the limits of its generalizability. Replication allows researchers to repeat a study using a slightly different sample to see how the results compare to the original study. For example, a study conducted using only male respondents may be replicated using a female sample to see if the findings change or remain the same. A study also may be replicated if the findings are particularly puzzling or unexpected; researchers might repeat the study to see if they get similar results. Replicating a study helps establish the reliability of the measures used in the research.

Reliability

In conducting research, investigators must construct measures to assess the variables being studied. Measures must be both reliable and valid. For example, a researcher interested in finding out if there is a relationship between family size and family dysfunction must devise methods to measure both family size and family dysfunction. Family size is not difficult to ascertain, but the researcher must also construct an instrument to assess how "dysfunctional" a family is.

Reliability thus refers to the *"accuracy* or *precision* of a measuring instrument" (Kerlinger 1973: 443). Synonyms for *reliability* include *dependability, predictability, stability,* and *consistency* (Kerlinger 1973: 442). Reliability is established when an instrument yields similar results after being repeatedly administered to similar populations. Returning to the earlier example, to be reliable, a measure of family dysfunction must consistently and accurately assess dysfunctional families when administered to similar populations over time.

It is difficult to establish reliability in family research because families and children are dynamic and ever changing (Copeland and White 1991). Researchers believe that families that are flexible and adapt well to change are healthy, or functional. Thus, as Copeland and White (1991) point out, a *healthy* family is one that may show inconsistent scores when a test is administered several times. Researchers must decide if such inconsistency indicates poor reliability of the measuring instrument or healthy flexibility in the family.

Validity

Measuring instruments must be valid as well as reliable. The definition of *validity* is presented in the form of a question: "Are we measuring what we think we are measuring?" (Kerlinger 1973). A valid instrument is one that measures what the researcher designed the instrument to measure.

Validity often is best understood in connection with reliability. As an example, consider an instrument designed to measure the concrete variable *speed.* Traditionally, speed is measured using a speedometer. Imagine that an automobile manufacturer has replaced speedometers with new instruments to measure speed called "computer chip MPH gauges." While driving a car with the new MPH gauge, a student is stopped for speeding. He is almost certain he was traveling the posted 30 miles per hour, but he sheepishly and apologetically accepts the speeding ticket when the officer explains she clocked him on her speedometer at 40 miles per hour. The next day, the student carefully monitors his speed, noting that the MPH gauge shows he is traveling at 30 miles per hour. Again he is stopped for speeding. This happens each day for a week. Is the MPH gauge reliable or valid?

Clearly, the instrument is reliable but not valid. The gauge consistently (or reliably) shows the student is traveling 30 miles per hour, but the gauge is not a valid measure of speed. Note that the validity of the instrument was evaluated by assessing how closely the readings on the MPH gauge compared with an accepted, standard measure of speed—a speedometer. Comparing how well the results of the instrument correspond to an already established measure of the variable usually assesses the validity of an instrument.

Unfortunately, establishing the validity of measures used in family research can be difficult. Few variables in family studies are as concrete as velocity. Although standard instruments are available to measure tangible variables such as height, weight, speed, temperature, and the like, there are few standard measures of family dysfunction, marital happiness, or parental effectiveness. Additionally, family research is a relatively new field of study, so "few standards against which one can assess the validity of one's measure" have been developed (Copeland and White 1991: 19).

Research Strategies

As noted earlier, social scientists have a variety of research strategies at their disposal: self-report methods, including surveys and interviews; clinical and participant observation; experiments; content analysis and archival research; and secondary data analysis. Each research strategy has inherent strengths and weaknesses. Some methods, such as surveys and secondary data analysis, emphasize **quantitative research,** which yields numerical and statistical data. Others, such as observational studies, are examples of **qualitative research,** which focuses more on describing data. Mentally compare and contrast the research strategies as they are examined. Try to identify the trade-offs social scientists make when they select one research method over another.

Self-Report Research Strategies

Debate has raged since the inception of family studies about the value of self-report data (Nye 1988). On one side are the scholars who argue that individuals do not give frank and honest answers to intimate questions about family life. The solution, they suggest, is to devise indirect measures from which inferences can be drawn concerning intimate relationships. Others argue that for some issues adequate information can be obtained only by asking respondents questions directly (Nye 1988). These scholars point out that often the only way to discover people's perceptions and attitudes is to ask them in a survey or interview (Copeland and White 1991). Although most family scholars concede the need for self-report data in some circumstances, they also acknowledge that caution must be used in interpreting these data.

The issue of accuracy and honesty of respondents' answers is a concern to researchers using self-report data. Any time a questionnaire or an interviewer asks respondents to describe an event, attitude, or behavior, the possibility arises that the answers are not completely accurate. The same is true when taking individuals' oral histories. However, participants in social science research seldom intentionally distort their responses. Nevertheless, answers may be unintentionally distorted for several reasons. For instance, answers to questions about past events may be distorted because of **inaccurate recall.** In a study of family violence, for example, Straus, Gelles, and Steinmetz (1981: 256) administered a questionnaire in which respondents had to recall how many times in the past year they had a dispute with their spouses in which they "discussed the issue calmly," "cried," "stomped out of the room or house," "slapped the other one," or "used a gun or knife." Responses may not have been entirely accurate simply because people could not remember exactly how many disputes they had with their spouses, much less how the conflict was handled.

Additionally, **selective perception** distorts memory. Some events remain vivid in memory years later, whereas others are quickly forgotten. Respondents in the family violence study, for example, probably recalled more accurately the number of times they "used a gun or knife" against their spouses than the number of times they "discussed an issue calmly."

Self-report data also may be distorted by **social desirability.** Human beings generally want to be perceived favorably by others. Participants may respond to questions in a manner that presents them in the most positive light, even if the response is not completely candid. For example, a friend who just registered her child for kindergarten reported that she had to answer a question about discipline on her child's "social history." Occasionally, this mother, who is an excellent parent, spanks her child, but she did not report this to the school counselor who administered the survey. As this friend explained, "I knew she would think I was a bad parent if I said I spanked my son, so I just told her I used 'time out.'"

Bias in self-report answers can be minimized by proper construction of questions. In Figure 2.1, Copeland and White (1991) provide some excellent guidelines for constructing self-report questions for surveys or interviews. Self-report studies vary in format. Respondents can be asked open-ended or closed-ended questions over the telephone, in person, or through an anonymous questionnaire. The format in which the self-report study is conducted also influences the quality of the data.

Survey Research

Surveys are preferred by researchers because they are easy to administer, save time, and are ideal for studying large numbers of people. As Kinsey argued in 1948, investigators "can secure a couple of hundred" questionnaires in the same amount of time that "another person, using a personal interview technique, needs to contact, win and secure" a single interview (cited in Broderick 1988: 575). Larger sample sizes yield results that are more **generalizable,** or applicable, to those in the population being studied. Questions on surveys tend to be closed ended (Copeland and White 1991). All respondents are asked the same questions in the same order, thus the data are consistent and comparable. Additionally, questionnaires can be completed anonymously, so respondents may feel more comfortable giving honest responses.

Figure 2..1

Guidelines for Writing Self-Report Items (and Examples of Some Failures)

1. All questions should be clear and unambiguous.

    Failure: How is your family?

2. The vocabulary used in the items should be appropriate to the educational level and experience of your respondents.

    Failure: I am interested in learning about families. Would you call your family enmeshed or disengaged?

3. The questions should not demand information your respondents do not have.

    Failure: How do you think your spouse *really* feels deep down inside about the way you make love?

4. You should present a clear frame of reference for the questions so that your subjects interpret the questions the way you do, or be prepared to elicit *their* frame of reference.

    Failure: I am interested in families. So, what is your spouse like? (The respondent has no idea whether you are interested in the partner's sex role, way of dealing with conflict, feelings about the marriage, and so forth.)

5. Focus each item on a single idea rather than touch on separate problems that might or might not evoke similar responses.

    Failure: Would you say you and your spouse have problems in communicating or do you have a pretty good marriage?

Source: From A. P. Copeland and K. M. White, *Studying Families*, p. 32, copyright © 1991 by Sage Publications. Reprinted by permission of Sage Publications, Inc.

However, surveys present special difficulties, as well. Answers on surveys do not reveal much detail about the respondent's attitudes. An *X* in a box labeled "strongly agree" does not tell the researcher why the respondent agrees or under what conditions the respondent may disagree. Participants have a tendency to complete surveys quickly, without carefully considering each question. Often, they will read the first few questions and then respond to the remainder of the survey with similar answers. Researchers have called this *yea-saying, nay-saying,* and *hugging the middle,* although the technical term for intentionally clustered answers is **response set bias** (Copeland and White 1991). Response set biases threaten the validity of the survey.

The questionnaire item that follows, designed to measure gender ideology, illustrates the methodological issues raised by surveys and self-reports. Respond to each statement with "strongly agree," "agree," "disagree," or "strongly disagree":

1. Wives should obey their husbands.
2. Men cannot respect a fiancée who has had sex before marriage.
3. Husbands should have the main say in marriage.
4. Women's liberation makes sense.
5. Women should not have authority over men.
   (Glaser and Polisar 1988: 668)

This gender ideology item can be administered to many individuals quickly and responses are easy to tabulate. However, responses could be biased by social desirability. (Few today would feel comfortable admitting they "strongly agreed" that "wives should obey their husbands.") Responses also could be inaccurate because of carelessness. For instance, participants may disagree with the first two or three statements and continue to mark "disagree" on other statements without noticing that statement number 4 is quite different from the others. Additionally, responses may give superficial information because participants cannot reveal the rationale behind their answers. Researchers might interpret agreement with the statement "Women should not have authority over men" as an expression of a conservative gender ideology. However, some respondents may agree with the statement because they believe that men and women should be equal and neither sex should have authority over the other. The validity of a measure is threatened when researchers cannot be certain of the reasoning behind the answers.

Interviews

When the field of family studies was first established, researchers were skeptical of interviews (Broderick 1988). Scholars were concerned that respondents would feel uncomfortable discussing private family issues with a researcher who is a virtual stranger. Additionally, family studies was heavily influenced by social workers concerned about correcting family problems rather than just studying them. Social workers argued that it may be unethical to interview a family, identify a set of problems, and then leave without conducting a therapeutic follow-up to correct the problems. Nevertheless, by 1938, when the first scholarly family journal was established, interviews already were "becoming part of the standard repertoire of the family researcher" (Broderick 1988: 575).

Interviews permit open-ended questions, which allow respondents to give elaborated answers (Copeland and White 1991). Questions can be asked in different ways to reduce misunderstanding and probe into answers. Open-ended answers may more accurately reflect the respondents' viewpoints, because participants can reply in their own words rather than choosing from a set of responses the researcher has constructed (Fowler 1984). Also, respondents can give answers researchers do not anticipate, leading to unexpected insights.

Data from interviews are difficult to compile because open-ended responses can be worded in a variety of ways. Researchers must be able to group diverse responses with similar meaning. Interviews also are unique and therefore difficult to replicate. Additionally, interviewers may inadvertently influence responses by their body language or vocal intonations (Gano-Phillips and Fincham 1992). Because interviews are more time consuming than surveys, fewer respondents are involved, which limits the generalizability of the findings.

Observational Research

The earliest workers to confront and study family issues were family caseworkers helping poor families as well as psychiatrists treating more affluent families (Broderick 1988). It is not surprising, therefore, that early family research was based largely on data collected from clinical observations and family case studies. At the same time, observational studies account for only about 4 percent of the family studies conducted over the past 50 years (Nye 1988).

One form of observational study in social science research is **participant observation,** in which researchers observe in natural settings and are a part of the situation without necessarily being identified as researchers. For example, a sociologist interested in the social worlds of children or the subculture of childhood might observe children interacting on a playground over a number of weeks or months, whereas a sociologist interested in parent-child interaction might observe many families with young children at the beach or the zoo. The researcher records observations as descriptive field notes for later analysis, which makes these data more subjective and less reliable and replicable than data from surveys. Participant observations, nevertheless, are valuable in family studies for identifying variables, providing content-rich accounts of authentic behavior, and stimulating further scientific inquiry. When you attempt to make objective observations of your family, you are acting as a participant observer.

Observation is advantageous to researchers because several family members can be studied simultaneously. Researchers can witness family dynamics and interaction patterns and discover how the behavior of one family member influences others. Observation allows researchers to learn "what family members actually do in relation to each other, and not just what they say they do" (Copeland and White 1991: 28). Because observational methods do not involve asking participants about themselves or their families, social desirability biases may be avoided.

Conversely, most participants in observational studies know they are being watched and may behave self-consciously rather than naturally (Copeland and White 1991). Additionally, observations may be structured artificially. For example, couples may be asked to discuss an assigned topic while being videotaped, but their contrived, self-conscious behavior may not accurately reflect how they interact at home. Assigning participants interesting tasks in which they become absorbed can minimize staged interaction (Copeland and White 1991). Recording equipment such as cameras and microphones should be inconspicuous to further minimize participants' self-consciousness (Copeland and White 1991).

Clinical observations are another form of observational research usually made in controlled settings using structured situations. Studies based on therapists' or social workers' clinical observations lack comparability because data are not collected systematically from case to case (Broderick 1988). In addition, samples are special populations of families in treatment, which limits the generalizability of findings to other populations. Finally, introducing a therapist or social worker automatically changes the natural dynamics of family interaction (Broderick 1988).

Experimental Research

The use of controlled experiments in family research began in the 1950s (Broderick 1988). Difficulty recruiting participants and the artificiality of experiments has hindered its use in family studies. Subjects are aware that they are being studied in an experiment and are therefore less likely to behave naturally. However, knowledge of parental behavior and child development has been significantly advanced through experimental studies.

All experiments involve an independent variable, a dependent variable, an experimental group, and ideally a control group. The **independent variable** is the variable that is manipulated by the researcher and is administered differently to the experimental and control groups. The **dependent variable** is the variable that is measured to see what impact the independent variable may have had. **Experimental groups** are subjected to the independent variable, whereas **control groups** are not subjected to the independent variable. Experiments are the only research strategy that allows researchers to determine if there is a **cause-effect relationship** between variables in which one variable causes the other to change or occur. Other research methods can establish a **correlation** between variables—that two variables are somehow related—but cannot be used to determine causality.

Most family studies professionals have observed children who appear to act more aggressively after viewing television programs that contain violent scenes. To empirically test whether violent programming causes children to behave aggressively, an experiment would have to be conducted. Many factors other than television programs can contribute to aggressive behavior in children, such as missing a nap, a lack of verbal skills, witnessing violence between family members, and individual temperament. Only in an experiment can researchers control the setting such that other explanations for aggression can be eliminated.

An experiment to determine whether violence in television programs causes children to behave aggressively might be constructed in the following way: A researcher recruits a group of children the same age (with their parents' consent, of course) from similar racial, ethnic, and socioeconomic backgrounds. The children are randomly divided into two groups. One group—the experimental group—is shown a program containing violence, such as *Power Rangers*. The other group is shown a program containing no violence, such as *Mr. Rogers' Neighborhood*. Afterwards, both groups of children are observed playing in a room. Researchers systematically record the number of aggressive acts each child engages in, and then determines if the children who saw *Power Rangers* displayed more acts of aggression than the children who watched *Mr. Rogers' Neighborhood.* Can you identify the independent and dependent variables in this experiment? If you said the independent variable was exposure to violent programming and the dependent variable was the number of aggressive acts the children displayed, you are correct.

Archival Research and Content Analysis

Self-selection and social desirability biases can be avoided completely by utilizing documents rather than people as data sources. Family studies can be conducted through **archival research,** the study of public documents such as birth, death, and marriage records (Jones 1985). Additionally, researchers can study the contents of texts such as diaries, speeches, newspapers, song lyrics, and magazine articles—a research strategy known as **content analysis.** Analysis of personal documents such as letters and autobiographies as well as oral histories helps us understand family interaction patterns in the past (Broderick 1988). Researchers must be aware, however, that the quality of the data depends on the consistency and accuracy of the records being studied.

Secondary Analysis of Data

Obtaining data from large, nationally representative samples is time consuming and expensive. As a result, researchers increasingly utilize existing data sets rather than collect their own data to examine research questions—a process known as **secondary analysis of data** (Copeland and White 1991). Secondary analysis of data is not simply reanalyzing data; it is using previously collected data to answer a question not intended in the original study (Copeland and White 1991).

The past 50 years have seen a dramatic increase in national surveys and the number of family studies involving secondary data analysis (Nye 1988). When family research was formally recognized as a field of scholarly inquiry in the 1930s, studies of nationally representative samples were rare; even the U.S. Census did not yet include much information valuable to family scholars, beyond basic demographic variables (Broderick 1988). The development of sophisticated computer and statistical technology has contributed greatly to the increased use of secondary analysis of data.

The primary advantage of secondary data analysis is that it adds value to data that were very time consuming and expensive to collect (Miller, Rollins, and Thomas 1982). Secondary analysis also takes advantage of high-quality data from nationally representative studies, often superior to what researchers could collect in their local areas (Miller, Rollins, and Thomas 1982). The large sample size from which the data are collected and the carefully constructed sampling process increase the generalizability of the findings. The primary disadvantage is that preexisting data may imperfectly fit the researcher's needs (Copeland and

White 1991: 78). Researchers must accept whatever measures of variables were used in the initial survey (Nye 1988), and questions asked of respondents cannot be reworded (Miller, Rollins, and Thomas 1982).

Secondary analysis of data involves sophisticated statistical procedures difficult for most readers to understand. Nye (1988) argues that only about 5 percent of the readers understand the statistical charts and mathematical calculations commonly used in reports of these studies. The conclusions or the significance of the findings are difficult to grasp.

Utilizing Multiple Methods

All research strategies inherently have strengths and weaknesses. By selecting survey research over interviews, researchers gain the ability to gather quantifiable data that are more generalizable than interview data. In return, the flexibility and detail that are inherent in interviews are sacrificed. In an experiment, researchers have complete control over the environment, but they must be wary that subjects will not behave as naturally as they would in their homes.

If possible, data should be gathered using multiple research methods. When several techniques are used to investigate a research question, the strengths of one method can overcome the weaknesses of another. For example, survey data supplemented with interview data can provide researchers with both quantifiable, generalizable data and detailed oral explanations. Unfortunately, time and budget constraints prohibit most researchers from utilizing multiple research strategies to gather data for a single project.

Additional Challenges Studying Families

As you have seen, family scholars must separate their personal biases from their scholarship and establish the reliability and validity of measures they use. Their work is affected by the dynamic nature of families and the often imprecise, or "soft," variables studied in family research (Adams 1988). Because the family is perceived as a private institution, problems of inaccurate responses and low response rate may be exaggerated in family scholarship. Additional methodological problems also must be addressed.

Defining Family

Throughout the research process, concepts must be operationally defined. An **operational definition** refers to how a researcher makes an abstract concept measurable for the purposes of a particular study. In family research, the most basic concept—family—can be defined in many ways. The operational definition of

What research strategies do sociologists use to gather data about families? How is the family defined and how does it operate as a unit of analysis? What special challenges do sociologists face in doing family research?

family adopted by a researcher establishes the parameters of the sample. In other words, who is included in the study depends on how the researcher has operationally defined *family*. The diverse and changing nature of families complicates constructing an operational definition. Copeland and White raise the following questions researchers must consider when defining the parameters of family:

1. Do the child-rearing adults in the family have to be married to each other to be included in the definition of a family? At what point does a mother's boyfriend become a father substitute? What about homosexual partners?
2. In single-parent families, does the "family" include the noncustodial parent? What if there is joint custody? If both parents have remarried, is the child considered to have two families?
3. In stepfamilies and reconstituted families, how soon after marriage is the new family considered the meaningful family for the members? Immediately? After a month? A year? (1991: 3)

In a particular study, the research question determines the operational definition used. For instance, the operational definition of *family* in a study of dual-career couples will differ from the definition used in a study of divorced mothers. Divergent definitions of terms used in research undermine comparisons between studies. For example, a study of child abuse in which *family* is operationalized as "parents identified by social services as abusive" probably will yield very different results than a study in which *family* is operationally defined as "randomly selected households in which one or more adults lives with one or more children."

The Family as the Unit of Analysis

Studying families—that is, using families as the unit of measurement—raises the question of how to construct valid measures of families. Much family scholarship has the individual rather than the family unit as the focus (Szinovacz 1983). Researchers also tend to use only one individual, usually the wife, to represent "couples" (Szinovacz 1983). However, data gathered from one person in the family cannot be a valid measure of the family as a whole.

Many researchers study several family members and combine their scores to represent the family. Although this approach comes closer to studying the family unit, it is not perfect. When family members give dramatically different answers, researchers must determine if the differences are due to ambiguous questions, inaccurate recall, social desirability, or more substantive reasons, such as differing perceptions of marital issues (Szinovacz 1983). Furthermore, every "family is greater than the sum of its parts," and using aggregate data fails to capture the family unit as it is experienced by its members (Walters, Pittman, and Norrell 1984: 497). Developing measures for studying the family as the unit of analysis remains a challenge.

Sampling Issues

Sampling is "a procedure by which we can infer the characteristics of a large body of people (called a **population**) by talking to only a few people (a **sample**)" (Backstrom and Hursh-César 1981: 52). A good sample is one that is appropriate to the research question and representative of the whole so that answers obtained from the sample are generalizable (or applicable) to the larger population. Generalizability and accuracy (reliability) of responses increase when the sample is selected by using the laws of mathematical probability (a *probability sample*) rather than the researcher's personal preference (a *nonprobability sample*) (Backstrom and Hursh-César 1981).

However, obtaining a random (probability) sample in family studies is often very difficult or impractical. As noted earlier, because the family is perceived as a private institution, many people refuse to be studied. Even the most carefully constructed random sample can be biased by a low response rate. Furthermore, random samples often are impractical because they may not yield many families with the characteristics under study. For instance, a random sample of several thousand households is likely to uncover very few homosexual couples who have adopted children. If homosexual couples who have adopted children are the focus of the study, a nonprobability sample of members of a gay and lesbian support group would be more fruitful.

All researchers must carefully draw their sample of respondents to avoid bias. However, even the most carefully planned random sample of respondents can be biased if the majority of those contacted refuse to participate in the study. Response rates tend to be very low in family research. Studies of divorce over the past two decades, for example, have reported response rates ranging from 11.5

percent to 39.5 percent. Response rates between 17 percent and 22 percent are common in family research (Braver and Bay 1992). **Low response rates** are problematic for researchers for several reasons. First, low response rates reduce the sample size and therefore limit the generalizability of the results. Second, low response rates can create a self-selection or nonresponse bias if participants in the study differ from nonparticipants on a variable significant to the study. **Self-selection biases** are particularly difficult to detect. Researchers have virtually no information about those who do not respond to a survey or refuse to participate in an interview, and therefore they have trouble ascertaining whether the respondents and nonrespondents differ on any of the variables being studied.

Several methods of detecting self-selection bias have been proposed. One suggestion is to ask those who refuse to participate to provide some basic demographic data and a brief explanation of why they declined to participate (Hiller and Philliber 1985). Alternatively, family researchers can utilize public records such as marriage, birth, divorce, and death records to detect self-selection bias (Braver and Bay 1992).

Comparison Groups

Comparison (or control) groups are necessary for researchers to establish that the independent variable alone is responsible for the change in the dependent variable. Ideally, researchers randomly assign individuals to either the experimental group or the control group to minimize bias. In family research, random assignment of individuals to groups is impossible when studying certain topics. For example, participants cannot be randomly assigned to "divorced" or "intact" families, "abusive" or "loving" parents, or "poor" or "wealthy" households. Therefore, researchers can never be certain that the independent variable, rather than some preexisting difference, accounts for the differences detected between groups.

Research Ethics

Researchers must follow an established set of principles when studying human subjects. At the most basic level, participants cannot be harmed either physically or emotionally. Participants must be informed of any risks involved in the research and must consent to participate in the study. All researchers must obtain **informed consent** from participants before including them in the study. Subjects must be given the right to refuse to participate or to terminate their participation at any time during the research process without penalty.

Furthermore, the **confidentiality** of responses and the **anonymity** of the respondents must be maintained. Researchers must avoid deception as much as possible and must tell participants at the end of the study exactly what they were investigating. Finally, scholars must demonstrate that the results of the study will make a significant contribution to knowledge or application.

Evaluating Family Scholarship: A Checklist

Scientific issues are common to all researchers as well as specific to family research. Keep these issues in mind as you evaluate the samples of family scholarship presented throughout this book and in media reports. The following questions should be considered when evaluating empirical research:

1. What is the topic being studied?

2. What has previous research revealed about the topic? How have other scholars studied the topic?

3. What is the research hypothesis in the present study? Is the theoretical rationale for the hypothesis clear?

4. How is the hypothesis being investigated? What research strategy is being used to gather data?

5. Who is being studied? How and why was this sample selected? How generalizable are the findings to the population the sample represents?

6. Are constructs and variables clearly defined? Are the operational measures of variables reliable and valid?

7. What are the potential sources of bias in the study? What measures have been taken to avoid bias?

8. How are the data analyzed? Are the results and conclusions communicated clearly?

9. Why are the conclusions important? What did the researchers find that was unique or surprising? What implications do the conclusions have for social policy?

10. Were the ethical principles guiding research on human subjects followed? What measures were taken to protect the rights of the participants?

Summary

Research on families is conducted using the scientific method, a five-step process in which researchers identify a topic, review the literature, formulate a hypothesis, collect and analyze data, and disseminate results. Researchers must strive to conduct studies that are objective, replicable, reliable, and valid.

Many techniques for collecting data are available, including self-report methods, observation, experiments, content analysis and archival research, and secondary data analysis. In deciding which method to use, one must consider the research question as well as the advantages and disadvantages of each strategy. Ideally, studies should be conducted using several research methods, although time and cost considerations often prohibit such thorough data collection.

Family scholars often face additional challenges conducting research. Constructing a precise definition of family, studying the family as a unit, obtaining samples that will yield generalizable findings, and having comparison groups are all difficult tasks in family research. All scholarship must be conducted ethically, taking extra care to protect participants' rights.

Readings for In-Depth Focus

The Personal Experiences of Divorced Mothers

Divorce is common in American society. Much research has been conducted examining the impact of divorce on children and low–socioeconomic status–women, but relatively little information has been available on divorce in middle-class families. Terry Arendell sought to fill that void with the research she describes in the following reading.

Ultimately, Arendell concludes that the primary problem middle-class, single-parent women face after divorce is a sharp drop in income. In fact, divorce caused 90 percent of the women in her study to fall immediately below the poverty line. Gender bias in employment and laws governing divorce, alimony, and marital property contribute to the economic decline. The women Arendell studied tried hard to help their children cope with the changes created by divorce, particularly the loss of the daily presence of a father, economic hardship, and an overburdened mother. Although most children adjusted well, the effort it took the women to provide financial and emotional support prohibited them from developing other intimate relationships and proved exhausting.

As you read the description of her research methods, notice the detail Arendell provides regarding each step in the data-collection process. Why is such detail necessary? Be sure to note how the sample was selected, the sample size, and the participants' characteristics. Consider why she selected that particular research strategy, and ask yourself if you would have approached the topic similarly. What are the strengths and limitations of her study?

■ ■ ■

Methods, Sources, and Research Needs

Terry Arendell

SUBJECTS

I began my effort to construct a random sample of divorced mothers by consulting the public records of the superior courts in two Bay Area counties. I collected the names of two hundred women who had received final decrees of divorce at least two years earlier and then sent each one a letter describing the project and inviting her participation. The response was poor, chiefly because so many of the recorded addresses were out of date; over half the letters were returned because the post office could find no forwarding address. From among the women I was able to make contact with, twenty ultimately met the criteria for being interviewed and were willing to participate in the study. In ideal circumstances (without constraints of time or money), all subjects would have been located through public records in order to avoid some of the dangers of self-selection by subjects. But after discussions with my dissertation committee and other researchers, I decided that other means of contacting divorced women could appropriately be used.

Subsequently, I contacted divorced women by leaving announcements of the project at various places: a child care center, a latchkey program, two workplaces that employed hundreds of persons in a wide variety of jobs, and two large urban churches that sponsored adult singles' groups. Unexpectedly, a newspaper story about the project encouraged interested persons to contact me, by telephone or through the mail, at my expense. The response became almost overwhelming, and I spent many hours on the telephone talking with women who were interested but did not meet the criteria for participation in the study.

I began formally interviewing women in 1983. I stopped interviewing after the sixtieth subject, because by then both the general and the particular aspects of the divorced women's accounts could be "more or less predicted," a strategy summed up by Jacqueline Wiseman (1979:282). The sixty women interviewed lived in six different Northern California counties in the San Francisco Bay Area and as far east as Sacramento. I found no substantial differences between the accounts of the women located through court records and through other means, and no differences that reflected county of residence.

Each interview subject met the following criteria: she was a legally divorced mother who

had not remarried; she had been divorced for more than two years; she had custody of at least one minor child; and she viewed herself as having been "middle class" during marriage. I used two years as the minimum time since divorcing because other researchers have shown that it takes most family units of women and children approximately two years to regain some kind of equilibrium. Because I was interested mainly in examining how divorced mothers had made new arrangements and reached new understandings of their lives, I decided to avoid the complications of studying women who were still caught up in the direct emotional effects of separation. And because I wanted to discover what divorced women with children had to say about their lives as single heads-of-household, I decided not to interview women who shared a residence with an adult male. (According to data from the U.S. Bureau of the Census, the majority of divorced mothers do not pool resources with an adult male.)

I chose to study women who had been "middle class" during marriage because much divorce research has traditionally focused on persons of low-income and lower-class status, with the result that many of the stereotypes about divorce reflect an assumption that divorce is not common to the middle class. Recent studies using descriptive statistical data, such as the University of Michigan's longitudinal Panel Study of Income Dynamics, have shown that the dramatic increase in the divorce rate has involved persons of all status groups, and that persons belonging to the "middle class" have been particularly affected by it. Therefore the need to study divorced women of "middle class" status is acute.

My attempt to select women of "middle class" socioeconomic status requires more explanation for it poses many conceptual and definitional difficulties. Family class status is typically measured by the educational and occupational position of the husband, not the wife; researchers have demonstrated that most people tend to rate their personal class status higher rather than lower; and patterns of occupational mobility and economic change tend to be obscured in personal reports. However most wives—and even those who are employed—are economically dependent on their husbands (U.S. Bureau of the Census 1985; Rainwater 1984). People's tendency to rate their socioeconomic class status higher than statistical criteria would suggest can be minimized by asking particular questions. Variations in socioeconomic class status can also be discovered by asking the respondents specific questions about their reports on class status. The women interviewed for this study were well educated and had been married to highly educated men, had economically comfortable family life-styles, and shared an understanding of themselves as belonging to the middle class. I declined offers to interview several women who reported a primary reliance on welfare by more than one generation of women in the family; again, I did this as a precaution, for I had no sure knowledge that they were not in fact "middle-class" women living in unusual circumstances.

Clearly I have not used a perfectly representative sample of all divorced women with children. I have studied the experiences after divorce of sixty individual women, each of whom was a custodial parent, considered herself to have been "middle class" during her marriage, and was a single head-of-household with no adult male in residence. It should be noted, however, that if the sample were truly representative of the general population, the portrayal of women's postdivorce experiences would probably be even more shocking. Census data and other statistics show clearly that divorce has the most devastating economic effects on lower-income and poverty-stricken families; and also that women deserted by husbands or separated without being divorced are the poorest of all categories of low-income women. By limiting my study to divorced women who had not remarried and were not living with an adult male, I have not taken account of all the ways in which women cope with the difficulties of being divorced with children. Divorced mothers living with an adult man, although they may well have other pressing problems in their lives, have more opportunities for relieving financial uncertainties and perhaps also for reducing stress overload, loneliness, and conflicts about "dating" and sexual activity.

INTERVIEWS

Early in my research, I also asked five attorneys who do divorce work (not all of them were specialists in family law) and ten public school teachers to give me their impressions of the effects of divorce on children and family life. These background interviews, which I did not include in the analysis, helped increase my sensitivity to some of the issues that emerged as I began interviewing the divorced mothers.

Before beginning the formal interviews, I developed an interview instrument, reviewed it with several qualitative researchers, and refined it. I pretested it by interviewing five divorced women acquaintances and then revised it again. The instrument listed all the basic questions I wanted to ask in the formal interviews; however, I quickly found that strict adherence to its structure tended to interfere with the interviewee's train of thought, and I soon accepted Norman Denzin's statement that "as a social process, the interview relationship assumes emergent and not wholly predictable dimensions" (1978:171). As a result, the interviews were hugely open-ended but followed a general pattern of questioning. I sought consistency among the interviews by checking to see that each of the particular areas covered by the instrument were discussed at some point in each interview.

I developed questions for the following specific areas: general background information, which included age, level of education, number and ages of children, age at marriage, length of marriage, time divorced, and family socioeconomic status; description of the marriage; the legal aspects of divorce; economic effects of divorce; sources of income, income level, and employment; parenting; domestic activities; leisure activities and dating; relations with the ex-husband and his involvement with the children; kinds of support found available and used; and a personal expression of hopes and fears for the future. I learned from pretesting the interviews that the weakest area of questioning in my early interview instrument was the one concerned with the legal aspects of divorce. Because my assessment was confirmed in the first two formal interviews, I subsequently gave more attention to this facet of divorce. The instrument otherwise proved to be more than adequate.

The interviews were long; most took more than three hours, and several lasted more than five hours. Follow-up interviews were done with five of the women. Fifty-one of the interviews were done in the women's homes, and nine were done either in my office or at the women's places of work. Each woman chose the site of the interview.

All of these women were volunteer subjects who came to the interview with some understanding of my research goals. They were informed that they could redirect the questioning at any point and even stop the conversation if they wanted. Anonymity was assured to the extent possible.

Children freely entered and left the interview situations in over two-thirds of the home interviews. I was usually introduced to them, frequently shown their bedrooms, and sometimes shown pictures of their fathers. Because of the limitations of this research project, I declined many invitations to interview children. However, their presence during parts of the interview sessions gave me an unexpected opportunity to observe parent-child interactions. My observations proved valuable in that they tended to support mothers' assertions about their children.

I tape-recorded the interviews (with the permission of the interviewees) and took some notes during the sessions. I asked questions and sought clarification when I did not understand what was being said, and I also tried to clarify apparent inconsistencies. However, I adopted the premise that the interviewee was the "only possible expert" regarding her own experiences (Schwartz and Jacobs, 1979:73). I actively sought to gain access to each woman's perspective and understanding—to each woman's picture of her own social reality. I recorded my own comments and observations immediately after leaving the interview, often while driving home or to my office.

The cooperation and interest I received from these women exceeded my earliest hopes. Although the subject of divorce and life after divorce was an emotionally painful one, many women told me they felt they had benefited from being able to talk about it with me.

As the interviews proceeded, I began to understand their eagerness and candor. In part, at least, they wanted to break through the sense of isolation they had felt as divorced mothers. The interview gave them an opportunity to express their frustration about social indifference to their situations; it gave them a ray of hope, however slight, that they "might be heard." Further, by sharing their experiences, they felt validated in them. I think this sense of validation was particularly important to most women in regard to their parenting. The desire to have some recognition for their parenting efforts and for their success at maintaining their families, even under adverse conditions, was what led them to invite me to interview their children and tour their homes.

DATA ANALYSIS

I transcribed the tape-recorded interviews in duplicate; one copy was left intact for ready reference to the total interview, and the other was cut apart and used for coding. I analyzed the data according to the procedures delineated by Barney Glaser and Anselm Strauss (1967) and further described by Howard Schwartz and Jerry Jacobs (1979) in their works on grounded theory. I found, as Schwartz and Jacobs have written, that "in grounded theory data collection, observation, coding and categorizing the data, and developing theories all tend to go on simultaneously and to mutually support one another" (28).

As core variables were discerned, I recoded and organized data by the emergent categories. The major categories of these divorced women's experiences were as follows: married and family life; economics and income sources; single parenting; life as a single divorced woman; children; the legal experiences of divorce; relations with family; relations with the ex-husband; sources of logistical and emotional support; and personal assessment. Each of these categories was then broken down into subcategories. Both the categories and the subcategories were revised as coding of the data proceeded.

RESEARCH NEEDS

From my experience with this project, I believe that two kinds of academic studies are needed most urgently: first, sociological studies geared toward the practical development, implementation, and evaluation of programs aimed at meeting the greatest needs of today's divorced mothers; and second, empirical studies of divorced men.

The specific needs of divorced women that ought to be addressed are as follows: a decent and protected minimum income, to be made possible through a variety of sources (themselves open for evaluation and reform), including adequate child support payments and supplementary sources of income; reentry training programs; health insurance and retirement conversion plans; affordable and quality child care; improvement of the work-family relationship by modifications of the workday and work structure; adequate housing; and community and social support programs. Ideally, this type of research will be augmented by continuing longitudinal studies of diverse groups of divorced women: only by following the experiences of women over several years will we be able to discern the short-term and long-term needs that require political action.

The second area in which research is most obviously needed concerns the lives of divorced men. Except for a few studies, which have used predominately psychological approaches to explore attitudes toward intimate relationships and remarriage, men have been ignored in divorce research. We need empirical data on the social and economic factors in men's lives after divorce. We also need to know how they interpret their own experiences of divorce, for many questions remain unanswered. For example, what have been the principal events and influences in divorced men's lives? How has divorce affected their sense of self, their objectives and priorities, their spending patterns? I believe that the actual choices divorced men make about social activity, living arrangements, and spending priorities deserve as much attention as the ways in which they think and feel. We also need more research on how divorced men relate to their children. How do they deal with the fact that their children, in most cases, are living with their former wives? Discovering the factors that contribute to satisfactory or unsatisfactory relations between divorced men and their children could be of great help in planning how to help families make the transitions required by divorce. We also need to know why some men pay child support even while most do not. What kinds of events or understandings alter men's payment patterns? And what kinds of family support resources and services would divorced fathers use if they were available?

Ideally, academic studies of family life and divorce will analyze data on both men's and women's experiences so that they can be contrasted and understood in relation to each other.

Specifically, we need studies of divorced men and women who are parents of minor children, and studies of men and women who divorce after long-term marriages. And of course, the effects of the social definition of gender on the experiences of family life and intimate relationships require continued analysis.

REFERENCES

Denzin, N. (ed.). *Studies in Symbolic Interaction*, vol. 1. Greenwich, CT: JAI Press, 1978.

Glaser, B., and A. Strauss. *The Discovery of Grounded Theory*. Chicago: Aldine, 1967.

Rainwater, L. "Mothers' Contributions to the Family Money Economy in Europe and the United States." In P. Voydanoff (ed.), *Work and Family*. Palo Alto, CA: Mayfield, 1984.

Schwartz, H., and J. Jacobs. *Qualitative Sociology*. New York: The Free Press, 1979.

U.S. Bureau of the Census. *Statistical Abstract of the United States. 1985. National Data Book and Guide to Sources*. Washington, DC: U.S. Government Printing Office, 1985.

Wiseman, J. *Stations of the Lost: The Treatment of Skid Row Alcoholics*. Chicago: University of Chicago Press, 1979.

Critical Thinking Questions

1. Discuss possible biases in Arendell's study.

2. What is the research hypothesis or research question being investigated in the study?

3. How is *socioeconomic status* operationalized? What are the potential biases in the way that social class is measured?

4. What other research strategies could the author have used to study the experiences of divorced women?

5. Do you believe Arendell's description of her research methods is thorough? Why or why not? Is there other information about the study that she should have included? Explain your answer.

3 Theoretical Perspectives in Family Sociology

T *heory*. As an undergraduate student, the word *theory* conjured images of professors endlessly droning on about esoteric ideas that only the elite few could understand. *Theory* was synonymous with *boring, dreadful,* and *useless*. Imagine my surprise to discover that theories offer explanations for a variety of interesting and perplexing questions. Why, in most societies, do women tend to do child care and men the economic labor? Why do some husbands abuse their wives and why do some wives stay in battering relationships? Why do some parents abuse their children? Why do many dual-income couples struggle over child care and household chores? Answers to these and an infinite number of other questions about families interested me. Theories became not only interesting but also exciting as soon as I saw how they were relevant to questions I had.

This chapter introduces three sociological perspectives used to explain family issues. In thinking about how to write a theory chapter that students would find interesting, informative, and engaging, I thought about my own experience. The historical context and the basic assumptions of each theory are explained in contemporary language so that they are easy to comprehend. Furthermore, each theory is applied to family issues in general so that they are not so abstract.

Countless theories are designed to explain family dynamics, but I decided to introduce only the three primary theoretical frameworks in sociology in this chapter: *symbolic interactionism, structural-functionalism,* and *conflict theory*. Each of these general theories is designed to explain a broad range of social phenomena and has generated much research on a variety of family issues. You will see these theories applied to topics in future chapters. Other middle-level theories in family studies also will be introduced in later chapters that discuss particular family phenomena, such as family violence or mate selection.

Theories: What Are They and Why Are They Useful?

"Theorizing is the process of systematically formulating and organizing ideas to understand a particular phenomenon. A theory is the set of interconnected ideas that emerge from this process" (Doherty et al. 1993: 20). As this quote suggests, *theory* can be defined as both a process and a product. *Theorizing* is the process of constructing, organizing, assimilating, and testing ideas. This process is intricately linked with empirical research, through which theoretical ideas are generated and tested. Thomas and Wilcox (1987: 93) describe the process of theorizing as "building increment on increment of one research project after another." The process of theorizing results in a product: theory.

All theories must contain clearly defined concepts. For example, the definitions of concepts (such as *conflict* and *marital satisfaction*) must have the same clear meaning to all researchers applying or testing the theory. Concepts are organized into theoretical statements (or propositions) that describe social phenomena and the relationship between concepts (Turner 1974). Propositions must be testable through empirical research so scholars can reject any assumptions that are not supported by facts (Wilson 1983).

The statement *High levels of marital conflict reduce marital satisfaction* is an example of a theoretical statement. Researchers can investigate whether marital satisfaction declines when marital conflict increases in a couple's marriage. Likewise, marital satisfaction can be compared in couples with high and low levels of conflict. (Notice that, as discussed in Chapter 2, the concepts *marital satisfaction* and *marital conflict* must be operationally defined by the researcher so that they can be measured.) In contrast, the statement *Couples shouldn't fight* is not a theoretical proposition; it is a value judgment. Relationships between variables are not clearly stated, and researchers cannot test this statement through scientific study.

Research and theory (as both process and product) are interdependent or reciprocal. Well-developed theory generates research, and the findings of scientific studies contribute to the further development of theory (Lavee and Dollahite 1991). Although research methods and theories are discussed in separate chapters, it is important to keep in mind that "the heart of any scientific activity rests in the important relationship between theory and research" (Eshleman 1969: 13).

It is also important to remember that neither the process of theorizing nor the theory is ever complete, because theories never can be proven. Although a theory may have been tested repeatedly, there is always the possibility that the next study will disprove it. Theories are constantly tested and revised based on the findings of studies.

Theories and theorizing serve several purposes. First and foremost, theories offer explanations for facts (Kerlinger 1973; Skidmore 1979; Wilson 1983). As sociologist George Homans once argued, "A theory is nothing—it is not a theory—unless it is an explanation" (cited in Gibbs 1972). Theories must offer testable explanations for why a particular phenomenon occurs. In family studies, for example, theories offer explanations for why conflict arises and how conflict can be reduced. Theories also offer explanations for broad questions such as Why do societies have families? and Why do men and women perform different roles in the family? Ultimately, the explanations offered by theories should help shape social policy and inform the decisions and recommendations made by educators and family therapists (Grunebaum 1988; Lavee and Dollahite 1991).

Theories can be both general and specific. Social scientists often operate from general theoretical frameworks or perspectives and the assumptions on which they are based. The three primary theoretical perspectives in sociology are symbolic interactionism, structural functionalism, and conflict theory. Symbolic interactionism first became prominent in family studies between 1918 and 1929, structural functionalism emerged as a dominant perspective between 1930 and

1945, and conflict theory was widely applied to family issues between 1960 and 1980 (Boss et al. 1993). The following time line summarizes the origin of each theoretical perspective in family studies:

1918–1929	1930–1945	1960–1980
Symbolic Interaction	Structural Functionalism	Conflict Theory

Symbolic Interaction Theory

Symbolic interactionism is a theoretical perspective in which human behavior is explained by examining social interaction (Charon 1998). The perspective emerged as a prominent sociological theory during the 1920s—a time in which there was a great deal of public interest in individual psychological health and interpersonal relationships (Doherty et al. 1993; LaRossa and Reitzes 1993). Many people wanted to learn about self-improvement as well as how to enhance family relationships. The emphasis in the symbolic interactionist framework on self-concept, communication, and the importance of relationships to individual well-being corresponded with the popular ideas of the time (Doherty et al. 1993; LaRossa and Reitzes 1993).

Symbolic interaction was also perceived as a refreshing change from other sociological and psychological explanations of human behavior that had been offered. Until symbolic interaction theory was developed, sociologists had explained human behavior as controlled either by biological, institutional, or economic forces. Psychologists argued that individuals were at the mercy of childhood experiences or were simplistic creatures of habit. LaRossa and Reitzes (1993) argue that the symbolic interactionist perspective flourished in the 1920s because it was the one theoretical approach that portrayed individuals as having some control over their lives rather than as being helplessly tossed about by biological, social, or psychological forces.

Sociologists who developed the symbolic interactionist approach, such as George Herbert Mead and Charles Horton Cooley, were reacting against psychologists of their day. During the 1920s, *behaviorism*, also referred to as *stimulus-response theory*, was gaining much attention in psychology. Early behaviorists assumed that all human behavior is a learned (conditioned) response to a stimulus. In other words, behavior was believed to be a "function of the environment" and "not a result of the individual's free will" (Franklin 1982: 132). Furthermore, behaviorists argued that behavior could be understood through objective scientific observation rather than thinking processes, which were deemed too subjective to study (Franklin 1982). Human behavior was portrayed as no different than any other animal's behavior; it was simply a conditioned response to a stimulus.

The classic experiment conducted by John B. Watson and Rosemary Rayner (1920) on Little Albert illustrates the assumptions of stimulus-response theory. In the experiment, an 11-month-old boy named Albert was brought into a laboratory and shown several furry objects, including a rat, a rabbit, a dog, and a mask. Initially, the child was curious and eager to touch these interesting objects. The researchers then placed the rat (the stimulus) in front of Albert, and, as he reached for it, they made a loud noise behind him by striking together two metal bars. The noise frightened Albert (his response). After being subjected to this procedure several times, Albert began to exhibit signs of fear (he cried, "turned, fell over, and crawled away as fast as he could") upon the mere sight of the rat, even when the researchers did not startle him with noise (cited in Zimbardo 1979: 243). Albert's learned fear of rats also extended to the other furry objects, supporting the behaviorists' argument that all behavior is learned.

Basic Premises of Symbolic Interaction Theory

Most symbolic interactionists accept the following propositions:

■ *Human beings are unique creatures because they can create and manipulate symbols.* Symbolic interactionists, unlike behaviorists, believe that human beings are different from all other animals because they have the ability to communicate through a sophisticated system of verbal and nonverbal symbols (Charon 1998). The ability to think in abstract symbolic terms allows individuals to classify their experiences, recall past events, and predict what might occur in the future (Hewitt 1997). In contrast to the simple stimulus-response model proposed by behaviorists, symbolic interactionists believe that human behavior is extremely complex, because it can be influenced both by events that occurred years earlier and by events that have not yet occurred that the individual believes might happen.

The ability to think symbolically also allows human beings to categorize people, objects and events. Hence, it is possible for people to think about themselves and others in broad social categories, such as Caucasian, Mexican, middle class, investment broker, or mother. Symbolic interactionists emphasize the importance of social roles.

■ *The meaning of symbols is created in social interaction.* Symbolic interactionists assert that all people, objects, and events, are, to some extent, social creations because they acquire meaning through the process of social interaction. Herbert Blumer (1969: 12), the sociologist who labeled the perspective *symbolic interaction*, argues that through interaction with others, "the meaning of anything and everything has to be formed, learned, and transmitted." This means that the meanings attached to objects and events are not permanent, but can change over time and in different situations (Blumer 1969). Furthermore, the meaning of objects may vary among individuals and groups. Blumer (1969: 11) offers the following examples: "A tree will be a different object to a botanist, a lumberman, a poet, and a home gardener; the President of the United States can be a very different object to a devoted member of his political party than to a member of the opposition; the members of an ethnic group may be seen as a different kind of object by members of other groups."

From a symbolic interactionist perspective, the meaning of objects to individuals is crucial because "human beings act toward things on the basis of the meanings that the things have for them" (Blumer 1969: 2). In other words, the way individuals perceive objects and events influences their behavior. Using Blumer's example, your perception of the president of the United States may not only influence your voting behavior but it also may determine whether you become actively involved in a particular civic cause, to whom you donate money, or even how well you conform to the policies of the administration.

Symbolic interactionists argue that to understand human behavior, social scientists must understand the meaning that objects have for individuals. Whereas behavioral psychologists believe that human behavior can be understood by observing the stimulus and the response, interactionists argue that the most crucial determinant of human behavior—the interpretation of meaning—occurs in thought after the stimulus and before the response.

■ *Perceptions of situations influence human behavior.* The idea that "human action cannot be understood apart from the subjective interpretations given to situations" (LaRossa and Reitzes 1993: 140) has been labeled the *Thomas Theorem.* Sociologist W. I. Thomas (with his wife Dorothy Swaine Thomas) argues that if *people define situations as real, they are real in their consequences* (Thomas and Thomas 1928: 572). In this statement, the Thomases point out that to understand human behavior fully, both the objective circumstances and the subjective interpretation of the situation (or the definition of the situation) must be analyzed (Franklin 1982). For example, a parent who perceives that a child intentionally broke a family heirloom will behave toward the child very differently than a parent who defines the child's behavior as an accident—regardless of the child's actual motive. Therefore, to understand completely the parent's behavior toward a child, one must know how the parent defines the situation.

By declaring that meaning is created in social interaction, symbolic interactionists acknowledge that human beings have control over their behavior and their environment. Unlike other perspectives, symbolic interactionists do not see individuals as controlled by biological, economic, or psychological forces out of their control. Instead, "human beings are active in shaping their own behavior" (Franklin 1982: 102).

■ *Human beings are born into an ongoing society.* Although symbolic interactionists argue that behavior and meaning are constructed in social interaction, they also recognize that individuals are born into a society in which social meanings have already been constructed (Charon 1998). Human behavior is therefore influenced by social norms and values that individuals learn through **socialization,** the process whereby people learn the norms and values of their culture. By interacting with parents, siblings, peers, teachers, coworkers, religious leaders, and others, people learn what is considered appropriate and inappropriate behavior in different situations, and what is expected of them as members of society.

Symbolic interactionists depict society and individuals as "two sides of the same coin" (Cooley, cited in Stryker 1964). Individuals are born into an ongoing society and are shaped, to some extent, by society. At the same time, individuals shape society through their behaviors, attitudes, and beliefs (Corsaro 1997).

■ *Individuals are not born with a sense of self but develop self-concepts through social interaction* (LaRossa and Reitzes 1993: 144). Symbolic interactionists believe that social interaction is an important process in the development of **self-concept.** Sociologist Charles Horton Cooley (1902) first articulated this view. Cooley argues that an individual's self-concept reflects or mirrors what the individual perceives others in society think of him or her. Hence, the self is a "looking-glass self" (Cooley 1902: 152–153). The looking-glass self has three principal elements: (1) our imagination of how we *appear* to others; (2) our imagination of how others *judge* our appearance; and (3) self-feelings, such as pride or embarrassment, that result from how we *imagine* others have evaluated us (Reynolds 1993).

You probably can recall times when you consciously thought about what others think of you. After being in a new or unfamiliar situation (a first date or a job interview, for example), you might stop to evaluate how you looked to others and how they may have judged you. Cooley argues that how you feel about yourself is shaped in an ongoing fashion by how you think others perceive you in both familiar and unfamiliar situations.

Cooley further argues that the self develops through interaction within **primary groups**—groups "characterized by intimate face-to-face association and cooperation" (Cooley 1909: 23). Cooley identifies the family as the most important primary group, for it is there that children first begin to see themselves as an important part of a social unit (Reynolds 1993). Additionally, family members such as parents, siblings, and other relatives appraise an individual's self-worth and begin to shape the individual's self-concept.

■ *The self is both a process and an object.* George Herbert Mead expanded on Cooley's concept of the self as a product of social interaction. Mead (1934/1962) argues that the self has two components: the *I* (self as process) and the *me* (self as object). The *I* is the acting, behaving human being; it is also the part of the self that is aware of whom we are (Elkin and Handel 1989). The *me* is the accumulated ideas about ourselves that we obtain from others. Thus, Mead argues that self-concept is constantly being acquired as we interact with others. We then can reflect on ourselves, thinking about our behavior and what others might think of us.

Mead also explains how the self develops through social interaction and language. As you have seen, social interaction is necessary for individuals to get appraisals of their actions. Language is necessary for two reasons: to understand others' appraisals of our behavior and to think about ourselves. According to Mead, self-concept is developed through the internal conversations we constantly have with ourselves.

The self develops in several stages. Following a brief period in which children mimic the language and behavior of others without any real comprehension, children enter a *play stage,* in which they learn to take the role of another person (Elkin and Handel 1989). During this stage, children see themselves as separate from others and can play at being someone other than themselves. Children pretend to be mothers, fathers, teachers, police officers, doctors, librarians, and so on. Mead argues that in pretend play, children learn what is expected of people in different **social roles.** Hence, they can pretend to be teachers and praise their pretend students for doing good work. Such play indicates that the child has learned some of the role expectations of teachers (to encourage achievement) and of students (to work hard and do good work).

In the next stage, the *game stage,* children learn to take the role of many others at once. Instead of thinking only about the expectations of their parents or teachers, children can think in broad abstract categories such as family or school. Mead calls this the ability to take the role of the **generalized other.** As LaRossa and Reitzes (1993: 139) explain, "By taking the role of the generalized other, a person is able to interpret the responses of others from the vantage point of societal norms and so more completely and accurately anticipate the responses of others to self behaviors." Children learn that it is not just their particular teachers who expect them to perform academically, but that all teachers expect this of students. By taking the role of the generalized other, children can anticipate how others will react to particular behaviors in different social settings.

Mead's description of the self and how it is acquired incorporates all of the premises of symbolic interaction discussed so far. He assumes that human beings are unique in their ability to communicate and he underscores the importance of language in the development of the self. The *I,* the active, spontaneous part of the self, permits meaning to be constructed in social interaction. However, Mead also acknowledges that much social meaning is a part of the culture into which we are born and that we learn these norms through socialization. For Mead, though, social norms and expectations are more than rules that must be blindly obeyed; they are incorporated into the individual's self (the *me*).

Critics say that symbolic interactionism lacks conceptual clarity, and that concepts such as *self, I,* and *generalized other* are ambiguous and vague, making it difficult to define terms operationally and to use the perspective in empirical research (Reynolds 1993). Critics of symbolic interactionism point out that the symbols and their socially constructed meanings ignore the importance of history, the economy, and power in human affairs (Reynolds 1993).

■   *Human beings must be studied in their natural environment and cultural context.* This final premise of symbolic interaction has three components. First, symbolic interactionists argue that because human beings are unique creatures, they must be studied directly. Unlike stimulus-response theorists, symbolic interactionists argue that the behavior of rats, monkeys, dogs, and other animals cannot be used to understand human behavior (Burr et al. 1979). Second, symbolic interactionists argue that to get an accurate picture of human behavior, people must be studied in their natural environments rather than in a scientific laboratory. Again, symbolic interactionists are reacting to behavioral psychologists who believed that only observable behaviors could be studied through objective experimental research. Third, symbolic interactionists argue that people's thoughts and behaviors cannot be understood separately from their cultural contexts.

From the symbolic interactionist perspective, explanations for much human behavior are not directly observable because they occur in the individual's mind. Human behavior is influenced by cultural constructions of reality and the way individuals perceive situations and themselves. Therefore the job of the sociologist is somehow to observe and understand mental activity (Franklin 1982). Cooley proposed that this could be accomplished only if researchers think like those being studied. In other words, investigators must get to know their subjects so well that they can begin to "see the world from the point of view of [the] subject" (Stryker 1964: 135). Therefore, symbolic interactionists tend to favor qualitative research strategies, such as interviewing and participant observation, which allow researchers to probe into the thought processes of subjects and to understand the motives for their behavior.

Application of Symbolic Interaction Theory to Family Issues

Symbolic interactionism may be used in a variety of ways to understand and explain family issues. The concepts of primary groups, socialization, social roles, self-concept, definition of the situation, and internal conversation are all used to examine family dynamics.

As you have seen, the family is a *primary group* and the primary agent of *socialization*. Symbolic interactionists are interested in how socialization occurs and the impact socialization processes have on individuals. For example, symbolic interactionists have been instrumental in studying gender socialization. They also investigate the impact of socialization in different types of family settings (such as single-parent families, violent families, economically advantaged or disadvantaged families, families of color, and gay or lesbian families) on individuals' behaviors and self-concepts.

What questions might a symbolic interactionist ask about the situation shown in this photograph? What assumptions of symbolic interactionism would be applied and with what outcomes for sociological research? How do the assumptions of the structural-functional perspective differ?

The appraisal individuals receive from family members is crucial in the formation of *self-concept.* Individuals want to be loved, valued, and respected, especially by those who are most important in their lives, such as spouses, parents, siblings, sons, and daughters. When family members evaluate each other positively, self-concept is enhanced; likewise, negative evaluation from family members can be devastating. One of the most important contributions symbolic interaction makes to family studies is "its assertion that individuals develop both a concept of self and their identities through social interaction" (LaRossa and Reitzes 1993: 136).

You probably know individuals who have negative self-concepts, who believe they are ugly or stupid or fat, when objectively this is far from the truth. Symbolic interactionists point out that negative self-concepts develop over time through interactions with others—particularly family members. As a friend, you can communicate to these individuals that they are attractive or intelligent or slender, but you probably will have less influence than a single positive comment from a valued family member.

As a primary agent of socialization, the family also is instrumental in teaching individuals *social roles,* the norms or expectations attached to social positions (Heiss 1981). Family social roles—such as wife, husband, mother, father, daughter, and so on—contain a host of expected behaviors that individuals learn by observing and interacting with family members. Individuals also perform these roles. Individuals know how people in family roles are supposed to behave, and although they do not always conform to these norms, their behavior is influenced by the norms nonetheless. Young mothers who are employed, yet have learned that it is best if mothers of young children stay home, may feel guilty or inadequate for not meeting the role expectations of mother.

The key to understanding the behavior of family members, according to symbolic interactionists, is knowing how the members *define the situation.* Often, family members perceive situations or events differently, which can lead to family conflict. The way family members perceive situations is influenced by their roles in the family. Wives may perceive events differently than husbands, for example, and children may perceive events differently than parents. Family dynamics can be improved and conflict reduced, according to symbolic interactionists, by improving communication between family members. Compromise and reconciliation are more likely when individuals understand how others perceive a situation.

Finally, symbolic interactionists also emphasize the importance of *internal conversations* in self-concept, motivation for behavior, and family dynamics. Frequently, individuals rehearse through internal conversations "an actual interaction that they intend to have, would like to have, or are anxious about having" (Rosenblatt and Meyer 1986: 319). These imagined interactions can help individuals identify their own feelings and gain self-control so they can approach actual interaction better prepared to present their perspective and listen to others' opinions. Most everyone has had an argument with a close friend or family member that left them absolutely furious. Following confrontations, people often spend hours or even days silently debating what they should say or do to respond. They rehearse different scenarios in their minds and imagine what they will say and how the other will respond. Internal conversations can improve family dynamics by allowing people to calm down and decide the most rational, least destructive way to resolve the situation.

Structural-Functional Theory

Structural-functional theory, also known as *functionalism,* emerged in Europe prior to the turn of the twentieth century. If traced back to its philosophical roots, functional theory is the oldest theoretical perspective in sociology (Turner 1974). Europe in the mid- to late 1800s, like the United States, was in the midst of the Industrial Revolution, and many scholars (who would later be called *sociologists*) were trying to explain the vast changes being witnessed in society.

Early functionalists also were influenced by the writings of Charles Darwin. In *The Origin of Species* (1859) and *The Descent of Man* (1871), Darwin proposed that living organisms evolve over time through a process of natural selection. Organisms that were well adapted to their environment survived and reproduced; those that did not survive removed maladaptive qualities from the gene pool. Although Darwin never intended to explain social phenomenon, many social scientists, including functionalists, used his evolutionary principles to explain social order and change.

Structural functionalism began to be used to explain family dynamics in the 1930s and remained prominent into the 1960s (Boss et al. 1993). Family sociologists reinterpreted some of the basic assumptions of the original perspective.

Basic Premises of Structural-Functional Theory

The most basic premise of structural functionalism is that *society is a system of interrelated and interdependent parts* (Winton 1995). Early functionalists, applying evolutionary theory to society, drew the basic analogy that societies are like living, biological organisms or systems. Like all organisms, *societies are comprised of many structures, each of which has unique functions.* The human body, for example, contains a heart, a liver, lungs, kidneys, bones, muscles, a brain, and so on, each of which is necessary to sustain the life and health of the organism. If any of these structures fails or becomes damaged, then the system's delicate equilibrium is disrupted and the body falls ill. Over time or with certain treatments, the body may heal, but if major changes have occurred, the body will never perform as it did before.

The structures of social systems include institutions, such as the family, economy, government, religion, and education. Each of these structures performs functions essential to the maintenance (or continuation) of the social system. A failure or drastic change in any of these structures disrupts the system's equilibrium, leading to social disorganization. Over time, the system may adapt to changes in a particular institution but it will never operate as it once did. Functionalists also argue that individual components of the social system operate as mini-systems. The family is therefore seen as a system consisting of parents, children, and spouses. Every structure, or role, in the family is believed to be essential to the smooth operation of the family unit. These propositions are basic to structural functionalism:

▪ *System components are interdependent.* Functionalism also rests on the premise that the structures within society are interdependent, just as all the organs (or structures) within the human body work together to sustain the organism. Functionalists emphasize the interdependence between parts of the social system. Just as the heart, lungs, liver, kidneys, and so on all work together to maintain the life of the human system, functionalists argue that the economy, family, religion, government, and education all work together to maintain society. Furthermore, the components of each social institution are interdependent. Functionalists argue that in the family, for example, the roles of husband and wife as well as parents and children all are interdependent. Since functionalists assume system components are interdependent, then (1) each part of the system influences all others and (2) when one part of the system changes, all the other components must adjust to this change.

The changes in the family during industrialization in the United States illustrate the interdependence of structures within a social system. As you will recall, prior to industrialization, the U.S. economy was primarily agricultural and families worked together at home. Sons were expected to learn the skills and occupations of their fathers and daughters were expected to train for homemaking like their mothers. Children received little formal schooling but learned to read and write in the home by studying the Bible. With industrialization, a major shift in the economy, all social institutions had to adapt. Education became more institutionalized and specialized to provide the workers with what an industrial economy requires. Factory jobs and formal education away from the home changed parental roles. Within the family system, fathers' involvement in children's lives and everyday interactions in the home decreased. Women no longer needed to help produce goods in the home and the role expectations of mothers changed. Mothers' primary responsibilities became the caregiving and nurturing of children. At the same time, childhood emerged as a distinct stage of life, especially after anti–child labor laws removed many children from factories in the late nineteenth century. Thus, a change in one structure—the economy—created changes in all of the other components of society.

Functionalists analyze social issues by identifying the structures (or components) of social systems, describing the functions each structure performs, and explaining "the relationship between the parts" and the relationship of the parts to the whole (Eshleman 1969: 17). Functionalists often are accused of using circular reasoning, because they tend to assert as fact the phenomenon they are trying to explain. For example, functionalists make the circular argument that the family is functional for society because it exists, and it exists because it is functional.

▪ *Social change affects the entire social system.* Functionalists consistently argue that because system components are interdependent, change in any part of the system will ultimately affect the entire system. However, functionalists' arguments about whether social change is positive or negative for society have evolved over time. Early functionalists, influenced by Darwinism, believed that social changes were inevitable consequences of evolution. Change was believed to be automatic, necessary, and functional (beneficial) (Thomas and Wilcox 1987). Prior to the turn of the twentieth century, functionalists viewed the family as an adaptable social institution that was continually evolving. Following the disruptions of World War I, the Great Depression, and World War II, functionalists began to define social change as troublesome and the cause of social disorganization and chaos (Thomas and Wilcox 1987). When functional theory was most prominent in family studies (between the 1930s and 1950s), functionalists argued that social change was harmful and disruptive to society and the family. In the 1960s, the concept of **dysfunction** was introduced to describe social structures and behaviors that disrupt social equilibrium rather than contribute to it (Merton 1968).

Functionalists' emphasis on the disruptiveness of social change was strongly criticized. They were accused of ignoring social change and failing to recognize social conflict (Farrington and Chertok 1993). Critics argued that functionalists failed to recognize that social change and conflict are not necessarily detrimental to society and the family. Social change and conflict can produce positive outcomes in society, such as the positive changes that resulted for people of color from the civil rights movement.

Functionalists today, as in the past, acknowledge that social change affects all parts of the social system. Yet, instead of pointing out only the functional or dysfunctional consequences of change, contemporary functionalists argue that change constantly occurs and cannot be avoided, but that social systems ultimately adapt to change (Vannoy 1991).

Application of Structural-Functional Theory to Family Issues

From a functionalist perspective, the family is "an essential subsystem within society" (Doherty et al. 1993: 10) that performs basic functions necessary for society to continue. The functions the family serves have been identified as the following (Winton 1995: 45):

1. Provide replacements for dying members of the society.
2. Produce and distribute goods and services for the support of the members of the society.
3. Accommodate conflicts and maintain order internally and externally.
4. Train human replacements to become participating members of the society.
5. Deal with emotional crises, harmonize the goals of individuals with the values of the society, and maintain a sense of purpose.

Families also are described as individual micro-systems in which family members perform different functions. Beginning with the ground-breaking work of Parsons and Bales (1955), functionalists have argued that women perform expressive roles within the family such as nurturing, caregiving, and maintaining harmony, whereas men perform the instrumental roles of providing food, shelter, clothing, and other essential survival needs through paid employment. Functionalists further assume that women are biologically better equipped for the expressive tasks of nurturing and caregiving because they bear children. Men, who do not bear and nurse children, are freer to specialize in the instrumental tasks of leadership and earning income (Parsons and Bales 1955: 23).

In the traditional functionalist view, biology is destiny. Women are wives and mothers and are also responsible for helping to maintain the social order. Women who choose to combine employment with motherhood upset the "natural balance" in their family and in society. Sociological research in the 1950s claimed to document the ill effects of women's employment; for example, juvenile delinquency and divorce were attributed to employed women.

Feminists often accuse functional theorists of reinforcing the subordinate role of women in the family and in society (Osmond 1987: 119). Functional theory suggests that the only way women can and should obtain any power is through their role as homemakers. As one functionalist explains, "Within the household, the mother is the instrumental leader so far as the homemaker is concerned. She directs servants, plans meals, furnishings, and decorations [and] organizes parties" (Pitts 1964: 74). Few people today, including functionalists, accept such limited ideas of women's role in society.

As you can see, the application of functional theory to the family was influenced by historical events and the sociocultural concerns of the day (Doherty et al. 1993). In the post–World War II era, when functional theory was widely applied to family issues, social scientists and the general public were "pre-occupied with issues of security (with the Cold War and the Bomb) and the desire to return to 'normal' gender relations that the war had interrupted" (Doherty et al. 1993: 9). In this sociohistorical context, it is not surprising that functionalists argued that traditional gender roles must be maintained to preserve stability within society.

Functional theory has long implied that the nuclear family, in which the man is patriarch and breadwinner and the woman is subordinate and the nurturer is the "normal" or "standard" family. Any variations—such as single-parent, dual-income, or ethically diverse families—have been considered "deviant" or "dysfunctional" (Scanzoni and Marsiglio 1993). Prior to the 1970s, for example, many social scientists described African American families as deviant (Scanzoni and Marsiglio 1993). However, no family structure is inherently stable or unstable, functional or dysfunctional. Single parent families, blended families, dual-income families, culturally diverse families, and traditional nuclear families all can be stable, functional units.

Functional theory was not widely applied to family issues in the 1960s and 1970s because it was considered dated and value laden. Recently, some sociologists have tried to revise the theory to make it more relevant to contemporary family issues. The work of Vannoy (1991) is an excellent example of how functional theory can be applied to modern society.

Vannoy (1991) accepts the functionalist premise that all elements of modern society are interdependent and operate as a system. However, she argues that the traditional homemaker/breadwinner roles within the family changed because they were no longer optimal (or functional) in the post–World War II era. After World War II, more service jobs were created that required good interpersonal skills to perform. Women were called into the work force partly by employers who desired their skills in service jobs and partly because the rising cost of living and living standards made it increasingly impossible for a man to support a family on his income alone. These economic forces led to changes in family and gender roles as men were called on to be more involved in household tasks and childrearing because women were no longer full-time homemakers. In the process, men began developing more nurturing skills while women began developing greater assertiveness and competitiveness. Vannoy's work, like that of other contemporary functionalists, acknowledges the interdependence of social institutions and the dramatic impact of social change, without labeling the changes as either positive or negative for society and families.

Conflict Theory

Conflict theory, also referred to as *radical* or *critical theory*, is a relatively new approach in family studies (Sprey 1979: 130). Although conflict theory is rooted in Marxist philosophy developed 150 years ago, it was not until the mid-1960s that researchers began examining family issues from this perspective (Farrington and Chertok 1993; Boss et al. 1993; Doherty et al. 1993). Again, social and historical factors help explain why conflict theory was ignored for so long in family studies and then was suddenly discovered in the 1960s.

Family scholars hesitated to use conflict theory prior to the 1960s because of its links to Marxism, socialism, and communism (Farrington and Chertok 1993). Particularly during the 1950s, few scholars dared write about the merits of conflict theory because of McCarthyism, the Red Scare, and the Cold War. Until the 1960s, scholars did not readily accept the assumption in critical theory that conflict could be beneficial in families (Farrington and Chertok 1993).

The 1960s were a time of dramatic social change and unrest, and traditional institutions and values were being questioned (Doherty et al. 1993). The sexual revolution, antiwar protests, the women's movement, and the civil rights movement all began in earnest and provided an "atmosphere in which the theoretical ideas . . . of conflict theory could be examined and accepted by many" (Farrington and Chertok 1993: 363). Even then, the Marxist and feminist perspectives were seen as radical. Many people in the rather conservative discipline of family studies are uncomfortable with the social and political implications of Marxist and feminist philosophies.

These social changes also had a direct impact on the family. Divorce rates rose, sex outside of marriage became more common, illegitimacy increased, and women entered the labor force in greater numbers (Doherty et al. 1993). Structural-functional theory no longer seemed relevant or adequate in the midst of these dramatic family changes (Farrington and Chertok 1993).

Basic Premises of Conflict Theory

▪ *Conflict is natural and inevitable in human nature and in society.* This is the first basic premise of conflict theory (also known as *critical theory*). Conflict theorists assume that human beings are essentially self-oriented and will pursue their needs over others' if necessary (Sprey 1979: 132). Furthermore, every individual is believed to have separate and distinct goals, values, and interests (Farrington and Chertok 1993). Conflict is bound to arise in social interaction as the goals and values of individuals clash with those of others.

Social conflict also can be explained by a scarcity of resources. Conflict theorists assume that societies never have enough resources for all of its members; therefore, individuals are constantly in competition for scarce resources (Sprey 1979). The resources that are in greatest demand but least supply in a modern, industrial, capitalist society are wealth, prestige, and power (Farrington and Chertok 1993).

▪ *The economy determines the structure of all other social institutions.* Conflict theorists assume that the economy is more important or influential than all other social institutions. Marx argues that the economy forms the substructure of society and influences the organization of all the other institutions in society. Thus, instead of biological forces determining the structure of society (the functionalist position), conflict theorists argue that economic forces do—a philosophy known as *economic determinism*.

According to Marx, societies develop through a "series of progressive states, beginning with a primitive period, followed by ancient, feudal, and capitalist stages, and ending with the communist period, which is the final state of human social development" (Farrington and Chertok 1993: 360). Marx describes each of these stages, with the exception of the first and the last, as *exploitative*. He argues that the economic arrangements in the exploitative social stage of capitalism create two social classes: the **bourgeoisie,** who own the means of production (such as land, factories, and machines) and the **proletariat,** who work for the owners (Farrington and Chertok 1993). Owners exploit workers for their labor and keep all the profits. According to the philosophy of economic determinism, this exploitation and oppression are reproduced in all the other institutions in society.

Marx was especially critical of capitalism, claiming that it breeds class conflict and inequality throughout society. He urged a social and economic revolution to move society from capitalism to communism, in which people would all be equal. People would contribute their talents to society and would receive their basic needs in return. If the economy was egalitarian, then it followed that equality would permeate the rest of society.

▪ *Conflict is necessary for growth and social change* (Sprey 1979: 132). In addition to portraying conflict as natural and unavoidable, critical theorists also believe that conflict can be beneficial for society. Social conflict and change are necessary for societies and social institutions to experience progress. However, *conflict* is difficult to operationally define for use in empirical research.

Application of Conflict Theory to Family Issues

As you have seen, conflict theorists assert that conflict is inevitable because of basic human nature and the scarcity of resources and that conflict can be beneficial and is necessary for progress. These assumptions have led to two distinct stances in conflict theory: one emphasizing the divisiveness of conflict and the other emphasizing the integrative consequences (or benefits) of conflict (Turner 1974). Both stances are evident in family studies.

Divisiveness of conflict is emphasized in the work of Frederick Engels, who applied Marx's basic ideas to the family and male-female relationships (Farrington and Chertok 1993). Using the principle of economic determinism, Engels attempted to show that the oppression and exploitation found in capitalism is duplicated in the family. For example, men, who control the economic means of production, have power over women in the family and enjoy superordinate status (Farrington and Chertok 1993). Women (and children) who do not have access to wealth and power are therefore subordinate.

Engels (1902) argues that private property, the accumulation of which is the cornerstone of capitalism, necessitated patriarchal, monogamous relationships. Capitalists who have accumulated private property need legitimate heirs to inherit their wealth. Monogamous marriages were established to ensure men the paternity of their children and the virtue of their wives. In societies with monogamy, marital fidelity of women usually is required as a symbolic extension of private property. Engels (1902: 90) explains, "[Adultery] is considered a crime for women and entails grave legal and social consequences for them, [but] is considered honorable for men or in the worst case a slight moral blemish worn with pleasure."

Engels reiterated Marx's call for a communist revolution, arguing that the eradication of capitalism would eliminate inequality in marriage and the family. Engels (1902: 100) describes what could be anticipated after the downfall of capitalist production: "A race of men who never in their lives have had any occasion for buying with money or other economic means of power the surrender of a woman; a race of women who have never had any occasion for surrendering to any man for any other reason but love."

Although few family scholars today still employ the rhetoric of Marxism, conflict theorists do take issues of gender very seriously. Conflict theorists argue that in most societies, the subordination of women is created in the economic structure as a by-product of the division of labor (Osmond 1987). Gender norms reinforce men's power and authority in families. Many conflict theorists advocate social and legal changes that would ensure women more access to economic resources.

However, when applied to family studies, conflict theory does not necessarily view men as oppressors and women as oppressed (Sprey 1979). The branch of conflict theory that emphasizes the benefits of conflict does not assume that any family member is exploited or oppressed. Scholars with this perspective point out the usefulness of conflict in relationships for addressing underlying problems in relationships and creating positive change (Farrington and Chertok 1993).

Conflict theory has generated less criticism than other perspectives because only recently has it been applied to family issues and is "employed by a relatively small minority of those who call themselves family theorists and researchers" (Farrington and Chertok 1993: 373). The introduction of the conflict perspective into family studies did not create a vast theoretical shift in the discipline, and therefore did not promote much criticism from other family scholars.

Multiple Theoretical Perspectives

With every article or book I assign in my Marriage and Family classes, I ask students to identify and discuss the theoretical approach the author used in the study. Students often report that they cannot figure out which perspective the author is using, because they see elements of all the theories in the study. Of course, this is the point of the exercise—to show students that most often researchers approach a study using multiple theoretical perspectives.

Symbolic interaction, structural functionalism, and conflict theory contain elements that complement one another. For example, symbolic interactionists emphasize the importance of the way individuals *define the situation,* and conflict theorists argue that *conflict can be beneficial.* In a study of family conflict, the researcher might suggest that family members must communicate how they perceive the problem (symbolic interaction) and that openly and constructively dealing with the conflict can improve the relationship (conflict theory).

Different theoretical perspectives offer scholars the opportunity to view the same problem through different lenses (Rank and LeCroy 1983). No perspective

What questions and assumptions might a structural functionalist have about the confrontation shown in this photograph? How would the premises and concerns of conflict theorists differ and with what outcomes for sociological research? Which of the three main theoretical approaches in sociology do you favor? How might you combine them to describe or explain the situation in the photograph at the beginning of this chapter?

is good or bad, correct or incorrect. Theoretical perspectives simply suggest different ways of analyzing problems and issues. As Rank and LeCroy (1983: 441) explain, "By utilizing more than one theory in framing hypotheses and interpreting results, a fuller understanding of family behavior may be achieved."

Unfortunately, in practice, many scholars conduct research with very little regard for the theoretical implications or relevance of the study. Nye (1987) found that over the past 50 years, only 1 percent of the published family studies contains any clearly stated theoretical perspective. Lavee and Dollahite (1991) identify two reasons that theory is avoided in empirical studies: the Theory Factor and the Research Factor. The *Theory Factor* includes problems inherent in theoretical perspectives that limit their usefulness in research. Some theories are very broad and include imprecise terms that are not easily testable. Additionally, theoretical assumptions may be outdated and unwieldy in guiding research on contemporary family issues and concerns.

The *Research Factor* involves problems in the research process that discourage scholars from using theory. Lavee and Dollahite (1991: 369) suggest that undergraduate and graduate students are "trained to be good researchers but not good theorists." Students take research methods and statistics courses to learn how to design studies and interpret results, but theory is taught as a separate course and is not emphasized as a necessary part of the research process. Scholarly work is evaluated on how methodologically sound the research design is rather than on the theoretical relevance of the study. To improve research and enhance theoretical development, "we need to sensitize ourselves and teach our students to 'think theory' while doing research and then to be clear and explicit about it when research is reported" (Lavee and Dollahite 1991: 370).

Summary

Theorizing is the process of generating, testing, and revising ideas that results in an explanation for a fact or phenomenon. Theories contain clearly defined concepts and propositions that describe how concepts are interrelated. The three primary theoretical perspectives in sociology are symbolic interaction, structural functionalism, and conflict theory.

Symbolic interactionism emphasizes the importance of communication, interaction, perception, and self-concept in human behavior. Unlike behavioral psychologists, symbolic interactionists believe that human beings are unique in their ability to create and manipulate symbols. The meaning of symbols is created in social interaction and is therefore culturally specific. Symbolic interactionists firmly believe that human behavior is influenced by the perceptions individuals have of social situations. Cultural norms and values, which are learned through the process of socialization, guide human behavior and allow for predictability in social interaction. Symbolic interactionists further argue that individuals' self-concepts are created in interaction with primary groups such as the family.

The self, which is seen as having both an active, dynamic *I* component, as well as a more stable *Me* side, incorporates perceptions of interaction episodes (definition of the situation), cultural norms, and social roles. Interactionists believe that since so much information about the motivation for human behavior is contained within an individual's self, human subjects must be studied using qualitative research strategies if possible.

Structural-functional theorists depict society and families as individual systems, comprised of interdependent structures that perform separate functions. The social system is comprised of structures such as the family, government, religion, economy, and education. Change in any one of these institutions will temporarily disrupt the social system and create changes in all other social institutions. The family is believed to serve the functions of procreation; providing productive workers; and contributing to social order by mediating conflicts, socializing individuals to cultural norms and values, and providing emotional support for individuals.

As mini-systems, families are comprised of members who perform interdependent roles. Functionalists have long argued that adult males perform the instrumental tasks in the family of providing food, shelter, and economic security, whereas women are said to perform the expressive tasks of nurturing and caregiving. Families that vary from this traditional role allocation, such as single-parent families or dual-worker families, are described as being deviant and as disrupting social order. The fact that functionalists endorsed traditional gender roles in the family led many sociologists in the 1960s and 1970s to question the usefulness of the perspective. Today, some scholars have revised functional arguments by showing how contemporary family arrangements are functional adaptations to social change.

Rooted in Marxist philosophy, conflict theorists assume that conflict is inevitable in society. Conflict naturally arises when individuals have competing values or goals or when there is competition for scarce resources. Conflict theorists believe that the economy is the central institution in society, influencing the structure of all other social institutions—a philosophy known as economic determinism. Karl Marx argued that a capitalist economy breeds inequality, oppression, and conflict between the bourgeoisie (wealthy) and the proletariat (poor). The principle of economic determinism suggests that in a capitalist economy, the family is a breeding ground for inequality, oppression, and conflict between the wealthy and powerful breadwinning husband and the subordinate homemaker. Conflict theorists acknowledge that social change and conflict can ultimately be beneficial for society, families, and individuals.

In the study of marriage and the family, two branches of conflict theory have developed. One branch of conflict theory emphasizes the divisiveness of conflict and stresses gender inequality in the family. The other branch emphasizes the positive outcomes of conflict resolution and stresses the importance of good communication between family members.

Although three distinct perspectives have developed in sociology, it is important to note that most scholars today blend the ideas from several of these theories to explain family dynamics. Unfortunately, some scholars become so consumed with developing good research methods to study and measure family issues that they fail to apply theoretical ideas at all.

Readings for In-Depth Focus

Understanding and Applying Theories

In recent years, several tragic incidents have occurred in schools in which teachers and students were killed and maimed by a fellow classmate or group of classmates armed with guns and homemade explosives. Naturally, people wonder why ordinary adolescents would be driven to such rage and violence, and so they create theories to provide answers. Some people theorize that overexposure to violent movies, music, and video games causes young people to behave aggressively; others propose that lax gun control is the root of the problem; still others believe that deterioration of the home and family is to blame for adolescent violence.

As Burr points out in the following article, human beings constantly create theories to explain social phenomena. Although every theory is unique in the explanation it provides, all theories have common characteristics. As you read the article, think about how Burr's arguments apply to the three sociological perspectives discussed in Chapter 3.

■ ■ ■

Using Theories in Family Science

Wesley R. Burr

We humans are a curious and meddlesome bunch. We are always asking what is happening around us and what we can do to make things better. *What* happens to the children when their parents divorce? *What* can we do to make divorce as constructive as possible? *What* is happening that leads one child in a family to turn out well and another to turn into such a brat? *What* can we do to create intimacy, peace, love, and closeness? And we don't ask these questions just to be asking. We want answers!

As we try to answer these questions, we develop *theories*. Our theories give us *explanations* and help us know how to *intervene*. For example, the question about why some children in a family are more difficult than others led Vogel and Bell (1960) to develop a theory of scapegoating. They reason that some families tend to blame one child for the family difficulties and that when this occurs it often sets up a vicious circle. The child who is the scapegoat tends to misbehave more than before, and the family may then be even more sure that he or she is the source of the family's problems. Gradually, the scapegoated child acts more and more rebellious, and the family treats him or her more and more as a problem child. The scapegoating helps some families operate fairly normally in other ways as long as they can put the blame for their difficulties on the one child, and as long as the rest of

From "Using Theories in Family Science," by W. R. Burr, in *Research and Theory in Family Science*, edited by R. D. Day, K. R. Gilbert, B. H. Settles, and W. R. Burr, 1995, Pacific Grove, CA: Brooks/Cole Publishing. Used with permission of the editors.

the family, and sometimes the child, believes that he or she is the root of the family problems. This "solution" helps perpetuate the problem.

The theory about scapegoating is a minor theory, but it is an example of the way the term *theory* is used in the sciences. Thus, as mentioned above, scientific theories can be defined as groups of ideas that give us explanations that can be used as the basis for intervening.

All scientific fields have a number of theories. In geology, for example, there are theories of sedimentation and theories of glaciation. The theories of sedimentation help geologists understand how layers of rock and dirt are formed. The theories of glaciation help them understand how large segments of earth have been scooped up and removed. Family science is just like all the other fields in that it has many theories about family processes.

SIX IMPORTANT ASPECTS OF GENERAL THEORIES

One way to understand the nature of theories is to recall the fable of the six blind men who approached an elephant. Remember that the men all had different "theories" about what they were encountering.

Theories Answer Questions about "What Is Going On"

Each of us constructs our private theory about "what is going on." The fable of the blind men helps us understand that the theory each man constructed gave him an explanation of what elephants were like. The man who felt the leg thought of how large, firm, and sturdy the leg was, and his insights satisfied his intellectual curiosity. The one who felt the side thought of how massive the "wall" was and how he couldn't move it when he pushed on it. His ideas accurately helped him understand one aspect of elephants. Each of the others had a different explanation because of his theory about elephants.

Theories about family processes help us understand what is going on in various aspects of the family realm. For example, some theories

help us know what is happening when 2-year old children are always saying "No!" Other theories help us understand what is going on when marriages succeed or fail, and others help us understand what is going on when some teenagers rebel and others cooperate.

Theories Are in the Minds of the Scientists

Another way the fable of the blind men helps us understand the nature of theories is that the theories were not part of the elephant. The blind men developed, or constructed, the theories. The theories were not "in" the elephant. They were "in" the *minds* of the six men.

It is the same in family science. Our theories about families are not "in" families; they are in the minds of the scientists who study families or the counselors or educators who try to help families. The theories are the sets of ideas that the scientists "think with" to help them understand and give them a basis for interventions.

Another way to describe theories is that they are intellectual "models," frameworks, or sets of ideas that exist in a scientific field. When students are learning any field, they learn a new language. They learn how to talk the "theory" language and think with the ideas that make up the field.

One way family scientists have described this aspect of theories is to observe that "the map is not the territory." If we have a map of a state or city, the map is not the state or the city; it is merely a description that people make to help them understand the state or city. Our theories about family processes are intellectual maps we use to describe families.

Theories Give Us Power

Good theories do more than just satisfy intellectual curiosity. They also help scientists and practitioners devise methods of changing things or solving problems so people can better attain their goals. Using the elephant analogy, for example, the man who felt the trunk and thought the elephant was like a rope had some "new" ideas in his head. He could then use these ideas to help him attain goals such as moving large logs or carrying other objects. Thus, as Sir Francis Bacon said over three centuries ago, *knowledge is power.*

How do family scientists use this power? It helps therapists know how to help families solve their problems and cope with difficult situations. It helps extension specialists know what to write in pamphlets. It also helps them know what to do and say in television and other educational programs that are designed to help the families improve their lives. And it helps people in business know how to make work environments more supportive of workers and their families. Thus, the ultimate payoff of theories is that they give us ideas that we can use to better attain our goals.

The Search for One Integrating Theory Is Futile

Another aspect of the elephant fable is also helpful in understanding theories in family science. Theorists and practitioners in family science are somewhat like the blind men in that we are all blind to many things. None of us is able to understand all of the aspects of the "elephant" in family science. Families are so complex, they interact in such complicated ways with their many environments, and they have such long and complicated histories, that it is impossible to understand all of their arms, legs, trunks, and tails.

Families are so complex that it is impossible for any one theory to explain everything. The result is that family science has different theories about different aspects of the elephant. One theory is about the trunk of families, and another theory is about legs. Other theories deal with the elephant's skin and eyes, the food it eats, and the oxygen it needs to stay alive.

Thus, we should not try to get one grand or great theory that will explain everything about families (Holman & Burr, 1980). It would be too large to manage, understand, and use. We mortals need to be satisfied with having several different theories that focus on different parts of our elephants.

Another implication is that it is helpful for family scientists to learn several different theories. Then we can use each of them when it is helpful. If we only have a theory about an elephant's tail, and the problem we are trying to deal with is in the leg, we are seriously handicapped. It is impossible for any one family scientist to learn all of the theories that can be used to understand family processes, but it is possible to learn more than one and then shift among them when it is helpful.

Usefulness Rather Than Truth Is What Matters

Since theories are analytic tools that scientists use to explain and understand, and they are "true" to the group of scientists that views them as true, it is therefore not very helpful to argue, debate, or bother to do research about whether theories are true or false.

If a theory makes sense to a group of scientists, it exists and is true to the scientists who think with it. In fact, to push this point further, a theory could be fairly untrue in some objective or ultimate sense, but if it is helpful to a group of scientists and if there is no better theory, it could be quite valuable.

Scientific theories are developed because a group of scientists make observations about a part of their elephant, and each theory, even if it is inconsistent with another way of thinking, is truth—as seen by that group of scientists. Thus, the truth or falsity of theories is fairly irrelevant, and worrying about it can actually get in the way of developing new and helpful ideas.

If the ultimate or objective truth of theories should not demand our concern and attention, what does matter? The important thing is whether theories help theorists, researchers, and practitioners accomplish their goals. Therefore, it is helpful to evaluate theories in terms of their utility, their practical value, their usefulness, and their helpfulness.

Thus, the theories that help scientists understand important questions and help them solve important problems are valuable. Valuable theories become widely known in the field, and they are taught in universities, research centers, and clinics. A large number of people learn them and use them to satisfy their intellectual curiosity and accomplish their goals. The theories that are not helpful or useful—or that are so unrealistic, irrelevant, or inconsistent with empirical observations that they are not helpful—are gradually ignored, and eventually they are forgotten.

The conclusion to this point is that there is a natural selection process in the rise and demise of theories, and it has little to do with truth or falsity. It is a selection based on the pragmatic value of theories. When theories are helpful in satisfying intellectual curiosity, providing explanations, or solving human problems, they remain part of scholarly fields. When old theories are replaced by better ones, the old theories, like old soldiers, fade away.

The moral: Good theories are helpful. Bad theories fade away, and trying to prove a theory bad or untrue is usually not worth the effort.

Theories Give Us Perspectives

Another helpful aspect of the elephant fable is that it illustrates differences in *perspectives*. When we understand the theory about the legs of elephants, it gives us a certain "point of view." We think differently than if we are thinking about the theory of the chemistry in the digestive system of the elephant.

In terms of family science, when we think with behaviorism, we assume that humans are malleable. We also assume that the environment can change humans a great deal by changing the rewards and punishments. This is a very different point of view from that of psychoanalysis, which assumes that all people have innate, biological drives that influence what they do. These two theories, behaviorism and psychoanalysis, make such different assumptions about the nature of humans and the nature of families that family scientists don't usually think with both of them at the same time. One is a theory about legs, and the other is a theory about tails. Both are true, but they deal with very different parts of the elephant. It is helpful to

know both of them, but they have very different perspectives, and they give us very different concepts, insights, generalizations, and ideas.

THE ESSENTIAL PARTS OF THEORIES

When we read something, how do we know if it is a theory? For example, does a set of ideas need to have mathematical formulas to be a theory? Does there need to be a large amount of research into some ideas before the ideas become a theory?

The answer to both of these questions is no. We don't need a mathematical formula, and we don't need a large amount of research.

What, then, are the minimal, essential components of a theory? The answer is that the ideas in a theory have six essential characteristics. One of these characteristics, that the ideas give us a *perspective*, has already been discussed. The other five are that the ideas have *concepts, assumptions, generality, explanations,* and a *history* of evolving in a scientific community.

Theories Have Concepts

The theories used by scientists have words, or terms, that are carefully defined. This helps all scientists think the same way when they learn the theory, and it minimizes misunderstandings and confusion. The terms in scientific theories are called *concepts,* and they are the basic building blocks of scientific thinking.

Theories Have Assumptions

The dictionary tells us that assumptions are facts or statements that are taken for granted, supposed to be true, or assumed to be true. Different theories make different assumptions. For example, behaviorism assumes that people are born with minds that are *tubulae rasae* (empty slates, blank chalkboards). This assumption is made in behaviorism. After the theorists made it, they were able to develop some new ideas about how people learn. They probably would not have developed their ideas or would not have been able to convince their colleagues that the ideas were valuable if they had not been able to assume a tabula rasa condition.

Family-systems theory does not assume that the mind is a *tabula rasa.* Why? The *tabula rasa* assumption is about the mind, and family-systems theory is not a theory about the mind. Using the elephant analogy, behaviorism is about one part of the elephant, and systems theory is about a different part.

When we want to think with family-systems theory, we assume that family systems can change and that the flow of information is an important part of the system. These assumptions then focus our attention on patterns of dealing with information rather than on how people learn.

What about the truth of assumptions? Do they need to be true? Do we need a lot of research into assumptions so we can have confidence that they are true? The answer is no. Assumptions merely identify the starting point for our reasoning. They identify what we want to begin with, what we want to take for granted while we think with or use a theory. They can be true, but they can also be hypothetical.

Theories Have Generality

Some theories are very narrow or specific. For example, Adams's (1979) theory of mate selection helps explain why people marry the people they do. Since it deals with a small part of the world, it is a fairly *specific* theory. Other theories deal with larger parts of the world. Behaviorism, for example, is an attempt to explain how humans learn, and it can be applied to any type of human learning. Since it can be used to explain more things than Adams's theory of mate selection can, it is a more *general* theory.

Systems theory is an example of a very general theory. It can explain why things happen in many different systems. It can be used to understand biological systems such as the circulatory or nervous system, and it can be applied to large and complex systems like armies and governments. Since it can be used to answer "why"

questions in a wide variety of situations, it is a very general theory.

The highly general theories are the most valuable because we can use them in many situations. If we have a very narrow theory, for example, such as a theory about why a 2-year-old child broke a window, it is not helpful in very many situations. A more general theory, such as a theory about why children obey and disobey, can help us understand the child's breaking the window and many other situations. Therefore, scientists try to develop theories that are as general as possible.

Theories Have Explanations

The payoff of theories is that they give us explanations. The explanations are true statements that satisfy our intellectual curiosity. These true statements are sometimes called generalizations, postulates, propositions, or laws, and they are the main reason we have theories.

The concepts and assumptions help provide the explanations because they provide the foundation for the true statements, or generalizations. The concepts give us words with which to think and communicate. The assumptions help us know what to focus on, what to assume, and where to start reasoning. But the payoff part, the fruit of all the work, is in the true statements that give us the explanations.

Theories Have a History

Theories are not static sets of ideas or perspectives. They are always changing. Theories change and grow as new concepts are developed, as new discoveries are made, and as new problems are encountered.

There is also a pattern in the way that most theories change. They grow in uneven cycles. There are periods of rapid change when a brilliant scholar makes some unusual contributions. These periods are then usually followed by some minor refinements or reactions to the innovations and a period of little or no change.

Sometimes the periods of stability in theories last for decades or even centuries. At other times periods of major development are fairly close together. In most of the general theories used in family science, the periods when major developments were made are not numerous. It is usually a matter of learning about the work of a few creative people at certain periods.

Since it is almost impossible to understand general theories in family science without being aware of the historical patterns of change, it is helpful to know some strategies for remembering these changes. The following three ideas can help this process:

1. *Remember the names of major theorists.* Science is a social phenomenon. It is groups of individuals trying to find answers to their questions. Also, advances are usually made by one or two main individuals, so it is not necessary to learn long lists of names.

2. *Remember the approximate dates of the major publications.* Most of the advances in theories are made in reaction to advances in other theories or as reactions to unique historical events. They are also usually published in a small group of articles or books, and they have publication dates. It is therefore helpful to be aware of a few publications and dates.

3. *Pay attention to the roots and branches.* Most of the ideas in the general theories have long histories, and it is helpful, whenever possible, to be aware of these intellectual roots. Many new developments in general theories are reactions to or modifications of previous theories, and it is helpful to see how theories divide and branch into new perspectives.

REFERENCES

Adams, B. (1979). Mate selection in the United States: A theoretical summarization. In W. R. Burr, R. Hill, F. I. Nye, & I. L. Reiss (Eds.), *Contemporary theories about the family,* chap. 11. New York: Free Press.

Holman, T., & Burr, W. R. (1980). Beyond the beyond: The development of family theories in the 1970s. *Journal of Marriage and the Family, 42,* 723–729.

Vogel, E. F., & Bell, N. W. (1960). The emotionally disturbed child as the family scapegoat. In N. W. Bell & E. F. Vogel (Eds.), *A modern introduction to the family.* Glencoe, IL: Free Press.

Critical Thinking Questions

1. Explain what Burr means by the following statements: "Theories are in the minds of the scientists" and "Theories give us power."

2. Why does Burr argue that the *usefulness* of a theory is more important than whether it is *true?* Do you agree? Why or why not?

3. Identify and discuss the six essential components of a theory.

4. Drawing on Burr's article and the information presented in Chapter 3, identify the concepts and assumptions of functionalism, conflict theory, and symbolic interactionism.

5. Using the information presented in Chapter 3, trace the history of functionalism, conflict theory, and symbolic interactionism.

4 *Understanding Family Diversity*

*P*eople often remark that they observe numerous variations in family types in the United States, compared to other societies. The wide variations of families within and between cultures makes it difficult to define *family.* How can we understand the variations that we see or hear about? What tools does the sociologist use to understand family in intracultural, cross-cultural, and global contexts? These questions frequently are asked in the university setting, and, with different wording, in popular media, as well.

My students like to make comparisons between family types. Often, they ask for guidance in finding ways to understand family in the United States and family elsewhere without passing judgment on societies or family types. That is, the students want to avoid being ethnocentric in their quests to understand family in larger contexts. **Ethnocentrism** refers to the tendency to judge other groups and cultures based on the standards and practices of one's own group or culture, operating with the assumption that one's own group is the best. What my students want are the tools for comparative analysis. Some of these tools, such as theoretical perspectives and methods of research, were discussed in Chapters 2 and 3. Three other tools are provided in this chapter: terminology, the comparative perspective, and the comparative approach. These three chapters together, then, give you the tool kit needed for investigating family issues.

With these tools, you can have a deeper and more objective understanding of cultural diversity as it is reflected in and transmitted by families. You also may understand better how historical forces, customs and traditions, as well as race, social class, and gender contribute to this diversity.

To say that there is **diversity** is to assume that there is **pluralism,** or more than one type of something, in a given society. The United States is quite pluralistic culturally, with different family cultures and life-styles by social class, race, and ethnicity, for instance. Other nations of the world also tend to be pluralistic, with variations, or diversity, based on class, caste or tribe, religion, ethnicity, and geographic region.

Sociologists are indebted to the accumulation of legal, sociological, and anthropological endeavors for the language and tools needed to address the questions of family variation and similarity. John Ferguson McLennan and Henry Lewis Morgan published the earliest known efforts. McLennan's *Primitive Marriage* (1865) introduced us to marriage types, the terms *endogamy* and *exogamy,* and ancient systems of kinship. Morgan's work on the Iroquois (see Morgan 1847), and his later work *Ancient Society* (1877) provided fertile fields from which to hone and refine comparative analyses of family systems. Since then, many scholars have refined the terminology and approaches to these types of endeavors. Therefore, you should not be surprised if some of the references in this chapter seem old. They are. These old references, though certainly not perfect, remain decidedly evergreen. Or, as Gary Lee (1984) argues, just because a cross-cultural study was conducted in 1880 does not mean that the study is obsolete so much as it may mean that the cultures have changed. All the same, the study can still be instructive when testing hypotheses in a current study, and "there is no reason to assume that these observations become less useful over time" (p. 527).

Understanding Family Patterns

The Family as an Institution

As a **social institution,** family is a recognized component of every known society. Along with religion, family tends to be seen as one of the most basic cornerstones for all societies. **Institution** refers to relatively stable clusters of statuses, roles, and norms. These clusters help transmit culture over the generations. They also serve as **agents of socialization;** that is, they help us learn about the structure, customs, beliefs, norms, and laws of our society, and help prepare us to be functioning members of society.

What sociological constructs would you use to describe this or any family as a social institution? Why is it difficult to define family? *Do you think the authors' definition of family—as a collection of people who form an economic unit; are related by marriage, ancestry, adoption, or affinity; and who have a unique identity as a unit and commitment to each other and any children that are part of the collection—would work in this case?*

Status refers to position or rank. Mother, father, and infant all are statuses in family compositions. There are two ways by which we attain a status. **Ascription** involves arbitrarily assigning status on socially significant grounds such as race, caste or tribe, sex, or social class of the family into which a person is born or adopted. **Achievement** refers to attaining a status based on a person's own merits and efforts. Attached to statuses are **roles,** which are the generally accepted rights, duties, obligations, privileges, norms, and expected behaviors, including personality characteristics, attached to that status. Roles emerge as the members of groups and societies conduct their everyday lives (Babbie 1990). They then become seen as **normative,** or what is generally acceptable and expected. **Norms** are generally shared social rules and expectations. **Prescriptive norms** are a society's "Thou Shalt" or "You Must" rules. An example of a prescriptive norm in the United States is that parents should take care of their children. **Proscriptive norms** are a society's "Thou Shalt Not" or "You Must Not" rules. In the United States, for example, a proscriptive norm is that parents do not physically harm their children.

Families are made up of people who have lived together or associated intimately with one another and who have myriad social, moral, and legal obligations to one another. Husbands and wives have an array of legal obligations to one another. Parents have moral obligations to their children. Across the generations, aunts, uncles, cousins, siblings, grandparents, and grandchildren develop various combinations of social obligations and affinity with one another.

Critically important to the understanding of the family as an institution is avoiding narrowly defining family by household composition. Simply put, a household does not make a family; a family is not neatly contained with one household. This would work if every newly united couple went off by themselves and never again conversed with, assisted, or sought the companionship of parents, siblings, and other kin. However, this usually does not occur.

Some households are **family households,** which means that only people who are related such that they are family—that is, though marriage, ancestry, affinity, or adoption—live in the household. Other households are **nonfamily,** which means that people unrelated to one another in the sense of family are living in the same households. Most families around the world live in several households but maintain their family associations and identities, further arguing against narrowly defining family by household.

The Family as a Social Group

A **social group** is "an interacting collection of people with interrelated statuses and roles, who share a common identity, and adhere to a set of special norms" (Larson, White, and Petrowsky 1998: 200). Cooley distinguished between primary and secondary groups. A **primary group** is intimate, characterized by face-to-face interaction, and pivotal in the development of the social self. A primary group contains people who are significant in your life, who help construct and sustain your sense of who you are. To Cooley, the family was **the most primary group. Secondary groups** are formally organized, impersonal, and anonymous (Larson et al. 1998). An example of a secondary group might be your volunteer group's steering committee. The members meet at a specific time at a specific location. They focus on the tasks that must be accomplished and then go their separate ways. Statements made during the sessions have little to no lasting significance on how you see yourself or your estimations of your self-worth.

While some (e.g., Troost 1996) argue that the most efficient way to analyze families today is by focusing on **dyads,** or two-person groups, and then the dyads' relations with others, my own perspective is that that is far too narrow. Societies have identifiable structures and institutions such as the family. Within family, there also is both structure and interaction. Families, no matter how composed, operate in relation to other people and to the larger society. Focusing on particular dyads might help us understand those individual dyads as entities unto themselves. However, if links to normative systems and the larger society are not made, the understanding has limited use. Regardless of whether one is discussing a family comprised of a heterosexual, cohabiting couple with no children, a lesbian couple with two children, or a family containing a married heterosexual couple in which the woman previously has been married and has two children from that union, the husband is a first-time married man with a child from a previous union, plus this couple's aging parents, one is still referring to a collection of people with tangible and intangible ties with one another, who enact identifiable roles, and whose interaction maintains a singularly unique identity. These elements, moreover, are connected to norms and other features of the larger society.

Families by Type of Authority

Family varies by authority systems. **Authority** refers to legitimate power or legitimate right to varying degrees of influence in and control over the lives of others. This power is legitimated through custom and law. The authority system of the family as an institution in a given society tends to reflect and reinforce the authority system of the larger society.

Worldwide, family systems have tended to be patriarchal. In **patriarchal systems,** men, because they are men, have greater rights and privileges as well as differential access to valued resources. Thus, men categorically have varying degrees of control over women and children. It is important to recognize that patriarchy is a matter of degree. It is not appropriate to define patriarchy simply as male domination. For instance, males may numerically predominate as decision makers in several or all of the institutions of a society. Domination, however, implies both force and coercion as well as absolute control.

Patriarchy exists on a sort of continuum. At one end, there are places in the world today where **absolute patriarchy** exists. In an absolutely patriarchal system, men have complete and arbitrary control over the lives of women and children. One can argue, for instance, that the Taliban of Afghanistan, which is a religious ruling system that forces all women to stay inside the dwelling place and to have no means of making money, is an illustration of absolute patriarchy. In an absolute patriarchy, at its most extreme, men may arbitrarily decide how women may dress, what they can eat and when, and when and how they should die. At the other end of the continuum would be merely vestiges of patriarchy, where men are seen as being somewhat better or more important than women and enjoy a modest amount of unearned advantages because they are male. Currently, it seems that some of the Nordic countries such as Sweden and Finland are moving toward vestiges of patriarchy. In these countries, women enjoy relatively higher status than do women in the rest of the world. At the same time, there still are some discrepancies.

In reality, most patriarchal societies tend to have a **dual patriarchy** operating. In a dual patriarchy, some men are "more equal" than other men. They have more rights, enjoy more prestige, and have differential access to valued resources in comparison to some other men. The slavery era in the United States is an example. If taking a conflict perspective on social class and race in the United States today, one could argue that a dual patriarchy still exists, with upper-class white men having a measure of control over men of color and men of the lower classes.

In patriarchal families, then, men have greater rights, higher prestige, and more influence in decision making than do women and children. Given their higher status and greater authority, men also have varying degrees of influence in and control over the lives of women and children.

Although there are no truly **matriarchal** societies in the world (Goode 1964), if there were one, it would be a society wherein women, because they are women, have greater rights and privileges as well as differential access to valued resources. They would therefore have measures of control over and influence in the lives of men. Perhaps you have heard the mythological tales of the Amazon women: tall, warrior women who dominate their societies. The first white explorers apparently generated these tales. These explorers came upon some very tall, slender people with long hair who had adorned their bodies with jewelry and paint or make-up. Their bodies and faces were rather hairless. From the perspective of these white people, the dark-skinned natives were some of the tallest, fiercest women in the world. Actually, though, these tall natives were men (Plotkin 1993). The whites applied interpretations from their own cultural experiences when viewing these natives. There was no matriarchy.

Some American Indian tribes and some groups in various parts of Africa afford women more social and political power than most Westerners are accustomed to doing. However, even in these cases, men categorically still have greater prestige and access to valued resources.

Some scholars also have assumed that matriarchies exist among groups where female-headed households predominate. This has been the case with previous research on U.S. lower-class black families, for instance. This is an erroneous assumption. As a general rule, female-headed households predominate in cultures of poverty. In cultures of poverty, which are associated with the lower classes, patriarchy tends to be pronounced and enforced, as is discussed in several other chapters in this book.

Individual families may be more strongly influenced by the primary female figure than by a male figure. These families can be described as **matrifocal;** that is, inside the home, deference is paid to the primary female figure. This figure wields considerable authority within the home and regarding domestic matters. Mexican American families, for instance, have been described as matrifocal.

Perhaps one of the most instructive recognitions to be drawn from discussing patriarchy and matriarchy is that sex is a status. In the United States today, so much attention is paid to *gender*—to the point that using the term *sex roles* is seen as archaic—that we sometimes fail to remember that stratification by sex is a social fact. Sex, then, is not merely about biology or a physical activity. Other chapters of this book present gendered realities and gendered divisions of labor, so you would probably do well to tuck into the back of your mind that these gender roles reflect at least the sex-status configurations of families as well as those of a given society.

In egalitarian authority systems, status is attained solely by achievement; there is no ascription involved. In a truly egalitarian society, for instance, race, sex, religion, and other factors would have no bearing on one's social esteem, access to scarce resources, or influence in the lives of others. In **egalitarian families,** then, all authority would be based on one's knowledge, skills, and abilities; being male or female would have no bearing. Egalitarianism is a virtue frequently espoused in nations such as the United States. However, fully egalitarian family systems are not yet the norm. As will become clear in Chapters 5, 10, and 11, efforts are being made to be less patriarchal and to create more egalitarian families at both the institutional and group levels, but it is premature to classify United States families as egalitarian. Thus, the norm of egalitarianism is seen as an ideal feature for families in the United States; movement in that direction is discernible but not universal.

Families by Descent Pattern

Families are organized into groups according to patterns of descent. **Descent** speaks to who is related to whom. Descent systems also detail who is obligated to whom, who has what duties to kin, and what one's name will be. Some societies trace descent primarily or solely through one bloodline, whereas others acknowledge both the male and female family lines. In **unilineal** systems, only one bloodline is acknowledged. The descent pattern may be **patrilineal,** tracing through the male lines or through a specific male ancestor, or **matrilineal,** tracing through female lines. Matrilineal descent, however, can be somewhat confusing and not all that definitive. Typically, in matrilineal groups, the woman and her children live with her brother or other designated male family members (Farber 1964). Boys, in particular, are partially responsible for their brothers. Sometimes, recognition of the father's contributions to family lineage also is acknowledged. Matrilineal descent is usually found in horticulturist societies in which women provide most of the economic labor. Patrilineal descent is common in societies in which the male is the primary economic provider, such as in Western industrialized societies and among pastoralists and intensive agriculturists (Haviland 1994).

Traditionally, Navajo society was matriarchal, matrilineal, *and* matrilocal. *What do these terms mean and why are they significant in understanding the cultural contexts of marriage and the family?*

Although patrilineal systems tend to be patriarchal, matrilineal systems do not tend to be matriarchal, nor are matrilineal systems promiscuous, as some early scholars believed. Matrilineal groups have marriage eligibility rules, and children born into these unions are legitimate. Although quite rare, family membership can be established through **double descent**—a system in which descent is reckoned matrilineally and patrilineally at the same time. **Ambilineal** descent, a double-descent pattern, allows individuals to choose to affiliate with either the mother's or the father's kinship line. Eastern European Jewish immigrants developed ambilineal descent patterns at the beginning of the twentieth century to preserve family ties and culture after relocating to the United States. Most of these family groups are still present today in New York City and other large cities with substantial Jewish populations (Haviland 1994).

In **bilineal systems,** ancestors and bloodlines on both sides are acknowledged. In the United States, tracing one's family tree is an example of a bilineal system, in that a child is related to both mother's and father's family and kin.

Families by Emphasis

Different family systems place different emphases on blood ties and marriage. In **conjugal systems,** the emphasis is placed on the marital relationship. In **consanquinal systems,** the emphasis is on blood ties. Conjugal systems are most common among groups and societies where high value is placed on the individual. Consanguinal systems are most common among groups and societies where the family, and more specifically, the immortal family, is seen as most important. In the United States, the heaviest emphasis is on the conjugal relationship, though the consanquinal system is given recognition.

Families by Residence Type

Families also can be described according to their residential patterns after marriage. The most common residential patterns are patrilocal, matrilocal, and neolocal. A **patrilocal** residential pattern is one in which a newly married couple moves in with the husband's family. A **matrilocal** residential pattern is one in which a newly married couple lives with the wife's kin. In the United States and other Western industrialized societies, **neolocal** residential patterns, in which a newly married couple establishes their own residence, are most common. Neolocal residence patterns are usually found in societies where geographic mobility and financial independence are considered desirable (Howard and Dunaif-Hattis 1992).

Although more rare, other residential patterns are possible. **Avunculocal** residential patterns occur when a newly married couple lives near the husband's mother's brother. **Ambilocal** residence describes a pattern in which the married couple may choose to live with or near the parents or kin of either the bride or groom. In a **bilocal** residential pattern, the newly married couple lives for a period of time near or with the bride's parents and then lives with or near the groom's family for a period of time.

Residence patterns reveal a great deal about who gets to have contact with which kin. In patrilocal systems, for instance, both the wife and the children may have limited or no ongoing contact with the mother's side of the family. In neolocal systems, contact with kin becomes more a matter of inclination and logistics, and less a matter of honoring one or the other side of the family.

Families by Marriage Type

As can be seen in Figure 4.1, there is more than one definition of *marriage*. Earlier definitions reflect an emphasis on cross-cultural studies in their formulation. The definition by Olson and DeFrain reflects an effort to be more inclusive—that is, a definition for marriage that could apply to same-sex couples and that would reflect efforts in the United States to acknowledge these unions as marriages (Olson and DeFrain 1997: 10).

Some cultures have given occasional acknowledgment to same-sex unions such as women marriages in parts of Africa (MacGaffey 1996). This is a rare occurrence, however, and in my discussions with African sociologists, I have come to learn that these unions also may not necessarily be sexual. Not infrequently, an older woman is literally taking in a younger woman, giving her a place to live, and perhaps expecting the younger woman to produce a son with her husband that the older woman can also claim as her son.

In the United States, more states are trying to recognize the social and legal rights and credibility of heterosexual cohabitation and other domestic partnerships such as gay and lesbian cohabitation. All the same, it seems appropriate to make a distinction between *marriage* and *marriagelike relationships.* Marriagelike relationships are alternatives to marriage. Based on previous cross-cultural work (e.g., Stephens 1963), it would appear that all cultures have a generalized norma-

Figure 4.1

**Some Definitions
of *Marriage***

> *"Marriage is the emotional and legal commitment of two people to share emotional and physical intimacy, various tasks, and economic resources."*
>
> —David H. Olson and John DeFrain (1997: 10)

> *"Marriage my be defined as a socially sanctioned union of one or more men with one or more women with the expectation that they will play the roles of husband and wife. Marriage implies a ceremony, a union with social sanctions, a recognition of obligations to the community assumed by those entering this relationship."*
>
> —Ernest W. Burgess et al. (1971: 5)

> *"Marriage is the complex of customs centering upon the relationship between a sexually associating pair of adults within the family. Marriage defines the manner of establishing and terminating such a relationship, the normative behavior and reciprocal obligations within it, and the locally accepted restrictions upon its personnel."*
>
> —George Peter Murdock (1949: 1)

> *"Marriage is a socially legitimate sexual union, begun with a public announcement and undertaken with a more or less explicit marriage contract, which spells out reciprocal rights and obligations between spouses, and between the spouses and their future children."*
>
> —William N. Stephens (1963: 5)

tive concept of marriage as well as a recognition for marriagelike relationships or alternatives to marriage. **Marriage** involves a socially recognized, sexually based relationship between at least one eligible female and one eligible male. Different societies decide who is and is not eligible to marry one another. Marriage entails both social and legal obligations between spouses. Marriage also entails a contract that operates on custom and tradition, and/or can be codified into law.

In some cultures, marriage establishes a situation where men have exclusive sexual rights with their wives, though whether wives enjoy a reciprocal exclusivity is variable. Worldwide, marriage entails a system of rights of inheritance for spouses and legitimate children. In the United States, marriage is a three-party contract. The three parties are the husband, the wife, and the state. Marriage is entered into with the intention of permanence, at least in the eyes of the third party. To terminate this contract, one or both of the spouses must petition the state. Usually, the petition is referred to as a *divorce petition* or *divorce plea*. Spousal rights and obligations are contained within the annotated codes for each state.

Marriagelike relationships refers to all coupled relationships wherein the parties are committed to one another, have an identity as a couple, and establish obligations toward one another and the relationship. These obligations typically include financial and social ones. Marriagelike relationships in the United States include cohabitating couples, both homosexual and heterosexual. Another alternative to marriage, which can be seen as marriagelike, would be group marriage. This would be a situation in which two or more men and two or more women see themselves as married to each other.

Polygamy refers to marriage systems where there are many marriages. Contrary to popular belief, polygamy is not practiced simply to provide sexual diversity; polygamy grows out of economic and demographic demands of societies (Reiss 1980). There are two basic types of polygamy. The more common is **polygyny,** which is a marriage system in which a man may have two or more wives and, depending on the culture, at least one concubine. A **concubine** is a woman who is not eligible or has not earned the relatively high status of wife, but is a socially recognized sexual partner of the man. Polygynous groups are found primarily in parts of Africa, the Middle East, and Asia and Southeast Asia.

Polyandry is a marriage system wherein two or more men may have one wife in common. Polyandry is exceptionally rare; it is known to be practiced in fewer than a dozen cultures, including Tibet, India, Sri Lanka, Nepal, the Marquesan Islands of Polynesia, and among the eastern Inuit (Eskimos) (Haviland 1994; Howard and Dunaif-Hattis 1992). This marriage form has been most strongly associated with a group's attempts to reduce temporarily their birth rates and the strain on their environment in order for the group to survive. It also may occur if societies are experiencing rapid and deleterious changes, such as chronic war combined with economic and environmental catastrophes. The interesting feature of polyandry is that, since disputes over who the genetic father of a child is are rather fruitless, the concept of **social fatherhood** is practiced—that is, one man is seen as the father and is held responsible for the child's care and well-being in the context of the group's norms and customs.

Monogamy is a marriage system wherein one and only one eligible man and one and only one eligible woman may enter into a socially recognized, sexually based contractual relationship with one another. In the United States and most European countries, monogamy is prescribed as the only legal and socially acceptable form of marriage (Howard and Dunaif-Hattis 1992). Monogamy is becoming common among groups for whom polygyny is an option. There are a number of reasons for this. First, polygyny can be expensive. Second, polygyny seems most compatible to situations, such as labor-intensive agriculture, that require many children and adult workers. So, once groups are beyond subsistence strategies, this marriage system might become cumbersome. Third, Western ideas of marriage norms and treatment of women are having their effects in other parts of the world.

Even though polygyny was outlawed in the United States in 1890, news stories about polygynous groups occasionally surface. Typically, what is happening is that so long as individual rights are not being violated (e.g., forced marriages, incestuous unions) and the group is basically comprised of citizens who pose no threats to others, no official interventions are made. However, rightly or wrongly, when there is a suspicion that rights are being violated, officials tend to investigate.

If an individual in the United States knowingly and willingly enters into more than one marriage at the same time, and has no religious rationale for doing so, that person may be found guilty of a felony called **bigamy**. Monogamy is seen as normative, as reflected in the laws of the country. Bigamy raises the possibility that children born in unions other than the first one may not have rights of inheritance. Spouses married to the bigamist are sometimes not aware that other spouses and children exist. Also, in some cases that tend to get a bit of media coverage, it may be that the bigamist is both sexually and financially exploiting the spouses.

In **serial monogamy**, people tend to remarry after a divorce or death of a spouse. Before childbirth and pregnancy became less life threatening, serial monogamy tended to involve a widowed man marrying again for the second or third (or more) time. Today, the primary catalyst for serial monogamy is divorce, though death of spouse still contributes to this pattern.

Families by Mate Selection Pattern

Groups and societies vary by which mate selection pattern they encourage or endorse. Some systems prefer **endogamy,** which is marriage to someone who is defined as being socially similar. Depending on the group, the endogamous rule might be that a person has to marry someone from his or her own village. Other groups may endorse **exogamy,** which is marriage to someone who is socially dissimilar, or not a member of one's group. An exogamous rule, for instance, might be that a person must marry outside the patrilineal group.

Discussions of endogamy and exogamy invariably lead scholars to discuss incest. **Incest** refers to "illicit sex or marriage between persons socially or legally defined as too closely related" (Vander Mey 1992: 885). Scholars writing in the 1800s sometimes confused endogamy with encouraging incestuous unions. Since kinship is socially rather than biologically defined, it is not always the case that endogamous groups set the stage for incestuous unions, or that exogamous groups' rules of mate selection render incest impossible. For instance, in a patrilineal group that traces kinship through one ancestor, while ignoring other unions' contributions to bloodlines over time, it is possible that exogamous rules to the effect that one must marry outside this ancestor's groups might make available as mates people who are actually closely related biologically.

The United States, in the strictest sense, encourages neither exogamy nor endogamy. There are rules regarding incestuous unions, but that aside, the United States has tended to encourage **free mate choice**—that is, selecting one's own mate based on availability, accessibility, and desirability. Nonetheless, it appears that norms about who is a proper mate are in place. This is reflected in the strong tendency toward **homogamy,** or marriage to socially similar others. Americans tend to marry people of their own race and ethnicity, people from similar or identical social class backgrounds, and people close to them in age.

Families by Household Composition

Regardless of the caution against confusing families and households, people nonetheless use household analysis in trying to understand family systems. Often, a distinction is made between two types of family: the family of orientation and the family of marriage. The **family of orientation** (also referred to as the *family of origin*) is the family into which a person is born. The **family of marriage** (or the *family of procreation*) is the family a person forms by marrying and having or adopting children. Each of these family types contains a **nuclear family** unit consisting of a father, a mother, and children. Murdock (1949) indicates that other family members also might be residing with this couple. The nuclear family is the most frequently found family household type in the United States. Variations on the nuclear family occur, of course. There are nuclear families (dyads) with no children present. There also are **attenuated nuclear families,** typically entailing having only one adult with children in the household. In addition, there are **augmented nuclear families,** wherein other or honorary relatives reside with the couple and their offspring.

This family has been extended into one household through horizontal ties between brothers. Who would be in a vertically extended family? These brothers married their wives exogamously through the custom of bride capture. Traditionally, in the event of a husband's death, a brother of the husband was expected to marry his widow. What might be some advantages of this practice in a traditional society? What principles do you think should guide the comparative study of marriage and the family?

Extended families are comprised of the nuclear family plus at least one other relative in residence with the family. Extended families can be comprised of several brothers and their wives and children living together. Extended families also can be three-generation households, with one or more grandparents as part of the economic and social unit.

As discussed in Chapter 1, the extended family has long been held as an ideal in the United States. In reality, life expectancies and other factors have kept this from being a prevalent family type. For all practical purposes, U.S. families today can be described as **modified extended** (Litwak 1960)—that is, households tend to be nucleated, but identification, interaction, and association with other family and kin is common. We visit one another, hold various social events together, sometimes baby-sit for each other or help each other in other ways, and identify ourselves as members of a unit much larger than the group present in our household. According to Litwak, this modified extended family "permits the nuclear family to retain its extended family contacts" (Litwak, 1960, p. 9).

Interestingly, however, anthropologist William Haviland (1994) reports that until recently, extended family organizations could be found in the United States along the coast of Maine, where families relied on a mix of farming and seafaring for economic survival. Since neither farming nor seafaring allowed families to be economically self-sufficient, they alternated between the two types of work. To provide enough labor to tend the farm and to furnish crews for sea vessels, a young married couple would settle on the farm of either the bride's or the groom's parents. Sociologists believe that the rise in single-parent families could make extended family arrangements more common in industrialized nations. As is discussed in Chapter 7, extended family arrangements are currently used by many racial and ethnic minority groups to ease financial burdens and provide social support.

The Comparative Perspective in Family Studies

A **comparative perspective** involves comparing two or more social systems (Lee 1987: 60). Comparisons can be made between family systems based on race, class, ethnicity, or nation, for instance. As shown in Chapter 1, a comparative perspective also can be used to give a sociohistorical accounting for family systems of one country over time.

Kenkel (1973) outlines the merits of using a comparative perspective to investigate or understand family systems and issues. These include the following:

> Developing an appreciation of cultural variability and uniformity with respect to the family; heightening one's objectivity as a social scientist and in particular as a student of the family; developing an awareness of various aspects of the family in one's own society; and, stimulating curiosity leading to the formulation of specific hypotheses concerning family relationships, and marriage and the family generally. (pp. 5–6)

When employing a comparative perspective, one stands outside one's own family system and culture, puts on new lenses, and asks new questions. The new "lenses" are the tools previously identified in this chapter. For example, one can identify the key features of family culture by social class. Then, for instance, one may be better able to understand why divorce varies by social class in the United States. This perspective makes it possible to steer clear of declaring one social class better than another or viewing divorce as good or bad. With the comparative perspective, a person is able to "stand under" aspects of family life and more clearly understand what factors are correlated with a phenomenon and why that phenomenon may vary.

Babbie (1990) argues that one of the greatest values of sociology for students is that, because it relies on empirical evidence, it helps students become more critical, objective thinkers and less ethnocentric. The comparative method is a key contributor to increasing objectivity and decreasing ethnocentrism. As Kenkel (1973) notes, the comparative perspective requires that we dissociate ourselves somewhat from our sometimes fierce loyalty to our own families or our own values, and investigate issues without prejudice or bias (p. 6). When we look at family patterns in other societies, we become more informed about patterns in our own. This can help lead us toward a sensitized awareness of factors contributing to family similarity and variation.

The Comparative Method

The **comparative method** involves investigating the properties of systems. The "primary objective is explanation: How and why do the properties of social systems affect human behavior?" (Lee 1987: 61). Lee asserts that knowing which societies practice which marriage types is of little value. Rather, what is valuable is understanding what properties of the systems give rise to these practices, and how these practices affect the people in the system.

In comparing family systems by social class, race, ethnicity, or nation, certain factors must be considered. There must be equivalence in surveys, for instance (Jowell 1998). As discussed in Chapter 2, surveys ideally should be based on representative samples. Therefore, if analyzing divorce rates by social class, for instance, researchers need to make sure that all social classes are statistically represented in the survey, that there is no over- or undersampling of one class or more. With research that crosses national boundaries, equivalence entails making sure that measurement instruments are as comparable as possible. In Chapter 13, for instance, comparative analyses of children of divorce in Great Britain and the United States are presented. In these studies, the authors strove to make sure that measurements were equivalent. Had they not done this, the results would have told different tales about different groups, but provided no means of knowing if divorce had similar or different effects among children in these two nations.

British social scientist Roger Jowell (1998) provides 10 rules for cross-national research. These include making sure that survey instruments are appropriately translated so that concepts are understood in equivalent ways among different groups and cultures; avoiding the tendency to compare so many countries at once that one ends up with leagues of tables but few understandings; recognizing that cross-culturally not every topic is equally open for investigation; and providing exact details of sampling, response rates, and procedures for each country involved in a study.

The comparative method, then, requires that all aspects of research be carefully scrutinized and reported. Researchers need to state clearly, for instance, how social class was measured, nation by nation. How these measures are equivalent also must be explained to readers. Additionally, in powerful nations such as the United States, it is critical that cross-cultural research not impose culturally inappropriate topics. For example, if researchers interested in studying marital adjustment of wives in polygynous unions in Cameroon encounter resistance from repondents, it is likely that this research topic is considered inappropriate in that part of Africa. It is imperative that researchers know more about a country and its cultures before attempting research in it.

Summary

This chapter has built on Chapters 2 and 3 in an effort to provide you with the complete tool kit for investigating family issues. This chapter provides the terminology used to explore family by such variables as household composition, patterns of descent, authority systems, marriage types, and mate selection patterns. The comparative method and the comparative approach, along with theoretical perspectives and the general tool kit of research methods, will assist you in investigating family issues without succumbing to ethnocentric assessments.

Readings for In-Depth Focus

Cultural Definitions of Marriage and Sex Roles

In the following reading, Harvard professor of social science Wyatt MacGaffey takes on at least two intellectual journeys. One is the journey into research, detailing rituals and role enactments of selected groups in Africa. The other is a journey to understand more fully the pitfalls of ethnocentrism, whether one is merely a visitor or researcher in another society. As you read about the seemingly genderless, or gender free, Shango, imagine that you are there, seeing the cult's members yourself. With what group, if any, would you compare them in order to avoid ethnocentrism? What variables would guide your analysis?

■ ■ ■

Husbands and Wives

Wyatt MacGaffey

Students of Africa have long known that in some societies a woman may marry one or more wives to whom she is "husband," and be the "father" to their children. Until recently, studies generally took for granted that one knew who "women" were, in opposition to "men," and also that sexual activity was fundamental to the definition of these categories; sex was given and universal, though cultures put their own constructions upon it. The anthropologist Melville Herskovits was one of the first to describe woman-woman marriage: writing about Dahomey in 1938, he said that it implied no homosexual relationship but added, offering no evidence, "it is not to be doubted that occasionally homosexual women . . . utilize this relationship to the women they marry to satisfy themselves." Reports of woman-woman marriage acquired a new audience in the early 1970s as feminist writers (and some anthropologists) undertook to compensate for anthropology's traditional neglect of women's roles, experiences, and perspectives. Woman-woman marriage seemed to provide a precedent for lesbian marriage; the poet and activist Audre Lorde repeats Herskovits's unsupported assertion that some of these unions have sexual content.

The Nigerian anthropologist Ifi Amadiume includes Western feminists—especially Americans—among other anthropologists in a sweeping indictment of the tendency to generalize about "African women" and to pass judgment upon their life situations as conforming, or more often *not* conforming, to supposedly universal criteria of liberation and self-fulfillment. The title of her book, *Male Daughters, Female Husbands* (1987), announces its concern with complex gender definitions among the Nnobi-Igbo of southeastern Nigeria. Female bonding is stronger among the Igbo than in the West, Amadiume agrees, but she denounces as prejudiced, shocking, and offensive to Nnobi women the imputation, by Lorde and others, that it connotes lesbian relationships.

This new imperialism, as Amadiume calls it, continues Europe's (and now America's) centuries-old preoccupation with sex, and with the difference between the normal and the deviant—a distinction used to map the world and to index the difference between Us and Them, whether "Them" means other Europeans, other classes, other races, or people from other climates. In *The Geography of Perversion* (1995), a survey of "male-to-male sexual behavior" as reflected in the European ethnographic imagination, R. C. Bleys documents the extraordinary zeal of some nineteenth-century scholars to scrutinize the penises and anuses of young African men and to develop technical vocabularies with which to assess the likelihood that "perversion" characterized this or that tribe.

Not content with documentation, Bleys seems at times to partake of this same enthusiasm. Dividing the world into regions, he regrets the fact that reports of homosexuality in sub-Saharan Africa (which he treats as a homogeneous area) are few and ambiguous, but instead of leaving it at that he frequently challenges his sources' alleged "reluctance to admit that same-sex practices occurred." Nor does he engage in any serious critique of the evident unreliability of these same sources, asserting despite the ambiguities that "same-sex practices [have] been observed" and therefore, "We can deduce with great probability that acts of homoerotic tenor were indeed suggested" (whatever that means). On a report from 1801 that in Congo a particular word meaning "partridge" referred to someone who had seduced the king's concubine, he offers the truly wacky comment, "Perhaps Karsch-Haack's claim that it was a nickname for a male person who engaged in sex with other men was justified, as Aristotle had perceived that male partridges easily mounted one another." Meanwhile, Bleys fails to notice that in several of the reports the transvestites and alleged homosexuals are described as ritual experts; he reduces the complexities of social representation to a question of sexual practice.

Even the best of causes often shelters nineteenth-century views. The campaign against female genital mutilation is one of these. In accounting for the horrifying form of mutilation known as infibulation—the removal of the external genitalia and the sewing together of what remains in order to close the vaginal opening—too many Western writers have recourse to myth. Hanny Lightfoot-Klein's *Prisoners of Ritual* (1989) signals by its title the author's rationalistic assumptions. "Man in primitive societies," she reports, secure in her Frazerian mythology, "was mystified by the fertility of the soil, the birth and death of animals and human beings, their sexual coming of age, and reproduction. In the course of time, he invented a variety of rituals whose intent it was to regulate, appease, or bribe the deities or spirits thought to control these phenomena. As a result, surgery is almost universally practiced in primitive tribal cultures." Circumcision, she supposes, is a substitute for an earlier practice of placating hostile spirits by human sacrifice.

In their egregiously narcissistic report of an expedition to West Africa, *Warrior Marks: Female Genital Mutilation and Sexual Blinding of Women* (1993), the novelist Alice Walker and her friend, the film-maker Pratibha Parmar, display a complacent disdain for African culture—and for

Africans, too, except those they consider to be on their side. Like colonial conquistadors, they barge in to interview reluctant African women, briefly and through semicompetent interpreters, and come away believing that they have acquired knowledge worth having. They *know* that female genital mutilation belongs with polygamy, child marriage, and other forms of universal patriarchal oppression. Mutilated women become mere vehicles for male sexual pleasure, they assert, ignoring their own evidence that infibulation not only decreases male pleasure but often renders it impossible. Their concern with the frequency and quality of women's orgasm and other secrets of joy insists on women's universal right to what Amadiume, on the other hand, disdainfully calls "recreational sex." Parmar (herself coauthor of an article deploring the tendency of Western feminists to universalize their own values) says that in making the film she "wanted to evoke a sense of women loving their own bodies, reveling in their capacity to enjoy sexual pleasure through oral sexual practices." When she and Walker notice that, in a ritual they leave unexamined and unexplained, some of the dancing women are dressed like men, the extent of their curiosity is to guess that the women may be lesbians, or that they cross-dress to identify with the patriarchal oppressor.

Janice Boddy is a Canadian anthropologist who has lived among the Hofriyati in Sudan. witnessed infibulation, and discussed it at length with the women who practice it (*Wombs and Alien Spirits*, 1989). Without in the least endorsing the practice, she says the argument that it is meant to keep female sexuality under control confuses cause with effects. Women say the purpose is to make their bodies clean, smooth, and pure, thus enhancing their femininity and preparing them for womanhood. "By removing their external genitalia, female Hofriyati seek not to diminish their sexual pleasure—though this is the obvious effect—so much as to enhance their femininity." Downplaying sexuality brings their fertility function into sharp focus;

the women insist that they are not the sexual or social servants of their husbands but powerful, valuable contributors to Hofriyati society, indispensable as mothers of men and guardians of its culture. Their closed bodies are microcosms of the home, the endogamous lineage, and the integrity of their world. Men's circumcision, in a complementary metaphor, opens them to the world outside.

Whatever its ancient roots, one should not assume that infibulation now has the same cultural significance in the western Sahara as Boddy has described for the east, still less that genital mutilations practiced on men and women elsewhere in the world are reducible to variations on it. Nor, though the inhabitants of these areas are predominantly Muslim, is it an Islamic practice, as Americans often assert in the context of the ongoing "clash of civilizations." Boddy reports that some Hofriyati men who travel to work in Saudi Arabia and other parts of the Muslim world are bringing back the news that Islam does not endorse the practice and urging women to abandon or at least moderate the operation—a suggestion opposed by most Hofriyati women.

In a recent report in the journal *Africa*, Melissa Parker, an English anthropologist, describes her participation in the lives of women in a Sudanese village. These women could not understand why infibulation, in their view so necessary to womanhood, was not performed on girls in England. Parker gives us her personal reactions as witness to the operation, but also comments with some distress on the universal rush to judgment against it by the English men and women, some of them anthropologists, to whom she described it. Without pausing to find out about the cultural context, one of them "had no compunction about applying a range of derogatory and insulting adjectives to the women who carried it out" and another thought, "General Gordon should have murdered the lot of them." Parker concludes: "The apparent need for many people in the West to make sense of themselves in terms that emphasise particular

aspects of their sexuality, and to require particular kinds of sexual gratification for their well-being, is not, of course, universal. In other parts of the world, and indeed for some people in the West, such ideas seem immoral, amoral, or bizarre." Future research on genital mutilation, she suggests, should acknowledge that the intense emotions aroused by the subject are largely influenced by Euro-American discourses having little or nothing to do with the populations under study.

J. Lorand Matory's *Sex and the Empire That Is No More* (1994) raises the question of how to understand gender in new and yet more challenging ways. Among the Yoruba of southwestern Nigeria, he tells us, *all* women are husbands to somebody and simultaneously wives to multiple others. Central to his study is the transvestitism of male priests in the Shango possession cult among the northern or Oyo Yoruba today, a phenomenon which has, Matory maintains, nothing to do with sex. He contradicts the prevailing doctrines in the study of transvestitism and transsexualism, denying that cross-dressing in the Shango cult affirms or subverts gender categories, mocks women, undermines power inequalities, or ritually inverts order in the interest of disorder. Shango initiations are not rites of self-fashioning but of collective healing and reproduction, processes that are inherently neither progressive nor conservative. "Transgressivist" or culturalist readings are predicated upon the assumed priority of "normal" gender. But what if there's no such thing? Matory denies, for the Yoruba at least, that gender is a given which provides symbolic material in which other social relationships may be represented; on the contrary, gender is negotiated politically, and is itself the object of metaphorical projections which can be read as historical residues.

Shango is said to have been an early ruler of Oyo, an eighteenth-century empire that owed its expansion to the use of cavalry, a military instrument introduced from the north and not available to southern, forest kingdoms where horses would fall prey to the tsetse fly. After his death, as the deity, or *orisha*, identified with thunder and lightning, Shango became Oyo's spiritual patron. His legend and his cult contrast with that of Ogun, a spirit associated with iron-working and with southern "republican" military regimes during the nineteenth century. Nowadays Ogun is the patron of truck drivers, mechanics, and the military government of Nigeria. The Ogun cult is consistently patriarchal, "ritualizing the divinity of men in groups": Ogun priests, all male, wear male-coded attire, the charm-laden shirts and trousers of hunters and blacksmiths. Shango priests, by contrast, are mostly female, and even the male priests wear women's clothing, cosmetics, and jewelry.

Shango ritual and iconography are dominated by the logic of complementary gender opposition. Shango's cult, unlike Ogun's, is one of possession, in which the priests are "mounted" by the god. This mounting (the Yoruba word carries the same dual equine and erotic connotations as the English) recalls the history and political organization of Oyo, the "empire that is no more" of Matory's title. In Oyo, as in the Fon kingdom of Dahomey, wives of the king, who could never hope to occupy the throne themselves, were entrusted with ministerial functions outside the palace. There were hundreds of such wives, palace staff who did not necessarily have a sexual relationship with the monarch. Oral tradition reports that men performing similar functions began to be called "wives of the king" and to dress accordingly in female garb; many of these "wives," as royal messengers, rode horses. Matory argues that the lordship of the king over his wives, and of the rider in turn over the horse, is antecedent to the ritual image of mounting in modern Shango possession ritual.

The transvestitism of Shango priests underlines the categories not of man and woman but of husband and wife, which are not sex-specific. In different contexts, both men and women shuttle not only between wifeliness and husbandliness but between motherhood and what Matory is forced to call "brideliness," where the

status of bride implies subordination but that of mother sometimes implies dominance—the threatening, postmenopausal figure of the witch. Given the history of women's participation in the Oyo-Yoruba state and the sexual complexity of the "husband" category, Matory observes, one could not describe this society as patriarchal without numerous qualifications.

Matory's work is immensely suggestive of new readings for other African religious cultures. The only Oyo-Yoruba men who wear corn-row braids are possession priests, and carrying water on the head is among the symbols of "brideliness." Among the Nnobi-Igbo, titled women might not plait their hair or carry anything on their heads, and the priest of the paramount female spirit with whom their titles are associated is a man who must dress like a woman. Among the Ndembu in Zambia, a priest mimes sexual intercourse with young male initiands; they are his "wives." At his installation, a Luba king's hair was dressed in a feminine style. Though the bellicose Queen Nzinga, the foremost slave-trader of late-seventeenth-century Angola, kept sixty young men as retainers, all dressed as women, and herself wore weapons like a man as she led her forces into battle, need we register "perversion"? Even in America, sex itself is not necessarily about sex.

When confronted with gender which is not gender as we know it, we are tempted to view it all as theater, so that we can hang on to our conviction that, underneath, the actors are *really* just men and women. Matory will not allow this escape. Cross-dressing, indicating potential or actual spirit possession, is the antithesis of theater, understood as an "act." According to Yoruba concepts of the person (which are in fact widespread in West and Central Africa), "subjects may occupy a person's body without being that person or a fiction that he or she is conjuring up"; possession is itself an act of cross-dressing by the god. Moreover, the book as a whole goes far beyond the domain of rituals practiced, after all, by a minority of Yoruba, to show how the political values they are built on also structure the struggles attendant on both modern bourgeois redefinitions of gender and modern Yoruba politics in what Matory calls the age of Abiola (the elected and then jailed president of Nigeria). In "the modern bourgeoisie" Matory sees a loose alliance of the military regime, the southern Yoruba states, Christianity, and Islam, all concerned to carry on the work begun by the British colonizer of sorting out traditional gender ambiguities and confining women to their "proper" place. Ritual organization of women's resistance to this pressure center on the possession cults of Shango and the goddess Yemoja, in which Muslim and Christian women can unite.

In English, "sexuality" in the sense of "possession of sexual powers, or capability of sexual feelings" dates only to 1879. In today's America, sexuality appears to be understood as a package of natural inclinations, to be "expressed" or perhaps "repressed." Though "talk of 'the natural' is America's favorite officializing discourse" (writes Matory, paraphrasing Bourdieu), for the Yoruba naturalness is not a desired state of the person, nor are cultural constructions upon gender considered violations of nature. On the contrary, the persuasive force of the husband/wife metaphor is that it predicates cultural order upon natural disorder. The violence and disorder that Nigerians see as characteristic of North America indicate that Westerners lack the cultural integument that contains wild powers in ordered vessels and converts them to social uses.

The South African anthropologist Eileen Jensen Krige anticipated part of Matory's argument in 1974, in an analysis of marriage among the Lovedu. The Lovedu believe that a woman is entitled to have a "daughter-in-law" live with her; if she has no married son in her household, she may marry a girl herself. If the woman has a son who is away at the mines, she may permit him to sleep with the girl on his visits home; without knowing the legal details, nobody can tell whether the girl is married to the man or to his mother. Although a male is necessary for the procreation of children, in marriage as the Lovedu think of it, "not one of the constituent units need be a male." Krige recommends that

the marital union be defined as "a union between the conceptual roles of male and female instead of as between a man and a woman." We should consider the set of male and female roles in a particular society before deciding that the female husband in woman-marriage is a "male" role.

Translations of others' meanings are necessary but not shameful compromises, as they go on to generate new, and hopefully more precise, meanings. As Nancy Jay reminds us (in *Throughout Your Generations Forever*, 1992), "The notion that because we cannot possess *the* meaning we fail is based on a mistaken notion of understanding. Trying to understand the meaning of a ritual is not an act of acquisition but a work of relating; the understanding is not an end point that can be reached so much as a movement of turning toward the social world of the ritual actors." Our psychological and political investments in particular cultural definitions of life and death, female and male, the decent and the deviant, make such movement difficult and incline us instead to the language of absolutes. There is a note of defeat, but also of wisdom, in Janice Boddy's remark, "The female ethnographer shares with female informants biology, but not necessarily an understanding of what it means to be a woman in another cultural context."

Ethnographies of life, death, gender, and what it is to be human are inevitably political because these fundamentally volatile concepts are culturally constructed, and therefore necessarily contestable and contested, in Hofriyat as in Washington. If ethnography were as free of politics as it sometimes pretends, it wouldn't sell. Matory pleads for "a new politics of ethnography" which recognizes the value of indigenous verbal and ritual tropes. "Local conceptions of action, responsibility and personhood," he writes, "regularly differ from those that organize indigenously Western constructions of global politics and change, such as 'class,' 'women,' 'patriarchy,' 'homosexuality,' 'dependency' and 'oppression.'" This is not, however, a reiteration of the old, impossible demand that the anthropologist should write "from the native's point of view." Matory's work is consoling to ethnographers who worry that their translations from African languages into English impose distortions, and he rejects Mudimbe's dichotomy (in *The Invention of Africa*, 1988) between allegedly primordial African discourse and anthropological reporting. "No dialogue simply reveals the predialogic understandings of the interlocutors," because epistemological bridges are already in place. Yoruba think and speak about themselves in terms already inflected by English, by Christianity, and, of course, by Islam. In turn, anthropology owes some of its most successful models to the self-representations of African peoples. In the Americas, the ethnographic "been-to" is not the only interpreter of Yoruba religion—an international phenomenon that has been the focus, Matory points out, of at least four world conferences of worshipers and scholars. Anthropology participates in an intercultural dialogue that has been carried on for 500 years already, and continues not only in Nigeria but in Bahia and Brooklyn, wherever the orishas have traveled. Clifford Geertz offered a much-quoted answer to his own question: "What does the ethnographer do?—he writes." True; but if he is any good, before he writes he listens.

Critical Thinking Questions

1. Identify at least three different instances of imposing Western ideals and frames of reference on Africans in general and African women in particular, as discussed by MacGaffey. What might future Western researchers do to avoid these mistakes?

2. Assuming that there is a legacy among British and American people to focus heavily on sexual aspects of behavior, or to attribute sexual motivations and factors to the behaviors of others, what is required to "desexualize" frames of reference so that behaviors and rituals not seen as sexual by the participants might be more fully understood?

3. Assuming that MacGaffey's account of Alice Walker's report of her visit to West Africa is accurate, why, do you suppose, Walker and her friend basically walked away, merely having had their preconceived ideas confirmed by their observations and interviews? What is your assessment of Walker's explanation for the women, who, from a Western perspective, were dressed like men?

4. Given your understanding of patriarchy, do you think that female genital mutilation (a Western term, by the way) is fostered by patriarchy? What is your assessment of reasons some African women give for endorsing and maintaining this practice? Is your assessment ethnocentric? If not, how did you avoid being ethnocentric?

5. Short of "writing from the native's point of view," what should researchers do so that their analyses of other groups and cultures are accounts that those studied would see as accurate? How might employing a symbolic interactionist perspective help or hinder an unbiased accounting?

Part II

Family Studies
The Perennial Sociological Variables

5 *Gender*

Your sister just had a baby. Your father calls you to tell you the good, much awaited news. "What is it?" you ask. "I just told you," replies your father, "It's a baby." "No, really, Dad. What is it?" you demand. "A human being," he answers. "What did you expect? A monster?"

Imagine that this charade continues indefinitely. You are never told whether the baby is a girl or a boy. You do not know whether you have a niece or a nephew. What kind of birthday and holiday gifts will you bring? What games will you play with this child? What topics will you discuss? Which t-shirt will you pick up as a souvenir at Disneyworld—Mickey or Minnie? Belle or Aladdin?

The scenario just described was the topic of a short story for children that appeared in one of the first issues of *Ms.* magazine (Gould 1972). The story—about a "Secret Scientific Xperiment" in which a couple raises X, a child that they never identify to anyone as being either a girl or boy— demonstrates how pervasive gender stereotypes are. In the story, X develops as a perfectly happy, well-adjusted child, but teachers, other children, and relatives have a very difficult time interacting with X because so much of social life is constructed around presumed sex "differences." The impact of sex and gender on family life is the subject of this chapter.

Sex and Gender

Although the words *sex* and *gender* often are used interchangeably in conversation, they have different, quite distinct meanings. **Sex** refers to the biological, genetic composition of the individual and normally is determined before birth (Caplan and Caplan 1999). **Gender** refers to "the attitudes, self-concepts, and conduct expected of a person of a given sex in a particular society" (Elkin and Handel 1989: 210) and is influenced by cultural norms and practices. Individuals are socialized (taught) to behave in ways that the culture defines as appropriate for males and females. The question that has plagued scientists for centuries is which of these two has the greatest influence on human behavior and attitudes: nature (sex) or nurture (gender)?

Unfortunately, you will not find in this chapter the definitive answer to the nature-nurture question. Most researchers today believe that biological and environmental influences are mutually reinforcing and cannot be separated. All human beings are influenced by their environments from the moment they are born (and to some extent even before they are born). At the same time, all humans are born with biological blueprints.

Nevertheless, many researchers persist in trying to disentangle the effects of biology and socialization. Because the two variables are virtually inseparable, much of the research on sex and gender is flawed. In addition, researchers are influenced by cultural norms about male and female characteristics. Therefore, the very research questions asked often reflect conventional ideas about male and female behavior (Caplan and Caplan 1999). If researchers assume that males and females differ on some dimension, such as intelligence or aggression, they probably will begin by asking why such differences exist rather than whether these differences actually do exist or under what conditions differences emerge.

Researchers' preconceived beliefs about male and female "differences" also influence their interpretations of research findings. The following example illustrates bias in the interpretation of research findings: "A girl playing with fire may be said to be demonstrating her inborn desire to cook, while a boy playing with fire would probably be called a natural fireman or naturally daring" (Caplan and Caplan 1999: 2).

Additionally, the research literature tends to exaggerate sex differences and to underestimate similarities between women and men. Researchers most often investigate whether males and females differ on some dimension instead of looking for similarities between the two. Often, studies that do not find sex differences are considered failures and are not submitted for publication or are rejected by publishers (Caplan and Caplan 1999). Consequently, the published literature on sex and gender is filled with studies that confirm differences between the sexes rather than those that discover similarities. Despite these biases, however, research on sex development and gender socialization continues and has important applications in the sociology of marriage and the family.

Sex Development and Differentiation

Although the sex of a child is identified by the external genitalia (either a penis or a vagina), physiological sex is actually far more complex than secondary sexual characteristics. Physiological sex develops in four stages that occur prior to birth: (1) chromosomal sex, (2) gonadal sex, (3) hormonal sex, and (4) morphologic (or genital) sex (Elkin and Handel 1989; Kilmartin 1994).

The first stage in sexual development, established at conception, is known as **chromosomal sex.** Humans have 23 pairs of chromosomes. Each chromosome contains genes and copies of genes that determine a variety of physical characteristics from height and hair color to intellectual potential. Sex is determined by one pair of chromosomes: "Unless there are genetic abnormalities, females have two X chromosomes (XX) and males have one X and one Y chromosome (XY)" (Kilmartin 1994: 48).

In the second stage of sexual development, **gonadal sex,** undifferentiated glands (gonads) develop into organs, either testes or ovaries. In the first few weeks after conception, XX and XY embryos are indistinguishable and have an undifferentiated pair of gonads (Kilmartin 1994). If the embryo is XY, around the seventh week after conception the gonads develop into testes. Gonads in the XX embryo develop into ovaries around the twelfth week after conception.

Hormonal sex is determined by the fetal sex hormones produced by the testes and the ovaries. Testes produce more *androgens* and ovaries produce more *estrogens* (Kilmartin 1994). Males and females produce both kinds of hormones, but in different quantities, with XY embryos producing more androgens and XX embryos producing more estrogens (Saprio 1999).

Fetal sex hormones determine the internal and external sexual anatomy that the embryo develops, known as **morphologic** or **genital sex** (Elkin and Handel 1989). The presence of testes and androgens "masculinize" the male embryo and lead to the development of male reproductive structures such as seminal vesicles, vas deferens, prostate, and penis (Kilmartin 1994). Interestingly, estrogens are not necessary to produce female reproductive organs. In the absence of androgens, female reproductive organs develop, including the uterus, fallopian tubes, upper vagina, and clitoris (Kilmartin 1994).

In the course of normal development, the four stages of sexual development and differentiation are linked. In rare instances, a baby may be born with what appear to be normal male or female genitals, but with the internal reproductive organs of the other sex (Beal 1994). For example, a baby may be born with a vagina but internally has testes rather than ovaries. In other cases, babies are born with ambiguous external genitals. Doctors cannot determine just by looking whether the child is a boy with a small penis or a girl with a large clitoris. Individuals with incongruent external and internal reproductive organs or whose genitals are ambiguous are known as **pseudo-hermaphrodites.** The term **hermaphrodite,** half male and half female, describes individuals who have one ovary and one testis, an extremely rare condition, with only 60 documented cases (Beal 1994).

Studies of pseudo-hermaphrodites have provided opportunities to assess the relative importance of nature and nurture (Money and Ehrhardt 1972; Money and Tucker 1975). In some cases, researchers have found socialization, or the way the child is reared, has the strongest influence on the child's behavior, attitudes, and gender identity. In one instance, a child whose genital sex was female all her life discovered during adolescence that she was a chromosomal male. Doctors discovered after she failed to menstruate that she had testes rather than ovaries. She continued to see herself as a woman and eventually married a man and adopted a child. In this case the way the woman was raised influenced her gender identity and behavior more than her gonadal and hormonal sex.

Other studies show the impact of biological sex on gender identity and behavior. Money and Ehrhardt (1972) report the case of parents who brought their twin boys in for a routine circumcision, but one boy's penis was accidentally burned off during the operation. The parents and doctors decided that it would be best to surgically make the child into a girl and raise him as such. At the age of 17 months surgery was performed, the child was given a girl's name, and the parents began "treating" the child as a girl. Hormone treatments followed. Early evaluations showed that the child developed as a happy, well-adjusted girl who loved to play with dolls and help her mother with housework, while her brother continued to display "masculine" interests and behaviors. Problems began, however, when the child reached adolescence (Basow 1992). She was considered unattractive and inappropriate as a girl, had difficulty making friends, and became unhappy being female. After attempting suicide, she learned how her sex and gender had been reassigned, and she decided to stop hormones and live as a man (Beal 1994). In this case, the child's gonadal and hormonal sex influenced development during adolescence more than socialization did.

Clearly, maleness and femaleness cannot be understood as the product of biology or learning. Many social scientists believe that "the sexes are much more alike than they are different, and that variations within each sex are far greater than variations between the sexes" (Shapiro 1990: 57). The extent to which males and females are different or similar is influenced in part by biological factors and in part by environmental factors.

Agents of Gender Socialization

A child normally is socialized according to his or her morphological (or genital) sex, beginning at birth (Elkin and Handel 1989). A child born with a penis and scrotum is treated differently than a child born with a vagina. Stop and think for a moment about ways in which males and females are treated from the time they are born. Differences come to mind fairly easily. Boys may be dressed in blue and girls in pink; girls may receive dolls and tea sets and boys may receive war toys and athletic equipment; girls take dance and boys play baseball; men are expected to provide the majority of income and women are expected to provide the majority of child care. Other differences are more subtle, such as the expectation that when a male and female travel in a car together, he is supposed drive and she should be the passenger—even if the car belongs to her. Teachers, like parents, have behavioral and educational expectations for all children, but tolerance for misbehavior may be greater for one sex, and expectations for academic participation and achievement may differ for male and female children.

Social institutions and individuals that directly or indirectly transmit cultural norms and values are known as **agents of socialization.** Significant agents of gender socialization include parents, peers, the educational system, and the media. Every culture has multiple sources from which norms regarding appropriate and inappropriate behavior for each sex are taught.

Parents

Parents or caregivers possibly are the most important socialization agents for young children. Children love and trust their parents and desire their approval, and children are impressionable and ready to learn. Therefore, the manner in which parents interact with and respond to their children has profound effects on their development.

Researchers have documented a variety of ways in which parents socialize girls and boys differently. From birth, parents perceive girls as more vulnerable and are therefore more protective of them than boys (Hoffman 1988). Parents play more aggressively with boys, believing that girls are more fragile. These perceptions influence the amount of independence parents allow their children. Parents tend to encourage boys to be more independent by allowing them to cross the street at earlier ages and leaving them unsupervised more often than girls (Hoffman 1988; Kronsberg, Schmaling, and Fagot 1985).

Although boys may be given more independence, girls tend to be given more responsibility. For instance, girls are assigned more chores than boys (Etaugh and Liss 1992). Additionally, parents tend to assign chores that correspond to gender stereotypes (Hoffman 1988; Etaugh and Liss 1992). Girls typically are assigned chores most often done by the mother, such as washing dishes, making beds, and baby-sitting, whereas boys are assigned the father's duties, such as taking out the garbage and cutting the grass (Hoffman 1988).

The sex of the child also influences how parents respond to misbehavior. Kronsberg and colleagues (1985) found that parents respond more quickly to a boy's misbehavior than to a girl's, possibly because they believe girls are more responsible, obedient, and trustworthy than boys. Parents punish boys more than girls (Kronsberg et al. 1985), possibly because girls are perceived as less in need of punishment or as more vulnerable to harm.

Caregivers also provide different toys and room furnishings for boys and girls. Boys' rooms tend to have more vehicles, sports equipment, toy animals, machines, and military toys, whereas girls' rooms generally have more dolls, doll accessories, and domestic toys (Etaugh and Liss 1992). Parents routinely reward children for gender-typical (or gender-appropriate) play and punish or discourage gender-atypical (or gender-inappropriate) play (Etaugh and Liss 1992).

Interestingly, parents reinforce masculine stereotypes for boys more strongly than they do feminine stereotypes for girls. Researchers Idle, Wood, and Desmarais (1993) asked parents what toys they believed were most appropriate for their children and then observed the parents playing with their children. Both mothers and fathers rated masculine toys as most desirable for sons and feminine toys as least desirable. However, parents rated "neutral" toys as most desirable for girls and masculine toys as least desirable. Parents may have less tolerance for boys playing with girls' toys because they fear this play will lead to homosexual behavior in adulthood. In contrast, tomboyish or "masculine" behavior in girls often is seen as a phase that they will outgrow.

Researchers found that parents of both sexes tend to select "feminine" toys (such as dolls and kitchen equipment) least often when playing with both boys and girls. Parents also played with "feminine" toys for shorter periods of time than either "masculine" or "neutral" toys, indicating that "feminine toys are the least entertaining" (Idle et al. 1993: 688). The children in the study rarely rejected the toys that their parents offered them. The children's enthusiasm for the toys was influenced by the parents' enthusiasm and not by the gender appropriateness of the toy.

The toys offered to children have important consequences for their social, intellectual, and physiological development. Children learn appropriate gender-roles through gender appropriate toys (Idle et al. 1993: 680). Additionally, toys assist children in developing physical and cognitive skills. Neuroscientists now know that the way the brain forms and functions—that is, the *landscape of the brain*—is profoundly influenced by experiences (Barnet and Barnet 1998). Just as teaching a child to play music at a young age permanently shapes the neural circuits in the sensory cortex (Begley 1996), teaching a child to throw, catch, or hit a ball permanently effects his or her hand-eye coordination. Some researchers suggest that males may develop better spatial and mathematical abilities because they are given construction toys and building materials (Elkin and Handel 1989). Similarly, girls may develop stronger verbal skills because they are given toys such as dolls and stuffed animals (Elkin and Handel 1989).

Parents' toy selections reveal that socialization is a complex reciprocal process. Parents both stimulate and respond to the wishes and demands of children, and children influence parents' responses. Thus, the socialization process is bidirectional. For instance, parents may buy children particular toys because those are the toys the children prefer (Idle et al. 1993). Researchers cannot assume that purchases of gender-specific toys reflect the parents' choices.

Etaugh and Liss (1992) investigated parent-child dynamics in the selection of toys. The researchers visited kindergarten children before Christmas and asked what gifts they had requested. After Christmas, the researchers returned and asked the children what presents they received and which they liked the best. Quite expectedly, they found that girls asked for more "feminine" toys and boys asked for more "masculine" toys. Both boys and girls also reported liking their gender-appropriate gifts the best but also typically did not receive gender-atypical toys they requested. Thus parents tend to give children gender-appropriate toys, which children also prefer (Etaugh and Liss 1992).

The role children play in their own gender socialization cannot be ignored. Researchers believe that gender identity—the perception of oneself as male or female—may begin to form as early as infancy but is certainly developing by age 2 (Beal 1994). During the critical period (or sensitive period) in the formation of gender identity, between the ages of 2 and 5, children engage in gender stereotyping, seeking out same-sex role models and playmates and carefully imitating their behavior. Very often, young children reject other-sex activities and even begin to regulate their speech patterns to "enhance their identity as a boy or girl" (Beal 1994: 110).

Child development specialists speculate that young children exaggerate gender differences in the process of learning gender norms to help them better understand these complex rules. Young children do not have the cognitive ability to understand exceptions to the rules and therefore ignore them. Intellectually, a 5-year-old child knows that some girls like to play basketball and some boys are dancers; however, the child ignores such exceptions and continues to focus on distinct differences between the sexes (Beal 1994). Stereotyping appears to be a part of the normal process of developing a gender identity.

Parents sometimes are frustrated by the degree to which children insist on reinforcing gender stereotypes, even when the parents consistently have tried to raise their child in a gender-neutral manner. My oldest son, who saw his mother receive her Ph.D. and his father cook dinner every night, insisted during a trip to the hospital when he was 5 that "nurses *have* to be women." It seems that children learn gender stereotypes even when parents make a concerted effort to teach and model **androgyny**—the ability to display both masculine and feminine characteristics as circumstances demand (Bem 1997; Sapiro 1999)

Gender stereotyping diminishes somewhat as children age, particularly in girls. As girls mature, they show increasing preference for male activities. Etaugh and Liss (1992) for example, found that kindergarten boys and girls tend to select occupations that are traditionally appropriate for their sex, but as girls get older, they begin to select gender-neutral or traditionally male occupations. Older boys and girls may understand that jobs traditionally held by women have less prestige, power, and pay, making men's occupations more attractive (Etaugh and Liss 1992).

Peers

Peers, or agemates, are another significant agent of gender-role socialization. Like parents, peers reward gender-typical behavior with positive reactions and punish gender-atypical play "by providing fewer positive interactions and more criticism" (Etaugh and Liss 1992: 130). Children quickly learn that if they want the approval of friends, they have to conform to rigid gender expectations.

Gender norms are transmitted by peers directly through overt criticism and indirectly in the choice of play activities. In a classic study of gender socialization, Lever (1988) documented the subtle ways that children learn gender norms through play. Lever studied 181 Caucasian, middle-class fifth-graders, ages 10 and 11, using a variety of research methods: observation of the children at play, interviews with the children, and questionnaires about the children's play. Additionally, Lever asked the fifth-graders to keep diaries of their leisure activities, describing "(1) what they had done the previous day after school, (2) who they did it with, (3) where the activity took place, and (4) how long it had lasted" (p. 326).

Lever (1988) distinguishes children's play from children's games. *Play* is defined as "interaction that has no stated goal, no end point, and no winners" (p. 328). Play usually occurs in small groups, is not structured by teams, and does not have formal rules. *Games*, on the other hand, are more complex and competitive than play and are "aimed at achieving a recognized goal" such as a touchdown or a checkmate (p. 328). Games require larger groups of participants to make teams and are governed by explicit rules.

After examining the observational and self-report data, Lever (1988) concludes that "girls played more while boys gamed more" (p. 332). Girls played in smaller groups in which all participants engaged in the same behavior, such as riding bikes and roller skating, or activities that required taking turns, such as jumping rope or hopscotch. Girls usually did not compete directly against each other. Often, girls played fantasy games such as "house," which requires cooperation to construct and maintain the activity. Boys most often played team sports. The games boys played required large teams and were very competitive. Boys also were extremely conscious of rules that govern games, and spent much time disputing what rules applied and when rules had been violated.

Sex differences in recreational activities reflect and reinforce gender norms (Lever 1988). Girls and boys learn different skills through their play and game experiences, which may affect adult opportunities. Through games, boys learn strategic thinking, leadership, self-control, and sportsmanship—skills that may be particularly beneficial in the competitive, bureaucratic work world. Girls develop social skills in their play, including verbal proficiency and emotional sensitivity, but may remain at a disadvantage in corporate environments where the skills boys have developed are most valued.

Schools

School systems tend to incorporate a hidden curriculum of gender messages to students. **Hidden curriculum** is defined as "things that may be taught consciously or unconsciously but are not part of the apparent lesson plan" (Saprio 1999: 158). Although the educational system is designed to teach subjects such as reading, writing, mathematics, science, and geography, much more than formal lesson learning occurs in the school experience. For example, students learn patriotism as a cultural value through recitations of the Pledge of Allegiance. They also learn how different racial and ethnic groups are perceived in society by seeing what is (and is not) written about them in textbooks. And, of course, they receive hidden messages about gender norms.

The stories teachers read to young children or assign to older students transmit messages about the roles of males and females in a culture. Researchers have found that females are less represented in literature at all levels of education, from primary and secondary schools to college and graduate courses (Orenstein 1994; Sapiro 1999). When females are portrayed in literature, they often are engaged in sex-typed activities such as cooking, cleaning, and caring for children (Hoffman 1988). Most often, males are the main characters in fictional works and are shown in active roles (Hoffman 1988).

The occupational structure within the school system sends messages to students about gender roles (Orenstein 1994). In elementary schools, most teachers are female, whereas most administrators, such as principals, are male. In secondary schools, students see males and females separated by subject; math, science, auto mechanics, and carpentry are taught most often by men, whereas literature, English, typing, and home economics usually are taught by women. Occupational segregation continues in college, where very few women teach architecture, engineering, and physics, and even fewer are college presidents.

The role models students see in school clearly reinforce gender stereotypes. The absence of females as school administrators suggests that males should hold positions of power and make policies and decisions. The absence of males as kindergarten and first-grade teachers suggests that women are more patient and nurturing with small children. Course assignments suggest that males excel in math and science and females in literature and writing. Therefore, it should come as no surprise that in adolescence, boys and girls develop preferences for different subjects in school. Boys tend to prefer mathematics, believe they are most competent in that subject matter, and select careers that require more math; girls prefer reading and art and believe these courses are their strengths (Etaugh and Liss 1992).

In their interactions with students, teachers often have different expectations of boys and girls and therefore treat them differently (Orenstein 1994). Teachers may perceive girls as better students than boys, meaning that they are more cooperative and better behaved than boys. Teachers' expectations affect academic achievement. Girls are described as more attentive and less disruptive than boys, but teachers often believe that boys are more intelligent than girls and therefore have higher expectations of boys. Boys are reprimanded more than girls, but also receive more praise than girls when they follow instructions (Beal 1994; Elkin and Handel 1989; Orenstein 1994).

Socialization, however, is a reciprocal process in which students are not passive recipients of teachers' expectations and behaviors. Teachers may respond to boys and girls partly on the basis of gender stereotypes, but they also may be reacting to actual behavioral differences between boys and girls that are present before they begin school (Elkin and Handel 1989).

Media

Television programming often reinforces stereotypes; women, especially, are portrayed in highly stereotyped ways (Vest 1992). Programming for children and adolescents may be even more stereotyped than programs targeted toward adults. In children's cartoons, male characters far outnumber female characters, and females often are shown as getting into trouble and needing rescue by males (Beal 1994). Consider some of the popular children's programming in the 1990s. Teenage Mutant Ninja Turtles—found in feature films, cartoons, and comic books—depicts four male turtles and one female (April), who is a television reporter. Although April is a single career woman, she also wears tight, short skirts and often needs rescuing by the turtles.

The wildly popular *Power Rangers* stars three male and two female teenagers. All of the Power Rangers are courageous, athletic, and strong. However, the two girls (dressed in yellow and pink) often spend their leisure time shopping, whereas the three male rangers (costumed in red, black, and blue) usually study or work out.

Sesame Street, considered one of the most ground-breaking shows in children's programming, has only one popular female Muppet—Miss Piggy, who is loud, conceited, and vain. Although the producers of the show make an effort to eradicate stereotypes about social class, race, ethnicity, and disabilities, the lack of female role models for children perpetuates gender stereotypes. Over two decades after the program began, a mother called to complain about the lack of female characters and was told that the producers "were still 'working on it'" (Beal 1994: 161).

Programming for teenagers is also highly stereotyped. Intelligent females are depicted as less attractive and the unintelligent female characters are portrayed as beautiful and preoccupied with shopping and their appearance. Con-

What agents of socialization can be inferred from this photograph? What other agents of socialization might influence these children's choices of toys, television programs, and entertainment? Do you think socialization is the strongest determinant of gender behavior? Why or why not? In what ways is gender socialization a complex reciprocal process?

sider *Step-by-Step*, a program that was a routine part of CBS's popular TGIF line-up for many seasons, which depicts a blended family with six children, including three girls. The "smart" sister, who is always studying, was cute but not beautiful. The beautiful sister was very shallow and concerned only about her routine trips to the mall. The youngest sister, a quick-witted "tomboy," was respected by boys for her athletic ability but rarely had any romantic relationships with them. Such programs send a clear message that women cannot be smart, pretty, and athletic simultaneously; by choosing to have one of these strengths, women must automatically forego the others.

Viewers are exposed to a multitude of socializing agents in addition to television, making it difficult for researchers to isolate the impact that television alone has on individuals. In addition, practically every home in North America has at least one television set, making it impossible for researchers to find a control group of people who have not been exposed to television.

Researchers have compared groups on the basis of the amount of viewing and found that heavy viewers have more stereotyped attitudes about gender roles than light viewers (Kimball 1986; Morgan 1982). However, cause and effect are difficult to determine. Stereotypical television programming may cause heavy viewers to develop gender stereotypes, but individuals with traditional gender attitudes may be heavy television viewers because they find stereotypical programming appealing.

Another way of studying the influence of television messages on viewers is to control the programming to which individuals are exposed. Beal (1994) describes a study of a group of 9- to 12-year-old children who were exposed to a

13-part series of half-hour programs, entitled *Freestyle*, in which males and fe-males were depicted in nontraditional roles. Researchers found that those chil-dren who viewed the *Freestyle* programs were open to more nontraditional ca-reers than those who were not exposed to the programs. Boys who watched the *Freestyle* series "even became more receptive to the idea that men could be secre-taries or nurses" (Beal 1994: 167). This type of research indicates that even though children and adolescents are not passive recipients of television program-ming, they are influenced to some extent by the images they view.

In summary, "gender-typing is a complex process in which children are both influenced by and in turn influence socializing agents" (Etaugh and Liss 1992: 145). Parents, peers, teachers, literature, and television all influence the gender-role expectations that children learn. Likewise, the ways that parents, peers, and teachers interact with children and the products and programs that are made for children are influenced by the behavior, attitudes, and interests of boys and girls.

Gender Socialization and Social Change

Socialization to gender norms is a process that constantly occurs in all cultures. However, the gender norms that children learn may vary between and within cul-tures. For example, gender ideals differ between social classes (Komarovsky 1967; Rubin 1976/1992). Generally, blue-collar, working-class men and women hold more traditional gender expectations than college-educated, middle-class cou-ples. Ethnic and regional differences also have been found. Mexican American families tend to accept more patriarchal values than Anglo American families (Queen et al. 1985). People in the Northeast and West Coast are believed to have more progressive attitudes on a variety of social issues, including gender norms, than people from the Deep South and Midwest, and urban residents tend to be more accepting of nontraditional sex-role behavior than rural dwellers.

Gender norms also tend to change over time. As you saw in Chapter 1, in-dustrialization significantly altered American men's and women's family roles in the nineteenth century as the homemaker/breadwinner distinction emerged. Then, during the latter half of the twentieth century, the homemaker/breadwinner gender-role expectations were challenged by the increasing number of women in the labor force. Between 1950 and 1991, the percentage of women over the age of 15 in the labor force jumped from 34 to 57 percent (Bloom and Brender 1993).

The dramatic rise in the number of employed women is important because it both reflects and creates changes in gender expectations and ultimately in the socialization of children. As women move into the labor force, children witness more egalitarian roles in their families. Although few men share equally in house-work and child care, men whose wives are employed take on more of these re-sponsibilities than men married to full-time homemakers (Hoffman 1988). Sons and daughters watch as fathers cook dinner and mothers contribute to the family budget. As gender roles begin to converge, "sex differences among children and future generations of adults can be expected to diminish" (Hoffman 1988: 302).

Twentieth-Century Trends in Women's Labor Force Participation

Since 1900, both the type of work women perform and the pattern of women's labor force participation has changed (Piotrkowski, Rapoport, and Rapoport 1987). At the turn of the century, most women worked as private household domestics, as manufacturing operatives, or in agricultural jobs (Marshall and Paulin 1987; Piotrkowski et al. 1987). Today, women are most heavily concentrated in clerical and retail jobs (Marshall and Paulin 1987). The change in the type of work women perform reflects the increasing technology and reduced reliance on agricultural and manufacturing jobs since World War II (Marshall and Paulin 1987).

Despite the changes in the type of work performed, women are still heavily concentrated in traditional occupations. In 1995, 99.4 percent of all dental assistants were women, whereas only 13.4 percent of dentists were women. Although over 90 percent of all registered nurses, preschool and kindergarten teachers, child-care workers, and clerical workers are women, fewer than 4 percent of airline pilots, auto mechanics, firefighters, and carpenters are women (U.S. Bureau of the Census 1996). Recently, there have been increases in the number of women in nontraditional fields such as medicine and law, but men still far outnumber women in these professions; only one-quarter of physicians and lawyers are women (U.S. Bureau of the Census 1996).

The pattern of women's labor force participation also has changed. From the turn of the century until World War II, women generally were employed prior to marriage (in their late teens and early twenties) and then dropped out of the labor force when they got married and had children (Masnick and Bane 1980; Oppenheimer 1970; Piotrkowski et al. 1987; Weiner 1985). After 1940, it became increasingly common for married women to remain in the labor force.

Weiner (1985) describes the changing patterns of women's employment by dividing the century into three periods: 1900–1940, 1940–1970, and 1970 to the present. From 1900 to 1940, the majority of employed women were single, widowed, and divorced. Caucasian middle-class married women typically did not work outside the home. At the turn of the century, only 6 percent of married women worked, compared to 41 percent of single women (Weiner 1985). Although single women often worked even when their families could financially support them, married women usually worked only because of severe economic need, and generally were poor women and women of color. In 1900, more than 25 percent of African American wives worked, but only 3 percent of native-born Caucasian wives were employed. The number of women in the labor force increased steadily from 1900 to 1940, but the pattern of women's labor force participation remained similar: Women worked when they were single and then dropped out of the labor force when they married unless they absolutely had to work for economic reasons (Oppenheimer 1970).

From 1940 to 1970, married women joined the labor force in vast numbers, eventually overtaking single women as the largest group of female workers (Weiner 1985). Employment rates for married women rose by 28 percent each decade during this 30-year period (Weiner 1985). Recall that during World War II, women were called to work in war industries and many married women who were formerly full-time housewives joined the labor force as part of their "patriotic duty." After World War II, women were expected to give up their jobs and return to being full-time homemakers. Many middle-class women did leave the labor force and devote themselves full time to raising their children and caring for their husbands and homes. However, many married women with older children remained in the labor force. Married women without small children could justify their employment as a means of contributing to their family's quality of life.

Keep in mind that poor women and women of color were in the labor force even when they were married and had small children. Dire economic circumstances made it impossible for these women to live up to the American ideal of the suburban housewife. However, as older middle-class married women moved into the labor force, the racial composition of married women workers changed. No longer were working wives almost exclusively women of color. The employment rates of Caucasian married women rose from 17 to 30 percent between 1950 and 1960 (Weiner 1985).

Clearly, the pattern of women's labor force participation began to change with the advent of World War II (Chafe 1972). No longer did middle-class married women permanently exit the labor force after marriage; now, many women temporarily left the labor force between the ages of 25 and 34 to raise small children and then returned to employment when their youngest child was in school (Teachman, Polonko, and Scanzoni 1987). Masnick and Bane (1980) describe the pattern of women's labor force participation in the decade following World War II as "M-shaped." If the labor force participation rates of women were graphed by age, an M-shape would be formed; employment rates for women rose from their late teens through their early twenties, fell during their mid-twenties to late thirties, and then rose again from their forties until their fifties when labor force participation rates again declined.

Men's labor force participation following World War II was described by Masnick and Bane (1980) as looking like an upside down U. Men entered the labor force in their late teens, had their highest participation rates between the ages of 25 to 54, and then exited from the labor force beginning about age 55. Marriage and the birth of children did not adversely affect the employment rates of men.

Since 1970, the labor force participation pattern for women has again changed. After 1970, there was a dramatic increase in the participation of married women with preschool-age children (Bianchi 1990; Weiner 1985). Whereas married women with older children joined the labor force in vast numbers after World War II, married women with young children have entered the labor force primarily since 1970. Only 12 percent of mothers with preschool-age children were employed in 1950, but by 1995, 59 percent of mothers with infants and 66.7 percent of mothers with children under the age of 2 worked at least part time (U.S. Bureau of the Census 1996). Given the number of women who remain in the labor force after the birth of children, it is not surprising that women's employment patterns now look much like men's (see Figure 5.1).

Figure 5.1   Labor Force Participation Rates by Age and Sex: 1995

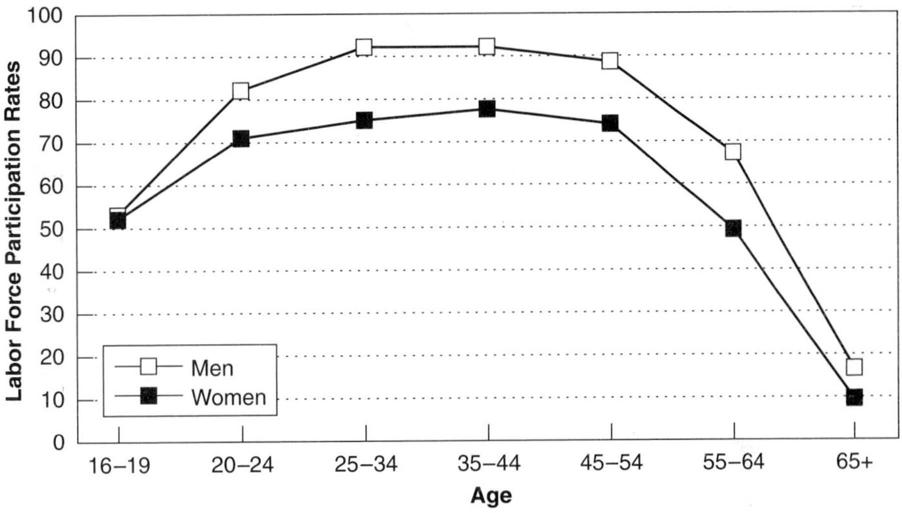

Source: Adapted from *Statistical Abstract of the United States, 1996* (116th ed., Table 615) by U.S. Bureau of the Census, 1996, Washington, DC.

Reasons for Women's Increased Labor Force Participation

Oppenheimer (1970) offers the theory of supply and demand to explain why both the type of work women perform and the demographic characteristics of the typical female worker changed after World War II. She argues that prior to 1940, the supply of single women—the type of female worker preferred by employers—kept pace with the demand for women workers. However, after World War II, the demand for women workers increased dramatically as the economy became more service based and less reliant on agricultural and manufacturing jobs. A service based economy requires a significant number of clerical workers, a job traditionally filled by women. But as the demand for women workers increased, the supply of young, single women decreased. In the first two decades following the war, the age at marriage dropped and the proportion of single women fell. The supply of women aged 18 to 64 who were single, widowed, divorced, or married with an absent husband was not adequate to fill the huge demand for female workers. Therefore, employers were forced to hire women who were previously considered inappropriate workers—married women with children.

Oppenheimer's explanation for the rise in the number of married women in the labor force is often cited because she examines the interaction of several social, economic, and demographic trends. There are, however, a number of social changes since World War II that Oppenheimer overlooks that also help explain the rise in the number of women in the labor force. Sweet (1973) suggests that the social factors that help explain the rise in female labor force participation can be divided into three conditions: enabling conditions, facilitating conditions, and precipitating conditions. *Enabling conditions* are factors, usually associated with family responsibilities, that give women more freedom to seek employment. *Facilitating conditions* are factors, such as increased education, that improve women's opportunities for finding employment. *Precipitating conditions*, like economic need, are factors that force women to seek employment. Each of these conditions will be examined more closely.

Enabling Conditions

Fewer family responsibilities enable women to participate in the labor force. Since World War II, several social changes have reduced family demands on women, freeing them to seek employment. First, many women are postponing marriage. Since the 1960s, there has been a gradual rise in the age of first marriage, reversing a trend of declining ages at marriage that had begun at the turn of the century (Teachman et al. 1987). Unlike women who marry young, women who postpone marriage several years have time to complete a college education and even become established in a career before assuming marital responsibilities.

In addition to postponing marriage, many couples also delay childbearing. Since the mid-1970s, the birth rates for women in their twenties have remained fairly stable, but birth rates for women in their thirties have increased sharply (Bianchi 1990). Just 10 or 15 years ago, women in their thirties saw themselves at the end of their childbearing years, but today, many women in this age group are just beginning to have children (Bianchi 1990). Women who delay childbearing have more time to be in the labor force without the distraction of parental responsibilities.

Demographers point out that couples also are having fewer children. The declining fertility rates are the result of a variety of factors, including the widespread use of the birth control pill. Oral contraceptives give women more control over the timing and number of children they bear than they had in the past (Hoffman 1988). Additionally, women's fertility begins to decline in their thirties, so women who postpone childbearing are likely to have fewer children. Finally, the ideal family size in American culture has shrunk as both the standard and cost of living have risen.

Declining fertility rates affect women's labor force participation (Smith 1979). Women who are childless or have only one child are significantly more likely to be in the labor force than other women and also are more likely to be employed full time (Hanson et al. 1984). Fewer children enable women to devote more time and energy to careers. However, Weiner (1985: 90) argues that the relationship between fertility and women's labor force participation "must be viewed with caution." Even during the height of the baby boom, employment rates of married women continued to rise. From 1940 to 1960, fertility rates rose from 72.9 to 118.0 births per 1,000, yet the labor force participation rates of married women increased by 88 percent (Weiner 1985).

Another enabling condition is the demographic trend toward increased life expectancy. Today, a Caucasian female born in 1990 can expect to live 79.5 years and an African American female can expect to live 73.7 years (U.S. Bureau of the Census 1996). People over the age of 85 are the fastest-growing age group in the country (Skolnick 1991: 15). In contrast, only 2 percent of the population in 1850 lived until age 65 (Skolnick 1991). The increased life expectancy, combined with declining fertility rates, means that women spend less of their life cycle actively engaged in parenting. The average woman in the postmodern era can expect to spend half of her life without having to care for small children and thus is free to work outside the home (Skolnick 1991).

Facilitating Conditions

Since World War II, several changes have occurred that have increased job opportunities for women. The dramatic rise in the number of women pursuing higher education is one factor that has facilitated women finding employment (Bouvier and Devita 1991; Hoffman 1988). As women become better educated they improve their opportunities for finding desirable jobs.

As Oppenheimer (1970) points out, the technological and economic changes following World War II also facilitated women's labor force participation. Because the number of clerical and retail positions have increased dramatically, women seeking employment are likely to find work in one of these fields. Economic and technological changes also have led to increased urbanization, which further facilitates women's employment. Women who live in cities have access to more job opportunities and higher wages than women who live in rural areas (Weiner 1985). As highway development and mass transportation have improved, more women have access to employment opportunities in urban areas.

Legislative changes also aid women in gaining employment. Title VII of the Civil Rights Act of 1964 makes it illegal for employers to discriminate against individuals in hiring, compensation, or conditions of employment on the basis of sex (or race, color, religion, and national origin). Furthermore, Executive Order 11246 encourages employers to take *affirmative action* to increase the number and percentage of women and minority employees. Such laws expand job opportunities for women and encourage them to seek employment.

Precipitating Conditions

While enabling conditions give women the freedom to seek employment, and facilitating conditions draw women into the labor force, precipitating conditions force women to look for work. Economic necessity is an example of a prominent factor precipitating women to seek employment. Inflation, recession, and higher unemployment rates for men help explain why many women, including those who are married and have small children, have moved into the labor force (Teachman et al. 1987). Although women generally earn less than men, the wife's income very often makes a significant contribution to the family budget.

Rising divorce and illegitimacy rates make many women the sole wage earner in the household. In 1993, 31 percent of births were to unmarried women (U.S. Bureau of the Census 1996). The rise in the number of single-parent families headed by women helps explain why many mothers of small children have been driven into the work force, especially following welfare system reforms.

In addition to economic necessity and rising numbers of single mothers, the increased standard of living in American culture also is a precipitating factor. Oppenheimer (1984) argues that today, Americans have increased life-style aspirations that require two incomes to sustain. For example, many parents want children to have their own bedrooms, requiring larger and more expensive apartments or homes. Many families also desire annual summer vacations and the ability to pay for higher education for their children. Although life-style expectations vary somewhat by social class, rising standards of living since the 1950s have made it increasingly difficult for couples to achieve their goals on the husband's income alone (Oppenheimer 1984).

Another precipitating force is the increased social acceptance of women's employment, particularly for married women (Hoffman 1988; Masnick and Bane 1980; Weiner 1985). In the past, the strong cultural prohibition against working mothers may have discouraged many married women from seeking employment. With the women's movement of the 1960s, cultural attitudes shifted so that women not only were allowed to work but they were encouraged to do so. The image emerged of the supermom who "strides forward, briefcase in one hand, smiling child in the other" (Hochschild 1989: 1), putting pressure on women to combine work and motherhood. The negative image of the homemaking role as unrewarding, boring, and unfulfilling also motivated many women to seek employment (Koerin 1985).

Correlations and Causes

A variety of social, economic, demographic, and historical factors contributed to the rise in the number of women in the labor force. Thus, no single factor or combination of variables caused more women to seek employment. Census correlations do not indicate cause-and-effect relationships. Causality is difficult to determine when studying complex issues in which factors are so interrelated that it is virtually impossible to discern which came first.

For example, we know that social attitudes became more accepting of working mothers at the same time that married women with young children were moving into the labor force. One must therefore ask which came first—more working mothers or greater social tolerance of working mothers? Social scientists cannot answer this question with any certainty, for it is likely that each factor is both a cause and an effect: Increased numbers of working mothers made the practice more socially acceptable, and the increased social acceptance encouraged even more mothers to move into the labor force.

Demographers also point out that some of the statistical increase in the number of working women during the century is a result of a change in U.S. census calculations (Folbre 1991; Folbre and Abel 1989). Prior to 1940, census data underestimated the number of employed women, and some of the increase seen since 1940 may actually reflect a more accurate measurement of the number of women in the labor force. Prior to 1940, the census asked about individuals' occupations, making the distinction between those who were gainfully employed and those who were not. Women who took in boarders, worked on the family farm, or engaged in production at home (such as sewing, crafts, and ironing) very often were not reported as gainfully employed.

Beginning with the 1940 census, however, the definition of labor force participation was changed to include family members "working for pay or seeking paid work in the preceding weeks" (Folbre and Abel 1989: 547). Under this modern definition, farm work and home-based employment are considered economically productive activities. Women who had been doing such work for decades and were not considered workers are now identified by the U.S. Census Bureau as "employed." Although some of the increase in the number of employed married women can be explained by the change in the way labor force participation is calculated, most social scientists agree that the rise in the number of working mothers after World War II is much more than an artifact of Census Bureau measurements.

Women's Labor Force Participation and Family Life

The increase in the number of women in the labor force, particularly married women with young children, has had a tremendous impact on family life. One of the most noticeable consequences is the dramatic rise in the number of dual-earner households. In 7 out of 10 of the 24.7 million two-parent families in the United States, both the husband and the wife are employed during some part of the year (Hayghe and Bianchi 1994). Dual-earner couples have become so common that they are "now the dominant family model among workers in the labor force" (Ahlburg and DeVita 1992: 25).

Family life in a dual-worker household can become quite hectic, especially in homes with several children. Men and women struggle to manage simultaneously the demands of three social roles—spouse, parent, and worker. Much research has been conducted to assess the impact that playing multiple roles has on individuals. Early researchers (e.g., Barnet and Rivers 1996; Goode 1960) believed that individuals have a limited supply of energy and that meeting the demands of several social roles rapidly depletes this scarce resource. Based on this model, dual-worker couples were believed to be constantly exhausted and haggard, their energy zapped by having so many role responsibilities.

Other researchers later challenged the notion that dual-income couples are drained and weary (e.g., Marks 1977). They argued that performing several roles simultaneously actually enhances the amount of energy an individual has, because success in one role restores or even generates energy for other roles. For example, a promotion at work could generate extra energy to meet family demands. From this perspective, dual-earner couples are portrayed as energetic and enthusiastic, constantly reaping rewards from several social roles.

Today, researchers recognize that performing multiple roles can be both stressful and rewarding. Dual-income couples certainly have many demands to meet, and at times the responsibilities are overwhelming. Other times, rising to the daily challenges of being a parent, spouse, and worker can be quite rewarding. Researchers have found that characteristics of both the work and family environment influence the amount of stress dual-income couples experience. Properties of the work environment that influence the degree of difficulty dual-earner couples have in combining work and family life include job satisfaction, work autonomy, job security, and income (Lambert 1990). Family characteristics such as the degree of happiness at home and the degree to which family responsibilities are shared also influence the amount of stress dual-income couples experience (Hochschild 1989).

Dual-Income Couples: Her Perspective

Well-known family sociologist Jessie Bernard (1972) wrote, "There are two marriages . . . in every marital union, his and hers. And his . . . is better than hers" (p. 15). She went on to argue that men and women tend to perceive marriages very differently because they have different degrees of authority in the relationship. Men, having greater economic and social power, perceive marriage as more rewarding than women. Although Bernard made this argument in reference to the traditional homemaker/breadwinner marriage, it is also true in dual-earner relationships.

Most Americans believe that husbands and wives in dual-income couples should share in household and child-care responsibilities (Amato and Booth 1995; Brannen and Moss 1987; DiBeneditto and Tittle 1990; Menaghan and Parcel 1990; Thornton 1989). However, egalitarian attitudes most often do not translate into egalitarian behavior. Employed women, like full-time homemakers, continue to "bear the bulk of the responsibility for children, for maintaining the child-care arrangements, and for housework" (Brannen and Moss 1987: 141). In dual-income couples, "most wives do two to three times more family work than their husbands" (Thompson and Walker 1989: 854). Women with egalitarian marital expectations are likely to experience greater marital instability the more they work because they become angry for being held responsible for the majority of household responsibilities (Greenstein 1995).

Hochschild (1989) argues that women in dual-earner couples work what amounts to an "extra month of twenty-four-hour days a year" doing the "second shift." Like their husbands, employed wives work the regular weekday workday at their jobs, but unlike the men, these women then come home to a "second shift" of work: cooking dinner; washing laundry; cleaning house; and feeding, bathing, and playing with the children. As the reading at the end of the chapter illustrates, women often feel angry and resentful that their husbands do not share or even help out with most of these second-shift responsibilities.

On the other hand, women often believe that household chores and child care really are primarily their responsibilities. Since the time they were little girls playing "house," women have been socialized to be wives and mothers foremost, so it is not surprising that adult women's identities tend to be more strongly tied to family than to work (Bielby and Bielby 1989). Many women feel guilty that because of their job they cannot keep their houses neater or spend more time with their children (Berg 1986).

In sociological terms, women who combine work and family experience **role strain**—"difficulty in meeting given role demands" (Goode 1960: 485). Role strain arises from both role overload and role conflict. **Role overload**, being overwhelmed by role expectations, occurs when women who work are also expected to do all of the so-called second-shift work. **Role conflict** is experienced when the demands of two social roles are contradictory, making it virtually impossible for an individual to perform both roles adequately. Many women in dual-income couples constantly face role conflict because the cultural expectations of motherhood—always being present and available for one's children—are incompatible with the demands of full-time employment.

Women in dual-career couples have several strategies to manage role strain. Many cut back on the amount of housework they perform so that they have more time to spend with their family and on work (Hochschild 1989). Other women reduce role strain by switching from full-time to part-time employment (Menaghan and Parcel 1990; Moen and Dempster-McClain 1987). Other women quit their jobs altogether (Hochschild 1989). Reducing the amount of hours in paid employment frees more time for family responsibilities, but it also places women in a precarious financial position. Women who cut back on or quit work become more economically dependent on their husbands and could be financially devastated in the event of divorce or widowhood.

Other women strive to maintain the same level of housework as full-time homemakers and the same amount of commitment to work as men and single, childless women. This can be accomplished in one of two ways. First, women can strive to perform all roles superbly by becoming the "superwoman" often epitomized in media presentations such as commercials (Hansen-Shaevitz 1984; Hochschild 1989). A recent airline commercial illustrates the common superwoman image. In the advertisement, a beautiful, well-dressed mother kisses her young daughter goodbye at a day-care center. She then hops on an airplane, flies to a meeting, gives a presentation, flies home, and returns to her daughter who waits for her with open arms. Amazingly, this woman, who may have just crossed several time zones, looks relaxed, refreshed, and energetic. Although superwomen in the media make combining career and family look effortless, most women find that trying to do it all is tiring and frustrating. Therefore, if they can afford it, many women use the second method of accomplishing all their tasks: hiring outside help (Hochschild 1989).

Many women try to reduce role strain by directly or indirectly convincing their husbands to do more around the house (Hochschild 1989). Some women demand that their husbands help with housework and child care and threaten to leave if the husbands do not help. Others nag by constantly reminding their husbands what needs to be done. Still others resort to more subtle strategies such as playing helpless or withholding sex to get their husbands to take on more family responsibilities (Hochschild 1989).

Dual-Income Couples: His Perspective

Men traditionally see "breadwinning" as their primary family responsibility (Lein 1979). Because being a good provider is a central expectation of both the father and husband role, men experience less conflict in combining careers and families than women do. Whereas women often feel torn between the demands of work and parenting, men tend to view their desire for a career and children as independent choices (Bielby and Bielby 1989; DiBeneditto and Tittle 1990). From this perspective, men in dual-income couples experience less role strain than their wives.

However, in some ways, men in dual-income couples experience at least as much role conflict as their wives. Men have been socialized to suppress emotions and to be aggressive and competitive in the workplace (Balswick and Peek 1971; Lewis 1978; Rabinowitz and Cochran 1994; Sawyer 1970). They may be admonished from the time they are very young that "big boys don't cry" and that affection and intimacy are "sissy stuff" (Balswick and Peek 1971; David and Brannon 1976; Kilmartin 1994). Yet, the norms of masculinity in American culture are increasingly at odds with the expectations of men in modern family life. With more women making an economic contribution to the family, men's roles as fathers and husbands have been expanded (Bernard 1989). Today's husband is expected to be emotionally expressive with his wife—sharing all his feelings and insecurities.

The contemporary husband also is expected to share in household duties (Bernard 1989). Most men continue to think of family responsibilities as "women's work" and thus resist their wives' attempts to get them to participate more fully in child care and housework (Hochschild 1989). Although men do not experience the degree of role overload that women do, the clash between husbands' attitudes and behaviors and their wives' expectations can contribute to both marital and role conflict.

Men's roles as fathers also have changed dramatically. Today, being a good father means providing more for one's children than material goods. The modern cultural definition of a good father is one who: "is an active participant in the details of day-to-day child care. He involves himself in a more expressive and intimate way with his children, and he plays a larger part in the socialization process that his male forebears had long since abandoned to their wives" (Rotundo 1985: 17).

LaRossa (1988) points out that men in dual-income couples often experience conflict between the cultural ideal of the good father and their actual conduct as fathers. He argues that although the cultural norms surrounding fatherhood call for men to be more actively involved with their children, few men actually are. The result is that many men feel ambivalent about their performance as fathers. When they compare themselves with their fathers and grandfathers, men may feel virtuous for being more involved than men of earlier generations. However, when men compare themselves to the standard of fatherhood set in the culture—the standard they see in the media and that their wives prefer—they may see themselves as failures (LaRossa 1989).

Why do so few men share equally in family responsibilities when wives and the new cultural ideal of the good father support greater involvement in family life? The answer is that both social and economic forces constrain men from being as committed to family as they are to work. Many men feel uncomfortable, even incompetent, in family roles. Few men were taught homemaking and child-care skills when they were young, so they feel ill-prepared to handle these responsibilities as adults (Pleck 1985). Additionally, they often receive little support from employers and colleagues for taking time off from work to meet family demands (Lein 1979). A carpenter in a dual-income couple described the reaction of his boss and coworkers when he occasionally had to take time off work to pick up his children from day care: "I sort of have had to shrug my shoulders and ignore it, but my co-workers and my boss are always, not always, but occasionally there's this, you know, 'taking off early again?' My boss makes a fair number of cracks about 'how do you expect to get it done if you're only putting in six hours a day?'" (Bidwell 1992: 74).

Practical economic considerations also make it difficult for men to fulfill the cultural ideal of the involved family man. Women contribute only about one-fourth to one-third of the total household income in dual-earner couples, making most families economically dependent on the man's income (Hanson 1991). Few men can afford to reduce their commitment to work to make more time for family roles. Many men who would like to spend more time with their wives and

How does this photograph suggest changes in twentieth-century trends in the family roles of men and women? According to sociological research, how will this dual-income couple view their roles as spouses and as parents after the birth of their child? What child-care arrangements are they most likely to make when they both return to work?

children recognize that greater family involvement means that they will probably have to be "less productive and ambitious in their paid work" (Pleck 1985: 158). For many, this is a choice they cannot afford to make. The new image of father is largely a middle-class cultural ideal (LaRossa 1988). Most men in other social classes still adhere closely to traditional gender ideals and feel little ambivalence or role conflict.

Child-Care Arrangements in Dual-Earner Families

As the number of mothers with young children in the labor force has grown, child-care arrangements have shifted. In 1958, when only 18 percent of married women with children under age 6 were employed, over half (57 percent) the children were cared for in their own homes, most often by their fathers or other relatives; 27 percent were cared for in someone else's home, usually by a friend or relative; and fewer than 5 percent were cared for in day-care centers (Bianchi 1990; Rapp and Lloyd 1989). By 1994, the majority of children of working mothers were cared for outside their homes by baby-sitters (31.3 percent) or in day-care centers or nursery schools (29.4 percent); only a third of children (33 percent) were cared for in their homes by relatives or baby-sitters (U.S. Bureau of the Census 1998; see Figure 5.2).

It is important to note that increasingly fathers are providing child care while their wives work. In 1993, one in four married fathers (1.6 million men) cared for their preschool-aged children while the mothers were at work (Casper 1997). Fathers who are most likely to provide care for their children are unemployed, work part time, or work nights. Since child-care costs can be quite expensive, it is not surprising that "fathers in families with lower incomes are more likely to care for their children than fathers in families with higher incomes" (Casper 1997: 5).

The dramatic rise in the number of children who are cared for outside the home by a nonrelative has led to national concern about *nonmaternal care*. Today, more than 9.7 million children under the age of 6 whose mothers are employed spend some time in nonmaternal care (U.S. Bureau of the Census 1998). Mothers are believed to be the best caregivers for their young children (Bianchi 1990), and many people fear that children who are cared for by others may be at greater risk for social, intellectual, and emotional problems. However, research on the effects of day care on young children does not support this belief (Elias 1999).

Day Care

When women with young children moved into the labor force in vast numbers in the 1970s, researchers began to evaluate the effect that institutionalized day care had on children's psychological well-being. Belsky (1990) explains that the research on day care occurred in several stages or waves. Different research questions were asked and different variables were included in each wave of research. Over time, the research became more complex, giving a better overall evaluation of the impact of day care on children.

Figure 5.2   **Primary Child-Care Arrangements for Preschoolers Whose Parents Are Employed**

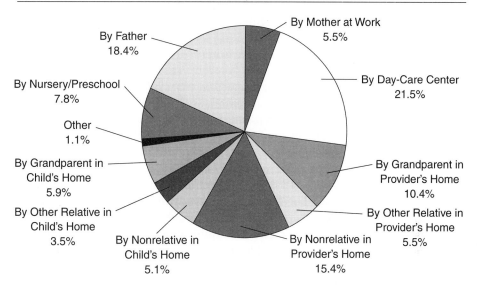

Source: Adapted from "Who's Minding Our Preschoolers? Fall 1994 (Update)," by U.S. Bureau of the Census, 1997, *Current Population Reports*, Fall 1994 (Update), Table 2, Washington, DC. <www.census.gov/population/socdemo/child/p70-62/tab02.txt7>.

In the first wave, researchers asked whether "extensive and routine non-parental care" in the first years of life "undermined children's psychological well-being" (Belsky 1990: 893). The research design was fairly simple: Investigators compared the scores on emotional, intellectual, and social development scales (dependent variable) of children who spent time in day care to children who were "home-reared" (independent variable). These early studies generally found that children in day care were well adjusted and that day care did not have a detrimental effect on children (Belsky 1990).

However, many of these studies in the first wave of research were criticized for having limited generalizability because of social class bias. Most of the data were drawn from high-quality, university-sponsored day-care centers. The finding that children who had high-quality care showed no ill effects from their day-care experience led researchers in the second wave of studies to identify factors that enhance or reduce the quality of day care (Belsky 1990). Researchers found a number of factors related to caregiver-child interaction, group size, and curriculum, which they suggested parents examine when selecting a day-care program.

Children benefit from one-to-one interaction with a consistent caregiver. Therefore, parents should look for day-care centers that have a low teacher-student ratio and low staff turnover rates (King and MacKinnon 1988). Children become attached to their caregivers and can become very upset when a teacher leaves. Parents also should strive to keep their child-care arrangements stable. Children who experience frequent changes in their day-care arrangements have little time to form attachments to their caregivers or friendships with their peers (King and MacKinnon 1988).

Parents also should observe the quality of adult-child interaction before selecting a day-care center. Caregivers should be responsive and attentive to children (MacKinnon and King 1988), have experience working with young children, and, ideally, have some formal child development training (King and MacKinnon 1988).

The quality of interaction that children have with their caregivers is influenced by group size. Children are most responsive and secure in small groups of less than 15 children, and teachers should spend time interacting with children individually in smaller groups (King and MacKinnon 1988). Additionally, children benefit from attending smaller day-care centers that are "more along the proportions of a large family than a small elementary school" (King and MacKinnon 1988: 395). Physical space for play is also important to children; preferably there should be 75 square feet per child, and the center should be well equipped, well organized, and free of hazards (King and MacKinnon 1988).

Parents also should inquire about the structure of the curriculum offered at the day-care center. Ideally, the center should strive to balance social interaction with activities that enhance cognitive development. Day-care centers that "focus exclusively on cognitive development tend to graduate children with good test scores but inadequate social skills" (King and MacKinnon 1988: 395). It is important that the curriculum be organized and scheduled consistently so that children know, for example, that after lunch time, they will have nap time or that after story time, they will be allowed play time.

In the third wave of day-care research, the focus shifted from the quality of day care to child-centered variables (Belsky 1990). Researchers asked what impact the age at which the child entered day care and the length of time spent in day care have on the child's psychological adjustment and attachment to adults. Many of the findings in this wave of research are inconsistent. Some researchers found that day care had no impact on the parent-child bond, regardless of the age at which children are placed in day care (MacKinnon and King 1992). Other studies indicated that infants who spend more than 20 hours per week in day care in the first year of life are at increased risk for insecure attachments to adults and are more likely to be aggressive between the ages of 3 and 8 (Belsky 1990). Infants in high-quality day care during the critical first year are less likely to suffer from attachment and behavioral problems (Belsky 1990).

In the first three waves of research, investigators failed to examine the interaction between the family environment and the day care-environment. Any problems detected in children who regularly attended day care were attributed to the day-care environment. Likewise, day care was credited for any social or intellectual benefits the children displayed. In the fourth wave of research, investigators began the more difficult and complex task of disentangling the impact of the family environment and day care on child development (Belsky 1990).

Researchers discovered that although both the family and the day-care environments affect the child, "the influence of family consistently supersedes the influence of day care variables" (King and MacKinnon 1988). Therefore, children who come from a nurturing, harmonious home environment are at little risk for developmental problems, even if they attend only mediocre day care (Belsky 1990). Researchers also discovered that "good and bad child care are not randomly assigned to families" (Belsky 1990: 896). Parents with little money and information have difficulty obtaining quality day care for their children, so children from lower socioeconomic backgrounds may be further hindered by poor-quality day care (Belsky 1990; King and MacKinnon 1988). However, high-quality day care can benefit children from lower socioeconomic status families by providing them with increased intellectual and social skills (King and MacKinnon 1988).

In sum, the research on the effect of day care on children indicates that day care can have both positive and negative consequences. Compared to home-reared children, day-care children are "more social, friendly, [and] popular with peers" (MacKinnon and King 1992: 230). On the other hand, day-care children also tend to be more aggressive and less obedient and compliant than home-reared children (MacKinnon and King 1992). The complete impact of the day-care experience on children can be assessed only after examining the quality of care offered at the center, the amount exposure children have had to day care, and the quality of the home environment.

Latchkey Children

Many parents believe their child-care worries will disappear when their children start school; instead, they find that circumstances worsen. As many as 10 million children need care before or after school, but few programs are available for older children (Creighton 1993). Formal after-school programs offered at day care and community centers often are extremely expensive and of low quality (Creighton 1993; Padilla and Landreth 1989). Additionally, many after-school programs do not offer transportation from school to the center, so parents must leave work to pick up their children (Padilla and Landreth 1989). The result is that between 2 and 15 million elementary school children are left completely unsupervised or in the care of an older sibling for several hours a day (Creighton 1993; Padilla and Landreth 1989). Such children are referred to as **latchkey children.**

The term *latchkey children* came into common use during World War II when fathers were away fighting and many mothers were working in war industries. Children were given keys, which they wore around their necks, so they could let themselves into their houses after school (Padilla and Landreth 1989). Today, between 7 percent and 10 percent of children ages 5 to 13 care for themselves either before or after school (Bianchi 1990; Schwartz 1987). Older children, between the ages of 11 and 13, are the most likely to be left unsupervised (Padilla and Landreth 1989; Bianchi 1990). Only 1 percent of 5-year-olds receive no adult supervision after school (Schwartz 1987). Latchkey children are most likely to come from Caucasian, middle-class families and live in suburban neighborhoods (Schwartz 1987; Bianchi 1990).

Despite the reports of neglectful parents, such as the Chicago couple who drew national attention by leaving their two children home alone while they vacationed in Mexico, most parents who leave their children unattended do so because they cannot find a suitable or affordable alternative (Creighton 1993). Although the majority of latchkey children are alone for less than one hour before school and less than two hours after school (Bianchi 1990), parents report that they constantly worry about their children's safety (Creighton 1993). Children left unattended report that they, too, fear for their safety, and are particularly afraid of getting hurt, being kidnapped, or getting involved with the wrong kinds of friends (Padilla and Landreth 1989).

As early as 1944, scholars expressed concern that latchkey children were "'problem adolescents-to-be in the 1950s and . . . maladjusted parents-to-be in the 1960s'" (cited in Padilla and Landreth 1989: 446). Although the doomsday predictions of the scholars 50 years ago were not entirely accurate, children who are unsupervised for long periods are at higher risk for substance abuse, precocious sexual activity, and lower grades in school (Creighton 1993). Additionally, children who have responsibility for younger siblings or household chores miss out on some of the care-free time of childhood and have fewer opportunities to interact with their peers (Creighton 1993; Padilla and Landreth 1989).

Educators have developed programs for survival skills and self-care to help latchkey children better care for themselves. Such programs generally involve teaching personal safety strategies (such as procedures for answering the door and telephone and dealing with strangers), first aid, fire safety, and guidelines for coping with emergencies. Many programs also include information on time management, proper nutrition, and ways to deal with fear, loneliness, and boredom. Programs tend to be most effective when they involve the students in role playing in addition to simply explaining proper procedures (Koblinsky and Todd 1989).

Although some experts feared that teaching children self-care would give parents a false sense of security and generate fear in youngsters, generally the opposite has occurred. Parents who have attended self-care programs with their children became more aware of potential dangers and often began reducing the time their children were unattended or arranging for adult supervision (Koblinsky and Todd 1991). Children attending survival-skills courses report increased self-confidence and are better prepared to face emergencies (Koblinsky and Todd 1989).

Theoretical Perspectives on Gender

Gender roles, dual-income couples, and working mothers are viewed quite differently when examined from each of the three theoretical perspectives in sociology (presented in Chapter 3). Structural functionalists stress that traditional homemaker/breadwinner roles are rooted in biological differences. Because women are biologically equipped to bear and nurse children, their primary function in the family is to rear children (Parsons 1964). The primary function of men is to support and protect the family as a social institution (Parsons and Bales 1955). Functionalists argue that these complementary sex roles must be maintained if the family is to remain cohesive and function smoothly.

Recall that functionalists further argue that the family, like society, is comprised of interdependent parts. When social change alters any of the components of the family, the entire structure is thrown into a state of chaos and may become dysfunctional. For example, traditional functionalism would interpret the increase of mothers in the labor force and pressures toward an egalitarian division of labor within the family as dysfunctional for the family. These changes can be linked to marital conflict in dual-income couples and latchkey children's increased risk. Contemporary functionalists focus on less judgmental explanations of social change in the family (Vannoy 1991; Scanzoni and Marsiglio 1993), arguing that as the economy has changed, family roles have had to adapt. Women provide much of the necessary labor in a service-based economy, and the rising cost of living makes it difficult for families to survive on one income. Vannoy (1991) contends that modern functionalists must acknowledge that the changing demands of the economic sector have made the homemaker/breadwinner roles obsolete and that flexible, egalitarian gender roles are now functional for the family.

Marxist and feminist conflict theorists emphasize that those who control economic resources have power and status in society, while those with fewer economic resources are exploited for their labor and have few privileges. Men have greater power in the family because they tend to earn more than women, even in dual-income couples. Because women tend to be economically dependent on their husbands, they have less power to negotiate role demands. Although women may want their husbands to assist with housework and child care, many often back down from their demands because they have a desperate fear of divorce (Hochschild 1989). Most women have seen friends or relatives suffer economic catastrophe as a result of divorce. Having little economic power, women suppress their anger and frustration and continue to do the majority of household and child-care duties in addition to their paid work.

Symbolic interactionists emphasize the power of socialization in shaping family roles. Women and men are socialized to adult family roles from the time they are very young. Little girls are given dolls and dishes to prepare them for mother and housewife roles, whereas boys are given trucks and footballs to prepare them for the competitiveness of the business world. However, rapid social change has made childhood socialization inadequate for today's adult roles. Although it is acceptable for women to work outside the home and for men to be emotionally expressive and nurturing, many adults are ill prepared to fulfill the responsibilities that have traditionally been given to the opposite sex. Women feel guilty about leaving their children to go to work because they have been socialized all their lives to know that "good mothers" stay home and bake chocolate chip cookies. Men feel awkward expressing their emotions to their wives and incompetent at changing diapers and doing laundry because as young boys they were not taught these skills. The discrepancy between yesterday's socialization and today's role demands often leads to role strain.

Symbolic interactionists further emphasize the importance of understanding husbands' and wives' perspectives in relationships. Symbolic interactionists argue that human behavior can be understood only in light of the subjective interpretation each individual has of the interaction. Much of the marital conflict in dual-income couples can be explained by looking at husbands' and wives' definitions of the situation. Most men believe that their primary family responsibility is to work hard at their jobs so they can be secure economic providers. Therefore, when a husband's work schedule conflicts with his wife's, he often believes that his work should take priority. When his wife indicates that he should contribute to household chores or child-care duties, he may become annoyed, for he believes that ultimately these are her responsibilities. Many women want to participate in the labor force as a source of economic and psychological reward in addition to being wives and mothers. They believe that if they are making an economic contribution to their families, their husbands should share in some of the household duties. When he resists her requests for help with housework or refuses to pick up the children from the baby-sitter so she can work late, she gets angry. From her perspective, it is only fair that he take on more family responsibilities; from his perspective, family responsibilities are primarily "women's work." These conflicting perceptions of the situation set the stage for marital conflict.

Summary

Sex, one's physiological composition, develops in four stages prior to birth: chromosomal sex, gonadal sex, hormonal sex, and morphological sex. Gender refers to the attitudes, behaviors, and roles expected in society of a person of a particular sex. Scientists have long debated whether biological sex or culturally assigned gender norms have the greatest impact on individual behavior and attitudes. Most researchers today believe it is impossible to disentangle the effects of biology and socialization; human beings are the product of the interaction of both forces.

Sociologists, however, are more likely to investigate environmental factors that influence the development of gender identity. Social institutions that directly or indirectly transmit cultural norms and values are called agents of socialization. Four agents of socialization—parents, peers, the educational system, and the media—are particularly important in conveying and reinforcing gender norms. Parents are likely to treat boys and girls differently, especially in the amount of independence they allow, discipline practices, and the toys they provide. Peers, through praise, criticism, and their choice of play activities, also transmit gender norms. Gender messages are conveyed in schools, as well as through the hidden curriculum. The books teachers use, the occupational structure within the school system, and teacher expectations are all parts of the hidden curriculum that socialize children to gender norms. The media also relay and reinforce gender stereotypes through sex-typed programming.

Gender norms are shaped in culture and are therefore likely to change as institutions within society change. The rise in women's labor force participation has influenced gender norms in society. Since 1900, there have been changes in the type of work women perform, as well as the characteristics of female workers. Women have become more heavily concentrated in retail and clerical jobs since the turn of the twentieth century. Furthermore, married women with young children have entered the labor force in record numbers.

The rise in women's employment can best be explained through a combination of enabling, facilitating, and precipitating conditions. Enabling conditions, such as postponing marriage and delaying childbearing, give women the freedom to seek employment. Facilitating conditions, such as increased education and legislative changes, improve women's opportunities for finding work. Precipitating conditions, especially economic necessity, force women to seek employment.

The increase in the number of married women with children has had an impact on women's and men's expectations and behaviors in marriage. Women struggle to balance traditional housework and child-care responsibilities with paid employment. Men struggle to participate more actively in household chores while maintaining responsibility as primary economic provider.

Children's lives also have changed as a result of both parents being employed. Children spend more time in nonparental care—with relatives, babysitters, or in organized day care. Although the research on the effects of day care is complex, we now know that the impact of day care on children is influenced by the quality of care they receive, the amount of time they spend in day care, and the quality of their home environments. Many older children are left unattended for parts of the day when parents are working. Educational programs have been developed to help these children, known as latchkey children, understand safety and personal responsibility.

Gender roles, dual-income couples, and working mothers are viewed differently when examined from the three primary sociological perspectives. Most structural functionalists believe that the drastic increase in women's employment has disrupted family life. Other functionalists contend that the changing economy and social structure necessitated more egalitarian gender roles, which are functional in modern society. Conflict theorists believe that increasing labor force participation will allow women to gain power and status in the family and society. Symbolic interactionists emphasize the role of socialization in shaping gender norms, as well as the importance of understanding women's and men's differing definitions of the situation in interaction.

Readings for In-Depth Focus

Conflicts in Gender Ideologies

People who have lived in dual-income households know the conflicts that arise between husbands and wives over who will do what chores. Responsibilities traditionally given to women—such as taking care of the children, cooking, and cleaning—must still be fulfilled, yet both spouses are out of the house a substantial part of the week. Some women expect that since they are contributing to the family finances, their husbands will share equally in the housework. These women have *egalitarian gender ideologies*. If their husbands also have egalitarian gender ideologies, there should be few conflicts over household responsibilities; both the husband and wife agree that housework and child care should be shared. What happens, however, when a husband has more traditional views, expecting his wife to take responsibility for housework and child care even though she is employed, but the wife has egalitarian views? This is the question Arlie Hochschild explores in the following excerpt from her book *The Second Shift*.

As you read, pay attention to (1) the way in which Nancy and Evan's gender ideologies are shaped by experiences from their past and (2) the tension created by their differing gender ideologies. Notice how Nancy first tries to resolve the tension and how Evan responds. What do Nancy and Evan finally do to resolve their ongoing conflict about the division of household labor? What does the resolution indicate about each partner's power in the relationship?

■ ■ ■

Joey's Problem
Nancy and Evan Holt

Arlie Hochschild

BEHIND THE FOOTSTEPS

Between 8:05 A.M. and 6:05 P.M., both Nancy and Evan are away from home, working a "first shift" at full-time jobs. The rest of the time they deal with the varied tasks of the second shift: shopping, cooking, paying bills; taking care of the car, the garden, and yard; keeping harmony with Evan's mother who drops over quite a bit, "concerned" about Joey, with neighbors, their voluble baby-sitter, and each other. And Nancy's talk reflects a series of second-shift thoughts: "We're out of barbecue sauce. . . . Joey needs a Halloween costume. . . . The car needs a wash. . . ." and so on. She reflects a certain "second-shift sensibility," a continual attunement to the task of striking and restriking the right emotional balance between child, spouse, home, and outside job.

When I first met the Holts, Nancy was absorbing far more of the second shift than Evan. She said she was doing 80 percent of the housework and 90 percent of the childcare. Evan said she did 60 percent of the housework, 70 percent of the childcare. Joey said, "I vacuum the rug,

and fold the dinner napkins," finally concluding, "Mom and I do it all." A neighbor agreed with Joey. Clearly, between Nancy and Evan, there was a "leisure gap": Evan had more than Nancy. I asked both of them, in separate interviews, to explain to me how they had dealt with housework and childcare since their marriage began.

One evening in the fifth year of their marriage, Nancy told me, when Joey was two months old and almost four years before I met the Holts, she first seriously raised the issue with Evan. "I told him: "Look, Evan, it's not working. I do the housework, I take the major care of Joey, *and* I work a full-time job. I get pissed. This is *your* house too. Joey is *your* child too. It's not all *my* job to care for them.' When I cooled down I put to him, 'Look, how about this: I'll cook Mondays, Wednesdays, and Fridays. You cook Tuesdays, Thursdays, and Saturdays. And we'll share or go out Sundays.'"

According to Nancy, Evan said he didn't like "rigid schedules." He said he didn't necessarily agree with her standards of housekeeping, and didn't like that standard "imposed" on him, especially if she was "sluffing off" tasks on him, which from time to time he felt she was. But he went along with the idea in principle. Nancy said the first week of the new plan went as follows. On Monday, she cooked. For Tuesday, Evan planned a meal that required shopping for a few ingredients, but on his way home he forgot to shop for them. He came home, saw nothing he could use in the refrigerator or in the cupboard, and suggested to Nancy that they go out for Chinese food. On Wednesday, Nancy cooked. On Thursday morning, Nancy reminded Evan, "Tonight it's your turn." That night Evan fixed hamburgers and french fries and Nancy was quick to praise him. On Friday, Nancy cooked. On Saturday, Evan forgot again.

As this pattern continued, Nancy's reminders became sharper. The sharper they became, the more actively Evan forgot—perhaps anticipating even sharper reprimands if he resisted more directly. This cycle of passive refusal followed by disappointment and anger gradually tightened, and before long the struggle had spread to the task of doing the laundry. Nancy said it was only fair that Evan share the laundry. He agreed in principle, but anxious that Evan would not share, Nancy wanted a clear, explicit agreement. "You ought to wash and fold every other load," she had told him. Evan experienced this "plan" as a yoke around his neck. On many weekdays, at this point, a huge pile of laundry sat like a disheveled guest on the living-room couch.

In her frustration, Nancy began to make subtle emotional jabs at Evan. "I don't know *what's* for dinner," she would say with a sigh. Or "I can't cook now, I've got to deal with this pile of laundry " She tensed at the slightest criticism about household disorder; if Evan wouldn't do the housework, he had absolutely *no* right to criticize how she did it. She would burst out angrily at Evan. She recalled telling him: "After work *my* feet are just as tired as *your* feet. I'm just as wound up as you are. I come home. I cook dinner. I wash and I clean. Here we are, planning a second child, and I can't cope with the one we have."

About two years after I first began visiting the Holts, I began to see their problem in a certain light: as a conflict between their two gender ideologies. Nancy wanted to be the sort of woman who was needed and appreciated both at home and at work—like Lacey, she told me, on the television show "Cagney and Lacey." She wanted Evan to appreciate her for being a caring social worker, a committed wife, and a wonderful mother. But she cared just as much that she be able to appreciate *Evan* for what *he* contributed at home, not just for how he supported the family. She would feel proud to explain to women friends that she was married to one of these rare "new men."

A gender ideology is often rooted in early experience, and fueled by motives formed early on and such motives can often be traced to some cautionary tale in early life. So it was for Nancy. Nancy described her mother:

> My mom was wonderful, a real aristocrat, but she was also terribly depressed being a housewife. My dad treated her like a doormat. She didn't have any self-confidence. And growing up, I can remember her being really depressed. I grew up bound and determined not to be like her and not to marry a man like my father. As long as Evan doesn't do the housework, I feel it means he's going to be like my father—coming home, putting his feet up, and hollering at my mom to serve him. That's my biggest fear. I've had bad dreams about that.

Nancy thought that women friends her age, also in traditional marriages, had come to similarly bad ends. She described a high school friend: "Martha barely made it through City College. She had no interest in learning anything. She spent nine years trailing around behind her husband [a salesman]. It's a miserable marriage. She hand washes all his shirts. The high point of her life was when she was eighteen and the two of us were running around Miami Beach in a Mustang convertible. She's gained seventy pounds and she hates her life." To

Nancy, Martha was a younger version of her mother, depressed, lacking in self-esteem, a cautionary tale whose moral was "if you want to be happy, develop a career and get your husband to share at home." Asking Evan to help again and again felt like "hard work" but it was essential to establishing her role as a career woman.

For his own reasons, Evan imagined things very differently. He loved Nancy and if Nancy loved being a social worker, he was happy and proud to support her in it. He knew that because she took her caseload so seriously, it was draining work. But at the same time, he did not see why, just because she chose this demanding career, *he* had to change *his own* life. Why should her personal decision to work outside the home require him to do more inside it? Nancy earned about two-thirds as much as Evan, and her salary was a big help, but as Nancy confided, "If push came to shove, we could do without it." Nancy was a social worker because she loved it. Doing daily chores at home was thankless work, and certainly not something Evan needed her to appreciate about him. Equality in the second shift meant a loss in his standard of living, and despite all the high-flown talk, he felt he hadn't *really* bargained for it. He was happy to help Nancy at home if she needed help; that was fine. That was only decent. But it was too sticky a matter "committing" himself to sharing.

Two other beliefs probably fueled his resistance as well. The first was his suspicion that if he shared the second shift with Nancy, she would "dominate him." Nancy would ask him to do this, ask him to do that. It felt to Evan as if Nancy had won so many small victories that he had to draw the line somewhere. Nancy had a declarative personality; and as Nancy said, "Evan's mother sat me down and told me once that I was too forceful, that Evan needed to take more authority." Both Nancy and Evan agreed that Evan's sense of career and self was in fact shakier than Nancy's. He had been unemployed. She never had. He had had some bouts of drinking in the past. Drinking was foreign to her. Evan thought that sharing housework would upset a certain balance of power that felt culturally "right." He held the purse strings and made the major decisions about large purchases (like their house) because he "knew more about finances" and because he'd chipped in more inheritance than she when they married. His job difficulties had lowered his self-respect, and now as a couple they had achieved some ineffable "balance"—tilted in his favor, she thought—which, if corrected to equalize the burden of chores, would result in his giving in "too much." A certain driving anxiety behind Nancy's strategy of actively renegotiating roles had made Evan see agreement as "giving in." When he wasn't feeling good about work, he dreaded the idea of being under his wife's thumb at home.

Underneath these feelings, Evan perhaps also feared that Nancy was avoiding taking care of *him*. His own mother, a mild-mannered alcoholic, had by imperceptible steps phased herself out of a mother's role, leaving him very much on his own. Perhaps a personal motive to prevent that happening in his marriage—a guess on my part, and unarticulated on his—underlay his strategy of passive resistance. And he wasn't altogether wrong to fear this. Meanwhile, he felt he was "offering" Nancy the chance to stay home, or cut back her hours, and that she was refusing his "gift," while Nancy felt that, given her feelings about work, this offer was hardly a gift.

In the sixth year of her marriage, when Nancy again intensified her pressure on Evan to commit himself to equal sharing, Evan recalled saying, "Nancy, why don't you cut back to half time, that way you can fit everything in." At first Nancy was baffled: "We've been married all this time, and you *still* don't get it. Work is important to me. I worked *hard* to get my MSW. Why *should* I give it up?" Nancy also explained to Evan and later to me, "I think my degree and my job has been my way of reassuring myself that I won't end up like my mother." Yet she'd received little emotional support in getting her degree from either her parents or in-laws. (Her mother had avoided asking about her thesis, and her in-laws, though invited, did not attend her graduation, later claiming they'd never been invited.)

In addition, Nancy was more excited about seeing her elderly clients in tenderloin hotels than Evan was about selling couches to furniture salesmen with greased-back hair. Why shouldn't Evan make as many compromises with his career ambitions and his leisure as she'd made with hers? She couldn't see it Evan's way, and Evan couldn't see it hers.

In years of alternating struggle and compromise, Nancy had seen only fleeting mirages of cooperation, visions that appeared when she got sick or withdrew, and disappeared when she got better or came forward.

After seven years of loving marriage, Nancy and Evan had finally come to a terrible impasse. Their emotional standard of living had drastically declined: they began to snap at each other, to criticize, to carp. Each felt taken advantage of: Evan, because his offering of a good arrangement was deemed unacceptable, and Nancy, because Evan wouldn't do what she deeply felt was "fair "

This struggle made its way into their sexual life—first through Nancy directly, and then through Joey. Nancy had always disdained any form of feminine wiliness or manipulation. Her family saw her as "a flaming feminist" and that was how she saw herself. As such, she felt above the underhanded ways traditional women used to get around men. She mused, "When I was a teenager, I vowed I would *never* use sex to get my way with a man. It is not self-respecting; it's demeaning. But when Evan refused to carry his load at home, I did, I used sex. I said, 'Look, Evan, I would not be this exhausted and asexual every night if I didn't have so much to face every morning.'" She felt reduced to an old "strategy," and her modern ideas made her ashamed of it. At the same time, she'd run out of other, modern ways.

The idea of a separation arose, and they became frightened. Nancy looked at the deteriorating marriages and fresh divorces of couples with young children around them. One unhappy husband they knew had become so uninvolved in family life (they didn't know whether his unhappiness made him uninvolved, or

whether his lack of involvement had caused his wife to be unhappy) that his wife left him. In another case, Nancy felt the wife had "nagged" her husband so much that he abandoned her for another woman. In both cases, the couple was less happy after the divorce than before, and both wives took the children and struggled desperately to survive financially. Nancy took stock. She asked herself, '"Why wreck a marriage over a dirty frying pan?" Is it really worth it?

UPSTAIRS-DOWNSTAIRS: A FAMILY MYTH AS "SOLUTION"

Not long after this crisis in the Holts' marriage, there was a dramatic lessening of tension over the issue of the second shift. It was as if the issue was closed. Evan had won. Nancy would do the second shift. Evan expressed vague guilt but beyond that he had nothing to say. Nancy had wearied of continually raising the topic, wearied of the lack of resolution. Now in the exhaustion of defeat, she wanted the struggle to be over too. Evan was "so good" in *other* ways, why debilitate their marriage by continual quarreling. Besides, she told me, "Women always adjust more, don't they?"

One day, when I asked Nancy to tell me who did which tasks from a long list of household chores, she interrupted me with a broad wave of her hand and said, "I do the upstairs, Evan does the downstairs." What does that mean? I asked. Matter-of-factly, she explained that the upstairs included the living room, the dining room, the kitchen, two bedrooms, and two baths. The downstairs meant the garage, a place for storage and hobbies—Evan's hobbies. She explained this as a "sharing" arrangement, without humor or irony—just as Evan did later. Both said they had agreed it was the best solution to their dispute. Evan would take care of the car, the garage, and Max, the family dog. As Nancy explained, "The dog is all Evan's problem. I don't have to deal with the dog." Nancy took care of the rest.

For purposes of accommodating the second shift, then, the Holts' garage was elevated to the full moral and practical equivalent of the rest of the house. For Nancy and Evan, "upstairs and downstairs," "inside and outside," was vaguely described like "half and half," a fair division of labor based on a natural division of their house.

The Holts presented their upstairs-downstairs agreement as a perfectly equitable solution to a problem they "once had." This belief is what we might call a "family myth," even a modest delusional system. Why did they believe it? I think they believed it because they needed to believe it, because it solved a terrible problem. It allowed Nancy to continue thinking of herself as the sort of woman whose husband didn't abuse her—a self-conception that mattered a great deal to her. And it avoided the hard truth that, in his stolid, passive way, Evan had refused to share. It avoided the truth, too, that in their showdown, Nancy was more afraid of divorce than Evan was. This outer cover to their family life, this family myth, was jointly devised. It was an attempt to agree that there was no conflict over the second shift, no tension between their versions of manhood and womanhood, and that the powerful crisis that had arisen was temporary and minor.

The wish to avoid such a conflict is natural enough. But their avoidance was tacitly supported by the surrounding culture, especially the image of the woman with the flying hair. After all, this admirable woman also proudly does the "upstairs" each day without a husband's help and without conflict.

After Nancy and Evan reached their upstairs-downstairs agreement, their confrontations ended. They were nearly forgotten. Yet, as she described their daily life months after the agreement, Nancy's resentment still seemed alive and well. For example, she said:

> Evan and I eventually divided the labor so that I do the upstairs and Evan does the downstairs and the dog. So the dog is my husband's problem. But when I was getting the dog outside and getting Joey ready for childcare, and cleaning up the mess of feeding the cat, and getting the lunches to-

gether, and having my son wipe his nose on my outfit so I would have to change—then I was pissed! I felt that I was doing *everything*. All Evan was doing was getting up, having coffee, reading the paper, and saying, "Well, I have to go now," and often forgetting the lunch I'd bothered to make.

She also mentioned that she had fallen into the habit of putting Joey to bed in a certain way: he asked to be swung around by the arms, dropped on the bed, nuzzled and hugged, whispered to in his ear. Joey waited for her attention. He didn't go to sleep without it. But, increasingly, when Nancy tried it at eight or nine, the ritual didn't put Joey to sleep. On the contrary, it woke him up. It was then that Joey began to say he could only go to sleep in his parents' bed, that he began to sleep in their bed and to encroach on their sexual life.

Near the end of my visits, it struck me that Nancy was putting Joey to bed in an "exciting" way, later and later at night, in order to tell Evan something important: "You win, I'll go on doing all the work at home, but I'm angry about it and I'll make you pay." Evan had won the battle but lost the war. According to the family myth, all was well: the struggle had been resolved by the upstairs-downstairs agreement. But suppressed in one area of their marriage, this struggle lived on in another—as Joey's Problem, and as theirs.

NANCY'S "PROGRAM" TO SUSTAIN THE MYTH

There was a moment, I believe, when Nancy seemed to *decide* to give up on this one. She decided to try not to resent Evan. Whether or not other women face a moment just like this, at the very least they face the need to deal with all the feelings that naturally arise from a clash between a treasured ideal and an incompatible reality. In the age of a stalled revolution, it is a problem a great many women face.

Emotionally, Nancy's compromise from time to time slipped; she would forget and grow resentful again. Her new resolve needed maintenance. Only half aware that she was doing so, Nancy went to extraordinary lengths to maintain it. She could tell me now, a year or so after her "decision," in a matter-of-fact and noncritical way: "Evan likes to come home to a hot meal. He doesn't like to clear the table. He doesn't like to do the dishes. He likes to go watch TV. He likes to play with his son when he feels like it and not feel like he should be with him more." She seemed resigned.

Everything was "fine." But it had taken an extraordinary amount of complex "emotion work"—the work of *trying* to feel the "right" feeling, the feeling she wanted to feel—to make and keep everything "fine." Across the nation at this particular time in history, this emotion work is often all that stands between the stalled revolution on the one hand, and broken marriages on the other.

It would have been easier for Nancy Holt to do what some other women did: indignantly cling to her goal of sharing the second shift. Or she could have cynically renounced all forms of feminism as misguided, could have cleared away any ideological supports to her indignation, so as to smooth her troubled bond with Evan. Or, like her mother, she could have sunk into quiet depression, disguised perhaps by overbusyness, drinking, overeating. She did none of these things Instead, she did something more complicated. She became *benignly* accommodating.

■ ■ ■

HOW MANY HOLTS?

In one key way the Holts were typical of the vast majority of two-job couples: their family life had become the shock absorber for a stalled revolution whose origin lay far outside it—in economic and cultural trends that bear very differently on men and women. Nancy was reading books, newspaper articles, and watching TV programs on the changing role of women. Evan wasn't. Nancy felt benefited by these changes; Evan didn't. In her ideals and in reality, Nancy

was more different from her mother than Evan was from his father, for the culture and economy were in general pressing change faster upon women like her than upon men like Evan. Nancy had gone to college; her mother hadn't. Nancy had a professional job; her mother never had. Nancy had the idea that she should be equal with her husband; her mother hadn't been much exposed to that idea in her day. Nancy felt she should share the job of earning money, and that Evan should share the work at home; her mother hadn't imagined that was possible. Evan went to college, his father (and the other boys in his family, though not the girls) had gone too. Work was important to Evan's identity as a man as it had been for his father before him. Indeed, Evan felt the same way about family roles as his father had felt in his day. The new job opportunities and the feminist movement of the 1960s and '70s had transformed Nancy but left Evan pretty much the same. And the friction created by this difference between them moved to the issue of second shift as metal to a magnet. By the end, Evan did less housework and childcare than most men married to working women—but not much less. Evan and Nancy were also typical of nearly forty percent of the marriages I studied in their clash of gender ideologies and their corresponding difference in notion about what constituted a "sacrifice" and what did not. By far the most common form of mismatch was like that between Nancy, an egalitarian, and Evan, a transitional.

But for most couples, the tensions between strategies did not move so quickly and powerfully to issues of housework and child-care. Nancy pushed harder than most women to get her husband to share the work at home, and she also lost more overwhelmingly than the few other women who fought that hard. Evan pursued his strategy of passive resistance with more quiet tenacity than most men, and he allowed himself to become far more marginal to his son's life than most other fathers. The myth of the Holts' "equal" arrangement seemed slightly more odd than other family myths that encapsulated equally powerful conflicts.

Beyond their upstairs-downstairs myth, the Holts tell us a great deal about the subtle ways a couple can encapsulate the tension caused by a struggle over the second shift without resolving the problem or divorcing. Like Nancy Holt, many women struggle to avoid, suppress, obscure, or mystify a frightening conflict over the second shift. They do not struggle about this because they start off wanting to, or because such struggle is inevitable or because women inevitably lose, but because they are forced to choose between equality and marriage. And they choose marriage. When asked about "ideal" relations between men and women in general, about what they want for their daughters, about what "ideally" they'd like in their own marriage, most working mothers "wished" their men would share the work at home.

But many "wish" it instead of "want" it. Other goals—like keeping peace at home—come first. Nancy Holt did some extraordinary behind-the-scenes emotion work to prevent her ideals from clashing with her marriage. In the end, she had confined and miniaturized her ideas of equality successfully enough to do two things she badly wanted to do: feel like a feminist, and live at peace with a man who was not. Her program had "worked." Evan won on the reality of the situation, because Nancy did the second shift. Nancy won on the cover story; they would talk about it as if they shared.

Nancy wore the upstairs-downstairs myth as an ideological cloak to protect her from the contradictions in her marriage and from the cultural and economic forces that press upon it. Nancy and Evan Holt were caught on opposite sides of the gender revolution occurring all around them. Through the 1960s, 1970s, and 1980s masses of women entered the public world of work—but went only so far up the occupational ladder. They tried for "equal" marriages, but got only so far in achieving it. They married men who liked them to work at the office but who wouldn't share the extra month a year at home. When confusion about the identity of the working woman created a cultural vacuum in the 1970s and 1980s, the image of the supermom quietly glided in. She made the "stall" seem normal and happy. But beneath the happy image of the woman with the flying hair are modern marriages like the Holts', reflecting intricate webs of tension, and the huge, hidden emotional cost to women, men, and children of having to "manage" inequality. Yet on the surface, all we might see would be Nancy Holt bounding confidently out the door at 8:30 A.M., briefcase in one hand, Joey in the other. All we might hear would be Nancy's and Evan's talk about their marriage as happy, normal, even "equal"—because equality was so important to Nancy.

Critical Thinking Questions

1. What is the "second shift"?

2. What strategies did Nancy pursue to get Evan to do more of the second shift? How did Evan respond to Nancy's "gender strategies"?

3. Describe Nancy's and Evan's visions of the ideal marriage.

4. What is the Holts' "family myth"? What purpose does a family myth serve?

5. How did Nancy sustain the family myth?

6. What theoretical perspective(s) is/are reflected in Hochschild's research? Explain your answer.

6 *Socioeconomic Status*

You are having dinner with a friend. During mealtime conversation, your friend begins telling you a story involving a person you have never met, so you interrupt and say, "I don't know who she is." Your friend quickly replies, "Oh, she's a lawyer who makes over $60,000 a year."

You are a teacher. During a unit exploring work and careers, you give your first-grade students the opportunity to tell the class what their parents do for a living. Samuel says, "My dad drives a big truck, so he's gone a lot." Martha says, "My mommy's a teacher. She works at the high school." Jack says, "My dad just lost his job at the factory, but my mom works. She's a, a, what do you call it? Oh, yeah. She's a secretary."

Your roommate sets you up with a blind date. You are a nervous wreck. You have been assured by reliable sources that your date is good looking, but still you are worried that you will not have anything in common with this mystery person. Your roommate, who reassures you that you two have a lot in common, begins telling you about your date. You are told about this person's hobbies, college major, and family. Included in the information your roommate shares with you is the comment that your date's father "makes big bucks" as a computer programmer for IBM.

All three of the above scenarios share a common theme. In each situation, a person's occupation is identified and his or her income is explicitly or implicitly described. Consider for a moment what this information tells you about the person and in what ways your perceptions of the person and his or her family life are shaped by knowing about occupation and income.

The Impact of Social Class

Clearly, occupation and income give some indication of social class. Upon learning a person's income or occupation, one almost unconsciously begins to form impressions about other characteristics of the individual and the individual's life-style. For example, one would probably assume that the successful lawyer and the computer programmer live in fairly large, relatively expensive homes in an upper middle-class neighborhood. Furthermore, one might predict that these individuals drive newer-model automobiles, wear stylish clothing purchased from department or specialty stores, and enjoy reading books on the best-seller list. Assumptions about the type of home, neighborhood, automobile, clothing, and preferred reading material would probably be quite different about Samuel's truck-driving father, Martha's schoolteacher mother, and Jack's parents.

Although the stereotypical assumptions one makes about individuals based on their social class may be inaccurate, it is an indisputable sociological fact that social class is one of the most important and defining characteristics of our lives. Social class influences quantifiable demographic characteristics such as age at marriage, fertility, and life expectancy. Furthermore, the position one holds in the social class hierarchy also determines life-style characteristics. Mantsios (1995) explains:

> [Class differences] have a profound impact on the way [people] live . . . [such as the] differences between playing a game of handball in the park and taking riding lessons at a private stable, watching a movie on television and going to the theater, and taking the subway to work and being driven in a limousine. More important, the difference in class determines where [people] live, who their friends are, how well they are educated, what they do for a living, and what they come to expect from life. (p. 137)

Social class, like sex and race, is a variable that sociologists consistently examine in research on the family. In both quantitative and qualitative studies, family scholars try to assess the role that socioeconomic status plays in family structure and interaction. Most often, social class is treated as an independent variable, where researchers try to assess the impact that class has on some family phenomenon, such as marital satisfaction, childrearing practices, or sexual behavior. However, social class also can be a dependent variable, in which researchers try to determine the impact that other variables, such as race and gender, have on social class. In virtually every study, researchers ask respondents to indicate their social class in some way, so that they can determine the relationship of social class to the topic under study.

A discussion of social class is important in a family textbook also because the opportunities and expectations of individuals are shaped to a great extent by the social class in which they are raised. To a certain degree, family dynamics are influenced by socioeconomic status. The interests, activities, marital expectations, and parenting practices of families in different social classes vary somewhat. Sociologists are fascinated with the ways in which socialization experiences are influenced by the resources to which families have access.

Defining Socioeconomic Status

All societies have some system of **social stratification**—the way individuals or groups are ranked hierarchically in society (Kornblum and Julian 1998). Those at the top of the stratification hierarchy have the most prestige, power, and privileges, whereas those at the bottom of what is commonly referred to as the *social ladder* have the least prestige, power, and privileges. The ways in which individuals can be stratified in societies are infinite. Conceivably, societies could stratify on the basis of hair color, eye color, ability to play racquetball, or knowledge of calculus (Williams 1952).

In the family literature and in the popular culture, many terms related to so-cial stratification—such as *social class, social status,* and *socioeconomic status*—are used interchangeably, although technically they have different meanings (Lang-man 1987). **Social class** generally refers to position in the stratification system based on income. Karl Marx believed social class was determined solely by indi-viduals' "relation to the means of production"—their occupation and property. Max Weber, another influential sociologist, argued that social stratification is not simply "reducible to variations in wealth" (Langman 1987: 212). Weber believed that social stratification is based on a complex relationship between wealth, power, and prestige, and that within society, people are divided into status groups that differ in nonmaterial aspects of their lives (Gecas 1979). Groups of individuals who are accorded similar levels of prestige within the community and who share similar cultural tastes, interests, patterns of consumption, and life-styles are said to have similar **social status.**

Weber's distinction between social class and social status is important, for although the two concepts often overlap, they are distinctly different compo-nents of social stratification. Consider, for example, a factory foreman and a bank executive who both earn $75,000 a year. Their identical incomes would place them in the same social class, yet they do not share the same social status because their jobs are accorded different amounts of prestige in the community and they most likely have distinctive life-styles, enjoy different hobbies, read different types of literature, and socialize with different circles of friends.

Social scientists have struggled to find a term that encompasses both the material and nonmaterial aspects of social stratification. The term **socioeco-nomic status (SES)** refers to the combined influence of income, occupation, ed-ucation, material possessions, cultural tastes, and prestige on social ranking (Brinkerhoff, White, and Ortega 1999; Gecas 1979).

Theoretical Perspectives on Social Stratification

Social stratification can be explained by all three sociological paradigms—func-tionalism, conflict theory, and symbolic interactionism. As macro-theoretical perspectives, functional and conflict theory offer competing explanations for *why* social stratification exists in society. Symbolic interaction theory, a micro-theoret-ical approach, is best suited to explain *how* social class differences are maintained in society.

The Functionalist Perspective

Functional theorists, you will recall, believe that every structure in society has a function. If some aspect of the social structure did not fulfill a function, then it would disappear. Functionalists point out that every known society has some form of social stratification whereby some individuals are accorded greater wealth, power, or prestige than others. Since social stratification is a component of all known societies, functionalists argue that stratification must meet critical human social needs. Because all structures in society are interdependent, when one aspect of the social structure changes or is neglected, the entire fabric of society is affected. The multitude of tasks necessary to keep society running smoothly are performed by individuals in their chosen or assigned occupations. Some individuals grow food, some harvest food, some sell food, and some cook food; some individuals maintain social order, others maintain health; some individuals invent technology, some manufacture technology, and some sell technology. Every occupation, from sanitation engineer to nuclear engineer, is important and necessary for society to function smoothly.

Although every job in society is equally functional, some jobs are regarded as more important or as easier to fill than others. Some work does not require special talents or training and can be performed by many people in society; other jobs require tremendous physical or intellectual abilities and years of specialized training and can be performed by relatively few people. Functionalists believe that to entice people to perform jobs that require a great deal of effort, training, and ability, society must offer greater rewards in the form of income and prestige. A system of social stratification results from allocating different amounts of wealth and status to different types of work. Social stratification thus provides incentive to people to work hard and strive for the more difficult, stressful jobs.

The Conflict Theory Perspective

Conflict theorists argue that social stratification is created and perpetuated by an economic structure in which wealth and power are maintained through oppression and exploitation. They argue that economic, social, and educational barriers prevent the poor from improving their socioeconomic status. Conflict theorists contend that the functionalist argument that societies grant economic rewards to those who perform the most difficult jobs is largely a myth. Numerous examples can be found in which income and prestige are not associated with education, skills, or the functional necessity of the work. Many people acquire their wealth through inheritance rather than occupational achievements. A schoolteacher, who must have a college degree and pass a licensing examination, may be paid less than the school custodian. Rock musicians, rap stars, professional athletes, and movie stars receive disproportionately high wages for work that is less essential for human survival than the low-paid, low-status work of farmers, garbage collectors, and day-care providers.

Conflict theorists also point out that wages often are paid on the basis of characteristics of the worker, not just the work performed. For example, women and minorities often are paid lower wages for performing the same work as white males. Feminist conflict theorists argue that women's subordinate status is both reinforced and reflected in the economy. Women are most often hired for low-paying, low-status jobs so they cannot gain access to power relative to men. Furthermore, women's occupational roles and degree of power reflect their family roles (Sapiro 1999). Most of the jobs deemed most appropriate for women are extensions of family roles. For example, secretarial work, nursing, elementary school teaching, and day-care work are low-paid jobs requiring many of the organizational and nurturing skills associated with the roles of housewife and mother.

The Symbolic Interactionist Perspective

Symbolic interactionists focus on the ways in which socialization maintains class distinctions. Symbolic interactionists argue that social norms are internalized in individuals through the process of socialization. As their cognitive abilities mature, children learn to view themselves and others from an abstract societal perspective. In the process, children learn the cultural belief system regarding social class and economic success.

Americans, in general, believe that one's position in the social hierarchy is based on "personal qualities and achievements" (Williams 1952: 91), and that anyone who is willing to work hard can make it to the top. The U.S. culture is filling with Horatio Alger–type rags-to-riches stories that reinforce the belief that those who put in the effort will be economically and socially successful (Coleman and Rainwater 1978: 25). People tend to view the poor with disdain, believing that they are personally responsible for their unfortunate position in society.

Social class influences the opportunities and values one is exposed to in the family. Lewis (1966) proposed an early theory of the way family socialization perpetuates class differences. Lewis believed that people who are poor and live in deprived, isolated environments develop a unique set of cultural values, different from middle- and upper-class values, that perpetuate poverty from generation to generation. Lewis claimed that people in poverty develop "a strong feeling of fatalism, helplessness, dependence, and inferiority . . . [and] a strong present-time orientation with relatively little disposition to defer gratification and plan for the future" (Gecas 1979: 391). According to Lewis's culture of poverty theory, the solution to poverty is simply to resocialize the poor to the middle-class values of optimism, empowerment, independence, future orientation, and delayed gratification.

The culture of poverty theory has been widely criticized for being judgmental and ethnocentric. Contemporary symbolic interactionists believe that, in general, people from all social classes have similar goals of education, occupational, and economic successes. However, the poor, who must overcome many obstacles to improve their socioeconomic status, perceive their chances of attaining these goals differently than the middle and upper classes. As Kohn (1990: 391) explains, symbolic interactionists believe that "members of different social classes, by virtue of enjoying (or suffering) different conditions of life, come to see the world differently—to develop different conceptions of social reality, different aspirations and hopes and fears, different conceptions of the desirable." These differences do not mean that the perceptions of any particular social class are superior or inferior. Symbolic interactionists focus on understanding how people from different social classes perceive situations and how their perceptions shape their behavior and family dynamics.

Measuring Social Class

In a classic study from 1971 to 1973, Coleman and Rainwater (1978) interviewed 900 adults in the Boston and Kansas City metropolitan areas, asking: "How would you describe social class in America? What class would you place yourself in and how would you make that determination?" Think for a moment about how you would have responded to those questions.

In general, respondents in the Coleman and Rainwater (1978: 18) study believed that social class "refers to differences between people in status reputation, in how they are rated and treated by the community." However, respondents varied widely in their descriptions of how social class should be determined. Some believed social class could be determined through a single measure: income. "Money, far more than anything else, is what Americans associate with the idea of social class" (p. 29). Other respondents believed that social class should be determined through a combination of income, occupation, and educational attainment.

"The finer points in social standing" included life-style variables, such as "moral standards, family history, community participation, social skills, speech, and physical appearance" (Coleman and Rainwater 1978: 22). Social class also was said to involve "the places you go," "what you wear and how you dress," and "the car you drive" (p. 79). One respondent explained:

> *I would suppose social class means where you went to school and how far. Your intelligence. Where you live. The sort of house you live in. Your general background, as far as clubs you belong to, your friends. To some degree the type of profession you're in—in fact, definitely that. Where you send your children to school. The hobbies you have. Skiing, for example, is higher than the snowmobile. The clothes you wear . . . all of that. These are the externals. It can't be [just] money, because nobody ever knows that about you for sure.* (Coleman and Rainwater 1978: 80)

Just as the American public could not agree on any single, standard measure of social class, neither can researchers. Several measures of social class have been developed, including the National Opinion Research Center's occupational prestige scale and the Duncan Socioeconomic Index (which are discussed later in the chapter). Each measure has its own unique strengths and weaknesses. The difficulties associated with measuring social class are compounded by the close relationship between social class, gender, and race. These methodological difficulties can lead to very practical difficulties for you as a student, citizen, and future policy maker. For example, you may receive conflicting information about social class in the United States from government representatives or the media in which it is reported that one study shows poor and middle-class families differ in some respect, whereas another study finds no class differences. To decide which study provides the most reliable, valid data, you must determine how social class was operationalized and assess the strengths and weaknesses of the measures employed.

Operationalizing the Concept of Social Class

In studies in which social class is a key variable, researchers must decide how they will operationalize and measure this complex concept. In the years following World War II, many researchers simply defined *social class* as respondents' own perception of their class standing. Social class was measured by asking individuals to describe their class position. Researchers found, however, that when asked whether they belonged to the upper, middle, or lower class, the vast majority of people described themselves as *middle class* (Williams 1952). People believed that if they labeled themselves as *upper class,* they would be perceived as snobbish, while the term *lower class* would suggest that they are deficient or deviant. When a fourth social class—working class—was added, the distribution of responses changed dramatically; far fewer people described themselves as middle class (Williams 1952). The impact of wording on responses leads to concerns that the measure of social class is not particularly reliable or valid.

Community Studies

An alternative to using individuals' subjective perceptions of class standing is the **community study** involving participant observation and interviews. In community studies, researchers immerse themselves in a particular community and observe for themselves the stratification system. Additionally, they interview members of the community, asking them to describe their own as well as other's social class ranking (Langman 1987).

Community studies have shown that members tend to agree about the class status of individual families, suggesting that local operationalizations of the concept of *class* can be reliable and valid, especially when respondents have a sophisticated understanding of stratification and base their judgments on a combination of factors, including "education, occupation, wealth, income, family [background], intimate friends, clubs and fraternities, as well as . . . manners, speech, and general outward behavior" (Warner et al. 1963: 38).

Community studies are effective only in small, rural communities. In larger metropolitan areas, people have a small circle of people with whom they are familiar, and therefore they cannot categorize the class standing of others (Williams 1952; Langman 1987).

Income

A direct, objective measure of social class is **income.** Income is a quantifiable variable important in data analysis, and respondents easily can be asked to report their annual income or to select a salary range that best represents their income. By using income as an indicator of social class, researchers—rather than respondents—decide whether a family is upper, middle, working, or lower class.

Operationalizing social class as annual income assumes that the amount of money earned corresponds closely with the material and nonmaterial life-style the respondent leads. Unfortunately, "income does not necessarily determine life-style" (LeMasters and DeFrain 1989: 104). For instance, families with substantial income may choose to live modestly and protect their money in savings, while families with lower earnings may affect a posh life-style by purchasing items on credit. Additionally, when income is used as a measure of social class, the cost of living in different regions must be considered. A family living in rural Mississippi earning $50,000 a year is likely to live in a newer suburban home, own two cars, and enroll their children in private schools. A family living in New York City with the same earnings probably lives in a cramped apartment, rides public transportation, and uses the public school system.

Income traditionally has been used to calculate whether a family is poor. By comparing a family's income to the U.S. government's official poverty line, researchers can determine if a family should be considered poor. In 1998, the official poverty line for a family of four was $16,450 (The 1998 HHS Poverty Guidelines). This absolute standard of poverty overlooks standard of living, however. It is hard to imagine that a family earning one dollar over the official poverty line lives much differently than the family just at or below the poverty line, yet the family earning that extra dollar technically is not considered poor. Many poverty experts today are calling for researchers to move away from income-based measures of social class to measures based on families' relative standard of living (McGregor and Borooah 1992).

An even more pressing problem for researchers is that most respondents are extremely cautious about reporting their income to strangers. Even after they have disclosed some of the most intimate secrets in their lives, most people will hesitate to report how much money they earn. Assuming that the respondent agrees to provide the information, there is always concern that the reported income is inaccurate. Some people may exaggerate or underestimate their income intentionally; others, especially those who are paid hourly wages and overtime, simply may not know exactly how much they earn in a year.

Occupation

Another common measure of social class is **occupation.** Jobs that require a high school education or less, involve physical labor, entail little authority or power, and pay hourly wages usually are labeled *blue-collar* or *working class.* Conversely, white-collar, middle-class, or professional jobs often require a college diploma, involve more mental than physical labor, entail decision-making authority, and pay an annual salary. The category *lower class* consists of families in which the primary earner is irregularly employed in unskilled labor and families that rely primarily on public assistance (Elkin and Handel 1989). The *underclass* is a label some sociologists use to identify those families who are chronically unemployed because they are isolated in inner-city ghettos away from good jobs and educational opportunities (Coleman and Cressey 1999; Kornblum and Julian 1998; Wilson 1987). However, the term *underclass* is controversial because some social scientists believe it has become a pejorative, vague term misused by the media (Gans 1990). The occupational category *pink-collar* includes the low-paying, low-status, nonmanual work, such as clerical and retail jobs, performed almost exclusively by women.

Occupation probably is the easiest, most convenient way of assessing respondents' social class (Elkin and Handel 1989). Most people will readily tell a researcher what they do for a living, and it is not difficult to determine whether a job is considered blue-collar, white-collar, or pink-collar. However, when occupation is used as an indicator of social class, the researcher is assuming that occupation corresponds closely with income and social prestige, and as you have seen, this is not always the case (LeMasters and DeFrain 1989).

Education

Education also can be used as a means of assessing social class, since people with higher levels of education generally have jobs that pay more income and have more prestige than people with less education. According to data from the U.S. Bureau of the Census (1998), adults with bachelor's degrees earned an average of $38,112 in 1997, whereas adults with only high school diplomas earned $22,154. Education correlates with individuals' life-styles and cultural tastes better than their occupations (Langman 1987). However, like occupation, education is not always correlated with income. A manual laborer with a high school education earning $19 an hour makes more money than many college professors with Ph.Ds. Asking respondents to indicate their levels of education (grade school, high school, college, or postgraduate) also does not indicate the quality of the education received (Langman 1987). Whether people were educated at public or private schools may influence both the material and nonmaterial aspects of their lives.

The National Opinion Research Center (NORC) and Beyond

Since income, occupation, and education each have distinct advantages and disadvantages when used separately, then why not combine them for a multifaceted measure of social class? In fact, researchers have done just that to form a composite measure of social class. In 1947, the National Opinion Research Center (NORC) sampled a cross-section of Americans to determine their perceptions of the prestige of occupations. Respondents were shown a list of 90 occupations "presumed to be representative of the entire range of legitimate occupations in the United States" (Powers 1982: 4) and were asked to rank the general standing of the occupation on a five-point scale from "excellent" to "poor." Researchers calculated the overall score for each job, then constructed a ranking scale from 1 to 90, with shoe shiner having the lowest rank and Supreme Court justice having the highest (Powers 1982). Although more a measure of social status than social class, the occupational prestige scale assessed the perceived status of occupations based on the type of work performed (occupation), the salary associated with the job (income), and the amount of training necessary to do the work (education).

Criticisms eventually were raised about the usefulness of the NORC occupational prestige scale, however. First, the scale does not contain any occupations that traditionally are performed by women. When the list of occupations was being constructed approximately a half century ago, researchers argued that in the interest of keeping the number of occupations "within practical limits," women's occupations such as nurse, secretary, and dressmaker would be eliminated from the list (Powers 1982: 4). When a breadwinning man and homemaking woman headed the majority of families, the NORC occupational prestige scale could be used to assess fairly accurately the social status of the family. However, as more women moved into the labor force, many of them single-parent heads of household, the absence of female jobs made it virtually impossible to use the NORC scale to assess social status.

Second, the initial finding that people's ranking of jobs are consistent has been called into question. It appears that there is strong agreement among people about the prestige rankings of jobs at the top and bottom of the scale, but there is less agreement about how to rank jobs in the middle (Powers 1982). Also, the occupation of respondents influences the prestige respondents assign to particular jobs. College-educated respondents rank professional jobs higher than respondents with less education, and those with no more than an eighth-grade education rank skilled jobs such as carpenter and railroad worker higher than respondents with more education (Powers 1982). The validity of the rankings has further been challenged by the finding that people rank the prestige of jobs such as nuclear physicist without knowing what these jobs entail.

To avoid the subjective biases of the NORC occupational prestige rankings, other researchers have constructed indexes of socioeconomic status based on the objective criteria of income and education combined with occupational prestige. Best known is the Duncan Socioeconomic Index (SEI). Researchers today also measure social class as a multidimensional concept through the use of sophisticated computer-generated statistical models. These programs assess the independent and combined effects of income, occupation, and educational level on the topic being studied.

Assessing Social Class in Dual-Income Couples

"The family is recognized as the basic unit in the stratification system of a society" (Hiller and Philliber 1986: 583). Hence, it is assumed that a husband, wife, and children living together in the same household share a common social status. Traditionally, the income, occupation, and educational levels of the primary earner, usually the husband, determined the socioeconomic status assigned to the family. This conventional method of determining a family's social class works well when husbands are the sole earners in the family. However, few families today are comprised of a breadwinning husband and a full-time homemaking wife, which raises the complex question of how social class should be determined in dual-earner households.

Measuring the socioeconomic status of a dual-income couple using the husband's occupation, income, and education alone is problematic. The most obvious criticism of this traditional approach is that it is sexist to ignore women's economic contributions and presume that the husband is the dominant earner. Failure to acknowledge women's work contributions in dual-income couples also can give an inaccurate picture of families' material life-styles. Consider, for example, a family in which the husband is a carpenter and the wife is a secretary. Using his occupation, income, and education, the family would be classified as working class. The income, prestige, and education associated with her work as a secretary also would qualify the family as members of the working class. However, their combined earnings may make it possible for the family to afford many of the material advantages that would be considered middle class. Because of the wife's labor force participation, the family may be able to live in a newer suburban neighborhood, regularly purchase new cars, and afford expensive vacations.

The importance of including women's earnings when assessing the socioeconomic status of dual-earner families is underscored by recent data that suggest that employed wives have contributed to a 150 percent increase in the income of married-couple families between 1947 and 1997. The proportion of married women in the labor force has almost tripled since 1951, which has led to a growth in real median income in married-couple families from $20,620 in 1947 to $51,591 in 1997 (U.S. Bureau of the Census 1995; 1998).

Women's work also can influence the socioeconomic status of families in less quantifiable ways. Women who are secretaries, for example, often work in professional settings such as doctors' offices, law firms, and universities. As such, these women and their families may socialize with their upper middle-class supervisors. As part of the benefits of their work, their families may have access to more middle-class facilities and benefits such as the company fitness center, a university-sponsored day-care center, or corporate profit-sharing plans. Family scholars will overlook many of these qualitative life-style differences if socioeconomic status is measured using only the husband's occupation. Clearly, "women's work experience has a demonstrable effect on various dimensions of family life" that cannot be ignored (Osborn 1987: 431).

The issues involved in studying the socioeconomic status of dual-income couples can become even more complex. In the earlier example, the husband's and wife's occupations both were classified as working class. Couples can, however, occupy jobs that place them in different social classes—a situation sociologists label **cross-class** or **mixed-class marriages** (Collins 1988). Commonly, men in middle-class occupations are married to women in working-class jobs, a situation sociologists call **traditional cross-class marriages** (Leiulfsrud and Woodward 1987). In these cases, the family is usually considered middle class based on the husband's social status.

But how should **nontraditional cross-class marriages,** those in which the wife is in an occupation with higher prestige and earnings than her husband, be treated? Some researchers contend that such families are so rare that they are not worth analyzing, and therefore believe it is perfectly acceptable to base a family's socioeconomic status on the husband's occupation alone (e.g., Erickson 1984; Goldthorpe 1983). However, for scholars interested in discovering subtle interaction differences between families, it is imperative that the occupation, income, and education levels of both spouses are assessed. By accounting for wives' work when assigning social class, it becomes possible to compare traditional and nontraditional cross-class families. For example, researchers have found that nontraditional cross-class families are more egalitarian than traditional cross-class families; husbands are more likely to help with child care and wives have more financial control (Leiulfsrud and Woodward 1987). Furthermore, in cross-class couples, the spouse with better verbal skills and greater occupational prestige, regardless of sex, is likely to negotiate with outside agencies, such as schools and banks. Previously, it was assumed that men were more likely to conduct such business because they have more power and are perceived as more aggressive. By examining the occupation and income of both the husband and the wife, it becomes apparent that family dynamics in dual-income couples are significantly influenced by the social status of both partners.

How, then, should social class be assessed in dual-earner couples? Osborn (1987: 431) argues that the measure of a family's social class depends on the research questions being asked. If the purpose of the study is to discover "how the occupational mobility of the main breadwinner affects the lives of family members," it is perfectly appropriate to use the occupation of only one spouse to determine social class. On the other hand, if researchers want to understand the "life-chances, life-styles, patterns of association . . . and modes of action of members of the family unit," it is important to account for both partners' occupations, incomes, and education in the measure of social class (Osborn 1987: 431).

Gender and Racial Biases in Measures of Social Class

Studies of socioeconomic status of dual-income couples that do not include measures of women's economic contributions are not the only form of gender bias in studies of social class. Another source of gender bias stems from the different perceptions that men and women have of socioeconomic status. Researchers have found that husbands and wives do not always agree on the social class to which they should be assigned, particularly in mixed-class marriages (Hiller and Philliber 1986; Simpson, Stark, and Jackson 1988; Vanneman and Cannon 1987). Women tend to adopt a *maximizing strategy* for class placement in which they identify with the higher social class in mixed-class marriages (Vanneman and Cannon 1987). Men, on the other hand, tend to adopt an *egocentric strategy* in which they ignore their wives' occupational achievements and base their class identifications on their work alone (Hiller and Philliber 1986; Vanneman and Cannon 1987). Studies in which social class is measured using the subjective perceptions of only one family member may be biased by the differing perceptions of men and women.

Researchers also must be sensitive to racial bias in measures of socioeconomic status. People of different racial and ethnic backgrounds may perceive social class somewhat differently. Some scholars have suggested that African Americans have a "middle mass" instead of a middle class (Vanneman and Cannon 1987); that is, African Americans define middle class more broadly to include professionals, white-collar workers, and skilled blue-collar workers. African Americans may see themselves as middle class if they are respected community members, regardless of their income, education, or occupational prestige. Those who adopt middle-class values and behaviors—such as emphasizing education,

How do occupation and income define and measure socioeconomic status? What other factors contribute to social class membership? What have been some gender and racial biases in measures of socioeconomic status? Why is social stratification such an important variable in family studies?

hard work, and church attendance—are often perceived by themselves and others in the black community as middle class (Vanneman and Cannon 1987).

Social class, like virtually every variable studied in the social sciences, is multidimensional and difficult to measure. Researchers have a responsibility to describe how they defined, operationalized, and measured social class and to acknowledge the limitations of those measures (Langman 1987). In family scholarship, you must be aware of the issues and problems in research on social class, and interpret the significance of the data accordingly.

Social Class Prototypes

Although debates about how social class should be defined and measured persist, all social scientists agree that "different groups possess unequal amounts of wealth, influence, prestige, and 'life-chances'" (Elkin and Handel 1989: 85). People who have access to similar degrees of wealth, education, power, and prestige tend to lead similar life-styles and have similar family interaction patterns. Drawing on studies of social class in American society, researchers have constructed portraits, or prototypes, of what family life is like at different class positions (LeMasters and DeFrain 1989). However, the danger in describing prototypes of families at different class levels is that the information could "easily deteriorate into scholarly versions of popular stereotypes" (Gans 1982: 281). To avoid stereotyping, it is imperative to remember the following:

An incredible variety of families and individuals are to be found at most every income level. . . . Images of the social order must be built around prototypes—families who fit general expectations of how education, occupation, and income go together. Prototypical families then become the core for each status level. But in the real world, prototypical families are only a fraction of the total. (Coleman and Rainwater 1978: 210)

Social class can be labeled and divided in a variety of ways. The following sections describe occupations, educational levels, life-styles, and marital relationships in four broad social class prototypes: upper, middle, working, and lower (or poor) class.

Upper-Class Families

Few empirical studies have been conducted about the most affluent social class. Most sociologists have little interest in studying upper-class families because they are so rare and do not represent how most people live. The elite nature of the upper class is revealed in statistics: The richest 5 percent of Americans earn eight times the income of the poorest 20 percent (U.S. Bureau of the Census, "Income, 1998").

Many upper-class families were born into wealth; others acquired their wealth through prosperous entrepreneurship or work in highly paid professions such as medicine and law, upper-echelon corporate positions, and the entertainment business. Many entrepreneurs in recent years have amassed fortunes through creative and innovative endeavors in the fashion, fast-food, electronics, computer, and retail industries (Langman 1987).

Upper-class families live in the most exclusive neighborhoods and can afford the best-quality automobiles, medical care, and schools. In their leisure time, upper-class families tend to enjoy the theater, classical music, museums, and art galleries. Membership in the most elite country clubs provides opportunities for recreation (Langman 1987).

Nuclear families generally live near extended kin and may schedule regular gatherings at a summer cottage or winter retreat. Control of inherited wealth often requires joint decisions between family members; therefore, it is important that extended kin maintain close contact (Langman 1987).

Parents in upper-class families generally have many professional and community commitments and spend little time at home. The children often are raised by governesses and nannies and are educated through private schools and supplemental private tutoring in music, language, and art (Langman 1987). Some children in affluent families are sent to boarding schools for private education with other children of the same social class. As a result, relationships between parents and children may be distant (LeMasters and DeFrain 1989).

Marital relationships in the upper class are generally characterized by traditional sex-role ideologies. Men are responsible for most of the business dealings while women attend to charitable and cultural activities (Langman 1987). Unlike most traditional relationships, however, women in upper-class marriages tend to have considerable economic resources and community influence.

Middle-Class Families

Middle-class families have been studied more intensively than any other social class, primarily because they represent the classic ideal of the American Dream (LeMasters and DeFrain 1989). Families can attain middle-class status through a variety of occupations, including teaching, science, engineering, accounting, law, and medicine. Mental-health workers, middle-level managers, members of the clergy, small-business owners, and administrators in government organizations also are considered middle class (Langman 1987). Most middle-class occupations require at least a college degree, and often some type of postgraduate or professional schooling is necessary.

Middle-class couples with young children typically live in spacious, but not palatial, homes in suburban neighborhoods (Elkin and Handel 1989). They usually own more than one vehicle, which they may regularly trade in for newer models. Culturally, most middle-class families enjoy "monthly book clubs, best-sellers, Broadway musicals, and pop or soft rock" (Langman 1987: 228). Discretionary income allows these families to enjoy regular family vacations and the financial security of modest investments and retirement plans. Most middle-class couples are involved in professional, business, and community organizations, which become an important part of their social network.

Occupational advancement and educational pursuits make middle-class families quite geographically mobile. Although extended kin may not live in close proximity, relationships with relatives are maintained through regular visiting and frequent communication (Langman 1987). Having limited access to kin, middle-class families often report that they rely on large friendship networks for social support and interaction (Gardner 1991).

With the exception of some slight generational differences, most middle-class married couples expect their relationships to be egalitarian and intimate, characterized by friendship and communication. Coming from college-educated backgrounds, both husbands and wives have been exposed to the rhetoric of the women's movement and therefore they expect that household responsibilities and decision making will be jointly shared (Perry-Jenkins and Folk 1994; Rubin 1976/1992). Furthermore, many middle-class wives are involved in busy careers, which they pursue for personal fulfillment and to allow the family to maintain its desired life-style, and they believe that they are entitled to an egalitarian relationship (Elkin and Handel 1989; Langman 1987).

Working-Class Families

Researchers often portray working-class families in extremes; they either romanticize their courage and determination or pity them for their life of hard work and disappointments. Rosen (1987: 3) argues that working-class life is "not always a bed of roses, neither [is it] always a 'world of pain.'" Members of the working class earn their living in jobs that usually require high school diplomas or degrees from technical schools. These jobs include work in construction, factories, mechanics, and low-status service jobs such as secretarial, retail, or food service work. In their classic study of Middletown, Lynd and Lynd (1929) argued that blue-collar workers manipulate things, whereas white-collar workers manipulate people and ideas.

Working-class employees often are paid hourly wages instead of a salary and they are more prone to layoffs during economic slumps, making their income less stable than that of most middle-class workers. In the past, many blue-collar jobs, especially unionized jobs, offered workers the opportunity to earn decent incomes. Sons often found work in the same factories that their fathers worked in all their lives. Since World War II, manufacturing industries and labor unions have declined, however, and well-paying blue-collar work is more difficult to obtain (Wilson 1996). Working-class families have grown increasingly reliant on two incomes for economic survival.

Working-class families tend to live in clean, respectable houses that are older and smaller than homes owned by the middle class (Elkin and Handel 1989). Birth rates are somewhat higher in the working class than in the middle and upper classes, so most homes afford less space and privacy to family members. Leisure time is usually spent in home-centered, commercial, sport, or craft activities that are inexpensive and readily available. Men often enjoy hunting and fishing together, whereas women enjoy informally socializing with friends and relatives (Langman 1987).

Research consistently shows that working-class families interact more with extended kin than middle-class families (Gardner 1991; Komarovsky 1967; Rubin 1976/1992). Working-class families often live close to relatives, making it more convenient to visit and interact with family members. Furthermore, working-class families may find the cost of formally entertaining friends prohibitive, but not feeling obligated to provide a fancy meal to relatives, they enjoy the company of family (Gardner 1991; Rubin 1976/1992).

Having kin within close proximity has its advantages and disadvantages. Relatives can be valuable sources of emotional support in times of crisis and can provide services such as baby-sitting and automobile and home repairs at little or no cost. On the other hand, relatives, especially in-laws, can be a source of marital conflict. In her ground-breaking study of working-class families, Rubin (1976/1992) found that in the early years of marriage, husbands may continue to spend a great deal of time with their parents, stopping by their parents' homes after work for supper or to help with home repairs. Wives, who traditionally have prepared nice meals for their husbands, become understandably frustrated and angry, while husbands report feeling torn between the duty to their parents and the desire to spend time with their wives (Rubin 1976/1992).

Much of the early research suggested that working-class couples did not enter marriage with the same expectations as middle-class couples (Komarovsky 1967; Perry-Jenkins and Folk 1994; Rubin 1976/1992). Unlike middle-class marriages in which spouses are expected to be their partner's best friend and closest confidant, working-class couples were said to expect less marital communication (Gans 1982). Communication about intimate and personal topics was believed to be more gender segregated in working-class relationships. Wives were found to disclose their feelings with their mothers, sisters, and female friends, whereas husbands talked to their brothers and male friends (Gans 1982; Komarovsky 1967; Perry-Jenkins and Folk 1994; Rubin 1976/1992). Additionally, working-class couples were believed to have and desire a much more traditional division of labor than egalitarian middle-class couples. Men, it was said, expected to be the primary earners in the household, and if it was at all possible, they preferred to be the only earner in the family. Wives were expected to take primary responsibility for housework and child care (Gans 1982; Rubin 1976/1992).

Although these gender-segregated, traditional relationships may have characterized working-class marriages at one time, research today suggests that marital expectations and interaction patterns in contemporary working-class relationships are quite similar to middle-class marriages. Twenty years after her initial study of working-class couples, Rubin (1995) reexamined marital dynamics in working-class families and discovered several significant changes. First, far more working-class women were employed in 1990 than were in 1970. Women reported feeling guilty that they could not be full-time wives and mothers, and men said they wished their wives did not have to work, yet these couples generally recognized that the changes they have experienced are the result of economic forces beyond their control. As one husband explained, "A guy should be able to support his wife and kids. But that's not the way it is these days, is it? I don't know anybody who can support a family any more, do you?" (Rubin 1995: 78).

Second, Rubin (1995) found that compared to 20 years ago, working-class couples today expect their marriages to be more egalitarian. The belief that household chores, child care, and economic labor should be shared tends to be a relatively new phenomenon among the working class, and therefore was much more prominent among younger couples, those under age 40, than in older couples. Nevertheless, it appears that as working-class women joined the labor force in significant numbers, the dynamics of the traditional working-class marriage become more egalitarian.

As in middle-class marriages, the egalitarian relationship in working-class families may be more of an ideal than a reality. Women continue to do far more housework and child care than men do (Rubin 1995). However, in many working-class families, men make a significant contribution to household responsibilities. Blue-collar work often is done in shifts, which makes it possible for husbands and wives to schedule their work so that one parent can provide child care. When couples work in staggered shifts, men are the sole child-care providers for part of the day, spending a substantial amount of time with their children (Rosen 1987).

Finally, Rubin (1995) found that women in working-class relationships have more power and control in the family today than in the past. Women who make a significant contribution to family income generally have more authority in their marriages than full-time homemakers or women who earn very little. In working-class families, women may earn as much as 40 to 50 percent of the total household income, allowing them greater input into financial decisions and other family matters (Rosen 1987).

Poor Families

According to 1997 U.S. Census data, 35.6 million Americans, or 13.3 percent of the population, live in poverty (Weinberg 1998; Dalaker and Naifeh 1998). Poor families have few economic, educational, or social resources. Unemployment is common in poor families, and those who are employed tend to work intermittently in low-paying, unskilled jobs. With a high school education at best, most families in the lowest socioeconomic stratum have few opportunities to improve their economic status. Poor families have weak social support networks because they move frequently, looking for work or following harvests (LeMasters and DeFrain 1989).

Poor families tend to have more children in the household than nonpoor families. Demographers refer to the relationship between socioeconomic status and fertility as an *inverse relationship*, meaning that as socioeconomic status declines, fertility rises. The birth rate for families earning less than $10,000 annually is 95 per 1,000 women, whereas the birth rate for families with incomes of $75,000 or more is only 43 per 1,000 (U.S. Bureau of Census 1994). An inverse relationship also can be found between socioeconomic status and divorce, health problems, and infant mortality. In other words, poor families have higher divorce rates, more health problems, and higher rates of infant mortality than wealthier families (LeMasters and DeFrain 1989; Mantsios 1995). A *direct relationship*—when one variable increases, the other increases, or when one decreases, the other decreases—is found between socioeconomic status and life expectancy. Without the statistical jargon, this means that those with the fewest economic resources have the shortest life expectancy.

Poor families, like all families, are diverse and difficult to characterize. They differ in family structure, living conditions, geographic location, and the persistence of their poverty. Some poor families contain an intact, employed parental unit, whereas others are comprised of a single, unemployed mother who is dependent on government assistance. Some poor families live in substandard rental property, others in public housing, and the most desperate poor are homeless. Geographically, poor families are quite different also. Inner-city, urban poor families have received considerable attention in political debates and the media, but many poor families live in rural areas. In 1986, when the economy was in a deep slump, the poverty rate in rural areas was equal to that of urban areas: 18 percent (O'Hare and Curry-White 1992). Unlike urban areas that offer an intricate network of federal, state, and private agencies to offer assistance to the poor, rural areas contain few sources of economic and social support for poor families (LeMasters and DeFrain 1989).

O'Hare and Curry-White (1992) found that poor rural and urban families differed in other ways, as well. First, fewer women are found in the rural underclass (47 percent) than in the urban underclass (60 percent). Second, the rural poor tend to be proportionately older than the poor in urban areas. Less than 48 percent of the rural poor were between the ages of 19 and 34 in 1990, while nearly three-fifths (59 percent) of the urban poor were in this age bracket. Finally, the racial distribution of poverty differs geographically. The urban poor tend to be disproportionately black (49 percent); however, in rural areas, 55 percent of the poor are non-Hispanic whites. These differences between poor families in urban and rural areas are significant for counselors, social workers, and policy makers.

Poor families also differ from each other in another important way—the persistence of their poverty. Contrary to popular belief, poverty is not a permanent condition for most people. Although some families experience chronic poverty over several generations, most families that are poor slip in and out of poverty fairly often, experiencing what are called *poverty spells*. According to the U.S. Bureau of the Census, one-half of all poverty spells last 4.6 months or less (Naifeh 1998). The two most important factors that cause families to slip into poverty and help them recover are changes in income and changes in family composition (Voyandoff 1990). Poverty spells can occur when there is a decline in or loss of income from a primary earner in the family or when the composition of the family changes through divorce, death of an earner, birth of a child, or when an economically productive young adult leaves home. Poverty spells are most persistent in single-parent homes headed by women (Bianchi 1990; Voyandoff 1990). People recover from poverty spells through a substantial increase in wages by obtaining better employment or through the addition of a wage earner, usually through marriage.

The number of families living in poverty increased dramatically between 1970 and 1990, jumping from 5.3 million families to 7.1 million families (Ahlburg and DeVita 1992). Poverty rates peaked in 1993 and have steadily dropped since then due to an economic recovery that led to increases in family income (Weinberg 1998). Unfortunately, economic gains do little to change the status of the chronically poor. Persistent poverty is rooted in structural changes in the global economy, and therefore it cannot be eradicated easily.

Since World War II, the economy has shifted from a manufacturing-based industrial economy to a service-based postindustrial economy. As a result, from 1961 to 1988, manufacturing as a percentage of nonagricultural employment decreased from 30 to 18 percent (Voyandoff 1990). The drastic decline in manufacturing jobs in recent years is further documented by Wilson (1996: 29–30):

> The manufacturing losses in some northern cities have been staggering. In the twenty-year period from 1967 to 1987, Philadelphia lost 64 percent of its manufacturing jobs; Chicago lost 60 percent; New York City, 58 percent; Detroit, 51 percent. In absolute numbers, these percentages represent the loss of 160,000 jobs in Philadelphia, 326,000 in Chicago, 520,000—over half a million—in New York, and 108,000 in Detroit.

Manufacturing jobs are being replaced by two different types of service-based work: (1) jobs with lower wages and fewer employment benefits than factory work, such as clerical and retail jobs, and (2) jobs requiring advanced education and sophisticated technological skills, such as jobs in health care and the computer industry. Workers who expected their high school diplomas and the local factories to provide a decent livelihood cannot earn enough to support their families in low-wage service jobs, and they do not have the education and skills necessary to obtain many of the better-paying jobs (Ahlburg and DeVita 1992).

Socialization and Social Class

As you have seen, socioeconomic status influences every aspect of our lives, from the number of years we are likely to live to the types of activities we are likely to enjoy in our spare time. In sociological terms, social class has a profound impact on our socialization experience. Every event encountered in life is a part of the socialization process, although some are more significant and lasting than others. Sociologists and psychologists have long recognized that the most basic and enduring socialization occurs during childhood with those people whom we value most—our families and peers. Additionally, experiences within the educational system, an inevitable part of childhood, also is an intrinsic part of the socialization process.

Socialization, Social Class, and the Family

Growing up in a spacious home with unlimited educational and material resources is certainly a far different experience from growing up in an overcrowded, dilapidated public housing project with few educational opportunities and few material possessions. In this respect alone, the social class of one's family of origin has a profound impact on childhood socialization experiences. But social class has an even more direct impact: Research suggests that social class influences parents' values and childrearing practices (Kohn 1990). The case can be made that social class probably is the single-most important determinant of parental values and behavior, having a greater impact than religion, national origin, and even race (Alwin 1984). The questions sociologists most often pose about social class and parenting styles are "(1) how does social class affect parental behavior? [and] (2) why does social class affect parental behavior" (Gecas 1979: 366).

How Social Class Affects Parental Behavior

In 1958, child development expert Urie Bronfenbrenner published a paper titled "Socialization and Social Class through Time and Space" in which he argued that working-class parents use physical punishment more frequently than middle-class parents. Middle-class parents, he argued, most often employ "reasoning, isolation, and . . . love oriented discipline techniques" (cited in Erlanger 1974: 68). This paper, which was based on data from six previously published studies, sparked widespread interest in the relationship between social class and parenting behaviors.

Subsequent research suggests that although "there are substantial differences in how parents of differing social class position raise their children" (Kohn

How would you describe this family in terms of social class membership? In this case how might occupation, income, and education influence the parents' values and behaviors in child-rearing? How might parental values and behaviors differ in urban families? In upper-middle-class families? In what ways and why might class differences in parenting be disappearing?

1990: 389), the differences are not so much in how parents discipline but rather why they discipline. Both middle-class and working-class parents usually begin disciplining their children by reminding them of the limits or the rules of the house, and resort to physical punishment only after other discipline techniques have failed. Furthermore, parents from all social classes have similar goals for their children; all parents want their children to be happy, honest, considerate, obedient, independent, and reliable (Kohn 1990).

The difference between social classes is in the emphasis that parents place on particular values. Middle-class parents are more likely to value self-direction, consideration, curiosity, responsibility, and self-control, and they are less likely to value conformity to authority (Gecas 1979; Kohn 1990). When they discipline their children, middle-class parents usually explain the reasons for their actions in complex sentences using sophisticated vocabulary. As a result, middle-class children may develop advanced language skills that help them in school and allow them to articulate and negotiate well (Elkin and Handel 1989). Conversely, working-class parents tend to value manners, neatness, respectfulness, and obedience (Kohn 1990). Working-class parents generally expect that their children understand that if they are disobedient, they will be punished. Therefore, they may see little need to offer their children elaborate explanations about punishments, a parenting style some have labeled *authoritarian* (Rubin 1995).

Kohn (1990) argues that the most consistent and significant differences between parental values are in the areas of self-discipline and conformity to external authority. Middle-class parents are likely to punish children for losing self-control, whereas working-class parents are likely to punish children for being disobedient. Kohn's findings are based on research he conducted with both working-class and middle-class mothers in which he presented them with eight conditions in which parents discipline children and asked them to report how they would handle each situation. The circumstances parents considered were when the child (1) plays wildly, (2) fights with siblings, (3) fights with other children, (4) loses his or her temper, (5) refuses to do what he or she is told, (6) steals something, (7) smokes cigarettes, and (8) uses language of which the parent disapproves (Gecas 1979). Kohn (1990) found that mothers did not differ significantly in the frequency with which they used physical punishment, but they did differ in the circumstances that prompted a spanking. Middle-class mothers were more likely to punish children physically for losing their temper than for playing wildly, but working-class mothers used physical punishment equally in both situations.

In examining these differences, Kohn discovered that middle-class mothers were responding to the intent of the behavior, whereas working-class mothers responded to the consequences of the behavior. Consider, for example, a situation in which a parent discovers that a child has just broken an expensive table lamp. According to Kohn's research, the middle-class parent is likely to rush in and ask "What happened?" If it is clear that the child broke the lamp in the middle of a temper tantrum—a situation in which the child has lost self-control—the parent is more likely to punish the child physically than if the child accidentally broke the lamp in the midst of a creative game of "flying ninja ballerinas." Working-class parents, on the other hand, are more likely to respond to the consequences of the behavior: The lamp is broken. From the working-class parents' perspective, the child disobeyed house rules that stated no wild play is allowed in the living room. Disobedience, regardless of whether the child intended to break the lamp, requires punishment.

Why Social Class Affects Parental Behavior

Although it is easy to describe different parental values and discipline techniques in various social classes, it is much more difficult to explain why these differences emerge. Kohn (1990) argues that the nature of parents' work influences the characteristics that parents ultimately value in their children. Middle-class parents—who typically work in jobs that are complex, nonroutine, and free from close supervision—come to value self-discipline because that is what they are rewarded for on the job. Working-class parents—whose work is closely supervised and who do less complex, more routine work, are rewarded for obedience and conformity to the authority of supervisors; therefore, they value these characteristics in their children. Anticipating that their children probably will be in jobs similar to theirs, parents also may enforce values consistent with their work to ensure their children's success in future occupational roles.

Are Parental Values Converging?

Recent research suggests that the differences in the values and childrearing styles of the middle and working class may be disappearing. Using data from 25 years worth of surveys, Alwin (1984: 359) found that there was a "clear and consistent

increase . . . in the valuation of autonomy for children and a decrease in preferences for obedience" across social classes. The most preferred parental value for
all of the years studied was "thinks for self" and the importance assigned to this
characteristic increased steadily over time. Parents also considered "obeys" and
"helps others" important, but preference for the value of obedience declined
steadily from 1958 to 1983 (Alwin 1984).

Why might parents be shifting away from valuing obedience and conformity
and toward the values of autonomy and independence? Alwin (1984) suggests
several possible reasons. First, average family size has declined since the 1950s.
When parents have fewer children in the household, they tend to be more tolerant
of expressions of individuality and autonomy and less concerned with obedience.
Second, more mothers have joined the labor force. Employed mothers have a limited amount of time each day to interact with their children, and they probably
prefer to spend the time in enjoyable activities rather than constantly enforcing
rules. Third, there has been a tremendous increase in the number of single-parent
families. Single parents, who must juggle work and family responsibilities, may
prefer to have their children become independent at a young age. Fourth, educational levels in the United States, especially among immigrant and minority families, have increased dramatically. Higher education is consistently associated with
an acceptance of individuality, independent thinking, and curiosity.

Finally, and probably most important, the mass media consistently trans-
mits middle-class values throughout American culture. Middle-class values of independence and autonomy filter into homes daily through television, popular
magazines, and child-care books. Television programs, from soap operas to situation comedies, almost exclusively depict upper middle-class families and values
(Macionis 1999). Women's magazines, which contain numerous parenting articles, are written for a middle-class audience. Child-care books, allegedly offering
expert advice on parenting, endorse a middle-class form of discipline and childrearing (LeMasters 1975).

Socialization, Social Class, and Education

Social class further influences individuals' socialization experiences in school.
The social class background of students affects teachers' perceptions of and interaction with students, students' perceptions of each other, resources available to
schools, and ultimately educational achievement.

Teachers' Perceptions of Students

The social class background of students influences the type of instruction they receive, contributes to the values and skills children learn, and ultimately affects
the occupational opportunities they have as adults (Anyon 1994; Bowles and
Gintis 1976). In her study of fifth-grade classrooms in four different schools,
Anyon (1994) found that the social class backgrounds of students influenced the
style of instruction adopted by teachers. Fifth-graders in all four schools were

taught the same material from the same textbook, but the method by which the topics were taught differed significantly, depending on the social class backgrounds of the students.

In the "working-class school," which was comprised of students whose parents generally worked in blue-collar jobs, teachers emphasized the procedure necessary to complete assignments rather than reasons for the procedure. For example, when teaching two-digit division, children were simply told the steps to follow and memorize without any formal explanation of why each step was necessary. At the "middle-class school," attended by children from families in which the parents were employed in well-paid blue-collar jobs, white-collar office jobs, or city employment, teachers emphasized learning how to get the right answers on assignments. Following the proper steps to complete two-digit division was seen as important, but teachers also wanted students to figure out for themselves why each step in the process was necessary. At the third school, an "affluent professional school," attended by children whose parents were primarily well-paid professionals such as doctors, lawyers, and engineers, class work was completed more independently with a greater emphasis placed on expressing individuality and creativity. Finally, at the "executive elite school," in which most children had fathers who were top executives at large corporations such as American Express or U.S. Steel, teachers emphasized developing analytical thinking skills in students. Class work often was completed in groups, with much discussion of the children's ideas.

Anyon (1994) concludes that teachers, like parents, emphasize docility and obedience in working-class students and stress initiative and personal assertiveness in middle- and upper-class students, reinforcing the values believed to be necessary to succeed in the type of work performed in their social class. Rote learning and an emphasis on obedience prepares children for work that is mechanical and routine, whereas children taught to think independently and analytically are prepared for work as corporate and societal leaders (Anyon 1994). Conflict theorists may go so far as to argue that American schools are designed not to educate children but rather to perpetuate the current system of social stratification by socializing children to the occupational values and skills necessary to perform the type of work their parents perform (Bowles and Gintis 1976).

In addition to teaching style, socioeconomic status influences teachers' perceptions of students' abilities. In a now classic study of an urban St. Louis school, Rist (1973) found that the socioeconomic status of students biases teachers' perceptions of the intellectual abilities of students. Using information about social class gathered from school records and assessments of the children's physical appearance, demeanor, and vocabulary, kindergarten teachers made judgments about students' potential for academic success. Children who came to school in torn, dirty clothes, spoke in informal street dialect, and had less developed social skills were judged to be lower achievers than students who were well dressed, articulate, and well mannered. Rist found that by the eighth day of kindergarten, teachers had already determined which children were high and low achievers without any objective tests of ability; students' abilities were determined based on subjective perceptions of their socioeconomic status.

Rist (1973), who followed a group of kindergarten students through the second grade, found that teachers' perceptions of students' abilities continued to influence their interaction with the children throughout the school year. Children from higher socioeconomic backgrounds, who were believed to be better students, were placed closer to the teacher's desk and were given more positive reinforcement and attention than children from lower social classes. Children from more deprived backgrounds were seated furthest from the teacher's desk and received the least attention and the most criticism.

The children in the class soon perceived the labels teachers placed on students. Children from lower social classes who were believed to be low achievers by the teacher were teased by their peers for being stupid. Furthermore, kindergarten teachers told first-grade teachers about the "abilities" of the students, so labels followed children from one grade to the next. It is not surprising that children of lower socioeconomic status who were labeled as low achievers in kindergarten actually demonstrated lower reading and math abilities in the second grade than students from higher socioeconomic background who were labeled high achievers in kindergarten.

Students' Perceptions of Each Other

Research shows that children become aware of social class differences at a very young age. First-grade children can accurately match a car style with pictures of the type of people who are likely to drive them (Elkin and Handel 1989). By the sixth grade, children can match pictures of people with the type of house they are likely to live in, the furniture they are likely purchase, and the type of people they would likely invite as party guests (Elkin and Handel 1989).

But children's understanding of social class extends beyond perceptions of life-style differences to judgments about the character of individuals. As they get older, children begin to believe that people from higher social classes have desirable values and behaviors, whereas people in lower social classes are disreputable. Children ages 8 and 9 have already learned the stereotypes associated with social class so well that they believe that rich children are popular and successful, and that working-class children have reading problems, lie to their mothers, and initiate fights (Elkin and Handel 1989). These findings hold true regardless of the social class from which the child comes. Therefore, not only do peers reinforce the positive labels attached to high social class and the negative labels associated with low social class but children also begin to evaluate their own self-worth based on their socioeconomic status. By the time they reach adolescence, the stereotypes associated with social class have been so thoroughly internalized that teenagers from wealthier backgrounds have higher self-esteem and greater confidence than teenagers from poorer socioeconomic classes (Wiltfang and Scarbecz 1990).

Resources Available to Schools

Social stratification influences the resources available to schools and ultimately the quality of instruction students receive. Public schools are largely funded through property taxes, which means that schools located in wealthier neighborhoods with higher property values receive more funds than schools located in poorer neighborhoods. Wealthier schools can afford to pay higher salaries to teachers, are able to attract and retain the highest-quality teachers, and can hire plenty of teachers to ensure smaller class size, many electives, and specialized courses. Furthermore, schools in wealthier neighborhoods have more money available for instructional materials such as library books, computers, and science equipment, and are able to offer students a variety of extracurricular learning opportunities, including athletic teams, academic clubs, and music instruction (Kozol 1991).

Educational Achievement

Researchers consistently find that children from higher social class backgrounds score better on college entrance exams such as the Scholastic Achievement Test (SAT), receive higher grades in school, and complete more years of formal schooling than children from lower socioeconomic classes (Mantsios 1995). The lower educational success of children from economically deprived backgrounds is no surprise, given the negative labels, criticism, poor self-concept, and lack of educational resources persistent throughout their school years. In addition, children growing up in poor families may not receive adequate nutrition or medical care and may be overwhelmed by family and community stress, making school work more difficult.

In his moving account of a poor family living in an inner-city housing project, Kotlowitz (1991) describes the many distractions from school that poor children experience. Children living in cramped, overcrowded housing find it more difficult to find a quiet place to study. Marital conflict, spouse abuse, and drug and alcohol addictions, which are statistically more common in poor families, also upset and distract children. Living in a neighborhood fraught with problems such as gang violence, drug abuse, and unemployment further contributes to children's inability to concentrate at school. Poor children even feel unsafe and afraid in the school building itself. Instead of the routine fire drills common in elementary schools, many urban schools require children to practice "duck and cover drills" to protect them from bullets fired in gang-related shootings (Kotlowitz 1991).

The Perennial Variables: Gender, Race, and Socioeconomic Status

Gender, race, and social class—the three variables that family scholars consistently examine—are both independent and interrelated. On the one hand, sexism and racism cut across economic boundaries. Women—whether they are well-educated professionals, manual laborers, or clerks—may be subject to stereotyping and discrimination. Similarly, racial minorities from all socioeconomic levels may experience harassment and be denied opportunities because of their race.

At the same time, both gender and race influence socioeconomic status; minorities and women are far more likely to be poor or working class than whites and males (Mantsios 1995). The impact of race on socioeconomic status is reflected in median household incomes, which, in 1997, was $40,577 for non-Hispanic whites, but was only $26,628 for Hispanic Americans and $25,050 for African Americans (U.S. Bureau of the Census, "Money Income" 1998). Asian Americans, as a group, have a greater median household income ($45,249) than the white majority, but these figures must be interpreted with caution. Asian Americans, who earn lower wages, on average, than whites, have a higher household income because they are likely to have two or more wage earners in the family (U.S. Bureau of the Census, "Money Income" 1998). Furthermore, Asian American families, who tend to live in urban metropolitan areas on the West Coast, where the cost of living is higher, may actually have more household income but a lower standard of living than whites (Kalish 1994).

Minority families have higher poverty rates than white families. In 1997, 26.5 percent of African Americans, 27.1 percent of Hispanic Americans, and 14 percent of Asian and Pacific Islander Americans lived in poverty, compared to 11 percent of whites (Dalaker and Naifeh 1998). Although minorities have higher rates of poverty relative to their size in the population, it is important to acknowledge that "more than two-thirds of all poor are white and 46 percent of all poor are non-Hispanic whites" (Weinberg 1998).

Gender also influences socioeconomic status. Women who work full time, year-round earn only 74 percent of what male workers earn (Weinberg 1998). This difference in the average annual earnings of women and men is commonly referred to as the **wage gap.** Although the wage gap has narrowed in the past three decades—women earned 58.5 percent of what men did in 1968—the gap persists despite antidiscrimination legislation, women's increasing educational attainment, and the increased participation of women in nontraditional occupations.

It is not surprising, therefore, that women are far more likely to live in poverty than men. For women who are single parents, the risk of poverty is extremely high; 31.6 percent of families headed by a single female are poor (Dalaker and Naifeh 1998). Single-parent families headed by women are more likely to be poor than any other family type (Naifeh 1998). When race and gender are considered simultaneously, the impact on social class is compounded, placing a double burden on women of color. Whites, as a group, have a 1 in 10 chance of being poor, whereas African American and Hispanic American single-parent women have a 1 in 2 chance of being poor (Mantsios 1995).

Summary

The hierarchical ranking of individuals or groups in society, known as social stratification, is found in all societies. Social status refers to groups of people who have similar levels of prestige and share similar life-styles. Social scientists refer to the combined influence of income, education, occupation, prestige, and lifestyle as socioeconomic status.

All three sociological paradigms can be used to explain social stratification. Functionalists describe social stratification as a necessary and inevitable by-product of providing financial incentives for people to work hard and fulfill the more difficult, stressful jobs. Conflict theorists believe stratification is created and perpetuated by an economic structure in which wealth and power is maintained through exploitation and oppression. Symbolic interactionists at one time endorsed the culture of poverty theory, which suggested that poverty was a by-product of adopting deviant values. Today, symbolic interactionists suggest that one's position in the stratification hierarchy influences one's perceptions, behavior, and family dynamics.

Social class can be measured and operationalized in a variety of ways. Community studies, which involve participant observation and interviews, can be effective measures of social class in small communities. Social class can be measured quantitatively using income, occupation, education, or some combination of all three variables. The measure of social class used in a study should be determined by the research question.

Assessing socioeconomic status is quite complex in dual-income families. Traditionally, researchers overlooked women's earnings in married-couple households. However, ignoring the income women contribute creates an incomplete picture of a family's socioeconomic status. Researchers also must be sensitive to racial bias in social class measures.

Family dynamics generally differ by social class. Middle-class couples tend to have more egalitarian relationships than upper-class or working-class couples. Extended kinship networks provide social support in all families. However, extended kin also are important for transferring and maintaining wealth in affluent families, and are important for leisure interaction in working-class families. Poor families struggle with poor-quality housing, education, health care, and a multitude of other problems. The majority of poor families experience temporary bouts of poverty, but the chronically poor have become increasingly economically marginalized.

Socialization experiences are strongly influenced by social class. Early research suggested that working-class and middle-class parents disciplined children differently, but research by Kohn suggests that social class affects what behaviors parents punish more than how parents discipline. Other research suggests that because parental values are converging, the impact of social class on parenting behaviors is declining.

Social class also influences a child's educational experiences. Teachers perceive and treat children differently based on social class. Children, too, perceive and treat each other differently because of social class. The economic resources available to schools, which are strongly related to parents' income, have a direct impact on the quality of education children from different social classes receive.

The interaction between the three perennial variables—social class, race, and gender—cannot be overlooked. Minorities and women suffer more economic hardships than whites and men.

Readings for In-Depth Focus

The Stigma of Being on Welfare

People who are classified as poor by state and federal governments generally qualify for some type of financial assistance. Food stamps, subsidized housing, and Medicaid are examples of *in-kind* welfare benefits in which recipients receive an essential good or service that they could not ordinarily afford with their low income. Temporary Assistance to Needy Families (TANF) is a program that allows families raising young children in deprived conditions to receive some supplemental cash benefit each month. TANF benefits replaced Aid to Families with Dependent Children (AFDC), the program with which more people are familiar.

Take a moment to think about what type of people you think receive welfare? What do these people look like? What do they act like? Have you ever been behind a person in the grocery store who is paying for purchases with food stamps? How did you feel about that person? Are the views you hold about welfare recipients primarily positive or negative? Are your views fairly typical of how most people view welfare recipients?

People who have never received welfare benefits generally have very negative views of those who do. If you have never received welfare benefits, you may never have thought about what it would be like to raise a family in such dire poverty that you had to rely on government assistance to avoid homelessness and starvation. Sociologist Karen Seccombe interviewed 47 women from several communities in Florida who received welfare benefits to learn what experiences led them to welfare and how the welfare system has had an impact on their family lives. In the following reading, welfare recipients discuss the stigma and discrimination they routinely face. As you read, consider how race and gender influence the negative stereotypes these women encounter. Also think about how constantly experiencing shame, ridicule, and embarrassment might affect their self-esteem as well as their children's.

■ ■ ■

Stigma and Discrimination

Karen Seccombe

Conjure up in your mind an image of a "welfare mother." What does she look like? How does she sound? Why is she on welfare? How does she feel about being on the system?

For many people, a woman like Dawn would come to mind. She embodies many of the stereotypical traits of a woman on welfare, yet, . . . Dawn is anything but typical of women who receive welfare. Nonetheless, she fits the largely negative images that we have of "welfare mothers"—images wielded by the mass media.

Dawn is a large, gregarious woman. She is African American, 31 years old, and has never been married. Her grandmother raised her, although her mother is alive and they have always been close. "Momma didn't live there, but we would always see her. She was always close by," said Dawn. "That's a trend in my family." Dawn's grandmother received welfare for her care. "Granny," as she affectionately called her grandmother, and to whom she referred to several times throughout the interview, recently passed away.

Dawn has four children, fathered by four different men. Her first child was born to her when she was only 13. "Me and my oldest daughter—we were both children growing up," she told me. Dawn had her second child when she was 18 years old, her third one at 20, and her fourth child at age 21. Her mother volunteered to raise her second child for her, a son, and her mother therefore receives welfare for him. Dawn sees her mother and her son regularly. She does not find the living arrangement odd; after all, it mirrors her own childhood. She's appreciative that her mother offered this help.

> I guess my life was going kind of fast, having children. By the time I was 21 I had four kids. And my mom, one day she came to me because by the time my son was one year old I had another baby and was pregnant. So my mom, she felt sorry for me. And so she asked me if she could take one of the kids. At first it was going to be a temporary thing. But she asked me if I wanted her to help out, to at least take one kid. She offered to take him or the other. And he was the one I chose. And that helped me out a lot. So, she raised him since he was about a year, or something like that. But I see him all the time freely. Me and my mom, you know, we're close family. He doesn't live in the household, but he knows. I wonder if I'll raise my grandchild?

I don't want to. But I don't know what will happen.

The children's fathers, in contrast, provide very little help. Only one pays child support to the county welfare office, but he pays only sporadically. When he does pay, Dawn is given an extra fifty dollars in her welfare benefits for that month. "But, he hasn't paid lately," she tells me. "I guess he's in jail or something. But when we don't get those checks, it's a long time until my kids get shoes." Without this added assistance, Dawn receives a $365 cash grant and $345 a month in food stamps for her and her three children who live with her. The rent on her modest but neatly kept single family home is subsidized and she therefore pays only $21 a month, plus approximately $150 a month for utilities. And, like virtually all AFDC recipients, she and her children receive Medicaid.

Unlike Dawn's early years, she told me that she really no longer has an interest in men or romantic relationships. She feels that a father figure for her children, at this point, is relatively unimportant. She didn't have a father, and as she sees it, that did not harm her. Dawn was not the first woman who, after bearing several children, flatly told me that she was not interested in any further relationships. Several women expressed discomfort around men. Some alluded to be being sexually abused. Dawn, however, was more vague.

> I didn't grow up around anyone but my grandmother. I had an uncle who lived in the house for awhile, my grandmother's house, and I just didn't like that man. When he wasn't there, it was good and I loved it. But when he was there, I just didn't like him. I didn't like him at all. So I guess that's a pattern that I had. When there was a man in the house, I don't know. That's why I don't have a husband. I can't. For some reason I have real big problems in that department. So when they aren't there, I just feel kind of content. More comfortable. So I guess I don't want a husband. I

wouldn't want him here all the time. Although sometimes I want a boyfriend to help out financially. And then, again, sometimes I say it's not worth it, just forget it and go back to the way it was.

Dawn has been off and on welfare for most of her life. She has also worked at a number of jobs as well, as a cashier, a nurse's aide, and she has washed cars. She works for a few months at a time, then gets "bored" and switches jobs or quits. None of the jobs have been particularly high-paying. Several times when she was employed she withheld her employment and income information from her caseworker, and continued to receive a welfare check in addition to her earnings. She did this, only temporarily, she told me, so that she would be able to pay off her bills at the first of the month. Once when she did it, she was caught, found guilty of committing welfare fraud, and given probation for 18 months. She now has a criminal record.

On first glance, Dawn is an easy target to use in the quest for welfare reform. She corroborates the negative stereotypes we have of women on welfare: She appears to be lazy, unmotivated, and dependent on the system. We assume that she lives in a culture of poverty, where her "deviant" family values and her criminal record for welfare fraud are normative, and perhaps even encouraged. No more information about her life is needed for judgment. Onlookers do not probe deeper. Instead, many people suggest that *she* is the precise reason why we need to reform welfare: We need to eliminate Dawn, and the suspected millions of women like her, from abusing the welfare system.

Dawn is, however, an atypical welfare recipient in most respects. Compared with an average welfare mother, Dawn has more children, she has been on welfare longer, and her racial background represents only a third of welfare recipients nationally. She is an anomaly. Yet, somehow, she fits the image that Americans have of women who receive welfare—an image that is inaccurate. Perhaps the principal way in which Dawn is typical of others who received welfare is

that her life is considerably more complex than acknowledged at first blush.

Stereotypes of women who receive welfare are fed to us regularly by multiple forms of media. It is not only the middle and upper classes who are bombarded with these negative images of welfare mothers. Poor women are bombarded as well. Are women on welfare, then, also aware of these stereotypes? If so, how do they justify being on the system, with welfare mothers so widely denigrated? How do they manage, or cope with this stigma? The poor make judgments not only from the same media and cultural influences as do the more affluent, but also from their very own personal experiences with limited employment opportunities, lack of available child care, and other constraints. . . .

AWARENESS OF SOCIETAL ATTITUDES TOWARD WELFARE RECIPIENTS

First, let us examine the issue of recipients' first-hand experience with stigma and discrimination. We know that distrust and hostility toward welfare recipients is widespread within the more affluent population. Do women who receive welfare know the extent of the negative sentiment felt towards welfare and welfare recipients? Do they have firsthand experience with stigma and discrimination?

Other studies indicate that many welfare recipients do indeed feel stigmatized for receiving welfare. Goodban (1985), for example, using a sample of 100 African American women on welfare, reported that nearly two-thirds claimed they experienced some sense of shame at various times for being on welfare. Rank (1994), in his study of welfare recipients in Wisconsin, found that the lack of privacy and the stigma associated with welfare, at least in part, fueled recipients' desire to exit from welfare. Another study focusing solely on African American mothers found that women felt stigmatized as nonworkers, single parents, and inner-city dwellers (Jarrett, 1996). Another study based on in-depth interviews with 10 divorced or separated women on welfare did not find stigma to be a constant entity, but found that it varied depending on the social audience, situation, and recipients' life history (Rogers-Dillan, 1995). Her analysis, which was based on food stamp use, a public acknowledgment of welfare receipt, suggests that stigma was not experienced in the same way, in all contexts, by all recipients.

Our interviews also revealed that welfare recipients tend to be well aware of their stigmatized status. When asked if they ever hear negative comments about people on welfare, answers were overwhelmingly "yes," and most claimed that criticism has been directed at them personally. Dawn told me of her experiences:

> Yeah, I have had people look down at me. And it makes me feel bad. I don't want to— oh, I don't know. I'd probably be the same way, I guess. I don't know. I think they should understand though, that if I didn't need them, I would not be embarrassing myself like that. You know what I'm saying? Maybe they don't understand because they've never had to have them. I wish I could feel that way. But, you know, I kind of know how they feel, but then again, if I didn't have this, me and my children wouldn't be able to eat. Then how would you look at it?

Most welfare recipients who were interviewed, African American and white, as well as young and old, reported that they hear considerable personal blame and criticism. For example, when asked what kinds of things they had heard said about welfare recipients, a 28-year-old white woman named Rhonda, who has one son, told me:

> I've heard One girl was going to quit working because all the taxes come to us. Plus, you know, they downgrade us in every kind of way there is. They say we look like slobs, we keep our houses this way and that way. And our children, depending on the way they're dressed, we're like bad parents and all sorts of things like that.

The theme of laziness, an image embodied in the individualist perspective, emerged frequently. Welfare recipients are well aware that mothers on welfare are criticized for being lazy, unmotivated, and for taking advantage of the welfare system. Leah, a 24-year-old African American woman with four children, commented:

> I've had people who didn't know I was receiving assistance and everything was just fine. But when people find out you're receiving assistance, it's like, "Why? Why did you get lazy all of a sudden?" People automatically just put you in this category of people that don't do anything except sit on their butts and do nothing. It's just all out there in the community.

Mandy, another African American woman, who is 20 years old with two young children, told me:

> They say you lazy. They say you lazy and don't want to work. You want people to take care of you. You want to sit home and watch stories all day, which I don't. And they say it's a handout.

Erving Goffman's book *Stigma* (1963) provides an insightful analysis of this phenomenon. He is interested in the gap between the image the individual wishes his or her public identity to be, "virtual social identity," and what the public identity actually is, "actual social identity." A person is stigmatized when there is a discrepancy in these identities. It can be a powerfully negative social label that radically changes a person's self-concept and identity. Goffman divided stigmatized individuals into two groups: Those whose stigma is known or easily perceivable (such as a paraplegic or someone who is disfigured), and those whose stigma is hidden or not easily identified. When it is identified, the stigmatized person can become deeply discredited, labeled as deviant, and deemed to be morally flawed (Gans, 1995). The label associated with stigmatization focuses on only one aspect of the individual's character. This one aspect is elevated to the level of a "master" status—it becomes the primary mechanism through which that person is identified. One suddenly becomes, "the cripple," "the lesbian," the "cross-dresser," "the person with AIDS," "the man in a wheelchair," or "the welfare mother." Other statuses, such as Sunday school teacher, school volunteer, swimmer, friend, and daughter are largely overlooked.

The stigma surrounding welfare is deep and widespread, and research has documented that it may even keep some eligible families from applying for aid (Yaniv, 1997). Because women are well aware of the ways in which welfare is denigrated, they are often embarrassed about being poor and receiving welfare. So are their children. Many women told me of this embarrassment, including Sarah. Sarah is a white, 30-year-old divorced mother who works part-time at a fast food franchise. She also attends college, and is working toward her Associate of Arts (AA) degree. Both she and her daughter are embarrassed at wearing hand-me-down clothing. She described an incident in which her daughter's only coat did not fit her because it was originally purchased for someone else.

> She inherited my mom's winter coat because we couldn't afford one. Her arm was up here, and the sleeve was down here, but hey, she wore it. She stayed warm. You do what you have to do. You try to make it so it's not as embarrassing. But it really is. I mean, the parents made more fun than the kids did.

Dawn, our "stereotypical" welfare recipient, also discussed her embarrassment about receiving welfare:

> First of all, I'm embarrassed about being on welfare. I'm not going to tell you no lie. Maybe I've been on it all my life, but maybe that's why I'm embarrassed about it. But the kids used to go, "Momma, the

check is here." And that was so embarrassing. Downstairs, upstairs could hear. I had to stop them from doing that. I had to tell them, "This is not good. Don't be happy because we're getting a welfare check. This is not nothing good."

Most women, like Sarah and Dawn, could not hide their stigma, and were publicly embarrassed by it. In Sarah's case, her family's poverty was on display every day in which the coat or other hand-me-down clothing was worn. In Dawn's case, despite living in a public housing project in which all of her neighbors were on welfare, she was embarrassed when her children loudly announced the arrival of the welfare check. By her children doing this, she lost all pretenses that she was not really receiving welfare.

RACISM AND WELFARE

One of the many reasons that welfare use is stigmatized is that it is associated with use primarily by African Americans. Welfare is put in racial terms because many whites incorrectly assume that the majority of the poor and the majority of welfare recipients are African American. They see welfare as a program primarily serving African American mothers who have never married. Yet, although African Americans are overrepresented among the poor and among welfare recipients given their proportion of the population in the United States, a nearly equal proportion of welfare recipients are white. . . . Whites and African Americans constitute 37 percent and 36 percent of welfare recipients, respectively. But because of this misperception, racist overtones were evident in the comments made to women on welfare. One woman heard welfare recipients referred to as "white and black niggers sucking off the system." The racist view that welfare is a program primarily for the African American community was epitomized in the comments made by Beth, a 27-year-old white woman with one child:

> Oh they say silly stuff, prejudiced stuff, "The black people are getting it, so we

might as well—you might as well go ahead and get it too while you can. They're driving Cadillacs," and this and that. It just shows how ignorant they are—to me.

Several African American women commented that the public unfairly labels welfare as a problem primarily within the African American community, ". . . they want to say that there are more black people on the system than white people." Dee is an African American woman, 24 years of age, with three children aged four and under, and she told us that the most negative comments she has heard come from white males:

That's mainly who I hear it from. I mean, I hear a couple of things from black guys, but a lot of black guys I know grew up on the system. You know, they are trying to get off that system. So you don't really hear it much from them. They have first hand experience with it. Those who don't have first hand experience have friends who have. So, the majority of them have come into contact with it sometime in their lifetime. As for the white males, a lot of them grew up in the upper middle class, you know, above the poverty line, so they never run across it, unless they had friends who were on the system. But there are as many white people on it as black people.

As Kluegel and Smith (1982) reveal, many whites see African Americans' experience as having improved significantly in recent years, and tend to deny that our social structure limits their opportunities. Many white Americans are resentful. They often feel that they themselves are victimized by policies of "reverse discrimination," while African Americans and other minorities reap employment and social welfare benefits. A survey from the National Opinion Research Center reveals that only 17 percent of the adult population in the United States strongly or somewhat agree to the statement "the government is obligated to help blacks,"

whereas nearly half disagree (National Opinion Research Center, 1993). Moreover, data from the General Social Survey indicates that less than 40 percent of whites support increased social spending to help African Americans (Bobo and Smith, 1994). African Americans are not seen as needing special treatment or privilege, and many whites are resentful that African Americans are receiving these privileges nonetheless.

Our nation tends to deny racial inequalities, and instead claims to embrace the idea that "we are all created equal." Consequently we oppose Affirmative Action programs that demand that we acknowledge the differences among us—the inequalities in earlier life circumstances that affect one's opportunities today. But can we really deny that adults and children are treated differently, and have different experiences and opportunities based on their skin color and position in our class structure? Even public education—supposedly the great equalizer by providing all children with the same quality education and chance for the good life, perpetuates "savage inequalities," according to author Jonathan Kozol (1991). In comparing two high schools, one poor and with a 99.9 percent black student population, and one consisting of mostly white upper-middle-class students, he found dramatic differences in school funding, in their facilities, and in personnel. For example, high school students in poor East Orange can afford few athletic facilities. The track team has no field, and they must do their running in the hallway of the school. Meanwhile, in nearby upper-middle-class Montclair, money is available to buy two recreation fields, four gyms, a dance room, a wrestling room, a weight room with a universal gym, tennis courts, a track, and indoor areas for fencing. Money is also available in Montclair High to hire 13 full-time physical education teachers for their 1,900 students. East Orange High School, by comparison, has four physical education teachers for 2,000 students. Drastic differences such as these not only provide different current experiences and future opportunities, but they also send a clear message about the value of education. It should come as no surprise that graduation rates from high school are race and class correlated. Students with lower family incomes and members of most minority groups in the United States are significantly more likely to drop out of high school than are more affluent whites.

Individual and institutional racism are prevalent in the United States. It is manifested in many ways, including hatred and distrust towards those African Americans most in need. William Julius Wilson suggests that young African American women are actually *more* likely to be blamed for their economic circumstances than are their white counterparts, and they are considered less worthy of government assistance (Wilson, 1996). Many Americans associate the Culture of Poverty perspective with African Americans, and criticize the supposed subcultural adaptations in the African American community as aberrant and antithetical with mainstream American values associated with hard work and family. Women's poverty, African American women's in particular, is blamed on a breakdown in women's moral virtue, which has resulted in declining marriage rates and rising illegitimacy.

These concerns stem, at least in part, from several important demographic factors, both of which can be seen in Dawn's experiences. First, African Americans are indeed less likely to marry than are whites; and second, they are more likely to have a child outside of marriage. National data show that race, ethnicity, and social class do affect marriage patterns in many critical ways. In 1996, 42 percent of African Americans age 18 and older were married, compared with 63 percent of whites and 58 percent of Hispanics (U.S. Bureau of the Census, 1997b, Table 58, p. 55). In addition, a higher proportion of African Americans, as compared to whites and Hispanics, have never been married (39, 21, and 30 percent, respectively). Critics are quick to implicate this as a subcultural adaptation at odds with American values. But here are two primary reasons for this. Both reasons are rational and pragmatic, and have little to do with a culture of poverty *per se*. First, high rates

of unemployment and underemployment discourage young adults from marrying. Unemployment among young African American males is more than twice that for whites their age. And, among those males who are employed, their earnings are significantly less than that of whites. Therefore, given high rates of unemployment and underemployment, young men are less eager to take on the responsibility of a family, and young women are less apt to see these men as desirable marriage prospects. The second reason for the lower rate of marriage among African Americans is sheer demographics. The number of eligible African American women for marriage far exceeds the number of available men. The statistics are alarming: one out of every 80 African American males is the victim of a violent death, and a disturbingly high percentage of men are incarcerated. Thus, for African American females, the search for a lifetime marriage partner can be a daunting task. There is a critical shortage of marriageable men. Like many other African American women, Dawn has not found a man to marry. Given her less-than-likely chance of finding a man to support herself and her four children, her reluctance to look for one is therefore not surprising.

Higher rates of nonmarital births among African Americans also influences the belief that a separate subculture exists that is antithetical to mainstream American values. The nonmarital fertility rate for African Americans is about 2.3 times that of white women (84 vs. 36 births per 1,000 women, respectively), and the nonmarital fertility rate among Hispanic women is about 2.6 times that of non-Hispanic whites, at 95 births per 1,000 women (National Center for Health Statistics [NCHS], 1995). Part of these differences can be traced back to income or education levels. Significant racial differences persist, however, even after the effects of socioeconomic status and other individual and family characteristics are accounted for. These nonmarital births are not simply the result of accidental pregnancies. Corresponding with these demographic trends, birth *intentions* also differ among racial and ethnic groups. Using a national sample of 12,686 males and females between the ages of 14 and 21 from the U.S. National Longitudinal Surveys of Labor Market Experience of Youth (NSLY), researchers compared birth intentions of African Americans, Hispanics, and whites. They report that African Americans were twice as likely to expect an adolescent birth as were whites (10.6 vs. 5.5, respectively), and were nearly four times as likely to expect a nonmarital birth (15.2 vs. 4.2, respectively). Hispanics fared somewhere between these two groups (Trent and Crowder, 1997). Dawn's pregnancies were not planned, but, at the same time, they were not particularly surprising to her either. Yet today, the rate of teen pregnancies alarms her. Her values, and those of many other women interviewed, were not at odds with conventional expectations. She did not hold separate subcultural values that encourage or tolerate teen pregnancy. Rather, Dawn is concerned about the high rates of teenage pregnancy that plague young women and severely limit the work and educational opportunities available to them. Consequently, she is actively trying to prevent her own daughters from becoming pregnant. Dawn, and other women, told me that they were trying to ward off teenage sexual activity, among both their daughters and their sons, through repeated warnings, keeping a watchful eye on them after school, and through a series of rewards and punishments. Referring to her oldest daughter, who is now 17 years old, Dawn said:

> I'm real proud of her, because she did not do like I did. She did not have a baby at 13, or 14, or 17. She's doing good. I told her not to. Oh, so many times. All the time, right up until this day. I don't remember how long ago I used to start talking with her. But now I have a 10-year-old daughter, and I see that she's maturing, so I know she must have been about 9 or 10 when I started preaching my little preach. Ten is not too early at all.

These two demographic trends—lower rates of marriage and higher rates of nonmarital births—have become the rallying cry for Individualists and Culture of Poverty enthusiasts. African American women, in particular, are assumed to be the cause of their own poverty. Supposedly, they are poor because of their own immoral and indiscriminant sexual behavior, and their failure to find suitable lifetime mates, or so the story line goes. "It is the moral fabric of individuals, not the social and economic structure of society, that is taken to be the root of the problem" (Wilson, 1996: 164). Poverty and welfare use is racialized by many white Americans because they are increasingly weary of social programs, they believe that racism has declined, and they blame African Americans as failing to expend the effort needed to improve their financial standing.

CONTEXTS IN WHICH STIGMA AND DISCRIMINATION OCCUR

Recipients commented that they heard criticism most often in public places such as grocery stores. In this context, one cannot hide being on welfare; food stamps are used in full view of anyone who cares to notice. Food stamps are what Goffman has termed "stigma symbols." Using them forces a welfare recipient to publicly acknowledge her devalued status; her use of welfare becomes a highly visible attribute. She becomes, in the eyes of the public, a "welfare mother" with all the negative connotations that title evokes. One African American woman named Lonnie, who has been on and off of welfare several times, and most recently has received welfare for two years, revealed the hostilities she encountered in the grocery store when using food stamps:

> And I've went in the grocery store, and when you get ready to buy your groceries, people have made nasty little remarks about the groceries you're buying. They'll go, "We're paying for that." Once there was some university students and I guess they felt like that. They had a small amount in their buggy, and I had large amounts. He

started talking, so his girlfriend kept trying to get him to be quiet. And he kept talking and talking. And then he said, "That's why the president is trying to cut off welfare because of people like that!" I turned to him and I say, I say, "Well, you know something? I have worked in my time too. And I will work again. It's not like I'm asking you for anything. And I hope you don't come and ask me for anything 'cause with me and my five kids I couldn't give you none anyway!" And he stomped out of there when I told him that. But I was being honest with him. I have worked. I felt real bad that day, I really did.

Cashiers and others who are looking for evidence of fraud or abuse closely scrutinize the foods that women purchase. "Welfare mothers who purchase steak with food stamps" is a classic metaphor used by many people to illustrate the supposed fraud and abuse within the food stamp program. One woman in our study described how the fellow students in her class at the community college believed the stereotypes about women on welfare, and criticized them for buying "steaks or shrimp with food stamps." The assumption is made that welfare mothers live "high on the hog" at taxpayer expense and must be closely monitored in order to prevent irresponsible behavior and abuse of the system.

One woman told us about an actual experience purchasing a steak with food stamps. She described the critical responses she received by other shoppers in line who witnessed it. Acknowledging that she was feeding the stereotype, she tried to not let it bother her:

I did have this instance where I was in the store, and I was buying groceries, and I got a thin three dollar steak, and this lady behind me said, "It must be nice to be able to buy steak. I can't afford to buy steak with my money!" And the lady behind her said, "Well, if you were on food stamps, you could afford to buy two or three steaks!" And I just shook my head. It really didn't

bother me, because I was, like, as long as I can feed my kids, I don't care what people say. And if food stamps help me buy my kids a steak every now and then, then so be it . . . I don't look at what somebody else gets and say, "Oh look what they got? A steak or pork chops." That's their business.

Using food stamps or other "stigma symbols" requires women to give up their privacy and their choices. Their lives, their shopping habits, and their food preferences are closely scrutinized. Welfare critics are quick to judge their spending habits as inappropriate and wasteful, and look for examples of this to verify these assumptions. They look for women who buy steak with food stamps, and are vindicated when they find them. Yes, she purchased a steak, but in order to do so, what else did she give up? In what other ways did she scrimp and save during the rest of the month? Purchasing a month's worth of food on the food stamp allotment provided to families takes resourcefulness and ingenuity. At a funding level of approximately 75 cents per person, per meal, wastefulness is unlikely.

The women interviewed responded in a variety of ways to using food stamps. Some were embarrassed about using them, and preferred to shop only in specific stores where they felt welcome. It was generally common knowledge which stores have cashiers who are less sympathetic to food stamps, and women tried to avoid shopping there. Other women were more defensive, saying, "What do they want us to do, starve?"

Interestingly, another common context, other than grocery stores, in which negative comments were routinely heard was the welfare office itself. Rather then being viewed as a place for help, the welfare office is viewed with disdain. It is run by people who are seen as self-serving and who have contempt for their clients. The caseworkers are the gatekeepers to welfare, and many welfare recipients resent this, and believe that caseworkers take their function far too seriously, "They act like it's their own money they're giving away." Women commonly reported ill feelings toward their caseworker. Two women specifically suggested caseworkers should be community volunteers or representatives from churches to insure that caseworkers' first concerns were humanitarian, rather than simply viewing welfare and welfare recipients as a routine and boring job. Welfare recipients felt demeaned by their caseworkers: "They think you ain't much of nothing . . . ," "They try and make you feel bad and say little mean things . . . ," "Some of them talk to you like dirt . . . ," were frequent comments. As one mother, a 41-year-old white woman named Denise, revealed:

> Some of them treat you like you got to take this, "Because I got your case in my hand and I'm the one who decides whether you get these stamps." And some of them talk to you like dirt and some of them are all right. It's like they have no respect for you, but you have to take it because you need it. You need that check, you need that Medicaid. It's like, if you make them mad, you can hang it up, because you ain't going to get it! One lady said, "I have 30 days to approve your case or not." It didn't matter if you had kids or not. I've heard some of the workers talk to the elderly people and some of them talk to the elderly people so bad. And they don't care, it's like, "I got my job."

Amy is a 23-year-old white mother of one child who attends a university full-time and plans to go to graduate school. She will earn her bachelor's degree next year, and plans to get a master's degree in physical therapy. She told me about her experience going into the welfare office to meet with her caseworker:

> It's a very humiliating experience—being on welfare and being involved in the system. You are treated as though you are the scum of the earth. A stupid, lazy, nasty person. How dare you take this money? It's a very unpleasant experience. I'd avoid it at all costs. But unfortunately, I can't avoid it right now.

Recipients felt stigmatized and discriminated against in other ways as well. They felt mistreated by public health clinics, for example. Several women mentioned that they have to sit many hours in the waiting room before being seen, or that doctors and nurses talk "down" to them, as though they are too ignorant to understand basic medical or health terminology. Others talked about the stigma they experience when applying for a job and revealing that they currently receive welfare. They felt that they had been denied job opportunities because they were labeled as "stupid" for being on welfare. Kim, a 29-year-old African American mother of three children, is employed part-time, and told me that she is diligently looking for full-time employment. She talked about her frustration in dealing with people when applying for jobs:

> Yeah, people in employment offices, when you go looking for a job and say you're on AFDC, they automatically look at you and assume you're a dummy, "Here's another drop out." . . . If you put all this stuff down on your application they, like, double question you about the information, like you're lying. And I don't think that's fair. I don't think that you should be judged, just for being on AFDC.

Other contexts in which stigma and discrimination occurred were more personalized. Women told me that their friends, neighbors, boyfriends, or family members were sometimes extremely critical of their use of welfare. Many told me of their anxiety with telling certain people, or of the ways in which they tried to keep it a secret from them.

But perhaps the disapproval from family, friends, or acquaintances hit the children the hardest. They don't understand the societal disapproval heaped on their families. Dawn revealed a story in which her daughter, unsuspecting that food stamps were stigmatized, pulled one out of her backpack on the school bus. She was teased unmercifully by her school mates, "the kids picked on her so bad, she came home crying." Likewise, Sheila's daughter Melanie, who was introduced in Chapter 1, is shy and a loner, and Sheila attributes this to feeling self-conscious among her peers at school about being poor and on welfare. "That's why she, Melanie now, she's a loner too. When she comes in that door, she don't go back outside." Criticism from peers is especially difficult for children and teens; peers are an important reference group. Teens, in particular, spend an inordinate amount of time trying to look, dress, and behave in certain ways that reflect those of the peer group. Criticism from them is a painful and blatant reminder of the stigma attached to welfare.

REFERENCES

Bobo, Lawrence, and Ryan A. Smith. (1994). Antipoverty Policy, Affirmative Action, and Racial Attitudes. In Sheldon H. Danziger, Gary D. Sandefur, and D. Weinberg (Eds.) *Confronting Poverty.* Cambridge, MA: Harvard University Press: New York: Russell Sage Foundation.

Gans, Herbert. (1995). *The War against the Poor: The Undercalss and Antipoverty Policy.* New York: Basic Books.

Goffman, Erving. (1963). *Stigma.* Englewood Cliffs, NJ: Prentice Hall.

Goodban, Nancy. (1985). The Psychological Impact of Being on Welfare. *Social Service Review.* 59, 403–422.

Jarrett, Robin L. (1996). Welfare Stigma among Low-Income African American Single Mothers. *Family Relations.* 45, 368–374.

Kluegel, James R., and Eliot R. Smith. (1982). Whites' Beliefs about Blacks' Opportunity. *American Sociological Review.* 47, 518–532.

Kozol, Jonathan. (1991). *Savage Inequalities.* New York: Crown Publishers.

National Center for Health Statistics. (1995). *Advance Report of Final Natality Statistics. 1993 Monthly Vital Statistics Report. Vol. 43, No. 3 (supplement).* Hyattsville, MD: U.S. Public Health Service.

National Opinion Research Center. (1993). *General Social Surveys, 1972–1993: Cumulative Codebook.* Chicago: National Opinion Research Center.

Rank, Mark Robert. (1994). *Living on the Edge: The Realities of Welfare in America.* New York, NY: Columbia University Press.

Rogers-Dillon, Robin. (1995). The Dynamics of Welfare Stigma. *Qualitative Sociology.* 18, 439–456.

Trent, Katherine, and Kyle Crowder. (1997). Adolescent Birth Intentions, Social Disadvantage, and Behavioral Outcomes. *Journal of Marriage and the Family.* 59, 523–535.

U.S. Bureau of the Census. (1997b). *Statistical Abstract of the United States.* 117th ed. Washington, DC: U.S. Government Printing Office.

Wilson, William J. (1996). *When Work Disappears: The World of the New Urban Poor.* New York: Alfred A. Knopf.

Yaniv, Gideon. (1997). Welfare Fraud and Welfare Stigma. *Journal of Economic Psychology.* 18, 435–451.

Critical Thinking Questions

1. How do welfare recipients feel about being on public assistance? How do cultural stereotypes of the poor affect welfare recipients' self-concepts?

2. According to Seccombe, how is racism related to the negative perceptions of welfare and its recipients?

3. Identify social factors that explain the declining rates of marriage and the rising rates of illegitimacy in African American communities. How are these social factors related to poverty and welfare?

4. In what social contexts do welfare recipients report feeling the most stigma and discrimination?

7 *Race and Ethnicity*

*F*amilies have unique interaction patterns, rituals, and norms. I first became aware of this fact in early childhood during the holiday season. Christmas Eve in my home was filled with excitement and anticipation. My brother and I each were allowed to unwrap one present before going to bed. The next morning, we jumped out of bed and hurried to wake our parents (who had sometimes just gone to bed after assembling Hot Wheels tracks and Barbie Dreamhouses). We were under strict instructions that we could not go into the living room to see what Santa had brought until we were formally summoned by Mom and Dad.

So we sat on their bed, waiting, not so patiently, for them to brush their teeth, get the coffee started, turn on the Christmas tree, and build a fire in the fireplace. Finally, we were called into the living room, where we pounced on all that Santa had brought.

The process of opening presents from relatives was slow. We had to take turns opening presents and had to examine what others had received before opening our next gift. We were not allowed to see what was in our stockings until after breakfast. Our Christmas morning ritual stretched out for several hours.

At first, I thought all families celebrated Christmas morning as we did. But in conversations with friends, I discovered that other families did things quite differently. Some of my friends were allowed to open all their presents on Christmas Eve and got their "Santa stuff" on Christmas morning (I didn't think I'd like that very much). Other friends reported that their parents slept in the morning while they and their siblings tore through presents (that idea sounded great). And still others did not celebrate Christmas at all, but received presents over eight days during Chanukah (eight days sure beat one day in my opinion). Some friends received far less than I did, and I was selfishly thankful that I did not live in their families.

After pondering this, I confronted my parents one evening early in December. I said I thought the Chanukah tradition of getting presents every day for several days was far superior to ours of having to wait until the twenty-fifth of the month. They explained that our family did not celebrate Chanukah because we were Christian, not Jewish, and then they launched into a lengthy explanation of the different events that each holiday commemorates.

Understanding that I had to stick with Christmas, I proposed that we do like Cindy's family did—tear through presents like mad animals. I went so far as to suggest that this practice would actually benefit my parents because they could sleep late. We wouldn't disturb them, I promised. However, this option was out of the question, I was told, for my parents firmly believed that Christmas should be savored—not rushed. I was further informed that, more than anything else, my parents enjoyed watching my brother and me open presents. They would much rather see us enjoy our gifts than open their own!

There was a lesson in this: Holiday practices differed between families because of both cultural heritage (Christian versus Jewish) and individual notions about how traditions should be celebrated (slow-paced pleasure versus frantic excitement). Families do not choose which holidays to celebrate simply on the basis of their gift-giving rituals; the holiday that is celebrated reflects and reinforces the cultural and religious heritage of the family. At the same time, families from similar cultural backgrounds can celebrate the same holiday quite differently, depending on the unique views and economic means of its members.

The same principles surrounding the celebration of holidays can be applied to the study of racial and ethnic family structures. Although members of a particular racial or ethnic group may share a common history, heritage, or heredity, they do not necessarily behave identically. The emphasis placed on racial or ethnic background and the practice of some customs and traditions differs among families. Additionally, socioeconomic status within ethnic and racial groups varies widely, yielding different patterns of behavior. This chapter examines these factors as they apply to racial and ethnic minority families in the United States.

Defining Diversity

In common language, people tend to use the terms r*ace, ethnic group,* and *minority group* interchangeably (just as they often do with the terms *sex* and *gender* that were discussed in Chapter 5). For social scientists, however, these terms are not synonymous. **Race** "is a category of persons who are related by common heredity or ancestry and who are perceived and responded to in terms of [genetically determined] external features or traits" (Wilkinson 1987: 185).

The U.S. Bureau of the Census has collected data on race since the first census, conducted in 1790. However, the labels applied to racial groups have changed over time. In the earliest censuses, respondents were classified as *white, negro,* or *other.* The racial classification schemes have been revised and expanded by the federal government throughout the years to allow for more accurate data collection. In 1977, the racial classification standards were revised to include four groups: *American Indian or Alaskan Native; Asian or Pacific Islander; black;* and *white* (U.S. Bureau of Census, "Findings on Questions" 1996). Beginning with the decennial census in the year 2000, the racial classification categories will contain the following five racial categories (*Revisions to the Standards* 1998):

■ *American Indian or Alaska Native:* A person having origins in any of the original peoples of North America and who maintains cultural identification through tribal affiliation or community recognition

- *Asian:* A person having origins in any of the original peoples of the Far East, Southeast Asia, or the Indian Subcontinent including, for example, Cambodia, China, India, Japan, Korea, Malaysia, Pakistan, the Philippine Islands, Thailand, and Vietnam

- *Black or African American:* A person having origins in any of the black racial groups of Africa

- *Native Hawaiian or Other Pacific Islander:* A person having origins in any of the original peoples of Hawaii, Guam, Samoa, or other Pacific Islands

- *White:* A person having origins in any of the original peoples of Europe, North Africa, or the Middle East

An **ethnic group** "consists of those who share a unique social and cultural heritage that is passed on from generation to generation" (Mindel and Habenstein 1976: 4). Ethnicity consists of attitudes and behaviors that are learned rather than inherited. Ethnic identities often are expressed through religion, dress, language, food, and shared customs and traditions (Mindel and Habenstein 1976). The U.S. Bureau of the Census first collected data on ethnicity in the 1970 census by asking respondents to indicate whether they were of Hispanic or non-Hispanic origin. Beginning with the year 2000 census, *ethnicity* will be defined as:

- *Hispanic or Latino:* A person of Mexican, Puerto Rican, Cuban, Central or South American, or other Spanish culture or origin, regardless of race

- *Non-Hispanic or Latino:* Persons who are not of Hispanic origin

Although the Bureau of the Census formally gathers data only on Hispanic ethnicity, there are numerous European American ethnic groups in the United States whose identities are rooted in a common homeland, including, for example, Polish Americans, Italian Americans, Irish Americans, Arab Americans, and Greek Americans (Mindel and Habenstein 1976). Other ethnic groups—such as Jews, Amish, Muslims, and Mormons—are based on common religious and cultural heritage (Mindel and Habenstein 1976).

It is important to recognize that the designation of a person's racial and ethnic heritage is subjective and self-defined, rather than scientific. Census statistics regarding racial and ethnic membership are based on self-reported data, where individuals are asked to indicate the group or groups to which they belong. Until now, people with mixed ancestry have been forced to label themselves with only one race or to leave the question blank. Beginning with the 2000 census, respondents will be allowed to mark more than one racial category. However, respondents will not be given the option of selecting more than one response to the ethnicity question (*Revisions to the Standards* 1998).

Many racial and ethnic groups also are regarded as **minority groups**—people who have unequal access to economic, political, and social opportunities or who possess characteristics that are considered "inferior" by the dominant group (Kornblum and Julian 1998; Staples 1988; Wilkinson 1987). Notice that the sociological definition of *minority group* makes no reference to numerical size. As is the case with African Americans in several U.S. cities, a group can be numerically the largest, yet be considered a minority group because of its comparative lack of access to economic, political, and social resources.

Studying Diverse Families

As with all family research, methodological problems plague studies of minority families (Dilworth-Anderson and McAdoo 1988). Four methodological issues in particular—sample selection, comparison groups, definitions of concepts, and units of analysis—are of particular concern because they have contributed to a negative and inaccurate portrait of minority families (Dilworth-Anderson and McAdoo 1988; Staples 1988).

In many studies of minority families, the **sample selection** is hapazard and convenient rather than random (Dilworth-Anderson and McAdoo 1988: 266), implying that within-group differences are not important. Data based on samples that are not drawn randomly also have limited generalizability, and the use of convenient samples instead of random samples often creates a distorted image of minority families.

To better understand how sample selection procedures can create a systematic bias in the data, consider for a moment how you might obtain a sample of minority families to study. Like most researchers, you might be tempted to draw your sample from neighborhoods where many minority group members live so that you would be sure of having a large sample. You might conveniently find your sample of minority families in low-income, inner-city areas, which would lead to a distortion or bias in the data you collect. Your sample does not fairly represent minority families from all social strata.

As in the preceding scenario, most studies of minority families have been based on samples from lower socioeconomic groups (Staples and Mirandé 1983). Some researchers have mistakenly concluded that family troubles associated with high rates of poverty, such as high divorce rates and high illegitimacy rates, are the result of belonging to a particular racial or ethnic group. A distorted or negative image of minority families emerged because researchers were ignoring middle-class and affluent minority families (Dilworth-Anderson and McAdoo 1988; Staples 1988).

Another methodological problem plaguing minority family scholarship involves the comparison groups that are used. Just as I assumed as a child that all families celebrated Christmas as mine did, many researchers often mistakenly assume that families from the same racial or ethnic background are all alike. As a result, researchers tend to use as comparison groups people from racial and ethnic backgrounds different from the group they are studying. For example, scholars studying African American families might compare their patterns of interaction to non-African American families. However, because family structure, values, and practices can vary widely within a minority group, researchers also should draw comparisons between members of the same group. Unfortunately, family scholars have tended to overlook differences within ethnic groups (Staples 1988).

Minority family scholarship also has been hindered by very narrow **concept definition.** The concept of *family* has been defined almost exclusively as a nuclear, two-parent unit throughout the marriage and family literature (Dilworth-Anderson and McAdoo 1988). The emphasis on the nuclear family makes ethnic families that rely on multigenerational, extended kin networks appear deviant and problematic simply because they differ from the nuclear family norm. Additionally, the tendency to ignore the unique structure in some minority families limits what we can learn about alternative family arrangements.

Closely related to the problem of narrow concept definition is the **unit of analysis** that is used in studying minority families. Scholars who use a narrow, traditional definition of family tend to use as their unit of analysis only members of the immediate nuclear family, such as fathers, mothers, and children. Many minority families may have *extended family* or *fictive kin*—nonrelatives who are considered members of the family. Scholars studying minority families must expand the unit of analysis to include extended kin, rather than solely focus on immediate, nuclear family members (Dilworth-Anderson and McAdoo 1988).

Racial and Ethnic Diversity in the United States

Time magazine ran a cover story about racial and ethnic diversity in April 1990 that opened with these words: "Someday soon, surely much sooner than most people . . . realize, white Americans will become a minority group. Long before that day arrives, the presumption that the 'typical' U.S. citizen is someone who traces his or her descent in a direct line to Europe will be a part of the past" (Henry 1990: 28). Census data support this assertion. The demographic composition of the United States has shifted dramatically during the twentieth century from a predominantly white population of European ancestry to a heterogeneous society comprised of a variety of racial and ethnic groups (O'Hare 1992). As recently as 1950, 75 percent of all minorities were African American, but 30 years later, less than half were African American, and it is believed that Hispanics will become the nation's largest minority group by the year 2010 (O'Hare 1992).

The changing demographic composition of the U.S. population has led to a tremendous growth in research on minority families. In the past, researchers tended to ignore minority families or to assume that they were dysfunctional, but contemporary scholars recognize the importance of studying families from all racial and ethnic backgrounds.

As you will see as different racial and ethnic groups are examined in detail in this chapter, minority families—from recent immigrants to those who have been in the United States several generations—struggle with assimilation into

U.S. culture. **Assimilation** refers to the process of blending into the dominant culture by gradually surrendering traditional cultural practices and beliefs. Most minority families do not want to abandon their cultural heritage entirely, so they struggle to integrate traditional values and practices within contemporary American culture.

Language is one of the central unifying elements of a culture; it both expresses and reinforces cultural values. Many racial and ethnic minority families in the United States speak a language other than English. Learning to speak English may be necessary to find employment (Constable 1998), complete an education, or simply read package labels. However, if one's native tongue is entirely replaced by English, the family may experience a loss of ethnic identity.

Parents and children in recent immigrant families often wrestle with unique assimilation dilemmas. For example, many Latin American parents come to the United States ahead of their children to search for employment, leading to long separations. The result is vividly described in the following passage:

> Some [immigrant women] come to the United States illegally, leaving their babies behind. They toiled at menial jobs, saving money, and dreaming of a glorious family reunion. Instead, when their children finally arrived, they were adolescent strangers—resentful, resistant to parental authority, and bewildered by competitive, freewheeling society. (Constable and D'Vera Cohn 1998)

Muslim families that have immigrated from conservative cultures such as Somalia or Afghanistan, where women are expected to cover themselves completely and are forbidden to shake a man's hand, often find it difficult to maintain these customs in the United States. For instance, some Muslim families may forbid their daughters to participate in gym at school to uphold their standards of modesty—a practice that may conflict with states' physical education graduation requirements (Constable and D'Vera Cohn 1998). Girls may further be told that they cannot walk with or talk to male classmates, making social interaction and adjustment difficult.

Immigrant women may especially feel the stress of the assimilation dilemma. As Constable and D'Vera Cohn (1998) explain:

> For immigrant women . . . life is sometimes an awkward tug of war between the excitement and opportunities of modern America and the familiar but usually confining customs of their homelands. This struggle is most intensely played out in the family, where women frequently are both the cultural guardians of the old country and the force pushing their children to do well in the new one.

Most immigrant women come from male-dominated family structures where their roles are restricted to the home. In the United States, these women encounter entirely different arrangements, in which it is common for wives and mothers to work outside the home, raise a family, and expect equality (Constable and D'Vera Cohn 1998). Women may experience confusion and guilt about how to fulfill most effectively their responsibilities within the family.

African American Families

African Americans are the largest racial minority in the United States and have been studied more than other racial and ethnic minority groups. African Americans comprise 12.7 percent of the U.S. population and number almost 34 million people (U.S. Bureau of the Census 1998). It is estimated that the black population will represent 12.8 percent of the total U.S. population in the year 2000, and by the year 2050, African Americans will grow to 15 percent of the nation's population (U.S. Bureau of the Census 1998). Although many African Americans share a similar cultural heritage, it is important to recognize that black Americans have different degrees of economic success, come from different countries, and have different cultural and regional values (Staples 1988). Southern blacks differ from northern blacks, just as first-generation Haitian immigrants differ from blacks whose families have lived in the United States since colonization or slavery.

History of African American Families

In 1790, approximately 750,000 Africans were owned as property in the United States (Carlson 1990). The practice and institution of slavery, along with diverse traditional African practices, influenced the structure and interaction patterns of early African American families.

Marriage between slaves was prohibited because slaves were not allowed to enter into contractual relationships (Queen, Habenstein, and Quadagno 1985; Staples and Johnson 1993). However, informal marriage ceremonies commonly were performed by masters or ministers or by couples themselves with the slave community as witnesses. Most individuals were allowed to select their spouses, but some were ordered by owners to cohabit to breed the next generation of slave labor (Staples and Johnson 1993).

Black couples lived together in nuclear family units whenever possible. Ideally, husbands and wives lived together with their children in a small cabin on the plantation, although some women lived in single-parent households because of the death or sale of their husbands (Queen et al. 1985). Husbands who lived on a nearby plantation usually were permitted to visit their wives and children, sometimes as often as once a week (Queen et al. 1985). In fact, many black men, recognizing that they could not protect their wives from physical and sexual abuse by owners, preferred to marry women from other plantations (Franklin 1988; Staples and Johnson 1993). One man wrote: "I did not want to marry a girl belonging to my own place, because I knew I could not bear to see her ill-treated" (cited in Franklin 1988: 24).

Black families living in slavery constantly had to contend with the insecurity of knowing that at any time a spouse or child could be sold. Women and small children generally were kept together, but husbands and teenage children were often separated from their immediate families. Nevertheless, most slaves on large plantations were surrounded by immediate and extended kin because plantation owners preferred to keep couples together so that they would naturally re-

What does recent research suggest about marriage, the family, and childrearing in conditions of slavery in the United States? What are some myths and facts about the legacy of slavery in the structure, function, interactions, and conflicts of African American families?

produce (Queen et al. 1985). Furthermore, plantation owners often bequeathed slaves to their grown children, who lived on a portion of the same plantation. Thus, even when they could not live with their immediate families, most slaves were able to keep in close contact with family members.

Slaves maintained family loyalty as a strong value in African societies, despite the efforts of owners to promote a casual attitude toward family ties (Franklin 1988). Families separated through sale struggled to be reunited, and many risked their lives by running away from the plantation to find a missing family member. One advertisement placed by a plantation owner during the antebellum period read: "I think it is quite possible that this [runaway] . . . has succeeded in getting to his wife who was carried away last spring out of my neighborhood" (cited in Franklin 1988: 23). Numerous other advertisements for escaped slaves suggest that adolescent children ran away to find their mothers, mothers escaped to find children, and men escaped to be reunited with wives and children (Franklin 1988).

Gender roles in black families during slavery have long been a source of debate. Some early scholars ignored or overlooked the role of the male in slave families, assuming that men had no function in the family because they could not serve as the family provider, as their white male contemporaries did (Billingsley 1992). Hence, black families were believed to be matriarchal and dysfunctional. Other early scholars recognized the strong male presence in slave families but assumed that "if a man was in the family, the man was dominant" and "that it is a good and proper thing when men are dominant in the family" (Billingsley 1992: 110).

Recent research suggests that relationships between black couples were neither matriarchal nor patriarchal but were instead dominated by white owners (Billingsley 1992). The oppressive conditions of slavery made it impossible for either husbands or wives to exercise power and authority in the family. Historical evidence suggests, however, that couples did manage to emulate ideal gender roles prescribed in the culture at the time for white slave-owning families. Black women could not devote themselves completely to their husbands and children like white women were expected to, but when they returned home at night from tending to the owner's family, wives worked in their own small gardens, prepared meals for their families, and performed other household duties (Strong and De-Vault 1992). Black men tried to serve as "providers" by supplementing the family's meager diet with fish and wild game (Queen et al. 1985).

The lives of black children were influenced by the status of their parents as "house" or "field" slaves (Strong and DeVault 1992). Children whose parents worked in the fields were treated more harshly and expected to work at a younger age. Children of "house" slaves often were permitted to play with the owner's children and usually did not have to work until they reached adolescence (Queen et al. 1985).

Records indicate that in 1798 there were 59,466 free blacks in the United States (Billingsley 1992). Little is known of life in free black families, but records indicate that the majority (approximately 85 percent) of free black adults were married (Billingsley 1992). Some married other free blacks, and others married slaves, Native Americans, or whites (Billingsley 1992).

The first few years after emancipation, known as *the traveling time,* freed slaves searched throughout the South for relatives who had been sold (Franklin 1988; Strong and DeVault 1992; Queen et al. 1985). The majority were not successful. Many who searched for their lost relatives never located them; others discovered that their spouses had given up hope of a reunion and had already remarried (Franklin 1988).

In the early Reconstruction period, the rights of African Americans to retain custody of their children was challenged (Anderson 1996). White plantation owners sought to keep older black children on their property to exploit them as unpaid laborers. Using antebellum apprentice statutes to argue that they should be awarded custody, plantation owners claimed that the parents were unable to support their children. White judges almost always ruled in favor of the landowners. African American women suffered tremendous emotional and financial harm when their children, especially their sons, were removed from their custody. These women were denied their valued identity as mothers and had their most significant relationships severed. Furthermore, with many husbands away searching for employment, African American women relied on sons as a source of income (Anderson 1996).

After emancipation, many intact couples hurried to make their marriages legitimate. For example, in 1866, 9,452 former slaves legally registered their marriages in 17 North Carolina counties (Franklin 1988). Farther north, in the District of Columbia, 843 couples were legally married between November 1866 and July 1867 (Billingsley 1992).

In 1890, 90 percent of all blacks lived in the rural south and worked as farmers (Billingsley 1992). Some freed slaves moved to northern cities, seeking work in manufacturing industries (Billingsley 1992) or went west. Most black men who were former slaves considered "a working woman . . . a mark of slavery," and therefore preferred that their wives become full-time homemakers (Staples and Johnson 1993: 11). However, widespread racism, prejudice, and discrimination made it difficult for most black men to find work that provided enough income to support a family. After emancipation, many black wives sought employment to supplement family income.

African American Families in the Twentieth Century

Events of the twentieth century affected white and black families differently. For instance, most black families did not feel the economic boom that many white families experienced during the Roaring Twenties, yet the economic hardships of the Great Depression had comparably greater impact on black families.

World War II gave men and women economic opportunities they never before had. African American men in the military received regular paychecks and some opportunity for advancement. African American women joined the war industries during World War II, as many white middle-class women did. While many white women entered the labor force for the first time solely as a patriotic duty, black women previously employed in domestic work joined the war industries because of the new economic opportunities they provided.

Racism and discrimination prevailed in both combat and industry during war, as in peacetime. Often, African American soldiers were assigned more dangerous duties because racist superiors regarded them as more expendable than whites. African American women also were assigned more dangerous, demanding work and were paid less than white women, even when they performed the same duties (Field 1987). After the war, 40 percent of black women with small children were employed, and two-parent black families had a poverty rate of over 50 percent (Coontz 1992).

African American Single-Parent Families

Demographic trends in family structure during the second half of the twentieth century changed profoundly. Marriage rates declined, and age at first marriage, divorce rates, and number of births to unwed mothers rose. These trends resulted in a dramatic increase in the number of single-parent households headed by women. Although similar changes in marriage, divorce, and birth rates occurred in families from all racial and ethnic backgrounds, African American families "disproportionately suffered" their impact (Taylor, Chatters, Tucker, and Lewis 1990: 1001), making single-parent households more common among African Americans than any other racial or ethnic group (O'Hare 1992). In 1997, 47 percent of African American families were headed by a single female, compared to 14 percent of white families, 13 percent of Asian American families, and 24 percent of Hispanic American families (U.S. Bureau of the Census 1998).

Sociologists believe that greater numbers of single-parent families in the African American community can best be understood as the result of *different pregnancy resolution strategies* and *unequal educational and economic opportunities* (O'Hare et al. 1991).

Young black women who become pregnant are less likely than white teenagers to terminate the pregnancy, give the baby up for adoption, or marry; thus, they are more likely to become single parents (Taylor et al. 1990). The choices teenagers make when confronted with an unplanned pregnancy are shaped by access to social, educational, and economic resources. Teenagers "who have the greatest economic disadvantage and lowest academic ability" are the most likely to become pregnant outside of marriage (Luker 1994: 169). African Americans, who are disproportionately poor and are more likely to attend inferior public schools, are at a greater risk for out-of-wedlock pregnancies. The availability of extended kin, particularly maternal grandmothers, in African American households may encourage single mothers to keep their babies (Kalmuss 1992).

Marriage is a less desirable option for African American teenagers because of limited job opportunities. Young males have exceedingly high unemployment rates, so they often cannot contribute to the economic support of a family (Edelman 1987; Staples 1988; Wilson 1996). Neither young black men nor young black women perceive marriage as economically advantageous. Greater opportunities for education, job training, affordable child care, and employment might make marriage a more attractive alternative than single parenthood (Wilson 1996).

African American Socioeconomic Diversity

Growth in low-income, single-parent households and the plight of poor blacks has overshadowed the socioeconomic diversity among African American families. In 1997, 23 percent of black families had incomes below $10,000, 29 percent earned between $10,000 and $25,000, 48 percent made more than $25,000 per year, and approximately 1 in 5 black families earned at least $50,000 annually (U.S. Bureau of the Census 1998). Expanded educational and economic opportunities for African Americans made it possible for the black middle class to double in size since the 1960s (Landry 1987). Although blacks tend to earn less than whites, in younger families headed by a college-educated married couple, African Americans earn almost the same as whites with similar characteristics (O'Hare et al. 1991).

Socioeconomic status is an important determinant of family structure and life-style. Using in-depth analysis of 18 case studies, Willie (1991) illustrates differences among African American families belonging to different social classes. He found that black families who become affluent usually do so as a result of the dual employment of the husband and the wife. Although many white families attain middle- and upper-class status solely through the employment of the husband, African American families generally rely on two incomes to achieve higher socioeconomic status (Willie 1991; Landry 1987; O'Hare et al. 1991). As Anderson (1996: 205) explains: "In all social classes, married African American women are more likely than white women to work for pay, whether their husbands are opposed to, neutral, or in favor of their employment."

Willie (1991) also found that many affluent black families worked in public-sector jobs, such as teachers in public schools and postal workers. Affluent black families tend to be well educated, with at least one spouse, often the woman, having a college diploma. Professional couples strive for an egalitarian marital relationship, restrict family size to two children, and stress the importance of education as a means to economic success. These parents save for and are prepared to spend lavishly on their children's education (Huttman 1991). Affluent and middle-class African American parents encourage their children to attend college immediately after graduating from high school.

Dynamics of African American Families

Socioeconomic diversity notwithstanding, common patterns of interaction in African American families can be identified. The dynamics between spouses and relationships with extended kin are somewhat different in African American families than in white families, and, unlike most white parents, many African American parents feel compelled to instill a unique racial identity in their children.

When African American and white families from the same socioeconomic class are compared, African American married couples generally are more egalitarian than white married couples (Taylor et al. 1990). Black husbands are more likely than white husbands to share housework and child care, but, like white women in dual-income couples, black women still perform more household duties than their spouses (Taylor et al. 1990).

Another pattern in African American families is a greater reliance on extended kin than is found in white families (McAdoo 1978; Taylor, Chatters, and Mays 1988; Taylor et al. 1990). Approximately 30 percent of African American families have extended kin living within the household, compared to only 18 percent of white families (Glenn and Yap 1994). Extended family serve important economic and social functions in African American families. Grandparents and other extended kin contribute to household income and also provide child care so single mothers can pursue employment and educational opportunities (Taylor et al. 1990). Extended family also serve as a source of strength and protection against racism and social isolation in society (McAdoo 1978).

Recently, family scholars interested in understanding how black children develop a distinctly African American identity have discovered that many parents deliberately socialize their children to take pride in their racial heritage. Approximately two-thirds of black parents report that they consciously teach their children about racial hostilities or African American heritage (Taylor et al. 1990). For these parents, "issues of race are a central concern in raising their children," and they explicitly prepare their children "for their unique situation and experiences as black Americans" (Taylor et al. 1990: 994).

Hispanic American and Latino Families

The terms *Hispanic, Latino,* and *Latina* all refer to Spanish-speaking populations from Latin American countries. The federal government coined the term *Hispanic* for purposes of data collection, but *Latino,* or its feminine form, *Latina,* is the self-designated term that many Latin people prefer (Zambrana and Dorrington 1998). These terms will be used interchangeably in this chapter.

Hispanic Americans are the second-largest ethnic minority group in the U.S., comprising 8.9 percent of the United States' population and numbering 22.8 million people (del Pinal 1995; Mattson 1992). Almost 74 percent of the Hispanic population live in California, Texas, New York, and Florida. The population of Latinos under the age of 18 in these four states is projected to increase from 11 percent at present to 28 percent by the year 2020 (Holman 1997). The Latino population is expected to grow 33 percent in the first decade of the twenty-first century (Ortiz 1995). Hispanic Americans are a diverse ethnic group, claiming ancestry from Mexico, Puerto Rico, Cuba, and Central and South American countries. The vast majority of Hispanic Americans (64 percent) are of Mexican origin, 11 percent are Puerto Rican, 4.7 percent are Cuban, 14 percent are from Central and South American nations, and the remaining 6.3 percent are classified as "other Hispanics" (Ortiz 1995). Vast differences between these Hispanic subgroups have emerged as a result of the time, political climate, circumstances under which they entered the country, and the region where they settled (Torrecilha, Cantu, and Nguyen 1999).

History of Hispanic Americans

The earliest known ancestors of Mexicans lived in the Southwest part of the United States and occupied large parts of Mexico centuries before Europeans arrived in America (Saenz 1999). The ancestral line of Mexican Americans was altered by the arrival of the Spaniards in 1519, who dominated the various indigenous groups through technology and military force. Following the Mexican-American war, Mexico was forced to give approximately half of its land to the United States in exchange for $15,000,000 (Saenz 1999). Mexicans who were living on the land that now belonged to the United States were given one year to decide if they wanted to become U.S. citizens—with protection of their land, language, and religious customs—or return to Mexico. The majority decided to remain in the United States, becoming the first generation of Mexican Americans. Later, Mexicans immigrated to the United States to work in agricultural or manufacturing jobs, and most recently they have come in search of service jobs (Rodriguez and Hagan 1999).

Puerto Rico is a Caribbean island situated in the central West Indies that has long been valued for its scenic beauty and strategic location (Torrecilha et al. 1999). The Spanish first colonized the island after it was "discovered" by Christopher Columbus in 1493. After the near total destruction of its indigenous population, the Spanish repopulated the island with African slaves. The United States acquired the island 400 years later, in 1898, after the Spanish-American war, and Puerto Ricans were granted U.S. citizenship. The island remains a commonwealth of the United States, although controversy continues as to whether Puerto Rico should be given independence or extended statehood (Torrecilha et al. 1999).

Cuban nationalism and a sense of rebellion against Spanish colonial authority in the 1830s led to the first wave of Cuban migration to the United States (Pérez 1994). The majority of this first wave of Cuban immigrants settled in New York and New Orleans. In 1868, a bloody insurrection against Spanish authority led to more Cuban migration, this time to Key West, Florida, and Ybor City on the outskirts of Tampa, Florida. The vast majority of these Cuban immigrants were men who worked in the cigar industry.

In 1959, Cuba's social, political, and economic structure was radically changed from one closely intertwined with Unites States capitalism to a centrally planned system guided by Communist principles. This dramatic upheaval prompted a mass exodus from Cuba, beginning with the wealthiest, most educated classes, which lasted for 30 years. It is estimated that more than one million people, one-tenth of the total Cuban population, left the island of Cuba since the revolution (Pérez 1994).

Most other Hispanic American groups have a more recent history of immigrating to the United States as political refugees. In the late 1970s, prompted by political instability in Central America, people from Guatemala, Nicaragua, El Salvador, Panama, Costa Rica, and Honduras came to the United States as political refugees (Torrecilha et al. 1999). Refugees include people from all class and educational backgrounds—from well-educated, wealthy landowners to unskilled, uneducated peasants.

Dynamics of Hispanic American Families

The diversity among Hispanic Americans makes it difficult to describe interaction patterns that characterize the entire ethnic group. Nevertheless, two traditional values are prevalent in most Hispanic groups: familism and rigid sex-role distinctions (Mirandé 1985; Ortiz 1995; Wilkinson 1987). *Familism,* described as probably the most significant characteristic of the Hispanic American family, is the expectation that family members will offer support to each other whenever necessary, even if it means subordinating the needs of individuals for the needs of the family (Mirandé 1985). Regardless of national origin, Latinos report a strong commitment to family (Ortiz 1995). In practice, the emphasis on familism means that family members, including extended kin, should be available to each other for emotional, economic, and social support (Queen et al. 1985).

Familism is in part a product of native Hispanic cultures retained by families when they immigrate to the United States. In addition, research suggests that familism is a pragmatic adaptation to the social and economic conditions in the United States (Baca Zinn 1994). The ability to turn to extended kin for social and

How would you describe racial and ethnic diversity among Hispanic Americans? What are some shared characteristics and values of Hispanic families, and how are they changing? How are Asian American families similar and different?

economic support can be invaluable to immigrants, who may not speak English fluently and initially may be unemployed or underemployed.

A unique feature of familism in Hispanic families is the *compadrazgo* system of godparents (Baca Zinn 1994). *Compadrazgo* refers to two sets of relationships with fictive kin: relationships between godparents and children, and relationships between the godparents and the children's parents. Godparents are expected to attend major religious celebrations in their godchild's life, such as baptism, first communion, and marriage. They also serve as co-parents by providing parents with emotional and economic support when it is needed, as well as help discipline the children (Baca Zinn 1994).

Traditionally, Latin American families are patriarchal and governed by strict distinctions between male and female sex roles and gender distinctions. Children are socialized at a young age that men are the ultimate family authority, serving as primary economic provider and decision maker in the family (Queen et al. 1985). Any evidence of feminine characteristics in males is strongly discouraged (Wilkinson 1987). Conversely, women are expected to be warm, nurturing, and loving and to take primary responsibility for housework and child care.

The dominant, masculine behavior encouraged in Hispanic men is referred to as *machismo*, which often is perceived negatively outside Hispanic culture as allowing men to be controlled by violent, brutal impulses (Staples and Mirandé 1983). However, the concept of *machismo* is seen in Hispanic American culture as based on "honor, respect, and dignity" rather than "power, control, and violence" (Staples and Mirandé 1983: 506).

Rigid sex-role distinctions traditionally valued and supported in Hispanic families are being challenged by social and economic changes. As more Hispanic women move into the labor force, because of rising divorce rates and the increased cost of living, the traditional patriarchal pattern of family interaction is upset (Queen et al. 1985). The economic power women receive from employment contributes to greater gender equality in the family (Baca Zinn 1994). Although employment does not guarantee women more power in marriage, many Hispanic families are more egalitarian than they were in the past (Vega 1990; Baca Zinn 1994). Today, a variety of gender-role relationships can be found in Latino marriages, ranging from patriarchal to egalitarian (Baca Zinn 1994).

Given the value placed on family and the women's roles as wives and mothers, it is not surprising that, as a group, Hispanics tend to have larger families than non-Hispanics. However, fertility rates among Hispanics vary widely, with Mexican Americans having the highest birth rates and Cuban Americans having the lowest (Bachu 1995). Cuban American women actually have slightly lower fertility rates than non-Hispanic white women (Pérez 1994; Vega 1990).

Hispanic Americans also have lower divorce and marital separation rates than non-Hispanic white families. However, census data suggest that rates of marital disruption are rising among the Hispanic population (Vega 1990). Among Latin American groups, Cuban Americans have the highest divorce rates, possibly because Cuban women have high rates of employment, which disrupt traditional gender-role relationships (Pérez 1994).

Hispanic Americans and Poverty

An overriding concern among Hispanic American families today is poverty. In 1992, 29.3 percent of Hispanic Americans lived in poverty, compared to 14 percent of non-Hispanics (del Pinal 1995). Although they make up only 8.9 percent of the population, more than 18 percent of people living in poverty in the United States are of Hispanic origin (del Pinal 1995). As such, Hispanic American children are more likely than non-Hispanic white children to live in poverty. In 1992, 39.9 percent of Hispanic American children lived in poverty, compared to 13.2 percent of non-Hispanic children (del Pinal 1995).

Low educational levels and high unemployment rates contribute to poverty within Hispanic American communities. In 1993, 60.4 percent of Hispanic adults were high school graduates, compared to 91.2 percent of non-Hispanic whites. That same year, only 9 percent of Hispanic Americans received college degrees, whereas 26.8 percent of non-Hispanic whites were college educated (del Pinal 1995). Within the Hispanic American population, Cuban Americans are most likely and Mexican Americans and Puerto Ricans are least likely to receive a college education. Hispanic Americans are also more likely to be unemployed (11.9 percent) than non-Hispanic whites (6.1 percent). Cubans have the lowest unemployment rate (7.8 percent) of any Hispanic group (del Pinal 1995). Hispanic males earn only 63.1 percent of what non-Hispanic white males earn, and

Hispanic females earn only 78.1 percent of what non-Hispanic white females earn (del Pinal 1995).

These bleak economic indicators contribute to family stress and instability. High poverty rates, combined with strong patriarchal values, contribute to higher drinking and wife abuse rates in Hispanic American households than in non-Hispanic households with similar degrees of economic stress (Jasinski, Asdigian, and Kantor 1997). Advocates are searching for ways to improve the economic, educational, and social position of Hispanic American families.

Asian American and Pacific Islander American Families

"In 1996, the Asian and Pacific Islander population was estimated at 9.6 million persons and represented 3.7 percent of the total population" (Bennett and De-barros 1997). In the past three decades, the Asian and Pacific Islander population has grown dramatically, rising 141 percent between 1970 and 1980 and another 98 percent from 1980 to 1990 (Lee 1998). Since 1990, the Asian American and Pacific Islander population has grown about 4.5 percent per year, with 86 percent of that growth due to immigration (Lee 1998).

Like the Hispanic American population, the Asian and Pacific Islander population is quite diverse, with groups differing in their language, culture, and recency of immigration (Bennett and Martin 1995). Asian Americans include people of Chinese, Filipino, Japanese, Asian Indian, Korean, and Vietnamese descent (O'Hare 1992). Within the Asian American population, some groups, such as Chinese Americans and Japanese Americans, have been in the United States for several generations, whereas others, particularly those from Southeast Asia, are more recent immigrants. Pacific Islanders, which comprise only 5 percent of the Asian and Pacific Islander population, include Hawaiians, Guamanians, and Samoans (O'Hare 1992). Hawaiians are native to this country, and, unlike Asian Americans, relatively few other Pacific Islanders are foreign born (Bennett and Martin 1995).

History of Asian American and Pacific Islanders before 1965

The earliest Asian immigrants were primarily "Chinese and Japanese men who worked as miners, railroad workers, farmers and laborers" (Lee 1998: 6). The first wave of Asian immigration began in the 1850s when Chinese men were brought to the United States as contract laborers to work in the California gold-mining endeavor. Although Hawaii was not yet a state, thousands of Chinese men were recruited to work on Hawaiian sugar plantations at the same time. When the gold rush ended in northern California, thousands more Chinese laborers were drawn to this country to help build the transcontinental railroad (Lin 1999).

With the completion of the railroad, white workers arrived on the West Coast, looking for work. Competition between white and Chinese men for work led to anti-Chinese rioting and lynchings in the western states in the 1870s and into the 1880s. As a result, the Chinese Exclusion Act of 1882 was passed, barring further Chinese immigration. The act was renewed every 10 years until 1943.

The exclusion of further immigration left Chinese men in "bachelor societies." Most men arrived in the United States without their wives and children because of the high cost and danger of transatlantic travel (Lin 1999). Prostitutes and slave girls were smuggled in to "service the sexual desires of the laboring men" (Lin 1999: 324). Brothels, gambling, and opium parlors were common in bachelor communities, contributing to the negative stereotypes and prejudice against the Chinese.

Japanese immigration began in 1884, two years after the Chinese Exclusion Act was passed (Fujiwara and Takagi 1999). Hawaiian plantation owners recruited Japanese laborers to work on the sugar plantations to replace the dwindling Chinese labor supply. Unlike the Chinese laborers before them, many Japanese laborers brought their wives and children with them. Plantation owners welcomed the family units, believing they would create a "civilizing atmosphere" on the plantation (Fujiwara and Takagi 1999). Ironically, the presence of family probably contributed to a quick shortage of Japanese workers, as most families moved to the mainland as soon as their labor contracts expired. Hawaiian plantation owners then recruited Korean and Filipino laborers (Fujiwara and Takagi 1999).

Over 120,000 Japanese Americans were interned in concentration camps in the United States during World War II. Families were forced to evacuate their homes within a week, with only the possessions they could carry, and move to concentration camps. Evacuees were not told where they were going, although efforts were made to keep families together. The property and assets the families left behind usually were not recovered after the war (Fujiwara and Takagi 1999). While many Japanese American soldiers were fighting for the United States, their loved ones were "incarcerated behind barbed wire under military occupation" (Fujiwara and Takagi 1999: 306).

History of Asian American and Pacific Islanders after 1965

In 1924, when the U.S. Congress passed the National Origins Act, Asian immigration was virtually halted. The act effectively banned all immigration from Asia (Lee 1998). Although the Chinese Exclusion Act was rescinded in 1943, and the War Brides Act of 1946 allowed wives of Asian American war veterans to join their spouses, Asian immigration remained severely limited until 1965, when the Hart-Cellar Immigration Act was passed. Under this new immigration policy, a top annual quota of 20,000 immigrants from any country were permitted into the United States. Additionally, the policy allowed immediate family members of Asian Americans—including parents, spouses, and children to enter the country as nonquota immigrants. Family reunification brought Asians from all social classes, but labor provisions in the immigration law brought more immigrants who were middle-class professionals and skilled workers (Lin 1999).

Beginning in April of 1975, a large wave of immigration from Southeast Asian began. With the establishment of communist rule in South Vietnam imminent, members of the South Vietnamese government and military came to the United States as political refugees. Most of this first wave of Southeast Asian immigrants were well educated and skilled workers (Espiritu 1999). As the economic and political conditions in Southeast Asia worsened, a second wave of refugees who were poorer and less educated arrived in the United States, including Vietnamese, Cambodians, Laotians, and Hmong (Espiritu 1999).

The "Model Minority" Stereotype

The combination of high earnings and educational attainment, along with seemingly stable family structure, has led to a stereotype that Asian Americans are a *model minority* group. Asian Americans have a higher median family income than whites, African Americans, or Hispanic Americans. In 1996, the median family income for Asian and Pacific Islanders was $43,000, more than $3,000 higher than non-Hispanic whites, $18,000 higher than Hispanic Americans, and almost $20,000 higher than African Americans (Lee 1998). Asian Americans also tend to be highly educated; in 1997, 42 percent of Asian Americans age 25 and older had a college or professional degree, compared to only 26 percent of non-Hispanic whites, 13 percent of African Americans, and 10 percent of Hispanic Americans (Lee 1998). Asian American men have higher education rates than Asian American women, owing to traditional cultural values that placed more emphasis on education for sons than daughters. Nevertheless, Asian American mothers are more likely than women from any other minority group to have a high school degree (Bennett and Martin 1995; Lee 1998).

The family structure of Asian Americans also has been considered highly desirable. Of the 2.1 million Asian and Pacific Islander families in the United States, 80 percent are married-couple households (Bennett and Debarros 1997). Compared to all other racial and ethnic groups, Asian American women are less likely to have a child out of wedlock, and Asian American children are more likely to be living with both parents (Lee 1998).

On the surface, it would seem that being described as a model minority based on statistics that show high income and educational levels as well as stable family life would not cause concern in the Asian American population. However, the model minority stereotype is a vast overgeneralization that ignores significant problems within the Asian American population and exacerbates prejudice. Asian Americans are likely to live in extended kin arrangements, with several adult workers per family, which helps explain the higher household income among Asian Americans. Using per capita income as a measure of financial resources, Asian American family members earn less than non-Hispanic whites (Lee 1998).

The model minority stereotype minimizes the discrimination and racism that Asian Americans continue to face, especially the so-called glass ceiling barrier to high-level executive and managerial positions (Fujiwara and Takagi 1999).

More importantly, there are considerable income differences within the Asian American population that are overlooked when the model minority stereotype is applied. Although Japanese Americans and Asian Indians have high household earnings, Vietnamese and other Southeast Asian immigrants have extremely low incomes (Lee 1998). According to the 1990 census, the per capita median income was $9,032 for Vietnamese, $5,597 for Laotians, $5,120 for Cambodians, and only $2,692 for Hmong (Espiritu 1999). Unemployment and poverty rates are much higher and educational levels are much lower for Southeast Asians, compared to other Asian American and Pacific Islanders.

Maintaining Cultural Identity

Although Asian Americans differ on many dimensions—such as country of origin, socioeconomic status, and degree of assimilation into American culture—several values that guide Asian family life have been identified. Typically, Asian Americans place greater value on the family than the individual. Asian Americans, like Hispanic Americans, believe individuals' needs are subordinate to the needs of the family and often have extended kin living in the home. However, the philosophy behind these similar sets of values are quite different. The Hispanic ideal of *familism* is believed by some to be rooted in Latin American culture, whereas others believe it is a form of adaptation to American culture. Asian devotion to the family, on the other hand, is rooted in the philosophies of Confucianism and Buddhism, which teach that individuals should subordinate their needs for the collective good of the family, village, or country (Shon and Ja 1992; Suzuki 1985). Self-discipline, unquestioning obedience to parents, and respect for the elderly are considered essential for achieving happiness in life and bringing honor to the family (Suzuki 1985).

The concept of *family* among many Asian peoples is not limited by time, as it is in Western cultures. Americans and other Westerners generally define *family* as including their living relatives. For many people of Asian descent, the concept of family extends backward and forward in time. An individual is seen as a product and reflection of all previous ancestors, and an individual's behavior is believed to influence future generations (Shon and Ja 1992). Hence, individuals have a tremendous responsibility to monitor their own behavior and consider how it will reflect on the image of the family and how it will influence family members yet to be born. Asian Americans often pride themselves on the "close, cooperative, caring relations between kin" that characterize their family structure, and consider those values as an important source of cultural identity (Espiritu 1999: 358).

Asian families generally are patriarchal. Traditionally, males are valued more highly than females, and gender-role expectations are quite distinct (Shon and Ja 1992). Men are considered the head of the household. They make the important family decisions and have responsibility for providing economically for their families. Women are expected to care for and nurture the children as well as take care of household duties. However, not all Asian American families have sufficient economic means for the man to be the sole economic provider. Many Asian American women, like African American women, historically have had high rates of labor force participation (Glenn and Yap 1994). Although Asian American families tend to be patriarchal, second- and third-generation Asian American families are somewhat more egalitarian than recent immigrant families (Fujiwara and Takagi 1999; Suzuki 1985).

Maintaining cultural identity and traditional family practices in contemporary American society can be difficult. Asian American women find that it is possible to challenge the traditional patriarchal family structure with the increased economic and educational opportunities available in the United States. Although most first- and second-generation Asian American women do not radically challenge tradition (Espiritu 1999), conflicts over gender roles are likely to erupt. Native-born third- and fourth-generation Asian American women are more likely to eschew the traditional roles of their cultural heritage in favor of the more egalitarian roles prescribed in contemporary American culture.

Concern about maintaining Asian and Pacific Islander cultural heritage has been heightened by the high rates of interracial and interethnic marriage within this population (Oyserman and Sakamoto 1997; Root 1997). Interracial marriage is most common among native-born Asian Americans. Third-generation Japanese American males, for example, have an out-marriage rate of 25 percent, and third-generation Japanese American females have an out-marriage rate of over 60 percent (Fujiwara and Takagi 1999). The majority of interracial marriages are to non-Hispanic white partners. Although the rate of interracial marriage dropped from 25 percent in 1980 to 15 percent in 1990, the rate of interethnic marriage climbed (Lee and Fernandez 1998). *Interethnic marriage* describes unions between Asians of different cultural backgrounds, such as marriages between Korean and Japanese Americans. The combination of ethnic diversity and high rates of interracial and interethnic marriages have prompted some researchers to speculate that Asian Americans have a multiethnic identity rather than a single cultural identity (Spickard 1997).

Native American, Eskimo, and Aleut Families

Native Americans comprise 0.9 percent of the U.S. population and number 2.3 million people. The Native American population has grown 12 percent since 1990, compared to a 3 percent growth in the non-Hispanic white population (U.S. Bureau of the Census 1998). Although as many as 500 tribes have been identified (Staples 1988), over half of all North American Indians identify with one of the eight largest tribes—Cherokee, Navajo, Chippewa, Sioux, Choctaw, Pueblo, Apache, and Iroquois (O'Hare 1992). Nearly half of all North American Indians live west of the Mississippi River, with 42 percent of the population living in Oklahoma, California, Arizona, and New Mexico (Paisano 1995). Family structure, values, and behaviors vary widely among tribes and nations, making it impossible to describe a typical North American Indian family. Some tribes are monogamous, others are polygamous; some are matrilineal, others are patrilineal. At one time, Native Americans spoke more than 170 languages (Staples 1988). Much of the diversity stemmed from the vast geographical areas where tribes lived that provided different natural resources and climates. Native American settlements have been divided into seven regions: Arctic, Subarctic, Northwest Coast, Far West, Southwest, Great Plains, and Eastern Woodlands (Haviland 1994). Different housing, economic, and family patterns developed within each region. The vast differences between Native American families prompted one set of authors to argue that "there is no such institution as a Native American family" (Staples and Mirandé 1983: 512).

History of Native Americans after Colonization

The history of Native Americans after colonization can be divided into six periods: discovery, conquest, and treaty making (1532–1828); removal and relocation (1828–1887); allotment and assimilation (1887–1928); reorganization and self-government (1928–1945); termination (1945–1961); and self-determination (1961–present) (Deloria and Lytle 1983).

In the early period of colonization, Native Americans had some economic and political power with the European settlers. The earliest settlers were faced with a land filled with unfamiliar vegetation. Since they did not know what plants were edible or how to prepare them, settlers bartered and traded with Indians for food (Murrin 1997). Additionally, the earliest European settlers needed Native American labor and materials in the fur trade, as well as their consent for land titles (Green 1999).

Settlers, and the slaves they brought with them, carried microbes that proved deadly to the Native people. With no immunity to smallpox, measles, or even simple bronchial infections, over 90 percent of Native Americans in any given region died within a century of colonization (Murrin 1991).

Removal and Assimilation

Under the guise of protecting Native Americans from white exploitation, the U.S. government began a policy in 1828 of relocating Native people to western territories. In the late 1840s, after whites began moving westward in great numbers, reservations were established for Native Americans so that all the remaining land would be available to white settlers. The establishment of reservations was seen as a peaceful way to take land from the Native Americans (Anderson 1996). The process of removal and relocation disrupted Native American social and family structure. Many tribes were moved from their homelands to an area far away with different (and usually fewer) resources.

In 1887, with the passage of the Dawes Severalty Act, the U.S. government abandoned its reservation policy in favor of allotting parcels of land to individual American Indian families. The act stipulated that "each [male] head of household was to receive 160 acres of allotted land, each single adult 80 acres, and each minor child 40 acres" (Anderson 1996: 28). The U.S. government would hold these lands in trust for 25 years and sell "surplus" Indian land.

This new policy was intended to acquire more land from Native Americans at a low cost. The act, which also was designed to "civilize" Native Indians by turning the men in tribes into farmers, had a devastating impact on Native Americans (Green 1999). The federal government did not give families the training, capital, or quality of land necessary to produce successful farmers. Furthermore, in many tribes, farming traditionally had been performed by women, so males often felt emasculated, frustrated, and embarrassed by being forced to farm (Anderson 1996).

Reorganization and Self-Government

During the New Deal era of the Great Depression, the government recognized the failure of allotment policies to incorporate Native Americans into mainstream society (Green 1999). A radical new approach was adopted with the Indian Reorganization Act (IRA) of 1934. The IRA was designed to revitalize tribal governments and increase the land holdings of Native Americans. Tribes were to be managed by tribal business corporations, modeled after the structure of the U.S. government, and would be given revolving credit to institute new economic activities (Green 1999).

Although seemingly a more beneficial policy, the IRA was criticized by many white politicians as "communistic" (Anderson 1996). Additionally, many Native American tribes had traditionally operated with informal, fluid leadership; the structured, formal system thrust upon them was unfamiliar and undesirable. The heterogeneity of tribes also made it difficult for them to unite into tribal corporations (Anderson 1996).

Renewed interest in assimilating Native Indians into mainstream culture, coupled with post–World War II economic concerns, led to yet another federal attempt to manipulate Native Americans. The government now tried to get Native Americans to relocate voluntarily to urban areas to look for work. Job placement programs with money for transportation, placement, and economic support were offered to Native Americans who relocated. This policy was combined with drastic cuts to funding for agricultural and industrial activities on reservations. The government also began terminating the legal recognition of some tribes, not surprisingly those that were most stable and economically successful, to minimize those eligible for relocation funds (Green 1999).

Self-Determination

While civil rights activists, women's rights activists, and antiwar protestors were gaining media attention in the 1960s, another, less visible, social movement began. Native Americans began protesting for the right to self-determination and against the harsh, racist termination policies of the government (Green 1999). Native Americans from a variety of tribes worked together in what has been dubbed the *Pan-Indian movement*. The result was the creation of the Indian Self-Determination and Educational Assistance Act (1975). Tribal governments were given control over federal funding for health care, education, and economic development. Tribes also were given more access to natural resources on reservations, such as oil, timber, and coal.

Contemporary Native American Family Dynamics and Issues

Clearly, governmental policies have disrupted the traditional economic, social, and family structure of Native American groups. As with other minority groups, many family issues that contemporary Native Americans face are a by-product of past and present prejudice and discrimination.

Native American families often struggle to maintain their cultural identity. Like African American, Hispanic American, and Asian American families, Native American families place emphasis on the importance of extended kin (McPhee, Fritz, and Miller-Heyl 1996; Staples and Mirandé 1983; Wilkinson 1987; Yellowbird and Snipp 1994). Furthermore, elders are respected and given much authority in decision making in Native American cultures. Elders are valued because they help preserve the heritage of the tribal community, provide strength and advice to individual families, and can offer access to tribal resources (Green 1999).

Beginning with the postwar termination policies, many Native Americans were separated from family and tribal members as they left reservations and moved to urban areas in search of better economic opportunities. The greater distance between family members has made it difficult for Native Americans to maintain ties with extended kin. Additionally, the transition to urban life often is quite hard without family nearby to offer social and economic support (Staples and Mirandé 1983). It is difficult to maintain traditional cultural practices and preserve one's Native American cultural identity when one is separated from extended kin, tribal elders, and tribal lands.

Socioceonomic Status and Economic Development

Poverty is another issue confronting Native American families. Thirty-two percent of Native Americans live at or below the poverty level, compared to 9 percent of non-Hispanic whites (Green 1999). Poverty rates found in the largest tribes range from a low of 17.3 percent among the Iroquois to a high of 47.3 percent among the Navajo (U.S. Bureau of the Census 1996). The median family income in Native American households is $21,750, only 62 percent of the $35,225 median income for all families (Paisano 1995). Proportionally, more Native Americans receive welfare benefits (51 percent) than any other racial group

(Green 1999). Poverty is further contributed to by low employment rates. Native Americans have the lowest work force participation rate (53 percent) of any racial or ethnic group tracked by the Bureau of the Census (Green 1999). Of those who are employed, only 43 percent work in white-collar jobs that generally provide the highest wages and benefits (Green 1999).

To combat high poverty rates, Native American Indian tribes are trying to find economic development opportunities. Recently, many tribes have turned to high-stakes gambling as a form of revenue and economic development. The 1988 Indian Gaming Regulatory Act allows tribes to negotiate with states for permission to operate any games of chance that are legal in that state. In 1994, gross revenues for Indian gaming exceeded one billion dollars (Green 1999). Gaming revenues have been used to provide improved health care, education, and jobs for tribal members. Foxwoods Casino in Ledyard, Connecticut, operated by the Machantucket Pequot Indians, reportedly employs over 10,000 people, including many nontribal members (Boudreau and Peppard 1994).

However, relying on gaming as a primary form of economic development is problematic in several ways. Public criticism has led to increased pressure for state legislatures to demand a share of gaming profits (Green 1999). Future gaming regulation may curtail the revenues tribes are allowed to keep. Furthermore, only those tribal members living on or near the reservation benefit from gaming revenues, leaving families that have relocated away from the tribal land with little gain. Furthermore, relatively few tribes are permitted to operate high-stakes gaming; two-thirds of all Native Americans are members of tribes that do not have gambling operations (Green 1999). Other avenues of economic development must be explored to reduce poverty among Native American families.

Single-Parent Families

Poverty is an especially acute concern in Native American single-parent families. Although 65 percent of American Indian families are married-couple households (U.S. Bureau of the Census 1998), the rates of single-parent families headed by women (27 percent) are far above the national average (17 percent) (Paisano 1995). Many single-parent mothers have several children because fertility and birth rates of Native American women tend to be high. Federal policies that disrupted traditional subsistence patterns, matrilocal residence patterns, and matrilineal descent patterns have made Native American women more economically dependent on males. A divorce or out-of-wedlock birth can leave single mothers economically devastated (Anderson 1996).

Many births in Native Indian communities are to single women under 20 years of age. The adolescent birth rate among Native Americans is twice as high as the birth rate of Anglo teenagers (McBride Murry and Ponzetti 1997). Several explanations have been offered for the high adolescent birth rate of Native American women. Regardless of race, teenage women who come from low-income, single-parent households are at the greatest risk for an early pregnancy. Many scholars believe that the high birth rates of Native American teenage girls is a by-product of the high poverty and single-parent household rates in their communities. Others argue that high teenage birth rates are a product of Native American cultural values. Children tend to be highly valued in Native American culture, so girls' parents or their partners may discourage contraceptive use. Among the Navajo, for example, pregnancy has traditionally been viewed as a normal part of a woman's life and should "be neither avoided nor sought, but rather accepted" (McBride Murry and Ponzetti 1997). Finally, tribal concerns and pressures can contribute to high teenage birth rates. Omaha Indians, for instance, were nearly destroyed by disease at one time, so the tribe has since encouraged large family size. To retain their tribal heritage, contemporary urban Omaha Indian women may continue to have many children, beginning at young ages (McBride Murry and Ponzetti 1997).

Native American Parental Rights

Both historically and in contemporary society, Native American parents have had to struggle for the right to retain custody of and authority over their children. The goal of much federal Native American policy has been to "eradicate the 'Indianness' in young people" (Mannes 1995: 266). This goal was first promoted by the 1819 Civilization Fund Act, which provided money to educate Native American children in mainstream European American cultural practices. In the early twentieth century, Native American children were placed in government-operated boarding schools designed to sever the parent-child relationship (Anderson 1996; Mannes 1995). In these schools, children were given haircuts, issued Anglo clothes, renamed, and punished for speaking their native language (Anderson 1996). The Native Indian children were not permitted to return home even during school vacations; instead, they were housed with Caucasian families (Mannes 1995). Native American parents routinely tried to hide their children from government officials so they would not be taken away. Government officials responded with roundups of Native American children (Anderson 1996; Mannes 1995).

After boarding schools were abandoned, Native American parental authority was further challenged by adoption policies. Social workers actively sought Caucasian families whenever adoption or foster home placements were required. In 1978, at a time when Native Americans were being given more self-determination, the Indian Child Welfare Act was passed, which gave tribal courts the ultimate jurisdiction over all Native American child custody placements (Mannes 1995).

In the wake of several recent custody battles, the Indian Child Welfare Act has become quite controversial. In California, a Native American grandmother used the act to block the adoption of her twin granddaughters to a white family, even though the children's biological parents approved of the adoption (Diamond 1995). In Kentucky, a judge ruled that an 11-year-old Native American girl should remain in the custody of her part-Cherokee, part-Choctaw adoptive mother. Citing the Indian Child Welfare Act, the Sioux Indian tribe demanded that the girl be returned to the reservation where she was born. Because of cases such as these, white legislators are increasingly putting pressure on the federal government to amend the Indian Child Welfare Act to limit its scope (Diamond 1995).

Theoretical Perspectives on Minority Families

The application of sociological theories to the study of ethnic minority families is a challenge because existing family theories were based on studies of white, middle-class families (Dilworth-Anderson, Burton, and Johnson 1993). Furthermore, researchers who focus on minority families have not developed or applied new theoretical frameworks specifically to explain family dynamics in minority families. In recent years, some scholars have attempted to explain how existing theoretical frameworks can be used to understand African American families, but efforts to relate theoretical perspectives to Hispanic American, Native American, and Asian American families "are virtually nonexistent" (Dilworth-Anderson et al. 1993: 639).

The Functionalist Perspective

Structural functionalists believe that every social structure and social institution, including the family, functions to make a society work as a whole. Two important functions of the family in modern society are the socialization of children and the stabilization of adult personalities.

In addition, within the family, husband and wife roles have traditionally distinct functions: Men are economic providers for their families and women are homemakers and caregivers of children. Parents are expected to raise their children to be independent and economically prosperous (Dilworth-Anderson et al. 1993). So long as individuals conform to normative roles and statuses, the family functions smoothly. Otherwise, the family becomes dysfunctional for its members, itself as a social institution, and society as a whole.

Using structural-functional theory, minority family life is often interpreted as disorganized and dysfunctional when it does not conform to the traditional, white, middle-class, two-parent, nuclear family structure. One result has been the characterization of minority families as somehow deficient or deviant.

Structural functionalism also can be used to interpret minority families as resilient and adaptive to social change. For example, female-headed households and greater reliance on extended kin in African American families can be viewed as functional adaptations to historically entrenched societal constraints.

The Conflict Perspective

Conflict theorists draw on Marxist or feminist philosophy and focus on sources of social inequality, such as economic oppression and sexual exploitation. Conflict theorists point out that racial and ethnic minority groups in the United States have lacked control over and access to economic and social resources. Minority group members earn lower incomes and have higher poverty rates than nonminorities with the same amount of education (O'Hare 1992). The proportions of African Americans, Hispanic Americans, and Native Americans living below the poverty level is three times higher than in the non-Hispanic white population (O'Hare 1992). The system further exploits minority workers by paying them low wages, thus concentrating wealth and power in the hands of nonminority capitalists. Minority women are seen as particularly vulnerable and exploited by the capitalist economic system and patriarchal social and family structures.

Conflict theorists argue that racial oppression and economic injustice influence family structure and dynamics. Minorities who are unemployed and underemployed are forced to live in the poorest sections of town, where educational and economic opportunities are scarce. Limited educational and occupational opportunities contribute to family instability, higher divorce rates, rising illegitimacy rates, and increasing numbers of single-parent families among minority groups.

The Symbolic Interactionist Perspective

Symbolic interactionists focus on the process by which individuals develop self-concept and self-esteem through interaction with others, particularly with members of a primary group such as the family. They examine interpersonal relationships, socialization practices, and identity development in racial and ethnic minority families. Symbolic interactionists ask how and when children begin to see themselves as a member of a particular minority group and how children learn to negotiate interracial encounters. Ethnic identity and family experiences influence how individuals perceive or define situations and how they behave.

Summary

Families in the United States come from diverse racial and ethnic backgrounds. The U.S. Bureau of the Census identifies four racial groups: American Indian or Alaskan Native, Asian or Pacific Islander, black, and white. Additionally, individuals are classified according to either Hispanic or non-Hispanic ethnic origin. It is often difficult to get accurate data on minority families due to biased sample selection, narrow concept definition, and inappropriate units of analysis.

Several common themes can be identified in the history and dynamics of African American, Hispanic American, Asian American and Pacific Island, Native

American, and Alaskan families in the United States. First, like white families, each racial ethnic group and subgroup is quite diverse. Differences in socioeconomic status, cultural background, and historical treatment have led to a variety of cultural practices, customs, beliefs, and values that shape family interaction. Second, ethnic minority families tend to emphasize family obligation and the importance of extended kin networks as an extension of traditional culture and a source of social and economic support in a wider society in which racism and discrimination are still quite evident. Third, social changes have altered traditional family structure in minority families as they have in Caucasian families. The three theoretical perspectives of structural functionalism, conflict theory, and symbolic interactionism help explain different facets of life in racial and ethnic minority families.

Readings for In-Depth Focus

A New Look at Black Families

Non-Hispanic white families are usually held up as the model of the ideal family in American society. Problems, rather than assets, of racial and ethnic minority families are highlighted in most public discourse. In the following excerpt from *A New Look at Black Families*, Charles Willie identifies changes in white family structure that were most likely modeled after African American families. As you read, compare African American and white family structures and consider how racial and ethnic diversity have an impact on all families.

■ ■ ■

Gifts to America from the Black Experience
The Equalitarian Family and Other Social Customs

Charles Vert Willie

The black family suffers as an object of research because it is difficult to get scholars to study this social institution on its own terms. White social scientists such as Jerold Heiss and Daniel Moynihan have presented the case against the black family. Moynihan's assertion that the family structure among blacks has seriously retarded their progress "because it is so out of line

From *A New Look at Black Families*, 4th ed., by Charles Vert Willie (Dix Hills, NY: General Hall, Inc., 1991), pp. 175–186. Printed with permission of General Hall, Inc.

with the rest of American society" has been widely publicized (Moynihan, 1965:29). Less well known is the "indictment . . . handed down against the black family" by Heiss. The key count of the accusation claims that blacks would be "better off if the differences in family form did not exist" (Heiss, 1975:3). His study, entitled *The Case of the Black Family*, sought to determine if "the characteristics of black families . . . differ from those of white families" (Heiss, 1975:5). In summary, states Robert Staples, social scientists who study the black family have been concerned primarily with its deviance from . . . middle-class white family behavior" (Staples, 1978:vii). Needed, in his opinion, are studies that "concentrate on the unique structure of the Black family and its evolution in meeting its own unique functional prerequisites" (Staples, 1978:v).

The Moynihan Report, although criticized by most knowledgeable family sociologists, nevertheless influenced the development of stereotypic notions about black families that are widespread today. The prevailing stereotype is that most black families are single-parent, matriarchal structures. Actually most blacks who ever marry continue to live with a spouse and two-parent black families are more equalitarian than patriarchal or matriarchal.

Middleton and Putney (1960) studied 40 families—10 white middle-class families, 10 black middle-class families, 10 white working-class families, and 10 black working-class families. Unlike many researchers, and to their credit, Middleton and Putney controlled for social class in their study. The families studied were matched on mean years of marriage and mean age of each spouse. A 15-item questionnaire was filled out separately by each spouse in a family. The questions had to do with child care, purchases and living standard, recreation, and attitudes. In the area of purchasing, for example, the spouses were asked: "If you were buying a house, would you prefer to buy a small new house or a larger but older house costing

the same amount?" After spouses had answered the questions separately, they compared their answers and then filled out the same questionnaires jointly. If their separate answers were different, the spouses in each family changed them on the family questionnaire that was filled out jointly.

If the husband won two-thirds or more of the "joint decisions" when joint decisions were different from those of one spouse—that is, if the wife changed her responses to those which the husband had given initially on his separate questionnaire—then the dominance pattern for that family was classified as patriarchal. If the wife won two-thirds or more of the "joint decisions," then the family was labeled matriarchal. If either parent won more than one-third but less than two-thirds of the decisions, the family decision-making pattern was classified as equalitarian.

The most interesting overall finding is that 17 of the 20 black families in the Middleton and Putney study made joint decisions that were classified as equalitarian. When the husband and wife differed, the husband tended to win about as often as did the wife in most of the black families. The findings indicate that, proportionately, more black families (17 out of 20) were equalitarian than white families (13 out of 20).

With reference to social class, middle class blacks were more equalitarian in family decision-making than any of the other race-class groups studied. Nine out of the 10 black middle-class households resolved their differences in a cooperative, give-and-take way that denoted dominance neither by the husband nor the wife. This was the experience for eight of the 10 working-class black families. A pattern of patriarchal dominance appeared in one of the 10 black middle class families and of matriarchal dominance in two of the ten black working-class families.

The findings from the Middleton and Putney study are similar to those derived from analysis of the case histories of families in this study. Black families do not constitute a monolithic pattern of relationships; such families vary in behavior by social class as do white families. Research must be sensitive to the variety found in black family life-styles and recognize that there is validity to varying life-styles, that there is no one best family structure for all people in all situations. The family, as well as other institutions, adapts to external as well as internal constraints. Those studying the family must recognize that it is a changing institution and they must take into consideration the qualitative adaptations families make.

Black families are often similar to other families, but they also may differ from white families in specific and fundamental ways due, in general, to their subdominant status in the nation's power structure. These differences should be acknowledged and studied for the information on strategies of adaptation that others may learn whose status, in time, could shift from dominant to subdominant, even as blacks may experience situations of dominance from time to time.

There seems to have been a calculated effort in the United States to doubt, denigrate, and deny the contributions of blacks and other minorities to the culture of this society. This I know because some whites have told me so. More than a quarter of a century ago in 1962, I was called to Washington, D.C., by the Kennedy Administration to serve as Director of Research for Washington Action for Youth—a delinquency-prevention project in the nation's capital that was sponsored by the President's Committee on Juvenile Delinquency and Youth Crime.

I surveyed the distribution of juvenile delinquency in Washington and discovered that two-thirds of the delinquency in that city at that time was committed by youngsters who lived in only one-third of the city's area. The area in which most of the juvenile delinquents lived was impoverished, dilapidated, and racially segregated.

One day, I addressed the Metropolitan Area Crime Council, gave the results of my survey and my interpretation of the findings. In the interpretation, I said, "We are not going to do anything about delinquency in our society unless we do something about poverty; and we are not going to do very much about poverty unless we do something about racial and ethnic discrimination."

A white businessman seated next to me at the head table did not like my remarks and wrote a letter expressing his displeasure. He wrote: "Dear Dr. Willie, You made a very able presentation at the luncheon . . . and you exhibit a substantial potential for . . . good among your race; . . . however, your perspective could stand some small adjustments. . . . Leaders of your race are never going to pull it up by inculcating in the minds of your people that their plight is caused by whites who 'discriminate' and 'alienate.' . . . Ghana, Kenya, Nigeria and all other African nations where the blacks predominate and control are undernourished educationally [and] impoverished. . . . Is there any areas where [Blacks] run their own show where the people are literate and prosperous? . . . You have got to do two things. One, you've got to fight for the curtailment of breeding in your low IQ and morally deficient group; and two, you've got to educate all of your race to stop expecting help of any sort. . . . When [Blacks] have earned acceptance, they won't have to ask for it. It will come to them. Sincerely, A Suburban White Businessman" (actually, he signed his real name) (Willie, 1969: 6–7).

This letter that doubted, denigrated, and denied the contributions of blacks was written in the 1960s. People were not as wise then as in later years. Yet I received a similar letter in the 1970s after I had addressed the West Tennessee Education Association in Memphis and had endorsed desegregation of the nation's public schools. This time it was a letter to the editor of the Memphis *Commercial Appeal* newspaper. The letter was addressed to the "Harvard educator."

The white male letter-writer said: "The first question that comes to mind after reading the remarks attributed to you [in the newspaper] . . . is how a possessor of such wild notions could long elude the man with the butterfly net. . . . To endorse and promote the forced association of widely disparate races . . . is to create abrasive situations in every area of daily existence and to deny human beings the benefits and pleasures of homogeneity. . . . History stands as proof that any white nation which crosses its blood lines with blacks sows the seeds of its own destruction. . . . It is the white race that has led mankind to its highest levels of achievement. To have race-mixing a sought-after desired result of education would ultimately lead to genetic changes and condemn civilization to the Dark Ages."

By the 1980s I assumed that my fan letters would be of a different sentiment, that citizens of this nation no longer had the need to doubt, denigrate, and deny the contributions of blacks and other minorities. My assumption was wrong. After an appearance on the McNeil/Lehrer television program of the Public Broadcasting System in the early 1980s to discuss standardized testing as an inappropriate way to assess the teaching competence of blacks and other minorities, I received this letter from San Francisco. It was addressed to "Professor or Doctor or whatever: Charles Willie" and stated these sentiments: "My wife and our two sons are Professors (real ones). They were in your Africa for five years teaching while I was there for electronic-engineering. The Blacks there are extremely stupid but those who are here are stupider to the extreme too! Here you are only good to parade grotesquely with stolen names which belong to White people. You don't see how the Americans are laughing when you tell them your [prestigious] names. Africa needs you and wants you very much. Here our White America doesn't at all!" Then my letter-writer suggested that I should go back to Africa.

There are, of course, whites and other residents of the United States who have sentiments that differ from those expressed by my letter-writers. But too many believe that blacks and their way of life in the United States is a distortion of American culture, a deviation from the mainstream.

My declaration is exactly the opposite: Blacks and other minorities are central to the purpose of this nation. Moreover, they are central to the capacity of this nation to fulfill its purpose. My conclusion is supported by one of the most eminent sociologists in this nation, Robert K. Merton, Professor Emeritus of Columbia University. He said, "It is not infrequently the case that the nonconforming minority in a society represented the interests and ultimate values of the group more effectively than the conforming majority" (Merton, 1968:421). Supreme Court Justice Thurgood Marshall said that "some of the oppressions of the past have been overcome today simply because some of the oppressed had sufficient faith in the Constitution to confront the anomalies in society and to insist that they conform with the basic principles upon which this nation was established" (Marshall, 1973:xii). Former U.S. Secretary of Transportation William Coleman echoed this view when he said, "American whites owe a debt of gratitude to American blacks for making the Constitution work" (quoted in Willie and Edmonds, 1978:3). Of course, when the Constitution works for the minority or the subdominant people of power it also works for the majority.

■ ■ ■

Always there are at least two norms in any social system—the norm of the dominant people of power and the norm of the subdominant people of power. It is well that there should be two norms. For the way of life of the minority identifies customs and conventions that could benefit the majority; and the way of life of the majority identifies customs and conventions that could benefit the minority. All of this is to say that Daniel Patrick Moynihan was wrong several years ago when he said, "it is . . . a disadvantage for a minority group to be operating on one principle, while the great majority of the population, and the one with the most advantages to begin with, is operating on another" (Moynihan, 1965:29). It is precisely because minority and majority groups operate on different sets of principles that each group can make a contribution toward social system self-correction. The majority without a minority is incomplete.

Middle-class whites have adopted the idea of individualism, freedom, and autonomy in the family. When there is conflict between the institutional family and an individual member, middle-class whites tend to resolve such conflicts in behalf of the individual because of their fundamental belief in autonomy. Middle-class whites understand individualism as the source of creativity that benefits not only a person but the total society. This is the wisdom of the white middle class that should be shared with others (Willie, 1985:16).

There is a down side to freedom, autonomy, and individualism. When manifested in the extreme, there is little corporate family activity and no sense of a common mission. Feelings of personal entitlement prevail in many white middle-class families. Each family member believes that he or she is entitled to happiness and personal fulfillment. Such feelings can lead to narcissistic attitudes and hedonistic behavior. There is little love and only limited support in a family where these attitudes and feelings prevail. Thus, the freedom that sustains individualism and its creativity sometimes shatters family solidarity among middle-class whites (Willie, 1985:118).

Middle-class black families have a way of life that is almost the opposite of that found among middle-class whites. Among middle-class blacks, maintaining the family in the style to which it has become accustomed is a team effort. Most middle-class black wives and mothers are gainfully employed in the labor force and their wages are a major source of household in-

come. A great stimulus for work by the parents in such families is to equip their offspring with skills and habits of behavior that will keep them from experiencing any deprivations. Thus, middle-class black parents insist that their children get a good education not only to escape possible deprivations but to serve as symbols of achievement for the family as well as for the race. Priming offspring to resist racism and overcome through personal achievement is the main mission of the black middle class.

Celebrations, vacations, and happy times are household affairs that include the extended family in the black middle class. The parental generation does not envy or compete with offspring, and the children honor and are not ashamed of their mothers and fathers. Each generation is expected to stand on the shoulders of the past generation and to do more. All achievement by members in black middle-class families is for the purpose of group advancement as well as individual enhancement. Thus, all family members bask in the reflected glory of any of its successful members. Cooperation rather than competition is the operative concept in black middle-class families.

This corporate activity, as wonderful as it is, has a down side for the black middle class. It stifles experimentation. Family members are urged to adhere to the tried and the true. Because success is a corporate outcome, failure is viewed this way too. Thus, the stress of failure is compounded when one realizes that dishonor has been brought upon the family as well as upon oneself. It is fair to say that the adaptations of middle-class blacks favor the group rather than the individual, including group goals. While black middle-class family members always have a collective cheering squad in the wing, such a group can be quite constraining and may even veto the interests of the individual; indications toward personal risk-taking are discouraged and the secure approach is advocated. Indeed, the individual is expected and has an obligation to forego or delay personal gratification for the sake of others in the black middle class (Willie, 1985:72–76). Creativity is limited under these conditions; experimentation is greatly controlled. Individual fulfillment is seen as a self-centered activity and therefore is less valued. What counts in the black middle class is how the family is faring.

Clearly the white middle class that emphasizes individualism could learn something about how to achieve a common family mission and corporate support from middle-class blacks. Such would overcome the fragmentation in family solidarity that is increasingly found in middle-class white families. Likewise, middle-class black families that emphasize group goals and collective effort could learn something about how to achieve freedom, personal fulfillment, and the creativity that flows therefrom. Too much creativity has been stifled in middle-class blacks who have been trained to put family needs above personal needs. And too many individuals have drifted aimlessly in middle-class white families who have been taught to place individual freedom before collective concern. Obviously, the customs and conventions the black middle class has discovered the white middle class has not; and the customs and conventions the white middle class has discovered the black middle class has not. These two groups need each other. It would be a disaster for our society if blacks had adopted the way of life of whites, as suggested by Moynihan; from whence would the source of societal self-correction have come? The complementary functions of black and white families in the middle class also appear in the working class and among the poor. This finding means that at all levels of society blacks and whites have something to teach each other and are therefore interdependent.

In addition to his inappropriate recommendation that blacks should act like whites, Moynihan also described his view of the ideal family. He said, "Ours is a society which presumes male leadership in private and public affairs" (Moynihan, 1965:29). This is a sexist remark. One wonders why the women's movement did not demand an explanation of his sexist orientation when blacks were challenging Moynihan about his inappropriate racial recommendations. To their credit, blacks rejected the Moynihan orientation that men should lead society. Blacks have opted for an equalitarian rather than an authoritarian family. In the black family, neither the husband nor the wife is always in charge (Willie, 1983:156–162).

The gift of the equalitarian or egalitarian family form to America is a common contribution by blacks of all social class levels. New family forms are emerging due largely to changing social circumstances. Andrew Billingsley has stated that "the family is a creature of society" (quoted in Myers, 1982:35). The family form in the United States under greatest attack is the patriarchal structure in which the husband-father is the dominant authority. D. H. J. Morgan has stated, "the patriarchal model of family and society is felt to be inappropriate" today (Morgan, 1975:211). "In most American families," according to Hector Myers, "the pattern of authority and power is differentially assumed by husband and wife in different areas, with different issues, and at different times" (Myers, 1982:57).

Blacks have been pioneers in the development of the flexible family form which distributes decision-making authority between husband-father and wife-mother. My studies and others mentioned of middle-class and working-class black families "confirm the presence of equalitarian decision-making" and reject the notion of female-dominated or male-dominated households (Willie, 1983:159). Furthermore, black parents tend to identify with the future and aspirations of offspring more so than parents in other families who prefer that offspring not forget customs and conventions of the past (Willie, 1985: 154-156, 188-192).

I found that a high proportion of nuclear families among middle-class and working-class blacks were equalitarian in household decision-making (Willie, 1983:15), that the equalitarian pattern of decision-making prevails among whites as well as blacks, but that "more residual practices of matriarchal or patriarchal dominance" are found among whites (Willie, 1983: 161). Therefore, the equalitarian family form is a major contribution by blacks to American society.

REFERENCES

Heiss, Jerold. 1975. *The Case of the Black Family.* New York: Columbia University Press.

Marshall, Thurgood. 1973. "Foreword." In C. V. Willie, B. M. Kramer, and B. S. Brown (eds.), *Racism and Mental Health.* Pittsburgh, Pa.: University of Pittsburgh Press.

Merton, Robert K. 1968. *Social Theory and Social Structure.* New York: Free Press.

Middleton, Russell, and Snell Putney. 1960. "Dominance in Decisions in the Family: Race and Class Differences." In C. V. Willie (ed.), *The Family Life of Black People.* Columbus, Ohio: Charles E. Merrill, pp. 16–22.

Morgan, D. H. J. 1975. *Social Theory and the Family.* London: Routledge and Kegan Paul.

Moynihan, Daniel Patrick. 1965. *The Negro Family: A Case for National Action.* Washington, D.C.: U.S. Government Printing Office.

Myers, Hector. 1982. "Research on the Afro-American Family." In Barbara Ann Bass, Gail Elizabeth Wyatt, and Gloria Johnson Powell (eds.), *The Afro-American Family,* New York: Grune and Stratton, pp. 35–68.

Staples, Robert (ed.). 1978. *The Black Family* (second edition). Belmont, CA: Wardsworth.

Willie, Charles Vert. 1969. *Church Action in the World.* New York: Morehouse-Barlow Co.

———. 1985. *Black and White Families.* Dix Hills, N.Y.: General Hall.

———. 1983. *Race, Ethnicity, and Socioeconomic Status.* Dix Hills, N.Y.: General Hall.

Willie, Charles V., and Ronald R. Edmonds. 1978. *Black Colleges in America.* New York: Teachers College Press.

Critical Thinking Questions

1. Compare and contrast black and white families.

2. Why have the contributions of African Americans and other minorities generally been ignored in American society?

3. What "gifts" does Willie identify that have been contributed by African American families?

4. Given what you read in the chapter, what family patterns may have been adopted by both African American and white families from other racial and ethnic groups?

5. How is the increasing diversity in the United States likely to affect family dynamics in the future?

Part III

Intimate Relationships

Issues in the Family Life Cycle

8 Love and Partner Selection

I n my years as a sociologist, I have learned of many different strategies people in various cultures use to select their partners. For example, in India, many marriages are arranged by the parents of the bride and groom. In Japan, a *nakado* (or "go-between") is often used to help form a match. In Jewish culture, a *shadkhan* (or *shadchan*), the equivalent of a professional marriage broker, can be paid to find a suitable mate for an eligible single (Mullan 1984). Of all of the mate selection practices I have seen and heard of, however, none is as unusual as the one I witnessed recently.

The ritual begins with a marriageable man or woman and 50 members of the opposite sex who compete to have the opportunity to mate with this person. A pair of hosts aid the person seeking a mate in narrowing down the field of potential partners from 50 to 1. Throughout the mate selection process, the person seeking a partner is not allowed to see any of the potential mates. In the mate selection ritual I witnessed, the person seeking a mate was a 20-year-old female. The process began when the host asked the young woman to pick from six categories: stomach, height, kissing style, age, nose rings, and hair. She first chose the *stomach* category and was asked if she liked partners with flat or flabby stomachs. She said she never wanted her partner to be thinner than she was, so she preferred flab. All of the men who had flat stomachs were disqualified from becoming her mate. Next, she selected *nose rings* and was asked if she believed they were "pretty" or "pretty icky." She responded with "pretty icky," so all the potential mates who thought nose rings are attractive were eliminated from competition.

The number of potential mates was narrowed to six through this initial process. In the second phase of the process, the young woman asks the men, identified only by number, to perform some task. If they perform the task to her satisfaction, they remain eligible partners. If not, they are eliminated. In the final stage of this elaborate mate selection ritual, three young men remain. They race to be the first to reach the young woman by having the most in common with her. The host poses questions to the men, then to the woman. The men who answer as she did advance one step toward her. The first man to reach her becomes her mate for at least one evening. It is only then that she is allowed to turn and view her partner.

In what kind of culture would such a bizarre procedure be used to meet potential mates? How successful can these unions be? If you are in tune with the youth culture in America, then you know that the mate selection ritual I just described is a television show on MTV called "Singled Out."

Dating and Mating in the United States

Although "Singled Out," like "The Dating Game," is not how most Americans choose their partners, elements of more traditional mate selection are present. In the game show, the person trying to select a partner is allowed to base mate selection partly on physical appearance by using categories such as height, stomach, and hair. Furthermore, the contestants remain eligible as partners as long as they have something in common with the chooser. As you will learn in this chapter, both physical appearance and similarity between partners are both very important facets of mate selection in American culture.

Love

One of the perennial questions in family sociology is: With whom do we mate? Initially, the answer to this question may seem quite obvious: We mate with someone we love. Although love is not the primary basis for marriage in all cultures and has not always been an important criteria in the United States, in contemporary industrialized countries, love is considered an important prerequisite for marriage (Allgeier and Wiederman 1991). Would you marry someone with all the right qualities if you didn't love him (or her)? Responses to this question, which was posed to college students across the globe, indicate that the United States "leads the world in its belief in romantic love"; 86 percent of American respondents said they would not marry without love, the highest percentage of any country (Levine 1993: 27). (India—a country where arranged marriages are the norm—had the greatest number of respondents [76 percent] who indicated that they would marry without love.)

Sociologists do not accept love as the sole explanation for mate selection, however. Love is a cultural construct that changes over time, differs between cultures, and is virtually impossible to measure, so it cannot provide an empirically satisfying answer to the question With whom do we mate? Furthermore, even if we accepted the answer that we mate with someone we love, then the next obvious question would be With whom do we fall in love? Contrary to the notion that Cupid's arrow can strike any two people randomly, sociologists have long recognized that if the background characteristics of one partner are known, it is not difficult to predict the characteristics of the type of person with whom he or she will fall in love.

Choice

Dating and mate selection in American culture can best be described in one word: *choice.* Throughout U.S. history, with the exception of some enslaved African Americans, individuals have had the freedom to select their mates. Although in the past, parents' approval of potential mates was considered important, children nevertheless were free to choose their own partners (Whyte 1990). This basic philosophy that individuals should choose their own mates has stood the test of time.

In colonial America, parents allowed young men and women to associate freely. However, romantic love was discouraged because marriage was defined as an economic arrangement, living conditions were harsh, and strict Puritan and Catholic morals emphasized practicality and duty over emotionality (Bardis

1964). Parents, especially fathers, had considerable power to influence mate selection in the colonial period because they owned the farms and businesses in which sons were given an interest upon marriage. If a father disapproved of his son's choice, he could refuse to give any land or status in the family business, making it difficult for the young man to support his bride.

Mate selection for enslaved African Americans prior to emancipation was not always characterized by free choice, as masters often forced particular men and women to unite as a couple. However, when permitted, African Americans exercised choice in mate selection. Courtship and mate selection rules for Native Americans—including people of Mexican, Inuit, and Hawaiian descent—were extremely diverse but also reflected many of the economic and social functions of marriage.

Functionalists would argue that allowing individuals choice in mate selection is functional in Western industrialized nations that strongly value individualism. One function of allowing people to freely select their own mates, they would suggest, is that unions should last longer because couples have formed a relationship based on mutual desire. In social systems in which individualism is valued, individuals are likely to resist being told with whom they must mate and would probably be unhappy with any partner they did not deliberately select.

The History of Courtship

A common form of courtship in the latter half of the eighteenth century was **bundling,** in which young couples were permitted to court in bed while at least partially dressed and often in the presence of other family members (Bardis 1964). Most commonly a couple was placed in a "bundling bed"—a bed divided by a wooden board down the middle. In other families, a "bundling bag" was used, in which women were placed in a large sack. Although less common, some families tied their daughter's feet together at the ankles to ensure her chastity while bundling (Eshleman 1997).

The practice of bundling, which was particularly common among lower socioeconomic status families, may have emerged in response to some practical considerations of the time. First, homes often were separated by great distances, which had to be traveled on horseback, so when a suitor visited, it was common for him to stay overnight. Second, bundling gave young couples some measure of privacy, which was difficult to obtain in the small, crowded dwellings of the time. Additionally, families often tried to conserve wood and candles—"commodities that required much time and labor" (Eshleman 1997: 295) by retiring early for the evening. The young couple was expected to quietly socialize under the covers. The warmest place in most homes in the cold New England winters was in bed under the covers. The practice of bundling was eventually abandoned as conditions changed and social norms called for more restraint.

The accepted, respectable form of courtship for white middle- and upper-class youth during the Victorian era was **calling.** Young women designated days when they would receive callers. Young men were eligible to call if they were invited by the girl's mother or the young woman herself or if they had been properly introduced at a private dance or dinner (Bailey 1988). When a young man came to call on a woman, he would present the young woman's card to the maid or butler who answered the door. The young man would either be admitted to the parlor or turned away with an excuse. During the visit, the couple would sit in the parlor with refreshments and talk or the young woman would play the piano.

A large body of literature on the etiquette governing calling emerged. Young women were advised in these books that the young man must return an invitation for a call within two weeks; she should focus their conversation on the man's interests, without being too personal; and when the gentleman caller was ready to leave, the young woman should never stand up or accompany him to the door (Bailey 1988).

Dating Then and Now

The modern practice of **dating** began to emerge in the late 1800s, and by 1910, dating was a part of middle-class vocabulary (Bailey 1988; Whyte 1990). The word *date* comes from lower-class slang and probably was introduced in 1896 by George Ade, who wrote a column for the *Chicago Record* called "Stories of the Streets and of the Town." In one of the stories, a male character asks his girlfriend, who has been unfaithful to him, "I s'pose the other boy's fillin' all my dates?" (Bailey 1988). Dating initially was considered unrespectable among the middle and upper classes because it was a custom originally practiced in the lower class. Poorer women, who lived in small, overcrowded residences without a parlor or piano, could not receive callers. The more practical way for poorer couples to court was in a public place, such as a dance hall, a diner, or eventually at the movie theater. The poor woman was dependent on a young man treating her to such commercial amusements, because her wages were too low for such extravagant leisure spending. Upper-class women began to see the dating model as preferable, for it offered more freedom and privacy than calling, and as the twentieth century began, it was no longer considered risqué to dine alone with a man (Bailey 1988).

The practice of dating—which was aided by the invention of the automobile, growing affluence in society, and the increased availability of leisure activities—transformed the dynamics of the courting relationship (Bailey 1988; Whyte 1990). First, dating removed much of parents' control of courtship. Couples could interact in the anonymity of a public place or the privacy of the family car rather than under the watchful eyes of a parent in the home. Second, the balance of power between men and women in the courtship process shifted. Under the calling system, women had all the power. They controlled who would be accepted and rejected and the visit took place in the woman's home. Dating is a courtship system in which men have the power and control. Traditionally, the man must take the initiative to ask the woman out; he pays for the activities and the date occurs in a place of his choice. Bailey (1988: 23), who has written an extensive history of dating in the United States, argues, "What men were buying in the dating system was not just female companionship, not just entertainment—but power. Money purchased obligation; money purchased inequality; money purchased control."

Bailey's analysis of men's economic power in dating reflects the arguments of conflict theorists as well as some feminist theorists. Conflict theorists argue that all social arrangements are determined by the economic structure in society. In a capitalist, patriarchal society in which men control wealth and power, even something as seemingly benign as dating will allow males to use economic power to reinforce their dominance over women.

Dating today can take a variety of forms. No longer are men solely responsible for requesting, planning, and paying activities. It is now socially acceptable for women to ask men for dates and to pay for events. Many couples share financial responsibility for dates by splitting the check or taking turns paying for activities. Furthermore, there are many more socially acceptable ways for individuals to meet dates. Creative entrepreneurs have developed a variety of services to aid singles in meeting partners. Today, individuals can meet companions by placing personal ads or using social introduction services. Increasingly, people also are meeting potential dates through the Internet.

Personal ads placed to meet partners can be found in most major newspapers and magazines. The *National Singles Register*, one of the oldest and largest singles publications, now has approximately 750 ads in its biweekly publication, compared to only 12 pages in 1970 (DeWitt 1992). Research conducted by Dr. Rosemary Bolig at Ohio State University indicates that there are significant gender differences in the characteristics sought and advertised in personal ads. She found that men tend to be more concerned with finding a physically attractive partner; in 40 percent of the ads placed by men, a request was made for a photograph of the respondent, compared to only 15 percent of the ads placed by women (DeWitt 1992). Additionally, women were more likely to mention children and less likely to mention their weight in personal ads than men (DeWitt 1992).

Ahuvia and Adelman (1992: 457) find that men get the greatest number of responses to their personal ads by (1) describing themselves as "being older and taller, (2) mentioning educational or professional success or a penchant for expensive cultural activities, (3) conveying an aura of masculinity, and (4) seeking an attractive woman but avoiding sexual references." Responses for women are increased by "(1) physical attractiveness (e.g., being younger and slimmer and mentioning a preference for sports), (2) providing positive or neutral self-descriptions, especially intelligence, and (3) mentioning or alluding to sex" (Ahuvia and Adelman 1992: 457).

Video dating services are another popular method to meet partners. Of the approximately 2,000 dating services available, about 600 use video technology (Ahuvia and Adelman 1992). Great Expectations, one of the largest video dating services, opened in 1976 and now has over 135,000 members across the nation (DeWitt 1992). Clients who visit video dating services are first given a set of fact sheets along with photographs of potential compatible partners. Clients may ask to see the videotapes, usually between 2 and 10 minutes long, of people who interest them. Those who are selected for dates are contacted by the agency and are given the opportunity of viewing a videotape of the suitor.

Social introduction services such as video dating companies are most often used by middle-aged, well-educated singles who have high incomes (DeWitt 1992). These types of single people tend to have demanding jobs that make it difficult to cultivate active social lives, and they have the income to afford the fees, which can be quite expensive. For example, Great Expectations charges between $1,000 and $2,000 for their services. LunchDates, a Boston area dating service used by over 10,000 singles, charges $350 to $695 for dating referrals without a videotape. The Patricia Moore Group in San Francisco, which targets wealthier, older clients, has fees starting at $5,000 (DeWitt 1992).

For those who do not have the money to use formal dating services, potential mates can be found at common locations such as fitness clubs, libraries, running clubs, theatrical groups, and even grocery stores. In Washington, DC, an area where 31 percent of all households are comprised of people under age 65 living alone, the supermarket at the Watergate Center is nicknamed the Social Safeway because it is such a prime meeting ground for singles ("The Singles Scene" 1992).

Cohabitation

After meeting a partner and casually dating for a while, some couples decide to cohabit. **Cohabitation** is the term used to describe couples living together in an intimate sexual relationship without being married. Estimates of the proportion of adults who currently live in nonmarital cohabiting relationships vary from 4 percent to 13 percent, with an additional 25 percent of adults reporting that they have cohabited at some time during their lives (Waite 1995; Waldrop 1990). The 1990 U.S. Bureau of the Census estimated that 2.9 million couples were cohabiting at the time (Seff 1995). Although the number and percentage of adults currently cohabiting is relatively low, the increase in rates of cohabitation in recent years is startling. The proportion of people who cohabited prior to their first marriage rose from 11 percent in 1970 to almost 50 percent today (Bumpass, Sweet, and Cherlin 1991). Between 1980 and 1990, cohabitation rates rose 80 percent (Seff 1995).

Why Have Cohabitation Rates Risen So Dramatically?

Cohabitation outside of marriage has become more common for several reasons. The increased sexual freedom, especially for young people, that accompanied the sexual revolution allowed couples to choose to live in an openly sexual relationship with less fear of social stigma (Glick and Spanier 1981). For many women who have completed college and embarked on careers, cohabitation may be more desirable than marriage, as it allows them to retain more economic independence and avoid some traditional role expectations. The rise in divorce rates that began in the 1960s may also contribute to an increase in cohabitation; couples may prefer to live together in nonmarital relationships to avoid both commitment and a potentially expensive, hostile divorce. Some researchers speculate that the AIDS epidemic may have contributed to the recent increase in cohabitation rates among heterosexuals. To decrease their risk of contracting the life-threatening sexually transmitted disease, individuals who are not ready to marry may be more prone to seek out one long-term sexual partner rather than numerous short-term partners (Buunk and van Driel 1989).

Who Cohabits?

The common stereotype of cohabiting couples is that they are primarily white middle-class college students. Cohabitation rates among this group did increase dramatically during the 1970s, drawing the attention of the media and scholars (Bumpass et al. 1991; Cherlin 1992a). However, college students were not the "innovators in cohabitation but rather the imitators" (Cherlin 1992a: 12). Cohabitation was a practice that began in the United States among a small minority of lower educational groups in the 1950s. In the late 1950s, cohabitation became fairly common among those who were less educated, and by the 1960s, cohabitation was on the rise among all groups (Bumpass et al. 1991).

As in the past, those who are most likely to live in nonmarital cohabiting relationships today tend to be younger, less educated, African American, with lower socioeconomic status. The majority (68 percent) of those living in cohabiting relationships are under age 35 (Laumann et al. 1994; Surra 1990). Cohabitation also is most likely among high school dropouts (Bumpass and Sweet 1989; Landale and Fennelly 1992); only 25 percent of college graduates have cohabited prior to marriage (Larson 1991). African Americans are more likely than whites to cohabit. Buunk and van Driel (1989) report that 29 percent of blacks, compared to 16 percent of whites, stated that they had cohabited in the past. Glick and Spanier (1981) report that rates of cohabitation among African Americans are three times greater than among whites. Given that cohabitation is most common among those who are young, less educated, and members of a minority group, it is not surprising that cohabitors also tend to be of lower socioeconomic status (Landale and Fennelly 1992). According to Bumpass and Sweet (1989), not only do cohabitors tend to earn less money themselves but they also are likely to have been raised in a family that received welfare.

In addition to age, educational level, race, and socioeconomic status, researchers have identified other common characteristics of cohabitors. Not surprisingly, most couples who cohabit have more unconventional attitudes toward family life (Surra 1990). They are more likely to have become sexually active before age 18 and report being less religious (Buunk and van Driel 1989; Laumann et al. 1994; Surra 1990). Cohabiting couples also are likely to come from single-parent families (Larson 1991; Laumann et al. 1994). Although we tend to think of cohabitation as occurring between people who have never been married, those who have been previously married are most likely to cohabit (Bumpass et al. 1991; Lilliard, Brien, and Waite 1995).

Why Do People Choose to Cohabit?

Couples decide to cohabit for a variety of reasons. Many report that they decide to live together for economic reasons (Larson 1991). It is less expensive to live together than to maintain separate households with two sets of rent, utility, and food bills. Some decide to cohabit as a precursor to marriage; these couples see cohabitation as a time to evaluate whether they could make a long-term marital commitment to each other (Larson 1991). Others cohabit for the opposite reason; they have no plans to marry, but still want to live in an emotionally and sexually intimate relationship. Some who cohabit have been previously married and are not yet ready to make that commitment again.

Using surveys and interviews, Macklin (1981) studied cohabiting college students at Cornell University in Ithaca, New York. She found that college students chose to live together for a number of reasons. Students reported that cohabitation allowed them to spend more time with their partners and was cheaper than living apart. Furthermore, moving in together was also more convenient. No longer did one partner have to leave in the middle of the night to return home nor were one's belongings scattered between two places. Like others (e.g., Buunk and van Driel 1989), Macklin found that most couples did not make a conscious decision to move in together. Instead, the cohabiting relationship seemed to evolve slowly over time as couples spent more and more time together and steadily brought possessions to one partner's residence. Very few cohabiting couples that Macklin studied were seriously considering marriage in the near future, and most spent a great deal of time apart from each other with separate friends.

What Are Cohabiting Relationships Like?

Cohabiting relationships are as diverse as the type of people who cohabit and the various reasons for deciding to live in such an arrangement. However, researchers have identified some common characteristics of most cohabiting relationships. First, cohabiting relationships tend not to last very long. The median length of a cohabiting relationship is 1.3 years (Surra 1990). Two-fifths of cohabiting relationships do not last more than one year, one-third last two years, and only 1 couple in 10 are still cohabiting after five years (Bumpass and Sweet 1989). The fact that a couple is no longer cohabiting does not mean that the relationship itself has dissolved; 60 percent of cohabiting couples eventually marry (Bumpass et al. 1991; Landale and Fennelly 1992).

What is the history of love and dating in the United States? What factors might influence a couple's decision to live together outside marriage? Does cohabitation lead to a more stable or happier marriage? Why or why not?

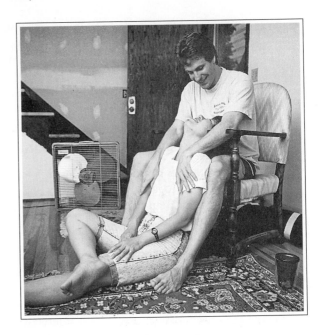

Cohabiting couples also tend to be more sexually active and engage in more sexual experimentation than similar married couples (Buunk and van Driel 1989). Blumstein and Schwartz (1983: 195) state that cohabitors are more likely than married couples to report having sex three or more times per week, leading the researchers to conclude that "no matter how long they have been together, more cohabitors are having sex more often than married couples." They go on to explain that sex probably plays a different role in cohabiting relationships than in marriage. Married couples are likely to see their relationship as more permanent than cohabiting couples and generally do not fear that a decline in sexual frequency will significantly disrupt the relationship. However, cohabiting couples do not have the security of a marriage license to "cement their relationship," so sex becomes a more important bond (Blumstein and Schwartz 1983: 206).

Cohabiting couples also tend to have more egalitarian values than married couples (Buunk and van Driel 1989). Blumstein and Schwartz (1983) report that cohabitors, especially women, believe that both men and women should work outside the home. Seventy-four percent of female cohabitors and 66 percent of male cohabitors believe that both partners in the relationship should be employed, compared to 39 percent of wives and 31 percent of husbands. Furthermore, cohabiting couples are more likely than married couples to believe that housework should be shared equally between men and women, although in practice male cohabitors "become no more involved with household duties than husbands," which ultimately may produce conflict in the relationship (Blumstein and Schwartz 1983: 147).

What Function Does Cohabitation Serve in Family Life?

Until recently, marriage and family scholars believed that cohabitation was just an additional step in the courtship process (Loomis and Landale 1994). This conclusion was reached because the vast majority of American cohabitors (90 percent) report that they plan to marry eventually—although not necessarily the person with whom they currently reside (Buunk and van Driel 1989; Larson 1991). A closer examination of the data suggests that this conclusion may not hold true for all groups, particularly minorities, the economically disadvantaged, and those cohabiting after marriage (Loomis and Landale 1994).

Statistics reveal that black women are more likely to cohabit than white women, but are less likely to make the transition from cohabitation to marriage (Manning and Smock 1995). Furthermore, black women are more likely to bear children in cohabiting relationships than white women (Loomis and Landale 1994). Manning and Smock (1995: 517) suggest that "it may be that cohabitation operates primarily as a precursor or a transitional stage to marriage among whites, but more as an alternative form of marriage among blacks."

For another minority group, mainland Puerto Ricans, cohabitation also appears to be an alternative to marriage rather than a step in the courtship process. Historically, except among social elites, cohabitation was widely practiced and accepted as a legitimate family form in Puerto Rico (Landale and Fennelly 1992; Manning and Landale 1996). Defined as *consensual marriage,* cohabitation was particularly valuable for those too poor to pay for a religious ceremony. In 1899, 33 percent of all unions in Puerto Rico were consensual marriages rather than formal ones (Oropesa 1996). Although less common on the island today (consensual marriages dropped to 4 to 5 percent in the 1970s), cohabitation among U.S. mainland Puerto Ricans is widespread (Landale and Fennelly 1992; Oropesa 1996). Almost half of all Puerto Rican first unions on the mainland begin as cohabiting relationships, and many women bear children in these relationships (Landale and Fennelly 1992). Marriage between mainland Puerto Ricans is probably impeded by low earnings and high unemployment. Noting the different role that cohabitation plays between races, Manning and Landale (1996: 74) remark that "the rise in cohabitation has taken place in very different family contexts for various racial and ethnic groups."

Cohabitation is also less likely to be a precursor to marriage among the economically disadvantaged, regardless of race. Cohabiting white women with low socioeconomic status are less likely to marry than wealthier white women. Additionally, poorer white women in cohabiting relationships have childbearing rates similar to married white women (Loomis and Landale 1994). As with African Americans and mainland Puerto Ricans, cohabitation appears to be a substitution for legal marriage among economically disadvantaged whites, as well.

In addition to being a step in the courtship process or a replacement for marriage, cohabitating relationships also can function as stepfamilies for those who have been previously married and their children. Between 30 and 50 percent of cohabiting couples have children, the majority from a previous marriage (Landale and Fennelly 1992; Loomis and Landale 1994). One-quarter of cohabiting households have children age 10 and over from a previous marriage (Bumpass et al. 1991). Children are so common in cohabiting relationships that Bumpass, Raley, and Sweet (1995: 433) argue that the currently accepted definition of *stepfamilies*, which focuses on remarriage, is too narrow. They point out that family scholars should include cohabiting couples with children from previous marriages in studies of stepfamily relationships: "We doubt that many observers would insist that a cohabiting couple and their [children] are a 'single parent' rather than a 'two parent' family. Something is added . . . by the couple's subsequent marriage, but surely such households do not become a family only at the ceremony."

The presence of children in cohabiting relationships means that many couples are addressing the issues and conflicts that arise from stepparenting. Thus, the perception that many people have of cohabiting relationships as free of responsibility and stress is inaccurate. The implications for children also are important. Children brought into cohabiting relationships already will have experienced the disruption of their parents' marriage, and since cohabiting relationships generally last fewer years than first marriages, many children also will experience the subsequent disruption of a parent's cohabiting relationship (Bumpass et al. 1995).

Prior to the mid-1970s, few cohabiting households included children. However, between 1975 and 1986, the number of cohabiting couples with children, most from previous marriages, increased dramatically (Buunk and van Driel 1989). In recent years, there has been an increase in the number of children born into cohabiting relationships. Approximately one-sixth of never-married couples have children in the cohabiting relationship, and such births account for approximately 25 percent of unmarried births in the United States (Bumpass et al. 1991). Cohabiting relationships in which children are produced generally last longer than cohabiting relationships without children (Wu 1995).

Does Cohabitation Lead to a More Stable Marriage?

What leads to a successful marriage? If posed this question, most people would say that getting to know one's partner rather than rushing into marriage is probably one of the best predictors of a successful marriage. Given this assumption, it would seem to follow logically that those who cohabited prior to marriage and got to know each other's personality and habits should have more stable, successful marriages than those who did not cohabit before marriage (Lillard et al. 1995). However, once again, social science research proves commonsense logic to be false. Research consistently shows that couples who cohabited prior to marriage have 50 percent higher divorce rates than couples who did not cohabit (Bumpass et al. 1991). Bumpass and Sweet (1989) report that of those couples who separate or divorce within 10 years of marriage, 36 percent had previously cohabited, whereas 27 percent had never cohabited.

Why is it that the statistics fly in the face of logic? Why are divorce rates higher for couples who previously cohabited than those who did not? The most common explanation for this phenomenon is that those who cohabit have less traditional values, are more accepting of divorce, and are less committed to marriage than those who do not cohabit (Axinn and Thornton 1992; Bumpass et al. 1991; Lilliard et al. 1995). Couples who choose to live together in a sexual relationship outside of marriage presumably have more liberal sexual values than couples who do not cohabit during courtship. Cohabiting couples may also have less traditional values about other family issues; they may see relationships as less permanent and in fact that is why they chose to cohabit in the first place. Therefore, when faced with the inevitable conflicts of marriage, couples who previously cohabited may be more willing to resort to divorce than those with more traditional values who did not cohabit prior to marriage.

Another reason that cohabiting couples may have higher divorce rates is that they may marry for the wrong reasons (Schoen 1992). Some cohabiting couples who are encountering trouble in their relationship may believe that if they marry, their present problems will disappear (Buunk and van Driel 1989). Obviously, getting married is not a way to save a relationship that is already in trouble, and it is likely that such unions would end in divorce.

The transition to marriage may disrupt the relationship, creating problems that lead to divorce (Schoen 1992). Cohabitors tend to desire more freedom and egalitarian sex roles than couples who do not cohabit (Seff 1995). Marriage may change the nature of the relationship the couple had when they were cohabiting outside of marriage. Partners may feel confined in marriage compared to when they were cohabiting and may believe they are being pushed into more traditional role expectations. Hence, they become dissatisfied with the relationship and resort to divorce.

As mentioned earlier, cohabiting couples tend to be more sexually active than married couples. Some researchers believe that the high level of sexual activity in cohabiting relationships may be mistaken for love and commitment (Kahn and London 1991). Once the couple is married and sexual frequency begins to decline, they may realize that they do not have much in common, which ultimately leads to divorce.

Others argue that because cohabitors begin living together sooner, they become dissatisfied earlier in marriage than couples who did not cohabit. For example, a couple who cohabited for two years prior to marriage has actually been living together that much longer than a married couple who did not cohabit. The cohabiting couple has had more time to have conflicts and disagreements and become unhappy in the relationship than the couple who did not begin living together until marriage. Thompson and Colella (1992) report that the longer a couple cohabits prior to marriage, the greater their risk for divorce. However, other researchers (e.g., Surra 1990) have not found empirical support for the argument that the time couples spent cohabiting is associated with marital dissatisfaction and divorce.

It is important to note that not all couples who previously cohabited have higher divorce rates than noncohabitors. Individuals who have been previously married and cohabit prior to a second marriage tend to have more successful marriages with greater marital satisfaction than couples who did not cohabit (Buunk and van Driel 1989). The relationship between prior cohabitation and divorce is strongest for cohabiting couples who have never been married.

Factors That Influence Partner Selection

Consider the following clichés: "Absence makes the heart grow fonder." "Out of sight, out of mind." "Opposites attract." "Birds of a feather flock together." These clichés describe ideas regarding mate selection in our culture. They illustrate the contradictory nature of commonly accepted notions about mate selection. "Absence makes the heart grow fonder" suggests that the longer couples are apart, the more deeply they love each other. On the other hand, "Out of sight, out of mind" suggests that once a couple is apart, they are likely to forget about each other. Which cliché is correct?

Sociology has as one of its primary goals the challenging of commonsense notions about behavior in culture. What factors have been identified through social science research as most important in selecting intimate partners?

Physical Appearance

The first thing people tend to notice about others is their physical appearance, and whether we like to admit it or not, physical appearance plays a key role in who we select as mates (Hatfield and Rapson 1996; Mullan 1984). Two people who initially find each other physically attractive are likely to interact, and interaction is essential for relationship formation. As the couple interacts, they learn more about each other, find common interests, and eventually physical appearance becomes less important in keeping the relationship going. However, upon first encounter, an individual's perception of another's physical appearance is the strongest determinant of whether future interaction will occur.

Not only do we tend to select mates whom we perceive as attractive but we also tend to select those whose levels of attractiveness our similar to our own. Sociologists refer to this phenomenon as the **matching hypothesis of mate selection.** Americans, who believe in romance, find the matching hypothesis appealing because it suggests that everyone has a chance to meet his or her ideal mate (Kalick and Hamilton 1986).

Cultural awareness of the matching hypothesis is reflected in the expression, "What does she see in him?" Also, couples might be told that they look like brother and sister or that they look more and more alike the longer they are together. These observations led researchers to ask whether similarity in physical appearance is a factor that is present when couples meet or whether couples become more similar over time. The majority of studies have found that couples tend to have similar levels of physical attractiveness when the relationship begins, which suggests that individuals are aware of and do consider their partner's level of physical attractiveness in relation to their own when entering relationships (Chambers, Christiansen, and Kunz 1983).

The matching hypothesis describes a social phenomenon, but sociologists want to understand why social patterns develop. Several explanations have been offered for the matching hypothesis. Matching may occur because individuals are attracted to people who resemble family members—their parents and siblings—because family members are people around whom they feel most comfortable (Chambers et al. 1983). Since family members tend to have some similar physical features, if individuals select as partners people who resemble their kin, it is likely that these partners also will look somewhat like themselves.

A second explanation for the matching hypothesis comes from social psychology research. Many studies have found that Americans tend to believe that people of similar degrees of attractiveness are happier than couples in which one partner is much more attractive than the other (Kalick and Hamilton 1986; Schafer and Keith 1990). Therefore, individuals may seek romantic partners similar to themselves in hopes that the relationship will be strong and lasting.

A third explanation for the matching hypothesis is that only those who are attractive themselves are able to compete for and win the affections of attractive partners. Physically attractive people confer status on their partners, and "are believed to possess all sorts of positive qualities such as being sensitive, kind, interesting, strong and sociable" (Mullan 1984: 179). Because physically attractive people are in such high demand, less attractive people are not successful in obtaining them as partners and must settle for someone less attractive (Lykken and Tellegen 1993; Schafer and Keith 1990). The result of this hierarchical mating is that people who form relationships tend to be of similar levels of attractiveness.

Age

The influence of age on mate selection can be understood through the concepts of homogamy and heterogamy. **Homogamy** is marriage between people having similar characteristics, either physical, psychological, or social (Theodorson and Theodorson 1969). **Heterogamy** refers to marriage between persons who are dissimilar in some respect (Theodorson and Theodorson 1969). As you have seen, mating tends to be homogamous in terms of physical appearance. Determining whether mate selection is homogamous or heterogamous with regard to age is a little more difficult, for people tend to select partners who are close to their own ages, but not necessarily the same age.

In first marriages today, people tend to marry partners who are within two to three years of their own ages (Small 1995; Vera, Berardo, and Berardo 1985). Most often, the male in the relationship is the older partner. "Age homogamy is in fact a type of age heterogamy since the norm is actually one of age difference, with husbands being expected to be older than their wives" (Vera et al. 1985: 556). The norm that men should be slightly older than their wives may be rooted in the patriarchal social structure. In a patriarchal society, men are expected to provide financially for their wives and children and to do so requires employment that provides economic security. Hence, traditionally, men who were in the work force for a few years had obtained some seniority, and had saved some money could begin to look for a young bride. As women become more economically independent, one would predict that the age differences between men and women at marriage would narrow. In fact, this has been the trend. The average age difference between women and men at the turn of the twentieth century was four years, but at the turn of the twenty-first century, the age difference has dropped to closer to two years (Vera et al. 1985).

Age homogamy seems to be most important in first marriages and when couples are younger. People who are entering second marriages and those who are approaching midlife are more likely to marry someone who is significantly older or younger.

It is often assumed that a large age gap between a couple will create instability in the relationship. People born a number of years apart may have different values and expectations, and this *generation gap* may lead to conflict in the relationship (Bumpass and Sweet 1972). Furthermore, a large age difference can produce an imbalance of power in the relationship—especially if the woman is older—which produces tension between partners. However, other studies have shown that a significant age gap does not affect couples' marital satisfaction or the number of marital problems they experienced (Vera et al. 1985).

Socioeconomic Status

In selecting romantic partners, we generally want someone who has similar cultural preferences, enjoys similar leisure activities, and shares common values. As you read in Chapter 6, socioeconomic status influences these qualitative aspects of life. Furthermore, most people prefer to marry someone who has at least as many financial resources as they do. Therefore, it is not surprising that individuals tend to marry those from similar socioeconomic status or class background.

One of the difficulties sociologists encounter in studying socioeconomic homogamy is in determining how socioeconomic status should be measured. The most direct way of measuring socioeconomic status in couples is to assess the income, occupation, and education of each partner. However, when studying mate selection, the subjects most often are young adults who may still be in school or just completing their education. As such, their earnings and occupation may not accurately reflect their social class. To counter this problem, some researchers measure young couples' social class using each partner's parents' (usually the father's) occupations or educational levels (Kalmijn 1991b). Some researchers simply ask respondents if their partners come from a higher, lower, or similar social class. Regardless of how class is measured, studies suggest that people tend to select mates from a similar socioeconomic background (Kalmijn 1991a; Kalmijn 1991b; Small 1995). When couples come from mixed socioeconomic backgrounds, the male in the relationship is most likely to be from the higher social class and the woman is more likely to be from a lower class.

Education

Individuals also tend to choose partners who are similar to them in their level of educational attainment (Kalmijn 1991b; Mare 1991). Educational homogamy occurs for several reasons. As was suggested earlier, we tend to prefer mates who share similar values, hobbies, and interests, and education shapes cultural tastes, leisure activities, and values. Therefore, "making a match on education enables spouses to develop a common lifestyle in marriage that enhances mutual understanding" (Kalmijn 1991a: 789). Additionally, education reflects future earning potential; when partners in a relationship have similar levels of educational achievement, they are probably qualified for occupations that pay similar wages and therefore will belong to the same social class (Mare 1991).

What factors will determine whom these individuals choose as mates? What are some facts and myths about partner selection? How can social exchange theory help us understand the complex process of mate selection?

Social networks and interaction opportunities also explain why people from similar educational backgrounds form intimate relationships. People who work together, go to school together, or live in the same neighborhood are likely to have similar levels of education and they also have the opportunity to interact with each other frequently (Mare 1991). The more opportunities people have to interact, the more likely they are to find common interests and then pursue a relationship. Conversely, it is unlikely that people with widely divergent educational backgrounds will have many opportunities to interact and form relationships, since they tend to perform different jobs, live in different neighborhoods, and share different leisure activities.

Another explanation for educational homogamy is that education, like physical beauty, is a desired characteristic in mates, such that those with more education are more desirable and can be more selective in choosing partners (Mare 1991). Those with less education cannot compete for the most educated partners and must settle for someone with at least as much education as they have.

Religion

Religion is considered an important characteristic in mate selection. Over 60 percent of all marriages are between people of the same religion (Small 1995). The similarity in religious background between partners becomes even more apparent when faiths are examined separately. Statistics show that 80 to 90 percent of Protestant marriages include partners of the same faith; in 64 to 85 percent of Catholic marriages, both partners are Catholic; and in 90 percent of Jewish marriages, both partners are Jewish (Kalmijn 1991a).

Religious norms often require marriage within one's social group under threat of negative sanction if one marries outside the religion (Theodorson and Theodorson 1969). Religious groups in American culture historically have advocated marriage to partners of the same religious background. For example, even today Reform Judaism opposes interfaith marriages. Most rabbis will not perform so-called mixed marriages of Jews to non-Jewish partners ("Reform's Position" 1999). Some rabbis, fearing that refusal to perform an interfaith marriage will drive the Jewish partner away from Judiasm, will preside over interfaith marriage ceremonies. However, many congregations will not extend membership to non-Jewish spouses. Furthermore, non-Jewish spouses are denied leadership roles and participation in many religious ceremonies (*Fallacy: Intermarried* 1999).

Although religious homogamy remains important, it declined over the twentieth century (Glenn 1982; Whyte 1990). Data on Protestant and Catholic marriages from 1920 to 1980 show that marriage outside one's faith has become increasingly common (Kalmijn 1991a). Protestant and Catholic clergy, family, and friends are less likely to oppose interfaith marriages today than they were in the past (Glenn 1982; Kalmijn 1991a). Protestants and Catholics also are less likely to be segregated into different schools, neighborhoods, and jobs, and therefore have more opportunities for interaction and intimacy. Protestant and Catholic values and behavior regarding ideal family size, marital fertility, and birth control also seem to be converging, making potential mates outside one's faith more attractive. In addition, many of the socioeconomic and educational differences that once separated Protestants and Catholics are disappearing, which led Kalmijn (1991a) to conclude that religious endogamy is being replaced by educational homogamy as a central element in mate selection.

Race and Ethnicity

Race is another important consideration in selecting a mate. An overwhelming 94 percent of marriages are between people of the same race (U.S. Bureau of the Census 1998). Historically, in American culture, couples who married outside their race faced social ostracism and ridicule and, in many states, were in violation of the law. It was not until 1967 that the U.S. Supreme Court declared laws barring interracial marriage unconstitutional (Norment 1994).

Although interracial marriages are still relatively rare, they are becoming increasingly common. The number of interracial couples in 1992 was more than six times the number in 1960. According to the U.S. Bureau of the Census (1998), in 1960, 99.6 percent of U.S. marriages were of the same race; in 1970, this figure dropped to 99.3 percent, followed in 1980 to 98.0 percent, and in 1992, to 95.1 percent. The growing number of interracial couples can be explained in part by increasing social acceptability. A *Washington Post* survey found that one-half of the respondents said they would date a person of another race, and almost as many respondents reported they would marry someone of a different race ("New Survey" 1995). Interracial relationships are most accepted by those who are younger and better educated, and African Americans are more accepting of interracial relationships than whites (Mills et al. 1995; "New Survey" 1995).

Increasing opportunities for interaction also account for the growth in interracial relationships. As workplace, residential, and educational segregation decreases, individuals have the opportunity to meet, get to know, and form intimate relationships with people of other races ("Why People Choose" 1992).

The term *interracial relationship* often conjures images of black/white relationships. However, it is important to keep in mind that there are numerous racial groups in the United States, including, for example, people of Eskimo, Japanese, Chinese, African, Filipino, Latin, Hawaiian, and Native American descent. Two of the states with the highest rates of interracial marriages are Alaska and Hawaii. However, sociological research has tended to focus on black/white interracial relationships. Although the number of these marriages has quadrupled in the past 25 years, they remain relatively rare (Taylor et al. 1990), as shown in Figure 8.1. Today, only 2 percent of all marriages in the United States, approximately 1.3 million couples, are comprised of an African American and a Caucasian partner (Norment 1994). Black/white intermarriage rates vary across the country, from a low of 0.6 percent in the South to 12.3 percent in western states (Taylor et al. 1990). Among African Americans, men are more likely than women to marry outside their race. In 1988, 4.6 percent of black men were married to someone outside their race, compared to 2.1 percent of black women (Taylor et al. 1990).

Figure 8.1   Percent of Specified Race Married to Whites, 1990

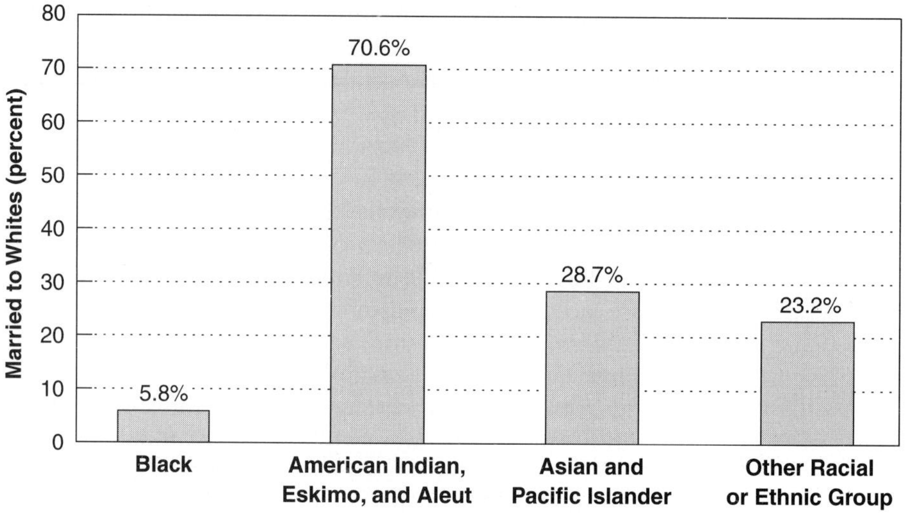

Source: Adapted from U. S. Bureau of the Census, "1990 Census of the Population, Housing, Public Use Microdata Samples," June 10, 1998. <www.census.gov/population/socdemo/race/interractab2.txt>.

As you may recall, African American women face what demographers call a *marriage squeeze;* that is, black women have a significantly smaller pool of eligible mates than black men. The marriage squeeze for African American women stems from a number of sources other than intermarriage. Young, single, African American males have comparatively high mortality and incarceration rates, which depletes the marriage pool (Spanier and Glick 1980). Furthermore, African American women tend to have higher levels of education and are more likely to be employed than African American men (Spanier and Glick 1980; South 1991). Norment (1994) reports that for every 100 black women, there are only approximately 35 to 45 single black men.

One way to counter a marriage squeeze is to become less selective in mate selection. When highly educated African American women cannot find black mates of similar age, educational level, and socioeconomic backgrounds, they might begin to consider men who are significantly older or younger, less educated, or in less prestigious occupations (Lichter, Anderson, and Hayward 1995).

However, recent data suggest that African American women do not lower their marriage preferences in response to the marriage squeeze. Studies have found that well-educated African American women respond to the shortage of eligible African American males by postponing marriage or remaining single instead of marrying heterogamously (South 1991; Lichter et al. 1995).

Propinquity

The mate selection factors discussed so far—physical appearance, age, socioeconomic status, education, religion, and race—are all factors people consider consciously. *Propinquity*, the physical nearness of a partner, is a factor of which most people are unaware. Yet, for a relationship to begin, people must meet and interact. The people you are most likely to see and interact with frequently are those who live near you (residential propinquity) and those with whom you work and go to school (institutional propinquity) (Davis-Brown, Salamon, and Surra 1987; Knox and Wilson 1981; Small 1995).

Modern computer technology reduces the importance of propinquity in mate selection, however (Jedlicka 1981). Today, it is possible to meet a partner who lives half-way around the world without ever leaving the comfort of one's home. Although the computer does not eliminate the need for face-to-face interaction, it does provide a means for individuals to learn about each other in a comparatively risk-free way. People can communicate personal information about themselves with less fear of rejection. Furthermore, computer interaction reduces the importance of physical attractiveness in the mate selection process because people can get to know about each other's interests and personalities before their physical appearance is revealed.

Several years ago, I had a student who came to me quite excited about a young man she had met in cyberspace. He lived and went to school in Great Britain. They communicated for hours every day via the Internet. She told me he was exactly the type of man with whom she wanted to spend the rest of her life. I must admit that I was skeptical that this relationship, formed in such a nontraditional way, would flourish. She flew to meet him during spring vacation and he returned to the United States with her. Several months later, they married, he became a U.S. citizen, and they now have a daughter. Although not all relationships formed in cyberspace work out as well as this one apparently did, I'm certain this student would point out that opportunities for computer interaction can be just as helpful in relationship formation as opportunities for face-to-face interaction provided by residential and institutional propinquity.

Third Parties' Support

Another characteristic that influences mate selection is the support of third parties, such as family and friends. Researchers have found that individuals are more committed to their romantic relationships and spend more time with their partners when friends and family approve of their mates (Surra 1990). Conversely, when family and friends disapprove of partners, the relationship is more likely to dissolve (Surra 1990). The opinions of others may help explain the high rates of racial homogamy discussed earlier. Although people of different races may have much in common, be of similar ages, share educational and socioeconomic backgrounds, enjoy each other's company, and be totally unconcerned about the color of their mate's skin, they may have difficulty maintaining the relationship in the face of opposition from family members and friends.

Methodological Limitations of Research on Mate Selection

Information on factors that influence mate selection is obtained through empirical studies, and data are gathered in a variety of ways. Many sociologists examine census data and track demographic trends in who marries whom and note any changes over time (Surra 1990). Surveys asking respondents what characteristics they desire in a partner also are a popular means of assessing mate selection preferences (e.g., Goodwin 1990). Another method is to perform content analysis of personal advertisements in print and electronic media (Davis 1990).

Whatever method is used, however, studies of mate selection preferences tend to rely on young, never-married respondents (Bulcroft and O'Connor 1986). Most survey data and experimental data, for example, are collected from unmarried college students. Very little is known about mate selection preferences in second marriages and among older people. In addition, data obtained through surveys and interviews may reflect a social desirability bias; respondents may describe their preferences inaccurately to avoid seeming odd or strange compared to others.

Another methodological limitation is that researchers tend to treat the characteristics of a potential partner as independent and of equal value (Feingold 1992). However, in real life, people consider several factors simultaneously when evaluating a potential mate, and some factors are regarded as more important than others. Although sociologists can ask respondents to list the characteristics they consider most important in a romantic partner and to rank those characteristics in order of priority, in reality, mate selection is much more complex. Some characteristics can have a *halo effect*; that is, one characteristic may influence how other facets of the person are perceived. For example, the halo effect accounts for people's tendency to find mates more attractive the more they get to know and like them. Sociological research does not capture the psychological complexities of mate selection (Feingold 1992).

Critics of mate selection research point out that it focuses almost exclusively on heterosexual romantic relationships (Huston and Burgess 1979; Surra 1990), opposite-sex partners (e.g., Mathes and Moore 1985), boyfriend-girlfriend relationships (e.g., Goodwin 1990), or heterosexuals of both sexes (e.g., Feingold 1992). In his study of classified personals ads, Davis (1990: 45) writes: "For the sake of this study, gay ads were not included." The most practical reason for purposely excluding homosexuals from the research is that mate or partner selection in family studies has been perceived as synonymous with marriage partner selection. Legally, homosexuals cannot marry; therefore, researchers have not looked at mate selection in the gay community. Furthermore, only recently have homosexuals begun living in openly gay relationships, allowing researchers easy access to a sample of homosexual respondents. Finally, researchers must have their projects approved by some type of review panel or human subjects research committee, which traditionally has rejected projects involving homosexuals on the grounds that research in this area would be too sensitive.

Do homosexuals select mates using the same characteristics and criteria as heterosexuals? This question cannot be answered without data from homosexual respondents. In one study, a comparison of homosexual men and women and heterosexual men and women on mate selection preferences found that homosexual men and women did not differ significantly from heterosexual men and women in the characteristics they desired in a partner (Bailey et al. 1994). However, one study is not enough to draw conclusions. More research on mate selection among homosexuals is needed.

Social Exchange Theory: A Framework for Understanding Mate Selection

At the beginning of this chapter, structural functionalism and conflict theory were used to explain various components of mate selection. Although these perspectives can be used to better understand particular elements of mate selection, sociologists most often rely on **social exchange theory,** which has many elements of symbolic interactionism, to explain mate selection and relationship formation (Aronson, Wilson, and Akert 1999; McDonald 1981).

Social exchange theorists, borrowing ideas from economics, argue that all interaction is an "exchange of goods, material and non-material," in which individuals try to maximize their profit by reaping as many rewards as possible while incurring the fewest possible costs (Homans 1958: 115). According to social exchange theory, the principles guiding human interaction can be summarized in the following equation: Profit (or Outcome) = Reward − Cost (Homans 1958: 122). Exchange theorists believe that people will enter into and remain in relationships as long as they are maximizing pleasure and reaping benefits; but as soon as their costs begin exceeding benefits, they will end the relationship.

The goods and services traded in social interaction can be either tangible or intangible. *Tangible* (or material) *goods* are those that can be seen and touched; *intangible goods,* such as affection and esteem, are more abstract but equally beneficial. What social goods are being exchanged in the following interaction? A student who has missed a class lecture approaches another student and asks to borrow the notes from the missed class. In social exchange theory, both the student who is asking for the notes and the student who has been asked the favor will consider what their likely rewards and costs in the interaction will be. Both will seek to maximize positive outcomes and minimize the costs. The key reward for the asker in the interaction will be tangible—a copy of the notes, which may be essential to doing well on the next exam. However, there are costs associated with the request. The asker may experience embarrassment or discomfort at having to ask for the notes (an intangible cost). The asker also incurs a debt because of the **norm of reciprocity,** in which people who extend favors to others expect that the favor will be returned in the future.

The loaner of the notes also must assess the rewards and costs in this exchange. The rewards might include being owed a future favor and feeling flattered to be chosen as someone who takes good notes. Costs to be considered might include the risk that the borrower will lose the notes and the negative feeling of being exploited. The outcome of this exchange will depend on the perceived rewards and costs for both parties.

In terms of mate selection, the characteristics that individuals consider in mate selection—physical attractiveness, socioeconomic status, common values and interests, and so on—are what social exchange theorists would consider as the "goods" being exchanged. That people tend to select individuals who are similar to them in a variety of ways can be explained by social exchange theory, as well. Matching occurs in mate selection because people exchange their personal and material assets with others of similar value:

> *Individuals seek the "best value" they can achieve in a mate. Each individual is assumed to carry an approximate "market value," depending on the degree to which he or she possesses valued traits such as beauty, intelligence, charm, wealth, and social status. It is assumed that if every individual seeks the best value in a mate, individuals of approximately equal value will tend to pair up. In this manner, individuals can be said to "exchange" their assets for those in a partner.* (Kenrick et al., 1993: 951)

What keeps people from choosing others who are significantly more attractive or wealthy than they are? Social exchange theorists might give these reasons: (1) one's value is not high enough to attract such a mate and (2) the costs would exceed the rewards. A less attractive (or less wealthy) person knows that acquiring a high-status mate would be a huge reward. However, the costs are high: Rejection is more likely. Even if the highly desired mate agrees to a relationship, the fear of losing this person to someone of higher status always will be present (Kalick and Hamilton 1986).

Huston and Burgess (1979) use social exchange theory to explain the entire relationship process from beginning to end. They divide relationships into three stages: initiation, relationship, and dissolution. The *initiation* of relationships can occur intentionally or unintentionally. When individuals seek out partners intentionally, they look for those with whom they believe they will have rewarding interaction. If the interaction does prove rewarding, the couple is likely to interact again. When partners meet by happenstance, they evaluate the initial encounter and decide whether it was beneficial. If so, they are likely to have future interaction.

Discovering common interests and similarities helps couples move from first encounter to the *relationship* phase. When couples share interests, they both receive the rewards of sharing mutually enjoyable activities. Couples who have similar social class, ethnic, religious, and educational backgrounds and who come from the same age cohort are likely to share common interests, which increases the rewards both partners obtain from the relationship. Furthermore, residential propinquity makes interaction more convenient, thus reducing the tangible costs of the relationship. Third parties, such as family members and friends, influence relationships by increasing rewards for the couples through social support or by adding to the costs through attempts to thwart the romance (Huston and Burgess 1979).

The costs and rewards of every encounter become less important as the relationship progresses, and couples begin to assess the rewards and costs of the relationship over time. Although the couple may experience some conflicts, they often continue the relationship because they remember the good times and believe they will return. Additionally, couples begin to evaluate their relationship by considering how well it meets their expectations (which sociologists call the **comparison level**) and whether there are opportunities for better alternative relationships with someone else (termed **comparison level of alternatives**) (Thibaut and Kelley 1959).

Some relationships eventually deteriorate and dissolve. *Dissolution* of a relationship occurs when there is a significant decrease in rewards or when the relationship becomes one-sided (Huston and Burgess 1979). In a one-sided relationship, one person is doing all the work to maintain the relationship while the other party enjoys all the rewards. Anyone who has been in a one-sided relationship can attest to the fact that the person who is least interested in continuing the relationship has the most power and can exploit the other partner; sociologist Willard Waller noted this phenomenon in 1938 and labeled it the **principle of least interest** (Eslinger, Clarke, and Dynes 1972). One-sided relationships often dissolve because the least interested party simply leaves or the most interested party finally decides that there are too few rewards and too many costs to continue maintaining the relationship.

Relationships high in costs and low in rewards often take a long time to dissolve (Huston and Burgess 1979). People often maintain unrewarding relationships because they do not want others to think that they failed. Additionally, many people hesitate to end unrewarding relationships because they would have to restructure their lives entirely. Ending a relationship with a significant other often means having to change living arrangements, friendship networks, and even personal identity.

From a social exchange perspective, mate selection, relationships, and even love are not spontaneous, emotional, and irrational; instead, they are the "product of a long history of interaction" (Huston and Burgess 1979: 12). Many people are uncomfortable applying the principles of exchange theory to intimate relationships, "because the basic tenets of exchange theory seem contrary to Western views about the nature of love and intimacy. Love is supposed to involve caring, altruism, communion, and selflessness. . . . The view that love is tied to the exchange of rewards seems crass" (Huston and Burgess 1979: 10). Social exchange theory also has been criticized because it is not easily testable. Concepts such as *profit, reward,* and *cost* are not easily measured, making it difficult to test social exchange theory empirically (La Gaipa 1977).

Gender: A Perennial Variable

Social exchange theorists insist that the evaluation of the costs and rewards in relationships must be understood from the participant's perspective. In other words, the individual's definition of the situation must be evaluated. This raises the question of whether men and women look for and perceive similar rewards in potential mates and relationships. Are there gender differences in mate selection preferences? If so, how do men's choices of mates tend to differ from women's? These questions have been examined quite extensively by researchers in the social sciences. It appears that there are some differences between men and women in partner selection preferences.

Gender differences appear particularly in the role that sexuality plays in choosing a partner and in the relative importance attached to physical attractiveness and socioeconomic status. Studies suggest that males and females differ in the degree of sexual experience they desire in mates, with men generally preferring more sexually permissive partners than women. Gender differences in the amount of sexual experience desired in a mate are most pronounced in less committed relationships. In selecting partners for short-term, uncommitted relationships, men generally prefer a female partner who has been quite sexually active, whereas women prefer a male partner with low to moderate levels of sexual experience (Oliver and Sedikides 1992; Sprecher, McKinney, and Orbuch 1991). However, when selecting partners for long-term, committed relationships such as marriage, gender differences begin to disappear; both men and women desire mates with low levels of sexual permissiveness in committed relationships (Kenrick et al. 1993; Oliver and Sedikides 1992).

The second area where gender differences in mate selection emerge is in the importance attached to particular characteristics of a potential partner. Examine the following characteristics that could be considered important in mate selection:

1. Dependable Character
2. Mutual Attraction
3. Education/Intelligence
4. Similar Educational Background
5. Desire for Home/Children
6. Favorable Social Status
7. Emotional Stability
8. Refinement/Neatness

9. Similar Religious Background
10. Good Health
11. Similar Political Background
12. Ambition/Industriousness
13. Pleasing Disposition
14. Sexual Chastity
15. Good Financial Prospect
16. Sociability
17. Good Cook/Housekeeper
18. Good Looks (Hill 1945: 554–558)

Decide which are important to you in choosing a partner, renumber them in order of priority, and then compare your answers with the following survey results. This list of characteristics was presented to college students in 1939, 1956, 1967, and 1990. Students in 1939, 1956, and 1967 rated "dependable character" and "emotional stability" as most important in a mate. Students surveyed in 1990 rated "mutual attraction" most important (Allgeier and Wiederman 1991).

Although male and female students agreed on the most important qualities in a mate, gender differences emerged in the importance attached to "good looks," to which men consistently attach more importance, and "ambition/industriousness" and "good financial prospect," which women rate as more important (Allgeier and Wiederman 1991). Other researchers have found a similar pattern: Males tend to emphasize physical appearance more than women, whereas females tend to emphasize characteristics associated with financial stability more than men (e.g., Davis 1990; Feingold 1992; Ganong and Coleman 1992; Townsend and Roberts 1993).

Explanations of Gender Differences in Mate Selection

Two very different explanations for gender differences in mate selection have been suggested, one emphasizing innate biological drives and the other emphasizing the role of social structure. The **sociobiological explanation** for gender differences assumes that mate selection preferences are genetically programmed into human brains from eons of evolutionary development (Small 1995). Sociobiologists argue that to ensure the survival of the species and our own individual genetic material, males and females have evolved different preferences for mates. Both males and females are biologically driven to maximize their reproductive success by having as many children as possible survive to adulthood. However, because males and females differ in their contribution to reproduction and parenting, they must adopt different strategies to accomplish this goal. Males normally have an abundant supply of sperm and can reproduce well into old age. Therefore, if they want to maximize their reproductive success, they should impregnate as many healthy, fertile women as possible (Hatfield and Rapson 1996; Small 1995). Sociobiologists suggest that males have evolved to be less committed to relationships than women to increase the number of offspring they produce. Physical attractiveness may be important to men because it is a sign of a woman's health and fertility (Allgeier and Wiederman 1991; Small 1995).

Females, on the other hand, have a limited number of eggs and a limited number of years in which they are fertile. Once a woman is pregnant, she cannot get pregnant again until she has given birth and resumed ovulation—a process that can take over a year. Furthermore, females must endure a nine-month pregnancy and then nurse their offspring. Sociobiologists argue that in an evolutionary context, females would not benefit reproductively by adopting men's strategy of indiscriminately mating with as many partners as possible; in fact, they risk producing "low quality" offspring if they do (Bailey et al. 1991: 1082). Instead, say the sociobiologists, females maximize their reproductive success by investing heavily in the few children they produce to ensure their survival (Allgeier and Wiederman 1991; Buss and Schmitt 1993; Small 1995).

One way for a woman to ensure that her children will survive is to select a mate who will continue in the relationship to help protect and provide for her and the offspring (Allgeier and Wiederman 1991). Women enter the mate selection process asking, "Is this a man who will continue to invest with me in any progeny he might father?" (Bailey et al. 1994: 1083). Sociobiologists believe females have evolved to be biologically compelled to value commitment in a relationship and to seek out a male partner who can be a good provider and protector.

From a sociobiological perspective, mate selection preferences are unconscious, biological urges that evolved, much as did food preferences (Buss and Schmitt 1993). The sociobiological perspective has been challenged. If mate selection is the product of human evolution, then preferences in males and females should be similar across cultures; yet, vast differences in mate selection preferences have been noted between cultures (Hatfield and Rapson 1996). One study found that cultural differences explained 14 percent of mate selection preferences, whereas gender differences accounted for only 2 percent (Hatfield and Rapson 1996). Furthermore, sociobiologists argue that physical attractiveness is a sign of a woman's reproductive fitness; cultural standards of beauty, however, vary tremendously across time and cultures. The contemporary standard of beauty for American women that emphasizes thinness actually can hinder fertility. Women who are extremely thin may fail to ovulate regularly or at all, making it difficult or impossible for them to conceive.

An alternative explanation for gender differences in mate selection preferences is a **social structural explanation.** Those who favor a social structural explanation look for elements of society that explain mate selection preferences. Using many of the assumptions of conflict theory (discussed in Chapter 3), the social structural explanation suggests that in male-dominated societies, females must acquire their social status and economic resources through marriage. Women are concerned with the financial stability of potential mates because marriage provides access to wealth and power (Hatfield and Rapson 1996). Both women and men desire power and money, yet structural obstacles, such as lower wages, may prevent women from having direct access to these resources. Therefore, women are forced to consider the socioeconomic status of potential mates more than men do (Small 1995).

The importance males attach to physical beauty also can be framed in a social structural argument. Men are free to evaluate women on the basis of appearance because men's financial security is not tied to the status of their partners. Additionally, men's access to power and wealth allows them to shape the beauty norms in culture. In her best-selling book *The Beauty Myth*, Wolf (1991) argues that the cultural preoccupation with women's thinness is a by-product of men's fear of competition with women in the marketplace. If women become preoccupied with diet and exercise and are undernourished, they become less successful and less threatening to men.

Gender Similarities in Mate Selection

Data on gender differences in mate selection must be interpreted with caution. The majority of researchers who compare women's and men's mate selection preferences are looking for differences and fail to notice similarities. In fact, men and women are quite similar in mate selection ideals. Consistently, both women and men rank personality traits such as kindness and honesty, as well as love and mutual attraction as the most important characteristics in selecting a partner (Townsend and Roberts 1993; Small 1995). Goodwin (1990) finds that both sexes want a partner who is kind, considerate, and honest. Men ranked physical characteristics as slightly more important than women did, but appearance was not their top priority in mate selection. Goodwin (1990: 510) concludes, "The results . . . indicate the existence of very few sex differences in partner preferences."

Kenrick and colleagues (1993) suggest that both men and women place high value on physical attractiveness in potential mates, but that the two sexes identify different traits as attractive. Women tend to find maturity attractive, whereas men are likely to find youthfulness appealing. Most research on mate selection does not allow respondents to make subtle distinctions in perception of attractiveness, so women's attentiveness to physical characteristics may not be revealed.

Consider also that great differences exist among men in mate selection preferences as well as differences among women (Bailey et al. 1994). Often, researchers are so busy comparing males and females that they fail to recognize that not all males are alike, nor are all females. In fact, the differences within each sex cohort may be far more dramatic than the differences between the sexes.

Summary

Dating and mate selection in the United States are characterized by freedom of choice. Although courtship practices have changed throughout American history—from bundling, to calling, to dating—individuals have been free to choose their own partners. After casually dating, some couples today choose to live together in an intimate sexual relationship without being married—a practice known as cohabitation. Cohabitation rates have risen in recent years because of increased sexual freedom, rising divorce rates, changing gender roles, and the AIDS epidemic. Cohabitation rates are influenced by age, educational level, race, and socioeconomic status. Cohabiting relationships are diverse, with some serving as replacements for marriage and others being precursors to marriage. Increasingly, cohabiting households include children. Cohabitation does not lead to more stable marriages, as cohabiting couples have a 50 percent higher divorce rate than couples who do not cohabit.

Sociologists have long recognized that physical appearance, age, socioeconomic status, education, religion, race, propinquity, and third parties' support influence who we select as mates. Most research on mate selection patterns, however, has focused on heterosexual romantic relationships; homosexual couples have been largely ignored in mate selection studies.

Social exchange theory is often used to explain why and how relationships form. Borrowing ideas from economics, social exchange theorists argue that people will enter into and remain in relationships as long as the rewards exceed the costs.

Gender differences in mate selection preferences have been discovered. Men generally prefer more sexually permissive and experienced partners than women. Men are likely to attach more importance to physical attractiveness of potential partners than women, whereas women tend to rate ambition and financial security as more important than men do. Both women and men rate mutual attraction as the most important characteristic in the mate selection process. Sociobiological theorists assume that gender differences in mate selection are genetically programmed into human brains from eons of evolutionary development. Those who favor a social structural explanation argue that gender differences are a product of the economic and patriarchal structure of society. It is important to recognize that women and men actually share many similarities in mate selection preferences.

Readings for In-Depth Focus

The Interdependent Relationship

Think for a minute about what type of intimate relationship you consider ideal. Is it the same type of relationship your grandparents or great-grandparents had? Unlike your older relatives, it is likely that the relationship you envision closely approximates what Francesca Cancian labels as *interdependent,* in which both partners are emotionally involved and share mutual interests. In the past, women were expected to maintain the emotional spark in a marriage. In the wake of the women's movement and radically changing gender roles, many couples became more independent of each other—sacrificing closeness for equality. Interdependence is an attempt to strike a balance between these two extremes.

■ ■ ■

Androgynous Love in Marriage

Francesca M. Cancian

. . . Within marriage, security is usually easier to achieve than freedom or interdependence. Married couples are pressured to stay together, and their lives are structured by a myriad of rules and expectations about how they should behave and feel. Emotional and material exchange and sharing also contribute to the security and commitment of marriage. Married couples usually live together, pool their money, have children, make love regularly, and share their meals and much of their leisure time. But the rules and exchanges that provide security often restrict freedom and channel men and women into rigid, overspecialized gender roles. On the other hand, couples that live together without being married often lack the security and commitment that is necessary for self-development and for maintaining the relationship. . . .

BECOMING INTERDEPENDENT

Interdependence is the cornerstone of a relationship that helps both partners develop an expanded, androgynous self. Both partners will have to move beyond the merging, demanding dependency of childhood—which is usually overt in women and covert or repressed in men. As they feel more interdependent and separate, they will be able to tolerate situations in which their immediate needs are not met without col-

lapsing in fear or becoming angry or withdrawn. They will experience themselves as powerful and in control within the relationship, at times, as well as weak and dependent, and will be able to empathically accept a broader range of their partner's self.

■ ■ ■

The development of greater interdependence in the marriage of Ann and Michael Gerrard illustrates these themes.[1] Ann . . . is a 42-year-old biologist and has been married to Michael, a hospital administrator, for nineteen years. They have two sons in high school. Ann's best features in Michael's eyes are "energy and enthusiasm" and "honesty and integrity, I mean I respect her." Ann values Michael's "physical attraction . . . it isn't just being sexy, it's also being very alive and strong but not frightening . . . it's just sort of there in his body . . . I respect him a lot." What she values most in her marriage is

> the sex, the house, the life, it's a whole life. I think of doing fun things together. I think of someone to hang on to when I get scared. I feel grounded. It makes me feel located and challenged. I mean nothing like trying to get close to someone to find out who you are.

Ann described the slow process of becoming less desperately dependent on her husband and more separate and able to share with him. Ten years ago Ann was unexpectedly fired from her part-time job with a large corporation. For several years, she had been working, raising her sons, and worrying about her marriage. "I was doing it all and being pretty successful . . . I was this macho, achieving, brilliant, tough person . . . But I felt somehow restless and boxed in. I thought it was something wrong with Michael, something he wasn't giving me." She joined an encounter group and had frequent meetings with a new woman friend, breaking her habit of spending all her time away from work with Michael or the children. She also had long arguments with her husband, reminiscent of the Gilmore's fights, in which she would pressure him to change, to come to the encounter groups with her, to talk with her more.

Then she was fired and unable to find another job. "My world crashed down around me"—her world of being a successful person, overtly independent but covertly very dependent on her husband, following a stereotypically masculine pattern. At her friend's suggestion, Ann entered therapy; she developed an intense bond with her therapist and slowly began to experience and integrate the dependent, split-off part of herself. Over the next four years, "all the creative, feminine parts, all that came out," and Ann began to play the harp and write poetry as her mother had done.

Why was it so tough to let that side out do you think?
Part of it is I didn't trust anybody. And because I learned to trust my therapist, I was able to not live my life as if I was a fortress constantly under siege.

You didn't trust Michael?
No, not that much. It was very hard. I was tense around him a lot. I always expected that anyone I was really close to was going to leave or betray me.

Ann developed a close friendship with two women, joined a feminist support group for women biologists, and eventually found a good new job. As she became more intimate with others, more aware of her own need to be taken care of, and more confident, she and Michael became less angry with each other and less dependent. "Now we're more separate and not as umbilically tied to each other . . . for all those years we were so tied," Ann comments. "I spent so much time thinking about him, and he spent so much time thinking about me, and lots of times it was a very angry thing, but we're very involved, passionately involved, even when it's awful." Michael describes how it used to be:

> She wanted to be working in the garden, I didn't want her in the garden. Why wasn't she paying attention to me? I wanted to watch a football game and she'd say why aren't you with the family? That kind of stuff, so we were giving each other incredibly little space.

Michael remembers how he began to feel more independent when he realized he could survive without Ann.

> I can remember in one of our particularly bad periods, being afraid of breaking up, and I was working with a counselor at this particular time and this was one of those dramatic experiences, realizing that I could do it. Because you get married and you kind of define yourself in terms of the relationship and you can't imagine yourself not being in it, ah, so it was really nice to know that I could do it, that is, I felt perfectly OK about the possibility of living alone and my own life.

"Michael and I started giving each other some room, " Ann remembers. "I started like not being home every weekend and every evening. I started having my own friends and doing things, and not hating him if he watched TV. Now we don't have to eat each other up all the time." Her struggles for independence and self-development are supported by her friends. "I go off and essentially take vacations by myself and trips by myself, and go out with friends, including sometimes men, and like that's really neat. I feel very free to do things. " Michael admits to being jealous of her friends at times: "I have certainly been jealous of her male friends, but we're both smart enough about relationships not to get into trouble blindly [have affairs]."

In Ann's words

> We trust each other more . . . I don't think it's so frightening any more. I can afford, we can afford to let each other get angry. We can afford to get out of touch, but we don't do that as much any more either . . . Just let go and the more you let go the closer we get.

Michael and Ann now share more at the same time that they spend more time apart. Michael has discovered that he likes to cook, and they enjoy making dinner for each other and discussing cooking techniques. Ann more often joins Michael in complaining about work—she no longer needs to be the master of every situation. And when their travels separate them, they can share their feelings of fear and sadness and phone each other. Their old pattern was to deny their fears about being apart, never phone, and have fights about some other issue before and after each trip. Michael and Ann seem less afraid that they will be rejected or controlled by the other and therefore less angry and demanding, and more able to support each other. They express more of their feelings, a style of relating that is supported by their circle of friends. "I'm still involved in this whole culture of human potential stuff." Ann comments, "all my very close friends are into this way of talking."

Ann still seems more dependent on the relationship than Michael, and she worries about

becoming too separate. When asked if there was something she would like to change about the marriage, she said,

> . . . We could confront a little bit more. We had this long period of confronting so much that I think we both just got burnt out. Then we had several years of peace-making. And now . . . we're a bit too careful. We tend to say, let's wait until tomorrow . . . you both go off in your separate directions, and cool off. It gets kind of chilly, distant.

Marriages such as the Gerrards' that have moved from Companionship to Interdependence seem traditional in many ways. Like couples in their parents' and grandparents' generations, Ann and Michael aspire to a life-long marriage, they are committed to support each other and to share their money and daily life. What makes this a modern, androgynous relationship is that both partners are responsible for maintaining the relationship; their balance of dependency and power is close to equal; and they are dedicated to developing themselves, working on their relationship, and communicating openly.

STAYING INDEPENDENT

Couples dedicated to Independence not Interdependence come closer to popular conceptions of the modern relationship. They emphasize their own freedom more than security or mutual support. Focusing on an independent couple clarifies how different the Independence blueprint is from the majority of long-term relationships.

For men and women who live together for many years without marrying, independence "is the most consistent theme of their relationship," conclude Philip Blumstein and Pepper Schwartz, after interviewing forty-eight cohabiting couples.[2] One of the couples was Lauren, thirty-nine, a speech pathologist in the city school system and Blair, thirty-eight, a social worker at the same school. They met seven years ago at work.[3] "I was impressed . . . by the way she was able to verbalize feelings and attitudes about education and social relationships," says Blair. "I just thought he was a fox," comments Lauren, "and then I found out he was married and decided that was too bad." Lauren, who was divorced and had two children, did not want an involvement with a married man, but Blair was unhappy with his wife, and the structure and commitment of marriage. "I was dissatisfied being married 'cause I didn't like that contract . . . The overriding feeling of commitment was something I really didn't want . . . My wife was a homebody. I wanted more freedom."

Blair and Lauren fell very much in love and one night had sex together. Ten days later, Blair spent several nights at Lauren's house, and he never left. Blair explains the almost casual way he ended his marriage and began a new commitment "for a while." After a few days at Lauren's

> there was kind of the next decision which needed to be made, which was: "I think I have to go home and get some more clothes." So I remember that day as being an incredibly intensive emotional day, because I knew then what I was really doing—which was moving out of my marriage. I knew at that point I was making a commitment.

He went home "with every intention of packing my stuff and sitting down with my wife and telling her that I'm getting out for a while." But his wife "didn't show up." Then "it started raining and there was no waiting around, so I hopped in the car and left. And got back here, and it was clear then—almost unspoken—that I was going to be here for a while."

From the start, Lauren and Blair tried to avoid permanent commitments and mutual dependence. They were both "just sure it was love," Lauren explains, but they didn't expect their bond to last very long, even after they had been living together for three years.

> We just sort of said, "This is the neatest thing that has ever happened to me. I place no limits on it. It may be over tomorrow and I'm not going to worry about it. I'm just going to enjoy it for what it gives right now." And love was used every other word.

Feelings of love and a willingness to communicate and work on the relationship are their positive bonds. "The neatest thing for me is that he is willing to work on the relationship," says Lauren. When a problem comes up, they talk about it until it's resolved. "We never quit till it's over if that means staying up all night . . . I don't feel insecure bringing anything up that bothers me, 'cause we can always work it out." Blair shares the value on communication, praising Lauren for being "incredibly out-front about all her feelings."

They also share the task of raising Lauren's two children, even though they have serious arguments about his standards of discipline, and they enjoy playing tennis and doing leisure activities together. Sexual exclusiveness may be another bond. After a "bad time" when Blair had sex with other women, "we have agreed on an exclusive intimacy" according to Lauren. Blair's version of their agreement on sex with other people is vaguer, following his pattern of avoiding definite commitments: "we agreed to sort of write it off" and tell the other person unless it's "a one-time sort of thing that may happen as a result of getting really stoned sometimes . . . " If one of them decided they would like sex with someone else, Blair says, "we have made a commitment to discuss that interest with the other before it is consummated, and the appropriate steps will have to be taken at that point—which may mean that we will have to break for a while."

Other parts of their lives they keep separate and equal. "We maintain very separate financial records," Blair explains. "I essentially make all the decisions about what I do with my money. She makes all the decisions about what she does with hers." "We keep all of our finances as separate as we can," Lauren agrees, and even when a friend gives one of them a gift, "if it's an *us* gift and it comes from my friends, it's mine, even if it's to both of us." They also attempt to divide housework equally, but Lauren "probably does a little bit more," Blair admits.

Staying independent, separate, and equal are primary goals for both of them partly because of problems in the past. When she was married, Lauren recalls, "I went through three years of psychotherapy thinking I was crazy for not being happy" and "that affects why I don't ever want to marry anybody again." With Blair she intends to remain more independent: "I know if Blair were to walk out and get hit by a truck, I would be devastated but I would be okay. I would make it, and I'd raise my kids and I'd still have things to do, and I lost all of that in marriage. I was either tormented or I was tormenting."

Blair feels he has learned from the failure of his marriage "to talk openly about problems as they occur rather than sandbagging" and to give each other more freedom to pursue separate interests. The key elements in making his new relationship work, he thinks, are "dealing openly and honestly with conflict" and "allowing each other space." Blair believes "the best relationships probably are made by people who don't really need them, just want them; don't have to have it, but since it's around I'm sure going to take advantage of it." And Lauren agrees, "if you ever need me, we're going to be in trouble."

Couples like Lauren and Blair avoid emotional and material interdependence to such an extent that it becomes almost impossible to have a committed, enduring relationship. Many of the cohabiting couples that Blumstein and Schwartz studied were more committed—about

85% of them were still together when they were recontacted eighteen months later, and couples that shared their money were especially likely to endure. Blair and Lauren were still "involved" when they were recontacted, but living in separate homes and exploring relations with other people.

SELF-DEVELOPMENT AND SUPPORT

Couples in an Interdependent relationship try to combine more mutual dependency and more commitment than Lauren and Blair have, with a great deal of freedom to develop themselves. The Gerrards illustrate some of the possibilities of developing an androgynous self at mid life, within the constraints of a stable marriage. A young engaged couple shows how an Interdependent relationship can foster self-development during the transition to adulthood.

Greg, twenty-four, and Lisa, twenty-two, have been dating for five years, and plan to get married soon, if they can overcome the objections of her family.[4] They both describe their relationship as a combination of secure nurturance and freedom to develop themselves. What Greg likes best about their relationship is that "she's always there no matter what, no matter what kind of mood I'm in or how bad a day it's been—she's always there to talk to, to help me, and over the years she has domesticated me a lot—she's made me into a more grown-up type person . . ." Greg describes himself as "the baby of the family" and is very close to his father— "I've always been under his wing." He has many friends including a best friend whom he sees every day, and who describes Greg as "outgoing, honest, funny and boisterous." When Greg met Lisa he had graduated from high school and was working in a gas station. "I had hair down to here (his shoulders). I was wild, crazy, into doing all kinds of stupid things," and Lisa helped him be "more grown-up." For example, she helped him conquer his bad temper. "She has developed that out of me, because for a while there I used to be the type that when I got mad I would see only red . . . I was uncontrollable, but with her around I am able to control my emotions." Now he has settled down, with some reluctance, into a job as a technician in a computer company, and has signed up for their management training course.

Lisa also has developed new ways of relating to others. "She has always been very sheltered" Greg said, "and I introduced her to a lot of fun things in life and she introduced me to a lot of responsibilities . . . Also she's just a damn awful lot of fun to be around all the time." With Greg, Lisa for the first time went water skiing, jet skiing, motorcycle riding, innertubing the rapids, and backpacking. "I'm a school principal's daughter, I was home every weekend. I have a very protective family. I mean it was a big deal to go to the grocery store alone! I have learned so many new things, and so many fun things . . ." With Greg's encouragement she is overcoming her internal restrictions. "I'll give anything a try, even though sometimes I get this radical fear that sweeps through me—I just have to put it out of my mind."

Lisa goes to college part time, works as a clerk, and has just started her own business, selling the ceramics she makes. Her best friend describes her as "outgoing, positive, understanding and very ambitious." Both Greg and Lisa say that they share equally in making decisions, but Lisa used to carry most of the responsibility for being emotionally supportive. "I'm not one that expresses my problems," says Greg, following the typical masculine pattern, and "she gets mad because I'm not as open with her as I should be." But mostly, he adds, "if there's ever anything that's bothering me or her inside or any problem we're having we can more or less bring it out and just talk to each other about it—problems about anything—that's why our relationship goes so well." From Lisa's perspective, "the first year or two I gave more, but now he gives more. I think with everything I'm doing—going to school, opening a shop—he's being the emo-

tional support which I need, and he's just really behind my decisions and my goals." They seem to be moving towards more androgynous gender roles, and there is a high level of mutual emotional dependence between them.

They are also financially interdependent, making joint investments in recreational equipment and in savings for their marriage. When Lisa was asked about her goals in relation to Greg, she answered with a mix of fifties familism and eighties consumerism:

> Marriage. We want a home and to be able to afford children and give them the best. We like a lot of toys and we like to do things like water ski and ride and we'd like to be able to afford to do these things. We are working really hard now, and hopefully it will pay off in the future.

Along with their mutual dependence, Greg and Lisa also seem unusually separate and autonomous for their age. Lisa describes herself as "a private person. I set aside time for myself every day . . ." Greg comments that "When we really disagree we'll say so, 'no, I don't want to do that.' And we can talk about it and work things out . . . We don't have to worry about stepping on each other's toes because even though we're coming together as one, we are still separate entities and there's always going to be times when we'll disagree."

Part of their separateness is that they have many other important relationships. They both live with their families and describe themselves as very close with their fathers and with their friends, and they both occasionally go off on a weekend trip without the other.

They also seem very much in love, especially Greg. "Normally when I'm my happiest is when I'm with her. Sometimes when I first appear around her, I'm a jerk to her . . . and she just takes it all in stride and gives it back in love, and that's the time when I can be as happy as I can be." His gratitude is remarkable and so is his mature recognition that he is "normally" happi-est with her, not "always." "I can feel her when she's there and I don't need her to touch me or anything . . . I enjoy her presence even when we say nothing. She's very soothing to me."

STRIKING A BALANCE

Interdependent couples try to strike a balance between opposing forces—to have a relation-ship of equality unconstrained by traditional gender roles and still depend on each other for emotional and material support, to be free to develop new capacities and still maintain a se-cure, committed relationship. Greg and Lisa, and Ann and Michael come close to achieving this balance. The material and emotional de-pendency between the woman and man is much more equal than many couples, such as, for example, the Gilmores, although the tradi-tional pattern of the woman being more emo-tionally and verbally expressive is still evident. Lisa supports herself economically, and Ann makes a good income at a prestigious job. Both women are energetic and ambitious and seem to have developed their "masculine" side more than the average female. Neither of them seems to think of herself as less competent or less pow-erful than her partner, nor do they express their individuality vicariously; each one is involved in her own projects. Moreover, the women have many other close relationships, which further decreases their dependency. The men also show few signs of supermasculinity. They do not deny their emotional needs, nor do they undermine their partners' moves towards independence and success. Greg seems more androgynous—more emotionally expressive and concerned with intimacy—than Michael, perhaps because he is younger, perhaps because he is not com-mitted to a job that encourages him to be imper-sonal and competitive. Finally, it is probably significant that neither couple has young chil-dren. In the early childrearing years, the burdens of marriage and parenting are so great that most

couples probably have little energy to focus on developing their selves or their relationship.

A less expected similarity among the cou-ples is the way they describe their love in terms of a reassuring physical presence. In Greg's words, "I enjoy her presence even when we say nothing." Their words are reminiscent of the at-tachment between mother and child and the re-assurance that a child feels from the physical presence of his mother or primary caretaker.[5] They suggest that transferences from early rela-tionships work in positive as well as negative ways, and that part of the somewhat mysterious bond that keeps some couples together while others separate is an unconscious conviction that they are connected and safe with their part-ner as they once were with their mothers.

These four individuals illustrate how self-development and enduring love can be mutu-ally reinforcing in a relationship that balances security and freedom. The rules and expecta-tions that make their relationships secure and supportive are relatively unconstricting. Instead of adopting the roles of Companionship mar-riage, they have developed their own more flexi-ble codes, so that Ann can have male friends and Lisa and Greg can go off with other people during the weekend. Each couple also belongs to a network or subculture that supports their rules for combining commitment and freedom, such as Ann's encounter group and Greg's fam-ily and friends.

Some conflict between developing oneself and marriage remains. As Ann comments "the bad part is it's limiting. Sometimes I'd like to go try somebody else, sort of, and you can't. I mean I don't because I don't want to run the risk . . . You don't know the road not taken and that's the cost of marriage."

But couples that choose Independence, like Lauren and Blair, seem to limit themselves more, cutting themselves off from the possibil-ity of enduring love and the self-development that can come from love. Given the alternative ideals in our time—Interdependence, Independence, and Companionship marriage based on polarized gender roles—Interdependence is the best blueprint for many couples.

ENDNOTES

1. The Gerrards were interviewed by Eileen Pinkerton.

2. Philip Blumstein and Pepper Schwartz, *American Couples* (New York: William Morrow, 1983), p. 412.

3. This case is from Blumstein and Schwartz (1983), pp. 436–447.

4. Greg and Lisa were interviewed by Kim Thompson.

5. See Winnicott's description of ego relatedness between mother and child in Guntrip, Harry, *Personality Structure and Human Interaction* (New York: International Universities Press, 1961), pp. 116–117.

Critical Thinking Questions

1. Compare and contrast *independent* and *interdependent* relationships.

2. How have changing gender-role expectations influenced the ideal type of relationships couples envision?

3. Why does Cancian believe interdependent relationships are preferable to independent relationships? Do you agree? Why or why not?

9 *Sexual Attitudes, Behaviors, and Relationships*

*T*hroughout much of U.S. history, sexuality was considered a taboo subject. Sexual relationships and acts were supposed to be reserved for the purpose of reproduction in marriage alone, and many myths were perpetuated in culture to control sexual behavior. One myth was that masturbation causes blindness, an idea first proposed by Swiss physician Simon André Tissot in 1758 (Schrof and Wagner 1994). Another less well known myth that frightened nineteenth-century Americans was the belief that "orgasm was more debilitating to the system than a hard day's work, and sex just for pleasure was certain to ruin the body's parenting capabilities" (Schrof and Wagner 1994: 77).

In today's society, such myths seem ludicrous. We find it difficult to believe how puritanical and naive people in earlier times were about sex. Yet, it was not so long ago that acknowledgment of sexual relationships, especially those outside of marriage, was considered scandalous. Consider the following incidents. In 1962, a male graduate student at Cornell University was suspended indefinitely for living with a female companion outside of marriage. Two years later at Cornell, a male student was reprimanded for staying overnight in a hotel with a woman who was not associated with the university (Macklin 1981). In 1968, a sophomore at Barnard College made national headlines when it was discovered that she had been, as the newspapers proclaimed, "shacking up" a with Columbia University undergraduate in an off-campus apartment. The sophomore's case was referred to the faculty-staff disciplinary committee at Barnard, for such behavior was a dismissable offense. Student protest dissuaded the disciplinary committee from recommending expulsion (Whitman 1997). As you read this chapter, consider how and why attitudes toward premarital sexual relationships have changed. Try to identify the social and family consequences of today's more permissive sexual values and behaviors.

Studying Sexual Attitudes and Behaviors

Before examining the data on sexual attitudes and behaviors in American culture, it is important to understand how such information is gathered. Think for a moment about how you would conduct a study of human sexual attitudes or behavior. What method would you use to collect data? What problems do you think you would encounter and how would you overcome them?

You probably ruled out research methods, such as observations and experiments, which might be ethically questionable in this context. Like sociologists and family scholars, you probably decided that survey research would be the most fruitful method to gather data on this sensitive topic, recognizing that you would have to find ways to help respondents be as candid and honest as possible. The majority of data on sexual attitudes has been gathered using experimental and survey research techniques (Sprecher and McKinney 1993), whereas data on sexual behavior have been gathered almost exclusively from surveys.

Experimental Research on Sexual Attitudes

Experiments designed to measure subjects' sexual attitudes often involve asking subjects to read a questionnaire supposedly completed by another subject and then to assess the permissiveness, likability, and intelligence of the subject. In reality, the questionnaire response has been created by researchers, who vary the characteristics of the hypothetical subject and his or her behavior. The goal is to determine if subjects' judgments change as information presented in the questionnaire changes.

For example, a group of subjects is randomly divided into two groups. Subjects in the first group read a questionnaire allegedly completed by a female, age 16, who has had three sexual partners. The second set of subjects reads the exact same questionnaire except that it was allegedly completed by a 16-year-old male who has had three sexual partners (Sprecher and McKinney 1993). Subjects are asked to make a variety of judgments about the fictional survey respondent. By manipulating the subject's gender, researchers can measure the extent to which a *double standard* regarding sexual behavior exists in culture. Researchers also can manipulate other characteristics of the hypothetical subject, such as the age at first intercourse or the duration and nature of the subject's relationship with his or her partner at the time of first intercourse. As with all experimental research, however, the setting and situations are contrived, and one must wonder if subjects would respond to real people as they do to anonymous, fictitious characters in a laboratory setting.

Survey Research on Sexual Attitudes and Behaviors

By far the most common research technique used to study both sexual attitudes and behaviors is the survey. Surveys can be administered to a large number of people relatively quickly and inexpensively, and larger sample sizes generally yield more generalizable data. An example is the well-known study by Blumstein and Schwartz (1983), *American Couples.* These researchers, who wanted to study cohabiting heterosexual and homosexual couples as well as married couples, sent out 22,000 38-page questionnaires to couples across the country. They received over 12,000 usable completed surveys, and supplemented these surveys with interviews of 300 representative couples. Such large-scale surveys yield a tremendous amount of information.

The most recent large-scale survey of American sexual attitudes and behaviors, conducted by researchers at Chicago's National Opinion Research Center, was called the *National Health and Social Life Survey (NHSLS).* This research illustrates some of the strengths and weaknesses of studying sexuality through surveys. In the NHSLS project, 3,432 English-speaking adults between the ages of 18 and 59 were administered a 210-page questionnaire. The results of this research have been published in two books—*Sex in America* (Michael et al. 1994) and *The Social Organization of Sexuality* (Laumann et al. 1994)—which are full of statistics regarding sexual attitudes and behavior. For example, researchers found that (1) most Americans have sexual intercourse 6 or 7 times a month; (2) married and cohabiting couples have the highest level of sexual activity, with 40 percent of married couples and 56 percent of cohabiting couples having sex at least twice a week; and (3) men report having sex an average of 6.5 times per month, whereas women report having sex an average of 6.3 times per month. But the most startling and controversial finding of this study was that the majority of Americans are monogamous; 83 percent of those surveyed reported having one sexual partner in the past year or more. Slightly over half of the respondents (53 percent) had only one sexual partner in the past five years. The researchers predicted from these findings "that there will not be a widespread breakout of AIDS in the heterosexual population" (Schrof and Wagner 1994: 76).

The NHSLS data also suggested that Americans mistakenly believe that others are far more sexually active than they are—misperceptions that can lead to numerous individual and social consequences:

> *America has a message about sex, and that message is none too subtle. Anyone who watches a movie, reads a magazine, or turns on the television set has seen it. It says that almost everyone but you is having endless fascinating varied sex. But, we have found, the public image of sex in America bears virtually no relationship to the truth. The public image consists of myths, and they are not harmless, for they elicit at best unrealistic and at worst dangerous misconceptions of what people do sexually. The resulting false expectations can badly affect self-esteem, marriages, relationships, and even physical health.* (Michael et al. 1994: 1)

This survey, like many others, is important because a vast amount of data were gathered from a large group of people. Critics charge, however, that respondents may underreport "behavior that has negative social consequences," such as having multiple sexual partners (Ingall 1995: 93). As was discussed in Chapter 2, this problem of social desirability bias is common in survey research. Furthermore, data from surveys may be inaccurate because respondents may have inaccurate recall or selective perception when responding to questions. Consider the findings on oral-genital sex: 31 percent of heterosexual males said their partners always or usually performed oral sex on them, whereas only 15 percent of heterosexual women said they performed this act on their partners. The wide disparity in responses between men and women about oral-genital sex suggests that one or both sexes is not recalling accurately or is selectively remembering (or forgetting) this type of sexual contact (Ingall 1995). The length of surveys also interferes with the validity and reliability of responses; how many of us could concentrate long enough to respond accurately to 210 pages of questions?

Research on Homosexual Sex

It is important to note that until the 1990s, much of the experimental and survey research on sexual attitudes and behaviors focused primarily on heterosexual respondents. Surveys on sexual behavior that incorporate data from homosexuals often focus on how common such relationships are rather than on the nature of homosexual relationships (the Blumstein and Schwartz study is a notable exception).

In 1948, Alfred Kinsey and colleagues estimated that 10 percent of white males are "more or less exclusively homosexual" (cited in Laumann et al. 1994: 288). This figure of 10 percent, repeated in a 1953 Kinsey publication, filtered into mainstream American culture. Critics later claimed that the Kinsey studies overestimated the number of homosexuals in the population because of the large number of participants who were prisoners in penal institutions or volunteers from gay organizations (Masters, Johnson, and Kolodny 1995).

Furthermore, the definition of *homosexuality* used to calculate the frequency of such relationships has varied and can include not only just sexual acts between persons of the same sex, but also respondents' desire for a same-sex partner and their gender identity. Using this more elaborated definition of *homosexuality*, the authors of the *Sex in America* survey found that only 2.8 percent of males and 1.4 percent of females identified themselves as homosexual, although 10.1 percent of males and 8.6 percent of females said that since puberty they had had a sexual experience or had been attracted to someone of the same sex (Laumann et al. 1994).

Trends in Sexual Attitudes and Behaviors

Prior to 1960, most heterosexual dating couples had fairly conservative attitudes regarding sexual behavior; they either believed in abstinence, in which the couple was expected to remain chaste until marriage, or in the double standard, in which men were permitted or expected to engage in premarital sex but not women (Sprecher and McKinney 1993). The 1960s marked a new era in sexual attitudes in the United States in which acceptance of premarital sex began to increase dramatically (Smith 1994). Both the approval and practice of premarital sex increased significantly between the mid-1960s and the mid-1980s (Robinson et al. 1991; Smith 1994; Roche and Ramsbey 1993). The changes in sexual behavior were particularly dramatic for women. Between 1965 and 1980, the number of males engaging in premarital sex increased 12.3 percent, whereas the number of females engaging in premarital sex rose 34.8 percent (Robinson et al. 1991). Kahn and London (1991) report that according to surveys, 40 percent of white women who married between 1960 and 1965 were virgins on their wedding nights, yet only 15 percent of white women married between 1980 and 1985 were virgins. African American brides report similar trends in behavior, although historically a smaller proportion of black women have been virgins at marriage (Kahn and London 1991). Keep in mind, however, that some of the increase in reported premarital sexual behavior may be an artifact of more honest responses; as premarital sex became more socially acceptable—especially for women—respondents may have become more honest about reporting their premarital sexual behavior.

Explaining the Sexual Revolution

This dramatic increase in the acceptance and practice of premarital sex that began in the mid-1960s and continued for two decades is usually referred to as the *sexual revolution*. Why did sexual norms and behaviors change so rapidly during this time? The wider availability of more **reliable contraception** is one of the most obvious explanations for the sexual revolution. The birth control pill, approved by the Food and Drug Administration in 1960, made it possible for couples to engage in premarital sex with far less fear of an unwanted pregnancy. The **women's movement,** which began in the 1960s, also contributed to the sexual revolution, for one of the messages of feminists was that women should shun the social constraints of the sexual double standard and be as free sexually as men are.

Furthermore, the 1960s was the decade when the first wave of **baby boomers reached young adulthood.** Not only were there more young adults than ever before, but record numbers of them attended college. In college, these young adults were independent of parents' watchful eyes and could experiment with relationships and sexuality, especially after colleges began to relax their strict regulation of students' sexual behavior. Until the latter part of the 1960s, most colleges' rules were based on a philosophy of *in loco parentis*, which means "in the place of the parent." Student conduct rules were supposed to be modeled after what parents would expect of their children if they were living at home. Hence, not only did colleges forbid open sexual relationships between unmarried students but they also had strict regulations about when and where male and female students could visit each other in their dorms and at what time students had to be in their rooms.

Students of the 1960s protested that they were legally adults—old enough to vote, marry, and be drafted into military service, so they certainly were old enough to make their own decisions about sexual relationships. As colleges and universities relaxed their regulations, many began to approve **coeducational dormitory facilities.** The first coeducational or mixed-sex dormitory was opened at Indiana University in 1956. Today, over 60 percent of college housing is coeducational, the most often requested type of housing by both sexes (Robertson 1996). Most coed dormitory arrangements involve the sexes sharing the same building but living on separate floors or in separate wings, but a few colleges—such as Antioch and Oberlin Colleges in Ohio—allow male and female students to share the same rooms (Robertson 1996). Although sharing the same residence hall or room facilitates sexual relationships between students, researchers have found that most students develop platonic, siblinglike relationships with members of the opposite sex with whom they live; students are most likely to develop sexual relationships with students who live in other dorms (Robertson 1996).

The sexual revolution also can be explained partly by an interplay of social and biological changes. Unlike the decade of the 1950s, when the median age at first marriage dropped to its lowest point in the twentieth century, the 1960s marks the decade when marriage age began to rise (Gatlin 1987). At the same time as marriages were being postponed longer, young people were reaching the age of sexual maturity earlier.

In females, puberty is signaled by *menarche*—the first menstrual period. The average age of menarche in 1840 was age 17, whereas today, the average age at first menstruation is between 12.3 and 12.8 years (Dworetzby 1990; Katcha-dourian 1985). Puberty in males, technically signaled when ejaculation of sperm becomes possible, is more difficult to identify with a single event. However, re-searchers believe that boys also reach sexual maturity at an earlier age today than in the past. Today, puberty in boys occurs between the ages of 13 and 15, and is marked by a growth spurt, deepening voice, and hormonal changes such as those that lead to the development of facial and body hair. Earlier sexual maturation is best explained by improvements in diet, health care, and sanitation.

The combination of delaying marriage and reaching sexual maturity at younger ages contributed to the erosion of the social norm prohibiting premari-tal sex. When sexual maturity is reached in early adolescence but people wait until their mid-twenties or even their thirties to marry, prohibitions against pre-marital sex becomes difficult to maintain and enforce.

During the sexual revolution, many people experimented with unconven-tional sexual relationships. Many young people who were part of the hippie counterculture established communes, in which individuals were free to change sexual partners whenever they wanted. *Free love*—sexual relationships without commitment, jealously, or possessiveness—was advocated in many communes. Some older middle-class married couples experimented with *swinging* (exchang-ing spouses) and *open marriages* (sanctioning extramarital sex). As you read in Chapter 8, many people began to live in **nonmarital cohabiting relationships,** the only commonly practiced and widely accepted life-style that remains today as a legacy of the sexual revolution (Thornton 1988: 506).

Sexual Behavior across the Life Span

Although human beings are sexual creatures at all ages, consensual sexual rela-tionships generally do not begin to develop until individuals have at least reached adolescence. Sexual behaviors change throughout the individual's life course with one's marital status and advancing age.

Nonmarital Sexual Behavior in Adolescence

Teenagers today are tolerant of a variety of sexual behaviors—from abstinence to oral sex and intercourse—and they feel entitled to make their own choices about whether and when to become sexually active (Rubin 1990). The term *sexually active* must be defined broadly when studying the sexual attitudes and behaviors of adolescents. All too often, researchers classify teenagers who have had sexual intercourse as *sexually active* and those who are virgins as *not sexually active*. However, these labels are not very useful in describing their behaviors. Many adolescents classified by researchers as sexually active often had engaged in sexual intercourse only once or had been abstinent for a year or more (Rubin 1990). On the other hand, students who had never engaged in intercourse were far from sexually inactive, many routinely engaging in genital fondling, mutual masturbation, and oral sex with their partners. Unfortunately, most large-scale surveys of teenage sexual behavior examine only whether adolescents have engaged in sexual intercourse; few statistics are available on the extent to which teens engage in other types of sexual behavior.

According to the 1994 report *Sex and America's Teenagers*, "Most adolescents begin having intercourse in their mid-to-late teens, about 8 years before they marry" (*Teen Sex & Pregnancy* 1997). It is uncommon for very young teenagers to have sex; only 9 percent of 12-year-olds, 16 percent of 13-year-olds, and 23 percent of 14-year-olds have ever had vaginal intercourse. Furthermore, 70 percent of females who had intercourse before age 14 and 60 percent who had intercourse before age 15 report that they did so involuntarily (*Teen Sex & Pregnancy* 1997). Voluntary sexual intercourse becomes more common in the middle to late teenage years. The Alan Guttmacher Institute estimates that 56 percent of women and 73 percent of men have had intercourse by age 18 (*Teen Sex & Pregnancy* 1997). Data from the 1995 National Survey of Family Growth (see Figure 9.1), a study of 10,847 women ages 15 to 44, indicate that 50 percent of women age 15 to 19 have engaged in sexual intercourse at some time (*Fertility, Family Planning, and Women's Health* 1997).

These most recent statistics actually show a decline in the number of teenagers engaging in premarital intercourse (*Fertility, Family Planning, and Women's Health* 1997). Throughout most of the 1980s, there was an increase in the number of unmarried teenagers having sexual intercourse and a decline in the age at which they first had sex ("Sexual and Contraceptive Behavior" 1997). Rates of vaginal intercourse among teenagers and the age at first intercourse began to level off in 1988, and declined throughout the 1990s.

Most of the increase in teenage intercourse in the 1980s was due to white teenagers from higher-income families initiating sexual intercourse at younger ages. Even so, men and women of racial and ethnic minorities still tend to initiate sexual activity at younger ages than white teenagers. Among never-married males aged 15 to 19 in 1988, 81 percent of blacks, 60 percent of Hispanics, and 57 percent of white men had ever had vaginal intercourse. In the female cohort, 61 percent of blacks, 49 percent of Hispanics, and 52 percent of whites reported having had intercourse ("Sexual and Contraceptive Behavior" 1997).

Researchers tend to focus on the proportion of teenagers who engage in sexual intercourse, yet it is important to note that many young people remain virgins. Data from the Alan Guttmacher Institute indicate that "1 in 5 teenagers do not have intercourse during their teenage years" (*Teen Sex & Pregnancy* 1997).

Figure 9.1 **Percentage of Never-Married Females Ages 15 to 19 Who Have Ever Had Sexual Intercourse (after menarche)**

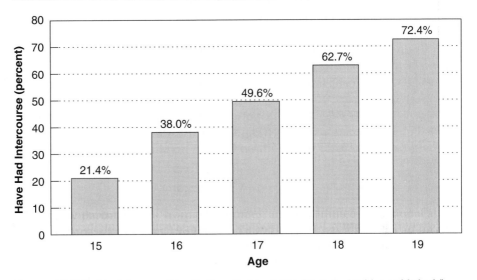

Source: 1995 National Survey of Family Growth, May 1997, "Statistical Tables, Published," Washington, DC: National Center for Health Statistics. <www.cdc.gov/nchswww/datawh/statab/pubd/2319_19.htm>.

Contraceptive Use Among Teenagers

Contraceptive use among teenagers has increased in recent years. Many teenagers use condoms as a contraceptive method, which reduces the risk of sexually transmitted infections as well as unwanted pregnancy. At least 70 percent of teenage women and their partners currently use contraception, and one-quarter of the 1.7 million women who use the birth control pill also use condoms (*Teen Sex & Pregnancy* 1997). Between 1982 and 1990, condom use among teenagers increased sharply, from 21 to 44 percent (*Contraceptive Use* 1997). In fact, sexually active youth ages 15 to 19 are the group most likely to use condoms. Only 13 percent of all American couples rely on the condom as their most common form of contraception, but 26 percent of teenage women use this method of birth control (Sexual and Contraceptive Behavior 1997).

Condom use is preferred by teenagers for several reasons (Sexual and Contraceptive Behavior 1997). First, adolescents believe that condoms are effective in preventing pregnancy, HIV infection, as well as other sexually transmitted infections. Second, condoms are easy and comparatively inexpensive to obtain and use. Unlike birth control pills, diaphragms, intrauterine devices (IUDs), and patches, condoms do not require a visit to a physician to obtain. Furthermore, they are not complicated to use, even for those with no sexual experience. Peer acceptance of condoms also contributes to their use. Teenagers perceive that their friends both approve of and use condoms.

However, many young people do not use any contraception, especially during their first intercourse. Planned Parenthood reports that "sexually active teenagers are more likely than any other age group to be nonusers of contraception, [with] one in five currently [using] no method of contraception" (*Sexual and Contraceptive Behavior* 1997). Sexually active teens who do not use contraception have a 90 percent chance of becoming pregnant within one year (*Teen Sex & Pregnancy* 1997). One-third of teens fail to use contraception during first intercourse (*Sexual and Contraceptive Behavior* 1997), which helps explain why one-half of all unplanned teen pregnancies occur within six months of the time the female first had intercourse (Masters et al. 1995).

Teen Pregnancy and Childbearing

The number of births to teenage mothers has declined in 46 states since 1991. Births to unwed teenage women dropped from a high of 62.1 per 1,000 females ages 15 to 19 in 1991 to 56.9 per 1,000 in 1995 (Vobejda 1996). Today, teenagers account for only 31 percent of nonmarital births, compared to 50 percent in 1970 (*Teen Sex & Pregnancy* 1997). Researchers are unsure of exactly why teenage birth rates have dropped, but given the trends examined in this chapter, one can speculate that reasons include the decline in teenagers engaging in sexual intercourse and greater contraceptive use. Researchers do know that abortion does not account for the decline in teenage births (Vobejda 1996).

What factors contribute to the incidence of unwanted pregnancies among adolescents? How does sexual behavior change after marriage? How do sexual relationships change over the life span?

Nevertheless, each year almost one million teenage women become pregnant, and approximately 85 percent of those pregnancies are unintended ("Pregnancy & Childbearing" 1997). Furthermore, teenage mothers and their babies are at greater risk for health complications. Children born to teenage mothers are more likely to be born premature and of low birth weight than babies born to older mothers. The higher risks associated with teenage pregnancies are due to two factors. First, young adolescent females' bodies are less mature, making full-term vaginal deliveries more difficult. Second, inadequate prenatal care and poor nutrition during pregnancy, both common among teenage mothers, further contribute to poor pregnancy outcomes.

Poverty and Teen Pregnancy

Prospects for the teenage mother and her child after birth are also discouraging. Teenage mothers are at far greater risk for a lifetime of poverty than women who delay childbearing until their twenties. The relationship between teenage childbearing and poverty is strong, but not as easily explained as social scientists once thought. In the past, researchers took it for granted that the relationship between teenage pregnancy and poverty was simple cause and effect: Teenage pregnancy caused poverty. It was logically assumed that the unwed teenage mother would have her high school education interrupted by the pregnancy, making it virtually impossible for her to find decent employment, thus confining her to a life of poverty.

More recent data, however, suggest that the relationship between poverty and teenage pregnancy is far more complex than originally believed (Geronimus 1991). In her article "Dubious Conceptions: The Controversy over Teen Pregnancy," Luker (1994) points out that teenage women who are at the highest risk for getting pregnant come from socioeconomically disadvantaged backgrounds. Furthermore, although it is true that teenage mothers are less likely to graduate from high school than other women are, it appears that many teenage mothers drop out of school before becoming pregnant. Luker argues that the combination of being socioeconomically disadvantaged and educationally discouraged puts teenage women at greater risk for becoming pregnant. Once they become mothers, it becomes even more difficult for these women to get out of the life of poverty in which they were raised.

Data from Planned Parenthood and the Alan Guttmacher Institute (see Pregnancy & Childbearing 1997; *Teen Sex & Pregnancy* 1997) support Luker's assertions. Teenagers who give birth are far more likely to come from low-income families (83 percent) than teenagers in the general population (38 percent). Almost 60 percent of teenage mothers are already living in poverty at the time their first child is born. Although more teenage mothers today are completing high school than they did in the past, the educational prospects for teenage mothers are still not good. Only one-half of women who have a child at age 17 or younger will complete high school by age 30, compared to 96 percent of women who delay childbearing until at least age 20.

Teenage Fathers

Researchers collect a tremendous amount of data on teenage mothers, but few study teenage fathers (Taylor et al. 1990). The little bit of information that is available on unwed teenage fathers suggests that the same factors that put teenage women at risk for pregnancy also put teenage men at risk for becoming fathers. Males at greatest risk of becoming unmarried teenage fathers are those who live in areas of high unemployment (Ku, Sonenstein, and Pleck 1993). In these areas, where prospects for economic success are few, there are not many incentives (e.g., a college education or the promise of a lucrative career) to postpone fatherhood. Teenage fathers, like teenage mothers, also are less likely to complete high school (only 39 percent of teen fathers receive their high school diplomas by age 20, compared to 86 percent of males who do not become fathers). Teenage fathers also are more likely to hold low-status, low-paying, blue-collar jobs than males who do not father children until their twenties (Pregnancy & Childbearing 1997).

Adult Nonmarital Sexual Behavior

Most of the social concern and political attention regarding nonmarital sexual relationships concerns adolescents, but it is important to note that more adults in their twenties have unplanned pregnancies than teenagers (Whitman 1997). In 1994, 22 percent of the children born out of wedlock had mothers 18 years old or younger, but more than 50 percent had mothers between the ages of 20 and 29 (Whitman 1997). Opinion polls indicate that although the majority of Americans believe that teenage sex is morally wrong, most people under age 45 today believe that adult premarital sex can be beneficial because it allows young people to "sow wild oats" before making a commitment to marriage and may make it easier for individuals to select compatible spouses (Whitman 1997).

The wide acceptance of adult nonmarital sex is reflected in the media. On prime-time network television, 8 acts of premarital sex are depicted for every 1 act of marital sex (Whitman 1997). Popular television shows (such as *Friends, Seinfeld,* and *Beverly Hills 90210*) have routinely depicted unmarried characters in sexual relationships. The characters are never condemned for engaging in sex outside of marriage, but issues of birth control and sexually transmitted diseases are rarely addressed.

Marital Sexual Behavior

Sex in marriage is both expected and approved of in society, so there are far less data on marital sexual behavior than on the sexual behavior of the unmarried (Sprecher and McKinney 1993). Available information on marital sexuality most often involves some measure of frequency of intercourse. Researchers consistently find that sexual frequency is greatest in the early years of marriage and declines with both age of partners and duration of the marriage (Blumstein and Schwartz 1983; Edwards and Booth 1994; Sprecher and McKinney 1993). During the first years of marriage, the vast majority of couples report having sex at least once a week and many have sex as often as 4 or 5 times per week (Frank and Anderson 1985). In her interviews with individuals who had been married five years or less, Greenblat (1985) reports a wide range of sexual frequency during the first year of marriage—from once a month to 45 times a month. Greenblat (1985: 361) argues that the wide variation in sexual frequency among newlyweds is due to the fact that "the marital sex domain has few cultural norms":

> *While the premarital sexual world is replete with proscriptions and prescriptions, there is little to guide the newlywed couple in how to develop a sexual pattern. . . . Bridal magazines . . . and sex manuals may endorse the idea that marital sex is important and may offer suggestions about good sexual technique . . . , but none of them say anything about how often to do it! Finally, few people talk with others to obtain the personal advice that on other topics is so abundant.*

Following the first year of marriage, sexual frequency tends to decline for married couples. Couples attribute the decrease in their sexual encounters to birth control, pregnancy issues, fatigue from children and/or work, and familiarity with each other (Blumstein and Schwartz 1983; Greenblat 1985; Sprecher and McKinney 1993). Particularly for women, pregnancy and the fear of pregnancy contribute to a decline in sexual intercourse in marriage. After the first few years of marriage, it is likely that a couple has children and is involved in establishing their careers. Both child-care and work responsibilities contribute to exhaustion and reduce the amount of time couples have to be intimate. Spouses also report that overfamiliarity with each other and the knowledge that their partners will be available for sex at another time also reduce the desire for frequent sex.

Although the frequency of sexual contact is far less in the middle years of marriage than in the early years, most couples still report that their sex life is satisfying (Frank and Anderson 1985). Sexual frequency is lowest for couples in the later years of their marriage. Only 20 percent of couples who have been married 20 years or more have sex at least once a week, compared to 59 percent of couples married 10 years or less (Frank and Anderson 1985). As will be explored in greater depth in the next section, the decline in sexual frequency in the later years of marriage is more a by-product of physical changes associated with aging than with role responsibilities.

Extramarital Sex

Extramarital sex—sexual infidelity in marriage—is relatively uncommon. Studies show that the vast majority of couples are sexually faithful in marriage. According to data from the National Health and Social Life Survey, more than 80 percent of women and 65 to 85 percent of men are monogamous in marriage (Michael et al.

1994). These statistics are corroborated by almost identical figures from the General Social Survey. Researchers believe that extramarital sex is relatively uncommon for several reasons (Michael et al. 1994). First, there are strong social pressures to remain sexually faithful in marriage. Second, married couples are usually so busy managing family life and work that they have little time or energy available for finding other sexual partners and maintaining extramarital affairs. Finally, husbands and wives may remain faithful because they do not want to jeopardize their marriage. As people get older, they realize that finding a new partner for a second marriage would not be as easy as it was the first time (Michael et al. 1994).

Sexuality in Later Life

Brecher (1984) surveyed 4,246 women and men 50 years old or older regarding their sexual behavior. He found that despite growing health problems—such as heart attacks, diabetes, and hypertension—older men and women continue to "engage in sex and to enjoy sex" (p. 406), with respondents in their eighties reporting a regular sex life and orgasms. Nevertheless, sexual frequency naturally declines with aging. As part of his analysis, Brecher compared healthy and less healthy participants and found a steady decline in sexual frequency decade by decade for both groups. All adults, regardless of health, experience physiological changes associated with aging that contribute to a decline in the frequency of sexual intercourse. Older adults have a decrease in blood flow, which makes getting and maintaining an erection more difficult for men and reduces vaginal lubrication in women. Also, nerve endings in the genitals become less sensitive, so it takes longer for older adults to become sexually aroused. The drop in estrogen levels in postmenopausal women not only contributes to vaginal dryness but also may reduce women's sex drive.

Fortunately, the decline in sexual function and frequency in older adults does not necessarily lead to a decline in sexual pleasure (Brecher 1984). Many older people report enjoying sex as much or more as when they were younger. Without the fear of pregnancy and stress from children and work, older couples are better able to relax and take more time with each other, which increases sexual pleasure and their sense of intimacy.

Sexuality and the Perennial Variables

Race and ethnicity, social class, and gender—the perennial sociological variables—affect sexual behavior and relationships. The influence of these variables on sexuality has been briefly mentioned in several places in this chapter. This section considers the impact of race and ethnicity, social class, and gender differences on sexual behavior and relationships in greater depth. Although the three variables are discussed separately, they are strongly interrelated, as you will see.

Race and Ethnicity

Sterk-Elifson (1994: 100) states, "Each racial group has some distinctive attitudes, norms, beliefs, and values regarding . . . sexuality." Unfortunately, until recently social scientists either ignored differences in sexual behavior and norms between racial and ethnic groups or simply compared minority groups to whites and described any behavior that differed from the white majority as deviant or dysfunctional. The most glaring example of such ethnocentrism can be seen in some of the information disseminated about African American sexuality. The consistent finding that African Americans tend to become sexually active at younger ages (65 percent of black males and 37 percent of black females report first having intercourse at age 15 or younger, compared to 32 percent of white males and 19 percent of white females) and have more sexual partners than whites (Cortese 1989; Sterk-Elifson 1994; Treboux and Busch-Rossnagel 1991) was seen by some social scientists as an indicator that blacks were sexual savages. Such racist and ethnocentric ideas left African Americans "stymied by . . . the prevailing myth that Blacks are unable to control their sex drives or satisfy their sexual urges" (Leavy 1993: 126).

Fortunately, most scholars today study and interpret racial and ethnic differences in sexuality differently. In terms of the research that is conducted, contemporary social scientists are more apt to make comparisons both between and within racial groups. In the past, racial minority groups were treated as homogenous, so the behavior of a small group of respondents was assumed to characterize the behavior of an entire race or ethnic group. Furthermore, researchers are more likely to control for social class when looking at race and ethnicity. Previous studies of race and sexuality routinely compared samples of lower socioeconomic-status minorities with middle-class whites (Cortese 1989). As a result, differences in sexual behavior that were a product of social class were attributed to race.

Improvements in research strategies have led to a more accurate understanding of the impact of race and ethnicity on sexual behavior and values. Sociologists now know that sexual attitudes and behaviors vary considerably within racial and ethnic groups. African American females of higher socioeconomic status tend to be less sexually permissive than poorer black women, a pattern quite different from white females, whose sexual permissiveness tends to increase with social class (Cortese 1989). Although scant data are available, it appears there also is much variation in the sexual behavior and attitudes of Hispanic and Latin Americans. Lower socioeconomic-status mainland Puerto Ricans are likely to have high cohabitation rates and low marriage rates, but poor Mexican Americans tend to reject cohabitation in favor of marriage. As Oropesa (1996) explains, the strong Catholic background in Mexican American culture has led marriage to be valued as an "affirmation of womanhood" and a "part of God's plan." Asians tend to be more sexually conservative than other groups (Lear 1997). Huang and Uba (1992) find that compared to whites, Chinese American men and women are less likely to engage in premarital intercourse and they are older when they have their first experience of sexual intercourse.

Many of the differences in sexual behaviors and attitudes once attributed to race are now known to be related to social class. The younger ages of sexual intercourse among African Americans are most common in urban, economically disadvantaged communities. African Americans living in such neighborhoods have few job or educational opportunities that would provide incentive to postpone sexual activity. Furthermore, African American youth growing up in poverty also are likely to return from school to a home with no adult supervision because both parents or single-parent mothers are working, allowing young people more opportunities to engage in sexual experimentation (Bowser 1994).

Social Class

As you have seen, lower socioeconomic status is linked with early first intercourse and higher rates of teenage childbearing. Rates of unprotected sexual intercourse and teenage pregnancy are lowest among adolescents who are "motivated to avoid early birth"—namely, young people from economically secure homes who have the opportunity to attain a good job and income by completing high school and attending college (Kalmuss 1992: 490). The fact that minority groups tend to be disproportionately poor helps account for their higher rates of premarital sex and out-of-wedlock births.

Social class affects sexuality within marriage, as well. In her ground-breaking qualitative study of working-class families, Rubin (1976) reports that attitudes regarding marital sexual practices differ between white middle- and working-class couples. Although the working- and middle-class couples she studied engaged in "essentially the same kinds of sexual behaviors in roughly the same proportions" (p. 138), working-class women were less comfortable with sexual experimentation, such as performing fellatio (oral sex) on their husbands, than middle-class women. Working-class wives reported that they felt awkward and guilty engaging in such acts, whereas middle-class wives had a more relaxed attitude about such practices. Rubin argues that middle-class women who have attended college are more comfortable with a wide variety of sexual practices because they learned in both the classroom and through their peers that behaviors such as oral sex are fairly common. Working-class females tend to see sexual acts other than vaginal intercourse as deviant, and furthermore are likely to hold more traditional sex-role attitudes, believing that so-called nice, respectable girls do not participate in such behaviors. Middle-class wives tend to hold less rigid gender stereotypes and therefore feel more comfortable engaging in a wide variety of sexual acts and positions with their husbands.

Gender

In summarizing the findings of their study, Sprecher and McKinney (1993: 149) point out that the one consistent theme that emerged from their research "was the many gender differences in sexuality in close relationships." The gender dif-

Do men and women view love and sex differently? How do the three main theoretical perspectives in sociology help explain gender differences in sexual attitudes, behaviors, and relationships?

ferences they found were in the areas of sexual permissiveness and the meaning attached to sexual relationships.

Gender and Sexual Permissiveness

Sexual permissiveness can be measured in a variety of ways, including age at first intercourse, beliefs about the appropriateness of premarital sex and sex acts, and attitudes regarding infidelity. On all of these measures, males tend to be more permissive than females. Males, regardless of race or social class, tend to experience sexual intercourse at younger ages than females. Statistics from Planned Parenthood reveal that among 15-year-olds, 27 percent of females and 33 percent of males have experienced vaginal intercourse; by age 19, 75 percent of females and 86 percent of males have engaged in sexual intercourse ("Sexual and Contraceptive Behavior" 1997). Men also tend to be much more accepting of premarital sex in casual dating relationships (Wilson and Medora 1990) and are more tolerant of infidelity in dating relationships (Sprecher and McKinney 1993) than women.

Gender, Sexuality, and Emotion

Sexual intercourse and sexual relationships are likely to have different meanings to men and women. Virtually all research on gender and sexuality shows that females desire emotional involvement in a sexual relationship more than men. In a survey of college students, 85 percent of women and 40 percent of men reported that emotional involvement was a prerequisite for participating in sexual intercourse "always" or "most of the time," whereas only 15 percent of women and a whopping 60 percent of men said that emotional involvement was "never" or only "sometimes" required for sexual intercourse (Ivy and Backlund 1994). Leigh asked 844 male and female subjects to rank in order of importance a list of reasons for engaging in sexual activity (reported in Ivy and Backlund 1994). Males rated "pleasure," "pleasing one's partner," and "relieving tension" as more important reasons for having sex than females did; females rated "emotional closeness" as more important in deciding to engage in sex than men did. Leigh further explored the meaning attached to sexual relationships by asking subjects what their primary reason for refusing sexual intercourse would be. The majority of women said they would refuse sex if there was "not enough love or commitment"; the majority of males reported they would "never neglect an opportunity [for sex]" (Ivy and Backlund 1994).

Gender differences in the meaning attached to sex tend to disappear in the later stages of dating relationships. When couples are described as in love or engaged, males and females are equally accepting of sexual intercourse (Wilson and Medora 1990). Men's and women's expectations regarding sexual intimacy are often "out of sync" in the early stages of dating, which can lead to disagreements, frustration, and conflict (Roche and Ramsbey 1993: 70). Other researchers have found that the best predictor of sex in the early stages of a dating relationship is conflict (Christopher and Cate 1988). Men, who desire sex earlier in the relationship and who may experience pressure from male peers to be sexually active, are likely to pressure women into sex earlier in the relationship than the women prefer.

The Phenomenon of Date Rape

Conflicts over the desired timing of sexual intercourse in dating relationships can contribute to date rape—a social problem identified in recent years. In one of the best-known studies of date rape on college campuses, Warshaw (1988) reports that 1 in 4 females had been victims of a rape or an attempted rape, 84 percent of the victims knew their attackers, and 56 percent of those rapes or attempted rapes occurred on dates. Another study reports similar findings: 22 percent of the women had been forced into a sexual act, and 96 percent of the victims knew the perpetrators (Schrof and Wagner 1994).

Several factors, in addition to couples' disagreements over the timing of sexual intercourse, help explain date rape (Ivy and Backlund 1994; Sprecher and McKinney 1993; Warshaw 1988). The use of drugs or alcohol by either or both partners increases the risk of date rape, because inhibitions may be lowered and it is more difficult for a woman to resist an attack while intoxicated. Warshaw (1988) reports that many males intentionally tried to get their dates drunk so they could more easily overpower them.

Male membership in peer groups, especially in fraternities where alcohol use is common, also can contribute to date rape. Males may encourage friends to "accept aggression as an acceptable way to obtain sex" (Sprecher and McKinney 1993: 140).

The socialization of women to be passive and men to be aggressive also helps explain date rape. Rather than forcefully and directly telling a partner *no*, many women try to communicate their lack of desire for sex indirectly and politely, leaving room for men to intentionally or unintentionally misinterpret their signals (Warshaw 1988). The media, which commonly depict sexual encounters in which the woman initially resists but eventually passionately succumbs, may encourage the male to persist in aggressively pursuing his partner, even after she has communicated her unwillingness to have sex.

At the root of all date rapes lies power inequality and males' desire for control. In American culture, as in most Western societies, men are vested with more economic and political power in relationships, which many males believe also entitles them to sexual favors. As with stranger rape, date rape is intended to control one's partner and express anger or hostility rather than to obtain sexual pleasure.

Gender and the Double Standard

At the turn of the third millennium, to what extent does a sexual double standard persist in American culture? Researchers today agree that the traditional double standard, which forbade women to engage in premarital sex but allowed men such freedom, has been relaxed. However, dual sexual standards for women and men still exist in American culture. Today, a conditional or transitional double standard exists in which it is considered socially acceptable for females to engage in premarital sex so long as they are in a monogamous, ongoing relationship and care about their partners; males continue to be allowed more sexual freedom— being free to have sex in casual, short-term relationships without acquiring a stigmatizing reputation (Rubin 1990; Sprecher, McKinney, and Orbuch 1987).

Evidence that a conditional, more subtle double standard exists can be found in much social science research. For instance, females who engaged in premarital intercourse at age 16 were judged more negatively than males who had done exactly the same (Sprecher et al. 1987). One study asked male and female subjects to evaluate the following statements (Robinson et al. 1991): (1) "A man who has had sexual intercourse with a great many women is immoral" and (2) "A woman who has had sexual intercourse with a great many men is immoral." Responses indicated that both men and women believe that a woman who has had multiple sex partners is more immoral than a man.

The three main theoretical perspectives in sociology can be used to help explain the persistence of a double standard. Structural functionalists would argue that the greater social control placed on women's sexuality serves the function of preventing unwanted out-of-wedlock pregnancies (Maccorquodale 1989). Men, who are believed to be biologically "driven" to be the sexual aggressors to ensure that their genes are reproduced, must have their sexuality held in check through women's unwillingness to participate in sexual intercourse outside of marriage for fear of ruining their reputations. Therefore, a social arrangement in which women are the sexual gatekeepers and males are the sexual aggressors evolved.

Marxist and feminist conflict theorists would argue that the greater social control over women's sexuality is just one more manifestation of the patriarchal power that men gain by virtue of controlling the economic assets in society and individual relationships. Marxists believe that with the advent of capitalism, males needed to ensure that the (male) children their spouses bore were indeed their own flesh and blood to whom they could pass down their surplus wealth. Therefore, women—who were dependent on marriage for survival—had their sexuality controlled with the threat of being deemed unmarriageable if they did not remain virgins until the wedding night. The loosening of the double standard in recent years would be attributed to women's increased economic self-sufficiency.

Symbolic interactionists would not try to explain the origins of the double standard, but rather its persistence in culture. Symbolic interactionists point to the role of socialization in keeping dual sexual standards alive. As Sprecher and colleagues (1987: 30) point out, "Men and women continue to be taught two sets of standards and values about sexuality—one for men's behavior and one for women's." From very young ages, individuals learn that the norms about when, with whom, and under what circumstances sex is appropriate differ for women and men. These norms are communicated and reinforced in a variety of ways. Women and men adopt different "sexual scripts" (Metts and Cupach 1989); women must subtly suggest or hint at their interest in sexual activity and men are supposed to interpret women's desires from their tone of voice, body language, and facial expressions (Ivy and Backlund 1994). Social rewards, such as prestige and admiration, are bestowed for conforming to sexual norms, and social penalties, including social rejection and stigma, are levied for rejecting sexual norms.

Sexuality and Sexually Transmitted Infections

Today, perhaps more than ever before, sexually active individuals must be aware of the risk of contracting a sexually transmitted disease or infection. Physicians make a distinction between *sexually transmitted diseases (STDs)* and *sexually transmitted infections (STIs)* (Laumann et al. 1994). Sexually transmitted infections lead to sexually transmitted diseases. One can have an STI without having the disease, such as those who are infected with the human immunodeficiency virus (HIV) but do not yet have the acquired immune deficiency syndrome (AIDS).

One can have an STI without having any symptoms and unknowingly spread the infection to others.

The risk of contracting an STI is influenced by three factors (Laumann et al. 1994): infectivity, partner risk, and practice risk. Infectivity refers to the likelihood of contracting an STI from a single exposure to an infected person. **Infectivity** rates of STIs vary dramatically. For instance, gonorrhea infectivity rates are extremely high. The risk of an infected man passing the gonorrhea infection to a woman in one episode of sexual contact is .50, which means there is a 50 percent chance a woman will contract the disease from a single exposure to an infected man (Laumann et al. 1994); the infectivity rate for men contracting the disease from an infected woman is .25 (Masters et al. 1995). Infectivity rates of HIV are relatively low; the probability of a woman contracting HIV from a single act of vaginal intercourse with an infected man is 1 in 500, and the probability of a man contracting the disease from a single act of vaginal intercourse with an infected woman is 1 in 700 (Masters et al. 1995).

Partner risk also influences the chances one has of contracting an STI. Familiarity with a partner's sexual history is important in reducing this risk. The better people know their partners, the more likely they are to be aware if the partners are infectious or at high risk for infection. Exclusivity also is a component of partner risk; the more partners either person in the relationship has had or currently has increases the risk of an STI being transmitted. For a person in a monogamous, long-term relationship with an uninfected partner, the risk of contracting an STI from sexual contact with that partner is zero (Laumann et al. 1994).

The third factor that influences the chances of contracting an STI is **practice risk.** Some practices decrease the risk of contracting an infection, whereas others increase the risk. Condom use is a practice that reduces the chance of contracting an STI, whereas alcohol use during or immediately prior to sexual intercourse increases the risk of infection transmission. The use of alcohol is a high-risk practice because people may exercise less caution in partner selection or condom use while intoxicated and may also engage in rougher sexual activity, which increases the risk of breaking the skin and transmitting a blood-borne infection. Anal intercourse is an especially high-risk sexual practice for spreading the HIV infection because of the physical trauma caused to the lining of the rectum. The risk of HIV transmission from a single act of unprotected anal intercourse with an infected person is between 1 in 50 and 1 in 100 (Masters et al. 1995).

The sexually transmitted disease that causes the greatest public concern today is AIDS, which was first identified in a 1982 publication by the Centers for Disease Control (CDC) ("Definition of AIDS" 1997). AIDS is caused by the human immunodeficiency virus, which destroys the body's ability to fight infections and some cancers (*HIV Infection and AIDS* 1997). Between June 1981 and December 31, 1994, there were 441,528 AIDS cases in the United States reported to the CDC. In that same time frame, 270,870 AIDS-related deaths were reported ("Quantifying the Epidemic" 1997). The World Health Organization estimates that by the year 2000, 30 to 40 million people worldwide will be infected with

HIV and 10 million people will have developed AIDS ("Quantifying the Epidemic" 1997).

HIV is most commonly spread through sex with an infected person. According to the United States Public Health Service, "The virus can enter the body through the lining of the vagina, vulva, penis, rectum, or mouth during sex" (*Transmission* 1997). The virus also can be spread through contact with infected blood or contaminated needles during intravenous drug use or blood transfusions. In 1985, a technique of heat-treating donated blood was developed that has made the risk of acquiring HIV through transfusions extremely small (*Transmission* 1997).

Although women have greater infectivity risks of contracting HIV through intercourse because of potential vaginal tears, males have higher death rates from AIDS. AIDS is now the leading cause of death among males ages 25 to 44 and is the fourth-leading cause of death among women of the same age ("Distribution of AIDS Cases" 1997; U.S. Bureau of the Census 1996). Higher rates of intravenous drug use and anal intercourse among men, both high-risk practices, account for the greater number of AIDS deaths in males. AIDS rates also vary by race and ethnicity (see Figure 9.2), with the epidemic spreading fastest among minority populations, particularly African American males. AIDS is six times more prevalent among African Americans and three times more common among Hispanics than among whites (*HIV Infection and AIDS* 1997). Higher rates of intravenous drug use and lower rates of condom use among minority populations help account for the more rapid spread of the disease.

The only way to prevent HIV infection is to avoid behaviors that put one at risk, particularly having unprotected intercourse and sharing needles. The Public Health Service recommends that individuals abstain from sex or use latex condoms during oral, anal, or vaginal sex with someone they do not know for certain is HIV free (Prevention 1997). Repeated blood testing or never engaging in any risky behavior are the only ways to be sure one is not HIV infected (*Prevention* 1997).

Figure 9.2

Distribution of AIDS Deaths by Race/Ethnicity, 1995

Source: U.S. Bureau of the Census, *Statistical Abstract of the United States, 1996,* Table 134, p. 99.

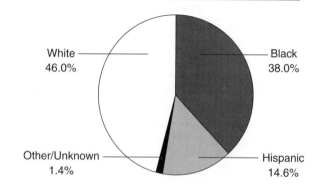

White
46.0%

Black
38.0%

Other/Unknown
1.4%

Hispanic
14.6%

Summary

Sexual attitudes and behaviors changed considerably in American society during the twentieth century. Researchers have measured and documented these changes through experimental and survey research. The increased acceptance and practice of premarital sex that began in the 1960s, known as the sexual revolution, is particularly interesting to sociologists. Several factors that contributed to the sexual revolution have been identified, including more reliable contraception, the women's movement, coeducational dormitory facilities, delayed marriage, and earlier sexual maturity.

Human sexual behavior varies considerably across the life cycle. Adolescence is a time of sexual experimentation for many. Age at first intercourse and contraceptive use among teenagers have increased in recent years, which contributed to the recent decline in unplanned teenage pregnancies. Adults are more likely than teenagers to engage in nonmarital sexual activity. Most research on marital sexuality focuses on the declining frequency of intercourse over the course of the marriage, which can be attributed to both biological and social factors. Extramarital sex is frequently portrayed by the media, but in reality is relatively uncommon. Older adults experience physiological changes that lead to a decline in sexual function and frequency, but most older people report they enjoy active, satisfying sex lives.

In addition to age, the perennial variables of race, social class, and gender have an impact on sexual norms and behaviors. It is important to recognize that sexual attitudes and behaviors vary within and between racial groups and social classes. Gender, perhaps more than any other variable, strongly influences one's sexual values. Sexual permissiveness, the meaning attached to sex within a relationship, and degrees of sexual freedom are influenced by gender norms within society.

Sexually transmitted diseases and infections are an acute problem in today's society. The risk of contracting a sexually transmitted infection is influenced by infectivity, partner risk, and practice risk.

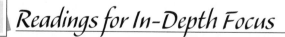

Readings for In-Depth Focus

Sexual Activity and Relationship Type

Sexual activity is an important part of intimate romantic relationships, but it is also very private. Most of us are curious about how often other couples engage in various forms of sexual activity because we want assurance that what we do and how often we do it is "normal." Although it is interesting to read what others reveal about their sex lives, very few of us would want to disclose this information about ourselves to others—especially strangers. Therefore, it is difficult to gather accurate, reliable data on human sexual behavior. In the following reading, Susan Sprecher and Kathleen McKinney summarize the available data on sexual frequency in married, cohabiting, dating, and homosexual couples. As you ponder the statistics, consider what types of people might be providing this information and how their particular characteristics may influence the researchers' findings. Compare the data on sexual frequency in the four types of relationships discussed and try to come up with as many explanations for why the rates of sexual activity differ. Think about what role sexual activity serves in each type of relationship.

■ ■ ■

Sexual Behaviors in Close Couples

Susan Sprecher and Kathleen McKinney

Most couples spend only a small portion of their shared time engaged in genital contact. As estimated by Ford (1980), "couples spend some 15 minutes per week actually copulating, which would amount to 99.9% of their time doing something else" (p. 49). Yet these 15 minutes, plus the time engaged in foreplay, afterplay, and preparation for sex, are an essential part of most sexually bonded relationships. . . .

MEASUREMENT OF SEXUAL FREQUENCY

Sexual frequency typically is measured in large survey studies by one direct question. For example, in their landmark survey study conducted with a national sample of 969 gay, 788 lesbian, and 4,314 cohabiting and married heterosexual couples, Blumstein and Schwartz (1983) asked the following question "About how often during the last year have you and your partner had

sexual relations?" The options ranged from 1= *daily or almost every day* to 7= *a few times.*

Other researchers have asked about sexual frequency without presenting a set of response options (an open-ended question). For example, the question asked of women in the National Fertility Studies (Trussell & Westoff, 1980; Westoff, 1974) was "In the past four weeks, how many times have you had intercourse?"

SEXUAL FREQUENCY IN MARRIED COUPLES

Although research on sex has increased dramatically in the past few decades, research on *marital sexuality* has not (e.g., Greenblat, 1983). One issue about marital sex that continues to be investigated, however, is sexual intercourse frequency. This issue has been of interest because of its association with fertility (a topic that interests sociologists in the field of demography) and because it is assumed that sex reflects the quality of the relationship (a topic that interests researchers in the field of marriage and the family).

Rates among Newly Married (Young) Couples

Many textbooks and popular books on sexuality and marriage state that young married couples in the United States have sex approximately two to three times per week (e.g., Crooks & Baur, 1990; Hyde, 1990). The data from the landmark sexuality studies conducted by Kinsey and his colleagues (Kinsey, Pomeroy, & Martin, 1948; Kinsey et al., 1953) and Hunt (1974) are most often cited as sources for this statistic. Kinsey and his colleagues interviewed 5,300 men for *Sexual Behavior in the Human Male* (1948) and 5,940 women for *Sexual Behavior in the Human Female* (1953). Although their sample was not random, they attempted to obtain respondents from all walks of life. Twenty years later, Hunt surveyed 2,026 adults randomly chosen from phone directories in 24 cities in the United States. Although Hunt's sample was a probability one, only 20% of those initially contacted agreed to participate. People who agree to participate in a sex study may be different (e.g., more sexually liberal) than people who decline (Morokoff, 1986). Thus one must keep in mind that these samples may not have been representative of the entire U.S. population.

Kinsey et al. (Kinsey, Pomeroy, & Martin, 1948; Kinsey, Pomeroy, Martin, & Gephard, 1953) found that the median frequency of marital sexual intercourse per week was 2.45 for respondents in the 16–25 age group and 1.95 for those in the 26–35 age group. Hunt (1974), more than 20 years later, found a higher level of sexual frequency for each age group than did Kinsey et al. For example, Hunt's youngest age group (18–24) had sex an average of 3.25 times per week. Hunt (1974) wrote: "The data show that there has been an important, even historic, increase in the typical (median) frequency of marital coitus throughout the population" (p. 189). As Hunt explained, various "contemporary forces" liberated marital sexuality over this period. These forces included more general sexual liberation, women's liberation, increases in erotic material (e.g., books, magazines, films), and the availability of more effective contraceptive methods (e.g., the birth control pill was introduced in the early 1960s).

Blumstein and Schwartz (1983) conducted their national (nonprobability) study 10 years after Hunt's study and also found that young married couples had sex relatively frequently. They reported that 45% of their heterosexual couples married for 2 years or less had sex three times per week or more, and another 38% had sex between one and three times per week. For couples married 2 to 10 years, comparable percentages were 27% and 46%.

Data on the frequency of marital sexual intercourse also have been obtained in large-scale studies that focus on childbearing decisions and fertility. These studies, conducted with national probability samples, have found rates slightly lower than those found in the sexuality studies described above. Westoff (1974) analyzed data from a probability sample of women under age 45, interviewed in 1965 for the National Fertility Studies (NFS), and reported that they had sex an average of 6.8 times over a 4-week period (or 1.7 times per week). He further found that a different national sample of women interviewed 5 years later, in 1970, reported that they had sex 8.2 times for a 4-week period (or slightly more than two times per week). This was an increase of 21% in intercourse frequency over 5 years, which provides further evidence that the frequency of marital sex increased in the 1960s. Trussell and Westoff (1980) extended this earlier study by including NFS data for 1975. They found a continued increase of sexual intercourse frequency between 1970 and 1975, although the increase was not as large as during the earlier period. In another study of fertility decision making, Udry (1980) conducted a longitudinal study of women who were all under the age of 30 at the time of the first interview. He reported that the mean frequency of sexual intercourse for a 4-week period was 10.01 in 1974, 8.45 in 1977, and 7.75 in 1978. Thus marital sex for these women declined from around 2.5 times per week to less than twice per week over a 4-year period.

The rates reported in the above studies were based on aggregate data; that is, the data were summarized across respondents. If we examine individual relationships in these samples, however, we find considerable variation in how often married couples had sex. Some married couples were celibate or had sex very infrequently (perhaps only on special occasions), whereas other couples had sex at least daily. This variation occurred even within the first year of marriage. Greenblat (1983) interviewed 80 persons married 5 years or less and reported that "the most striking finding concerning the frequency of intercourse during the first year of marriage is the wide *range* of responses" (p. 291). The monthly intercourse frequency reported by the respondents for the first year ranged from 1 to 45.

The Decline of Marital Sexual Intercourse over Time

> It's declined. As a friend of mine used to tell me, if you took a piggy bank and put a nickel in for every time you had sex during the first year of your marriage, and then did it for the second year, you would have saved less and less money as the years went on. It's declined considerably, but for reasons of strength, not a lack of interest. We just get tired and preoccupied with things and pressures here and there. We used to make love every night and now we don't. But our relationship hasn't decreased. As I said, the spirit is willing, but the flesh is weak. (a husband interviewed by Blumstein & Schwartz, 1983, p. 200)

A decline in sexual frequency over the course of a relationship and over the course of

one's lifetime is probably one of those "sure" things in life—like death and taxes. One sex researcher stated, "It has been observed since ancient times that frequency of intercourse declines with age in human beings" (Udry, 1980, p. 320). It should be noted, however, that although frequency may decline with age, the ability to have and enjoy sexual activities extends across the life span.

In all studies on marital sexual frequency that have included respondents from different age groups and/or respondents married for different lengths of time (*cross-sectional studies*), it has been found that respondents who were younger and/or married for a shorter length of time had sex more frequently than couples who were older and/or were married for a longer period of time (e.g., Blumstein & Schwartz, 1983; Edwards & Booth, 1976; Greeley, 1991; Hunt, 1974; James, 1983; Kinsey et al., 1948; Kinsey et al., 1953; Trussell & Westoff, 1980; Westoff, 1974). For example, Figure 1 shows the decline with age found among married respondents (both first marrieds and remarrieds) from the National Survey of Family and Households, which is a large survey study of a national, representative sample of adults, conducted in 1987–1988 (Call, Sprecher, & Schwartz, 1992). *Longitudinal panel studies* (the same people are surveyed more than once over a period of time) also have documented a decline in marital intercourse frequency (e.g., James, 1981; Udry, 1980). Finally, *retrospective studies*, in which couples or individuals are asked how often they have sex now and how often they had sex at earlier times in their relationship, also have documented a decline (e.g., Greenblat, 1983). The decline in sexual frequency may be greatest over the first year of marriage. This phenomenon has been called the "honeymoon effect." For example, James (1981) analyzed diaries kept by newlyweds and found that the median frequency of sex in the first month of marriage was over 17 times, but frequency declined to approximately 8 times per month by the end of the first year.

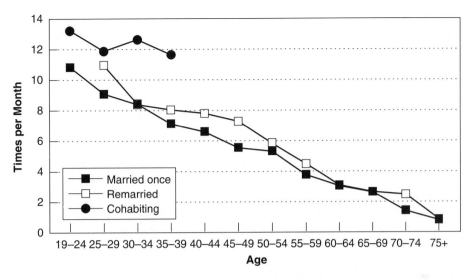

FIGURE 1 **Frequency of Sexual Intercourse by Age** (data from Call, Sprecher, & Schwartz, 1992)

James (1981) hypothesized that the rate declines by approximately one-half across the first year and then takes another 20 years to halve again.

In most of the research examining the decline of marital intercourse frequency over time, the partners' ages and the length of the marriage are treated somewhat interchangeably because age and marriage length are highly correlated in the general population. Therefore it is difficult to know whether a decline over time in sexual intercourse frequency is due to factors associated with the aging process or to factors associated with being in a relationship for a long time (e.g., the novelty wearing off). The following fable suggests that novelty wears off over time in one particular relationship:

One day President and Mrs. Coolidge were visiting a government farm. Soon after their arrival they were taken off on separate tours. When Mrs. Coolidge passed the chicken pens she paused to ask the man in charge if the rooster copulates more *than once each day. "Dozens of times," was the reply. "Please tell that to the President," Mrs. Coolidge requested. When the President passed the pens and was told about the rooster, he asked, "Same hen every time?" "Oh no, Mr. President, a different one each time." The President nodded slowly, then said, "Tell that to Mrs. Coolidge."* (Bermant, 1976, pp. 76–77)

This fable suggests that if people found a new partner (or several new partners) later in life, they may return to a sexual frequency rate similar to what they experienced at a younger age. On the other hand, we also know that, later in life, ill health and physiological changes can reduce sexual frequency and, in some cases, even can lead to the cessation of sexual activity (Riportella-Muller, 1989). One physiological change that has been blamed for the decline of sexual frequency with age is the decrease in production of androgen, the hormone linked to sexual interest in both males and females (e.g., Udry, Deven, & Coleman, 1982).

In reality, probably both factors—duration of marriage and age of partners—contribute to the decline of sexual intercourse frequency over time. Blumstein and Schwartz (1983) were able to examine the unique effects of both factors in explaining the decline in sexual intercourse frequency. They found that for married couples the impact of age and duration of the relationship were approximately equal. Both negatively affected sexual intercourse frequency and to about the same degree.

Some research has looked at whether the man's age or the woman's age contributes more to the decline in sexual intercourse frequency. Blumstein and Schwartz (1983) reported that the husband's age seemed to have a slightly greater (negative) impact on sexual frequency than the wife's age. Other research has found that the husband's age is more highly associated with the decline (James, 1974; Kinsey et al., 1948; Kinsey et al., 1953), although some research has shown just the opposite (e.g., James, 1983; Udry et al., 1982; Udry & Morris, 1978).

How do couples account for the decline of sexual intercourse over their marriage? Greenblat (1983) examined the accounts that married men and women gave for changes in frequency of sex over the first few years of their marriage. For those married more than 1 year, 69% reported that their current rate was lower than their first-year rate (only 6% reported an increase). She reported that, after the first year, "almost everything—children, jobs, commuting, housework, financial worries—that happens to a couple conspires to reduce the degree of sexual interactions while almost nothing leads to increasing it" (p. 294). The accounts that the respondents provided for the decline in sexual intercourse frequency fell into four major categories: (a) birth-control and pregnancy-related reasons (e.g., "I wasn't interested for a while after the pregnancy, and he got used to it less often"), (b) children (the resulting fatigue and lack of privacy), (c) work (e.g., heavy work schedules, work-related fatigue), and (d) famil-

iarity. Greenblat reported that the most common response in the accounts was familiarity, which sometimes was presented in a negative way (e.g., "We've gotten into a routine with each other, and it's not as exciting anymore"), sometimes in a neutral way, and sometimes in a positive way ("There are other things that satisfy us besides sex: reading to each other, listening to music together . . .").

Rubin (1990) also addressed the question of "What happens to sex in marriage over time?" in her recent interview study conducted with almost 1,000 people from all over the United States. She concluded:

> On the most mundane level, the constant negotiation about everyday tasks leaves people harassed, weary, irritated and feeling more like traffic cops than lovers. Who's going to do the shopping, pay the bills, take care of the laundry, wash the dishes, take out the garbage, clean the bathroom, get the washing machine fixed, decide what to eat for dinner, return the phone calls from friends and parents? When there are children, the demands, complications and exhaustion increase exponentially. And hovering above it all are the financial concerns that beset most families in the nation today. . . .
>
> Even when relative harmony reigns, the almost endless series of tasks, demands, and needs unfilled do nothing to foster the kind of romantic feelings that tend to stimulate sexual desire. "Christ, by the time we get through dealing with all the shit of living who cares about sex? I sometimes think it's a miracle that we still want to do it at all," said 28-year-old Brian, a Detroit factory worker, married nine years, the father of two small children. (p. 165)

Other Factors That Affect Sexual Frequency in Marriage

As described above, the number of years married and the ages of partners strongly affect how often married couples have sex. Very few other factors have been found to affect sexual intercourse frequency consistently or strongly. Some social background factors that have been found to modestly decrease sexual intercourse frequency, at least in some studies, include pregnancy, number of children (especially small ones), demanding jobs, being Catholic, living in a rural area, traditional attitudes about sex roles, the female working out of necessity rather than because of career motivations, and not using effective contraceptive methods (e.g., Call et al., 1992; Edwards & Booth, 1976; Trussell & Westoff, 1980; Westoff, 1974).

SEXUAL FREQUENCY IN COHABITING COUPLES

The number of unmarried heterosexual couples who live together has increased dramatically in the past few decades. In a number of studies, sexual frequency in cohabiting relationships has been compared with sexual frequency in marital relationships. One problem with making these comparisons, however, is that cohabiting cou-

ples eventually either marry or break up, which makes it difficult to find cohabiting couples who have been together for a long period of time. Thus cohabiting couples most often are compared with married couples who are in their first years of marriage.

Blumstein and Schwartz (1983) found that cohabiting couples had sex more frequently than married couples. For example, although 45% of the married couples married 2 years or less had sex three times or more per week, the measure for cohabiting couples was 61% (shown in Figure 2). Other studies also have found that cohabitors have sex more frequently than marrieds. Newcomb (1983) reviewed findings from several studies (e.g., Perlman & Abramson, 1982) conducted in the 1970s and early 1980s on cohabiting relationships and reported that cohabitors had a greater frequency of sexual intercourse than married couples. In fact, Figure 1, based on the data from the National Survey of Family and Households (Call et al., 1992), also shows that cohabiting couples have

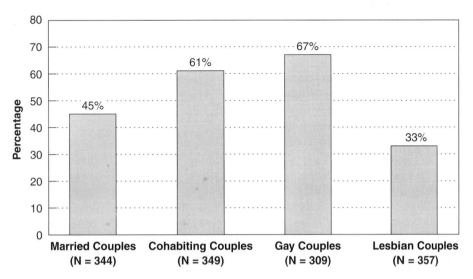

FIGURE 2   Percentage of Couples in Their First Two Years Together Who Have Sex Three Times a Week or More (data from Blumstein & Schwartz, 1983)

sex more frequently than married couples. Co-habiting couples also experience a decline in sexual intercourse frequency with increasing age.

Cohabiting couples also may have sex more frequently than dating couples. Results of the Boston Dating Couples Study indicate that, of the 40 couples who were living together, approximately 40% reported having sex six times or more per week. Among the dating couples, however, the measure was 12% (Rigman, Hill, Rubin, and Peplau, 1981).

There are at least two explanations for why cohabiting couples may be more sexually active than married couples (and dating couples). First, the individuals who are the "kind of people" who cohabit may be different from people who do not cohabit in ways that would explain the differences in sexual frequency. For example, cohabitors are likely to be sexually liberal and to have liberal sex roles, attitudes that are associated with more frequent sex. Second, a cohabiting relationship may be a "sexier" living arrangement (Blumstein & Schwartz, 1983). Fewer constraints and inhibiting factors in cohabitation, plus the uncertainty of the future of the relationship, may make the relationship more exciting and passionate.

SEXUAL FREQUENCY IN DATING COUPLES

We have very little data on how often dating couples have sex. Most studies on sexuality in dating relationships have examined the incidence (whether or not the couples engage in sex) but not the frequency. There are some exceptions, however.

Above, we reported that Risman et al. (1981) found that 40% of the cohabiting couples but only 12% of the dating couples from the Boston Dating Couples Study had sex six times or more per week. In the major report on the sexuality of the couples from this study, Peplau et al. (1977) reported that the "early-sex" couples, those who had sex relatively early in the relation-

ship (e.g., after 1 month), had sex at a median frequency of four to five times per week. The "later-sex" couples had sex at a lower frequency, about two to three times per week. In another recent study of sexuality in dating couples, a lower frequency was found. From an analysis of the data from a sample of 94 sexually active couples described in Simpson and Gangestad (1991), Simpson (personal communication, February, 1992) reported that the frequency of sex per month for these dating couples was slightly over seven times per month (or less than twice per week). Dating couples may have sex less frequently than cohabiting couples because they have fewer opportunities and less privacy to do so.

If we consider all types of sexual activity (not just sexual intercourse), however, we may find that dating partners have their hands on each other more than do even cohabiting partners. On the basis of her recent interview study, Rubin (1990) wrote:

> Sexual interest and activity are at their height during dating and courtship, take a drop when people begin to live together, then another fall after marriage, and show the most precipitous decline after the first child is born. It may be more or less dramatic, more or less troublesome to the particular individuals involved, but the patterning of the response is undeniable. (p. 163)

SEXUAL FREQUENCY IN HOMOSEXUAL COUPLES

Figure 2 presents data from the Blumstein and Schwartz (1983) study on the percentage of lesbian and gay couples who had sex (genital or oral) very frequently (three times or more per week) during their first years together. As seen in Figure 2, the gay couples had sex more frequently than all other couple types, whereas the lesbian couples had the least frequent sex. Lesbian couples, however, engaged in more nongenital physical contact, such as cuddling, touching, and hugging. Blumstein and Schwartz (1983) also reported that by the time they had been together 10 years or more, gay couples had sex less frequently than the married couples. The gays in more long-term relationships were still very interested in sex, but many now were having sexual contacts outside of their primary relationship. Although Blumstein and Schwartz (1983) reported that lesbians had the lowest frequency of sex of all couple types in their study, not all studies have found low sexual frequency among lesbians. For example, Coleman, Hoon, and Hoon (1983) found that lesbian women had sex more frequently than heterosexual women.

As discussed, marital sexual intercourse frequency declines with number of years married. It also declines in homosexual couples over time (Blumstein & Schwartz, 1983; Peplau, Cochran, Rook, & Padesky, 1978). For example, Blumstein and Schwartz (1983) found that the percentage of gay and lesbian couples who have sex three times or more per week after being together 10 years or more is 11% and 1%, respectively.

REFERENCES

Bermant, G. "Sexual Behavior: Hard Times with the Coolidge Effect." In *Psychological Research: The Inside Story*, edited by M. H. Siegel and H. P. Zeigler. New York: Harper & Row, 1976.

Blumstein, P., and P. Schwartz. *American Couples.* New York: William Morrow, 1983.

Call, V. R. A., S. Sprecher, and P. Schwartz. "The Frequency of Sexual Intercourse in American Couples: A National Sample." Paper presented at the Annual Meeting of the National Council on Family Relations, Orlando, FL, November, 1992.

Coleman, E. M., P. W. Hoon, and E. F. Hoon. "Arousability and Sexual Satisfaction in Lesbian and Heterosexual Women." *Journal of Sex Research,* 19 (1983): 58–73.

Crooks, R., and K. Baur. *Our Sexuality.* Menlo Park, CA: Benjamin/Cummings, 1990.

Edwards, J. N., and A. Booth. "Sexual Behavior In and Out of Marriage: An Assessment of Correlates." *Journal of Marriage and the Family,* 38 (1976): 73–81.

Greeley, A. M. *Faithful Attraction: Discovering Intimacy, Love, and Fidelity in American Marriage.* New York: Doherty, 1991.

Greenblat, C. S. "The Salience of Sexuality in the Early Years of Marriage." *Journal of Marriage and the Family,* 45 (1983): 289–299.

Hunt, M. *Sexual Behavior in the 1970's.* Chicago: Playboy Press, 1974.

Hyde, J. S. *Understanding Human Sexuality.* New York: McGraw-Hill, 1990.

James, W. H. "Marital Coital Rates, Spouses' Ages, Family Size, and Social Class." *Journal of Sex Research,* 10 (1974): 205–218.

———. "The Honeymoon Effect on Marital Coitus." *Journal of Sex Research,* 17 (1981): 114–123.

———. "Decline in Coital Rates with Spouses' Ages and Duration of Marriage." *Journal of Biosocial Science,* 15 (1983): 83–87.

Kinsey, A. C., W. B. Pomeroy, and C. E. Martin. *Sexual Behavior in the Human Male.* Philadelphia: W. B. Saunders, 1948.

Kinsey, A. C., W. B. Pomeroy, C. E. Martin, and P. H. Gephard. *Sexual Behavior in the Human Female.* Philadelphia: W. B. Saunders, 1953.

Morokoff, P. J. "Volunteer Bias in the Psycho-Physiological Study of Female Sexuality. *Journal of Sex Research,* 22 (1986): 35–51.

Newcomb, M. D. "Relationship Qualities of Those Who Live Together." *Alternative Lifetyles,* 6 (1983): 78–102.

Peplau, L. A., S. Cochran, K. Rook, and C. Padesky. "Loving Women: Attachment and Autonomy in Lesbian Relationships." *Journal of Social Issues,* 34 (1978): 7–27.

Peplau, L. A., Z. Rubin, and C. T. Hill. "Sexual Intimacy in Dating Relationships." *Journal of Social Issues,* 33 (1977): 86–109.

Perlman, S. D., and P. R. Abramson. "Sexual Satisfaction Among Married and Cohabiting Individuals." *Journal of Consulting and Clinical Psychology,* 50 (1982): 458–460.

Riportella-Muller, R. "Sexuality in the Elderly: A Review." In *Human Sexuality: The Societal and Interpersonal Context,* edited by K. McKinney and S. Sprecher. Norwood, NJ: Ablex, 1989.

Risman, B. J., C. Hill, Z. Rubin, and L. A. Peplau. "Living Together in College: Implications for Courtship." *Journal of Marriage and the Family,* 43 (1981): 77–83.

Rubin, L. B. *Erotic Wars: What Happened to the Sexual Revolution?* New York: HarperCollins, 1990.

Simpson, J. A., and S. W. Gangestad. "Individual Differences in Socio-Sexuality: Evidence for Convergent and Discriminant Validity." *Journal of Personality and Social Psychology,* 60 (1991): 870–883.

Trussell, J., and C. F. Westoff. "Contraceptive Practice and Trends in Coital Frequency." *Family Planning Perspectives*, 12 (1980): 246–249.

Udry, J. R. "Changes in the Frequency of Marital Intercourse from Panel Data." *Archives of Sexual Behavior*, 9 (1980): 319–325.

Udry, J. R., F. R. Deven, and S. J. Coleman. "A Cross-National Comparison of the Relative Influence of Male and Female Age on the Frequency of Marital Intercourse." *Journal of Biosocial Science*, 14 (1982): 1–6.

Udry, J. R., and N. M. Morris. "Relative Contribution of Male and Female Age to the Frequency of Marital Intercourse." *Social Biology*, 25 (1978): 128–134.

Westoff, C. F. "Coital Frequency and Contraception." *Family Planning Perspectives*, 6 (1974): 136–141.

Critical Thinking Questions

1. What problems do researchers encounter when studying sexual behavior? How do those problems affect the validity and reliability of the data they receive?

2. What explanations do Sprecher and McKinney offer for the decline in sexual frequency among married couples? Discuss any other explanations they have overlooked.

3. Compare the sexual frequency rates of married and cohabiting couples. What factors account for the different rates of sexual activity?

4. Compare the amount of research and data available on the sexual behavior of married couples to the amount of information regarding the sexual habits of cohabiting, dating, and homosexual couples. Why are sexual habits in marriage studied so much more than in other relationships? How do social norms regarding sexual behavior in society influence what and who scholars study?

10 *Marital Relationships and Domestic Partnerships*

*W*hat is a *relationship?* The term is used so cheaply these days. In my mind, a relationship speaks to people in relation to each other. I am related to my husband. We relate to and with each other. We share. We fuss. We laugh. We drink from each other's beers. He does most of the "hunting and gathering," my term for grocery shopping. I mow our 3-acre yard, plant trees, and dabble at gardening. We engage in "domestic beautification" together—forget calling it *housework*. Crank up the music and have a cleaning party! We handle finances and all manner of decisions together. We have dealt with the death of friends and family members together. He helped me give birth to our child. We're turning gray together and still act like we're dating. As my students might say, "Go figure."

This chapter will focus primarily on the concept and measurement of marital adjustment, correlates of marital quality and adjustment, relationship challenges over the life course, factors related to marital conflict, and communication in intimate relationships. Not all marriages are alike, and individual marriages see changes with the passage of time and stages of its life-cycle. These and related issues will be explored in this chapter. Attention will be paid primarily to work conducted in the United States, but will be balanced by work in other countries and cross-national studies, as well.

Marital Adjustment, Relationship Satisfaction, and Quality

Do you perceive yourself to be satisfied in your current relationship? Are you happy in and with this relationship? Are you adjusted to your partner? Adjusted to the relationship? How would you rate the quality of your relationship? Am I asking the same thing in just slightly different ways?

Lewis and Spanier (1979) probably were on target when they wrote that the concept marital quality can be used to encompass the various terms used above. **Marital quality** "is defined as a subjective evaluation of a married couple's relationship" (Lewis and Spanier 1979: 269). Marital quality embraces a number of aspects of marriage, including communication, interaction, and functioning. Marital satisfaction, marital adjustment, and marital happiness can be seen as dimensions of marital quality (Lewis and Spanier 1979).

The emphasis on marital quality in the United States is roughly correlated with a shifting view of marriage. As marriage became less a matter of pooling resources or merging bloodlines and more a voluntary, romance based relationship, the intensity of such an arrangement became noteworthy to sociologists and other social scientists. Sociologists became keenly interested in what made these arrangements happy or unhappy ones. Since the 1930s, academic and everyday interest in the relative happiness or unhappiness, success or failure, and level of quality of relationships, marital and other, have continued if not escalated.

Measuring Marital Quality

Marital quality, adjustment, and marital happiness have proven to be some of the most difficult concepts to measure—at the same time that they have become some of the most important matters in marriages and marriagelike relationships. Work on measuring successful marriages began in the 1920s, with the work of Hamilton. The better known and more sustained work was conducted by Burgess and Cottrell and Burgess and Wallin, primarily in the 1930s and 1940s and into the early 1950s (Locke and Wallace 1959).

Burgess and Cottrell (1939: 47) studied 526 Illinois couples in the mid-1930s. They defined a **well-adjusted marriage** as "one in which the patterns of behavior of the two persons are mutually satisfying." They argued that indicators of problems in martial adjustment "will be found in those items of behavior and attitude which reflect a weakening, or a disturbance, or a disintegration of this relationship" (p. 47). To measure marital adjustment, they created sets of questions that tapped into agreements and disagreements in key areas of married life, such as handling finances, demonstrations of affection, and relationships with in-laws. They also included items regarding loneliness, depression, and feeling miserable or irritable. The assumption was that these feelings might be indicative of problems in the relationship. Other items included frequency of shared activity, assuming that this would provide a measure of how coidentified, or bonded, the couple was in their relationship. Burgess and Cottrell exhaustively studied just about every factor one could think might be related to marital adjustment and happiness. This included an inventory of husbands' and wives' family backgrounds (social class, residence, relationship with parents and siblings, birth order), school experiences of spouses (including grades), history of the courtship, quality of the honeymoon, current occupational status of spouses, frequency of agreement on key matters, and feelings about oneself at the current time (Burgess and Cottrell 1939: 420–429). They were trying to create a "method of predicting before marriage its outcome in marital happiness or unhappiness" (p. 15). The reason for such an exhaustive approach was because they thought that single-item indicators (e.g., How happy are you in your marriage? Very Happy, Somewhat Happy, Happy, Somewhat Unhappy, Very Unhappy) simply would not reveal much or be very useful in predicting marital success or helping couples with problems. The significance of this research is that a general concept of marital adjustment emerged from it (Leslie, 1982).

Just as research on marital quality continues to be criticized either conceptually or on measurement grounds, these early works also met with criticism. These earlier researchers used **scales,** which are sets of categories containing varying numbers of items. Although these early works tended to be clear conceptually, at the same time they varied in their ability to adequately show reliability and validity (Spanier 1976: 17). These earlier studies also focused on married individuals and married couples. It would be a few decades before scales would be created for other relationships, as well. However, it must be said that the sustained work in this area substantiates the idea that science is a self-correcting enterprise. As the decades have gone by, more—in fact, incredibly more—attempts have been made to measure and study marital quality. By 1990, there was so much written on marital quality in the United States that Norval Glenn, charged with the unenviable task of providing the decade review for this area, declared that the work that had been done in the 1980s alone was immense, "far too large to be summarized in one short review article" (Glenn 1990: 818).

The Spanier Dyadic Adjustment Scale

Numerous marital quality scales are in regular use today. By far, the most frequently relied upon is the **Spanier Dyadic Adjustment Scale (DAS)**. This scale is "a mainstay in both marital functioning literature and couple treatment literature" (Hunsley 1995: 236). The DAS (see Figure 10.1 on pages 302–303) is intended for use not only with married couples but other couples, as well. It is for couples who have a meaningful relationship with each other, where there is identification as a couple, and where there is commitment to each other and to the relationship. I am making this clear in order that you garner the gist of what is intended in this chapter when the term *relationship* is used, and to emphasize that this instrument was developed for coupled relationships. This instrument will be of little value to someone trying to measure the quality of a two-week fling, for instance. Said another way—the DAS is designed for use with bonded **dyads**, which are two-person groups.

The DAS was developed with a clear recognition that relationship adjustment is first and foremost a process. People do not become **adjusted**—able to communicate effectively, to handle conflicts, and to be satisfied with a particular relationship—and stay that way. Relationships are real life. People change, people age, and circumstances change. The DAS provides a measure of the process of at least one point in the relationship, though encouragement is given to use it in longitudinal studies in order to map the quality of relationships over time among different people.

Several things can determine the outcome of dyadic adjustment. These include "troublesome dyadic differences, interpersonal tensions and personal anxiety, dyadic satisfaction, dyadic cohesion, and consensus on matters of importance to dyadic functioning" (Spanier 1976: 17). The DAS tries to capture the extreme complexity of dyadic relationships. Testing the instrument has led to refinement. The refined instrument is presented in Figure 10.1 so that you will know exactly which questions are used and how they are scored. The four areas that this refined instrument encompasses are dyadic consensus, dyadic cohesion, dyadic satisfaction, and affectional expression. **Dyadic consensus** is a measure of the level of agreement couples have regarding important issues. For dyadic consensus questions, look at items 1–3, 5, and 7–15. **Dyadic cohesion** refers to degree of sharing interactions and exchanges with one another, being socially intimate and working on things together. Items 24–28 are used to tap this dimension of intimate relationships. **Dyadic satisfaction** refers to the overall level of satisfaction with this relationship, as opposed to another or no relationship at all. Items 16–23 are used to measure dyadic satisfaction. Finally, items 4, 6, and 29–31 are used to tap the affectional expression dimension of dyadic adjustment. **Affectional expression** refers to the affectionate and sexual components of intimate relationships.

The Short Marital Adjustment Test

Another instrument that has stood the tests of time, critics, as well as reliability and validity is the Locke-Wallace **Short Marital Adjustment Test (SMAT).** Building on previous efforts to create an efficient yet valid and reliable marital adjustment instrument, Locke and Wallace (1959) created a 15-item short marital adjustment test. Many of the consensus items found on the Spanier scale are included on the SMAT. In addition, the short test includes length of courtship; a few childhood background questions, such as whether the person attended religious services and whether the couple lived in the country or in town or some other setting; degree of conflict with parents prior to marriage; a happiness rating of childhood; and parents' approval or disapproval of the marriage (Locke and Wallace 1959: 252–253). An assessment of this instrument relying on a sample of 281 couples revealed that it was still applicable when focusing on marital adjustment in a broad sense, and concluded that the test was still relevant (Freeston and Plechaty 1997).

The DAS and the SMAT measure some of the same and yet some different elements that are part of or influence a relationship. The Spanier scale taps the psychological and social lives of the couple themselves, whereas the Locke-Wallace test also taps childhood factors that may have some bearing on current relationship dynamics. The Spanier scale identifies components of relationships. Again, this draws attention to complexity. The DAS can be and is used to identify problem areas in relationships.

Factors Related to Relationship Quality and Adjustment

As previously noted, literally reams of studies have been conducted on marital quality, relationship adjustment, and factors related to these. The following sections provide an overview of consistent findings over the decades and newer areas of inquiry, as well.

Figure 10.1   The Spanier Dyadic Adjustment Scale

Most persons have disagreements in their relationships. Please indicate below the approximate extent of agreement or disagreement between you and your partner for each item on the following list.

	Always Agree	Almost Always Agree	Occa-sionally Disagree	Fre-quently Disagree	Almost Always Disagree	Always Disagree
1. Handling family finances	5	4	3	2	1	0
2. Matters of recreation	5	4	3	2	1	0
3. Religious matters	5	4	3	2	1	0
4. Demonstrations of affection	5	4	3	2	1	0
5. Friends	5	4	3	2	1	0
6. Sex relations	5	4	3	2	1	0
7. Conventionality (correct or proper behavior)	5	4	3	2	1	0
8. Philosophy of life	5	4	3	2	1	0
9. Ways of dealing with parents or in-laws	5	4	3	2	1	0
10. Aims, goals, and things believed important	5	4	3	2	1	0
11. Amount of time spent together	5	4	3	2	1	0
12. Making major decisions	5	4	3	2	1	0
13. Household tasks	5	4	3	2	1	0
14. Leisure time interests and activities	5	4	3	2	1	0
15. Career decisions	5	4	3	2	1	0

	All the time	Most of the time	More often than not	Occa-sionally	Rarely	Never
16. How often do you discuss or have you considered divorce, separation, or terminating your relationship?	0	1	2	3	4	5
17. How often do you or your mate leave the house after a fight?	0	1	2	3	4	5
18. In general, how often do you think that things between you and your partner are going well?	5	4	3	2	1	0
19. Do you confide in your mate?	5	4	3	2	1	0
20. Do you ever regret that you married? (*or lived together*)	0	1	2	3	4	5
21 How often do you and your partner quarrel?	0	1	2	3	4	5
22. How often do you and your mate "get on each other's nerves?"	0	1	2	3	4	5

	Every Day	Almost Every Day	Occasionally	Rarely	Never
23. Do you kiss your mate?	4	3	2	1	0

	All of them	Most of them	Some of them	Very few of them	None of them
24. Do you and your mate engage in outside interests together?	4	3	2	1	0

How often would you say the following events occur between you and your mate?

	Never	Less than once a month	Once or twice a month	Once or twice a week	Once a day	More often
25. Have a stimulating exchange of ideas	0	1	2	3	4	5
26. Laugh together	0	1	2	3	4	5
27. Calmly discuss something	0	1	2	3	4	5
28. Work together on a project	0	1	2	3	4	5

These are some things about which couples sometimes agree and sometimes disagree. Indicate if either item below caused differences of opinions or were problems in your relationship during the past few weeks. (Check yes or no)

	Yes	No	
29.	0	1	Being too tired for sex.
30.	0	1	Not showing love.

31. The dots on the following line represent different degrees of happiness in your relationship. The middle point, "happy," represents the degree of happiness of most relationships. Please circle the dot which best describes the degree of happiness, all things considered, of your relationship.

0	1	2	3	4	5	6
Extremely Unhappy	Fairly Unhappy	A Little Unhappy	Happy	Very Happy	Extremely Happy	Perfect

32. Which of the following statements best describes how you feel about the future of your relationship?

  5   I want desperately for my relationship to succeed, and *would go to almost any length* to see that it does.

  4   I want very much for my relationship to succeed, and *will do all I can* to see that it does.

  3   I want very much for my relationship to succeed, and *will do my fair share* to see that it does.

  2   It would be nice if my relationship succeeded, but *I can't do much more than I am doing* now to help it succeed.

  1   It would be nice if it succeeded, but *I refuse to do any more than I am doing* now to keep the relationship going.

  0   My relationship can never succeed, and *there is no more that I can do* to keep the relationship going.

Source: From "Measuring Dyadic Adjustment: New Scales for Assessing the Quality of Marriage and Similar Dyads" by Graham B. Spanier, 1976, *Journal of Marriage and the Family, 38,* pp. 15–28. Copyright 1976 by the National Council on Family Relations, 3989 Central Ave. NE, Suite 550, Minneapolis, MN 55421. Reprinted by permission. Scale and manual available from MultiHealth Systems (800-456-3803).

Marital Status

For decades, research conducted in the United States has documented that being married is positively related to global happiness. Overall, married people have been reported as being healthier, happier, and better off financially than their single, separated, or divorced counterparts (Stack and Eshelman 1998). Much of this research was conducted using white subjects (Kamo and Cohen 1998). By the early 1980s, research consistently revealed a pattern wherein married whites showed the highest levels of well-being when compared with widowed and single people as well as separated and divorced people, in that order (Ball 1983).

Since the mid-1980s, more research also has paid attention to African American married people in the United States. One of the earlier studies with black subjects relied on a sample of women. The study revealed that black married women had the highest life satisfaction, followed by widowed, divorced, single, and separated women (Ball 1983). The pattern for blacks, however, is generally the same as it is for whites. That is, married people tend to be happier than people who are not married, with married men being happiest of all.

Women's levels of happiness in marriage have been changing over the decades. Some of this is related to their experiences in employment out of the home, which appears to be enhanced when husbands are supportive and compromised when they are not. Overall, it appears that the happiness of married women varies considerably, depending on work circumstances, husbands' sex-role attitudes, and other factors (Wilkie, Feree, and Ratcliff 1998). Many of the earlier studies had relatively large samples of housewives as opposed to women who were employed outside the home. Housework tended to be devalued, and housewives tended to be unhappy. Truly, these earlier studies generally revealed that couples lived in two marriages together: his marriage and her marriage (Bernard 1972). However, and it must be emphasized, housewives still had higher levels of happiness than did single, divorced, or separated women.

Cross-national studies on marital status and happiness are worthy of note, as well. In a study of marital status and general well being in eight industrialized nations, including the United States, Ryan, Hughes, and Hawdon (1998) report that married respondents tended to have the highest levels of general life satisfaction. However, in Finland, both married and never-married people had the greatest life satisfaction, in contrast to the divorced, separated, or widowed respondents. The link between being married and having higher levels of general life satisfaction tended to be weakest among the various welfare states, such as Finland, Sweden, and the Netherlands. It is contended that in welfare states, marriage has declined in significance. The findings for Finland may be indicators of what is to come for other nations, as parental leave, the secularization of marriage, the elevation of women's status, and changing gender roles become elements of everyday life in other nations, as well (Ryan et al. 1998).

Another study yielded slightly different results. Stack and Eshelman (1998) looked at the relationship between marital status and happiness in 17 industrialized nations. While conceding that marriage may not be the most important correlate of happiness, since health and financial satisfaction were rated above marriage, it also is the case that healthier people are more likely to get married in the first place (p. 535).

For the United States, studies that compare married couples with cohabiting couples have begun appearing. This is a newer area of study, so much more research must be conducted before any definitive pattern can be identified as an acceptable truism. In addition, comparative, and especially comparative longitudinal, studies are somewhat hampered by the fact that many cohabiters in the United States only cohabitate for 12 months (Larson 1991). However, in one study, it was found that relationship quality was identical for married and cohabiting couples when cohabitors had marriage plans (Brown and Booth 1996). Previous research on cohabitation focused on the strong relationship between premarital cohabitation and divorce in the United States and in Canada (Krishnan 1998; Lillard, Briend, and Waite 1995; Hall and Zhao 1995). It could be that this relationship will dissipate. Historically, Americans who cohabited tended to be from single-parent homes, from poor homes, and had limited educational attainment (Bumpass and Sweet 1989; Larson 1991). There has also been an increase in the proportion of college-educated persons who cohabitate. In addition, more cohabitors are cohabiting for longer periods of time (Wilhelm 1998). Thus, it is likely that more comparative data will be available regarding relationship quality of married and cohabiting couples (see also Figure 10.2 on page 306).

We also should start seeing more research comparing heterosexual married couples' marital quality with the relationship quality of homosexual couples. This will primarily be due to increases in the number of homosexuals who are disclosing their sexual identities, combined with greater legal recognition of domestic partnerships. Previous research has indicated that heterosexual couples reported about equal levels of satisfaction with their sexual relationships. Gay couples tended to report more sexual intercourse and more partners than did either lesbian or heterosexual couples (Murphy 1997). Earlier work focused only or primarily on sexual behavior and not specifically on the quality of the relationship. A more recent, though not representative, study compared heterosexual married, lesbian cohabiting, and gay cohabiting couples on five dimensions of marital quality over a five-year period. These dimensions were intimacy, autonomy, equality, constructive problem solving, and barriers to leaving (Kurdek 1998: 553). The study revealed that these five dimensions of marital quality were meaningful for all couple types studied. The study also revealed that the links between relationship quality and relationship outcomes were equivalent for all three couple types (p. 567).

Length of Marriage

A cohort analysis revealed that marital quality might be declining for American couples (Rogers and Amato 1997). Information on components of marital quality among 2,033 married persons aged 20 to 35 years was gathered in 1980. Interviews were then conducted in 1992 with one child of each of the 1980

Figure 10.2

Marital Satisfaction
among Women in
Polygynous Unions

Martial satisfaction research has focused primarily on monogamous unions, whether constituted by marriage or cohabitation, whether homosexual or heterosexual. Studies have been conducted almost exclusively in Western nations. (For an exception, see the Japanese study conducted by Kitamura et al. 1998.) Marital satisfaction has virtually gone unstudied in Africa, for instance.

Gwanfogbe, Schrum, Smith, and Furrow (1997) have broken that mold, however. They conducted a study of marital satisfaction among women in polygynous unions in Cameroon, West Africa. This was not easy to do, for several reasons. In some cases, villagers refused to participate, and in others, women refused to participate. This is really not surprising, given the rather personal, intrusive nature of this study (something many Americans may not fully appreciate).

Nonetheless, the authors found that junior wives tended to be happier than senior wives, perhaps because they were younger or still bearing children. Children and childbearing both are highly valued in Cameroon. Therefore, these younger wives might be getting more positive attention and affection from their husbands, which would influence their assessments of happiness.

The researchers also discovered a ranking system of wives, with a graduated system of seniority. The most senior wives were happier than the senior but younger wives (perhaps akin to being vice-president rather than president of an organization or company). The older, most senior wives may actually have welcomed the younger wives, who provided companionship and help with child care and other wifely tasks. The more junior senior wives may have been less happy, however, because they were still relatively young and in the midst of their childbearing years. An additional wife may have detracted from their relationships with their husbands.

Perhaps the most important finding was the strong relationship between husbands' supportiveness and wives' marital satisfaction. This relationship was found even among women struggling for the very basic necessities. Wives with more education rated their satisfaction with husbands' supportiveness lower than did wives with less education. The authors speculate that husbands might expect educated wives to work outside the home. If the wife does not, the husband might "withdraw his support with respect to her traditional domestic tasks in order to reestablish equity, as he perceives it" (Gwanfogbe et al. 1997: 67).

The authors draw attention to the fact that they interviewed women living in a Muslim culture. The norms in that part of Cameroon follow traditional patterns associated with Islam, including one that requires women to stay at home and men to go out and do the shopping and other domestic work.

Source: Philomina N. Gwanfogbe, Walter R. Shrum, Meredith Smith, and James L. Furrow, "Polygyny and marital life satisfaction: An exploratory study from rural Cameroon," *Journal of Comparative Family Studies,* 28 (1997): 55–71.

respondents, when these children were in the same age range as their parents had been when they had been interviewed. It was found that though educational attainment level and women's ages at first marriage had increased from 1980 to 1992, this 1992 cohort reported more marital conflict and marital problems, and less marital interaction than had their parents. At the same time, the respondents in the 1992 cohort did not report higher divorce proneness or marital happiness than that reported by the 1980 cohort (Rogers and Amato 1997). Moreover, the younger cohort had a stronger commitment to staying married than did the 1980 cohort. Rogers and Amato (1997) suggest that the marital decline documented to have occurred between these two cohorts may have to do with the greater challenges younger people are facing in a rapidly changing world. These findings seem consistent with another national study that revealed that both marital happiness and divorce are lower the longer people are married (White and Booth 1991). At least one study indicates that the percentage of people rating their marriages as "very happy" decreases steadily with the length of the marriage (Glenn 1990: 825).

Children

In general, marital quality tends to decline with the arrival of children, reach a low point when children are teenagers, and increase when children start leaving the home. It is theorized that these dips might be a function of having numerous roles to enact during these phases of life, resulting in role strain that creates barriers to quality enactment of one's role as a marriage partner (Rollins and Galligan 1978).

However, dips in marital quality have been found to be similar for couples who are nonparents, as well. Thus, it is not clear if it is the presence of children creating this dip, or if larger concerns that typically must be faced, such as work demands and taking care of aging parents, perhaps combined with dealing with one's own aging, make the larger contribution to this general pattern (Glenn 1990).

In addition, research shows that marital adjustment may be affected when children have special needs or are handicapped or disabled in some way. A critical factor is whether the marital relationship was solid before the birth or diagnosis of the child with disabilities or challenges (Howard 1978). The severity of the disability, as well as access to, affordability of, and satisfaction with services for the child and family may have some bearing (Korn, Chess, and Fernandez 1978). Research indicates, for instance, that parents of a child who is deaf experience quite a bit of stress in handling this situation and in making sure that the child's special needs are met. Another study indicates that if all members of the family learn sign language, there tends to be less stress within the family. Likewise, families with children with learning disabilities face additional stress. Depending on the condition, the parenting couple may have to continue taking care of the child throughout the couple's life. This is common with mental retardation, for instance. Overall, it appears that when the parenting couple has support from kin and uses formal services and support networks, coping abilities of the parents are stronger and more effective, and marital quality is less compromised (Pearson and Chan 1993; Kluwin and Gaustad 1994; Hornby and Ashworth 1994; Trute 1995; Meadow-Orlans 1995; Hayden and Goldman 1996; Costigan et al. 1997; Judge 1998).

Jobs and Careers

Research results on the effects of jobs and careers on marital quality are mixed. One U.S. study using a national probability sample found no relationship between women's employment and marital quality. Another smaller study, comprised of a sample of highly educated U.S. women, also found no negative effect, especially when the husband was supportive of the wife's career (Glenn 1990). A comparative analysis of 1,989 dual-income couples and single-parent employed adults conducted in the U.S. revealed that women had more work/family overload than did men. Single parents had about as much work/family overload as did married couples (Duxbury, Higgins, and Lee 1994). When comparing levels of work/family conflict between men and women over the life course, it was found that men had lower work/family conflict across the life course, whereas women had notably higher levels of conflict in the early stages of the life course (Higgins, Duxbury, and Lee 1994). Using Locke and Wallace's SMAT, a study based on a sample of professional psychologists found that work/family conflict had an effect on marital adjustment. This effect was moderated, however, if people were enjoying spousal support for their efforts (Burley 1995).

Much of the earlier work on employment's effects on marital quality and on children focused on women. However, the 1990s saw an increase in more comparative analyses. For instance, a study looked at occupational stress and uncertainty among men farmers in the United States. Family farming nests employment and family within each other, making it worthy of careful consideration. Family conflict, hence lower marital quality, is highly possible in situations where work and family are intertwined rather than separated. The study found that one mechanism by which farm men decreased work/family conflict was by taking consolation when other farmers experienced even worse problems (problems of crop production due to bad weather, bad credit, foreclosures, etc.) than they were experiencing (Swisher et al. 1998).

Numerous studies have found that marital satisfaction increases with income (Berry and Williams 1987). In addition, having an adequate income has been found to be positively correlated with family satisfaction. Inadequate income and economic distress are related to lowered marital quality (Voydanoff, Donnelly, and Fine 1988).

Research based on a sample of 94 women employed as receptionists, secretaries, and front-line tellers at a large financial institution in midwestern United States found that although marital status by itself had no effect on women's commitments to their jobs, women who had children were less committed to their jobs than were women who did not have children. At the same time, however, the study did not show a relationship between having children and not working as hard as others did in the workplace (Campbell, Campbell, and Kennard 1994). It might be that women with children work just as hard as those without because they really need the money. It also might be that the women give work a lower priority than their families because this is, in fact, their ranking. Though this study does not address the issue, one could surmise that placing work second to one's family is an effective way of setting up boundaries. With boundaries established, one can do one's job at work and do it well, but at the same time ensure that work stays at work; work issues and worries do not come home and intrude on marital and family relationships. In addition, it is reasonable to assume that women ranked children and family ahead of work because that is what is culturally expected. To be blunt, given the normative system of the United States, how do you think most people would respond if mothers went around openly stating that their first priority was work, and children and husbands/partners came in second?

Thus, when thinking about work's possible effects on marital quality, it is important to remember that not just hours spent at work or hours spent on work taken home must be considered. Other factors include such things as relationships with others at work, uncertainty of one's employment future, gendered realities, and the priorities given to work and family.

As with many other nations of the world, efforts are underway in the United States to work with employers and corporations so that family/work conflicts are mediated. This might include allowing flexible work times and providing day care and after-school care. It appears that some companies are responsive. Perhaps this is due to the fact that work/family conflict is costly. People sometimes do not show up for work or leave early. People also may only work for a short while with a firm that has no flexibility (Glass and Estes 1997). Although the United States does not have social welfare policies to the extent that nations such as Finland do, it appears that some movement is being made to decrease the conflict or strain that working parents experience. If more family-friendly provisions are made in the American labor market scene, it is likely that work's potentially negative effect on marital quality will dissipate. Likewise, as more couples and partners share the burdens of work and home, marital quality should be less affected, as well.

A growing body of information on work/family conflict and marital quality is being conducted in countries other than the United States. One example is a study conducted in Finland, in which 501 employees from four different work organizations participated. It was found that, for women, work/family conflict was a function of how many children were in the home, whether spouses were employed full time, and whether spouses had poor relationships with their superiors. For men, the key factors contributing to work/family stress were having several children at home and being highly educated. Overall, for men and women alike, family/work conflict negatively affected family well-being and occupational well-being. In addition, those who had high levels of work/family conflict also had lower levels of satisfaction with their parenting roles (Kinnunen and Mauno 1998).

A cross-national study involving respondents from five different nations found that cultural differences in gendered expectations explained patterns of work/family conflict. The nations represented were the United States, Australia, Bulgaria, the Netherlands, and Israel. Australians and Americans had the highest role conflict, but these also are nations where people have tended to see little benefit from combining roles. Bulgarians tend to have what Americans would consider to be a traditional division of labor. That is, the man's primary role is an occupational one; the woman's primary role is housewife/mother. Among Bulgarians, women professionals devote more time to their traditional roles and less to their occupational roles in order to reduce conflict. At the same time, Bulgarians included in this study tended to perceive that they were suffering from greater work/family conflict (Moore 1995).

Gender Issues and Housework

Blood and Wolfe (1960) were among the first sociologists to study decision making and division of labor among U.S. couples. They found that when women worked outside the home, men tended to help with child care and domestic tasks. That study has been followed by numerous other studies regarding gender and housework. Most of these studies focused solely on gendered divisions or sharing of housework. What generally has been found is that there have been some increases in men's contributions to domestic affairs, varying by gender ideology, work and time constraints, and perceived abilities or inabilities. Overall, women still do more of the housework, even when they work for pay outside the home. Generally, the **traditional division of labor** entails a system in which women do the bulk of the indoor tasks and men do the bulk of the outside tasks (Baxter 1997). Sex-typed tasks for men include gardening; automobile repair and maintenance, such as changing the oil; and home maintenance, such as removing leaves from rain gutters. Sex-typed tasks for women include cooking, doing laundry, and cleaning the house (Baxter 1997). Child care, of course, has been seen as primarily a woman's responsibility.

Other studies have found that household labor divisions spark more conflict than does paid work. The major bone of contention tends to be the fact that women spend more time on housework than they perceive husbands do or should do (Kluwer, Heesink, and van de Vliert 1996). This could be because who has to do what—for example, taking the children to the park versus cleaning the toilets—may speak to power distributions in the relationship.

Using data from a national survey conducted in the United States, it was found that satisfaction with the division of labor, for women, was more important in terms of its effects on marital quality than were factors such as educational attainment, occupational status, and age (Suitor 1991). Comparing results of national surveys conducted in 1975 and again in 1995, it was found that there is no truth to the rumor that women no longer enjoy housework or place importance on a neat house. In fact, it was found that the younger women in the 1995 study were putting in about four more hours per week on housework than did their counterparts in 1975. However, it also was found that there was a negative relationship between the combined roles of mother, wife, and worker and satisfaction with household cleanliness (Robinson and Milkie 1998). It might be that homes are less clean today than they were in 1975, but it also might be that in an effort to be satisfied in one's marriage and with one's relationship to one's children, women are putting up with houses that do not meet their cleanliness standards. This draws attention to the need for more research focused on the relationship between dissatisfaction in the level of household cleanliness and marital quality.

Using data from the National Survey of Households and Families, researchers sought to find out if there were differences between black and white U.S. couples in their gendered division of labor. As noted in Chapter 5, black couples tend to be more egalitarian than white couples. This national study supported this assertion in relation to housework. In fact, it was found that black men spend more time on housework than do white men. However, when the total number of hours spent doing housework and working for money were calculated, it was found that white women spend less time than black women for both of these areas and white men spend slightly more time than do black men. Overall, black women spend 10.5 more hours per week on these combined areas than do their male counterparts, whereas white women spend 4 hours more per week than do their male counterparts. Domestic egalitarianism among black couples is compromised by women's greater number of hours engaged in paid employment (Kamo and Cohen 1998).

An area in need of further study regarding housework and marital quality focuses on perceived fairness of the division of household tasks. The question then becomes not so much who does what and how much time is invested, but rather the question becomes: Is this fair? The fairness concept recognizes that couples vary in their expectations regarding divisions of labor. It is possible that some couples might declare that everything has to be split 50-50—the income generated outside the home, the time and quality of time spent with children, and the time and expertise put into making the appliances shine. Others, however, might have different viewpoints.

One of the first studies to explore this area relied on a sample of 239 couples living in the Chicago area. Of these couples, 136 were dual employed; in the other 103 couples, the husband was the sole breadwinner. The results were that for women and men alike in both types of couples, there was a statistically significant relationship between marital satisfaction and perceptions of fairness in family work (Yogev and Brett 1985: 614). The researchers point out, however, that this is not a causal analysis. It could be that the couples had high marital quality before needs to resolve domestic work issues arose. This high marital quality may have set the stage for the establishment of arrangements perceived to be fair to both parties.

Another study relied on a sample of 382 dual-earner couples only. It was found that both the division of labor and role preferences had an effect on marital quality (Wilkie, Feree, and Ratcliff 1998). Both a disproportionate share of housework on the part of wives and a disproportionate share of breadwinning on the part of husbands had negative effects on marital satisfaction and heightened perceptions that there was unfairness. The study revealed that "housework is not a 'bad' that makes those who do more of it necessarily more unhappy, nor does performing housework automatically indicate less power. Conversely, paid work is not a 'good' that automatically empowers and satisfies each spouse" (Wilkie et al. 1998: 593). Perceptions of appropriate domestic roles are very gendered. In addition, those gendered lenses reflect ideas of fair and unfair divisions of labor. Unfair divisions of labor, then, are related to lower marital satisfaction.

A newer area of study is the relationship between gender-role attitudes and marital satisfaction. The few studies published in the 1980s revealed that marriages in which husbands' attitudes were traditional but wives' attitudes were more contemporary had low marital quality (Glenn 1990). A study relying on a national sample of U.S. respondents from the Study of Marital Stability Over the Life Course found that when women's attitudes became less traditional over time, marital quality tended to decline. However, marital happiness and interaction increased when husbands' attitudes became more egalitarian. The researchers concluded, "Men lessen the stress in contemporary marriages when they, too, have attitudes that support role-sharing and gender equity" (Amato and Booth 1995: 65).

A cross-national study focused on gender attitudes, household structure, age, employment patterns, and presence of children in relation to the division of labor in the United States, Canada, Australia, Norway, and Sweden (Baxter 1997). Some variation across nations was found—for instance, in the Nordic countries, there was less gap in the division of labor and gender attitudes—but overall, the patterns for these five countries were very similar. When wives significantly contribute to the household income, both spouses are employed outside the home, and both hold liberal sex-role attitudes, the division of labor is more egalitarian. In general, older women do more housework than do younger women. Women with children also do proportionately more housework than their husbands or women without children. It was concluded that especially given that these findings held for the more egalitarian nations such as Norway and Sweden, broader levels of gender equality do not necessarily translate to gender equality in the home (Baxter 1997: 239).

Heterosexual couples in the United States tend to have a more discernible, gender-driven division of labor than do either gay or lesbian cohabiting couples. In general, gay couples tend to allocate tasks based on ability and interest, taking work constraints into consideration. Lesbian couples, generally more sensitive to equality, try to divide tasks equally, though attention is paid to ability and interest (Kurdek 1993).

Other Factors Related to Marital Quality

Age at marriage has fairly consistently been found to be related to marital happiness and quality. In general, people who marry when they are relatively young tend to have more conflict in their marriages. This is probably best reflected in the divorce statistics. As will be discussed in Chapter 13, age at marriage is a key factor in predicting divorce proneness.

What factors relate to the quality of this couple's relationship? What factors contributed to their adjustment as a married couple? What do you think are the three most important factors in a successful marriage?

Just as the earlier researchers in the area of marital adjustment suspected, family background characteristics appear to influence marital quality. For instance, marital quality tends to be lower for persons whose parents divorced when they were children and for people who never lived with their fathers than for persons who grew up in intact homes (Webster, Orbuch, and House 1995). One study indicates that the loving style of the wife, but not of the husband, also may affect marital quality. It was found that there was a positive relationship between wives having an altruistic loving style and couples' marital adjustment scores. On the other hand, the study revealed a negative relationship between wives having a selfish loving style and couples' marital adjustment (Martin et al. 1990).

Undoubtedly, there are other contributors to marital quality. These include personal maturity, mutually shared personality traits, and spousal assessments of one another's positive traits and overall contributions to the relationship. However, the key factors consistently found to be related to marital quality have been overviewed, and these key factors often are related to or nested with each other.

Marital Adjustment over the Life Cycle

Rollins and Feldman's (1970) study of 799 middle class families revealed that there tends to be a **U-shaped curve (curvilinear)** between marital happiness and stage of the life cycle. That is, marital happiness tends to be high during the newlywed stage, drop with the arrival of the first child, level back out until children became teens, improving as children are being launched out of the home, and becoming somewhat higher in the retirement phase. Levels of happiness varied somewhat for men and women in these stages, with women most negative during the years when dependent children were present in the home. Companionship between husbands and wives, however, was high when children were infants and preschoolers and leveled off after that. This led Rollins and Feldman to conclude that marital satisfaction is associated with the stages of the family life cycle and that marriage has "different meanings for husbands than for wives" (p. 27). This curvilinear relationship has been found in numerous subsequent studies (Glenn 1990).

This section will examine the **family life cycle perspective** to marriage over the life course. This perspective assumes that there are generally recognizable stages and transitions in marriage and family. It also assumes that the family is a unit that begins with marriage and ends with the death of both spouses; families and marriage change according to life processes, changes in milieu, and stage-associated sociocultural expectations; each marriage and family goes through identifiable stages over time, because of maturation, the passage of time, and aging; and that at each stage there are certain developmental tasks to be resolved or mastered while preparing for and adjusting to the next stage (Mattessich and Hill 1987). **Developmental tasks** are circumstances, problems, or necessary requirements that have to be met. These tasks are tied to what is conventionally expected of people in a particular culture in a particular era (Elder 1998).

At the level of the individual, the life course perspective assumes that "the life course of individuals is embedded and shaped by the historical times and places they experience over their lifetime" (Elder 1998: 3). Undergirding that assumption is the **principle of historical time and place.** Two other assumptions guiding the life course perspective are critical to understanding the presentation here. These are that "lives are linked interdependently" and that "individuals construct their own life course through the choices and actions they take within the opportunities and constraints of history and social circumstances" (Elder 1998: 4). These two assumptions are based on the principles of **linked or interdependent lives** and **human agency,** respectively (Elder 1998).

The life course perspective socially locates individuals and couples in cultural, biological, historical, and social contexts. In using this perspective, it is important to realize that larger social forces such as war, economics, cultural traditions, and prevailing ideology have bearing on the life courses of individuals and couples. In addition, how much choice people have is first and foremost a function of the stratification system of their respective countries and the opportunity structures that exist. Finally, it is important to remember that not everyone has the same ability to recognize opportunities even when they do exist. Although some find this model unsatisfying, it is fairly adequate as a general frame from which to anticipate and understand challenges and transitions over the course of life.

Reservations about the coverage of the life cycle in the phases of newlywed, parental, middle age, and retirement might include the fact that the presentation focuses on couples with children and married or "coupled" couples. These are reasonable exceptions to take. In fact, the validity of this model of development has been challenged and tested. The family life cycle model has been challenged on the grounds that the stages do not apply to all families, not all marriages include children, some marriages end in divorce, some people get remarried, and some people never marry (Mattessich and Hill 1987). As presented, the model applies to some 50 to 67 percent of all married couples. As previously indicated, married couples with and without children tend to experience the same dips over the life course. The difference is that the dips are deeper for couples with children than for couples who do not have children. Research testing the appropriateness of this model has revealed that beyond the first stage of the life course model, blended families more or less align with this model. Other circumstances—such as parenthood with no marriage, or marriage, parenthood, and then divorce not followed by a remarriage—follow slightly different paths and challenges. In both of these cases, the parental stage is still a shared phenomenon with many of the same tasks and challenges. Thus, overall, the model is more or less appropriate for the vast majority of families and marriages or domestic partnerships (Mattessich and Hill 1987).

The Newlywed Stage

The **newlywed stage** is the period between the marriage and the birth of the first child. Given delays in births, the newlywed stage for some actually refers to the first two or three years of marriage. The transition or preparatory stage for the newlywed stage is engagement. **Engagement** begins when a couple decides to marry one another and ends when they get married. This period offers the couple time to get used to the idea that they will become married, and gives them the opportunity to begin sorting out their values and preferences—for example, when and if to have children, how many children, where to live, what types of birth control to use, how to handle money, and so on. This also is an important period because during this time, others provide socialization into the status of married. In addition, others will provide social support for this significant life decision. Finally, since one never marries just an individual but into other families, this is an important time to begin adjusting to in-laws and making decisions about the nature and degree of influence that in-laws should have in marital lives.

Developmental Tasks of the Newlywed Stage

Tasks during the newlywed stage include adjusting to a sexual relationship, handling finances in ways with which both are comfortable, adapting to the new social and legal status of married (or cohabiting), relating to each other as married individuals, becoming comfortable regarding sex-role expectations and behaviors, and deciding on such things as where to live, how to equip the home, which birth control to use, how to balance work and relationship needs, how to handle disagreements, whom to have as friends, and appropriate relationships and activities with friends. Many of these issues will have been given attention during the engagement period; however, now the couple is really married or really cohabiting. This changes the context and fiber of meanings and interactions.

Many of these tasks can be subsumed under a category of moving from *I* and *me* to *us* and *we*. Couples must decide how *we* want to live *our* shared lives, and what is most important to *us*. Looking at the number and types of developmental tasks associated with this stage, it is a wonder how couples tend to score so high on marital satisfaction. The answer is probably that the change in status itself is so exciting that it tends to buffer actually registering the stress. In addition, there tends to be social support and encouragement for couples who have decided to assume this more socially revered status.

Marital Distress and Marital Adjustment in the Newlywed Stage

A very small study, comprised of 25 heterosexual newlywed couples, supported the contention that marital adjustment in the earliest stage of marriage is, in part, related to husbands' and wives' abilities to identify less strongly with their parents and more strongly with their new roles as married people (Haws and Mallinckrodt 1998). Another study, based on 310 couples, found that when wives had high emotional investment in the earliest stages of the marriage, the marriage tended to be more stressful for them. Wives also were distressed when stepchildren were present at the beginning of marriage. Men scored highest on marital distress during the first few months of marriage and also when they were part of a couple who did not pool financial resources. The percentage of couples found to be distressed in this study, however, was very small—only 8 percent of the men and 14 percent of the women (Kurdek 1991: 627.) A study based on 49 newlywed couples found that expressing one's feelings was related to positive marital adjustment for men and women alike (Teichner and Farnden-Lyster 1997). All of these studies were based on very small samples, but all support previous research in these areas.

The interaction patterns and their relationship to marital happiness and stability among newlyweds has been given a bit of attention in the social science research. For example, a study of 199 black and 174 white couples found that regardless of race, men's avoidance of conflict and women's coidentification has bearing on their relative marital well-being. When compared with white couples, black couples had higher levels of self-disclosure, fewer areas of disagreement, and reported more positive sexual interactions (Oggins, Veroff, and Leber 1993: 494). Another study, based on a racially and ethnically representative sample of newlywed childless couples in Seattle, found that a key problem area in the newlywed stage emerged when husbands refuse to be influenced by their wives. This tends to help escalate problems in the marriage, which obviously is negatively related to marital adjustment (Gottman et al. 1998).

Finally, research is beginning to identify some differences between black and white newlyweds that might not only further our understanding of cultural differences in marriage but should also give guidance to marital therapy programs. Illustrative of this is a study conducted in Michigan using 343 newlywed, first-time married couples. The results of the study indicated that blacks and whites tend to share several narrative themes, or emphases, in their early years of marriage. These are achievement, family, and couple relations. The authors see this as reflective of the very real issues with which young couples in urban areas have to contend. The white couples emphasized the work theme more, whereas the black couples emphasized a couple growth theme more. The authors speculate that the white couples may be more oriented toward external indicators of marital success, such as one's success in one's job. Further, the authors wonder if black couples, who do not find work to be as important as whites do, emphasize their marital relationship more because success there is more attainable or because of the long history of an emphasis on family and kin. In addition, black couples emphasized religion more than did white couples. This is not surprising, given the historical significance of religion in the meaning and organization of African Americans' lives. Overall, there were greater similarities than differences by race in terms of focal areas in the newlywed stage. With regard to the differences found, the authors note that this points to a need to avoid a universal approach to these types of issues (Chadiha, Veroff, and Leber 1998). That is, couples basically have the same challenges to face. Not only may they face these somewhat differently but they also may have different priority systems for these challenges.

The Parental Stage

The **parental stage** begins with the first pregnancy. In a sense, the parenting stage never ends until the parents die. However, in the context of a life course perspective, it is assumed that the active parenting stage ends when the last child leaves the home. The parental stage typically lasts for two decades or more. Past conventional wisdom had it that the birth of the first child constitutes a crisis, as discussed in Chapter 11, but this usually is not the case. Furthermore, marital quality after the birth of the first child appears to be most strongly related to marital quality and satisfaction before the birth of the first child.

Developmental Tasks of the Parental Stage

Some of the developmental tasks associated with this stage in the life course interact with children's stages of development. Parents literally will parent differently when children are infants than when they are teenagers, for instance.

Tasks associated with this rather lengthy stage of the life course include adjusting to being parents, organizing work and family roles and schedules, becoming more engaged in community and civic activities as these relate to the well-being of children, understanding and trying to meet children's developmental needs, planning for the children's future, and striving toward economic and employment stability.

Marital Adjustment in the Parental Stage

In a study of 69 couples before, during, and after the transition to parenthood, it was found that during the transition, wives' division of child-care tasks began more and more to resemble that of their husbands. One possible reason for this is that with the advent of children, women are more likely to focus on the "labor of love" as part of being mothers and wives. Hence, they would be more likely to agree than disagree with husbands at this crucial stage (Johnson and Huston 1998).

Relying on responses from black participants in the General Social Surveys in 1980 and 1982 to 1986, it was found that the presence of minor children was associated with lower marital happiness for wives but not for husbands (Ball 1993). Wives' marital happiness was higher when the children were younger. The older the children, generally, the lower the marital satisfaction of wives. It is speculated that given the cultural emphasis on the mother role in black communities, the presence of young children has an affirmative value to it. However, as children get older, there is more stress involved in rearing them, preparing them for the larger world, and keeping them safe. At the same time, husbands' happiness increases when the children are teenagers. It may be that mothers of teens are given disproportionate caregiving duties of them, while fathers have less hands-on obligations but focus instead on the children's accomplishments (Ball 1983).

In a comparative analysis of 40 black and 65 white professional middle-class mothers who were married and employed outside the home, it was found that black mothers reported more marital conflict over work and family life, even though black women saw more rewards than costs to motherhood than did their white counterparts (Bridges and Orza 1996). Overall, black and white mothers had very similar roles and responded to them in similar ways. This included feelings of regret when leaving small children in someone else's care.

Late Parenthood

Earlier life cycle theorists assumed that parents who enter parenthood "late" would have difficulty and find parenthood less satisfactory than those who enter parenthood "on time," but a recent study casts doubt on these assumptions. Using a sample of American couples in which the women had their first child after age 35, and comparing them with a sample of on-time couples, it was found that the delayed parents reported less marital satisfaction with the sexual aspects of their marriages (frequency and quality). However, delayed parents also reported less stress as parents, the parents themselves were less depressed than the on-time parents, and fathers in the delayed couples reported less stress regarding their relationships than did fathers in the on-time group (Garrison et al. 1997).

Homosexual Couples and Parenting

In a comparative analysis of lesbian and heterosexual parents, it was found that the parenting dyads were similar in their levels of dyadic adjustment. The only significant difference found between the couple types was that lesbian couples scored higher on parenting awareness skills (Flaks et al. 1995). A study of 34 lesbian couples in northern California revealed that couples tended to share tasks equally. That is, the "Ozzie and Harriett" heterosexual pattern of primary breadwinner/primary caregiver was not very common (Sullivan 1996). In a review of literature on lesbian parenting published from 1980 to 1996, it was revealed that lesbian parents operate in a climate of concern that heterosexual couples typically do not have to consider. Lesbian parents worry about the effect that their life-style will have on the way their children are treated. The greatest threat that lesbian mothers face is child custody. Overall, lesbian parents tend to be healthy and secure and their children well-adjusted and socially tolerant (Parks 1998). Support from family and friends tends to strengthen the couple and parent-child relationship.

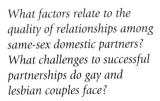

What factors relate to the quality of relationships among same-sex domestic partners? What challenges to successful partnerships do gay and lesbian couples face?

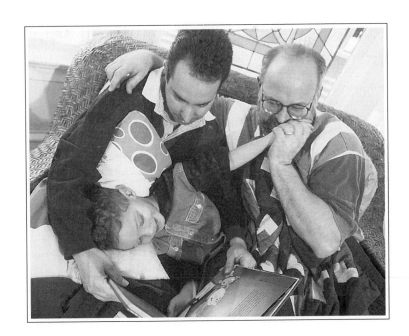

The Middle-Age Stage

The middle age stage begins when the last child has left the home, and ends when partners retire from employment. Increasingly, Americans are seeing this as a time to be enjoyed. It is a time when couples are no longer intensely responsible for children, have either made it or not in their careers, and have time to spend with each other. It is a time of looking back, reflecting, and looking forward.

Tasks of the Middle-Age Stage

Developmental tasks associated with middle age include readjusting as a couple, preparing for retirement, planning for the rest of one's career based on an assessment of past performance and prognosis for future occupational involvement, coping with physiological and psychological changes, dealing with aging parents and the deaths of friends, and dealing with one's own mortality.

Menopause and Male Midlife Crisis

Historically, menopause was seen as a time when women lost their social value. They no longer could become pregnant, they were aging, they were becoming asexual, and they were no longer attractive or interesting. In Western cultures, menopause was something to be dreaded (Chomesky 1998). Although the women's movement of the 1960s and 1970s challenged this double standard of aging, and scientific (Ferguson and Parry 1998) and popular media (e.g., advertisements for vitamins and cruises) challenge it today, research indicates that women still experience accelerated stress and anxiety as they approach menopause. In part, this is due to losing their childbearing abilities and their childrearing roles (Chomesky 1998). Midlife is a time of taking stock, a time of dealing with myriad social, psychological, and physical changes: wrinkles, gray hair, elderly parents in need of care, friends dying, and adult children coming and going. These changes are dealt with within a particular cultural context. In the United States, that still means that women may experience doubts about their social value, their attractiveness, and their changing roles.

Men also go through social, psychological and physical changes at midlife. They, too, have changes in sex hormones, typically with a decrease in testosterone. Although not exactly analogous to female menopause, male midlife does bring with it wrinkles, gray hair, diminished sex drive, and with drops in testosterone, some bone mass loss and muscle weakness (Sternbach 1998). For some decades in the United States, there was a general expectation that male midlife would also bring a **crisis**. This would be a period wherein the male actively sought to have his prowess reinforced by some younger female(s), and he would go through a crisis of not knowing who he was and what he wanted to do with the rest of his life.

Is this what normally happens to men in the United States? The answer, apparently, is no. **Male midlife crisis** is a catchy, even entertaining, phrase. For most men, however, midlife is a transition. As with other transitions, it has stress points to it. Men who perceive that they have a good relationship with their children and their wives tend to have the least stress (Julian, McKenney, and Arnold 1990). Overall, the midlife crisis was great stuff for sitcoms and advertisers of sports cars, but few men actually experience a life-altering crisis at this time. As one researcher put it, "The construct of the midlife crisis is a contemporary social construct that has outlived its usefulness" (Kruger 1994: 1299). Thus, just as the purported **empty nest syndrome,** theoretically a time of depression for a woman because children have left the home and she is bereft of direction and meaning, has not been supported by research (Glenn 1975), likewise the male midlife crisis has made it past the talk shows but not past empirical research. All said and done, midlife is a turning point for men and women alike. They have to accept their own mortality and the mortality of others. Children are grown up, but often still need their parents in various capacities. Their bodies are changing and the changes must be tended to. Increasingly, middle-age couples can look forward to many years together when both still are in good health and they have more time for each other. This can be, and often is, a very positive time for many couples.

Boomerang Kids

In recent decades, it has become increasingly common for adult children to return to their parents' homes after a few years away from it and on their own (Settersen 1998). A Canadian study indicates that this is due to younger people having difficulty finding jobs, while parents gain financial and emotional support from returning children (Boyd and Norris 1995). But what happens to the parents' marriage when the children return home? In a study of 172 families with "boomerang kids," the answer was, it depends. Marital happiness was higher among couples with boomerang kids when the couples were in their first marriages. It was lower if the children were returning to a parent who had remarried. Parents who were in poor health were happier with having the boomerangs than were parents in good to excellent health. Children who leave, return, leave again, and repeat this pattern several times put a strain on the parents' marriages. A critical factor affecting marital happiness in homes with returning children is whether the adult children get along with the mother figure. If not, then marital satisfaction diminished for the couple (Mitchell and Gee 1996).

Caring for Older Parents

With greater life expectancy comes also the expectation that one may have to care for one's parents in their later years. Usually, this caring comes at midlife. Adult children feel more obligations to biological parents than to a relatively new stepparent. In addition, how much and what types of help to extend generally are related to the length and quality of the relationship with the older parents (Ganong et al. 1998).

Results from the National Long-Term Care Survey revealed that when it came to helping elderly parents with their daily living activities, older parents usually were cared for by children of the same sex, especially if the parent was chronically ill (Lee, Peek, and Coward 1998). Another study found that although aging parents make use of formal service providers, black aging parents expect more assistance from children than do white aging parents (Lee, Willets, and Seccombe 1998). Among Asian Americans, it appears that Korean American adult children are more likely to assist and support their aging parents than are Chinese or Japanese American adult children. Among all three groups, less support is given if the parents frequently interact with friends and other relatives. In addition, for all three groups, adult children were most likely to help older parents they lived closer to if the parents' needs were great. Overall, Asian parents who lived some distance from their children and needed financial assistance were not likely to get it from their children (Ishii-Kuntz 1997). A study of women caregivers revealed that marital satisfaction during times of caring for seriously ill parents depended on husbands' support of the wife's caregiving. A husband's support was based on his attitude toward the particular tasks the wife performed (Suitor and Pillemer 1994).

The Retirement Stage

The **retirement stage** begins with the retirement of at least one partner from paid work, and ends with the death of the partners. With greater life expectancy has come a healthier and more active retirement stage. Research emphasizes that the retirement stage may have a lot of strain as couples adjust to a different economic status as well as adjust to being with each other more. At the same time, some research emphasizes that this stage can be very positive because retired couples tend to be healthy for a long time after retirement and have dispensable incomes that they can use to stay active and entertained. Comparative analyses reveal that retirement usually is not disruptive for U.S. couples, but that some problems in husband-wife role adjustment may appear in the early years of retirement (Ekerdt and Vinick 1991). All the same, very real issues must be dealt with at this stage of life.

Developmental Tasks of the Retirement Stage

Tasks associated with the retirement stage include adjusting to one's sexuality, as it has been affected by personal growth and physical changes (as discussed in Chapter 9); making decisions about where and how to live; maintaining a locus of control; preparing for one's own and one's partner's death; deciding on one's grandparenting style if there are grandchildren; and making financial changes, as needed, because of decreased income or health problems.

Timing of Retirement

A study based on data from the 1960s and 1970s revealed that there was a high incidence of joint retirement among married couples (Blau 1998). In a study of 228 couples from six different organizations that participated in the Cornell Retirement and Well-Being Study 1994–1995, it was found that wives tend to influence husbands' timing of retirement when husbands discuss retirement with their wives and when retirement is presented as a way to enter a new life stage. For women, the factor most influencing their retirement is their husbands' retirement (Smith and Moen 1998). Most couples try to retire at roughly the same time so that they can jointly decide what to do with their time and have more time together.

Grandparenthood

Grandparenthood appears to have changed over the past few decades. Grandparents and grandchildren tend to live farther apart, and opportunities for face-to-face interaction tend to be limited. A longitudinal study of grandparents and grandchildren in California found that emotional closeness tended to be somewhat curvilinear. Grandparents and grandchildren tend to be emotionally close during the child's first 14 years, and then tended to have less close ties and contact until the grandchildren become adults. As grandchildren became middle aged and grandparents became advanced in age, the relationship between them is likely to become more meaningful, especially for the grandparents. Affection between them begins to increase. Gender of grandchild and grandparent was of no consequence in this study (Silverstein and Long 1998).

Spousal Caregiving in Old Age

Research abounds to the effect that caring for one's infirm older parent is stressful for middle-age children. Less attention has been paid to the effects on marital quality when an aging spouse cares for an infirm spouse. One study that looked at this relationship found that caring for a spouse who was functionally impaired (e.g., one who needs help walking) had no negative effects on the caregiving spouse or the relationship, but that caring for a spouse who was cognitively impaired (e.g., one who suffers from memory loss or is in the early stage of Alzheimer's) did have negative effects. Spouses caring for cognitively impaired spouses perceived that their caregiving was ineffective. Unlike those caring for a functionally impaired spouse, those caring for a cognitively impaired spouse felt that the relationship had lost some of its closeness and that positive interactions with the spouse had been disrupted (Townsend and Franks 1997).

It appears that more research and practical attention is needed regarding aging spouses caring for one another. Researchers have tended to focus on the **sandwich generation,** the middle-age children who are launching their families, dealing with middle age, and also caring for older parents. Thus, there is a lack of understanding what factors influence this elder spouse caregiving, the degree to which it is helpful or harmful to each partner's physical and mental health, and what social support and other services this special population might need.

Widowhood

Due to differences in life expectancies and the tendency of women to marry men older than themselves, there are more widows than widowers in the United States. Widowhood tends to create financial strains for women. More women than men survive their spouses, some for many years. Men also are more likely to marry after the death of spouses than are women. In addition, widowed men have more health problems than do widowed women. Widowed women tend to have larger and more accessible social support networks than do widowed men. A study conducted in Florida and Kansas revealed that widowed men are more likely to be depressed than are widowed women, even though women have more financial strains. The death of one's spouse also more adversely affects men's health than that of women. It may be that women anticipate being the surviving spouse and are more ready to deal with this by relying on their social support networks. Men are less likely to expect surviving their spouses, and do not have many role models from which to pattern their lives. Practically speaking, there probably is a need for greater social service outreach to widowed people in general and widowed men in particular (Lee et al. 1998b).

Dealing with Marital Conflict

Conflict is inevitable in all intimate relationships. There is much about which to argue. Housework and child care are two major areas of potential conflict. Other areas of conflict include money, friends, sex roles, religion and religious commitments, social isolation, what to do on the weekends, whether to changes jobs and places of residences, and who is in charge of the remote control (Dortch 1994; Lawson and Thompson 1995; "The Big Picture" 1998).

Not all conflict or disagreements lead to violence in relationships; however, some do. Results from the National Survey of Families and Households revealed that 5 percent of the women respondents and 6 percent of the men respondents reported that marital arguments lead to physical violence (Sorenson, Upchurch, and Shen 1996). And some marital violence leads to death.

Spouse Abuse

Wife abuse has been more extensively studied than has husband abuse. At the macro-level, research reveals that in the United States, violence against wives is highest in the states where women's status is the lowest (i.e., South Carolina, Alabama, and Mississippi). The findings from this national analysis support feminist theories that violence toward wives is a function of male dominance in society. Battered wives and their batterers tend to be young, urban, less educated, and of lower income than nonbattering couples (Sorenson et al. 1996). Episodes of violence tended to have occurred prior to marriage, while either dating or cohabiting. More blacks than whites report violent episodes in their relationships. Most research on wife abuse focuses exclusively or primarily on urban couples, but one study focused on an ethnically diverse rural sample of battered women. This study found that regardless of ethnicity, battered women tended to be relatively young and had limited employment and educational experience. More Hispanic than white women reported violence during pregnancy, but more white than Hispanic women reported that their batterers were under the influence of alcohol and/or drugs at the time of the abuses. More whites reported that their batterers had had a childhood history of violence than did the Hispanic wives (Krishman et al. 1997).

While much research focuses on younger victims and perpetrators of domestic violence, it should be recognized that elderly spouses also sometimes are abusive. Research indicates that the risk factors tend to stay the same across the ages. That is, elderly who are abused by their spouses tend to be abused by partners who are poorly adjusted to the marriage, who perceive themselves to be under a lot of stress, who abuse alcohol, and who perceive that the victim is being verbally aggressive with them (Harris 1996).

When Steinmetz released her report entitled "The Battered Husband Syndrome" in 1977, the academic community met it with harsh criticism and scrutiny. Charges were made to the effect that she had manipulated data and that no battered husband syndrome existed (Hien and Hien 1998). At this time, it still is difficult to obtain valid and reliable samples of women who are domestically violent. Some of this may be due to the fact that at the national level, some 45 percent of men and 40 percent of women indicate that marital disagreements escalate to the point that *both* parties engage in violent acts (Sorenson et al. 1996). It is suggested that since women's rates of violent crimes in the society are increasing, more attention should be paid to women as perpetrators of violence in the home.

Spouse abuse and other forms of relationship violence are examined in detail in Chapter 12.

Couple Communication

Obviously, many couples argue and fuss with one another. The majority, fortunately, do not resort to violence. Over time, it appears that most couples learn various ways to communicate their emotions, points, and attitudes without hurting one another—at least physically. Compromise and the passage of time no doubt are two key ingredients here, along with mutual respect and placing a value on sustaining the relationship. Pundits have it that the way to avoid communication clashes is by understanding men's and women's gendered realities in the arena of communication. That is, generally speaking, men take a *status* orientation to communication. For them, life is a competition. Communication involves spewing forth facts and asserting one's knowledge. For women, who tend to have a *connect* style of communication, life is about networks of relationships. So, women conduct themselves more modestly and try to reach agreement and cooperation (Baher 1994). An elaboration on this is to the effect that men and women communicate slightly differently in the public versus the private spheres. Men deal with hierarchical networks at home in their communications and deal with competitive market networks at work. Women tend to be egalitarian in their communication, trying to give everyone a fair say, or else they are fatalistic, assuming that frustrations to connectedness, isolation, and powerlessness are part of what life has dealt them (Franzwa and Lockhart 1998). These, at least, are the theories.

Research indicates that the more egalitarian the relationship between spouses, the greater the quantity and quality of marital communication and the higher the levels of marital adjustment (Pollock, Die and Marriot 1990). Thus, for less egalitarian marriages, marital communication and marital quality tend to be lower. In terms of longitudinal research on handling marital conflict and communicating with one another, a study based on 60 ethnically diverse marriages that had lasted more than 20 years is instructive. For African Americans, marital conflict remained fairly stable from the beginning of marriage through the childbearing years. For whites, marital conflict during this time was triple what it was for blacks; for Hispanics, it was double the rate for blacks. However, among all three ethnic groups, marital conflict decreased after the children left home. For all groups in the early years, wives tend to be confrontational and men tried to avoid face-to-face confrontation. In general, black husbands tended to be more confrontational than Hispanic or white husbands. As these couples entered their empty nest years, open confrontation on the part of wives and avoidance on the part of men tended to be replaced by less destructive means of communication on the part of wives and less avoidance on the part of husbands. None of the couples had sought clinical intervention, and it is assumed that their evolving healthful ways of communicating their differences and frustrations may be instructive to therapists and everyday people alike (Mackey and O'Brien 1998).

Summary

Marital quality, adjustment, and happiness have proven to be some of the most difficult concepts to measure, yet they have become some of the most important matters in marriages and marriagelike relationships. Two frequently used scales for measuring marital relationship quality and adjustment are the Spanier Dyadic Adjustment Scale and the Short Marital Adjustment Test.

Factors related to relationship quality and adjustment include marital status, length of marriage, presence or absence of children, jobs and careers, gender roles, and perceived fairness of housework and child-care responsibilities. Children and housework are two major issue areas affecting relationship quality. Children can add strain to the relationship, and teenagers bring extra worries for parents. If there is a perception that housework and child care are not being fairly shared by partners, conflict and decreased relationship quality may occur.

Over the life course, marital happiness tends to be somewhat curvilinear, with higher levels of happiness before and after children are present in the home. While the newlywed stage is filled with seemingly daunting tasks, happiness levels tend to be high, nonetheless. Research shows that black and white newlyweds tend to be similar in their focal areas during the newlywed stage, but may differ in terms of which areas have higher priority.

The parental stage is a relatively lengthy stage in which couples typically find themselves working to balance work, family, and other obligations. Although the birth of the first child typically is not a crisis, it does appear that marital quality after the first birth is a function of marital quality before the first birth.

The middle-age stage is increasingly seen as a positive time for most American couples. The myths of the male midlife crisis and empty nest syndrome aside, many couples find this to be a time when they are healthy and can spend more time with one another. At this stage, also, most Americans must anticipate having to provide some type of care to their aging parents. In recent decades, middle-age parents also have had to contend with boomerang kids. These returning children seem most welcome if parents are still in their first marriage or if the parents are in poor health. Boomerang kids who leave home, return, leave again, and then repeat this pattern over and over again tend to put strain on their parents' marriages.

Today, retired couples tend to enjoy more years of good health together than ever before. For most couples, retirement is not disruptive, though there may be a few problems of adjustment during the earliest years of retirement. An area not well researched yet focuses on older spouses taking care of each other in times of ill health or infirmity. From the research available, it appears that marital quality is not affected when a partner is caring for a functionally impaired spouse. However, partners caring for a cognitively impaired spouse tend to feel that the relationship has lost some closeness.

Although most marital or relationship disagreements and conflict do not result in physical violence, violence occurs in about 25 to 35 percent of heterosexual and lesbian relationships and in about 20 percent of gay relationships. Wife abuse is highest in the states where women's status is the lowest as well as in the states with the greatest levels of social disorganization. Battered wives and their batterers tend to be young, urban, less educated, and have lower incomes than do nonbattering couples. Although husband abuse does occur, research has not yet adequately addressed this issue. Lesbian and gay partners remain in battering relationships for many of the same reasons that heterosexual partners do. In addition, those in the homosexual community may not be willing to acknowledge abuse for fear of further stigmatizing the life-style.

It appears that, over time, most couples learn various ways to communicate their emotions without hurting one another. Women tend to become less confrontational and men tend to decrease their levels of avoidance. The more egalitarian the relationship, the greater the quantity and quality of marital communication and the higher the levels of marital adjustment.

Readings for In-Depth Focus

Women's Views on Midlife

Most research and theory on the midlife stage has been written by and based on men. In her article "Women at Midlife," social work professor Sharon McQuaide argues that research on women's experiences of midlife is needed. One of her rationales is that without more research, the negative images and stereotypes of middle-aged women can become self-fulfilling prophecies. As you read this article, reflect on the evening television shows that you have seen most recently. Were there any middle-aged women in leading roles? In any roles at all? How were middle-aged female characters depicted? Think of middle-aged women you know. Do they have a fairly positive sense of their own relevance? Do they "put themselves down"? What else is going on in their lives that may be affecting how they see and feel about themselves?

■ ■ ■

Women at Midlife

Sharon McQuaide

With the exceptions of investigations of estrogen replacement therapy (ERT), menopause, the "empty nest," and other topics related to a woman's fertility or care of others, women's midlife aging experience has been understudied. The major studies of midlife development have been by male investigators looking at male subjects. The results of these studies, like those of research on heart disease, have been applied to women with the assumption that what was true for the gander was true for the goose. Another source of information for many women searching for understanding about midlife has been popular literature, such as Gail Sheehey's (1992) *The Silent Passage* and Germaine Greer's (1992) *The Change.* Not only were these works not research based, but they focused on menopause, leading to more constructions of a woman's midlife experience that are biologically oriented.

Several other factors limit the value of earlier research. First, the experience of midlife for women is changing rapidly. The generation of women now entering midlife differs from previous generations. Raised "traditionally," they have lived through the historical shift to a feminist self-view in adulthood. They gained control of reproduction, and they are the first generation in which so many have worked outside of the home and built identities based on value in the workplace.

Beyond this, most of the few research studies of women in midlife focus on "problems" women face at midlife (for example, physical changes, children leaving home) and how women "cope" with them. But midlife is not just about mortality, crumbling bones, and hot flashes. Most studies of mental health implicitly, at least, define "wellness" as not being sick and as an absence of anxiety, depression, or other mental disorders.

New conceptions of psychological well-being emphasize positive characteristics of growth and development, such as caring and trusting ties with others, a purpose in life, self-acceptance, and personal growth. The distinction is not trivial; although mental health research using a psychopathology model has often documented a higher incidence of psychological problems among women than among men, when positive well-being is the focus, women often show higher scores than men (Ryff, 1995). Identifying factors related to a woman's midlife satisfaction can provide a guide for women, as well as goals. The profile of a woman at midlife who feels satisfied with her life provides a role model to any woman who

wishes to transcend the negative stereotypes of her culture.

Research into women's midlife experience is clearly needed. From the perspective of the individual woman, the invisibility of women in midlife in the research literature leaves a woman at the mercy of cultural stereotypes and media portrayals, or lack of portrayals. Negative images of aging women abound and, without alternative images, serve to elicit a woman's own internalized ageism and sexism. Images of miserable empty nesters, women being left for younger women, menopausal madness, and dowager's humps can become self-fulfilling prophecies. A woman without alternative models and images may see her future in a limited way.

The lack of positive images of women in midlife affects others as well. For instance, without images to contradict the over-the-hill image of aging women, employers are more likely to pass over these women for employment or promotions. Add age discrimination to sex and color discrimination, and the challenge of having a purposeful vision of the future becomes enormous. Women at midlife, if kept invisible and isolated because their stories are not heard and their experiences are not researched, will be disadvantaged in a competitive labor market.

A need for sociologically and psychologically oriented research on woman at midlife exists. Social workers working with midlife women need to know not only what may aid in the prevention of osteoporosis, but also what factors are associated with midlife psychological well-being and with prevention of the marginality that can result from aging in an ageist, sexist society—a problem that women of all economic strata face.

It is also important for women to have accurate images of what a woman's experience of midlife is. Just what, if anything, do women like about midlife? What do they dislike? What are their stereotypical images of midlife women? What do midlife women see as their strengths and vulnerabilities? The participants in the study discussed in this article were eager to share their experiences and hear what other women were going through. They were eager to construct new images and build new knowledge. Not only will their stories help women struggling in isolation with the emotional, psychological, social, and physical changes that they feel no one talks about, they will help women enter the next stage of adulthood in a more confident, validated way.

LITERATURE REVIEW

The most influential theorists in conceptualizing midlife transitions have been Jung, Jaques (who coined the term "midlife crisis"), Erikson, Vaillant, and Levinson—all men writing about men. Their writings suggest that midlife satisfaction is related to having a sense of generativity and giving to future generations (Erikson, 1950); to being able to accept one's age, find meaning and purpose, and not yearn for the activities of youth (Jung, 1933/1983); to having resolved the fear of death (Jaques, 1965); to loosening up and seizing one more chance of rebirth (Vaillant, 1977); and to forming a realistic picture of oneself and the world (Levinson, 1978).

The theoretical and empirical literature focusing specifically on the midlife experiences of women is much thinner. Heilbrun (1988) contended that meaningful work is critical to a woman's well-being as she ages. Apter (1995), one of the few scholars to examine the actual experience of midlife women, found the greatest challenge for a woman was integrating the images formed in adolescence of being female with that of being a woman in midlife. In addition, she found that a woman's most important insight was that she could at last listen to her own voice.

The literature on resilience and on coping with stress also provides potential insights into factors that might be associated with successful passage through midlife. Pearlin and Schooler (1978) pointed to a correlation between coping well and low self-denigration, high self-esteem, and high self-effectance. Self-in-relation theorists (Miller, 1976) emphasized the importance to a woman's identity of having connections with others. Other researchers have identified the importance of a friendship network and a confidante to women's emotional health (Baruch & Brooks-Gunn, 1984). Studies of temperament indicate that certain traits are stable and consistent over the life cycle. The existence of temperamental traits associated with resilience and vulnerability (Wolin & Wolin, 1993) suggests that personality factors contribute to women's midlife satisfaction.

HYPOTHESES

The theoretical suggestions discussed, as well as clinical experience with a large number of midlife women, led me to make several hypotheses about psychological sources of well-being in midlife for women (see McQuaide, 1996a). I hypothesized that a woman who was experiencing midlife (defined as ages 40 to 60) as a period of well-being would be more likely

- to have the ability to grieve and let go of the past
- to have the ability to construct a new midlife self
- to believe in a protective, spiritual force outside of her self
- to have the ability to find purpose and meaning in her life and to have a vision for the future
- to believe that she has a right to a life and is not obligated to a life of self-sacrifice
- to be accepting of herself, self-forgiving, and have a benign (not harsh) superego
- to be accepting of her own body.

This article describes the results of a research study testing these hypotheses and identifying the demographic, situational, and psychological factors associated with midlife well-being for women.

METHOD

A questionnaire on attitudes, beliefs, and feelings about midlife was distributed by mail to midlife respondents recruited through posters in doctors' offices and university buildings, announcements in organizational bulletins, and advertisements in local newspapers; 103 women, ranging in age from 40 to 59, completed the survey. All of the women were white and lived in the New York City area. Detailed characteristics of the sample are given in Table 1.

The questionnaire had three parts. First, respondents were asked to describe their current psychological state in several ways: They were asked to rate themselves on a five-point Likert-type scale with regard to how happy or unhappy they were feeling at this time in their life, whether they were having an easy or difficult time coping, and whether they were finding this time in their life confusing or not. They were also asked to give themselves a grade from A (excellent) to F (very poor) in terms of 17 areas of life: having friends, dealing with fear and anxiety, dealing with depression, dealing with anger, dealing with guilt, family relationships, job and career, spirituality, intimacy, money management, creativity, leisure time, finding satisfaction, finding contentment, self-acceptance, acceptance of their body, and coping with this stage of life. The scores on the 17 areas were summed to provide an average grade or index of well-being reflecting their overall rating of themselves at this time in their life. Finally they were asked to indicate the current and recent sources of stress in their lives.

Second, the women were asked to indicate their level of agreement with 122 statements about themselves, using a five-point Likert-type scale, ranging from 1 = strongly agree to 5 = strongly disagree. Over half of the items made

TABLE 1   Characteristics of the Sample

Characteristic	*%*
Health	
Good or excellent	94.1
Other categories	5.9
Menopausal status	
Postmenopausal	44.3
Premenopausal	55.7
Education	
Four years of college	58.3
Less than four years of college	33.0
High school	8.7
Marital status	
Married	67.6
Living with significant other	6.7
Separated or divorced	18.6
Widowed	1.0
Single	5.9
Family income ($)	
<30,000	9.1
30,000–49,999	18.4
50,000–99,999	41.8
≥100,000	30.6
Reported sexual orientation	
Heterosexual	97.1
Homosexual or bisexual	2.9
Labor force status	
Full-time paid employment	59.4
Part-time paid employment	20.8
Homemaker	6.9
Student	4.0
Disabled, unemployed, or involuntarily retired	8.9
Occupational status*	
Managerial, professional, and technical	67.7
Skilled or semiskilled blue-collar	6.3
Clerical, sales, or other white-collar	26.0
Family responsibilities	
Taking care of own or spouse's parents	11.9
Children still living at home	35.0
Attitude toward feminism	
Describe self as a feminist	17.6
Describe self as a "traditional" woman	5.9
Describe self as a mix of both	76.5
Age: M = 49.82	
Range: 40–59 years; SD = 4.87	

*Of those in paid labor force.

up 10 scales designed to measure the various psychological constructs that I had hypothesized would be relevant to midlife well-being. These included self-esteem, lack of self-denigration, self-effectance, optimism, the ability to grieve, the belief that one has a right to a life, having a vision or goal and a sense of meaning in one's life, being aware of constructing a new identity in midlife, having a positive narrative about one's life, and having a benign (not overly harsh) superego. Additional scales measured such issues as the women's sense of their own spirituality, their feelings about their own appearance, the degree to which they felt marginal, whether or not they had positive images of midlife, feelings about their sex life, and feelings about their ability to manage their finances. I developed the scales on a rational-empirical basis. For each construct, a number of items were written that, on their face, appeared to reflect that construct. (The items for the initial self-esteem, self-denigration, and self-effectance scales were derived from those presented in Pearlin & Schooler, 1978.) After gathering data on 50 women, the responses to the items provisionally making up each scale were factor analyzed. Items were then eliminated so the remaining items on each scale constituted a monofactorial scale, with all items having loadings of at least 0.60 on a single factor.

Third, the questionnaire contained a series of qualitative questions. The participants were asked what they liked and disliked about midlife, how they saw themselves as changing in midlife, what their images of "typical" and "ideal" midlife women were, what the best times in their own lives had been, what their weaknesses and strengths in dealing with life were, and when they felt strongest or most vulnerable. They were also asked about how well understood they had felt as they were going through midlife, what their emotional needs were at this time, and what areas they would like to see more midlife research on; they then had space for open-ended comments.

QUANTITATIVE FINDINGS

Overall Well-Being at Midlife

In general, the women surveyed expressed high degrees of well-being: 72.5 percent ($n = 74$) indicated that at this time in their life they felt "very happy" or "happy," and 64.3 percent ($n = 65$) felt that they were finding this time in their life "not very confusing" or "not confusing at all." By contrast, only 13.7 percent ($n = 14$) of the women indicated that they were "unhappy" or "very unhappy," and a somewhat larger number, although still a clear minority, 27.7 percent ($n = 28$), indicated that they were finding this period "confusing" or "very confusing." Being happy and unconfused did not necessarily mean that they were not finding midlife a time of turmoil and struggle: Only 41.2 percent ($n = 42$), far fewer than the number reporting happiness, wrote that they were having a "very easy time" or "easy time" coping, whereas 39.2 percent ($n = 40$) reported a "difficult" or "somewhat difficult" time coping. The same pattern appears with respect to how the respondents rated themselves on specific areas of their lives. On the "report card," more than half the 103 respondents (56.2 percent) gave themselves an overall grade of B (good) or better. Only 9.7 percent gave themselves a C (fair) or lower.

The several measures of well-being measured by the survey were highly intercorrelated (for example, for the aggregate grade on the 17 areas of a respondent's life and the average of the respondent's self-ratings with respect to happiness, case of coping, and confusion, $r = .78$, $p < .01$). In the analyses reported below, the aggregate grade was used as an index of well-being.

Demographic and Situational Correlates of Well-Being

The responses of the women were first analyzed by separate one-way analyses of variance (ANOVAs) for each of the demographic and situational variables: health, income, having a confidante, having a group of friends, employment status, menopausal status, education level, occupational group, marital status, sexual orientation, and feminist versus traditional orientation. The ANOVAs indicated that women who reported high levels of well-being at midlife were distinguished from those who reported lower levels of satisfaction by several demographic and situational variables: good health, annual family income above $30,000, having a confidante or group of friends, and being employed or a homemaker were good predictors of well-being. The better a woman's health, the more likely she was to report high Levels of well-being [$F(3, 98) = 7.183, p = .0002$]. Menopausal status was not related to well-being, however [$F(1, 95) = .586, p = .4459$]. Whether or not a woman reported menopausal symptoms (for example, hot flashes) was also not related to well-being [$F(1, 98) = .919, p = .3401$].

Low family income was associated with low levels of well-being [$F(3, 94) = 3.594, p = .0165$], because of the problems faced by women at the bottom of the income scale. As long as family income was above $30,000 per year, income made no difference, but those with incomes below $30,000 were less satisfied than the other income groups. Occupational group had no effect [$F(3, 98) = 1.371, p = .2563$], and women who were homemakers or who were students and not in the paid labor force were no more and no less likely to express satisfaction than women who worked in the paid labor force. However, being out of the paid labor force involuntarily (for example, because of being laid off, forced into early retirement, or because of physical disability) was associated with lower levels of well-being [$F(4, 96) = 3.766, p = .0069$]. Educational level was not associated with differences in level of satisfaction [$F(4, 97) = 1.462, p = .2197$].

Marital status [$F(5, 96) = .443, p = .8169$], whether or not a woman had children living at home [$F(1, 91) = .062, p = .8044$], whether she had children at all [$F(1, 100) = 3.082, p = .0822$], and her sexual orientation [$F(2, 100) = .394, p = .6748$] had no significant effect on well-being, nor did whether or not a woman perceived herself as a feminist, a traditional woman, or a mix of the two [$F(2, 99) = 1.421, p = .2464$]. However, women who responded positively to the question, Do you have a confidante to whom you can speak freely and honestly about yourself? were significantly more likely to express a positive sense of well-being than women who did not [$F(1, 101) = 6.029, p = .0158$], and women who reported having a group of women friends with whom they were close also reported significantly greater satisfaction with their lives [$F(1, 101) = 13.843, p = .0003$]. Finally, the number of current and recent sources of stress was negatively correlated with well-being ($r = -.42$).

To explore the significance of the situational and demographic variables further, a multiple regression analysis was undertaken. A model comprising four variables—the number of stressors, health status, family income (below or above $30,000 per year), and whether or not a woman had social supports (having either a confidante or a group of friends or both)—accounts for 38.9 percent of the variance in well-being associated with demographic and situational factors (Table 2). Distinguishing between whether a woman has an intimate, a close group of friends, or both does not appreciably change the amount of explained variance. Labor force status also failed to explain additional variance, despite its first-order association with well-being. The latter situation appears to result from the fact that being involuntarily out of the labor force is often caused by having health problems and results in low family income. Hence, adding labor force status to health and family income does not add to the explanation of well-being. An alternative model using stress, labor force status, and social supports alone (and omitting health and income) explains somewhat less of the overall variance in well-being

TABLE 2   Multiple Regression Analysis: Demographic Variables

Independent Variable	β	SE	t	r
Stress	−1.6208	.4452	−3.641	.0005
Health	−4.2005	1.2468	−3.369	.0005
Income	2.4980	.8356	2.9894	.0036
Social support	−6.9358	2.6073	−2.6602	.0093

Dependent variable: Index of well-being (grade)
Constant: 74.1268. Multiple $R = .6172$; $F(4, 89) = 13.5354$, $p < .0001$

(30.1 percent) than the stress, health, income, and social support model, however.

Psychological Correlates of Well-Being

A woman's score on several of the measures of psychological function was, as was hypothesized, strongly related to whether or not she reported high levels of well-being. High self-esteem, lack of self-denigration, and a benign superego showed the highest correlations with the overall self-rating ($r = .70$ to $r = .73$). (With the exceptions specifically noted below, all correlation coefficients were significant at $p < .0001$.) Having the ability to grieve one's past, having a vision of the future and being able to create meaning in one's life, being able to construct a positive self-narrative, having a high sense of self-effectance, being optimistic, and believing one had a right to a life also predicted well-being, although not as strongly ($r = .56$ to $r = .64$). However, contrary to my hypothesis, feeling one was constructing a new identity in midlife was only weakly related to well-being ($r = .27$, $p = .005$).

Women who reported doing well at midlife also reported that they had a sense of their own relevance. They did not feel marginal or useless ($r = .61$). There was a less strong although significant correlation between well-being and positive feelings about one's own appearance ($r = .54$) or having positive images of midlife women ($r = .44$). Satisfaction with one's sex life was also moderately associated with well-being ($r = .47$). Confidence in one's ability to manage finances was not, however ($r = .22$, $p = .0269$). Surprisingly, a sense of spirituality was completely irrelevant to feelings of well-being ($r = −.06$, $p = .6623$).

To further elucidate factors associated with well-being, a multiple regression analysis was undertaken. A model containing four psychological variables—lack of self-denigration, having a vision of the future and being able to create meaning in one's life, being able to construct a positive self-narrative, and not feeling marginal or useless—accounts for the largest proportion of variance in well-being (Table 3). Together these four variables explained 62.9 percent of the variance, a substantially larger proportion than the 38.9 percent explained by the situational and demographic variables.

The failure of the other psychological variables to add appreciably to the prediction of well-being is the consequence of the high degree of correlation among these variables. To take the most extreme example, lack of self-denigration, a benign superego, and self-esteem all have correlations with each other above $r = .85$. Reflecting this, a number of other models, almost as good at explaining well-being as the optimal model, can be constructed by substituting, for

TABLE 3   Multiple Regression Analysis: Psychological Characteristics

Independent Variable	β	SE	t	r
Self-denigration	−.4035	.1054	−3.8302	.0002
Vision of future	−.3651	.1679	2.1741	.0321
Positive narrative	.4061	.1538	2.6402	.0097
Lack of marginality	−.6810	.2812	−2.4217	.0173

Dependent variable: Index of well-being (grade)
Constant: 59.1811. Multiple $R = .7931$ $F(4, 97) = 41.1276$, $p < .0001$

instance, having a benign superego or good self-esteem for lack of self-denigration, a high sense of self-effectance for having a vision of the future, and a sense of optimism or the ability to grieve one's past for having a positive self-narrative. A model combining even some of the relatively poorer predictors of well-being, such as feeling one has the right to a life, having positive images of midlife, having positive feelings about one's appearance, and being satisfied with one's sex life, can explain over half of the variance in well-being, although the contribution of these variables to explaining well-being is drowned out when they are combined with the better predictors with which they are correlated.

From a clinical and a theoretical perspective, the significance of such psychological constructs as superego strength and self-esteem should not be discounted because they are pushed out of the regression model by the marginally more powerful ability of lack of self-denigration (with which superego strength and self-esteem are correlated) to predict well-being. The different constructs reflect different underlying theoretical explanations, each of which would appear to be effective as a tool for understanding midlife well-being. The superego construct reflects, of course, a psychodynamic perspective, whereas the self-esteem construct may reflect more of a phenomenological viewpoint and the lack of self-denigration construct more of a cog-

nitive viewpoint. Having goals and a vision of the future, having a sense of self-effectance, being able to grieve the past, and being able to construct a meaningful narrative may reflect more of a cognitive constructivist viewpoint. The present study was not systematically designed to test the adequacy of models of midlife well-being coming explicitly from the differing theoretical perspectives, but it suggests the potential value of doing so.

Qualitative Findings

The qualitative responses to the questionnaire of the 10 women who had the highest overall self-rating of well-being (the aggregate score on the 17 areas of functioning) and those with the 10 lowest were compared impressionistically.

Both the group scoring highest in midlife satisfaction and the group scoring lowest in satisfaction were unanimous in reporting that what they liked best about midlife was increased independence and freedom—freedom from worrying about what others think, from responsibility for children, and from menstrual periods and freedom to develop an identity based on pursuing their own and not others' interests. High scorers were more likely to feel freedom "to" do something new (for example, develop relationships with women friends, build a career) whereas low scorers were more likely to report freedom "from" (for example, menstruation, pregnancy, and appearance worries). Low scorers were also more likely to report enjoying watching their children and grandchildren grow; high scorers more frequently reported that they most enjoyed doing things in a larger world beyond the family. All high scorers reported feeling their physical and emotional changes were understood by those around them, whereas not a single low scorer felt understood.

Both high and low scorers disliked the physical changes of midlife the most, especially the decrease in energy and in the ability to do things they once could do. Also frequently mentioned by both groups were gray hair, wrinkles, memory difficulties, and extra weight. The high scorers were more likely to mention disliking the discrepancy between how they saw themselves (very positively) and how they imagined society saw them (as unattractive). Low scorers were more likely to mention that they disliked the sense of life winding down, mortality, fear of the future and being alone, and mood swings. One woman reported feeling like midlife was the neglected middle child of adulthood: she felt she was too old to get hired for a job with benefits, yet too young for Medicare. Both groups noted that men do not lose social value as they age the way women do, and that gray hair and wrinkles are not seen as unattractive in men. They saw the double standard of aging as unfair.

High scorers had generally positive images of midlife (for example, less stress caused by children, open-mindedness and positive anticipation of the future, confidence in their potential to grow and contribute to the world), although these were often mixed with some negative images (depression, loss of libido, fatigue, and overweight). Low scorers reported predominantly negative images (a tired has-been, a woman struggling with a job she does not like, depression), although they saw the typical midlife woman as finding pleasure in children and grandchildren.

The high scorers were more task oriented and saw their weaknesses as traits such as procrastination, disorganization, and overextending themselves. The low scorers were more aware of issues related to self-esteem, fear, and being ruled by others' wishes. Doubting the self and not valuing the self were mentioned by every woman who reported low satisfaction with midlife. Both groups mentioned perfectionism—with parenting, career, or being a woman—as being a problem.

Both high and low scorers saw perseverance as their greatest strength. High scorers emphasized traits that enabled them to move forward (learning from mistakes, letting go of negatives that they could not change, self-forgiveness). Low scorers emphasized survival ("taking care of myself because no one else will," "I can appear in control even when I'm going to pieces," "I'm there for others in a crisis").

High scorers saw themselves as feeling strongest when they felt challenged and had a sense of high self-effectance. Low scorers also felt strongest when accomplishing something independently, however, they also mentioned feeling strongest when not beset by doubts, when not in the presence of a negative. Both groups felt most vulnerable when in love, when they or someone they loved was sick, and when there were financial problems. Both high and low scorers saw the most important psychological needs at midlife as being valued, productive, loved, accepted, understood, attractive, and independent, and as having inner resources to replace the losses of midlife.

Respondents with high satisfaction and those with low satisfaction identified similar kinds of research as being potentially helpful for midlife women. Women were most interested in research on hormone replacement—especially "natural" sources of estrogen—and on ways that modern women are going through midlife that differ from the ways their mothers and previous generations negotiated "the change." Several women wondered whether research could help identify whether all the changes stereotypically associated with menopause and midlife were real or whether they occurred because they were "supposed" to happen and thus were just a self-fulfilling prophecy. One woman stated emphatically that what was needed was not midlife research but midlife PR! Changing society's outdated attitudes toward aging was reflected in most subjects' enthusiasm for research on women.

CONCLUSIONS AND IMPLICATIONS FOR SOCIAL WORK PRACTICE

Society's Attitudes

First, social workers working with midlife clients should not adopt the negative stereotypes that currently prevail because of the lack of positive images of midlife women. To assume that midlife women are developmentally programmed to experience menopausal instability and depression or empty nest loneliness would be inaccurate and may lead to a self-fulfilling prophecy. Results of this study indicate, for instance, that menopausal symptoms and the empty nest are irrelevant to well-being in midlife for certain women. Midlife, for white middle-class and upper middle-class women, at least, is not a time of torment. Most of the women participating in this study were satisfied with themselves and their lives. Despite their happiness, they did find it a challenging stage of life. Almost three-quarters reported that they were happy, yet barely half that number reported that they were having an easy time coping. For some people, having stressors to cope with does not prevent them from being happy.

The women who reported most satisfaction with the 17 areas of their lives examined differed from those with the least satisfaction in a number of ways. Their annual family income was above $30,000 (how much above $30,000 did not seem to matter), they were healthy, and they were not involuntarily out of the labor force. Menopausal status and symptoms, caring for parents, an emptied nest, educational level, marital status, occupation, and feminism were not correlated to midlife well-being. It seemed that it was not so much what the women had but what they did with it that made the biggest difference to their well-being. If the woman was "blocked from being in the world" (through disability, poor health, involuntary unemployment, limited spending power), then she was less likely to be happy. "Being a player" seems to be critical to well-being. On a macro level, social work interventions that help women maintain their health and employment, avoid marginality, and maintain an adequate income would benefit midlife women.

The most satisfied women unanimously reported that this was the best or happiest time of life. They were actively participating in what the world has to offer and looking forward to a future filled with new opportunities as enjoyable as the opportunities of the past. Women not doing well yearned for earlier days when there was a sense of possibility—for a happy marriage, wonderful children, an exciting career. The present lacked a comparable sense of wonderful possibility. Opportunities in midlife were either invisible or inferior to those of earlier days. The women lacked positive images for vision building or meaning making, and they were finding dreams from the past an ineffective solace. Social workers can help women by enabling their active participation in the world and helping them find a sense of meaning and opportunity in the world.

Involvement with Others

Being able to participate in a social world by having a confidante or a group of women friends, as well as having positive models, was also predictive of midlife satisfaction. The women who reported doing well were involved with others and felt that the changes they were going through were understood by others. The women doing poorly felt isolated and were angry about being misunderstood. Social workers' ability to offer empathic individual and group treatment to help strengthen a woman's connection to a social network has the potential to offer precisely the help struggling midlife women need.

Women doing well and those not doing well reported feeling vulnerable under similar circumstances (when in love or when sick), and they reported their emotional needs as being the same (wanting to be loved, valued, respected), but their responses to vulnerability differed. Women doing well responded to vulnerability and emotional need by being challenged and becoming active in the world, resulting in increased self-effectance and power. Women having a more difficult time responded by feeling self-doubt rather than challenge, and they were frustrated in their attempts to get their needs met. For them the most rewarding aspect of the social world was children and grandchildren, a kind of vicarious enjoyment of the sense of possibility.

The Self

Women doing well were aware of a troubling discrepancy between the positive way they saw themselves and the social devaluation they perceived, and they felt challenged to live lives that contradicted the "over the hill" stereotype. Their sense of "personhood" was stronger than ever, yet society and the media were fading them into an invisibility that does not sit well with the baby boomer generation. They were aware of dissonance between the increased freedom and power they felt and negative cultural stereotypes and media portrayals. Women not doing well reported less dissonance, seeming to comply with cultural messages about obsolescence. Unlike women with greater satisfaction, they lacked alternative images of midlife aging.

All the women bemoaned the loss of physical capabilities and attractiveness and, to varying degrees, were astonished that so many areas of life were actually changing. Feeling more freedom yet more physical limitations was a source of frustration. Women doing well did not turn against the self. They reported being able to grieve old images of themselves (a constructive grief), value who they were becoming, construct a life story that was balanced toward the positive, feel positive about their appearance, and feel like important contributors in the world. They had a dream and were pursuing it armed with feelings of self-effectance, self-acceptance, and self-esteem. They reported believing that they had a right to a life, or a right to have power. They did not have to live vicariously or wait until everyone else was taken care of before their own needs mattered. Hopefully these research findings can guide social work practitioners in their collaborative treatment planning with clients who come for help during midlife.

On a micro level, social workers can help midlife women enormously. The clinical interventions in which social workers are trained are precisely the interventions that would develop characteristics associated with midlife well-being. Women who feel that the changes they are going through are empathically understood and who have a group or individual to confide in have some protection against midlife dissatisfaction, according to the results of this study. Social workers, using group or individual treatment skills, can help women raise self-esteem, break the habit of self-denigration, develop goals for the future, grieve the past, and compose a positive life narrative.

One surprising result of this study was that spirituality did not correlate highly with high midlife coping for this sample. My guess would be that this is because, although for a subgroup of women spirituality contributes to well-being, there is another group, which cancels out the effects of the first group, for whom spirituality is either neutrally unimportant or actively rejected.

This investigation has examined characteristics of women who are doing well at midlife. Both for social policy and for clinical work with women, these observations suggest some of the goals that would facilitate midlife well-being (for clinical examples of individual and group approaches see McQuaide, 1996a, 1996b). This current study focused on middle-class white women. Whether these findings also apply to women from other racial or ethnic groups or to poorer women remains a topic for future research and is currently being investigated.

What we have learned is that a woman needs a decent job and a decent income. She needs to stay actively involved in the world, not just the social world, and she needs to keep herself challenged. More than ever, having a supportive social environment and not denigrating oneself are critical. For social workers involved politically and clinically with the midlife woman these issues are central.

REFERENCES

Apter, T. (1995). *Secret paths: Women in the new midlife.* New York: W. W. Norton.

Baruch, G., & Brooks-Gunn, J. (Eds.). (1984). *Women in midlife.* New York Plenum.

Erikson, E. H. (1950). *Childhood and society.* New York: W. W. Norton.

Greer, G. (1992). *The change: Women, aging, and the menopause.* New York: Alfred A. Knopf.

Heilbrun, C. G. (1988). *Writing a woman's life.* New York: Ballantine Books.

Jaques. E. (1965). Death and the mid-life crisis. *International Journal of Psychoanalysis, 46,* 502–514.

Jung, C. G. (1933/1983). The stages of life. In A. Storr (Ed.), *The essential Jung.* Princeton, NJ: Princeton University Press.

Levinson, D. J. (1978). *The seasons of a man's life.* (with C. Darrow, E. Klein, M. Levinson, & B. McKee). New York: Alfred A. Knopf.

McQuaide, S. (1996a). Keeping the wise blood: The construction of images in a mid life women's group. *Social Work with Groups, 19,* 131–145.

McQuaide, S. (1996b). Self hatred, the right to a life, and the tasks of midlife. *Clinical Social Work Journal, 24,* 35–47.

Miller, J. B. (1976). *Toward a new psychology of women.* Boston: Beacon Press.

Pearlin, L. I., & Schooler, C. (1978). The structure of coping. *Journal of Health and Social Behavior, 19,* 2–21.

Ryff, C. (1995). Psychological well-being in adult life. *Current Directions in Psychological Science, 4,* 99–105.

Sheehey, G. (1992). *The silent passage.* New York: Random House.

Vaillant, G. E. (1977). *Adaptation to life.* Boston: Little, Brown.

Wolin, S. J., & Wolin, S. (1993). *The resilient self: How survivors of troubled families rise above adversity.* New York: Ullard Books.

Critical Thinking Questions

1. What makes today's middle-aged women so different from those of a generation or two ago? Do you think the differences are enough to justify research on them? Why or why not?

2. Overview the methodology employed for this study. What suggestions do you have for changing the sampling so that subsequent studies will be more reliable?

3. Why do you think no relationship was found between menopausal status and menopausal symptoms and well-being?

4. Why do you think that neither marital status nor whether one thought of herself as a feminist had no relationship on well-being? What other factors appear to be working here?

5. How do images of midlife relate to midlife satisfaction? Do these findings support McQuaide's original reason for conducting the study?

6. Based on the findings in this study, what aids women in counterbalancing the negative images of middle-aged women in this society? What could be done to help diminish these negative images?

11 Fertility Patterns and Challenges of Parenthood

*W*hy do some people in other countries have so many children? Why doesn't everyone use birth control? Isn't the use of fertility drugs unsafe and unethical? Why do people in some countries take risks with unsafe abortions? Why don't they just use birth control instead? What happens to marriages after children are born? These are questions students have posed to me over my teaching years. Most of the students asking these questions are genuinely curious and confused. For many, family experiences have been limited to their own families and the families of a few close friends who tend to be similar to them in social class, race, and religion. Some assume that everyone knows about fertility control and contraception and that everyone everywhere has the same access to information and technologies related to family planning. Often, students also believe that once children arrive, marriages whither on the vine. But are these assumptions and beliefs true?

To find answers to these questions, one must examine facts about population trends and fertility patterns in the United States and globally. For example, how does fertility control relate to maternal and infant mortality? What are the facts about contraception and abortion rates worldwide? One needs also to look at sociological research on couples' decisions to become parents or not and the effects of parenthood on marriage. What are the alternatives if a couple cannot have children?

Population Patterns and Trends

Deciding if and when to have children goes beyond the visions of a particular couple. When it appears that "everyone" is having large families, for instance, couples may perceive having several children as normative, the thing to do. Likewise, when public discourse bemoans increases in population or promotes the small family as ideal, or when the social acceptability of birth control is high, couples' decisions may be affected by this public opinion.

Population Growth, Environmental Quality, and Quality of Life

Each day, the world's **population**—the total number of persons occupying a designated geographical area—grows by 250,000 people (Motavalli 1996: 28). As of October 11, 1999, there were 6 billion people living in this world (McFalls 1998: 21). This figure is twice what it was in 1960, and it is expected to reach 9.4 billion by 2050 (Mitchell 1998: 21). Depending on death and birth rates, the world population could be as high as 27 billion by 2150 ("United Nations World Population" 1998).

By 1996, 10 nations had exceeded the 100 million mark: China (1.232 billion), India (945 million), the United States (269 million), Indonesia (200 million), Brazil (161 million), the Russian Federation (148 million), Pakistan (140 million), Japan (125 million), Bangladesh (120 million), and Nigeria (115 million) ("Population 2050" 1997: 72). By 1997, the developing countries of the world accounted for 98 percent of world population growth ("World Population Data Sheet 1997: 23). The population growth in developing countries is partially a function of greater abilities to control or cure diseases that previously were fatal. About 80 percent of the world's population live in developing regions, such as India, China, Central America, and Africa ("Population 2050" 1997). Furthermore, over half of the world's population is under the age of 25.

It is expected that by 2150, the world population of those under age 25 will drop to 17 percent, and the proportion of people over age 60 will increase (from 9 percent in 1995) to 30 percent ("United Nations World Population" 1998: 189). Much of the increase in the elderly population in the United States has been the result of longer life expectancies, especially in the developed Western nations. The so-called graying of America is largely a product of a bulge in the population following World War II. This bulge is referred to as the **baby boom.**

In the United States, population growth throughout the twentieth century was phenomenal. The U.S. population stood at 100 million in 1917 and at 200 million in 1967. The U.S. may have a population of 500 million by the year 2100 (Motavalli 1996: 29).

A number of key issues relate to population growth. In developing countries, for instance, soils are rapidly degrading and it is more and more difficult to find and access land suitable for growing foods. Through environmental degradation, overpopulation, and political and economic inequality, most of the world's hungry people are in the developing world (Motavalli 1996; Raloff 1996; "Third World" 1997; Kleine 1997; "But Severe Poverty" 1997).

In nations such as the United States, a key concern is the cost of population growth to the environment in relation to the comparatively high standards of affluent nations. Heavy reliance on fossil fuels and lavish life-styles that require manufactured goods and nonrecyclable materials lead to a rapid depletion of nonrenewable resources to sustain this affluence (Raloff 1996). It is estimated that only 20 percent of the world's population live in industrialized nations, but these nations account for 74 percent of the world's greenhouse emissions (Dunn 1998: 19).

When summits are held regarding the state of the world's environment, population issues always emerge and the debate never stops. The Western industrialized nations tend to point the finger at developing nations and demand that people in those nations reduce their birth rates, whereas developing nations argue that the industrial postmodern societies are placing the greatest demands on the environment (Raloff 1996; "Gets Worse for Who?" 1994). Who is right?

All nations must address issues of population growth. Is there enough arable land to feed a given population or the world's population? Can biotechnology and alternative agriculture meet the challenges for safe and efficient food production for expanding populations? How many children are too many children? How many are enough? Who decides how many children a particular couple may or should have? And, once the children are born, can they be fed? How long will they live? How well will they live? Will there be jobs for them in this ever-changing world?

Issues of Population Control

Population control refers to all policies, measures, and methods a society uses to maintain the population within a desired numerical range. Methods of population control include **birth control** (any strategy, device, or technology that prevents birth), **abortion** (the artificial termination of a pregnancy), and **infanticide** (the killing of infants). Methods of birth control increasingly in use around the world today are **contraceptive;** that is, they prevent conception. Birth control pills, condoms, diaphragms, IUDs (intrauterine devices), and hormonal patches or injections such as Depo-Provera are forms of contraception. Surgical procedures such as sterilization, vasectomy, laparoscopy, and hysterectomy also prevent conception.

Population control can be forced on a country by its government, as is the case in China. China limits family size to one son. If the first born is a son, then the couple is forbidden to have other children. If the first born is a girl, couples may try one more time to have a son. Governments also can try to control the legal age of marriage and encourage or force schooling for girls (Riley 1997). On the other hand, governments can discourage population by banning or severely restricting access to the most effective means of birth control. For instance, in Japan regulations favor the use of condoms over the use of birth control pills as a public health effort at controlling sexually transmitted diseases (Mitchell 1998). However, birth control pills are more effective contraceptives than are condoms. At the same time, of course, condoms provide protection from AIDS for spouses and fetuses.

Population control is influenced by policy statements, media campaigns, and well-publicized summits, such as the 1994 International Conference on Population and Development, held in Cairo. In countries such as Brazil, Kenya, India, and Mexico, televised soap operas illustrate the advantages of delaying marriage and childbirth, spacing births more widely, and having fewer children (Westhoff 1995). People also voluntarily reduce birth rates when future survival is uncertain. Wars, epidemics of fatal diseases, massive natural disasters, and famines also control population.

Individual participation in population control is a function of several factors. Cultural traditions may encourage or discourage fertility control. For instance, in some societies, a woman's fertility is the basis of her value as a spouse, and population control is unwelcome. Other factors include social class, individuals' knowledge of and access to effective means of birth control and abortion, and opportunities to delay first marriage and childbirth (Westhoff 1995; Riley 1997). In 60 countries, women may not be sterilized unless their husbands give formal permission. In some countries, husbands' permission is needed for all types of birth control (Mitchell 1998).

Husbands' disapproval has been noted as a barrier to fertility control in some countries. For instance, two national studies in Kenya found that when men wanted no more children, couples' contraceptive use is two to three times more likely than when men want more children (Dodoo 1998).

Studies conducted in Ghana also have found that male domination of decision making and male disapproval of fertility control are both related to higher fertility rates (Takyi and Oheneba-Sakyi 1997; Kannae and Pendleton 1998). Whether a couple engages in fertility control is significantly related to the husband's approval.

Depending on the country, religion also may play a role in fertility control. For instance, Catholics, Muslims, and Traditional Religionists tend to have more children than do Protestants in Ghana. Traditional Religionists carry with them generations of encouragement and kin support for large families. These groups also are patriarchal, with men holding the view that women and children are property (Nazzar et al. 1995). Ghanaian Catholics adhere strongly to papal decrees on birth control and abortion. Ghanaian Muslims, though tolerant of alternatives to their views and life-styles, tend to favor childbearing and disapprove of childlessness. Protestants are not as patriarchal as the other groups. Women are encouraged to be employed outside the home and to improve their quality of life (Oheneba-Sakyi and Heaton 1993).

For men in some developing countries, large families are a way to attain relatively higher status and more prestige. At the same time, women sometimes want fertility control urgently enough that they will secure it anyway, hopefully without getting caught by their husbands. For instance, it has been found that in Gambia, some women prefer using the injectable contraceptive Depo-Provera because their husbands, who disapprove of fertility control, probably will not be able to detect it (Riley 1997).

Fertility Patterns and Trends

The term **fertility rate** means the average number of births per woman between the ages of 15 and 49, or childbearing age (McFalls 1998: 8). Social and historical factors have played a role in every country's fertility trends. In addition, fertility patterns within a country vary in relation to social class, ethnicity, and age. One constant finding across countries is the fact that fertility rates are higher in rural than in urban areas. Rural residents tend to hold more strongly to a traditional ideal of large families. In many countries, children are still part of the rural family labor force, and there often is limited access to and knowledge about birth control.

Fertility in the United States

Until the first few decades of the nineteenth century, American women averaged seven children. Subsequently, the fertility rate gradually declined. This decline in fertility continued until the baby boom following World War II between the years 1945 and 1960 (McFalls 1998). Women averaged 3.4 to 3.6 children during this period of postwar affluence, when it was both financially possible and socially acceptable to have relatively larger families. In addition, contraceptive options were limited and access to them was not easy. The baby boom served as a catalyst for promoting the prevention of unwanted births and the education of women in an effort to curb potential overpopulation, bring the U.S. fertility rate down to replacement level only, and help women avoid unwanted pregnancies (Westhoff 1995).

By the 1970s, the U.S. was in a **baby bust** era, in which far fewer children were born. In 1976, U.S. fertility reached its record low, 1.74 children per woman. Fertility then increased to a baby boomlet fertility rate in 1990 of 2.08. Since 1996, the fertility rate has remained at 2.03. Several factors encourage lower fertility in the United States, especially the high cost of having and raising children and greater access to relatively inexpensive methods of birth control. The postindustrial economy and structure of employment in the United States favors

Figure 11.1   **Birth Rates in the United States, by Age of Mother and Age Groups, 1955 to 1996**

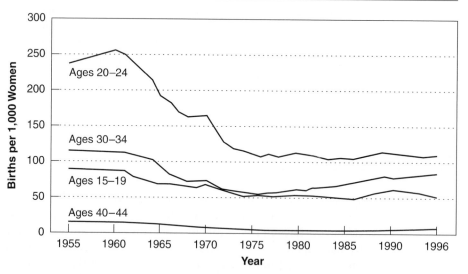

Source: From "Population: A Lively Introduction" by Joseph McFalls, 1998, *Population Bulletin*, *53* (3), p. 9. Used by permission of the Population Reference Bureau, Inc. (Based on National Center for Health Statistics, *Monthly Vital Statistics Reports* 46, no. 11 [1998]: table 4; and *Vital Statistics of the United States, 1990*, vol. 1 [1994]: table 1–9.)

women who delay childbirth. A pattern has emerged in which women delay marriage, delay childbirth until they are older, and either have fewer children than they originally intended or have no children at all (McFalls 1998: 9). Figure 11.1 illustrates the development of this pattern.

As you can see in Figure 11.1, from the 1960s and 1970s onward, the United States has seen a sharp drop in fertility among women ages 20 to 24—due to delaying marriage and first birth—and a corresponding increase in fertility when women are between the ages of 30 and 34. Interestingly, by 1996, the birth rate for women between the ages of 40 and 44 was below the levels recorded in the 1960s. Equally notable is that although the proportion of teenagers who are sexually active increased from the 1960s through the 1990s, the teen birth rate was comparatively low (McFalls 1998). Thus, in the United States, the fertility pattern by age tends to be low in the teens and early twenties, increasing through the twenties and early thirties, and then declining in the forties.

As with other countries, U.S. fertility levels vary by social class, race, and ethnicity. In general, fertility rates decrease as women's income and educational levels increase. Typical of this pattern are the statistics on U.S. fertility in 1995: Women who did not hold high school diplomas had an average of 2.7 children, whereas women with five or more years of college education had an average of 1.4 children (McFalls 1998: 11).

In 1996, the fertility rate for black women was 2.2; for Hispanic women, 3.0; and for Asian and Pacific Islander women, 1.9. The rate for white women was 1.8 (McFalls 1998).

Fertility in Ghana

In 1984, officials from Africa's many nations met in Tanzania to prepare for the International Conference on Population and Development sponsored by the United Nations. This meeting marked the first time that African leaders officially identified the need for reduced population growth and fertility rates and for greater availability of family planning services in order to achieve social and economic development for their respective countries and the entire continent (Goliber 1997: 4). Subsequently, many African nations officially created policies promoting family planning, lower fertility rates, and better health for women and children. In 1992, African delegates met again to discuss policies and strategies for economic and social development, with a focus on population. The conference, held in Senegal, encouraged leaders to review their policies regarding population reduction, fertility control, and environmental issues. One goal was to increase the prevalence of contraceptive use from 10 percent in 1992 to 44 percent by 2010 (Goliber 1997: 4).

Sub-Saharan West Africa's population was growing at a rate of 2.7 percent by the mid-1990s, which, if unabated, will double the population in 25 years (Goliber 1997). By 1998, 15 sub-Saharan countries had total contraceptive prevalence and 7 countries had modern contraceptive rates at 10 percent of their female population (Kannae and Pendleton 1998: 114). **Total contraceptive prevalence** means that contraceptives are available and accessible throughout a country. In most developing nations, if birth control is used, it is one of several traditional methods (Carr and Way 1994). **Traditional methods** include coitus interruptus (withdrawal), herbs, prolonged breast feeding, and abstinence or periodic abstinence (the rhythm or calendar method). Often, there is not enough money for the modern methods of birth control. Evidence suggests that "socio-cultural values seem to play an even greater role than financing" in the family planning arena in Africa (Kannae and Pendleton 1998: 114).

In 1960, the fertility rate for sub-Saharan Africa was 6.7 children per woman. In 1990, it was 6.0 (Goliber 1997: 16–17). Fertility rates in sub-Saharan Africa are the highest in the world (Kirk and Pillet 1998: 1). From 1960 to 1964, Ghana's fertility rate was 7.2 (Takyi and Oheneba-Sakyi 1994), but by 1993, it had dropped to 5.5, making it one of the lowest fertility rates in sub-Saharan Africa. Uganda, for instance, has a fertility rate of 6.9 and Rwanda's rate is 6.0 (Kirk and Pillet 1998).

Ghana's traditional culture placed a high value on having large families. Reasons include that family members' assistance is needed in farming, having many children offsets inevitable losses through infant and child deaths, and children are sources of insurance in old age (Takyi and Oheneba-Sakyi 1994). In parts of Ghana, people reject fertility control because of the problem of infant mortality (Nazzar et al. 1995). **Infant mortality** rates are expressed in terms of the numbers of children under the age of 1 year who die per 1,000 babies born. Ghana's infant mortality rate is 66 per 1,000, the lowest rate of all West African nations. In contrast, Burkina Faso, Ghana's neighbor to the north, has a rate of 103; Togo, Ghana's neighbor to the east, has a rate of 91; and Ghana's western neighbor, Cote d'Ivoire, has a rate of 89 (Goliber 1997: 7). The U.S. rate, by contrast, has been hovering between 7 and 8 infant deaths per 1,000 live births.

In Ghana, as in the United States, age at first marriage, educational attainment, and occupation are inversely related to fertility rates. That is, older, more educated, urban and professionally employed women have fewer children. Although there has been an influx of uneducated poor people into Ghana's cities, urban women tend to have higher educational attainment levels; more educated and professionally employed women tend to delay birth at first marriage; more middle- and upper-class people live in the urban versus the rural areas; and middle- and upper-class people tend to have smaller families.

Higher fertility rates in rural areas can be explained by cultural factors. Husbands and wives in Ghana's rural areas may encourage large families to help with labor-intensive agriculture. In addition, women in agriculture may have greater work flexibility and fewer difficulties with child care than do women in professional occupations (Oheneba-Sakyi and Heaton 1993; Takyi and Oheneba-Sakyi 1997; Kirk and Pillet 1998). Rural women tend to be illiterate, and, as with other low-income groups, for rural poor women in Ghana, motherhood is a desirable and attainable social status. The relationship between female literacy and infant mortality and fertility rates is clear. As female literacy increases, fertility and mortality rates decrease (United Nations 1997: 53). Fertility and mortality also decrease as more health facilities operate in rural areas so that women can easily secure pre- and postnatal care and medical care and vaccinations for their children.

Maternal Mortality: A Pressing Concern in Ghana

As fertility control levels increase, infant and mother mortality decrease. **Maternal mortality** is the number of mothers per 100,000 live births who die from complications of childbirth. The rate for the United States is 12. The rate for Ghana is 740 (UNICEF 1996). Sub-Saharan Africa accounts for 40 percent of maternal deaths worldwide. It is reported that the risk for pregnancy-related deaths is 100 times higher in sub-Saharan Africa than it is in Europe (World Health Organization 1996).

In Ghana, maternal mortality is a result of inadequate health care during pregnancy and childbirth, and some reflect the fact that mothers often are too young when they become pregnant. Other deaths were attributable to complications caused by female genital mutilation. This can involve several types of mutilation, the most severe of which is **infibulation,** which involves the removal of the clitoris and sewing closed the labia so that there is just a small opening for the vagina. Ideally, women will get to hospitals and have the labia unsewn prior to delivery of their children, but this does not always happen. Although female genital mutilation was outlawed in 1994, there are still millions of girls and women of childbearing age who have undergone this procedure. Other maternal deaths

What cultural and technological factors affect fertility and maternal mortality in Ghana, West Africa, and the United States?

are related to successive, closely spaced pregnancies combined with poor nutrition and weakened bodies. Unsafe abortions as a means of birth control also increase mortality rates (DaVanza, Parnell, and Foege 1991; Kulczycki, Potts, and Rosenfield 1996; "World Population Data Sheet" 1997). It is estimated that in Ghana, 25 percent of maternal deaths are caused by unsafe abortions (Panafrican News Agency 1997). Although some of the abortions are being sought by teenagers for whom contraceptive services have not been made available, research shows a lack of fertility control knowledge and access among married women, as well (World Health Organization 1996; Panafrican News Agency 1997; Conly 1998).

Among many groups in Ghana, husbands have control over wives' reproductive decisions and behavior. Inroads to greater fertility control among rural women slowly are being made, but these efforts have not yet yielded results in terms of decreased maternal mortality or convincing drops in fertility.

Use of Birth Control and Abortion

Worldwide, including the United States, the most common form of modern birth control is sterilization (DaVanzo et al. 1991; Piccinino and Mosher 1998). For men, this is the *vasectomy*, which involves a severing of the vas deferens, the conduits for sperm, by making a small incision in the scrotum. For women today, it frequently is a *laparoscopy* procedure. This involves making an incision at the navel, inflating the abdomen with gaseous substances, and using microscopic instruments to cut and tie off the fallopian tubes. You may have heard this procedure referred to as *Band-Aid surgery*, due to the Band-Aid placed on the navel at the end of the procedure. A more radical form of sterilization is the *hysterectomy*, which, if fully conducted, involves removal of the uterus and other internal reproductive organs. Hysterectomy is major surgery. Because less intrusive sterilization options are available for women, hysterectomy tends only to be used when medical conditions such as cancer deem it necessary.

It is reported that the highest rate of contraceptive use occurs in China, where 83 percent of women of childbearing age using some form of contraceptive. Great Britain reports the next-highest rate, with 82 percent of childbearing-age women using contraceptives (Golini 1998). In the United States, the figure is 64 percent, which reflects an increase from 56 percent in 1982. This increase occurred in all age groups and among white, black, and Hispanic women (Piccinino and Mosher 1998).

National data on U.S. women's contraceptive behaviors in 1982, 1988, and 1995 reveal that the most popular methods of birth control remain female sterilization, the pill, and the male condom. However, changes in preferences were noted between 1988 and 1995. From 1988 and 1995, use of the pill decreased and condom use increased among never-married women and black American women under the age of 25. Condom use, which also increased among formerly married women, reflects concerns about AIDS and other sexually transmitted diseases.

Even with the drop in use, the pill still is primarily used by women under the age of 30 who intend to have children later, who have at least one year of college education, and who are unmarried. Female sterilization is most common among women in their thirties and forties, blacks and Hispanics, and those with the least income and education. Although married white women's contraceptive preferences (female sterilization, male sterilization, the pill, and the male condom) have changed little, there was an increase in female sterilization among blacks, from 37 percent in 1982 to 54 percent in 1995 (Piccinino and Mosher 1998).

Risks accompany contraceptive options. Oral contraceptives (the pill) may increase the risk of cardiovascular disease among women who smoke by four to eight times that of pill users who do not smoke. Of course, smoking also carries the risk of cancer. However, high-dose oral contraceptives were removed from U.S. and other markets in 1989. The newer lower-dose pills have reduced this risk, though women who smoke are still encouraged to stop smoking if they also want to take oral contraceptives (Sadovsky 1998). The first large-scale, longitudinal study of pill use and health complications shows that pill-related risks of heart disease and cervical cancers are negligible 10 years after users stop taking the pill (Reuters 1999). A British team comprised of researchers from the Imperial Cancer Research Fund and the Royal College of General Practitioners recorded the health of 46,000 women from 1968 through 1993. They found diminished risk from going off the pill was evident for women who had taken the pill for 10 years or more, and for women who had taken the pill for less than 2 years. In addition, the death rate among the study's participants was lower than the death rate for the British population. This is an important study, especially since some 300 million women worldwide have used the pill since it became available in 1959 (Reuters 1999).

At the same time, oral contraceptives may decrease users' risks of uterine fibroids, ovarian cysts, and iron deficiency anemia. Studies in both developed and developing nations have revealed that oral contraceptives reduce the risk of **pelvic inflammatory disease (PID).** Oral contraceptives inhibit ovulation and therefore also reduce the risk of **ectopic (tubal) pregnancies.** It is suggested that since rates of ectopic pregnancies are high in developing countries, this benefit of oral contraceptives should not be ignored (DaVanzo et al. 1991).

Although intrauterine devices have been shown to reduce the risk of ectopic pregnancy by 60 percent, they carry risks, as well, one of which is pelvic inflammatory disease (PID). PID is associated with tubal infertility, an increased risk of contracting sexually transmitted diseases, and perforation of the uterus. Women who have more than one sex partner are not encouraged to use an IUD (DaVanza et al. 1998). Logically, one could add that women whose partners have more than one partner also should be advised against the IUD.

Condoms, of course, are well recognized for their **prophylactic** (disease preventing, health promoting) potential. Less recognized is the fact that the **diaphragm,** in conjunction with **spermicide** (substances that kill sperm), is not only an effective method of contraception but also another prophylactic method (DaVanzo et al. 1998).

When unwanted pregnancies occur, abortion rates increase. Worldwide, it is estimated that about 50 million abortions have been induced since the 1970s. Of these abortions, about 20 percent probably were illegal. Illegal abortions account for between 50,000 to 100,000 deaths a year, and occur mainly in poor and developing countries (Kulczycki et al. 1996: 1663).

The worldwide yearly abortion rate is estimated to range from between 32 to 46 abortions per 1,000 women of childbearing age. The Netherlands, which has the most liberal family planning provisions and safe legal abortions, has the lowest yearly abortion rate, at about 5 per 1,000 childbearing-age women. Russia has the highest rate, with about 186 abortions per 1,000 women of childbearing age (Kulczycki et al. 1998). Resorting to abortions, and particularly to unsafe ones, is highly related to lack of access to, or poor understanding of, effective contraception. **Unsafe abortions** are those performed by persons who lack the appropriate medical training. Typically, these abortions are performed under unsanitary (**septic**) conditions. Unsafe abortions are common in countries that do not legally permit abortions.

In industrialized Western nations, such as the United States, unmarried and poor women under the age of 25 obtain at least half of the abortions. Among these nations, there appears to be a relationship between being a young and ineffective contraceptive user, having difficulties accessing contraception, being too poor to afford children, being single, and securing abortions. In countries such as the Netherlands, family planning information and contraceptives are readily available to teenagers and unmarried people, and the abortion rate is the lowest in the world. In Japan and in eastern and central Europe, older married women seek abortions. This is because women in these regions tend to reject sterilization but use less effective contraceptive methods. All over the world, rural women are less likely to secure abortions, whereas educated women living in urban areas are more likely to secure abortions than their rural and/or less educated counterparts. This finding is somewhat in contrast to the trend in the United States (Kulczycki et al. 1998). According to a national survey conducted by the National Center for Health Statistics, women in the United States who have completed only high school have higher rates of abortion than do women with any other levels of educational attainment (Henshaw and Kost 1996: 143–144).

A national survey was conducted of 9,985 women who secured abortions in the United States during 1994 and 1995. As variables permitted, comparisons were made with a previous national study conducted in the United States in 1987. This comparison showed that abortion rates have increased for Hispanic women and that minorities and poor women are about two times more likely to secure abortions than are whites and women with adequate incomes. A consistent finding was that young women (ages 18 to 24) and never-married and separated women were about twice as likely to secure abortions than were older and married women. However, the proportion of those who were using a contraceptive during the month that they conceived rose from 51 percent in 1987 to 59 percent during 1994–1995 (Henshaw and Kost 1996: 140). Those securing abortions tended to use less effective or reliable measures, such as the condom.

Deciding to Become a Parent

In the developed world, in particular, having children increasingly has become seen as a choice. Likewise, voluntarily not having children is perceived as a choice in many countries today. It is projected that from 1990 to 2120, the number of childless couples in the United States will increase from 22 million to almost 31 million, an increase of about 44 percent (Edmonson et al. 1993). Much of this increase will be accounted for by baby boomers who initially delayed parenthood, and then either decided that parenthood was not an option or else became infertile and opted neither to adopt children nor to seek infertility treatment. Some of the increase will be due to people choosing never to have children in the first place and by non-baby boomers who delay having children until parenthood is no longer a viable option. Many of these will be women who received college educations, delayed marriage, and focused on their jobs and careers (Ambry 1992).

People choose to be childless for many reasons. These include worries about the negative effects on the marriage, concerns that jobs and careers might be compromised, a desire to focus the marriage on the marital relationship, concerns that children will financially strain marriages and life-styles, and a belief that children are not necessary for happy marriages (Ambry 1992).

When asked why they chose to have children, responses from mothers and fathers typically include wanting to experience children growing up, wanting to have the love and affection that children bring, wanting to experience the sense of family that children create, affirming moral or religious beliefs that having children is the right thing to do, believing that having children enriches a marriage, and believing that becoming a parent is a way of achieving adult status (Hoffman and Manis 1979; Cowan and Cowan 1992; DeWitt 1993).

The Transition to Parenthood

For those who become parents, the realization of the first pregnancy brings one of the most significant transitions of adulthood, the transition to parenthood. Simply put, everything changes. Time must be reorganized. Monetary priorities and allocations must be rearranged. Work outside the home takes on different meanings. Human energy becomes a valuable commodity. Dyads expand to triads or more if multiple births occur. The status of parent brings with it a new role identity.

Parenthood involves more than what parents do; it defines who they are. Research indicates that for parents, identity as a parent ranks as more important and significant than one's role as a marriage partner or one's occupational role (Rogers and White 1998). So, the quandaries begin. What does it take to be a good father? A good mother? Unlike a microwave, children do not come with directions for operations or neat recipes with guaranteed successful outcomes.

The area of parenthood that has received a great deal of attention is marital quality after the birth of the first child. This has been the case since LeMasters

(1957) published his work indicating that the birth of the first child constitutes a crisis in marriage. His research was based on interviews with 46 couples. Mothers reported being very tired as well as frustrated with confinement to the home and baby care. The crisis was most severely felt among mothers who had professional training and experience. Fathers said that they were strained by new financial worries and that wives were not as sexually responsive as before the birth.

LeMasters's study was very intensive, but the sample was quite small. The work was significant in that it was the first time research indicated that parenting is not always joyful and gratifying. Since the LeMasters's bombshell, numerous studies have been conducted to see if birth of the first child is indeed a crisis, what factors are related to marital happiness after the first birth, and whether children cause marital unhappiness. What has been found?

Wallace and Gotlib (1990) studied 97 couples during the first pregnancy and at one month and six months after the birth. They measured marital adjustment using the Spanier Dyadic Adjustment Scale and parental stress using the Parenting Stress Index. They also measured infants' temperaments using the Infant Characteristics Questionnaire, which asked parents questions about the child's temperament. They found that couples' global happiness was higher at one month after the child's birth than at six months after. There were no significant differences in men's and women's happiness, however. Infants' temperaments and characteristics had no bearing on marital adjustment and happiness.

Belsky and colleagues have extensively studied marital adjustment after the birth of a child. Illustrative of this work is a study conducted of 128 couples during pregnancy and at several points through the first three years of parenting (Belsky and Rovine 1990). The results showed that couples who experienced the sharpest declines in marital quality after the birth also had scored high on romanticism before the birth. It may be that the highly romantic couples had unrealistic notions about the realities of caring for infants. Although most couples experienced some decline in marital quality after the birth, there was considerable variation among the couples.

In a study based on self-report questionnaires completed by 454 Minnesota couples whose first child was between the age of 5 and 11 months, it was found that mothers and fathers who had been helped by others to prepare for becoming parents experienced less stress than those who had not received such help. In addition, the parents who received social support (a listening ear, advice, etc.) with their socialization as parents also had higher levels of personal and family well-being than did parents who did not receive this socialization support (Gage and Christensen 1991). Another study approached some of the questions differently. Relying on national U.S. panels of interviews with parents in 1988 and 1992, Rogers and White (1998) found that satisfaction with the parent role was related to the degree of commitment to that role. In addition, it was found that satisfaction with the parent role was "significantly higher for married parents with high marital quality" (p. 293). This relationship held for both fathers and mothers. This study suggests the likelihood that the mere presence or characteristics of children may not be the key factors in marital quality after the birth of a child.

Rather, parents' own commitment to and assessment of successful enactment of their parental roles may determine marital quality. Taken together, these studies imply that people who are adequately socialized into, and supported in, their parenting roles probably will be more satisfied with their role adjustment. Just as parenting affects marriage, marital quality affects parental role satisfaction. Decreased stress in the parental role, which social support can help provide, contributes to both marital quality and parental role satisfaction.

Overall, these studies support previous and accumulating research to the effect that although parenting the first born infant tends to be stressful, couples' **post partum** (after the birth) marital adjustment and marital happiness are related to their marital adjustment and happiness prior to the birth. This finding also challenges the notion of the first birth as a crisis.

Changing Roles for Mothers and Fathers

A growing number of books and articles focus on roles and identities of mothers and fathers as well as analyses of gendered participation in children's lives (Hays 1996; Coltrane 1996; LaRossa 1997; Sanchez and Thomson 1997; Brandth and Kvande 1998). Many of these writings borrow from the symbolic interactionist framework and focus on how motherhood and fatherhood are socially constructed today compared with the past. Contemporary trends include greater engagement of fathers in their children's lives. This shift to "daddying" did not just happen in the past few decades, however; important ideological changes in concepts of family, marriage, children, and gender laid the foundation back in the 1920s and 1930s. Marriage was becoming more of an intimate partnership. Children were less an economic asset to the family and more individuals in their own right. A diverse array of father role types was available. Some fathers were more traditional, hence patriarchal and authoritarian, whereas other fathers were more intimately involved in the lives of their children. As concepts of masculinity and femininity, marriage, family, and children have changed over the decades, concepts of fatherhood have changed as well (LaRossa 1997).

While there appear to have been many, even monumental, changes in motherhood and fatherhood over the past several decades, one constant remains. Parenthood and parenting remain gendered. The male and female statuses continue to organize the doing of parenthood. Fathers, even when on parental leave so that they can build relationships with their children, still do not measurably increase the housework that they do (Brandth and Kvande 1998). Mothers still tend to do more of both child care and housework. However, labor force participation changes under some circumstances. A national study reveals that initially after a birth, women's labor force hours decrease while their housework hours increase. For men who are taking care of more than one child, hours of labor force participation tend to increase (Sanchez and Thomson 1997).

Another national study relied on the 1987–1988 and 1992–1993 National Surveys of Families and Households. It was found that men spend more time and engage in more activities with sons than with daughters. This study revealed that fathers spend more time talking with children about their school worries than do mothers. In general, fathers who were actively involved in their preschoolers' lives, as indicated in the 1987–1988 survey, remained active in their children's lives. Interestingly, among couples where fathers spent little time with their children, the mothers spent less time with them, too. Other findings support previous research on gendered parenthood. For instance, women's financial contributions to the family did not decrease the time they spent with children and doing domestic tasks. Even when both parents were employed, women still spent more time with the children (Aldous, Mulligan, and Bjarnason 1998). Overall, it appears that motherhood and fatherhood remain "under construction," with some genuine effort not only toward more father engagement with children but also toward greater gender equity in married lives (Coltrane 1996; Brandth and Kvande 1998).

Infertility Issues and Options

Infertility is the inability to conceive after one year of unprotected intercourse (Lovin 1997). Relying on data collected for the National Survey of Family Growth in 1982, 1988, and 1995, it was found that the proportion of American women with fertility impairment rose from 8 percent in 1982 to 10 percent in 1995 (Chandra and Stephen 1998). The primary reasons cited for this was that

What reproductive technologies are available today for treating infertility? What are some ethical concerns associated with these technologies? What are some issues and problems with adoption today?

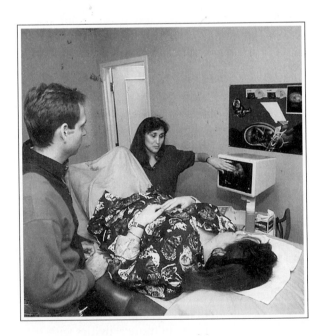

women in the large baby boom cohort were getting older, and as women age, fertility impairment is more common. In developed countries, it is estimated that 10 to 15 percent of adults are infertile. Overall, about 11 percent of American married couples have trouble conceiving. Half of all fertility problems are attributed to women, 40 percent to men, and 10 percent to both (DeWitt 1993; Trantham 1996).

Infertility in women is associated with advancing age, hereditary diseases and pituitary hormone deficiency, ovulation problems, endometriosis, adhesions in the reproductive system, complications caused by sexually transmitted diseases, uterine abnormalities, and fibroid tumors (Lovin 1997; Trantham 1996). Male infertility is related to sexually transmitted diseases, impotence, alcohol and drug use (including anabolic steroids), physical injury to the testicles, chromosomal abnormalities, varicose veins in the scrotum, blockage of the ducts that carry sperm, side effects of serious illness (e.g., cancer and hepatitis), and deficiency of pituitary hormones (The Endocrine Society 1998; Phillips 1998). Some infertility among older couples is due to having previously been sterilized, but now wanting to have children. Some infertility may be caused by exposure to chemicals in the workplace, the environment, and the home ("Environmental Toxins" 1996).

Infertility Treatment

Women are the primary recipients of fertility treatment (DeWitt 1993). Fertility drugs are used either to stimulate hormones or cause ovulation. Sometimes, the most effective infertility treatment is surgery to repair damaged fallopian tubes, ovaries, or the uterus. In cases where conception will have to occur without intercourse, as in the situation where the male partner cannot ejaculate normally during sex, the option may be to rely on artificial insemination. With **artificial insemination (IA),** a hollow tube, called a *catheter,* is used to place semen in the vaginal canal or the uterus (Nordenberg 1997). Artificial insemination is sometimes used in conjunction with fertility drugs (Hope 1998).

For other situations, more technically sophisticated alternatives may be prescribed. These approaches usually are classed as **assisted reproduction technologies (ART),** and include **in vitro fertilization (IVF),** usually used if a woman has blocked fallopian tubes. In IVF, the ovaries are medically stimulated so that multiple eggs will be produced. Then, when the eggs have matured, they are suctioned out and put in a petri dish and combined with sperm. Two to five days later, the **embryos** (fertilized eggs) that have formed are placed in the woman's uterus. **Donor egg IVF,** in which eggs from another woman are used, is indicated when a woman has a genetic defect that would be transmitted to her offspring or when her ovaries are too impaired to permit egg production. In **gamete intrafallopian transfer (GIFT),** three to five eggs along with sperm are placed in the fallopian tube and fertilization takes place inside the woman's body. **Zygote intrafallopian transfer (ZIFT)** borrows from both IVF and GIFT. Multiple eggs are fertilized in a petri dish and then placed in the fallopian tube, where one or more may travel to the uterus for implantation. Unless only a single fertilized egg is being used, multiple births are always possible. Furthermore, multiple births are becoming more common, especially when women use fertility drugs.

For men who cannot participate in conception because they have a condition known as **congenital absence of the vas deferens (CBAVD),** pregnancy may be achieved using a procedure called **intracytoplasmic sperm injection (ICSI).** The **vas deferens** are conduits in which sperm travel from the testicles to the penis. When these are missing, ICSI is used. Sperm are extracted and then injected into an egg for fertilization, and the egg is reimplanted in the woman (de Kretser 1997; Hope 1998).

Replacement of hypothalamic or pituitary hormones is used if these hormone deficiencies are the cause of infertility (The Endocrine Society 1998). Artificial insemination also may be an option if the man's sperm count is too low. **Intrauterine insemination (IUI)** may be advised if the man has low sperm counts but the sperm are viable. In this type of artificial insemination procedure, sperm are placed into the uterus through a catheter. In some cases, men may have to undergo microsurgery to correct varicose veins in the scrotum. In other cases, a vasectomy reversal is in order. It is estimated that there are about 500,000 vasectomy reversals in the United States every year (*Fertilitext* 1998).

Controversies in Infertility Treatment

A number of controversies surround infertility treatment. There is a concern that much scientific expertise and research money are spent on infertility treatment rather than on efforts to prevent infertility. There is also the concern that more attention has been focused on cures for infertility than on improving prenatal care and educating people on sexually transmitted diseases (Henifin 1993: 61; Wagner and St. Clair 1989).

Another area of great debate is whether fertility treatments should be covered by medical insurance. In the United States, insurance coverage of infertility treatments varies from state to state and from company to company. Three states—Massachusetts, Rhode Island, and Illinois—have mandated coverage of approved infertility treatments and several other states have mandated limited coverage under certain conditions. Federal and state laws hold that insurance companies cannot be made to cover anything that is not mandated by law. Many insurance companies have refused to cover infertility treatments on the grounds that assisted reproductive technologies are experimental and unnecessary and that infertility does not qualify as an illness (Gilbert 1996). The controversy facing the United States is a very challenging one. The Americans with Disabilities Act (ADA), passed in 1990, recognizes infertility as a disability (Gilbert 1996). However, although the ADA is legally recognized, recognition of infertility as a disability is not legally recognized in many states. The reason that insurance companies win court cases when challenged is because the ADA, though addressing all manner of discrimination against the disabled, did not clearly and specifically address situations under which insurance provisions, or selective lack thereof, would constitute discrimination (Gilbert 1996).

The greatest controversies, however, focus on the ethics of infertility treatments that result in multiple births and whether taxpayers should be footing the bill for the outcomes of fertility treatments. In 1997, septuplets were born to the McCaughey family. All the babies survived their first year, but many infertility experts vowed to do everything they could to prevent such dangerous events in the future (McCullough 1998). In December 1998, eight children were born to Nkem Chukwu and Iyke Louis Odobi. At the time of this writing, one baby had died and the surviving babies required extensive hospital stays. It is estimated that the medical care of the octuplet infants will come to two million dollars. Both Mrs. McCaughey and Mrs. Chukwu required extensive medical attention during their pregnancies, and extensive pre- and post-partum hospital care.

Both mothers had the option of **selective reduction** of the number of fetuses they were carrying. This means selective abortion. For religious reasons, neither mother chose this route. Had selective reduction been employed, however, the fewer infants born would have been healthier.

These spectacular events of multiple births to mothers who had taken fertility drugs moved the discussion of the ethics of infertility treatment into the public domain. The unnaturalness, medical risk, and financial costs of these births staggers the imagination, especially when multiple birth babies sometimes have lifelong health complications. It is known that women carrying more than triplets have a very high miscarriage rate, and the babies have high risks of physical and mental disabilities (McCullough 1998).

Other than simply accepting infertility and doing nothing about it, the primary alternatives to infertility treatment are surrogacy and adoption. **Surrogacy** involves finding a woman to agree to gestate a couple's embryo in her body. Surrogacy is fraught with legal and ethical controversies. Who are the real parents of the baby? Does the surrogate have visitation rights? Are surrogate mothers being exploited and turned into reproductive slaves (Henifin 1993; Grayson 1998)? All things considered, surrogacy is probably the least satisfactory and messiest alternative to infertility treatment available today.

Adoption is an ancient alternative to infertility and is practiced in every society. **Adoption** makes children legally part of a family in which they were not born. In 1998, President Clinton declared November "National Adoption Month." He stated that every year there are over 100,000 children in foster care in the United States who need to be adopted. Adoption Month was designed to help meet a national goal of doubling the number of adoptions by 2002 (*Weekly Compilation of Presidential Documents* 1998).

Exactly how many children are available for adoption is hard to pin down. Estimates tend to vary by whether writers are focusing on the adoption of U.S. infants, U.S. children in foster care, or children potentially available from other countries. Thousands of children are posted for adoption on the Internet. One report places the number of children in foster care in the United States at 500,000 (Rosenfeld et al. 1997).

Persons seeking to adopt usually prefer to have healthy infants. Adoptive parents tend to be older than other first-time parents. They also tend to have special needs as they go through the adoption searches and procedures. For instance, they already have had to cope with their infertility and weigh all the advantages and disadvantages of becoming the parents of an adopted child. Most lack experience in dealing with children and may perceive themselves to be in need of assistance (Sobol, Delaney, and Earn 1994). As a result of experiences that some children have had prior to adoption, couples may have to find professional assistance. For instance, some children may have been sexually abused, medically neglected, or otherwise harmed or traumatized. In some situations, the children may have experienced not only war but also the death of family members (Smith and Howard 1994; Nickman 1996; Rosenfeld et al. 1997; Mainemer, Gillman and Ames 1998).

Adoption can be expensive and the waiting period can be long. For parents wishing to adopt a U.S. child, the wait can be as long as seven years. The cost for securing an adoption through a public agency usually ranges from $5,000 to $25,000. If a private adoption route is taken, or if one uses a lawyer to secure the adoption, the wait usually is shorter, nine months to two years, and the cost is less, between $10,000 and $15,000. International adoptions take about as long as adoptions with private agencies, but there can be hidden legal fees, depending on the institution. The waiting period on international adoptions is usually from 6 to18 months (Gallagher 1998: 50). However, just as there are numerous counseling programs available to help adoptive parents and their children, the government also provides tax breaks for adopting. In addition, the Family and Medical Leave Act permits adoptive parents to take up to 12 weeks of unpaid leave after adopting, which protects parents' jobs (Gallagher 1998).

Adoption Issues and Outcomes

One controversy regarding adoption among U.S. citizens is whether only same-race adoptions should be permitted. In 1972, the National Association of Black Social Workers declared that transracial adoption constitutes cultural genocide (Bower 1994). Leslie Doty Hollingsworth (1998), a professor of social work, contends that contrary to popular portrayals, there are plenty of black families who can afford to adopt black children. She argues that in a racist society, only black parents can adequately prepare and socialize black children. Hollingsworth conducted a review of research on same-race and different-race adopted children and their self-esteem (Hollingsworth 1997). Her analysis revealed a negative relationship between transracial adoption and children's self-esteem. However, longitudinal research indicates that children reared in transracial families grow up to be emotionally and socially well adjusted and feel very much a part of their families (Simon and Altstein 1987; Simon 1995). These research outcomes suggest that new laws protecting against discrimination in adoption due to race or other factors serve the children's best interests (Simon 1998).

Individuals and couples considering adoption may be concerned about children's adjustment, regardless of race or ethnicity. A comparative study involving 48 adopted and 72 nonadopted (residing in the home of biological parents) young adults revealed that adopted respondents perceived their fathers as having been closer to them than did the nonadopted respondents. It was found that the closer the members of the adoptive family were to each other, the less different from nonadoptive families they saw themselves. In addition, the closer the family members were, the more prepared they were to talk about adoption if the issue arose (Sobol et al. 1994). A national study focused on children from 715 adoptive homes in the United States in comparison with nonadopted children. This study revealed that adopted adolescents showed only slightly poorer behavioral and psychological adjustment (Sharma, McGue, and Benson 1998). Another study using data from the National Survey of Families and Households in the United States found no statistically significant differences between adopted and biological children on measures of behavioral, psychological, and educational functioning (Borders, Black, and Palsey 1998: 237).

Open adoption has become a reality in many parts of the United States. In **open adoption,** adopting parents and adopted children have access to birth parent information. This access represents a move away from the secrecy that shrouded adoption for so long (Siegel 1993). Open adoption outcomes are just beginning to be studied, but the news thus far seems positive (Bauman 1997). Research indicates that open adoption has opened doors for birth and adoptive parents to communicate with one another. One comparative study showed that adoptive parents who had fully open adoption maintained communication with the birth parents. They also scored higher on attachment to their adopted infant than did adoptive parents whose adoption information was not as open (Mendenhall, Grotevant, and McRoy 1996). Another study focused on the participation of 171 children in open adoption. The study concluded that children are not confused by information about their adoptive status and their birth parents and that knowledge is not associated with lowered self-esteem (Wrobel et al. 1996).

Summary

Larger social forces often influence fertility decisions of individuals and couples. These include cultural beliefs and values in relation to economic factors, government policies and control measures, public opinion surrounding population trends and ideal family size, and knowledge about and access to fertility control methods.

The population in the United States grew from 100 million in 1917 to 200 million by 1967, after which fertility rates declined. Through the baby boom era after World War II, women of childbearing age averaged 3.4 to 3.6 children. Currently, the fertility rate in the United States is 2.0.

The main concern in population trends and patterns is the problem of overpopulation in relation to food supplies, nonrenewable resources, and quality of life. Western nations are identified as having less population but more negative impact on the environment.

Correlates of fertility control include social class, women's educational levels, and race and ethnicity. As a developing nation, Ghana also has other factors influencing fertility patterns such as knowledge of and access to birth control, rural residence, traditional ideals favoring large families, and husbands' control over wives' reproductive decisions. Of pressing importance to developing nations are infant and maternal mortality, both of which can be reduced somewhat by fertility control.

Fertility control is achieved through traditional methods and contraception, but the most common form of modern birth control worldwide is sterilization. Contraceptive use in the United States stands at 64 percent of all women of childbearing age. The greatest change in birth control patterns in the United States is that more unmarried women are using the condom rather than the pill, reflecting concerns about sexually transmitted diseases.

Abortion is a controversial alternative to childbearing. The Netherlands has the lowest abortion rate and Russia has the highest. In the United States, about half of all abortions are secured by unmarried, poor women under the age of 25. Low-income minority women are two times more likely to secure abortions than are higher-income white women.

The number of childless couples in the United States is increasing as women delay marriage and birth. Some people forego children out of concerns about possible negative effects on their jobs and relationships. Reasons for having children include wanting the experience of childrearing and believing children will enrich their marriages.

One of the most significant transitions of adulthood is the transition to parenthood. Parenthood initially is stressful but it is not a crisis. Although marital quality is affected by the birth of the first child, marital happiness and adjustment after the birth is primarily a function of marital quality and happiness before the birth. Parenthood remains gendered, despite the fact that more males are actively involved in their children's lives. However, women still do more of the housework and child care, even when they are employed full time.

It is estimated that 11 percent of U.S. couples have impaired fertility or are infertile. An array of drug and surgical options exists for persons wishing to be fertile. Fertility drugs, however, are under harsh scrutiny, due to medical and ethical issues associated with multiple births.

Surrogacy and adoption are alternatives to infertility treatment. Research contradicts the folk wisdom that adopted children have more educational, social, and psychological problems than nonadopted children do. A major controversy is transracial adoption. Research suggests, however, that transracial adoption is not detrimental to children's adjustment and well-being.

Readings for In-Depth Focus

The Effects of Fetal Ultrasound on Expectant Parents

Reproductive technology is having a profound effect on who we are and how we experience ourselves. In this reading, Margarete Sandelowski provides a structured look at one technology and its effects on parenthood. Parents who use fetal ultrasonography (ultrasound) learn the sex of their children and tend to alter their parenting expectations and behaviors accordingly. Little attention has been given, however, to how ultrasound affects expectant motherhood and fatherhood. As you read this selection, ask yourself what role ultrasound and similar technologies have on becoming a parent. Do you think that having the father see the baby on the screen helps shorten the "distance" between him and his developing offspring?

▪ ▪ ▪

Separate, But Less Unequal
Fetal Ultrasonography and the Transformation of Expectant Mother/Fatherhood

Margarete Sandelowski

Ultrasonography is the imaging technique that permits the paradox of "seeing with sound" (Yoxen 1987). When employed for fetal surveillance and diagnosis, sound waves sent through amniotic fluid bounce off fetal structures to produce a two-dimensional and cross-sectional picture of the fetus on a video display screen (Gold 1984). By providing visual access to an animated fetus while still in utero, fetal ultrasonography has transformed pregnancy into a "media spectacle" (Petchesky 1987, 58) and contributed to the development of the two-patient model of obstetric medicine in which the fetus is conceptualized and treated as a patient in its own right, separate from its mother (Mattingly 1992). Indeed, the technique has made it possible to talk about the fetus as if it were a baby and, more specifically, about the fetus in each of the three trimesters of pregnancy as if they were all separate patient categories, for

AUTHOR'S NOTE: This study was supported by Grant #NR01707 from the National Center for Nursing Research. I gratefully acknowledge Betty G. Harris and Beth Perry Black for their assistance in data collection and preparation. I also thank the anonymous reviewers of an earlier version of this article for their helpful critique.

Margarete Sandelowski, *Gender & Society*, 8 (2), pp. 230–245, copyright © 1994 by Sage Publications, Inc. Reprinted by permission of Sage Publications, Inc.

example, "second trimester fetus" (Corson and Kazazian 1985, 189).

■ ■ ■

Although both women and men are advantaged by fetal ultrasonography, deriving pleasure and parental feeling from seeing the fetus on screen, expectant fathers' experience of the fetus is always enhanced, whereas pregnant women's experience may be enhanced or attenuated. Ihde (1990) observed that technology can simultaneously magnify or amplify and reduce or place aside what is experienced through technology. For men, fetal ultrasonography is always enabling, permitting them access to a female world from which they have been excluded by virtue of their limited biological role in reproduction; it may be seen as a kind of prosthetic device compensating for a deficit of the body. Like the couvade, which attempts to redress socially a biological imbalance between the sexes (Meerabeau 1991), fetal ultrasonography may also be seen as serving to redress technologically the inequality in men's knowledge of, and access to, the fetus. In contrast, for women, fetal ultrasonography may also be a disabling mechanism that disrupts the privileged access to the fetus that only being "with child" (Rothman 1989, 90) confers.

METHOD

The interpretation that follows is based primarily on a secondary analysis of information obtained from multiple interviews conducted with 62 white, middle-class childbearing couples during pregnancy.[1] Between 1987 and 1993, these couples participated in a longitudinal field study, the primary purpose of which was to explore the transition to parenthood of infertile couples. Major findings and methodological details of this study have been described elsewhere (Sandelowski 1993; Sandelowski, Holditch-Davis, and Harris 1992). In the course of this study, couples provided information about fetal ultrasonography that stimulated the deliberate

search of the interview data for whether and how fetal ultrasonography influenced the pregnancy experiences of expectant mothers and fathers.

Of the 62 childbearing couples participating in the study, 42 couples were infertile. Thirty-nine of these couples conceived their babies through biomedical means after an average of four years of effort; two of these couples conceived a second child spontaneously. The three remaining infertile couples conceived spontaneously after two or more years of effort. Twenty of the 62 couples were normally fertile, having conceived their babies after an average of only three months of effort. These couples were interviewed conjointly two to three times, once in each trimester of pregnancy they were in the study. A total of 167 interviews were conducted during pregnancy.

All of these couples had at least one ultrasound examination, but the infertile couples often had two or more ultrasound examinations; they had more of these examinations earlier in pregnancy to confirm its existence and to detect multiple pregnancy, a common sequela to infertility therapy. By virtue of biomedical conception and ultrasound examinations, as well as of amniocentesis (36 percent of infertile pregnancies versus 25 percent of fertile pregnancies) and cesarean birth (47 percent of infertile couples' births versus 20 percent of fertile couples' births), the childbearing experiences of the infertile couples as a group could be described as more technological than those of their fertile counterparts; yet, no substantive differences in attitude toward, or acceptance of, technology between fertile and infertile couples solely attributable to fertility status or variables related to infertility (such as type of diagnosis and mode of conception) were discerned. Both fertile and infertile couples and women and men typically shared a favorable view of technological intervention in childbirth; alternatively, there were couples in both groups and women and men who expressed reservations about such intervention. Whether fertile or infertile, couples tended to view fetal ultrasonography as a benign, non-invasive, and even pleasurable technique, as opposed to the intrusiveness and threat they perceived in amniocentesis.

Conclusions drawn here are limited by the original purpose of the study and, therefore, by the information obtained from the couples to fulfill that purpose. Until further studies are conducted deliberately examining the influence of class and culture on the experience of fetal ultrasonography, the interpretation presented here applies only to the experiences of the middle-class group of couples on which it was based. Despite these important limitations, the information the couples provided was of sufficient quality to permit the interpretation of fetal ultrasonography that follows and to further our understanding of the interaction between gender and technology in preserving and transforming the nature of human relations and experience. Given the rapid increase in the United States in the use of diagnostic, surveillance, and management technology in all pregnancies, an analysis that includes the experiences of a group of couples with varying degrees of exposure to technology can illuminate the effects of the technological reality and rituals that have been described as the major characteristic of mainstream American obstetric practice (Davis-Floyd 1990).

GENDER AND THE EPISTEMOLOGY OF EXPECTANT PARENTHOOD

Expectant parenthood can be usefully conceptualized as having a distinctive epistemology. When viewed in a heterosexual context and apart from any medical context, there are two principal knowers in pregnancy and one knowable: expectant parents and the fetus. Although both pregnant women and expectant fathers have a relationship with the fetus, they occupy different epistemological standpoints as knowers of the fetus. The pregnant woman has a privileged relation to the fetus because she carries it in her body. That is to say, because her knowledge of the fetus is embodied (corporeal and

concrete), she has a tactile and kinesthetic awareness and an overall sense of knowing the fetus that her male partner cannot have. She alone has "access to (fetal) movements from their origin, and it is only under her direction that others can feel these movements." Only she can "witness this life within" her (Young 1984, 48). She alone has the experience of *me/not me* and of *me/but separate from me* that places her in the unique position of getting to know *herself-with-another* and *another-within-herself* (Bergum 1989; Rich 1976; Young 1984).

In contrast, the expectant father has traditionally been a vicarious knower in the sense that his knowledge of the fetus has been limited to external visual and tactile sources of information. He may sense the fetus, but only via his pregnant partner's body and only then with her permission (Stainton 1990). His knowledge of the fetus is disembodied and, therefore, more disconnected and abstract than hers. Whereas maternity has traditionally been an experience providing women with reproductive continuity from conception through gestation to birthing and nursing a child, paternity is only an "abstract idea" (Corea 1985; O'Brien 1981). Biological fatherhood is a discontinuous experience, the genetic/inseminator role separated in time and space from the nurturer role. As will be described later, both women and men recognized this reproductive deficit in men, but it was most poignantly illustrated by one infertile woman waiting to adopt a child. (A group of adopting couples also participated in the study described previously.) She felt like an expectant father rather than an expectant mother. Waiting for a child but not herself with-child, she was, in her words, "reduced to the same status as the father."

ULTRASONOGRAPHY AND THE NEW EPISTEMOLOGY OF EXPECTANT PARENTHOOD

Fetal ultrasonography is a technique that has altered the epistemology of expectant parenthood by emphasizing seeing as the principal mode of fetal inquiry and by extending the sensory capabilities of nonpregnant inquirers. During ultrasound examinations of the fetus, pregnant women, their male partners, and the clinicians/technicians producing and/or interpreting the fetal image are variously involved in relations of scanning and being scanned.

Spectator and Spectacle

The parental and professional knowers of the fetus are spectators, engaged in acts of looking.

■ ■ ■

With the exception of the expectant father, all of the individuals involved in the ultrasound examination are spectacles: objects at which to be looked. In the typical case, where only the sonographer and couple are in the ultrasound examination or viewing room, the expectant father is the only one who is not on display. Only the expectant father typically escapes being a spectacle. The fetus is the primary object of scanning and the primary subject of the fetal sonogram, and it is the pregnant woman's body that must be scanned to gain visual access to the fetus. Sonographers are not just scanners but are also often watched by the childbearing couple performing the operations of scanning, including moving the scanning device over the maternal abdomen to locate the fetus or the desired fetal body part and watching the screen. One expectant father described watching the technician for any indications that something was wrong with the fetus. As he recalled:

> We go in to have the ultrasound and you know we are sitting there watching it. I can't tell if there is any problem on the ultrasound. I don't know but, you know, you are sitting there looking for any indications from the technician—any sign in her eyes of any alarm and then she says: "Well, I'm going to go show it to the radiologist." And, we are sitting there and we are talking casually and in my mind I'm sitting there thinking: "I don't want her to be back there

any more than three or four minutes because if she is, you know this is terrible. I don't want the radiologist to call us back there to talk to us."

■ ■ ■

Including Men

Fetal ultrasonography emerged in the descriptions of the couples as a new kind of spectator sport for men and as an integral part of the cultural script of expectant fatherhood. The technique served to expand men's physical and emotional involvement in childbearing beyond their biological role in conception and their supportive role during childbirth. The ultrasound examination was an opportunity for men to become more involved in the pregnancy itself. By further legitimating their presence during their partners' prenatal visits, it made the conventional prenatal visit seem less gynecological or for women only. The ultrasound examination also legitimated a man's absence from work. As one woman implied, in the absence of any obstetric complications, the ultrasound examination was really the only good reason an expectant father could be expected to miss work. As she observed:

> We had the ultrasound in the first two months to see how far along I was. And since then, there hasn't been any need for that. That was the only time he's gone. I hate for him to go because he has to leave work and all to go up there. I had rather him not have to do that—to miss time out of work and all. And, I haven't done anything special. I just go in and they measure my tummy and they listen to the heartbeat and weigh me. And they took one blood sugar test. And that's it. I'm not there that long. It's not necessary for him to go.

■ ■ ■

Both men and women viewed fetal ultrasonography as a way to get men more involved in pregnancy and with their mates; it was a technique seen to enhance not only the father-child bond, but also the marital relationship by bringing wives and husbands closer together. For one man who had watched his wife undergoing in vitro fertilization techniques, fetal ultrasonography made him feel less like an observer and more like a participant in childbearing. As he remarked:

> I was more isolated from the process . . . I can't claim it as mine or ours because it's more hers because she has been going through the procedure. Now I am being pulled into it . . . there is more of an assimilation of our two into one.

Men were often fascinated by the fetal image and, at times, even more intrigued with the technological feat that made that image possible than with the image itself. As engineers, two expectant fathers "enjoyed" and found "amazing . . . technological things." One man was especially proud of the fact that he could converse intelligently with the obstetrician and even anticipate some of his findings from the ultrasound screen. Another man indicated some pride in knowing his way around inside his wife's body as projected on screen.

Women felt especially solicitous of their partners' experiential deficits in having children and viewed fetal ultrasonography as a way to make up for what "he doesn't have." Both women and men agreed that men lacked the sensations of pregnancy and, in one expectant father's words, the "emotion of knowing he is going to be a father" that comes from having the fetus inside one's body. One expectant father admitted:

> At times, I've talked like I was envious of not being able to have those changes going on inside of me, you know. Lately, we've been talking about how it's harder for the guy to accept this, what's going on, and being all excited about it.

Another expectant father, who especially craved involvement in pregnancy, remarked:

> I would really like to know how she feels. I want her to tell me throughout this whole thing what's different. Do you feel like you have a beer gut? What movements and things like that? It's something that there is no way that I can experience, but I sure would like to hear about it.

The fetal sonogram helped men see the fetus, and it helped women to help their partners to see, thereby reinforcing women's roles as gatekeepers to the fetus and the experience of pregnancy, and as altruistic gift-givers (Lorber 1989, 1993; Raymond 1990). One woman described how she was having an ultrasound examination done "at my request" because her husband "just wanted to see" the fetus.

Although both women and men derived great comfort and pleasure from seeing their babies, fetal ultrasonography seemed to be more important to some men than to their wives in confirming the existence of a baby and their impending parenthood. For women, the transformations of their bodies, feeling the fetus, and, especially, quickening remained important or more important than viewing the fetal sonogram as a stimulus of maternal feeling (Roberts 1986).

■ ■ ■

For many of the men, the fetal sonogram was a kind of proxy for female experience; it was a way for them to become more relevant and to move to center stage beyond their stagehand role in reproduction vis-á-vis their pregnant partners' leading-lady role (Jordan 1990). For the women, the fetal sonogram was a way their partners could feel less deprived and more involved as expectant fathers and partners. As one woman told her husband, "it was just kind of cool . . . to see you so excited. That was nice."

Women derived a kind of vicarious pleasure from observing the pleasure their partners derived from watching the fetus on screen.

Excluding Women

. . . With fetal ultrasonography, it is now possible for women to be and to feel left out in pregnancy by virtue of the supine position ultrasound scanning necessitates. This can obstruct their view of the screen. Other studies have suggested that women can also feel excluded by sonographers who fail to provide any or enough feedback concerning the fetus (Hyde 1986; Reading et al. 1982), a failure that may contribute to the feeling that strangers know more about their own baby than they do.

ULTRASONOGRAPHY AND THE TRANSFER OF EPISTEMOLOGICAL PRIVILEGE

As suggested by couples' descriptions, fetal ultrasonography transfers epistemological privilege from the pregnant woman to the expectant father and to an additional category of knowers: the health professionals who obtain, clinically interpret, and control access to the fetal sonogram. This imaging technique serves to make the positions of expectant fathers and sonographers as knowers of the fetus more equal to that of the pregnant woman because her knowing is made less exclusive and singular and more dependent on technology. By emphasizing the "scopic drive as the paradigm of knowledge" (Braidotti 1989, 153), fetal ultrasonography places a greater value on experience at a distance—on surrogate or voyeuristic, as opposed to direct bodily experience of the fetus. The dissociative mind's eye prevails over the connective body's eye (Keller and Grontkowski 1983, 209). Women's privileged access to the fetus by virtue of pregnancy is also made secondary to non-pregnant viewers' access to the fetal sonogram; the advantages and prerogatives of biology are made secondary to those of technology.

During the ultrasound examination, as spectators, but never as spectacles, expectant fathers acquire the power and entitlement of looking. One expectant father remarked that seeing the fetus on screen made it his; seeing the fetus permitted surrogate possession or appropriation of the fetus. Women, in turn, continue to be objects to be looked at (Doane, Mellencamp, and Williams 1984) and are placed in the somewhat bizarre position of looking at themselves inside out and from a distance.

Although a new mode of parental and professional inquiry, fetal ultrasonography tends to preserve a certain patriarchal arrangement of power and authority. Arney (1982) described the technological surveillance of pregnancy as constituting a new but familiar order of control over women. Women's bodies are made transparent to the male gaze. Men (whether expectant fathers or obstetricians) find pleasure and a new sense of capability in seeing a private world once denied them. Women's embodied knowledge of the fetus may even be viewed as less valuable than the knowledge obtainable from the fetal sonogram (cf. Oakley 1986). Several of the women interviewed, who knew exactly when they had conceived, described incidents where their physicians insisted on sonographically dating the fetus. In a recent study comparing maternal perceptions and ultrasound observations of artificially induced fetal movement, women's perceptions were found to be less reliable and "poor," leading the researchers to conclude that maternal reports were no substitute for ultrasound examination in producing accurate and clinically useful information (Kisilevsky et al. 1991). In some cases, as when a woman is obese, women can even be seen as impeding visual access to the fetus because sonographic visualization of the fetus is made more difficult.

Although fetal ultrasonography requires a female body to see through, an additional effect of the fetal sonogram is to make pregnant women so transparent as hardly to be seen at all. The fetal sonogram depicts the fetus as if it were floating free in space: as if it were already delivered from or existed outside its mother's body. Fetal ultrasonography creates the fiction of the independently viable fetus by erasing the pregnant woman without whom the fetus cannot exist (Oakley 1986; Petchesky 1987). One expectant father conveyed something of this fiction of fetal autonomy this way:

> [The baby is] a separate entity within C. It's not C. being pregnant. It's C. and the child. It's like you visualize the baby within C., not the external large tummy. We see baby is cramped, all folded up, in a small cave. . . . You see these nature films where they have the cutaway of the cave and there's the bunny rabbits in the cave. This is a cutaway of the cave and the baby in the cave.

For this man, his baby was inside his wife when he was looking at her, but it was at home and alone when he viewed the fetal sonogram.

GENDER AND HUMAN-TECHNOLOGY RELATIONS

The differences between pregnant women's and expectant fathers' experiences of fetal ultrasonography may be further illuminated by conceptualizing them as on a continuum of human-technology relations. Ihde (1990, 107) argued that there are three sets of such relations. At one end of the continuum are embodiment relations, where the operations of a technology are transparent enough to be experienced as "quasi-me." The technology "withdraws" (1990, 74) to the point that the human being whose sensations or capabilities are expanded by it may forget it is there, thereby experiencing it as part of the self. In the case of fetal ultrasonography, the artifice of the fetal sonogram eventually gave way to couples' perception that they were looking directly at a live baby, almost as if vision were naked, as if there were no technology present or necessary to see through a woman's body to the fetus inside.

The fictionalizing reality of the fetal sonogram caused both pregnant women and expectant fathers to feel like they were interacting with and even touching their baby when they were simply seeing an image of a fetus on screen. The static ultrasound picture took the fetus out of its uterine context and so-called real-time ultrasonic images created the "cinematic view" of the fetus (Sanders 1984, 29), which, in turn, created the illusion that the fetus imaged was in actual and natural motion, like a newly born baby. In embodiment relations, the fictionalizing operations of the fetal sonogram withdraw, the way the corrective and enhancement operations of eyeglasses withdraw from the experience of someone who is used to wearing them. This withdrawal further reifies the separation between mother and fetus (Rothman 1989, 158).

At the other end of the human-technology relations continuum are *alterity relations*, where the operations of a technology are so lacking in transparency as to be experienced as "quasi-other" (Ihde 1990, 107). In alterity relations, technology does not withdraw but remains in the foreground and is experienced as discontinuous with the self and with the world it reveals. In the case of fetal ultrasonography, the very artificiality of the technology intrudes, as evidenced by couples' descriptions of the initial difficulty they had seeing the snowy, decolorized, and defleshed fetal image as a familiar baby.

Finally, in between embodiment and alterity relations are *hermeneutic relations*, where the operations of a technology are experienced as part of the world made transparent by it. In the case of fetal ultrasonography, reading a fetal sonogram is an "analogue" of getting to know the fetus.

Fetal ultrasonography may have the effect of transforming men's experience of pregnancy from a relation of disembodiment to a human-machine relation of embodiment. This machine-generated relation of embodiment, which stands in contrast to the embodied relation of pregnant woman and fetus, involves the extension of their vision and, thereby, permits them an additional mode of sensing the fetus. Although the fetal sonogram, like the pregnant woman's body, still mediates men's experiences, the sonogram seems less of an impediment and more of an extension of their body. Once they learn to "read" the fetus on screen—to make sense of the garbled images there—men's experience of fetal ultrasonography may be closer to "perfection" than women's. Ihde observed that "the closer to invisibility, transparency, and the extension of one's own bodily sense [a] technology allows," the more it is experienced as "perfection in design" (1990, 74). By enhancing their eye view of the fetus and reinforcing vision as the primary mode of inquiry, the fetal sonogram is "perfected along a bodily vector" that seems particularly "molded" to fit and enhance men's experience of pregnancy.

In contrast, fetal ultrasonography may have the effect of subtracting from women's experience of pregnancy as an embodied relation with the fetus by adding relations with a machine. Fetal ultrasonography puts something in between pregnant women and the fetuses they carry—namely, the fetal sonogram. Fetal ultrasonography appears less molded to women's experience of pregnancy by its operations as a visual, as opposed to tactile and kinesthetic, device and by its potential (Ihde 1990, 108) to disrupt a pregnant woman's sense of oneness with self and fetus.

ULTRASONOGRAPHY AND THE DEMOCRATIZATION OF FETAL EXPERIENCE

Ultrasonography places both expectant parents and clinicians/technicians in a voyeuristic relationship to the fetus. Commonly depicted as promoting attachment to the fetus, the tech-

nique emphasizes a certain distance and detachment; it makes seeing and getting a picture of a fetus at least as significant as carrying the fetus. This potential effect makes it seem all the more nonsensical to emphasize men's limited role in reproduction as a deficit. Fetal ultrasonography furthers a long-standing patriarchal inclination to maximize the male role in reproduction by minimizing the differences between expectant motherhood and fatherhood (Rothman 1989).

Technological innovation typically involves both advantages and disadvantages, necessitating an "equity analysis" of who benefits and who loses (Bush 1983, 164). The democratization of fetal experience that ultrasonography can engender, by providing access to the fetus even to people who are not or can never be pregnant, has enhanced the experiences of men by enlarging their vision. It has also enhanced the experience of women by permitting them to realize their desire to share pregnancy; but, it may also trivialize the experiences women alone have. When an experience becomes universally accessible through technology, it often loses its uniqueness and miraculousness. Its new accessibility also raises the questions: What kind of and whose experience is it? (Boorstin 1974).

NOTE

1. I have also drawn from informal observations as a nurse present during ultrasound examinations and from formal observations I have conducted in a preliminary longitudinal study of couples obtaining positive prenatal diagnoses.

REFERENCES

Arney, W. R. 1982. *Power and the profession of obstetrics.* Chicago: University of Chicago Press.

Arras, J. D. 1990. AIDS and reproductive decisions: Having children in fear and trembling. *The Milbank Quarterly* 68:353–82.

Bergum, V. 1989. *Woman to mother: A transformation.* Massachusetts: Bergin & Garvey.

Blank, R. H. 1992. *Mother and fetus: Changing notions of maternal responsibility.* New York: Greenwood Press.

Boorstin, D. J. 1974. *The Americans: The democratic experience*. New York: Vintage.

Braidotti, R. 1989. Organs without bodies. *Differences: A Journal of Feminist Cultural Studies* 1:147–61.

Bush, C. G. 1983. Women and the assessment of technology: To think, to be, to unthink, to free. In *Machina ex dea: Feminist perspecitves on technology*, edited by J. Rothschild. New York: Pergamon.

Clinton, J. F. 1987. Physical and emotional responses of expectant fathers throughout pregnancy and the early postpartum period. *International Journal of Nursing Studies* 24:59–68.

Conner, G. K., and Denson, V. 1990. Expectant father's response to pregnancy: Review of literature and implications for research in high-risk pregnancy. *Journal of Perinatal and Neonatal Nursing* 4:33–42.

Corea, G. 1985. *The mother machine: Reproductive technologies from artificial insemination to artificial wombs*. New York: Harper & Row.

Corson, V. L., and Kazzazian, H. H. 1985. The impact of ultrasound on prenatal diagnosis. In *The principles and practice of ultrasonography in obstetrics and gynecology*, 3d ed., edited by R. C. Sanders and A. E. James. Norwalk, CT: Appleton-Century-Crofts.

Davis-Floyd, R. E. 1990. The role of obstetrical rituals in the resolution of cultural anomoly. *Social Science and Medicine* 31:175–89.

Doane, M. A., P. Mellencamp, and L. Williams, eds. 1984. *Re-Visions: Essays in feminist film criticism*. Frederick, MD: University Publications of America.

Gold, R. B. 1984. Ultrasound imaging during pregnancy. *Family Planning Perspectives* 16:240–43.

Hyde, B. 1986. An interview study of pregnant women's attitudes to ultrasound scanning. *Social Science and Medicine* 22:587–92.

Ihde, D. 1990. *Technology and the lifeworld: From garden to earth*. Bloomington: Indiana University Press.

Jordan, P. L. 1990. Laboring for relevance: Expectant and new fatherhood. *Nursing Research* 39:11–16.

Keller, E. F., and C. R. Grontkowski. 1983. The mind's eye. In *Discovering reality: Feminist perspectives on epistemology, metaphysics, methodolgy, and philosophy of science*, edited by S. Harding and M. B. Hintikka. Dordrecht, Holland: D. Reidel.

King, P. A. 1991. Helping women helping children: Drug policy and future generations. *The Milbank Quarterly* 69:595–621.

Kisilevsky, B. S., H. Killen, D. W. Muir, and J. A. Low. 1991. Maternal and ultrasound measurements of elicited fetal movements: A methodologic consideration. *Obstetrics & Gynecology* 77:889–92.

Lorber, J. 1989. Choice, gift, or patriarchal bargain? Women's consent to in vitro fertilization in male infertility. *Hypatia* 4:23–36.

——. 1993. The dynamics of maritial bargaining in male infertility. *Gender & Society* 7:32–49.

Manning, F. A. 1989. Reflections on future directions of perinatal medicine. *Seminars in Perinatology* 13:342–51.

Mattingly, S. S. 1992. The maternal–fetal dyad: Exploring the two-patient obstetric model. *Hastings Center Report* 22:13–18.

May, K. A. 1980. A typology of attachment and involvement styles adopted during pregnancy by first-time expectant fathers. *Western Journal of Nursing Research* 2:445–61.

——. 1982a. The father as observer. *MCN: American Journal of Maternal Child Nursing* 7:319–22.

——. 1982b. Three phases of father involvement in preganacy. *Nursing Research* 31:337–42.

Meerabeau, L. 1991. Husbands' participation in fertility treatment: They also serve who stand and wait. *Sociology of Health and Illness* 13:396–410.

Oakley, A. 1986. *The captured womb: A history of the medical care of pregnant women*. New York: Basil Blackwell.

O'Brien, M. 1981. *The politics of reproduction*. Boston: Routledge and Kegan Paul.

Petchesky, R. P. 1987. Fetal images: The power of visual culture in the politics of reproduction. In *Reproductive technologies: Gender, motherhhod, and medicine*, edited by M. Stanworth. Minneapolis: University of Minnesota Press.

Raymond, J. G. 1990. Reproductive gifts and gift giving: The altruistic woman. *Hastings Center Report* 20:7–11.

Reading, A. E., S. Campbell, D. N. Cox, and C. N. Sledmere. 1982. Health beliefs and health care behavior in pregnancy. *Psychological Medicine* 12:379–83.

Rich, A. 1976. *Of woman born: Motherhood as experience and institution*. New York: Bantam.

Roberts, E. J. 1986. Aspects of patient care: The consumer's view of ultrasound in pregnancy. *Radiography* 52:29–94.

Rothman, B. K. 1989. *Recreating motherhood: Ideology and technology in a patriarchal society*. New York: Norton.

Sandelowski, M. 1993. *With child in mind: Studies of the personal encounter with infertility*. Philadelphia: University of Pennsylvania Press.

Sandelowski, M., D. Holditch-Davis, and B. G. Harris. 1992. Using qualitative and quantitative methods: The transition to parenthood of infertile couples. In *Qualitative methods in family research*, edited by J. F. Gilgun, K. Daly, and G. Handel. Newbury Park, CA: Sage.

Sanders, R. C. 1984. *Clinical sonography: A practical guide*. Boston: Little, Brown.

Schodt, C. M. 1989. Parental-fetal attachment and couvade: A study of patterns of human-environment integrality. *Nursing Science Quarterly* 2:88–96.

Stainton, M. C. 1990. Parents' awareness of their unborn infant in the third trimester. *Birth* 17:92–96.

Weaver, R. H., and M. S. Cranley. 1983. An exploration of paternal-fetal attachment behavior. *Nursing Research* 32:68–72.

Young, I. M. 1984. Pregnant embodiment: Subjectivity and alienation. *Journal of Medicine and Philosophy* 9:45–62.

Yoxen, E. 1987. Seeing with sound: A study of the development of medical images. In *The social construction of technological systems: New directions in the sociology and history of technology*, edited by W. E. Bijker, T. P. Hughes, and T. J. Pinch. Cambridge, MA: MIT Press.

Critical Thinking Questions

1. How may fetal ultrasonography change the social construction of pregnancy and parenthood?

2. According to Sandelowski, how do ultrasonography sessions bring men more fully into their father role and how does this involvement affect women's experiences of their pregnancies?

3. What are the limitations of the sample used in this study? Do you think different results would be obtained if the sample were larger? Why or why not? Do you think the fact that so many couples previously had been treated for infertility may have affected the results? Explain.

4. To which sociological perspective does this analysis most align? What other theoretical perspectives are present in this analysis? If this article were written from a functionalist perspective, what would be different? Explain.

5. Based on Sandelowski's analysis, what suggestions do you have for women who feel "robbed" or alienated when sharing the ultrasonography sessions with their partners?

12 *Family Violence*

1 n some ways, this is probably the most difficult chapter to write because of the horrific ways family violence tears families apart. I recently returned from a trip to Denver, Colorado, where I delivered a presentation on battered women. The presentation was part of an annual series on domestic violence that honored a young woman named Margo Green. A week before she was scheduled to graduate from the University of Colorado at Denver, Margo was murdered by her husband, who then killed himself. Her mother, still struggling to recover from the grief of losing her daughter to such an untimely and violent death seven years ago, told me that Margo planned to open an accounting firm with her father upon graduation. They were going to call their family business "Green and Father"—Margo's idea, which her father embraced. That family has been shattered by domestic violence.

Students often share with me stories of abuse they endured or witnessed in their homes—both physical and sexual—and they know the lasting scars these experiences have left on their lives. Recently, during a class discussion about how the criminal justice system should handle child sex offenders, a student broke into tears and revealed that she and her twin sister had endured years of sexual abuse, first at the hands of a family friend, and later by an older brother. The parents refused to address the problem with either the neighbor or their son, although they knew their daughters were telling the truth, so the girls lived in constant fear and shame for years. The student said she remembered a "family life education" lesson in which her fifth-grade teacher described how girls got pregnant. The student went home hysterical, believing she was pregnant, since what the teacher said led to pregnancy was exactly what her older brother had been doing to her. To this day, she is intimidated by men and struggles to establish healthy intimate relationships.

Defining and Studying Family Violence

Family violence is a very difficult topic to study. First, most people want to portray their families as loving, safe, and warm, so they will hide violence from officials and researchers. Second, it is very difficult to define **family violence.** Some define *abuse* as an act that results in injury; others define it as any act in which a person intends to inflict harm, regardless of whether bodily injury occurs; and still others consider acts abusive if they could result in injury, regardless of motive or actual harm inflicted. Some limit their definitions of abuse to physical acts, others include sexual and or psychological maltreatment in their definition of abuse. No consistent definitions of abuse have been developed, which leads to widely divergent estimates of how prevalent family abuse is.

Studying family abuse is further complicated by the variety of data sources available. Much family violence research has relied on official records from criminal justice agencies, mental health workers, or social workers (Weis 1989). All official records, regardless of the source, underestimate the prevalence of domestic abuse because it very often is unreported and undetected by outside agencies. Additionally, abuse that does get reported may differ significantly from that which continues undetected.

Official data sources often are used simply because it is so difficult to gain access to families to study domestic violence. Sociologists often quip that one cannot simply approach a respondent and ask, "How many times a week do you beat your wife or child?" In all sincerity, few families would agree to participate in a study if they knew researchers were interested in studying abuse. To circumvent that problem, Straus, Gelles, and Steinmetz (1981) developed the **Conflict Tactics Scale** to allow them to study numerous types of family violence—including child abuse, spouse abuse, parent abuse, and sibling abuse—in representative random samples of families. This scale, which they used in two National Family Violence Surveys (see Gelles and Straus 1988; Straus and Gelles 1986, 1990), has become a standard data collection method among family violence researchers.

The Conflict Tactics Scale

Since so much data on family violence are gathered using the Conflict Tactics Scale (CTS), it is important to understand how the scale is administered and the strengths and weaknesses of the method. Respondents participating in studies using the CTS usually are told that researchers want to study "conflict resolution techniques" used in families. Researchers ask respondents to estimate how often, in the past year, they have utilized a variety of conflict resolution techniques. These techniques range from the most socially acceptable ("discussed the issue calmly") to the least socially acceptable ("used a gun or knife"). Although the CTS allows respondents to report nonviolent conflict resolution strategies, researchers usually analyze data only from the violence indexes (Straus et al. 1981: 259). The violence indexes include the following behaviors: threw something at the other one; pushed, grabbed, or shoved the other one; slapped the other one; kicked, bit, or hit with a fist; hit or tried to hit with something; beat up the other one; threatened with a knife or gun; and used a knife or gun.

The authors of the scale point out numerous advantages of this data collection technique. First, because the scale is presented "in the context of disagreements and conflicts" between family members, which most people recognize is a normal part of family life, respondents are less likely to resist participation (Straus et al. 1981: 257). Second, respondents are allowed to tell researchers about normative conflict resolution strategies (such as discussing an issue calmly) before admitting to more deviant, violent behaviors. This may increase the honesty, and hence the reliability and validity, of the instrument. Third, the scale may be used to study virtually any type of family violence. In their National Family Violence Surveys, an adult respondent was asked about conflict resolution strategies with a spouse (to measure wife and husband abuse), with children (to measure child and parent abuse), and between siblings (sibling abuse). A single respondent can admit to being both a victim and a perpetrator of family violence.

The CTS is not without flaws. Critics point out that the CTS deals with acts of abuse only. Researchers have no measure of the consequences of the violence, so they do not know if a person was injured or how severely. Furthermore, there is no measure of the events preceding or following each act. If a respondent reported slapping a spouse, there is no way to tell if that person was slapped first or if the respondent was the initial aggressor. Whether the slap was followed with further violence also is unknown. Another criticism of the scale is that categories are not mutually exclusive. For example, one category includes "kicked, bit, or hit with a fist." It might be important to know how many respondents reporting behaviors in that category were hit with a fist compared to bit or kicked. Another category, "hit or tried to hit with something," not only includes more than one type of behavior but it is also quite ambiguous. Researchers do not know what the object was (a brick or a pillow) or whether the intended victim was actually hit with the unidentified object. Respondents are asked to limit their responses to behaviors within the previous year but they may have trouble accurately recalling when events occurred. Additionally, since the scale is presented in the context of conflict resolution, adult respondents are asked to report behaviors dealing with children ages 3 to 17. Obviously, one cannot report that they "discussed an issue calmly" with a nonverbal infant. The CTS, therefore, cannot be used to measure abuse of infants and toddlers. Finally, the scale does not include a measure of sexual abuse.

In response to the criticisms of the original CTS, Straus and colleagues (1995) have revised the scale. However, because the revised version is relatively new, most of the data that have been collected on family violence to this point is based on the original CTS.

Theories of Family Violence

A story in the *New York Times* reported that following an argument between a husband and wife, their 6-week-old son began crying. "As the mother changed the boy's diaper, his father became enraged and jammed his finger down the boy's throat, fracturing his pharynx. . . . When the baby continued to cry, his father shook him hard, breaking two ribs, . . . and he later smashed the child's skull against the back of the crib" (Schemo 1992). Fortunately, this baby survived his life-threatening injuries. As we read this, and other horrifying stories of family violence, immediately we wonder how a person could inflict such malicious harm on an innocent child. Many theories have been advanced to explain family violence, including biological theories (Burgess and Draper 1989), psychological theories (O'Leary 1993), exchange/social control theory (Gelles and Cornell 1990), feminist theory (Dobash and Dobash 1979; Yllö 1993), and the intergenerational transmission of violence theory. Domestic violence is a complex social problem that cannot be explained easily by any single theory.

Biological and Psychological Theories

Biological and psychological theories of abuse assert that chemical, neurological, or mental disorders cause family violence. The research on biological roots of abuse is relatively new. Some studies show that neuropsychologically related disorders, such as antisocial personality disorder and attention deficit disorder, may increase the likelihood of physical child abuse (Milner and Chilamkurti 1995). Abusers also may be hypersensitive to stimuli, making them less tolerant of frustration and stress (Milner and Chilamkurti 1995). Intellectual deficits in parents have been related to child neglect, and head trauma, organic disorders, and birth complications have been linked with spouse abuse (Barnett, Miller-Perrin, and Perrin 1997). Psychological explanations focus on personality traits of the abusers. Psychological characteristics—such as impulsiveness, low self-esteem, and high levels of hostility and aggressiveness—have been identified as possible predictors of abuse (Friedrich and Wheeler 1995; O'Leary 1993).

Biological and psychological theories have been criticized on the grounds that there is not strong scientific evidence to support them. Gelles and Cornell (1990: 111–112) assert that "fewer than 10 percent of instances of family violence are attributable solely to personality traits, mental illness, or psychopathology." They contend that biological and psychological theories continue to be accepted without much supporting data because these explanations allow individuals to believe that they are incapable of abuse if they have not been diagnosed with a disorder.

Exchange/Social Control Theory

"People hit and abuse family members because they can." That is how Gelles (1983: 157) summarizes the exchange/social control theory, which combines ideas from social exchange and social control theories. Social exchange theory asserts that people engage in behaviors so long as rewards outweigh the costs. Social control theory suggests that deviance occurs in the absence of formal and informal social controls. Hypothetically, family violence could be costly to offenders if victims hit back, if abusers lost their community standing, or if batterers were arrested. However, Gelles argues that batterers rarely fear such negative consequences because victims generally are not as strong as offenders; victims' dependence and fear of embarrassment keep the abuse hidden from the public; and police, prosecutors, and judges historically have not punished family violence severely. The rewards of violence, such as getting one's way or getting revenge, are not offset by greater costs, so the behavior continues.

Exchange/social control theory suggests that increasing the informal and formal costs of abuse will reduce family violence. Media campaigns encouraging victims to report abuse, mandatory child abuse reporting laws, mandatory arrest policies, and stiffer penalties all are means of increasing the potential costs of using violence, and may lead angry family members to find alternative, more peaceful means of resolving conflict.

Feminist Theory

Feminist theorists believe that family violence cannot be understood without considering gender and power relations in society (Yllö 1993). From the feminist perspective, violence is rooted in the patriarchal social structure. Men's greater access to economic, political, and social resources gives them more power than women. Males are socialized that violence is a legitimate means to assert power. Women, who are economically dependent on men, have little power to oppose or leave the violence. Women are further hampered from challenging men's aggression by a criminal justice system that historically has ignored or tolerated wife abuse.

Dobash and Dobash (1990), pioneers in feminist theory, argue that this perspective is valuable because it demonstrates how family violence is insidious in culture. They write, "Violence against wives is not a result of aberrant individuals or sick marriages but is an extension of some of our most respected traditions, beliefs, and institutional responses" (p. 127). Therefore, solutions must go beyond individual counseling. Social institutions, such as the criminal justice system, must be more responsive women victims. Furthermore, male batterers must be forced to take responsibility for their actions and change future behavior. The tolerance for male aggression must be opposed by challenging the proliferation of violence in the media—including cinema, video games, television, and the Internet.

Critics of feminist theory contend that the theory does not adequately explain all forms of family violence, and is especially difficult to apply when men are victims. Additionally, some of the solutions generated by feminist theory, such as changing gender norms and cultural tolerance of violence, cannot be accomplished quickly or easily.

Intergenerational Transmission of Violence Theory

Egeland (1993: 197) argues that the **intergenerational transmission of violence theory**, which suggests that witnessing or experiencing abuse in childhood leads to abuse in adulthood, is the premier hypothesis in the field of family violence. Combining ideas from behavioral psychology and social learning theory, the intergenerational transmission of violence theory argues that violence is learned through the processes of conditioning and modeling. Behavioral psychologists argue that behavior is learned through a process of conditioning to reinforcement and punishment. Behavior that is reinforced is likely to be repeated, whereas punishment is likely to extinguish behavior. Applied to family violence, the theory suggests that violent behavior is reinforced by the victim's compliance. Furthermore, family violence is kept so secret that offenders rarely are punished. According to social learning theory, children imitate the behavior of role models they love and respect, particularly their parents. Thus, children who witness or experience abuse learn that physical violence is an appropriate method to handle

Is this child more likely to become a wife batterer when he grows up? Why or why not? What sociological perspectives help explain marital violence and child abuse? What social and cultural factors are involved in the incidence, frequency, and distribution of domestic violence in the United States? How does family violence vary according to the perennial sociological variables of gender, race and ethnicity, and social class?

conflict and get one's way. At the same time, children do not learn effective non-violent means of resolving conflicts or relieving frustration.

Although the intergenerational transmission of violence theory is a widely accepted explanation of family violence, we cannot lose sight of the fact that the vast majority of children who grow up in abusive homes do not become abusers as adults (Gelles and Cornell 1990; Pagelow 1984; Kaufman and Zigler 1993). Nor does being raised in a nonviolent home guarantee one will not be an abusive parent or partner. The intergenerational transmission of violence theory is an important reminder, however, that "a violent background is an important contributor to the *likelihood* that a person will be violent" in adulthood (Gelles and Cornell 1990: 60).

Child Maltreatment

The term **child maltreatment** refers to the entire range of ways children can be mistreated, including physical abuse, neglect, sexual abuse, and psychological abuse. Behaviors are considered a form of child maltreatment if they are both damaging (or potentially damaging) *and* violate contemporary social norms (National Research Council 1993). In American society, parents permit a variety of behaviors that harm children but that are not considered maltreatment. Circumcision, ear piercing, feeding children high-cholesterol diets, and allowing children to play full contact sports are all examples of behaviors that are damaging or potentially damaging to children but are within the social norms of acceptable parental conduct (Garbarino 1989). As social norms change, so do the behaviors that are considered forms of maltreatment. Consider the situation in which an infant who was not restrained in a car seat is killed in an automobile crash. Today, such a death is considered the result of parental neglect; a decade ago, it would have been considered a "preventable accident"; and several years before that, it would have been considered a "random accident" in which the parent was blameless (Garbarino 1989).

Beginning in the 1970s, Congress mandated periodic studies of the magnitude of child maltreatment in American society through National Incidence Studies conducted by the National Center on Child Abuse and Neglect (see Sedlak and Broadhurst 1998). The first National Incidence Study of Child Abuse and Neglect was published in 1981; the second was published in 1988. Data for the third National Incidence Study of Child Abuse and Neglect (NIS-3) were collected in 1993 and the results were published in 1996. Much of the information regarding the prevalence of child maltreatment presented in this chapter comes from that most recent study, so it is important to understand how the data were collected.

Data for the NIS-3 were gathered from over 5,600 professionals in 842 agencies in the United States (Sedlak and Broadhurst 1998). Child Protective Service (CPS) agencies in 42 sampled counties provided demographic data on all children who were "reported and accepted for investigation" during the study period. A representative sample of these cases were further examined to determine the details of the maltreatment and the outcome of the CPS investigation. Because much maltreatment is not reported to Child Protective Services, professionals who were likely to come into contact with abused and neglected children were recruited as "sentinels" to provide additional data. Sentinels from police and sheriffs' departments, public schools, day-care centers, hospitals, voluntary social service agencies, mental health agencies, public health departments, and county juvenile probation offices submitted information regarding maltreated children they encountered during the study period.

Two definitional standards of maltreatment were used in the NIS-3: the Harm Standard and the Endangerment Standard. The *Harm Standard,* which has been used in all three national incidence studies, is a strict standard requiring that an act of commission or omission "result in demonstrable harm in order to be classified as abuse or neglect" (Sedlak and Broadhurst 1998). The *Endangerment Standard,* developed during the Second National Incidence Study, is a broader and slightly more lenient category that includes all children who meet the Harm Standard, but it also adds others. The Endangerment Standard "allows children who were not yet harmed by maltreatment to be counted in the abused and neglected estimates if a non-CPS sentinel considered them to be endangered by maltreatment or if their maltreatment was substantiated or indicated in a CPS investigation" (Sedlak and Broadhurst 1998). Furthermore, the Endangerment Standard includes sexual abuse by teenage caregivers and maltreatment by adult caregivers other than parents in some categories.

Physical Child Abuse

Physical child abuse refers to acts of commission by a caregiver that have the potential to cause a child physical harm. Physical abuse includes burning, beatings with an object, severe physical punishment, punching, kicking, and biting (Landes, Quiram, and Jacobs 1995). **Munchausen Syndrome by Proxy,** a rare form of abuse in which an adult causes or feigns an illness in a child to get attention and support from the medical community, also is a form of physical abuse (National Research Council 1993; Rosenberg 1987).

According to the NIS-3, 381,700 children were physically abused under the Harm Standard, which represents a 42 percent increase from the 1988 Second National Incidence study. Using the endangerment standard, 614,100 children were physically abused, an astounding 97 percent rise from the previous National Incidence Study. The vast majority of children (78 percent) were physically abused by their birth parents (Sedlak and Broadhurst 1998). However, Tudge (1997) found that stepparents were "far more likely to *fatally* abuse their children than biological parents."

Consequences of Physical Child Abuse

Physical child abuse has numerous consequences for children. According to the National Child Abuse Coalition, in 1995, an estimated 1,215 children died from abuse. The National Committee to Prevent Child Abuse reported that child abuse fatalities increased 39 percent between 1985 and 1995. Additionally, many children suffer permanent injury. The U.S. Advisory Board on Child Abuse and Neglect stated in a 1995 report that near-fatal abuse leaves 18,000 children permanently disabled each year. Many other long-term consequences of physical abuse have been identified. Physically abused children tend to be more aggressive and have poor peer relations, developmental delays, poor school achievement (Kolko 1996), low self-esteem (Kaufman and Cicchetti 1989), lower verbal and cognitive skills (Friedrich, Enbender, and Luecke 1983), and higher rates of depression (Allen and Tarnowski 1989) than nonabused children.

Researchers disagree as to whether physically abused children are more likely to become delinquent. A 1992 U.S. Department of Justice study reported that 68 percent of juveniles arrested had a prior history of abuse and neglect, and that childhood abuse "increased the odds of future delinquency and adult criminality . . . by 40 percent" (National Child Abuse Coalition 1998). The National Council on Crime and Delinquency asserts that "youths with histories of severe abuse and neglect are much more likely to become chronic and serious juvenile offenders" (National Child Abuse Coalition 1998). However, these findings have been challenged on several grounds. First, correlations between abuse and delinquency usually are found in retrospective studies in which identified delinquents are asked whether they have ever been abused, rather than from longitudinal studies in which abused children are tracked over time (Kolko 1996). Second, many abused children obtain the label of delinquent for behaviors they engage in as a response to abuse. For example, many abused children become truant to avoid facing teachers and peers or they run away from home to escape the violence. Such behaviors, known as *status offenses*, are classified in the criminal justice system as delinquency although they are nonviolent, "victimless" crimes (Pagelow 1984). Knudsen (1992: 77) concludes that "the relationship between abuse and criminal behavior is ambiguous at best."

Risk Factors for Physical Child Abuse

Reports of physical child abuse always raise the same question: How could parents do such a thing? Although countless studies have been conducted to determine what *causes* child abuse, no simple answers have been found. Child abuse is the result of complex individual, family, and social dynamics; no single factor causes a parent to be abusive. However, research has helped identify **risk factors** for child abuse. Risk factors are characteristics of parents, children, and families that increase the probability abuse will occur in a family. It is important to distinguish risk factors from the situations that triggered the parents' rage, or what Gelles (1973) calls *immediate precipitating events*.

To help distinguish between risk factors and immediate precipitating events, consider the following media accounts of child abuse. A *USA Today* story stated that a Chicago couple was accused of killing their 16-month-old daughter "because she wouldn't go to sleep." In a *New York Times* article, it was reported that a Bronx man was accused of killing his girlfriend's 18-month-old daughter "when she blocked his view by crawling in front of his television." Failing to fall asleep and crawling in front of television sets are not risk factors for abuse; they are the immediate precipitating events that led the caregivers to become physically violent. The vast majority of parents who experience these normal frustrations respond calmly and lovingly by simply rocking their children a little longer or removing them from in front of the television set. Unlike the immediate precipitating event, risk factors are characteristics that help explain why these particular adults responded violently to such ordinary parenting situations. It is important to keep in mind, however, that observing any single risk factor in a family is not a cause for alarm (Vander Mey and Neff 1986). The risk for child maltreatment escalates significantly when several risk factors are present in a family.

Several **demographic characteristics of parents**—including the age, socioeconomic status, and sex of the parent—have been identified as risk factors for abuse. Young parents, especially teenage parents, are more likely to be abusive than older parents (Barnett et al. 1997; National Child Abuse Coalition 1998). *Age* is most likely a risk factor for abuse because young parents have less knowledge of child development and are less mature. Additionally, young parents may not have planned or desired the pregnancy and resent the child for interfering with their future plans. Some teenage women view motherhood unrealistically, expecting to have a darling infant to love them and fill a void in their lives, but are unprepared for the responsibility and frustrations associated with being a parent (Tower 1993). Young men may feel forced into an unwanted relationship because of an unplanned pregnancy and therefore resent the child (Tower 1993). Furthermore, young parents generally have little economic security, and because of their incomplete education, they have few prospects for finding good jobs and earning a decent income, which creates family stress and further increases the probability of abuse.

Low socioeconomic status is another risk factor for abuse. Data from the NIS-3 revealed that children whose parents earn less than $15,000 a year are almost 16 times more likely to be a victim of physical abuse using the Harm Standard and 12 times more likely to be physically abused under the Endangerment Standard (Sedlak and Broadhurst 1998). Several explanations for the correlation between poverty and child abuse have been suggested. The most common explanation is that parents who are struggling financially are under a great deal of stress. Parents may be worried about having enough food to last until the next check, paying bills and rent, and staving off creditors. Such stress makes them less patient, so they are more likely to respond to a child's misbehavior harshly. Others argue that child abuse is not necessarily more common in low-income families; rather, it is detected more easily. Low-income parents regularly come into contact with social workers if they are receiving any governmental assistance, such as food stamps, subsidized housing, or supplemental income. Social workers are trained to detect signs of abuse and are mandated to report suspected child abuse. Unlike middle- and upper-income families, low-income parents often have to use emergency rooms or clinics rather than a regular family physician for medical care. Doctors who are unfamiliar with a child's history may order more extensive diagnostic tests and in the process detect abuse.

The directors of the NIS-3 firmly believe that the correlation between income and child abuse is not an artifact of selective observation, but is a real difference. Sedlak and Broadhurst (1998) argue that over two million more children in families earning over $15,000 would have to be being abused without it being detected to substantiate the claim that income is not associated with child abuse. They contend that problems associated with poverty (e.g., poorer education, higher rates of substance abuse, and inadequate social support systems) explain the higher rates of child abuse in low-income families.

Gender also has been identified as a risk factor. Females are more likely than males to be reported for physically abusing children. Among children physically abused by birth parents in the NIS-3 study, 60 percent were abused by mothers, compared to 48 percent abused by fathers. As Gelles and Cornell (1990) explain, mothers spend more time with their children and are therefore more likely to experience frustration that they respond to with abuse. In many families, men are not present to be at risk for abuse. Pagelow (1984: 187), who argues that women often are unfairly suspected for abuse because they are primary caregivers, points out that if one examines only families in which "both parents are present and thus both are available to abuse, 76 percent of the abusers are fathers."

Socialization experience of the parent is another risk factor for abuse (Gelles 1973). As suggested by the intergenerational transmission of violence theory, parents who were abused as children are more likely to abuse their children than parents who were not abused (Gelles and Straus 1987). Kaufman and Zigler (1987) estimate that 30 percent of abused children become abusive parents. The obvious question is: Why do some parents continue the cycle of violence they learned in childhood, when the vast majority of parents who suffered childhood abuse provide loving care for their children? Parents who are likely to break the cycle of abuse are those who (1) had a supportive, loving adult who they could trust in their childhood; (2) had a supportive partner when they became parents; and (3) received therapy to help resolve their troublesome childhood (Egeland 1988; Main and Goldwyn 1984).

Substance abuse and dependence are strong risk factors for physical abuse (Kelleher, Chaffin, and Hollenberg 1994). Addictions to alcohol, illicit drugs, and even inhalants (Fendrich, Mackesy-Amiti, and Wislar 1997) are associated with an increased risk for child maltreatment. Researchers speculate that substance abuse interferes with parents' judgment and increases anger and irritability with their children (Kolko 1996). However, Milner and Chilamkurti (1995) argue that more research is needed before we know exactly how substance abuse is linked with physical child abuse.

The risk for physical child abuse also increases with **situational stress in the family.** Stresses within the family can stem from a variety of sources. *Unemployment* and *constant marital disputes* create stress that can increase the risk for physical abuse (Gelles 1973; Knudsen 1992). Families who are *socially isolated* and do not have relatives or friends they can turn to when child-care frustrations and other stresses become overwhelming also have a greater risk for being abusive. Gelles (1973) argues that some situational stress in families is child-produced stress. Children with *difficult temperaments*, who cry consistently or are difficult to discipline, create stress that some parents respond to with abuse. Having *unplanned* or *unwanted children* also is a risk factor for abuse (Tower 1993). Parents may resent unplanned children and have few economic or personal resources to deal with an infant. *Premature infants*—who cry more, are harder to comfort, and do not respond socially as early as full-term infants—also have an increased risk for being abused.

Children with disabilities also are at an increased risk for physical abuse (Belsky and Vondra 1989). In 1991, the reported incidence of abuse was 35.5 per 1,000 children with disabilities, compared to 21.3 per 1,000 children with no disabilities (Goldson 1998). Maltreatment of children with disabilites is becoming an increasing problem, because advancing medical technology allows children with serious trauma or disabilities to survive even though they may require a tremendous amount of care at home. Such care can be exhausting and costly for families. Parents who lack the personal, social, financial, and educational resources to handle such stress may become physically abusive toward children with disabilities.

Psychological disturbances are another risk factor for physical child abuse. Parents who have a hostile personality, are extremely irritable or aggressive, or suffer from depression are at increased risk for being abusive (Kolko 1996). However, Gelles (1973) cautions that although mental illness often is perceived as the sole cause of child abuse, multiple factors contribute to child abuse, only one of which is mental illness.

Child Neglect

Two stories of neglect appeared in the February 10, 1993, edition of *USA Today*. The first story, which made international headlines and has become a remembered part of American culture, was about neglect and abandonment charges being brought against David and Sharon Schoo for leaving their two daughters, ages 9 and 4, home alone for 9 days—including Christmas Day—while they vacationed in Acapulco. The Schoos were dubbed by the media as the "Home Alone Couple" because this incident had such striking similarities to the movie *Home Alone,* in which wealthy parents forgot to bring their son with them to Paris for Christmas. The second story of child neglect, buried deep in the newspaper, simply read: "San Antonio authorities said 13-month-old Matthew Gonzales died Monday after a house fire [was] started by his 4-year-old brother when the two were left home by their working mother, Linda Gonzales, 24. [A neighbor] said [Ms.] Gonzales couldn't find affordable day care. Police said they were considering possible charges."

Child neglect is different from other forms of maltreatment because it involves behaviors parents fail to do rather than acts they commit. As illustrated in the two contrasting news stories, parents can be neglectful for different reasons with different outcomes. Two important issues that often are considered in defining child neglect are *parental intent* and *harm to the child* (Erickson and Egeland 1996). Child protective service workers, police, and scholars all struggle with whether and how to distinguish between intentional, malevolent neglect and neglect that occurs because of dire socioeconomic circumstances. Both sets of children in the preceding news stories were left alone at ages most people would consider too young. However, the Schoos could have afforded appropriate care for their children, whereas Gonzales apparently could not. Therefore the intent of the parents' actions differ. Erickson and Egeland (1996) point out that legal culpability may hinge on intent, but the outcome to the children who are neglected is very much the same, regardless of the parents' intent. Therefore, they argue that any definition of neglect should center around the unmet needs of the children, rather the intent of the parents' behavior.

Harm is another issue that arises in constructing a definition of child neglect. The question that is raised is whether children must suffer immediate, identifiable harm as a result of the negligence or whether threat to the child's well-being is sufficient for the parents to be labeled neglectful. Certainly, the immediate consequences for the unattended children described in the newspaper articles were quite different. Matthew Gonzales died and his 4-year-old brother suffered the trauma of a fire and the death of a sibling. The two Schoo children were frightened and lonely, but suffered no physical harm. Most practitioners and scholars today agree that the effects of child neglect may not be recognizable for months or years (Erickson and Egeland 1996). Therefore, children can be considered neglected in the absence of any immediate signs of physical or emotional harm. A caregiver's act of omission that substantially risks the well-being of children, regardless of intent, is considered neglect.

Child neglect is the most common form of child maltreatment reported (Utech 1994). The National Center on Child Abuse and Neglect reports that 49 percent of all substantiated cases of child maltreatment involve neglect, which is more than twice the rate of the next most common form of child maltreatment—physical child abuse (Kemp 1998). According to the Third National Incidence Study of Child Abuse and Neglect, the number of children who were neglected under the Harm Standard increased from 474,800 in 1986 to 879,000 in 1993. Using the Endangerment Standard, the number of neglected children rose from 507,700 to 1,335,100 children (a 163 percent increase).

Consequences of Child Neglect

The consequences of child neglect vary tremendously and depend on the type of neglect endured. Children who suffer from educational neglect may be inadequately prepared for employment and independent living as adults. Medical neglect can leave children with permanent physical disabilities, including deafness and blindness (Knudsen 1992). Physical and emotional neglect can cause low self-esteem, poor social skills, and developmental delays (Erickson and Egeland 1996; Knudsen 1992). Infants who are physically and emotionally neglected can develop a medical condition known as **nonorganic failure to thrive (NFTT).** Doctors diagnose infants with NFTT—which is characterized by failure to gain weight, extremely low weight and height (below the 3rd to 5th percentiles), small head circumference, and significant delays in psychomotor development—when all biological causes have been eliminated (Kemp 1998; Utech 1994). In addition, babies with NFTT also resist being cuddled, suffer from sleep disturbances, and do not smile. Inadequate nutrition due to intentional malice or because of a lack of knowledge of how to feed or how much to feed babies, as well as diluting formula to save money can cause the condition (Tower 1993). Furthermore, NFTT can be caused by consistent failure to nurture and respond to an infant's emotional needs.

The most horrific consequence of neglect, of course, is death. Half of all children who die because of maltreatment are victims of neglect (Kemp 1998). Many of these fatalities happen because of house fires, drowning, and poisonings that occur while children are unsupervised. Physical neglect and medical neglect also can lead to starvation and untreated illnesses that become fatal.

Risk Factors for Child Neglect

As with physical child abuse, several factors that put children at risk for neglect have been identified. *Low socioeconomic status* is the most commonly noted risk factor for neglect. In fact, neglectful families tend to be the "poorest of the poor"

(Knudsen 1992: 149). Data from the NIS-3 reveal that compared to children whose families earn $30,000 or more per year, children from families with annual incomes below $15,000 were 44 times more likely to be neglected using either the Harm or Endangerment standard (Sedlak and Broadhurst 1998). However, it is important to note that much neglect in low-income families is a consequence of the social circumstances rather than parents' malice. Families who live in dire poverty also tend to live in substandard housing, where children may be exposed to health hazards such as lead paint. Lack of heat and environmental pollutants put poor children at risk for more illnesses, yet low-income families may not have access to adequate health care, so chronic and acute diseases go untreated. Parents also may run out of food before welfare checks, food stamps, or paychecks arrive, which contributes to nutritional deficits in children. Low-income parents who work often cannot afford adequate child care and may therefore leave children unattended.

Another commonly cited risk factor for neglect is *social isolation.* Parents who lack social support do not have people whom they can call when they need financial assistance or child care. In the absence of a strong support network, children may go hungry or be left unattended. Poverty and social isolation tend to be strongly correlated, as well. Poor neighborhoods generally are unsafe, so residents often are distrustful of each other and do not develop a sense of community, which leaves many parents socially isolated (Kemp 1998).

Family structure and *family size* also have been identified as risk factors for neglect. As with physical child abuse, neglect is more common in single-parent families than in two-parent families. The NIS-3 data show a 165 percent greater risk of experiencing any form of neglect in single-parent families (Sedlak and Broadhurst 1998). Barnett and colleagues (1997) report that 51 percent of children identified as neglected come from single-parent homes. The best explanation for the higher rates of neglect in single-parent families is linked with the risk factors mentioned earlier—poverty and social isolation. Single-parent households headed by women are likely to be low-income households, and single parents often lack the social support they need to care adequately for their children. Additionally, neglect is most common in larger families—those with four or more children—and least common in families with two or three children (Sedlak and Broadhurst 1998). Children without siblings have a higher risk for neglect than those in families with two or three children, but a lower risk than children in larger families. Sedlak and Broadhurst (1998) explain that the risk for neglect in larger families is explained by the greater stress and responsibility parents have. The higher rates of abuse in families with only one child may be explained by the fact that many of these families are in their early stages of development with younger, less experienced parents who eventually will have additional children (Sedlak and Broadhurst 1998).

Additional factors that put children at greater risk for neglect include having parents who are *young,* have *low education levels,* suffer from *depression,* and have a *substance abuse problem* (Barnett et al. 1997; Kemp 1998). Younger parents and those with less education may lack knowledge about proper parenting behaviors.

Depression can interfere with parents' judgment as well as their energy to care properly for children. Chemical addictions can contribute to neglect in several ways. Parents who are drunk or high may be unable to care adequately for children. They also may spend so much money on their addiction that they cannot afford to feed, clothe, or house their children properly. Some alcohol- and drug-addicted parents leave their children unattended for long periods while they are on binges. Increasingly, child welfare advocates are asserting that consuming significant amounts of alcohol during pregnancy, which can lead to **fetal alcohol syndrome,** characterized by physical deformities and mental retardation, or using illicit drugs such as cocaine or heroin, should be considered a form of child neglect. Several states have prosecuted women for child endangerment or neglect after giving birth to babies with measurable amounts of illegal drugs in their systems (Farr 1995; Madden 1993; Peak and Del Papa 1993).

Child Sexual Abuse

The National Center on Child Abuse and Neglect defines *child sexual abuse* as

> *contacts or interactions between a child and an adult when the child is being used for the sexual stimulation of the perpetrator or another person. Sexual abuse may also be committed by a person under the age of 18 when that person is either significantly older than the victim or when the perpetrator is in a position of power or control over another child.* (Barnett et al. 1997: 73–74)

Four key components of this definition of child sexual abuse are noteworthy (Barnett et al. 1997). First, the definition is broad enough to include sexual abuse by relatives and those outside the family. Second, the definition allows sexual experiences that involve physical contact as well as noncontact activities to be considered sexually abusive. Using children in pornographic movies is an example of a noncontact sexually abusive behavior. Third, the adult's exploitation of power to achieve sexual gratification is emphasized. Children are considered incapable of giving informed consent to sexual acts, since they cannot fully understand the consequences of those actions. Adults, who always have more authority and power than children, often use threats or promises of rewards to coerce the child's cooperation. Finally, the definition recognizes that differences in age or maturational level between the perpetrator and victim are as important as chronological age itself. Adolescents and even children can be perpetrators of abuse when they exploit differences in age, size, or intellectual abilities to obtain sexual gratification.

Despite the concrete definition of child sexual abuse provided by the National Center on Child Abuse and Neglect, it is often difficult to determine whether certain behaviors are abusive. Bathing with children and touching children's genitals are examples of behaviors that could be considered either abusive or not abusive. *Intent* is a key variable in determining whether a behavior is abusive. Parents who bathe with small children to save time or for safety reasons and parents who must touch children's genitals for hygiene purposes are not being abusive. However, if the intent of the parent is to obtain sexual gratification, those same behaviors could be considered sexual abuse (Conte 1993).

The NIS-3 data suggest that 217,700 children were sexually abused under the Harm Standard (an 83 percent increase from NIS-2) and 300,200 children were sexually abused using the Endangerment Standard (a 125 percent increase) (Sedlak and Broadhurst 1998). Girls are sexually abused three times more often than boys (Sedlak and Broadhurst 1998). Preadolsecents between the ages of 9 and 11 are at the greatest risk for abuse (Barnett et al. 1997), although the NIS-3 data suggest that there is "a very broad age range of vulnerability from preschool age on" (Sedlak and Broadhurst 1998). The majority of cases of sexual abuse involve a single incident. However, perpetrators often begin grooming victims for abuse long before the actual sexual incident by gradually moving from nonsexual to sexual touches. Perpetrators tend to select vulnerable children—those who are unhappy, lonely, starved for attention, passive, and quiet—as victims (Barnett et al. 1997).

Consequences of Child Sexual Abuse

The consequences of child sexual abuse are complex and numerous. Gomes-Schwartz, Horowitz, and Cardarelli (1990) point out that the impact of the abuse on the victim varies, depending on when the abuse began, how long it lasted, and the way in which the child was violated. Children who experience a single incident of sexual abuse at a very young age are least likely to suffer long-term damage because they do not understand adult sexuality. Older children suffer many negative consequences because they understand that such behavior is taboo. Sexual abuse during adolescence is particularly damaging because teenagers are mature enough to comprehend how they have been victimized, and they may feel guilt, as well. Consequences of sexual abuse include behavioral disturbances; emotional disturbances; destructive behavior; anger; fear; hostility; depression; withdrawal, regressive behaviors, such as bedwetting and thumbsucking; sleep disturbances; changes in eating behavior; and sexualized behavior, such as precocious sexual knowledge, inappropriate sex play, compulsive masturbation, and sexual promiscuity (Barnett et al. 1997; Gomes-Schwartz et al. 1990; Kemp 1998).

As adults, victims of childhood sexual abuse are likely to suffer from depression and to harbor guilt. Some professionals contend that memory of child sexual abuse may be blocked from the victim's memory for many years and not recalled until adulthood. **Delayed or recovered memories of sexual abuse** often occur after a person has begun therapy to deal with personal troubles (Zerbe Enns et al. 1995). Critics, who dub such recollections **false memory syndrome,** contend that remembrances of child sexual abuse in adulthood are not accurate and may be planted by therapists (Loftus 1993).

Risk Factors for Child Sexual Abuse

Several risk factors for child sexual abuse have been identified, some of which are risk factors for other types of maltreatment and some of which are unique to sexual abuse. Like physical abuse and neglect, *low socioeconomic status* is a risk factor for sexual abuse (Vander Mey and Neff 1986). According to the NIS-3, children from families with annual incomes below $15,000 were almost 18 times more likely to be sexually abused using either definitional standard (Sedlak and Broadhurst 1998). As with other forms of maltreatment, a *high level of stress in the family* also is a risk factor for sexual abuse. Stressors such as unemployment and financial difficulties may "function as a disinhibitor of sexual impulses" (Wurtele and Miller-Perrin 1992: 33).

A *history of childhood sexual abuse* is also a risk factor, as it is with other forms of maltreatment (Wurtele and Miller-Perrin 1992). Although researchers are uncertain why adults who have been molested are more likely than others to be abusive themselves, several explanations have been offered (Barnett et al. 1997). Perpetrators with a history of abuse may continue the cycle in an effort to resolve anxiety from previous abuse or to regain a sense of power and control in their lives by exploiting others. Alternatively, children who are sexually abused may fail to develop empathy or sympathy for others, which allows them to engage in cruel behavior without feeling guilty or remorseful. Gilgun (1991) found that males who had been sexually abused as children who did not repeat the cycle of abuse were likely to have had people in whom they could confide and trust. Most men did not disclose the history of abuse to their confidant, but were able to discuss how to have healthy adult sexual relationships as well as disclose feelings of depression and anger.

Social isolation and *family structure* are two other risk factors for abuse that are common to other forms of maltreatment. Social isolation can contribute to the risk for sexual abuse because perpetrators are more confident that they will not get caught, and without family and friendship networks, victims have few people with whom they could share their secret (Wurtele and Miller-Perrin 1992). Sexual abuse is more prevalent in families in which a child is living without both biological parents (Barnett et al. 1997; Vander Mey and Neff 1986; Wurtele and Miller-Perrin 1992). Children who live with a stepfather or father substitute (e.g., a mother's boyfriend) are at greater risk for abuse than those children living with both parents. Unlike other forms of maltreatment, sexual abuse is most likely to be perpetrated by someone other than a birth parent (Sedlak and Broadhurst 1998).

One risk factor for child sexual abuse that is different from other forms of maltreatment is the *sex of the offender*. Females are statistically more likely to commit physical abuse and neglect, but males are far more likely to sexually abuse children. NIS-3 findings show that 89 percent of children were sexually abused by a male, compared to only 12 percent by a female (Sedlak and Broadhurst 1998). Interestingly, although fathers are more likely to sexually abuse their children, mothers often have been accused of contributing to the problem. In the past, it was believed that mothers consciously or unconsciously encouraged sexual abuse by being unavailable to their husbands or by responding inappropriately when told of the abuse. Gomes-Schwartz and associates (1990) label this belief the **myth of the mother accomplice.** They found that more than 80 percent of the mothers in their study took some action to protect their child from the abuser, and the majority were not angry with their child for revealing the incident. Furthermore, the belief that father-daughter incest is simply a role reversal in which the daughter assumes the role of wife by caring for siblings, cooking, cleaning house, and performing sexual duties because the mother is emotionally or physically unavailable has not been supported through empirical research (Conte 1993).

Conte (1991, 1993) argues that fathers who have sexually abused their daughters have been perceived as less deviant and dangerous than other sex offenders. Rather than being punished through the criminal justice system, fathers who commit incest are often referred to community-based treatment programs for "rehabilitation" because they are considered less threatening to the community. Conte (1991, 1993) suggests that incestuous fathers are no different from other pedophiles. He found that 49 percent of incestuous fathers abused children outside the family during the same time period they were abusing their own children.

Although less common than father-daughter incest, brothers also can be sexually abusive. Male sibling sexual abusers are more likely than nonincest adolescent offenders to engage in sexual intercourse with the victim (O'Brien 1991). Additionally, brothers generally do not confine their abuse to one sibling but are likely to molest all younger sisters.

Psychological Maltreatment

Although everyone has had their feelings hurt by a parent at some point in their lives, not everyone has been a victim of psychological maltreatment. Isolated incidents of hurt feelings or harsh words do not constitute a form of abuse. **Psychological maltreatment** refers to *patterns* of psychologically or emotionally abusive behaviors, including both acts of omission and commission, that can cause mental injury (Kemp 1998). Behaviors such as rejecting, degrading or devaluing, terrorizing, isolating, corrupting, exploiting, confining, denying essential stimulation, and unreliable and inconsistent parenting all constitute psychological maltreatment (Kemp 1998: 75). Schaefer (1997: 626) argues that consistent comments such as "You dummy," "You're never going to amount to anything," "You're the reason we are getting a divorce," as well as cursing at and threatening children also are forms of psychological maltreatment.

Psychological maltreatment is the most underreported form of child maltreatment. Psychological or emotional abuse is the primary form of abuse in only 3 percent of reported cases of child maltreatment (Barnett et al. 1997), although psychological maltreatment often accompanies other forms of abuse. As with other forms of child maltreatment, parents with the fewest financial, social, personal, and psychological resources are most likely to be psychologically and emotionally abusive (Knudsen 1992). Poverty, social isolation, and a poor understanding of child development are all risk factors for psychological maltreatment.

The consequences of psychological maltreatment vary, depending on the age of the child, the age at which the maltreatment began, and the severity of the maltreatment. Hart, Germain, and Brassard (1987) outline the consequences of psychological maltreatment for children at different developmental stages. Infants who have been psychologically or emotionally abused have difficulty trusting others. In early childhood, psychological maltreatment can cause guilt, difficulty with toilet training, and suppressed emotions. School-age children who have been psychologically maltreated have low self-esteem, poor academic achievement, and difficulty making friends.

What Can Be Done about Child Maltreatment?

Programs to combat child maltreatment can be categorized as either primary, secondary, or tertiary prevention (Knudsen 1992). **Primary prevention,** usually conducted at the societal level, is designed to prevent maltreatment before it occurs. Programs conducted in schools to teach children to distinguish between good and bad touches are examples of a primary prevention against sexual abuse. Children learn to recognize sexual abuse and that it is appropriate to say no. Also, children may be more likely to disclose sexual abuse after attending sexual abuse educational programs (Wurtele and Miller-Perrin 1992). Offering education in high schools about child development and parenting skills is a form of primary prevention against physical abuse and neglect (Tower 1993). Between 1988 and 1992, the U.S. National Committee for the Prevention of Child Abuse ran an advertising campaign to educate the public about the damage of emotional child abuse. Slogans such as *Words hit as hard as a fist* and *Stop using words that hurt. Start using words that help* were broadcast on television, in magazines, and on billboards (Browne and Herbert 1997).

Secondary prevention programs are designed to reduce the chances of abuse occurring in families identified as being at high risk for maltreatment. The Minnesota Early Learning Demonstration (MELD) project is an example of secondary prevention against physical child abuse and neglect (Tower 1993). Mothers identified as being at risk for abuse were provided with intensive parent training for two years. Mothers met twice a week for three-hour sessions to learn coping skills, family management techniques, and child development information. Many secondary prevention programs involve bringing health care or social workers into the home to teach and observe. Olds and colleagues (Olds et al. 1986; Olds, Henderson, and Kitzman 1994) found that high-risk mothers who received home visits had more positive perceptions of their infants, punished less, and had fewer incidents of physical child abuse than high-risk mothers who did not participate in the program.

Tertiary prevention is intervention after abuse has taken place that is designed to prevent further incidents. This most common type of prevention includes education on nonviolent discipline techniques and child management for parents who are currently maltreating their children (Kolko 1996). Parents Anonymous was originally formed to provide education and social support for parents who physically abuse their children. An abusive parent was paired with a partner on whom they could call when they felt angry with their children. The partner could temporarily provide child care to relieve the parent or simply help calm the parent over the telephone. Today, Parents Anonymous also attracts parents who were victims of maltreatment who do not want to repeat the cycle of violence (Tower 1993). Tertiary prevention also involves helping adults who were abused as children to deal with the problems stemming from abuse. Many formerly abused adults need individual therapy or group therapy to help overcome the difficulty they have in trusting others as well as depression, low-self esteem, and substance abuse problems resulting from childhood abuse (Tower 1993). In extreme cases of maltreatment, children may be temporarily placed into foster care until social workers believe the parent can safely resume child-care responsibilities.

Abuse in Intimate Relationships

Parental relationships with children are, by definition, different in very important ways from relationships between consenting adults. Parents have some authority over their children's behavior, making the parent-child relationship inherently unequal. Today, experts strongly discourage parents from using physical punishment to assert control, yet tolerance exists for spanking as a form of discipline in American culture. On the other hand, expectations of intimate relationships between adults call for mutuality between partners rather than power struggles. Physical violence between adults who share a consenting sexual relationship, whether formalized through marriage or not, is culturally defined as deviant behavior.

Partner Abuse, Social Class, and Race

Data from several sources suggest that family violence is more prevalent in lower income families (Moore 1997). Straus (1980) estimated that families living at or below the poverty line have a rate of marital violence that is 500 percent greater than the wealthiest American families. The U.S. Department of Justice (1995) reported that "women in families with incomes below $10,000 per year were more likely than other women to be violently attacked by an intimate." Sociologists speculate that part of the reason violence rates are higher in families with lower socioeconomic status is because of the higher levels of stress—particularly financial stress—that low-income couples experience. Frustration and anxiety regarding finances lead to bickering and arguing, which may escalate into physical conflict.

Statistics can be deceiving, however. Much violence in middle- and upper-class families is kept hidden for a variety of reasons. People who live in middle-class and upper-class neighborhoods often have more privacy, including greater distance between their homes. Neighbors are less likely to hear a domestic disturbance in a wealthier neighborhood and to call the police. In addition, middle- and upper-class victims may be reluctant to call for help for fear of social stigma. Both the victims and the perpetrators are likely to hold prestigious jobs and may be well respected in the community, with the result that victims may not want to tarnish their reputations or their spouses' reputations by calling the authorities for help. Although the police respond quickly and do not charge a fee for their services, they arrive with sirens blaring and lights flashing, which is certain to draw attention to the home. To avoid the embarrassment and social stigma, wealthier victims may choose to deal with marital violence by seeking private counseling for themselves or visiting their private physicians, strategies that keep domestic violence hidden from the public and out of official statistics.

The data on the association between race and domestic violence is both contradictory and controversial. It is widely acknowledged that domestic violence cuts across all racial lines. Although minorities may show up in official statistics more often, for many of the same reasons that lower socioeconomic families do, all women—regardless of race—are vulnerable to violence at the hands of their partners. Drawing on information from the National Crime Victimization Survey, in which over 100,000 individuals from approximately 50,000 U.S. households participate, the U.S. Department of Justice (1995) found that "women of all races, as well as Hispanic and non-Hispanic women, were about equally vulnerable to attacks by intimates."

Partner Abuse, Gender, and Age

Since the late 1970s, when Steinmetz began writing about "battered husband syndrome," controversy has raged over the seriousness and scope of marital violence against men (see Steinmetz 1977, 1978, 1980). Advocates for women fear that acknowledging violence against men in intimate relationships will deplete desperately needed resources for battered women and their children. Others argue that it is unfair to ignore violence against men because of a political agenda.

Here is what we do know about gender and marital violence: First, although surveys using the Conflict Tactics Scale (discussed earlier) generally reveal little difference in the *frequency* of violence committed by women and men against their partners (Straus 1993), it is widely acknowledged that males are far more likely to inflict serious physical injury than are women (Browning and Dutton 1986; Saunders 1989). Second, men rarely feel the fear and intimidation from the violence that women do. As Pagelow (1984: 274) states, "Men perceived their wives' serious attempts to hurt them as amusing, or at most, annoying." Barnett, Miller-Perrin, and Perrin (1997: 191) concur, writing, "Whereas battered women report being very afraid of their violent partners, batterers report little fear of physical assault from their female partners." Third, there often is a gender difference in motive for the violence; physical assaults perpetrated by women against their husbands often are committed in self-defense or in retaliation for violence he used against her earlier. Men's motives are more often to intimidate or control (Pagelow 1984). Finally, men are usually less dependent on women economically and therefore can leave battering relationships more easily than battered women can (Pleck et al. 1978).

Thus there are significant differences in the severity, perception, motives, and consequences of men's violence against women, compared to women's violence against men. While acknowledging these differences does not justify or condone women's violence, it does suggest that battering of wives is a more serious social problem than husband battering.

Age is also a factor sociologists have studied in relation to marital violence. As with most other crimes, domestic violence occurs most frequently among partners between the ages of 18 and 30 (Barnett et al. 1997). According to Gelles and Cornell (1990: 74), "The rate of marital violence among those under 30 years of age is more than double the rate for the next older age group (31–50)." Additionally, newer marriages are at the greatest risk for abuse. Roy (1977) found the highest rates of abuse in couples married from 2.5 to 5 years; couples married 16 years or more are least likely to be violent.

Marital Violence against Women

Some measures of the prevalence of violence in marriages are based on official police records; others are based on reports from surveys. However the data are gathered, one fact is indisputable: Millions of women in the United States are beaten every year by the men who claim to love them. The FBI Uniform Crime Reports show that at least one woman is battered every 15 seconds (Bureau of Justice Statistics 1992). An article published in the *Journal of the American Medical Association* estimated that two to four million women are abused physically each year. Approximately 6 of every 10 married couples have experienced violence at some time during their marriage, suggesting that domestic violence may occur in more than half of American families (Novello 1992).

Marital Rape

Abuse in intimate relationships can take several forms. Psychological abuse, which almost always accompanies other forms of relationship violence, includes threats, persistent criticism and belittling, and constant lying. Physical abuse or battering can range from mild slaps to severe beatings. Sexual abuse also can occur in intimate relationships. Although in recent years awareness about date rape has increased, many find it surprising to learn that husbands can and do rape their wives.

Marital rape was long ignored in society and in the criminal justice system because it was believed that women agreed to sex on demand when they took their marriage vows (Field and Bienen 1980). Therefore, until recently, every state had a **spousal exemption** in their criminal code that specifically excluded husbands from being charged with raping their wives. On July 5, 1993, wife rape became a crime in all 50 states and the District of Columbia (Bergen 1996). However, in 33 states, husbands are still exempt from prosecution in some situations, such as when the couple has not separated or legally filed for divorce.

Marital rape is not an infrequent problem, with approximately two million incidences occurring annually (Bidwell and White 1986; Griffin 1980; Groth and Gary 1981). Bowker (1983) estimates that marital rape occurs more frequently than all other forms of rape combined, affecting one in eight wives. In her ground-breaking study, Russell (1982) found that 14 percent of respondents had experienced at least one completed or attempted rape by their husbands. Marital rape almost always is accompanied by other forms of violence (Klein 1983) and usually occurs more than once. Bergen (1996) found that 55 percent of her sample had been raped 20 or more times by their husbands.

The consequences of marital rape are devastating. In addition to physical injuries, victims of wife rape suffer from guilt, low self-esteem, and severe psychological trauma (Davidson 1978; Finkelhor and Yllö 1985; Frieze 1983; Russell 1982). Although conventional wisdom may suggest that stranger rape is more traumatic than marital rape, empirical evidence indicates otherwise. Griffin (1980) and Bowker (1983) found that the trauma following marital rape can be more severe because the victim is in a long-term relationship with the offender and therefore constantly lives in fear of another sexual assault. Furthermore, the offender is a man she loved and willingly had sex with in the past, so she must cope with the loss of trust in her marriage. Karen, a respondent in Bergen's (1996: 43) study of wife rape, describes the trauma she endured:

It was very clear to me. He raped me. He ripped off my pajamas, he beat me up. I mean, some scumbag down the street would do that to me. So to me it wasn't any different because I was married to him, it was rape—real clear what it was. It emotionally hurt worse [than stranger rape]. I mean you can compartmentalize it as stranger rape—you were in the wrong place at the wrong time. You can manage to get over it differently. But here you're at home with your husband, and you don't expect that. I was under constant terror [from then on].

Why Does She Stay?

Inevitably when people hear of a woman who has or is currently enduring abuse from her partner, they ask, Why does she stay? However, I believe that asking why she stays is an inappropriate focus. As one battered woman eloquently stated, "It's not illegal for me to stay, but everybody always asks why I stay. It is illegal for him to beat me, but nobody ever asks why he is abusive."

Before beginning a discussion of why some women stay with their abusive partners, it is important to point out that not all battered women do so. Many battered women leave their abusive partners permanently. Many others leave several times, but for a variety of reasons feel compelled to return. In fact, a Virginia court judge recently revealed that the average battered woman leaves her abuser seven times before leaving him permanently.

Leaving often imposes significant hardships on battered women. Because many battered women are economically dependent on their spouses, leaving an abusive partner often means giving up a warm place to live. It has been estimated that up to 50 percent of all homeless women and children in this country are fleeing domestic violence (National Coalition Against Domestic Violence 1997). Furthermore, leaving an abusive partner does not guarantee one's safety. The most dangerous time in a battered woman's life is when she decides to leave her partner, because that is the time when men are most likely to commit the most serious, even fatal, attacks. Divorced and separated women—those who have taken the step to leave the abuse—are attacked 14 times more often than abused women who still live with their partners (Klaus and Rand 1992). Ironically, while the public criticizes battered women for remaining with their abusers, in many cases it is economically and physically safer for them *not* to leave.

Economic Dependence

One of the most often cited reasons married women remain with their abusive husbands is economic dependence. They do not have the means to support themselves and their children and thus feel trapped in the relationship. To illustrate the desperation of an economically dependent battered woman, think about how much money you usually carry in your wallet or purse. Now imagine that you are being violently attacked by your spouse and your children are crying in the bedroom. You grab your children, your wallet or purse, and your keys, and then you run out the door. How far will you get with the amount of cash on your person? Will you be able to afford dinner for the kids, a hotel room, and gas for the car? What about credit cards and checking accounts? Most abusive husbands maintain complete control over the family finances to prevent their wives from having economic independence. They may stop the credit cards or drain the checking accounts. The cash you had when you ran might get you through a night or even a few days, if you were lucky to have a lot with you, but it probably would not be enough to allow you to stay away permanently.

Several studies have found that "the probability of staying in . . . violent relationships was highest for women whose husbands were the sole breadwinners" (Barnett et al. 1997: 221). Abusive men who have economic power over their wives know that their wives are not free to leave at any time. Therefore, many batterers try to prevent their wives from obtaining or keeping employment. They may use physical force or threats to prohibit wives from working outside the home. Some even go to the extent of taking the car keys so their wives will not have transportation to work.

Many batterers harass their employed wives so much at work that eventually the women lose their jobs. Zorza found that "abusive partners harass 74% of employed battered women at work, either in person or over the telephone, which results in their being late to work, [or] missing work altogether, and eventually 20% lose their jobs" (National Domestic Violence Fact Sheet 1998). The Department of Labor reported that in 1992, "approximately 20% of the women killed in the workplace were murdered by their husbands or male partners, current or former" (National Domestic Violence Fact Sheet 1998).

Fear

Many women stay in battering relationships because they are afraid of what their husbands will do to them or their children if they leave. Batterers often threaten to harm their wives, withhold money for food for the family, or harm or kidnap the children. A battering husband's threats are real, for he has inflicted physical pain on his wife in the past, and she knows he is capable of doing everything he threatens to do. And her fears of his violence are not unfounded. Barbara Hart from the National Coalition Against Domestic Violence reports that "women who leave their batterers are at a 75 percent greater risk of being killed by the batterer than those who stay" ("Myths and Facts" 1997).

No Place to Go

Many women remain with their abusive partners because they feel they have no place to go. Thinking about leaving, wives probably entertain several ideas of where to go with their children. Moving out on their own would be the ideal choice if they were not economically dependent. The next option would be moving back home to live with parents. However, going home may not be an option. Parents may not live close by, requiring relocation to a different city or state, which may not be permissible with children involved. The parents may be struggling financially and unable to take on additional economic strain. The battered woman's parents may be getting old and may not be comfortable with children running around the house again. Some parents may forbid their daughter to move home because they fear her husband's violence will follow her to their home. The daughter may not have a good relationship with her parents. The abuser himself may be responsible for the wedge between her and her parents, or she may have been a victim of abuse at home as a child, but for whatever reason, she just knows she cannot go home.

Moving in with a good friend may be a temporary solution, but the battered woman knows she and her children will wear out their welcome. It is a lot to ask of a friend. She will have to find a more permanent place to live. There is always the local shelter.

The option of going to a shelter is not as readily available as most people think. There is a severe shortage of shelters across the country. In 1990, there were only 1,500 shelters for battered women in the United States ("Myths and Facts" 1997). Women who live in rural areas are least likely to have access to a shelter. Where a shelter is available, there usually is a waiting list, and applicants can stay for only a limited time—usually six weeks. Again, the battered woman may see the shelter as a short-term alternative in an emergency, but only rarely will she be strong enough financially and emotionally to move out on her own in six weeks. One study found that "after being sheltered, 31 percent of abused women in New York City returned to their batterers, primarily because they could not locate longer-term housing" (National Coalition Against Domestic Violence 1997). Many women who do not return home to their batterers face homelessness.

Shame and Self-Blame

Physical violence is virtually always accompanied by verbal abuse. Batterers tell their victims that they are ugly, stupid, poor wives, poor mothers, and poor lovers, and that all of these shortcomings make them deserving of abuse. Most battered women feel partly responsible for the abuse, especially early in the relationship. Barnett and associates (1996) found that 53 percent of battered women still involved with their abusers blamed themselves for causing the violence. "If only I'd had dinner on the table at 6:00 like he asked, this wouldn't have happened" she reasons. "If only I'd been able to keep the kids quiet so he could rest." "If I hadn't spent so much at the grocery store." The list of things she thinks she did wrong to deserve the abuse goes on and on, and her partner helps her blame herself. He continually tells her he *has* to correct her. It is *her* fault. *She* needs to change. And she tries, but no matter what she does right, he finds some other excuse to beat her.

Love and Hope

Ask any battered woman who stayed in a battering relationship for any length of time why she stayed and she will probably say, "I still loved him and hoped he would change." Those not living in abusive relationships often find it difficult to understand how a battered woman could continue to love the man who is inflicting so much physical and emotional pain. Consider, however, an intimate relationship in which your partner said or did something that angered or hurt you. Did you immediately give up on that person and stop loving him or her? Probably not, and battered women are no different. They can be angry and hurt by the way they are being treated but still love the man.

Additionally, the battered woman remembers good times in the relationship. She remembers when he was loving and attentive and gentle. She fell in love with that man. She knows he was like that before and keeps hoping that if *she* tries hard enough, the man she fell in love with will return. Her love for him and the hope she harbors that he will change are reinforced by the complex nature of battering relationships. In her 1979 book *The Battered Woman*, Lenore

Walker identified what she called the **cycle of violence** in battering relationships. The cycle occurs in three stages, beginning with tension building, which leads to an acute battering, followed by a honeymoon phase.

In the *tension-building* phase, the batterer is moody and nitpicking. He withdraws affection from the woman, puts her down, yells at her, criticizes her, and threatens her. He is annoyed by little things and may react by pushing her, slapping her, or destroying items in the house. He is sullen and he may be drinking heavily. She responds by being either silent or talkative, whichever she thinks he wants. She stays away from her family and friends because she is embarrassed by his behavior and because he does not want her out of his sight. She tries to keep the children quiet, reasons with him, cooks his favorite meals, agrees with whatever he says, and nurtures him. In general, she does everything she can to keep the peace.

The tension-building phase may last several weeks, days, or hours. The longer the relationship continues, the shorter this phase lasts. Eventually, the tension builds and results in *acute battering*. During the explosive battering, he beats and verbally abuses her. He may also choke, rape, imprison, or use weapons against her. Her only response during this time is to try to protect herself any way she can. She may call the police or neighbors, or the children may call for help. She may try to reason with him or calm him or she may try to fight back.

After the acute, explosive battering, the couple enters what Walker calls the *honeymoon* or *apology phase* of the cycle. In this stage, the batterer sees the damage he has done; he sees the bruises and cuts and he senses the emotional damage he has caused. He begs her forgiveness, buys her flowers, promises to get counseling or attend church or go to Alcoholics Anonymous meetings—whatever she has asked him to do in the past. He promises he will never do it again, cries, begs her not to leave, asks the children to tell their mother not to leave, and declares how much he loves her. He is convincing, because he really believes he will change and he honestly, desperately wants her to stay.

Now the battered woman is confused. She is hurt and angry, but at the same time feels hopeful that he really is going to change. She feels she may get her old love back. He has been very sweet and kind, so she knows it is possible for him to behave this way toward her. She feels it would be a shame to give up on their relationship when he is finally coming around.

The apology phase enables many battered women to continue to love their abusive partners and keeps alive the hope that they will change. In a study of 140 couples conducted over eight years, Jacobson (1998) found that one of the strongest factors keeping battered women in abusive relationships was the hope that their husbands would change.

For the Kids

Traditional American values maintain that it is best for children to grow up with two parents. We want couples to try to work out their marital problems so that children will not suffer. The battered woman hears these same messages. She wants her children to have a father. Parents and friends may reinforce this belief by discouraging her from leaving. "Think about the kids," they caution her. Often, she is the only one being beaten, so she believes that staying in the abusive relationship harms only her and not her children.

But she is wrong. Children who witness marital violence tend to exhibit more behavioral problems than children who have not been exposed to marital violence. Additionally, they often suffer developmental and educational delays, experience nightmares, develop more health problems, including depression, and have higher aggression and lower self-esteem (Kolko, Blakely, and Engleman 1996). Boys who witness their fathers beating their mothers are learning that violence is an appropriate way to handle conflict and disagreements and to assert one's will. These boys are most likely to continue the violence in their own intimate relationships when they grow up (Pagelow 1984). Witnessing abuse may be a more powerful predictor of a boy's future violence than actually being physically abused by a parent.

Children in violent marriages often become victims of physical violence themselves. Straus and Gelles (1990) found that children experience a 300 percent increase in physical violence by a male batterer as the violence against their mothers becomes more severe and frequent.

Fear of Loneliness

Most battered women have very low self-esteem, reinforced as their partners tell them that they are worthless, stupid, and so unattractive that no one else would ever desire them. Many are afraid that if they leave their abusive partner, they will be alone for the rest of their lives. They believe that no one else could ever love them or want to be with them. Women who do leave their partners often become lonely, which reinforces their fear. Some 70 percent of the battered women interviewed in one study returned to their husbands because of feelings of "loneliness and loss generated by the separation" (Barnett et al. 1997: 222).

Why Does He Abuse?

No single factor causes men to abuse their partners, but several factors have been identified in batterers that help explain their behavior. These factors include witnessing abuse as a child; substance abuse problems; poor communication skills; poor problem-solving skills coupled with stress, jealousy, and insecurity; and a strong belief in the culture of male dominance.

The intergenerational transmission of violence theory also has been used to explain why some men use violence against their wives. Recall that this theory suggests that male children who witness domestic violence repeat the cycle because they have a role model for aggression; learn to solve conflicts using violence; do not learn effective verbal skills for resolving conflict; and learn that abuse "works" (when dad beat mom, he got his way). Sociologists believe the powerful learning that takes place in childhood helps explain why male children who grow up witnessing their fathers beat their mothers are more likely to repeat the cycle of violence in their own marriages.

Emotional Dependence

Abusive men tend to be extremely jealous, insecure, and emotionally dependent on their partners (Barnett et al. 1997). They also have high needs for control in the relationship. Early in a relationship, the woman may mistake his jealousy and possessiveness as a sign of love. But as the relationship progresses, the jealousy is no longer flattering; it becomes oppressive. He constantly questions her whereabouts and does not believe her when she tells him where she has been. He is always convinced that she is lying to him or cheating on him. He may limit her interaction more and more so that she cannot work, go shopping, or visit family or friends without him at her side.

Substance Abuse Problems

Alcohol and drug abuse show up often in studies of domestic violence. Anecdotal evidence, such as impressions of police officers, also tend to support the notion that alcohol or other chemical abuse problems contribute to domestic violence (Flanzer 1993). Gorney (1989) found that 60 to 70 percent of abusive husbands attack their wives while they are drunk, and 13 percent are violent while high on other substances. Additionally, substance abuse increases both the frequency and severity of the abuse in a relationship (Barnett et al. 1997). Perhaps substance abuse lowers inhibitions or elicits anger more quickly.

Many researchers, however, believe that alcohol abuse or other chemical addictions may be used by abusers as a convenient excuse for their otherwise unacceptable or deviant behavior (Gelles 1993). "I was drunk," he claims, as he begs forgiveness. "It was the alcohol that made me do it." Abused women may see alcoholism, defined in our culture as a disease, as the root of the problem rather than accept that their husbands are abusive. Intoxication among abusers may show up more often in statistics because police are more likely to make an arrest when the abuser is drunk or high (Buzawa and Buzawa 1996). Alcohol or other chemical substances probably are not the cause of the violence in the relationship. Men who batter when drunk also batter when sober.

Poor Communication and Problem-Solving Skills

Men who batter tend to have difficulty stating their opinions and making requests orally (Barnett et al. 1997). They also are likely to misinterpret communication from others. They may resort to violence because they are frustrated by their inability to get what they want by asking for it, and they may anger easily because they misinterpret their partners' verbal and nonverbal messages. She says, "I'm sorry dinner is cold, but I thought you'd be home by 6:30. Since you didn't call, I went ahead and prepared dinner." He responds, "So you think I need to report in to you any time I do anything. I'm the man of the house and I don't need to ask your permission to go out for a quick beer with my friends." If the couple is in the tension-building phase of the cycle of violence, the discussion may end there or continue in a verbal argument. In certain circumstances, a misinterpretation of the wife's benign statement could result in an explosive battering.

Men who abuse their wives also experience stress outside the relationship that they are not skilled at handling (Barnett et al. 1997). Unemployment, for example, is a common stressor found among men who batter. "Unemployed men have rates of wife assault that are almost double the rates for employed men" (Gelles and Cornell 1990: 75). Abusive men have difficulty finding strategies to resolve their problems and to manage stress effectively.

Masculine Stereotypes

Batterers are likely to have strongly internalized the masculine stereotypes that are part of American culture and the belief in male superiority. Violence is tolerated among males in our culture and is even promoted. Television, movies, and video games show strong men shooting each other, blowing up buildings, and resolving issues aggressively. The sports culture, with violence both on and off the playing fields, further reinforces the idea that real men solve their problems using violence. The violence against women portrayed in pornography and organized prostitution also strongly reinforces the idea that men should control women for their own physical pleasure.

What Can Be Done about Marital Violence?

Several approaches can be taken to address the problem of domestic violence, including individual counseling, working through the criminal justice system, and implementing comprehensive community programs.

Individual Approaches

Seeking counseling is certainly one way to deal with abusive relationships. Although some couples are encouraged to seek marriage counseling, this is considered a controversial response to domestic violence, for in marriage counseling, the problems are attributed to the relationship. Batterers are not forced to take responsibility for their actions and women are forced to accept part of the blame.

Batterers often are mandated into counseling as a condition of probation to deal with anger and accept responsibility for their actions. When counseling is tied to court sentencing, abusers are forced to attend a program for a specific period of time or perhaps face jail time. The advantage of such compulsory atten-

What can be done about domestic violence? What prevention strategies might be effective? What are the strengths and weaknesses of intervention programs such as counseling, community-based support programs, and criminal prosecution and correction? What social changes or social reforms in the United States might contribute to the reduction of family violence?

dance is that abusers cannot simply join a program when the couple is in the honeymoon phase of the cycle of violence and then drop out as tensions arise (Buzawa and Buzawa 1996). However, Gondolf and Foster (1991) found only a 1 percent completion rate in an eight-month individual treatment program for batterers. Court-mandated counseling has drawbacks, as well. Generally, to keep costs low, only group counseling is offered. Completion rates of mandated programs are not significantly greater than voluntary programs because it is expensive and difficult for the court system to monitor attendance (Buzawa and Buzawa 1996).

The success of counseling programs, whether voluntary or court mandated, remains debatable (Barnett et al. 1997). The success of counseling programs in reducing repeat offending is influenced by how long the program lasts and characteristics of the offender (Syers and Edleson 1992). Generally, the longer the program continues, the greater the success rate. Also, counseling programs tend to be most effective with men who have little experience with the criminal justice system and who do not have deeply rooted personality disorders and substance abuse problems (Saunders 1993). Buzawa and Buzawa (1996: 222) conclude that "evaluation of counseling programs do not hold great promise except to suggest that some work for certain types of offenders."

Victims often need counseling to heal from the trauma of the violence and to gain the self-confidence to leave their abusers. Effective counseling for women includes encouragement to be economically independent. Economic independence gives battered women more power in the relationship and more options to get away from the abuse. Employment also decreases women's isolation from the outside world and gives them self-confidence. Wilson and colleagues (1989) believe that working away from home is essential to a battered woman's survival.

Criminal Justice Approaches

Advocates for battered women long decried the poor response of the criminal justice system to domestic violence. Police officers often did not take domestic abuse seriously or feared for their own safety more than that of the victim. Many officers believed that men had the right to use physical force to control their spouses, so they refused to make arrests when appropriate. Additionally, because most officers did not understand the dynamics of battering relationships, they became frustrated after repeatedly responding to the same residence. Police policies also limited the effectiveness of officers' responses. Most domestic violence offenses are classified as misdemeanors, and in the past, officers were required to witness the violence before an arrest could be made in a misdemeanor offense. Batterers who knew this could beat their wives until the police arrived, calmly wait for them to leave, and then resume the attack.

Pressure from advocacy groups, legislators, and some social science research led to reforms in law enforcement. Police departments instituted either mandatory arrest or presumptive arrest policies in cases of domestic violence. *Mandatory arrest policies* require officers to make an arrest if there is probable cause to believe a crime has been committed. *Presumptive arrest policies* give officers more discretion but strongly encourage officers to make an arrest if victims appear visibly injured or afraid. Initial experimental research (Sherman and Berk 1984) indicated that arrest was more effective at lowering recidivism (repeat offenses) than either separating the parties or mediating at the scene. Although subsequent studies found that arrest did not deter future assaults (Dunford, Huizinga, and Elliott 1989; Hirschel et al. 1991), the results of the initial research had been so widely publicized that mandatory arrest continued to be perceived as effective.

With mandatory arrest policies, police officers cannot ignore domestic violence, but there are drawbacks, as well. Battered women have no control in the decision to arrest. Although women may call the police to stop the violence, they may not want the abuser arrested for fear of retaliation when he is released or because of economic dependence. If the batterer is arrested and loses his job, the victim may not be able to buy food or pay the rent. Research indicates that mandatory arrest is not an effective deterrent against domestic violence; only men with no prior arrests are likely to be intimidated by this type of arrest (Buzawa and Buzawa 1993).

In addition to mandatory arrest policies, many police departments are retraining male and female law enforcement officers to make them more aware of the constraints that battered women face. It is hoped that such training will make them more sympathetic and effective on the scene. Prosecutors and judges are being encouraged to take domestic violence seriously and to prosecute and sentence offenders. Offenders need to know that prosecution and conviction will follow an arrest and that they will pay a serious price for the crime.

Community-Based Approaches

As a society, we are becoming increasingly aware that a comprehensive communitywide approach is needed to address domestic violence and create long-term change. A community-based approach involves police, lawyers, clergy, counselors, magistrates, prosecutors, judges, medical personnel, social workers, educators, and victim advocates all working together. Many communities are establishing *coordinated response networks*, or **community intervention projects** (CIPs) with representatives from all of these areas to develop a response to domestic violence at many levels (Edleson 1991; Kemp 1998). Doctors, for example, often are among the first to see battered women. They need to ask appropriate questions and make appropriate referrals. Staff and volunteers at CIPs disseminate information to physicians, hospital staff, and others about resources for battered women in the community. Social workers are essential in addressing family violence. They must help women find economic resources, jobs, and housing to ensure that they can adequately provide for themselves and their children.

In San Diego, California, an integrated community response has been instituted that includes teaching children the importance of calling 911 and how to give appropriate information over the telephone (Domestic Violence 1996). This knowledge empowers children to help stop the violence in their homes. Prosecutors say that there is no more damning evidence against a batterer than replaying before a judge and jury the 911 call of a child crying hysterically that "Daddy is going to kill Mommy."

Violence in Dating Relationships

Violence between intimate partners is not limited to marital relationships. Physical violence and sexual assaults can be a part of dating relationships as well.

Physical Assaults

"At least one third of those who date have experienced physical aggression at some point in their dating history" (Stets and Henderson 1991: 29). That was the conclusion Sugarman and Hotaling (1989) drew after extensively reviewing over 20 studies that examined the frequency of violence in dating relationships. In a study of high school students, 59.1 percent reported having experienced violence in past or current dating relationships (Jezl, Molidor, and Wright 1996). However, violence is often defined differently among studies, which helps explain why dating violence rates range from as low as 6 percent to as high as 65 percent (Sugarman and Hotaling 1989).

Although these statistics are alarming, they may be only the tip of the iceberg, for only a small portion of dating violence incidents are ever reported. Harris (1996) reports that only 4 percent of those who experience dating violence ever tell an authority figure about the incident. Teenagers may be particularly reluctant to report dating violence because they "don't want their parents to think that they have poor judgement" and punish them by restricting their social activities (Harris 1996: 5). Furthermore, teenagers who date are seen as more popular among their peers. They may not want to tell anyone about dating violence for fear that they will be pressured to break up and ultimately lose some of their social status (Harris 1996). Many others do not report dating violence because they perceive it as a sign of love. One-third of victims of dating violence believe the abuse indicates their partners' love for them (Lloyd 1991; Mayseless 1991).

Lloyd (1991) argues that the cultural construction of courtship encourages violent behavior and discourages reporting such incidents. She contends that the importance attached to women having steady dates and the economic control that men have in dating relationships creates an environment in which women are likely to be victimized without reporting it. Women may be socialized to believe that "any man is better than no man" (Lloyd 1991: 16). Furthermore, the cultural ideal that love conquers all may encourage couples to ignore violence in the dating relationship, believing that (1) violence and jealously are signs of love and (2) the problem will disappear as the relationship progresses.

One of the most controversial and unexpected findings in the literature on dating violence is the involvement of both sexes (Makepeace 1997). Research suggests that physical violence in dating relationships is reciprocal. In other words, both males and females report being perpetrators and victims of physical violence (Thompson 1991). Some studies indicate that males report being victims of violence more often than females. A study of high school students found that 67.5 percent of the males and 50.8 percent of females experienced violence in a dating relationship (Jezl et al. 1996). A study of violence in African American dating relationships found a similar pattern: 41 percent of males and 35 percent of females reported being victims of physical aggression at the hands of a dating partner (Clark et al. 1994). Not only did males more often report being victims, but females also reported being perpetrators more often than males; 47 percent of the women surveyed admitted to using agression against a partner, compared to 35 percent of the men (Clark et al. 1994).

Researchers caution that the data on gender and dating violence must be interpreted carefully. Males may underreport their own violent behavior because they do not perceive their conduct as abusive. Although both women and men agree that females use physical aggression, very often the acts are not considered as serious for several reasons. First, male violence more often leads to injuries because of their greater size and strength (Clark et al. 1994; Jezl et al. 1996; Miller and Simpson 1991). Second, it is more socially acceptable for females to slap their partners, so the behavior is not perceived as negatively.

Both the consequences and intent of the violent acts must be considered. Male violence clearly has greater consequences for women (Clark et al. 1994).

Men and women also report somewhat different motives for their violent behavior. The primary reasons men give for violent behavior in dating relationships are to show anger and to intimidate, frighten, or force their partners into giving them what they want (Sugarman and Hotaling 1989). Women report that the primary motives for their violence are to show anger, to retaliate for being hurt previously, or to act in self-defense (Follingstad et al. 1991; Sugarman and Hotaling 1989). Although both males and females resort to violence out of anger, men are more likely to use violence to gain power, whereas women are more likely to be retaliating or acting in self-defense from violence previously directed toward them.

Activists for men's rights believe that violence by women against men is minimized and trivialized. Feminists counter that violence perpetrated by men against women is more damaging and serious than women's aggression. One conclusion to draw is that "both men and women need to be educated in how to monitor their behavior and act in ways that are non-violent" (Stets and Henderson 1991: 36).

Few studies have examined the link between race and dating violence. Those that have (e.g., Clark et al. 1994) indicate that rates of dating violence in minority couples are comparable to rates among white couples (Harris 1996). Socioeconomic status does appear to be linked with dating violence. Couples with incomes below $10,000 a year report the most violence; as income and educational levels increase, reported rates of dating violence decline (Harris 1996). It is important to keep in mind, however, that violence among poorer couples is likely detected and reported more often, especially if it occurs in lower-income neighborhoods, where police may patrol regularly. Thus, rates of dating violence among couples of higher social status may be much higher than indicated in official reports.

Statistics show that dating violence most likely occurs on weekends in private settings and tends to recur (Sugarman and Hotaling 1989). Couples report that violence most often erupts because of jealousy, uncontrollable anger, and drinking or disagreements about drinking (Carlson 1987; Stets and Henderson 1991). Female victims also cite sexual denial as a source of violence (Sugarman and Hotaling 1989).

Studies suggest that if dating violence occurs once in a relationship, it is likely to happen again (Sugarman and Hotaling 1989). Unfortunately, very often, victims of violence continue in the relationship only to be victimized again. Between 30 and 50 percent of those who have been abused remain in the relationship after a violent incident (Mayseless 1991). Carlson (1996) reports that most college students believe that a relationship should end after an abusive incident, and they believe that a relationship will deteriorate once violence has occurred; yet, when confronted with violence in their own relationships, most students do not leave.

The factors associated with dating violence are somewhat different from marital violence. For example, witnessing family violence is not a strong predictor of dating violence (Carlson 1987; Sugarman and Hotaling 1989). Thus, the intergenerational transmission of violence theory does not appear to help explain abuse in dating relationships. One of the strongest predictors of violence in dating relationships is the length of time the relationship has lasted and the degree of intimacy involved. Carlson (1987: 19) reports that "intimate, committed, long-standing relationships are more likely to contain violence." Having a sexual relationship is an important predictor of violence—and may be almost a "prerequisite" for dating violence (Carlson 1987). Short-term relationships without sexual intimacy are least likely to be abusive.

Women who are battered by their boyfriends often stay for many of the same reasons that married women stay with their abusers. They are afraid of what their partners will do if they leave; they believe the violence is their fault; they love their boyfriends and hope they will change; and they fear being alone. Furthermore, women often mistakenly believe that once they get married, things will change. However, if a boyfriend is beating his girlfriend before they get married, the violence will only escalate when he has marital control over her, and then it will be much more difficult for her to get out of the relationship.

Date Rape

Dating violence also occurs in the form of sexual assaults. In the first large-scale study of date rape, sponsored by *Ms. Magazine*, over 6,100 undergraduate students on 32 college campuses were surveyed. The results are published in a book titled *I Never Called It Rape* by Robin Warshaw (1988). This survey revealed that one out of four college women surveyed had been victims of rape or attempted rape, and 57 percent of those rapes occurred on dates. For every 12 male college students surveyed, 1 had committed acts on dates that met the legal definition of rape, but few males perceived themselves as rapists. Although the survey revealed that date rape is common, it often goes unreported; only 5 percent of victims surveyed in the *Ms.* survey reported the rape to the police. Victims often hesitate to report such attacks to the police because they feel guilty, worry others will not believe them, and often do not immediately believe what happened was rape since the attacker was not a stranger. Although the *Ms.* survey data have been criticized, subsequent research confirms that rapes that occur between dating partners or acquaintances are more common than stranger rape (National Victim Center 1992).

Researchers have identified several factors that increase the risk of date rape (Lundberg-Love and Geffner 1989). Alcohol use is the most commonly cited risk factor for date rape. Men who are intoxicated may be more aggressive and have fewer inhibitions about forcing women to comply with their desires. Intoxicated women are less able to defend themselves from an attack and are more likely to be held responsible for the rape by others (Richardson and Campbell 1982). Miscommunication about sex is another factor that contributes to date rape. Men may perceive women's cuddling, kissing, or petting as a prelude to sexual intercourse, whereas women may see these behaviors as expressions of affection not meant to go further.

Going on a date in a secluded location is another factor that increases the risk for rape. Men may perceive women's willingness to go to such a place as an indication of the women's desire for sex. Other men use secluded places, such as an empty apartment, to set up a situation where women are powerless to call for help (Warshaw 1988). Men who have very traditional attitudes toward women, accept violence toward women, and believe that women are responsible for rape are more likely to be sexually violent. Finally, men who take control of dates by initiating the date, paying for all the expenses, and driving are more likely to be sexually aggressive (Lundberg-Love and Geffner 1989).

Recently, a drug with the brand name Rohypnol (flunitrazepam) has been used to facilitate date rape. The drug, referred to on the streets by a variety of names, including *roofies, rope, Mexican Valium,* and *R-2,* is a colorless, odorless, tasteless depressant that is 10 times more powerful than Valium, which causes drowsiness, memory impairment, and confusion (Rohypnol 1998). Taken in combination with alcohol, Rohypnol can cause complete blackouts and amnesia. The effects of the drug begin within a half-hour and can last eight hours or longer, depending on the dosage. The pills can be purchased on the streets for less than five dollars per tablet. According to the Drug Enforcement Administration, Rohypnol is not manufactured or approved for medical use in the United States, but is smuggled in from Europe or Latin America, where it is sold legally by prescription for use as a preanesthetic medication and short-term treatment for insomnia (Rohypnol 1998).

Cases have been reported where men have raped dates or acquaintances after slipping the drug into the women's drinks. When the effects of the drug wear off, the women know they have been assaulted but cannot remember any details, so criminal prosecution becomes impossible. In response to the growing number of cases of rape in which Rohypnol has been used to render the woman defenseless, Congress recently passed legislation that imposes harsh penalties for using a controlled substance to commit a sexual assault.

Preventing Dating Violence

Experts suggest that the best way to prevent dating violence is to teach couples positive communication skills and problem-solving skills (Riggs and O'Leary 1989). Ineffective communication skills, such as "withdrawing, being especially disagreeable, insulting, or swearing" often lead to violence (Bird, Stith, and Schladale 1991: 48). Couples who learn to discuss issues calmly and to listen to one another's concerns can avoid physical violence. Additionally, couples often need to be encouraged to seek advice, understanding, and sympathy from family members, friends, or counselors rather than keep their problems between themselves (Bird et al. 1991).

The importance of preparing young people for intimate relationships by training them in effective communication and problem-solving skills is illustrated in an experiment conducted by Krajewski and associates (1996). These researchers divided high school students enrolled in a health class into two groups.

The experimental group was taught a curriculum entitled Skills for Violence-Free Relationships, which emphasized healthy communication and offered alternative solutions to conflict; the control group took a regular health class without the relationship skills component. One week after the curriculum was presented, students in the experimental groups showed significantly more knowledge and had less violence-prone attitudes than those in the control group, indicating that the program did have at least a short-term impact on the participants. However, five months after the curriculum was presented, there were no significant differences between the two groups of students. The researchers argue that effective communication and problem-solving skills must be taught consistently and continuously in schools and other social insititutions to truly reduce the amount of violence in dating relationships (Krajewski et al. 1996).

Violence in Homosexual Relationships

Little research has been conducted on violence in homosexual relationships. Only recently has homosexuality been discussed openly, giving gay and lesbian couples the freedom to acknowledge publicly their relationships. The dynamics of homosexual relationships, both healthy and unhealthy, could not be studied until scholars had access to respondents who were willing to discuss their life-style openly. Even today, when homosexuality is somewhat more accepted than in the past, it is still difficult to get an accurate estimate of the extent of violence in gay and lesbian relationships. In the struggle to gain acceptance, many homosexual couples have hidden violence in their relationships. Most studies of violence in homosexual couples use small nonrandom samples, which severely limits the generalizability of the findings (e.g., Kelly and Warshafsky 1987; Lie et al. 1991).

Given these limitations, the available data suggest that violence rates for homosexual couples are similar to rates in heterosexual couples. Renzetti (1992) estimates that, as with heterosexual couples, violence occurs in 25 to 35 percent of lesbian relationships. Island and Letellier (1991) estimate that between 11 to 20 percent of gay men are abused by their partners each year. Alcohol and substance abuse are associated with violence in gay and lesbian relationships (Coleman 1990; Kelly and Warshafsky 1987), although, as with heterosexual couples, substance abuse may be used as a rationalization for the violence (Renzetti 1997). There is no consistent evidence that the intergenerational transmission of violence theory explains violence between gay and lesbian couples (Renzetti 1997).

Lesbian and gay partners may remain in battering relationships for many of the same reasons heterosexual partners do. However, victims of violence in homosexual relationships face additional obstacles to leaving that relate to their life-style (Wallace 1996). Gay men, who constitute the largest group infected with AIDS, may have increased difficulty leaving abusive relationships for fear of being exposed to the disease with a different partner. Victims who have AIDS may remain in an abusive relationship because they are physically and financially dependent on their partners. Furthermore, if the abuser has AIDs, the victim may rationalize the abuse or feel guilty about leaving an ill or dying partner (Island and Letellier 1991).

Additionally, abusive partners may use the threat of blackmail or "outing" (publicly disclosing another's homosexuality) to keep the victim from leaving the relationship (Renzetti 1997; Wallace 1996). Abusers may threaten to tell victims' employers or families about their sexual preference if they leave or disclose the violence. Those within the homosexual community may not be willing to acknowledge abuse for fear of further stigmatizing their life-style. Therefore, victims are less likely to have support services or shelters to aid in their escape (Wallace 1996).

Elder Abuse

Older adults being cared for by their children or other relatives are also vulnerable to violence and abuse. Elder abuse is particularly difficult to define and measure. Researchers generally divide elder abuse into self-neglect, institutional elder abuse, and domestic elder abuse (Tatara 1996). *Self-neglect*, which is the most common type of abuse social workers see, occurs when an elderly person fails to care for his or her own needs (Kemp 1998). *Institutional elder abuse* occurs "in a nursing home or other facility that is paid to care for the elderly person" (Kemp 1998: 273). *Domestic elder abuse*, maltreatment by a caregiver with a special relationship to the elderly person (such as an adult child or spouse), will be the focus of this section (Tatara 1996).

Unlike child abuse, elder abuse has no universal mandatory reporting, so official reports of this type of abuse are incomplete (Kemp 1998). According to the National Center on Elder Abuse (NCEA), in 1994, there were approximately 241,000 reported cases of elder maltreatment, about half of which were substantiated (Kemp 1998). Drawing on information obtained from 2,000 noninstitutionalized elderly respondents, Pillemer and Finkelhor (1988) estimate that slightly over 3 percent of elderly people are abused by caregivers.

Elderly persons are most likely to suffer neglect at the hands of a family caregiver, followed by physical abuse, financial exploitation, and psychological maltreatment (Kemp 1998). However, it can be difficult to determine what constitutes *abusive treatment*. As Phillips (1986: 213) points out, it may be considered maltreatment for an elder to be required to live in a filthy room without indoor plumbing, but whether it should be called *abuse* "if the elder *chooses* to live in that place after alternatives have been presented" is questionable. Is tying an elderly person to a chair or bed *abuse*? If the person is tied down as a form of punishment or for the caregiver's convenience, one might answer yes. However, if the person is restrained to prevent injury, the behavior may not be considered abusive. Many factors, including the situational circumstances, the caregiver's motives, and the elder's response must all be considered in deciding if behavior is abusive.

Why Are Elders Abused?

The factors that contribute to domestic elder abuse also are unclear. Early researchers speculated that elder abuse was a result of the intergenerational transmission of violence—that is, caregivers who had been abused as children retaliated for past abuse by maltreating their parents in old age. However, this explanation blames the victim by unfairly holding abused elders responsible for their plight. The little research that has tested the intergenerational transmission of violence theory has failed to find a connection between past abuse and elder abuse (Barnett et al. 1997).

Other theories focus on the stress, frustration, and burden of caring for sick, dependent, elderly parents or spouses (Steinmetz 1993). Elderly persons often resist being cared for because they do not like feeling helpless and dependent. They may refuse to bathe, refuse to take their medicine, and criticize caregivers (Steinmetz 1988). Furthermore, patients with Alzheimer's disease or other forms of dementia may require constant care and supervision. The cumulative effect of the constant stress and pressure on the caregiver may result in neglect or abuse of the elderly relative.

Pillemer (1985, 1993) argues that domestic elder abuse is not caused by the elderly person's illness and frailty, but rather by the caregiver's dependence on the elderly family member. After surveying and interviewing 42 abused and 42 nonabused elders, Pillemer (1985) found that abused elders are no more likely than nonabused elders to be seriously ill or to have difficulty with daily functions such as bathing, dressing, or shopping. The biggest difference was that abusing caregivers are significantly more dependent on their elders for housing, household repair, financial assistance, and transportation. Abusive, dependent caregivers also are more likely to suffer from mental health problems or chemical addictions.

What Can Be Done about Elder Abuse?

How society should respond to elder abuse is controversial. Although 42 states have mandatory reporting laws that require professionals to report suspected abuse of elderly adults (Kemp 1998), many advocates for the aged argue that such laws are patronizing and treat older people like children. Furthermore, if social workers or police intervene to remove the elder person from the abusive spouse or adult child, they may "cut the elder off from the only people who provide meaning in the elder's life" (Barnett et al. 1997: 267).

The first step to solving the problem is identifying elders who are being abused. Quinn and Tomita (1997: 150) have developed specific protocols that professionals, such as doctors and social workers, can use to "identify and assess the possibility of mistreatment." Once identified, victims should be encouraged to enter counseling. Counselors will have to aid elders in overcoming their resistance to seeking help and may find the **staircase model** developed by Breckman and Adelman (cited in Biggs, Phillipson, and Kingston 1995) useful. The staircase model divides intervention into three stages: *reluctance*, in which victims deny mistreatment has occurred; *recognition*, where victims recognize the problem is serious and help is necessary; and *rebuilding*, when victims realize they do not have to tolerate abuse and begin to regain control of their lives. Unless the offender is jailed, most elder abuse victims will continue their relationship with the abuser (Quinn and Tomita 1997). Therefore, it is essential that abusers also receive counseling in which they take responsibility for their actions and learn more appropriate ways to interact with the elderly.

Elder abuse, like any other form of family violence, can involve both criminal and civil sanctions against the offender. Finkelhor and Pillemer (1988) remind us that some elder abuse is spouse abuse that has been occurring for many years. Treatment of elder spouse abuse can be handled similarly to other cases of spouse abuse, although prosecutors often are sensitive to the fact that offenders may be the person's only caregiver and the offender also may be suffering tremendous stress from caregiving. As such, professionals prefer to handle elder abuse through adult protective services rather than the criminal justice system when possible (Biggs et al. 1995). Elders with extensive social networks are far less subject to abuse than those who are isolated (Biggs et al. 1995). Therefore, something as simple as befriending an elder and allowing the caregiver some relief can prevent abuse.

Summary

Family violence encompasses many different types of acts and relationships, making it difficult to define and study. The Conflict Tactics Scale was developed to measure every form of family violence in random samples of families. Competing explanations for family violence have been developed, including biological and psychological theories, as well as exchange/social control, feminist, and intergenerational transmission of violence theories. Child maltreatment—which includes physical abuse, neglect, sexual abuse, and psychological abuse—has devastating consequences for victims. Risk factors, which increase the probability child abuse will occur in a family, have been identified for each type of maltreatment. Primary, secondary, and tertiary prevention programs have been developed to combat child maltreatment.

The perennial variables of social class, race, and gender as well as age have an impact on the risk for violence between intimate partners. Those women who stay in violent relationships do so for a host of reasons, many of which are linked to the social and economic structure of society. Likewise, social factors such as a history of childhood abuse and cultural norms regarding masculinity help explain why some men abuse their partners. Combating relationship violence requires a variety of approaches, from counseling to mandatory arrest policies to broad community intervention projects.

Violence also can occur in dating relationships in the form of battering and date rape. Abuse in gay and lesbian relationships, a largely overlooked problem, is often kept secret because of the stigma attached by some to living a homosexual life-style. Elder abuse such as neglect, physical maltreatment, financial exploitation, and psychological abuse can be contributed to by caregiver stress as well as the caregiver's dependence on elders.

Readings for In-Depth Focus

How the System Treats Children Who Have Been Sexually Abused

An individual accused of a crime has the constitutional right to face his or her accuser in a public trial. This right poses unique problems in child sexual abuse cases because the accuser is most often a young child. Defense attorneys often argue that young children are unreliable witnesses. Prosecutors worry that putting children on the witness stand to answer questions about the sexual abuse incident will further traumatize them. In the following article, Michael J. Martin identifies the problems encountered in prosecuting child sexual abuse cases and poses some ideas for how to improve the process. As you read, consider how the rights of the accuser and the accused conflict. If you were the parent of a child who had been sexually abused, would you allow your child to testify? What protections would you want for your child?

■ ■ ■

Child Sexual Abuse

Preventing Continued Victimization by the Criminal Justice System and Associated Agencies

Michael J. Martin

The past 10 years have seen a sharp increase in the number of reported cases of child sexual abuse. For instance, Illinois has experienced a 213% increase in confirmed cases from 1982 to 1989 (Illinois Department of Children and Family Services, 1990). This increase in the

An earlier version of this article was presented to the 1990 National Council on Family Relations Annual Conference in Seattle, WA. The author would like to thank Lynn Atwater and Karen Polonko for their contributions to the development of this article.

number of reported cases which has also occurred nationwide has resulted in a similar increase in the number of child sexual abuse cases adjudicated through the criminal justice system (Higgins, 1988). Because of the attention this phenomenon has attracted, there has been renewed speculation on the impact that the criminal justice system itself might have on the trauma experienced by the child victims. In addition, there has been further speculation on ways which the criminal justice system and the policies of investigatory agencies might be modified to reduce the traumatic nature of the process and still guarantee the legal rights of the accused (Bainor, 1986; Berliner & Barbieri, 1984; Goodman, 1984; Libai, 1969). Clearly, practitioners working with families need to become more aware of the specialized needs of families and children who are being exposed to the criminal justice and protective services systems so that they can better reduce the trauma those individuals experience.

LIMITATIONS OF THE CRIMINAL JUSTICE SYSTEM

Berliner and Barbieri (1984) have suggested that criminal cases of child sexual abuse involving children's testimony are difficult to prosecute for four main reasons. First, the evidence in the case often is dependent on the degree to which the child's testimony is believable. This may be influenced by the age of the child and the perceived competence of the child to testify. Although false reports are rare, particularly in very young children, adults are often skeptical when children report having been molested. (For a more thorough review of current information on children's ability to provide accurate testimony see Bolton & Bolton, 1987; Goodman, 1984; Saywitz, Goodman, & Myers, 1990.) A second important factor suggested by Berliner and Barbieri (1984) is that many people believe that sexual abuse is caused by a mental disorder

and thus should be dealt with in the mental health system rather than the criminal justice system. The criminal justice system is seen by those individuals as being too punitive and as providing little in the way of therapeutic intervention to change the offending behavior.

A third reason for the difficulty of prosecution is that people fear the child will be so traumatized by the process and the outcome of the criminal justice system that to prosecute would only further victimize the child. This may be especially true when the perpetrator of the abuse is a family member or a trusted friend. Criminal prosecution may result in lack of economic and emotional support for the victim or the rest of the victim's family. A fourth reason for the difficulty of prosecution of child sexual abuse cases is the reluctance on the part of many prosecutors to undertake a case which rests primarily on the child's testimony without corroborating physical evidence. Investigatory and court procedures which may emphasize the rights of the accused over the rights of the victim often make a clear, uncontaminated testimony difficult to obtain.

A key element of the debate of the defendant's rights versus the victim's rights are the Constitutional guarantees of the Sixth Amendment. This Amendment states that the defendant in a criminal prosecution is entitled to a public trial and an opportunity to confront the accuser (Higgins, 1988). Ironically, the victim has very few constitutional rights to protection during the investigation or trial in the United States (Parker, 1982).

Libai (1969) reports that Israel and the Scandinavian countries differ significantly from the United States in their investigatory and trial procedures. In Israel a trained interviewer takes down the child's testimony and testifies in that child's place in court. This procedure both reduces the number of times the child must tell the story of the abuse and also spares the child from the potentially traumatic experience of the court process. In Scandinavian countries, specially trained policewomen are used to interview the child and make a tape recording of her/his testimony to be presented in the place of the child at the trial (Libai, 1969). This procedure has the added advantage of capturing some of the nuances in the child's testimony that would make the account of the event more believable in court. In the United States there is some concern that the Israeli system of testifying in the child's place would violate the hearsay rule. There is also concern that the defendant's Sixth Amendment rights might be violated by the Scandinavian approach of allowing taped testimony, particularly if the defendant and/or the defense counsel are not allowed to participate in the questioning.

In some cases, U.S. criminal courts may allow hearsay testimony to be presented. In a recent Supreme Court decision *White v. Illinois* (1992), the court did not require a 4-year-old child to testify and allowed the testimony of her babysitter, her mother, an investigating officer, an emergency room nurse, and a doctor to whom she had disclosed the events of the abuse. The court held that this information "was admissible under state-law hearsay exceptions for spontaneous declarations and for statements made in the course of securing medical treatment" (p. 4094). In another recent U.S. Supreme Court opinion, *Idaho v. Wright* (cited in Myers, 1990), a pediatrician was allowed to give testimony on what a 2 1/2-year-old child had disclosed. In their ruling in *Idaho v. Wright*, the Supreme Court gave a partial list of factors which were necessary to establish reliability—"spontaneity, consistent repetition of the same story, the child's mental state when hearsay statement was made, the child's use of terminology unexpected of a child of similar age, and lack of motivation to fabricate" (Myers, 1990, p.3).

The Supreme Court has also begun to address issues relating to reducing the trauma that children experience when they testify. In *Maryland v. Craig* (1990), it was held that the child witness was permitted to testify via one-way video upon the finding that the witness if forced to testify would suffer serious emotional distress preventing her from reasonably communicating. The child was placed in a room outside the courtroom with the prosecutor and the defense counsel and allowed to give testimony while the judge, jury, and defendant watched via one-way video. These cases and others currently pending in the U.S. courts are likely to challenge the necessity for the child victim to testify in the presence of the alleged perpetrator and thus reduce the potential amount of trauma to which the child is exposed. Although likely to be further challenged on Sixth Amendment grounds, nearly 40 states have laws which allow for child testimony in sexual abuse cases by closed circuit television or videotaped pretrial testimony or some combination of both (Wilson, 1989).

Libai (1969) has suggested the development of a special "child-courtroom" in an effort to reduce potential trauma for children who must testify in court. This special courtroom would separate the child from the accused perpetrators and the jury by means of a one-way glass. During testimony the child would only be in the presence of the judge, the prosecutor, the defense attorney, and the child examiner. The accused would be able to communicate with his defense counsel by means of a two-way audio system. Although this child-courtroom would seem to be a reasonable approach to reducing the child's trauma in testifying in open court, the legal admissibility has not as yet been tested in the courts.

LIMITATIONS IN THE INVESTIGATION SYSTEM

For many years, cases of child sexual abuse have been investigated by a dual investigatory system which has often been poorly coordinated. Both the criminal justice system and the child protective services systems have become involved with the cases. The goal of the criminal justice system has frequently been more oriented toward prosecuting and punishing the offender than in protecting the child (Libai, 1969).

In many cases the child protective services systems may be experiencing a conflict in their joint goals of maintaining the family unit and protecting the child. This may be difficult to resolve when the sexual abuse perpetrator is a family member. As a result of somewhat different orientations to the cases and a certain amount of competition for control, the criminal justice system and the child protective services system often increase the number of persons interviewing the child and thus increase the trauma and confusion. Children may have to relate the events of the case to police officers, prosecuting attorneys, defense attorneys, child protective services personnel, medical care staff, and family members. Many of the interviewers may have little training in child development or specific instruction on how to interview young children and may actually cause the child's description of the event to change because of suggestive and leading questioning. As a result the child is subjected to needless trauma that could be eliminated by effective coordination and training. In addition, although research on children's memory for sexual abuse victimization has given some suggestions on how to interview young children (Saywitz et al., 1990), further research needs to be done which provides clear strategies for investigative questioning.

POTENTIAL TRAUMATIC EFFECTS OF THE INVESTIGATION AND COURT PROCEDURE ON THE CHILD

Although systematic research studies of the influence of the legal process have not been done, anecdotal accounts of severe psychological reactions to the trial process have been reported (Higgins, 1988). Goodman (1984) suggests that court related involvement may add additional stress to an already traumatized child, thus fur-

ther endangering the child's mental health. Weiss and Berg (1982) report that "emotional reactions suffered by the child are often prolonged or intensified whenever legal proceedings are involved" (p. 514). Further, Krieger and Robbins (1985) report that the effects of the judicial system on adolescent girls who were molested by their father or stepfather tend to create "a sense of insignificance, hopelessness and guilt" (pp. 419, 420).

Burgess and Holmstrom (cited in Higgins, 1988) have suggested four common psychological reactions to the trial process by child victims and their families. First, the family may become preoccupied with the assault and legal process which can drag on for a long time and make it difficult to get on to normal activities. Second, the investigation and trial process may require the child to recapitulate the traumatic event in his/her mind many times in settings which may be fear producing by themselves, such as hospitals, police stations, and courtrooms. Third, the child may come to realize that not everyone believes that he/she is telling the truth. This may negatively affect the child's self-esteem. Fourth, the child and family may feel betrayed by trusted support figures which are involved in a traumatic legal environment. The American Academy of Child and Adolescent Psychiatry (AACAP, 1986) has also indicated that testifying in public can add additional emotional stress to a child victim of sexual abuse. In addition, they suggest that "insensitive and repetitious cross-examination of abused children can be misperceived by them as further abuse" (p. 1).

Even though information on the impact of the investigatory and legal process on the child and his/her family is limited, theory and research in the area of factors which influence the long-term impact of sexual abuse on children's development may yield some information on those children who are most at risk for serious negative outcomes. Finkelhor and Browne (1985) have developed a four-factor theory which attempts to explain the characteristics of child sexual abuse events and their aftermath which are most likely to lead to traumatic outcomes for the child. They suggest that traumatic sexualization, betrayal, powerlessness and stigmatization are important traumagenic dynamics. In this author's opinion, these traumagenic dynamics can be exacerbated by the investigation and adjudication process, particularly in the areas of betrayal, powerlessness, and stigmatization. According to Finkelhor and Browne, betrayal occurs when someone on whom the child has placed a significant amount of trust has caused him/her harm. This may occur when the abuse perpetrator is a family member or trusted friend. It may also occur when persons involved in the investigation and the adjudication process promise positive outcomes for the child, such as protection for the child and punishment for the offender, and are not able to deliver on those promises because of the inability to win a conviction in court. In such cases the child may feel further betrayed by the system which she/he trusted to protect her/him.

Another of Finkelhor and Browne's (1985) traumagenic dynamics, powerlessness, may also be exacerbated by the investigation and adjudication process. This occurs when the child feels that she/he has little control over what is happening to her/him. When the child is barraged by a multitude of individuals asking complicated and highly sensitive questions, she/he may indeed lose most of the control over events in her/his life. This may include undesired foster care placement. As a result, the child may feel disempowered by the whole process.

The last of Finkelhor and Browne's (1985) traumagenic dynamics, stigmatization, occurs when the child is made to feel shameful or guilty as a result of the abuse. This may occur when the perpetrator or the defense counsel suggests that the child is in some way responsible for his/her own abuse. It may also occur while publicity surrounding the case causes persons in the child's environment to treat him/her in a derogatory manner. He/She may be made

to feel that he/she has been somehow "contaminated" by the abusive incident.

To summarize, current literature suggests that the investigation and court adjudication of a sexual abuse case may add additional stress and trauma to an already vulnerable child and family. Because the goal of these systems is presumably to "protect" the child, it would seem that some modification of the existing procedures would be desirable.

SUGGESTIONS FOR IMPROVED CRIMINAL JUSTICE AND INVESTIGATORY PROCEDURES

Several procedures have been suggested in child sexual abuse cases in an effort to minimize the risk to the children involved. First, it is important that the staff of the investigatory systems as well as the court adjudication system be well trained to deal with their difficult task (AACAP, 1986; Berliner & Barbieri, 1984). The staff should have clear knowledge of sexual abuse dynamics as well as information on child development. In addition, the staff should have direct "hands on" instruction on how to interview child victims of various ages in ways that will elicit the necessary information, but will provide a nonthreatening supportive environment for the child.

Second, the criminal justice system should be modified to more directly accommodate the needs and the limitations of the child witness (AACAP, 1986; Berliner & Barbieri, 1984). To limit the number of times a child must be interviewed, each community should have a specialized unit which includes law enforcement and protective services personnel who are specially trained to interview child victims of sexual abuse (Berliner & Barbieri, 1984). Those interviews should be videotaped for inclusion as evidence, if a criminal court case is to be brought against the alleged perpetrator. Extreme care should be taken to limit the number of times the child is subjected to questioning. This will help reduce potential contaminating factors in the child's recall of the event(s) and will also help reduce the feeling of powerlessness which many victims feel when they are continually required to submit to questioning.

To further empower the child in the process, the child should be given a court appointed special advocate (Berliner & Barbieri, 1984). The court appointed special advocate (CASA) would oversee the rights of the child in the criminal justice and protective services systems. Far too often the child's rights are in conflict with prosecutor's desire for a conviction, the defense attorney's desire for favorable treatment of his/her client, and the protective service system's desire to maintain the family unit. In addition, the protective services system may lack the resources to provide adequately for the child either before, during, or after the court process. A CASA can provide a voice for the child in the complex legal system.

Another needed accommodation of the criminal justice system to the needs of the child relates to the process by which the child gives evidence in a criminal court proceeding. Young children who have been subjected to the trauma of sexual abuse at the hands of an adult should not have to experience the added trauma of testifying in open court in front of their abuser (Berliner & Barbieri, 1984). Legally acceptable methods, such as the closed circuit testimony previously mentioned in *Maryland v. Craig* (1990), or a constitutionally acceptable form of pretrial hearing which can be videotaped and placed into evidence, or Libai's (1969) child-courtroom, must be developed to spare children from needless suffering and also insure that the rights of the accused are protected.

IMPLICATIONS FOR PRACTICE

Both the criminal justice system and the protective services system have not always done an adequate job of looking out for the best interests of the child in many cases of child sexual abuse. Continued victimization by the organizations charged with the child's protection is likely to exacerbate an already emotionally damaging experience. Practitioners in the family studies field who work with children or adults who have been sexually abused must realize that the traumatic aspects of the situation do not necessarily end when the abuse is identified. The investigation and court adjudication process may also be extremely traumatic for the individuals and families involved, requiring continued support from the family professional. In such a situation the practitioner may be the only individual working with the family who is not seen as being connected to the criminal justice system and thus, seen as a potential threat.

Drawing from the traumagenic dynamics discussed in Finkelhor and Browne (1985), family professionals can be extremely important in reducing the amount of betrayal, powerlessness, and stigmatization experienced by the child. In the area of betrayal, the family professional must be a consistent support figure for the child. This is particularly necessary when the child is not receiving adequate support from his/her own family. Care must be given to present a realistic picture of future events for the child rather than an unrealistically positive or negative one. Because of the necessity of creating a secure bond of trust between the family professional and the child, the family professional may need to focus increased attention on the child during times of particularly high stress, such as during the trial process.

In the area of powerlessness, the family professional must create a family intervention that is designed to empower the child. This may include encouraging the child to express angry feelings toward the alleged abuser and the investigatory and criminal justice systems. It may also include giving the child some control over the manner in which she/he is questioned by outside authorities or giving testimony in court. The focus of the intervention should be on the child as survivor rather than the child as victim.

It is perhaps in the area of stigmatization that the family professional can be most influential. A major focus of the treatment intervention should be to reduce the amount of shame or guilt that is associated with the event. The child must be encouraged to feel that she/he is in no way responsible for her/his own abuse and that she/he is a person of worth and value, regardless of what has happened to her/him or what is being said in court.

In working with families in which a child has been sexually abused, the family professional must also pay attention to issues of betrayal, powerlessness, and stigmatization. In cases in which the abuser was a family member, conflicting loyalties within the family may make it extremely difficult for individuals to provide emotional support for each other. In addition, family members may feel betrayed by the family member who has engaged in a deviant act. Similar to the reaction of the child, the family may also feel powerless in its attempts to cope with the complex legal system into which it has been thrust. Stigmatization may occur in the family as it deals with the fact that it failed to adequately protect the child from victimization. In addition, in cases which become known to the community, considerable shame may be involved as individuals within the community treat the family differently. Just as with the child victim the family professional needs to focus on issues of survival with the family rather than encouraging them to assume the role of victim. This may include focusing on some of the positive characteristics of the family as well as the areas in which improvement is needed. It may also include enlisting the family's help in providing support to the child as she/he goes through the traumatic experience of the investigation and court adjudication process.

In conclusion, there is a clear need for a more carefully coordinated approach to child sexual abuse intervention which better meets the needs of the child victims and their families. Professionals interested in family policy should focus on improving the investigation and adjudication systems. Practitioners who work directly with the children and families should provide interventions which protect the child and reduce the amount of betrayal, powerlessness, and stigmatization that is experienced.

REFERENCES

American Academy of Child & Adolescent Psychiatry. (1986). *AACAP statement for protecting children undergoing abusive investigations and testimony.* Washington, DC: Author.

Bainor, M. H. (1986). The use of video taped testimony of victims in cases involving child sexual abuse: A Constitutional dilemma. *Hofstra Law Review, 14,* 995–1018.

Berliner, L., & Barbieri, M. K. (1984). The testimony of the child victim of sexual assault. *Journal of Social Issues, 40,* 125–137.

Bolton, F. G., & Bolton, S. R. (1987). *Working with violent families: A guide for clinical and legal practitioners.* Newbury Park, CA: Sage Publications.

Finkelhor, D., & Browne, A. (1985). The traumatic impact of child sexual abuse. *American Journal of Orthopsychiatry, 55,* 530–541.

Goodman, G. (1984). The child witness: Conclusions and future directions for research and legal practice. *Journal of Social Issues, 40,* 157–175.

Higgins, R. B. (1988). Child victims as witnesses. *Law and Psychology Review, 12,* 159–166.

Illinois Department of Children and Family Services. (1990). *Child abuse and neglect statistics: Annual report—fiscal year 1989.* Springfield, IL: Author.

Krieger, M., & Robbins, J. (1985). The adolescent incest victim and the judicial system. *American Journal of Orthopsychiatry, 55,* 419–425.

Libai, D. (1969). The protection of the child victim of sexual defense in the criminal justice system. *Wayne Law Review, 15,* 977–1032.

Maryland v. Craig, 110 S. Ct. 3157 (1990).

Myers, J. E. B. (1990). Legal update: 1990—A bellwether year for the abused child in the U.S. Supreme Court. *Violence Update, 1,* 349.

Parker, J. (1982). The rights of child witness: Is the court a protector or perpetrator? *New England Law Review, 17,* 643–667.

Saywitz, K., Goodman, G., & Myers, J. (1990). Can children provide accurate eyewitness reports? *Violence Update, 1,* 1, 4, 10, 11.

Weiss, E. H., & Berg, R. F. (1982). Child victims of sexual assault: Impact of court procedure. *Journal of the American Academy of Child Psychiatry, 21,* 513–518.

White v. Illinois, 60 L W 4094 (1992).

Wilson, C. E. (1989). Criminal procedure-Presumed guilty: The use of videotaped and closed-circuit televised testimony in child sexual abuse prosecutions and the defendants right to confrontation—Coy v. Iowa. *Campbell Law Review 11,* 381–396.

Critical Thinking Questions

1. How can the investigation and court procedures in child sexual abuses cases further traumatize a child?

2. How have some courts tried to reduce the trauma for children testifying in sexual abuses cases? How are these solutions likely to withstand legal challenges?

3. What does Martin suggest can be done in child sexual abuse cases to minimize risk to the children involved?

4. What issues do counselors need to be aware of in dealing with child sexual abuse victims?

13 Divorce and Remarriage

*D*ivorce rates in the United States have declined. This comes as a surprise to most of my students. They keep hearing that one out of every two marriages will end in divorce. They also tell me that they have heard that every one getting married today has a 50 percent chance of becoming divorced. Although I tend to be rather data driven in the first place, it is especially here that I bring in the charts. Fortunately, since news of the divorce decline is getting around a little more, fewer charts are needed than before.

I suspect that some students have been exposed to, at the least, text-books and professors who have failed to stay current. No doubt, many students also have listened to talk shows or political and/or religious leaders decrying the death of the family and pointing to the so-called epidemic of divorce in the United States—usually from the peak figure given for 1979 (5.3 per 1,000 population) as a sure indicator that all is lost.

Of course, it could be that students are growing up with the notion that "no good news is good news"—that is, if one sees a decline in divorce rates as good news. Certainly, there are those who interpreted the divorce increases of the 1960s and 1970s as signs that things were improving for women. Goode's (1956) analysis of the *theoretical importance of divorce* must not be ignored just because rates have declined. For some people, divorce is a painful and sometimes very long experience. The United States does not offer a formal mechanism, such as a funeral, to help people deal with the losses and pain associated with divorce (Goode 1956). Yet, the fact that the crude divorce rates have declined is documented. Now, we need to figure out why and project what the future will likely hold.

Divorce Trends

Divorce, the legal dissolution of marriage, occurs all over the world. This fact often goes unnoticed, perhaps because divorce rates in non-Western societies are overlooked due to the ethnocentric tendencies and international domination of the Western media that focus primarily on Western societies and issues (Jones 1997). However, comparing the United States and other Western societies with non-Western societies usually proves very instructive. Is divorce in the United States a social problem, or is it merely a facet of the culture, patterns of adaptation to larger social forces, and societal change? By looking at divorce in other countries, we may be more equipped to answer these questions.

Ernest W. Burgess, one of the first family sociologists to teach a course on the family in the United States (Farber 1964) tried to identify systematically the effects of urbanization, industrialization, and changing ideologies on marriage, family systems and types, and divorce. Burgess (1947/1963: 15) argues that the family was transformed by urbanization, increased freedom for women, higher rates of mobility, and greater secularization. Accordingly, the family as an institution no longer was based on custom and law but on love and companionship (Burgess, Locke, and Thomas 1945/1971; Burgess and Cottrell 1939). Thus, increases in divorce and remarriage should not be uncommon.

Some analysts interpret high rates of divorce as a signal that Western family systems are becoming disorganized (Goode 1963: 81). However, sociologist William J. Goode (1963) attributes the rise in divorce rates in the United States and other Western countries by the early 1960s to factors such as decreased stigma surrounding divorce and remarriage, changes in laws, and alternatives to marriage. He also argues that as industrialization expands, family patterns change. The family system becomes more conjugal, with more independent nuclear units. However, Goode proposes that "the relation between the conjugal family and industrialization is not yet entirely clear" (p. 10). Goode also recognizes that family systems began to change prior to industrialization rather than as a function of larger social change. In fact, in nations with high divorce rates prior to industrialization, industrialization processes tend to prompt declines in divorce rates (Goode 1993).

In the United States, debates continue over whether divorce should be seen as an indicator of social disintegration, social instability, and moral decline or as a function of such factors as longer life expectancies, stress and strain in family life, female employment, urbanization, increased emphasis on the conjugal (marital) relationship over the consanguineal (bloodlines, kin) family, increasing numbers of alternative partnerships, changes in divorce laws, the advent of no-fault divorce, and increasing focus on self-interest (Goode 1993).

Studies Comparing Divorce in Different Countries

Jones (1997) compared the divorce trends in Southeast Asia with those of the West, and especially the United States, to see what effect, if any, urbanization and industrialization had on divorce rates. He was testing Goode's (1993) assertion that industrialization can actually lead to a decline in divorce rates in high-divorce systems. Jones found that, fundamentally, the divorce rates in Islamic Southeast Asia and the West have been going in opposite directions since the 1960s (Jones 1997: 95). That is, divorce rates in the West, with some variations among nations, tended to increase from the 1950s through the 1980s, while in Southeast Asia, divorce rates declined dramatically. Declining divorce in Southeast Asia parallels the rapid increase in industrialization and urbanization of countries such as Malaysia, Singapore, and Indonesia. Why did this divergence occur?

Increases in women's labor force participation, typically an outcome of industrialization, have been associated with increasing divorce rates. Both Western and Southeast Asian countries saw increases in female employment from the 1950s on. Jones points out, however, that there is no clear causal connection between women's employment and rising divorce rates.

According to Jones (1997), industrialization in the West is associated with an increased emphasis on the individual and self-gratification as well as an erosion of the centrality of the family. Divorce, then, becomes socially more acceptable. In much of Southeast Asia, there had been patterns of tolerance toward divorce, kin support systems for divorced women and their children, ease of divorce, easy remarriage, and relatively youthful first marriages. Ease of divorce by itself, according to Jones, reflected a cultural predisposition toward divorce (Jones 1997).

However, the government became concerned over the divorce rates. Women's groups also put pressure on the government to make divorce more difficult to obtain—at a time when, religiously, more people were becoming negative toward divorce. **Polygyny,** a marriage system wherein men can have two or more wives simultaneously, also was officially discouraged. These factors, coupled with an increase in age at first marriage and greater freedom of marriage partner choice, appear to have contributed to a decline in divorce. At the same time (i.e., 1960s and 1970s), many of the Islamic Southeast Asian countries were experiencing rapid industrialization, urbanization, and increases in both female employment and education. With the exception of Singapore, tightened regulations regarding divorce and increased stigma attached to divorce contributed to declining divorce rates in Southeast Asia, even in urbanized areas (Jones 1997). This is the case, despite an increase in women's employment outside the home.

Jones's analyses of declines in divorce in Southeast Asia run counter to linkages made earlier by Burgess and Goode in that the forces of modernization do not always result in higher divorce rates. Goode (1993: 281) documents that Indonesia was a stable high-divorce country prior to industrialization. No government plan was forced on the people in an effort to reduce divorce rates. Rather, divorce rates dropped *because* of socioeconomic development (p. 280). In addition, the traditional notion of divorce as acceptable and normal has been replaced with the idea that divorce is "rather uncouth" (p. 316). Thus, Goode's (1993) more recent proposition that industrialization might be accompanied by declines in divorce has been given some support.

On balance, based on the evidence discussed thus far, it would appear that deeper norms and ideologies should not be overlooked when trying to understand what effect, if any, industrialization might have on marriage, family, and divorce. Relying on the worldwide sample of preindustrial societies provided by Murdock and White's standard cross-cultural sample, Hendrix and Pearson (1995) explored the relationships between spousal interdependence, female power, segregated divisions of labor, and divorce. Data were not available in comparable forms for all nations. Thus, for some variables, their study included as few as 80 nations or as many as 95. All the same, it represents an important contribution to cross-cultural analyses of divorce and factors presumed to be related to divorce.

Hendrix and Pearson (1995) provide a very complicated series of analyses of the factors that they were able to analyze, given the data available. For our purposes, a brief summation of key findings will do. First, they found that ease of access does not always translate to high divorce rates. That is because a group's norms may discourage divorce. Said another way, easy access to divorce is one thing; a group's acceptance of divorce may be quite another. Second, there appears to be a relationship between high divorce rates and rigid separation of men's and women's tasks when combined with little or no involvement of fathers in childrearing.

Hendrix and Pearson (1995) speculate that this higher divorce rate is due to spouses having little in common. That is, the more separated are the roles, the more likely there are two different realities—his and hers—regarding marriage. So, higher levels of marital conflict are to be expected. In this setting, and assuming access to divorce, lifetime rates of divorce tend to be relatively high (Hendrix and Pearson 1995).

Regarding the United States, Hendrix and Pearson (1995) point out that female employment might not be a very powerful predictor of divorce. Rather, female employment in interaction with the degree of labor division within marriages is worth further exploration. Hendrix and Pearson also note that industrialization by itself may not provide answers to predicting divorce rate and proneness. It might be that other factors such as gendered divisions of labor contribute to divorce. What is the bottom line? One isolated reason can not be attributed to the rate of divorce. Large social forces, economic trends, and prevailing norms all must be taken into consideration.

Divorce in China

The **traditional family of China** is associated with the Ch'ing dynasty, which lasted from 1644 until 1911 (Leslie 1982). Briefly stated, the traditional family of China was characterized by an agrarian life-style. The majority of the people were peasants; very few were gentry. The gentry family was **patriarchal,** with males having greater rights and privileges; **patrilocal,** with married couples living with or near the husband's kin; and officially **monogamous,** with each man and each woman having only one spouse at a time. The monogamy was of a modified sort, with concubinage also practiced. **Concubinage,** akin to having an acknowledged mistress in residence, coexisted with prostitution. Both were seen as conducive to family stability. The ideal family system among the gentry was a very large and extended one, ideally with several generations living together. Wives had relatively high status and power compared to concubines. All the same, all women basically existed in a social system characterized by female subordination.

Beyond this family system was the clan, or *tsu.* The *tsu* contained numerous families and a group of elders serving as committees of overseers for families. The council of elders in the *tsu* arbitrated disputes, collected taxes for the government, intervened in individual family matters that family members themselves could not resolve, and served as mediators between families and the government (Leslie 1982).

Divorce was possible but rarely practiced in traditional China. The poor could not afford it, and the gentry disdained it as a sign of weakness and instability. Family welfare was prized more than individual needs; thus, couples did not often resort to divorce. When divorce did occur, it generally was seen as a tragedy for women (Leslie 1982). A divorced woman's only recourse was to be returned to her family of origin; she had no other options. A divorced woman was seen as a source of shame to her family. Furthermore, it was not acceptable for divorced women to remarry. As for men, alternative sex partners were readily available without divorce, so divorces were seen not only as disgraceful but also as unnecessary (Leslie 1982).

Divorce in the People's Republic

Since the emergence of the People's Republic of China in 1949, tremendous social and economic changes have occurred. In essence, government policies were formulated in opposition to the traditional family system. One goal of these policies was to break the power of the *tsu,* thus assuring the fulfillment of the Communist government's own objectives and goals.

Of this new government, emancipation of women was a primary objective (Bullough and Ruan 1994). Freedom of choice in marriage was made law in 1950 with the passage of the Marriage Law. This law also stipulated that citizens were to practice monogamy without concubinage, that both sexes had equal right of inheritance, that individuals had the right to free mate choice, that divorces could be obtained upon mutual consent or upon the insistence of one of the partners, and that children had protected rights (Leslie 1982; Bullough and Ruan 1994). At the same time, leader Chairman Mao Zedung forced people to dress in unisex fashion, gave officials the power to deny marriages, and jailed people found guilty of adultery (Pappas 1998).

In line with Goode's (1963) contention that indigenous sources of social change in a country typically exist prior to industrialization, evidence suggests that changes in Chinese marriage and family systems were occurring prior to the Communist takeover (Goode 1963, 1993). For instance, arranged marriage systems were modified before the takeover, and dating had been allowed as a trial period prior to marriage (Bullough and Ruan 1994).

One of the goals of the Communist Revolution was the modernization of China based on Western models (Goode 1963). Starting as early as 1907, and reflected in the Civil Code of 1911, various policies and laws introduced the ideas of individual rights, a wife's right to a divorce, divorce by mutual consent, equality of the sexes, and freedom of marriage. These earlier precedents were present in the Kuomintang Civil Code of 1931, but, "even in the 1950s the new policies had not succeeded in winning the allegiance of the ordinary Chinese" (Goode 1963: 275). Moreover, Chinese men were threatened by equal rights for women and women's rights to divorce. These policies were most resisted by the leaders of the Community party and rural peasants (Goode 1993: 305). On the other hand, even in the

1920s and 1930s, the more educated and more urban residents of China were freely selecting their marriage partners, and some had come to believe in romantic love and in newer, more Western ideals of marriage and family (Goode 1963).

Additionally, the divorce rate in China was on the rise prior to the Communist takeover and it continued to rise after the takeover. Officials were alarmed that in 1957, for example, women took the initiative in divorce in 82 percent of the cases, and that most divorces were being sought by people who had been married a short while and had perhaps married out of haste and a desire for material things (Goode 1963: 317). The officials had assumed that by allowing free mate choice, people would no longer have an excuse for marital unhappiness and divorce (Goode 1993: 304).

The 1980 Marriage Law and Divorce

Although China's Marriage Law of 1950 legally abolished the traditional, dynastic systems of marriage, it apparently was not 100 percent effective (Engel 1984). Although marital couple (conjugal) relationships and nuclear families had become more important and more prevalent in China, the more traditional version of the Chinese family had remained fairly stable, despite government efforts to replace it with more Western versions (Engel 1984: 960). In 1980, the government passed a tougher marriage law that forbade marriages as contracts between families rather than individuals, prohibited concubinage and polygamy, and legislated free choice in selecting a marriage partner. This new law also raised the minimum age at marriage to 22 for men and 20 for women (Engel 1984: 958). Efforts to postpone marriage were intended to help control population growth.

In 1980, China ratified the Convention on the Elimination of all Forms of Discrimination Against Women (*WIN News* 1995: 65). This convention stipulated that women have equal rights to men in all spheres of life, including the family. In 1985, the Inheritance Law clearly stated that women have equal rights of inheritance. The Compulsory Education Law of 1986 requires that at age 6, all children, regardless of sex, race, or nationality, attend school for a set number of years.

By the early 1980s, one could see that the younger generations in China had developed a fairly strong materialistic orientation and were enthusiastically embracing modernization—most strongly associated with urban dwellers in China (Chen 1985). This trend began weakening some of the bonds with the traditional system. Young urban couples started living in small, neolocal households and became more or less receptive to the one-child policy. However, the urban young's bonds with the more extended systems were not completely severed. For one thing, the young tend to spend all their money and sometimes need help. In addition, both independent living and extended households can be sustained in the rural areas. Finally, "the overarching extended traditions and reciprocal relationships undoubtedly will continue to exert a binding force on divided conjugal units in both urban and rural contexts" (Chen 1983: 201).

Based on a survey of families in China's five largest cities in 1982, Tsui (1989) found that the young tend to have a fairly strong individualist, consumption tendency, which runs counter to traditional ways. Some even ask for financial help from their parents when they have overextended themselves (p. 741). Also, there is a generation gap in China in relation to attitudes about premarital sex and divorce. A survey of factory workers found that 20 percent of the respondents saw nothing wrong with premarital sex. Further, unmarried women secured the majority of the abortions in one of the larger cities. In addition, divorce rates went from 0.33 per 1,000 population in 1979 to 0.88 per 1,000 in 1985. Individuals under the age of 35 sought 70 percent of these divorces (Tsui 1989).

The elevation of women's status is having an impact on Chinese family life. Since the beginning of the twentieth century, women started having more power in their marital relationships rather than being subordinate to their husbands and mothers-in-law. Changes in laws since 1950 have removed even more of this subordination. The five-city survey revealed that by 1982, 81 percent of all married women were gainfully employed. On average, their earnings comprised 42 percent of the household income (Tsui 1989: 744). Among the younger couples, and especially those who are more urban, families tend to be nuclear. **Stem family systems,** a modified extended system wherein adult male children and their families live near the parents and function as one large economic unit, are more common among older and rural residents. However, given the low wages of young people, and the tendency to encourage at least one child to stay with the parents, combined with other socioeconomic pressures, the stem family is in a transitional phase. Moreover, some young couples are opting for the stem system for practical reasons (i.e., they have little or no money). Although there are strong preferences and trends toward the nuclear family, there still are pressures favoring the stem system. However, on balance, there also are ideological pressures favoring the nuclear system (Tsui 1989: 746).

Since 1980, China has continuously undergone a liberalization of sexual attitudes. Women's status has been increasing at the same time that rates of industrialization and urbanization have been escalating. Although they indicate that it has been difficult to get accurate information, Bullough and Ruan (1994) report that in 1982, there were 110,930 divorces in China. This figure rose to 500,000 in 1986. Divorces are difficult to obtain in China. The obstacle for most persons is that they must have the permission of government officials. In 1989, for example, 1,307,000 couples sought divorces in China, but only 725,000 received divorce certificates from the officials (Bullough and Ruan 1994). Women initiated most of these divorces. Most individuals seeking divorces are urban, relatively young, and well educated.

Currently, China is rethinking its divorce provisions. With the divorce rate approaching 25 percent of all married couples, government officials in Beijing are working on laws that would make it more difficult to get divorced. According to a *Newsweek* article (Pappas 1998: 36), proposals being drafted include waiting periods for divorce, stricter definitions of what constitutes grounds for divorce, and even a three-year separation prior to divorce. Proposals also are calling for loyalty in marriage and the outlawing of adultery, single motherhood, and marriage among those who have AIDS or other sexually transmitted diseases. These proposals reflect the belief that divorce and family instability are associated with moral decline.

Divorce in Ghana, West Africa

Ghana's divorce rate is comparatively low (Takyi and Oheneba-Sakyi 1994). Divorced Ghanaians tend to be reintegrated into kin systems and the larger society and to remarry. Furthermore, given the prevalence of kin support systems for children, father or mother absence due to divorce (or any other cause) is buffered by this extensive network (Nukunya 1992). With the greater emphasis on kin, divorce may not be the great personal tragedy that it sometimes is perceived to be in nations such as the United States.

In 1960, Ghana became the first African nation to break from colonial rule. After decades of economic and political toil and strife, Ghana became a democratic republic in 1992. As with many other developing nations, Ghana faces difficult social, economic, and environmental challenges. Improvement in the quality of life for girls and women, primarily through education and participatory economic development strategies, is a recognized national priority (Vander Mey et al. 1998). Ghana is incredibly pluralistic ethnically, with many subcultures, traditions, and customs. Interwoven into everyday life are complicated combinations of traditional and contemporary ways and laws. There are incredible variations by region of the country (Assimeng 1981 1986; Nukunya 1992; Benneh 1994; Vander Mey 1999).

Females suffer a literacy gap, compared to males; women's legal rights are not always clear, given a confusion between traditional and provincial laws; and girls and women disproportionately suffer more the crushing effects of rurality and poverty. At the same time, Ghana has been very straightforward in passing laws that protect the rights of females and make it possible for more females to become literate (Vander Mey et al. 1998).

In Ghana, women are legally equal to men. However, in reality, traditional laws and norms sometimes take precedence. Thus, how much protection and rights women experience in terms of marriage, access to earnings, child support, and access to land vary widely ("The Status of Women in Ghana" 1992; Palumbo 1992; Dodoo 1994). For instance, men enter into many of the contracts about land agreements. Although the number of women farmers is increasing, tradition often asserts that women first work their husbands' fields and gain access to pieces of land by benevolence of their husbands rather than through official, protective channels (Panuccio 1989; Aseno-Okyere, Atsu, and Obeng 1993; Takyi and Oheneba-Sakyi 1994; Vander Mey 1999). In addition, kinship systems will hold sway at times. In systems where sons and daughters both inherit, the tendency is to give less land to daughters than to sons (Aseno-Okyere et al. 1993).

Marriage in Ghana

Divorce in Ghana must be approached by understanding the types of marriages available (Takyi and Oheneba-Sakyi 1994) and the fact that kinship is emphasized over nuclear family systems (Benneh 1994). Furthermore, regional variations exist in the degree to which monogamy versus polygyny predominates. Both polygyny and monogamy can be found all over the country, but generally polygyny predominates, along with the Islamic religion, in the northern portions of the country, whereas monogamy, along with Christianity, predominates in the middle and southern portions of the country. However, it must be noted that polygyny is not restricted to the Islamic religion (Takyi and Oheneba-Sakyi 1994).

Marriages in Ghana can be contracted in one of three ways: Customary Law, the Ordinance, and the Mohammedans Ordinance (Takyi and Oheneba-Sakyi 1994). Over 80 percent of Ghanaian women contract their marriages through Customary Law. **Customary Law** is part of the "personal law of the Ghanaian" and was the only recognized marriage law until 1884 (Takyi and Oheneba-Sakyi 1994: 261). This law permitted personal preferences in marriage rituals and practices, and allowed either monogamous or polygynous unions. With its continued emphasis on enhancing the status of women, the government has strengthened its Customary Registration and Divorce Law (*WIN News* 1996) in an effort to provide formal recognition to the marriage contract, to provide for just allocations should divorce occur, and to protect women from inequitable property settlements upon divorce.

Takyi and Oheneba-Sakyi (1994) assert that polygyny and issues regarding women's rights are not terribly problematic in Ghana because of the Ghanaian tradition of recognizing myriad types of unions as consensual, thus binding. However, the rights of cowives and their children in polygynous unions are not clearly protected, though the government is moving in that direction (Aseno-Okyere et al. 1993). While waiting for the clarifications, some second wives have organized themselves and are mobilizing their resources to ensure that protection becomes a reality.

Marriage under **the Ordinance** became law in 1884. These marriages are strictly monogamous and are similar to U.S. marriages legally. This marriage type also is similar to U.S. marriage in that usually there is a celebration of the marriage in a church. Typically, Ghanaians first contract their marriages under Customary Law and then refile it as marriage under the Ordinance (Takyi and Oheneba-Sakyi 1994).

Marriage under **the Mohammedans Ordinance** also became law in 1884. It allows for the registering of Islamic marriages that are contracted following the stipulations of the Ordinance. The Mohammedans Ordinance, in addition, permits multiple wives (Takyi and Oheneba-Sakyi 1994).

However, regardless of how marriages are contracted, most Ghanaians view marriage as less a personal matter and more a family matter. That is, marriage unites at least two family systems. Thus, most Ghanaians do not see a marriage as valid until their kin have recognized the union (Assimeng 1981; Nukunya 1992;

Takyi and Oheneba-Sakyi 1994). Given these views, Ghanaians generally see divorce as a last resort rather than a first resort when difficulties arise within the marriage.

Divorce Then and Now

Historically, divorce could be sought by Ghanaians for infertility on the part of the man or the woman, inhumane treatment, laziness, immorality, or incompatibility (Sarpong 1974). Typically, a divorce ceremony publicly acknowledged that the woman was no longer married to or associated with her former husband. If the woman was found at fault, then the **bride wealth** (money, land, cattle, and other valued gifts given by the husband's family to the wife and wife's family for use) had to be returned to her former husband's family. If the husband was at fault, then his family would have to forfeit the bride wealth. Bride wealth has helped maintain low divorce rates among patrilineal groups (i.e., those groups that trace ancestry through the male lines only; Sarpong 1974). Among **matrilineal** groups (i.e., those who trace lineage through the female lines), the bride wealth is very small or insignificant. Divorce rates in matrilineal groups typically have been much higher than in patrilineal groups. Another reason for discrepancies in divorce rates between patrilineal and matrilineal groups is the greater emphasis placed on kinship, in general, among the patrilineal groups (Nukunya 1992).

Other grounds for divorce in Ghana today include infidelity, marital rape, failure to consult with the senior wife before taking another wife, and failure in domestic duties and obligations (Takyi and Oheneba-Sakyi 1994: 269). Failure in domestic duties and obligations is similar to some of the desertion provisions in U.S. law—for instance, a failure to provide for one's family or failure to satisfy the wife emotionally or sexually.

How much divorce is there in Ghana? The 1993 Ghana Demographic and Health Survey estimates a 27 percent dissolution rate of all first marriages (Takyi and Oheneba-Sakyi 1994). The rate of divorce in Ghana is higher among the matrilineal groups and higher in urban areas. In addition, divorce in Ghana today is correlated with higher educational attainment rates of women. Higher divorce rates among more educated women is seen, in part, as a function of increased strain in everyday life, more alternatives outside of marriage, the influence of Western ideals, and the weakening of kin ties among the more educated (Nukunya 1992; Takyi and Oheneba-Sakyi 1994: 268). The lower divorce rate among the less educated and more traditional couples is seen as a function of women's reliance on traditional wisdoms for keeping marriages intact, combined with the strain-reducing effects of kin associations, such as help with child care, financial support, and marriage counseling (Takyi and Oheneba-Sakyi 1994). Lower divorce rates among less educated women may reflect their greater social and economic dependency on their husbands and husbands' kin.

According to Customary Law, upon divorce, one may take whatever one has acquired through one's own efforts. Thus, among the groups that permit women to hold property and accumulate money independently of their husbands, women retain that property and money after divorce. In some patrilineal systems, divorced women can hold property accessed or acquired while married, but cannot transfer it, because their children belong formally to a different kin group. For couples married under the Ordinance, law courts may decide property settlements according to the principle of equity and preferences of the couple (Takyi and Oheneba-Sakyi 1994).

What about the Children?

Upon resolution of Ordinance-contracted marriages, the custody of children follows the concept of the best interest of the child. Typically, younger children are placed in the custody of their mothers, and husbands are required to assure child support. In general, however, child custody follows lineage patterns. Thus, in the matrilineal systems, mothers tend to have custody, and in the patrilineal systems, fathers tend to have custody. There are exceptions, however, in this complicated society. For instance, among the patrilineal Ewe, children do not automatically go with the father because the Ewe do not assume that the husband was given reproductive rights over the woman (Takyi and Oheneba-Sakyi 1994). Thus, decisions will have to be made between the spouses, or between the spouses in conjunction with advice from kin and elders. Regardless, both parents are seen as having rights of access to and visitation with their children (Takyi and Oheneba-Sakyi 1994).

There is no welfare program comparable to Temporary Assistance for Needy Families to assure a minimum level of living for children in Ghana. However, the Maintenance of Children Decree of 1977 does give the government the right to intervene on behalf of children when parents, or the extended kin system, cannot or will not meet their financial obligations (Mensa-Bonsu 1994). This decree prescribed the Family Tribunal, which has jurisdiction in the areas of child welfare, paternity, custody, and maintenance. The Tribunal must assure that children are not neglected in terms of basic physical needs and education. It requires that both parents provide for children, regardless of whether they are the custodial or noncustodial parents. In cases where parents are indigent, the Tribunal often provides a small monthly stipend to the custodial parent (Mensa-Bonsu 1994).

Divorce in the United States

The Puritan rebellion against the Church of England included recognizing absolute divorce (Leslie 1982: 196). Plymouth, Massachusetts, was the first place to permit **absolute divorce,** permanent legal dissolution of marriage, in 1639 (Nock 1992). Other New England colonies soon followed. In general, the eastern colonies permitted absolute divorce, which meant that husbands' and wives'

What are today's patterns and trends in divorce and remarriage in the United States? How do current patterns and trends compare with those of the past? How do they compare with developments in other countries, such as China and Ghana? What sociological factors are associated with the incidence of divorce?

obligations—financial, social, and sexual—were severed. The southern colonies did not permit absolute divorce, but would recognize separation from bed and board. The middle colonies, such as Pennsylvania, tended to pattern themselves after the southern colonies (Leslie 1982; Nock 1992).

Regardless of regional differences, divorce and separation from bed and board remained very rare during the colonial period. During the 1600s, Massachusetts saw 54 divorce petitions, 44 of which were granted (Nock 1992: 505). From 1739 to 1760, the colony granted only 3 divorces, 2 separations from bed and board, and 5 annulments (Leslie 1982: 196). Women initiated most of the divorce suits during the colonial period.

After the American Revolution, states began considering allowing divorce. The eastern and middle states made divorce the province of the courts. The southern colonies made divorce a legislative matter until about the mid-1800s (Nock 1992). Although the southern states remained reluctant to permit absolute divorce, by the middle of the 1900s, all states had such provisions. Fundamentally, all states established an adversarial system for divorcement; that is, a lawsuit had to be filed. There had to be a plaintiff and a defendant, and official grounds for divorce had to be declared and proven. In the earliest days of absolute divorce in the United States, grounds were few and quite serious. Adultery, prolonged absence, and bigamy were some of the earliest grounds (Nock 1992; Leslie 1982; Weitzman 1985). Cruelty and lack of support were added during the Victorian period, suggesting that decision makers had begun to view marriage as a partnership in which emotional and intimate aspects were not to be violated (Nock 1992).

On January 1, 1970, the nation's first **no-fault** law went into effect in California (Jost and Robinson 1991: 355). The grounds for divorce using no-fault are irreconcilable differences. No-fault legislation initially was passed in order to stem increases in divorce; to remove the acrimony, hostility, and trauma that fault-based divorce caused; to recognize that, over time, some divorces simply are inevitable, so mechanisms must be put into place to make divorcing less problematic for couples and their children; and to make divorce laws that would not end up with husbands being hard hit by alimony and child support. No-fault divorce proposed to treat men and women more fairly (Weitzman 1985: 16–17). Whatever the rationale, by 1985, every state but New York had passed some version of no-fault divorce (Schimmerling 1997).

Divorce Increases and Declines in the United States

By 1860, the U.S. divorce rate had reached 0.2 per 1,000 population (Jost and Robinson 1991: 355). By 1881, the rate was high enough to prompt individuals to create the New England Divorce Reform League. In that same decade, the National League for the Protection of the Family was created to "promote an improvement in public sentiment and legislation on the institution of the family, especially as affected by existing evils relating to marriage and divorce" (Farber 1964: 19). In 1889, the first national survey of divorce in the United States was published. It reported a 150 percent increase in divorce over the preceding 20 years (Jost and Robinson 1991: 355). Throughout the early 1900s, divorce rates continued to increase, though recognition must be given to the fact that during this period more states began to allow divorce.

Official divorce rates dropped during the Great Depression. One should be cautious in forming explanations for this. It is possible that families stayed together through these tough times. It is also possible that official divorce was somewhat replaced with so-called **poor man's divorce**—that is, desertion. Likewise, divorce rates dropped during war times, only to increase at war's end. Overall, however, the U.S. divorce rate continued to increase steadily through mid-century (Nock 1992). Since the 1960s to very recent years, the divorce rate then rose rapidly (Glenn 1991), with a peak in 1979 at 5.3 divorces per 1,000 population (Jost and Robinson 1991: 355). Some would argue that Americans tended less and less to view marriage as a permanent or lifetime commitment (Glenn 1991). Some attribute the increase to changing views of divorce and marriage as well as more lenient divorce provisions, especially no-fault divorce (Jost and Robinson 1991).

Carlson (1995), a conservative critic, claims that no-fault divorce has destroyed the sanctity of marriage. In his promotion of family values, Carlson calls for, among other things, changes in the tax system, such that divorce would be financially discouraged, and changes in the legal system, such that divorce would become once again a rare occurrence and difficult to obtain. Further, he insists that the legal processes of divorcement change, such that the state would necessarily side with the party trying to keep the marriage intact.

Blaming no-fault divorce for high rates of divorce has become so prevalent that some state lawmakers are considering changing divorce laws to make divorce tougher to obtain. Some are considering disallowing no-fault divorces, in particular (Gatland 1997). Thus far, only the state of Louisiana has succeeded in returning the divorce provisions back to fault as the sole or alternate basis for divorce (Schimmerling 1997: 33).

Ironically, moves toward abolishing no-fault and toughening up on divorce are occurring at the same time that the U.S. **crude divorce rate** (divorces per 1,000 in the population) has begun to decline. The decline was evident by the late 1980s. By 1994, the divorce rate was 4.6 per 1,000 population, the same as that for 1993 and lower than the 4.7 rate for 1990 (De Vita 1996: 32). Given the trend toward later age at first marriage, combined with a graying of the population, most experts predict that this lower rate will hold stable or even continue to drop for the next decade or so.

Although the United States still has the highest divorce rate of all Western nations (see Table 13.1 on page 438), most Americans who divorce eventually remarry. Other research has begun to show high stability rates in remarriages (Clarke and Wilson 1994). In contrast to some other Western nations, the United States has lower cohabitation rates but higher marriage rates, which contributes to the relatively high divorce rates of the United States, compared to other Western nations (see Table 13.1). However, as De Vita (1996: 30) notes, "From an international perspective, married life remains a very durable institution in contemporary American life."

Why the Decline?

In part, the decline in the U.S. divorce rate may be a function of the graying of the population. Median age in the United States now hovers around 43 years (Wolfe 1998). Baby boomers now have reached a stage where if they were going to become divorced, they have done so (De Vita 1996). If they have entered another marriage, odds are that they will not divorce again (Clarke and Wilson 1994; Glenn 1991). In addition, the later age at first marriage in the United States may be contributing to this decline. In 1950, the median age for American men and women at first marriage was 22.8 years and 20.3 years, respectively. By 1994, median age at first marriage for men stood at 26.7 years, whereas for women it was 24.5 years (De Vita 1996: 31).

It is presumed that older people are more mature and more able to handle the responsibilities and stresses of marriage (De Vita 1996). Wolfe (1998) contends that another possible reason for the decline in divorce rates is the death of the youth culture, replaced by the middle-aged culture, with its own sets of values, such as being more spiritual and seeking to find meaning in life. According to Wolfe, the "psychological center of gravity" of the United States has shifted to-

Table 13.1   Marriage and Divorce Rates for Selected Countries, 1960–1992

Country	Marriages per 1,000 Population, Ages 15–64				
	1960	1970	1980	1990	1992
United States	14	17	16	15	14
Canada	12	14	12	10	N/A
France	11	12	10	8	7
Germany*	14	12	9	9	8
Italy	12	11	9	8	8
Japan	15	14	10	8	N/A
Sweden	10	8	7	7	6
United Kingdom	12	14	12	10	N/A

Country	Divorces per 1,000 Married Women				
	1960	1970	1980	1990	1992
United States	9	15	23	21	21
Canada	2	6	10	11	11
France	3	3	6	8	N/A
Germany*	4	5	6	8	7
Italy	N/A	1	1	2	2
Japan	4	4	5	5	N/A
Sweden	5	7	11	12	12
United Kingdom	2	5	12	13	12

Note: N/A is not available.

*Data for 1960 to 1990 refer to western Germany.

Source: From "The United States at Mid-Decade" by Carol J. De Vita, 1996, *Population Bulletin, 50* (4), p. 30. Reprinted by permission of Population Reference Bureau. (Based on U.S. Bureau of the Census, *U.S. Statistical Abstract, 1991*, table 1439; and *1995*, table 1366.)

ward a more moral, kinder, gentler, less materialistic, more introspective worldview. This shift is associated with declines in both crime rates and divorce rates (Wolfe 1998).

Patterns of Divorce in the United States

Regionally in the United States, divorce tends to increase from north to south and from east to west. Thus, divorce rates are relatively higher in the South and the Mountain States, and lower in the Northeast and Midwest (De Vita 1996). The reasons for this persistent pattern are not entirely clear but may relate to socioeconomic factors and population mobility. The Mountain States tend to have more mobile populations, and the South tends to have relatively poorer people who marry at earlier ages.

Divorce rates also tend to be higher in urban areas in comparison to rural areas. Large and medium-sized cities have about twice as much divorce as do nonurban, open-country areas (Shelton,1987). One possible reason for this might be that the larger the city, the less socially integrated people tend to be. Thus, the norms against divorce may be weaker at the same time that there are more alternatives to marriage.

Black Americans have higher divorce rates than do white Americans. The reasons are not exactly clear, however. Among blacks, sex ratios, age at marriage, and fertility do not account for the higher rate, nor does social class (White 1990). As noted in Chapter 5, all American families have seen dramatic changes in marriage, divorce, and birth rates. However, Black American families appear to have disproportionately experienced these changes. It may be that African cultural patterns influence the patterns of Black Americans. That is, there is a greater emphasis on family closeness and kin networks over the marital relationship. These cultural factors, compounded by economic hardships, may partially account for the lower marriage yet higher divorce rates among black Americans in contrast to white Americans (Cherlin 1998).

As noted in Chapter 5, Hispanic families tend to have lower divorce rates than do non-Hispanic groups, with Cuban Americans having the highest rate among Hispanic groups. However, the divorce rate has been increasing for Hispanics. Female employment outside the home may account for these increases among Cuban Americans (see Chapter 5). The 20 percent increase in divorces among Mexican Americans during the 1980s (Becerra 1998: 164) may partially be accounted for by poverty, migration from rural to urban places, and increases in nuclear households.

Asian Americans tend to have very low and stable divorce rates. Reasons for this are alluded to in Chapter 5. Families tend to place a stronger emphasis on the family than the individual—specifically, the family in an immortal sense. Marriage brings lineages together. These lineages are stabilized through intact marriages. Culture itself is the key to understanding Asian American life (Staples and Mirande 1980). Cultural norms, combined with greater conservatism about marriage and delayed age at marriage, help explain the low rate of divorce among Asian Americans.

Divorce varies by social class. There tends to be an inverse relationship between social class and divorce rates. That is, the lower the social class, the higher the divorce rates; this pattern has been observed for decades (White 1990). The relationship here is probably due to the tendency for lower- and working-class people to marry at younger ages. In addition, lower- and working-class couples begin having children at relatively young ages, thus adding to the strain in their lives. On the other hand, middle- and upper-class individuals tend to delay marriage until their mid- to late twenties, and begin marriages after completing the desired amount of advanced education or job training. These couples also tend to delay childbirth. All of these factors, combined with an emphasis on communication and problem solving, probably help reduce the risk for divorce.

What Causes Divorce?

If you ask individuals what caused their divorces, you probably would hear about disagreements over sex roles and gender-based tasks, alcoholism and drug abuse, infidelity, physical and psychological abuse, or recurring financial problems (White 1990). However, studies that rely on personal accounts of reasons for divorce have very small, unrepresentative samples (White 1990). In addition, because these studies focus on divorced persons, they do not help much in making predictions about divorce and its causes. Based on larger samples of both divorced and nondivorced couples, research tends to show that women's employment, the distribution of economic power and authority, and age at first marriage appear to be significant factors.

Women's Labor Force Participation

A popular myth is that women's labor force participation causes divorce. Research, however, does not fully support this claim (White 1990), and this factor is complicated by others such as hours worked and the wife's relative financial contribution to the family. White (1990) reviewed research that showed that American women's labor force participation as a factor by itself actually tended to reduce marital instability. However, as the number of hours worked increased, so did the likelihood of divorce. As seen in an earlier section of this chapter, cross-cultural studies also have yielded a mixed review of women's labor force participation as a factor in divorce rates.

An analysis of the impact of several indicators of the wife's employment on marital disruption was conducted using a national probability sample of all U.S. women who married for the first time between 1968 and 1982. It was found that the lower the income category of these women, the higher their divorce rates. Women who worked 35 to 40 or more than 40 hours per week were at greatest risk for divorce, compared to those who worked fewer hours. However, women's relative financial contributions to the family had no effect on divorce risk (Greenstein 1990).

Income Dependency

Data from the 1986–1989 Panel Study of Income Dynamics (PSID) for prime-age couples in their first marriages (2,030 persons) were used to analyze relationships between wives' employment and divorce. It was found that traditional couples, with the husband as the sole or primary breadwinner, were least likely to divorce. Among these couples, the greater the wife's dependency on the husband's income, the lower the likelihood of divorce. In addition, the more hours women spent on housework, the lower the divorce probability. Nontraditional, dual-career couples in which the wife earned 50 to 75 percent of the family income were most likely to divorce. Among couples where the wife earned 75 to 100 percent of the family income (reverse traditional couple), there was very low divorce proneness and high husband dependency. In this case, husbands were economically dependent on wives. They tended to be stay-at-home husbands. However, not all the husbands were staying home voluntarily; many were unemployed. The wives tended to take care of the husbands and the children (Heckert, Nowak, and Snyder 1998).

Thus, we probably need to focus more attention on the other realities of couples rather than simply determining if it is the wife or the husband who makes more money. This especially seems justified when we see that in the study by Heckert and colleagues, the nontraditional couples tended to have relatively high divorce proneness. The wife contributes 50 to 75 percent of the family income and is also expected to do the bulk of the child care and housework. Among these couples, it is likely that the strain on the woman is too much. For the reverse traditional couples, however, it appears that the wives' caregiving compensates for the husbands' dependency (Heckert et al. 1998).

At any rate, the relationships between wives' employment and divorce are not simple and there may be many more factors involved. For example, it could be that husbands' employment, or lack thereof, relates to divorce proneness. In addition, husbands' engagement or disengagement from parenting may minimize or add strain on working wives.

Age at First Marriage

Most sociologists would agree that if there was only one predictor of divorce, it would probably be age at first marriage. The older one is at first marriage, the less likely one is to divorce (White 1990). Perhaps it is because older people are, in fact, more mature and more able to handle the responsibilities and commitments associated with marriage. It also may be that by being a little older, one has reduced some financial and personal strains, such as completing the desired amount of schooling and training as well as establishing one's self in the work world.

Effects of Divorce

Incredible numbers of essays, opinion pieces, journal articles, and books have been written about the effects of divorce on children. Less has been written regarding the effects of divorce on college students and former husbands and wives. There is no doubt, however, that opinions and findings tend to vary widely. We will take a quick inventory to survey the empirical landscape in this area.

Effects of Divorce on Children

Based on a longitudinal study of 60 middle-class divorced families in the San Francisco area, Wallerstein (1983) and her colleague Blakeslee (Wallerstein and Blakeslee 1989) reported that 10 years after the divorce, only 34 percent of the children were doing well, whereas 37 percent of the children were depressed, did not do well in school, and were suffering myriad behavioral problems as a result of the divorce. Critics of this research pointed out that the findings were based on an extremely small and nonrepresentative sample. The families were middle class, all had been referred to a clinic for counseling, and all had extensive histories of psychiatric problems (Furstenberg and Cherlin 1991). Nevertheless, Wallerstein's work is heavily cited and has received much publicity. To balance these overwhelmingly negative findings from an extremely limited sample, let us take a look at a few other studies.

Amato and Booth (1991) used a national sample of 2,033 married adults to compare those who had and had not experienced their parents' divorce as children. In their 12-year longitudinal study, they tested three theories that address the effects of divorce on children. The first is the **socialization model,** which assumes that the "negative effects of divorce are due to dysfunctional learning experiences associated with single-parent families" (p. 896). The second is the **economic deprivation model,** which assumes that children of divorce will suffer very little if their mothers remarry or their fathers have custody of them and if the time spent in a one-parent family is relatively short. The third theory is the **family stress model,** the model that Wallerstein and her associates have employed. According to Amato and Booth (1991), the family stress model "views divorce as a major strain for children" (p. 897). The strain includes having to relocate, losing contact with grandparents, and changing schools.

When compared to the adults who had not experienced parental divorce as children, the adults from divorced families had lower levels of well-being (Amato and Booth 1991). However, adults who grew up in unhappy yet intact families also tended to suffer long-term negative consequences. In contrast to the adults who recalled their parents' marriages as happy ones, these adults scored lower on social, family, and psychological well-being (p. 910). Thus, the researchers concluded that although parental divorce appears to contribute to social, marital, and psychological difficulties in adulthood, these consequences are only modest and not severe (Amato and Booth 1991: 912). Furthermore, adults who grew up in low-stress homes where parents had divorced were just about as happy as adults who grew up in low-stress, intact homes. Both of these groups were happier than those who grew up in unhappy yet intact homes. This led Amato and Booth to conclude that children suffer minimal long-term effects if their parents' divorce causes minimal disruption in the child's life.

Amato and Keith (1991a) conducted a meta-analysis of 92 studies that compared children of divorce with children living in continuously intact families. They found modest differences between these groups. By a small margin, the children of divorce tended to have lower academic achievement, more conduct problems, lower scores on relationships with their mothers and fathers, and lower scores on self-concept, social relations, and psychological adjustment. Amato and Keith (1991b) then conducted a meta-analysis of studies comparing adults who had and had not experienced parental divorce as children. This analysis also revealed small but consistent differences between the groups. The adults from intact homes scored higher on marital quality, had a lower risk of divorce, and had higher psychological well-being and socioeconomic attainment.

A number of studies have been conducted that more or less support the work of Amato and his colleagues (Bynum and Durm 1996; Clark and Clifford 1996; Cherlin, Chase-Lansdale, and McRae 1998). Other studies, while generally supporting Amato's work, also bring additional variables into play. For instance, Howell, Portes, and Brown (1997) conducted a study on children whose divorcing parents had been remanded by the Family Court in a mid-southern state to participate (with their children) in the Families in Transition (FIT) program. Included were 213 boys and 218 girls ranging in age from 5 to 16. In addition to using the Child Divorce Adjustment Inventory and the Self-Perception Profile for Children, the researchers interviewed some of the children. They found that older children fared better than younger children during the parental separation phase and that the father-headed families fared better both before and after the separation. Girls had higher adjustment ratings than did boys, which is consistent with previous research. Also, the higher the socioeconomic status of the parents, the higher the self-esteem of both boys and girls.

It should be noted that the findings from the study by Howell and colleagues (1997) are supported by other research. For instance, a consistent finding is that children whose parents divorce before they are 6 years of age tend to have greater adjustment problems than do children whose parents divorce when the children are over six years of age (Pagani et al. 1997). However, boys whose parents divorce when they are between the ages of 10 and 14 tend to have greater relationship problems as adults than children who are younger when their parents divorce (McCabe 1997). Children without siblings may be more likely to experience divorce adjustment problems than those with siblings (Kempton et al. 1991). Finally, mother-child conflicts are more common in divorced than in intact families, and the conflict often spills over from conflict between the divorced parents (Forehand et al. 1991).

The research fairly consistently reveals that younger children tend to suffer the greatest negative effects and boys tend to suffer more than girls. However, some children are not affected at all. In addition, children do well following divorce if they are cared for by an effective parent—that is, one who is loving, is nurturing, and provides a predictable routine and consistent but moderate discipline (Furstenberg and Cherlin 1991).

Most studies on divorce's effects on children (and everyone else for that matter) have no predivorce measures to go by. A valuable contribution here has been made by Cherlin and his colleagues (1991). They conducted longitudinal studies of 2,279 children in the United States and over 11,600 children in Great Britain. For the British children, the researchers used interviews (included filling out the Rutter Home Behavior Scale) with mothers taken as part of the National Child Development Study (NCDS), interviews with the children's teachers using the Bristol Social Adjustment Guide, and children's reading and math test results. The Rutter Home Behavior Scale inventories behaviors such as temper tantrums, fighting with other children, sleep disorders, disobedience at home, reluctance to go to school, and problems with concentration. For the American children, the researchers used data from the National Survey of Children (NSC), mother interviews using items similar to those used in Great Britain, and children's test scores. They controlled for variables such as class and race. In addition, they controlled for the physicians' ratings of the children's physical and mental health.

Taking preseparation conditions into account, Cherlin and colleagues found that boys of divorced parents scored as high as boys from intact homes on academic and behavioral tests. This held for both American and British boys. Results for the girls were a little different. British girls from divorced families scored lower on behavioral and academic measures than did their counterparts from intact families, but no differences appeared among the American girls (Cherlin et al. 1991).

Based on their analyses, Cherlin and colleagues conclude that much of children's adjustments to divorce can be predicted by factors present in the family milieu prior to divorce. Thus, a shift toward analyzing the processes leading up to divorce, and their effects on children, appears warranted (Cherlin et al. 1991).

After all is said and done in this area of study, it remains safe to say that the most negative and long-term effect of divorce for many children is poverty (Seltzer 1994). Even if a child were not living in a poor family at the time of the divorce, children of divorce typically live in a family that must contend with a reduction in income after the divorce. Parents who divorce tend to have less money than do parents who stay married. Poverty, of course, is correlated with an array of personal and social woes. The true costs of poverty to individuals and a society are probably incalculable.

It has been documented that "divorce does not automatically result in poor child functioning" (Plunkett et al. 1997: 33) although it is a stressful time for children. It is suggested that professionals work with parents so that parents understand that inconsistent visitation, inconsistent parenting, and family conflict have detrimental effects on children's adjustment to divorce. It also is suggested that families use counselors to help children adjust to divorce and that professionals work with children to prevent self-fulfilling prophecies (Plunkett et al. 1997). An example of a self-fulfilling prophecy would be expecting that the child will have behavioral and academic problems due to being from a divorced family.

Thus, the psychological effects of divorce on children might not be as severe as Wallerstein and colleagues have contended. The child's social class, the degree of conflict in the family before and during the divorce process, the child's sex and age—all of these factors must be taken into consideration. Children in families that are not experiencing psychiatric problems—unlike the families in Wallerstein's study—probably are not going to suffer such severe and long-term negative psychosocial effects.

Effects of Divorce on Children of College Age

A study of 188 college students (Landis-Kleine et al. 1995) found no relationship between parents' marital status and students' attitudes toward marriage and commitment, but other studies are beginning to appear to the contrary. For instance, in a small sample of 46 students from divorced families and 66 from intact families, it was found that students from divorced families had more worries about becoming parents than did the students from intact families. Likewise, more students from divorced families reported witnessing father-to-mother violence while growing up. A relationship was found between divorce and physical abuse by the father and harboring negative thoughts about parenthood (Langhinrichsen-Rohling and Dostal 1996). Another study compared 40 students from divorced families with 184 students from intact families. It was found that if students could choose a living arrangement following divorce, the students from divorced families preferred sole custody arrangements, whereas students from intact families preferred joint custody arrangements (Derevensky and Deschamps 1997).

A study using a sample of 737 university students revealed that students from divorced families reported more conflict while growing up than did students from intact families. Furthermore, students from divorced families were more sexually active than were students from intact families. Students from divorced families also scored lower in altruistic loving and trust in relationships (Sprague and Kinney 1997).

Effects of Divorce on Former Spouses

In a decade review of the research in this area, it was reported that although divorced women tend to feel more distressed after the divorce, they also feel more positive about being divorced than men do. In general, it appears that women feel more distress prior to the separation and men feel more distress after the separation, despite the fact that women tend be paid less, get little if any child support, and experience more economic decline for longer periods after a divorce than do men (Kitson and Morgan 1990).

In a study of 268 divorced men and women in Marion County, Indianapolis, it was found that more women than men reported that exercising their independence was a major coping mechanism for them following divorce. More females than males also thought it important to have children help with chores, to share their feelings with children, and to have child-care assistance from family and friends. However, there were no real differences between the men and women on their economic adjustment to divorce, rate of sexual contact with former spouses, and adjustment to dating after divorce (Colburn, Lin, and Moore 1992).

Recognizing that among some divorced couples, attachment to each other will continue after divorce, Serovich and associates (1992) conducted a study of 46 divorced men and 71 divorced women, none of whom had been married to each other. They found that there were no significant differences in levels of communication with former spouses and that the communication tended to focus on shared children. Few of these male respondents had much direct contact with their children, but kept current with their children's lives by communicating with their former spouses. An implication here also is that the noncustodial fathers were able to adjust to the divorce because they could still have contact with former wives due to their shared interests in their child.

Child Custody, Child Support, and Visitation Patterns

Mothers tend to get custody of children following divorce (Arditti 1992; Cancian and Meyer 1998). Though there have been some increases in child custody awards to fathers, typically these fathers take custody of sons and older children. Though the research is mixed, it appears that fathers with higher incomes are more likely to seek sole custody. **Joint custody** of children, estimated to be at about 13 percent (Cancian and Meyer 1998), refers to the "legal right to make decisions about a child's life, regardless of where or with whom that child might be living" (Seltzer 1998: 135). Parents involved in joint custody arrangements tend to be well educated, urban, and well paid (Seltzer 1998). Home ownership also seems to be a feature of couples who opt for joint custody (Cancian and Meyer

What impact do divorce and custody conflicts have on children? How can divorcing or disputing parents protect their children from harm? Why do fathers' contacts with their children often decrease significantly after divorce, even when they have joint custody? What factors contribute to successful stepfamilies?

1998). Based on an analysis of 160 divorced families, for example, it was found that fathers with joint legal custody, compared to noncustodial fathers, pay more child support, spend more time with their children, and also have more overnight visits with their children (Seltzer 1998).

Visitation and Deadbeat Dads

Noncustodial father visitations tend to follow a downward spiral after divorce. In this spiral, noncustodial fathers who are dissatisfied with the scheduling, duration, and nature of their visits tend to visit less often and may stop visiting altogether (Arditti 1992). It may be that some noncustodial parents were not close to their children prior to the divorce and therefore tend to visit their children less after the divorce. On the other hand, noncustodial fathers who still have positive feelings toward their ex-wives tend to pay child support and visit with their children (Arditti 1992). Fathers with joint custody tend to visit their children and honor their support payments.

An analysis of the factors related to the downward trend in child support payments during the 1980s (Hanson et al. 1996) revealed that the trend was related to decreases in fathers' incomes, reductions in the numbers of children eligible for child support, and increases in custodial mothers' incomes. The mean real dollar value of child support payments in the United States declined by 25 percent from 1978 to 1985. It is argued that the decline was due to increases in custodial mothers' incomes. Rather, these real declines were due to declines in the real value of awards to custodial parents in terms of purchasing power (Graham 1995).

In 1988, Congress passed the **Family Support Act,** which mandates states to update periodically their existing child support awards and the guidelines used to set awards (Graham 1997). In addition, the act stipulated that all states would create computer systems to collect and disburse child support payments. Apparently, however, only 22 states are in compliance with this law, with the result that noncustodial parents who, for whatever reasons, fail to provide child support cannot be tracked adequately and forced to pay (Thibodeau 1998).

As previously noted, most noncustodial fathers tend to disengage from their children following divorce. In an analysis of 180 divorced custodial mothers, it was found that noncustodial parents who pay child support also visit their children more than those who do not pay child support (Seltzer, Schaeffer, and Charng 1989). However, using data from the National Survey of Families and Households, another study revealed that fathers tend to have limited contact with children after the divorce. This relationship held, even when marriages had been of longer duration. Contact decreased over time, especially after the fathers developed new relationships or remarried. Interestingly, this analysis revealed that contrary to conventional thought, fathers of boys were not more likely to visit than were fathers of girls. Finally, the fathers who spent more time with their children tended to be better educated and had relatively higher incomes than those who did not (Stephens 1996: 486).

Much of the research on fathers' postdivorce contact with children focuses on fathers' contact with minor children. However, at least one study looked at divorced fathers' contacts with their adult children. Using data from the National Survey on Families and Households, Cooney and Uhlenberg (1990) found that among their ever- and never-divorced fathers between the ages of 50 and 79, twice as many of the never-divorced fathers as compared to the ever-divorced fathers, had an adult child living with them. Over one-third of the divorced fathers had completely lost contact with one or more of their children (p. 685). About 10 percent of the divorced fathers had completely lost contact with all children during the fathers' later years of life. On the whole, the more educated the divorced father was, the more likely he had maintained some contact with his children in their adult years (Cooney and Uhlenberg 1990).

Furstenberg and Cherlin (1991) also have documented father disengagement after divorce, but they went a step further. They argue that society should help the custodial parent recover from divorce, especially financially. In addition, society must find ways to engage fathers more directly in their children's lives before a divorce occurs. Perhaps with more father engagement early on, husbands and wives will share more equitably, wives will not be so strained, and divorce might be resorted to less often.

Remarriage

Most Americans who divorce will remarry (De Vita 1996). Although the United States does have a relatively high rate of divorce, it also has the highest remarriage rate in the world (Coleman and Ganong 1990). In addition, the last few years have also seen a growth in **partial remarriage,** marriages between a never-married person and a formerly married person (Clarke and Wilson 1994). The best estimates are that at least 40 percent of all marriages in the United States are remarriages for one or both of the spouses (Coleman and Ganong 1990; Clarke and Wilson 1994). Roughly 25 percent of all children born in the United States in the 1980s grew up in homes with a stepparent present (Mason and Mauldon 1996). Thus, in a real sense, remarriages and stepfamilies, or blended families, are relatively normative family forms in the United States.

Historically, however, remarriages and stepfamilies created after a divorce have been treated as deviant. There has been a strong tendency to take a problems-oriented view of stepfamilies. With this approach, we see the remarriage and the stepfamily as fractured, vulnerable, and not a "real" family (Coleman and Ganong 1990). Is this realistic? Let's take a look.

As early as 1964, Burchinal compared five different types of families. These included unbroken, single parent (mother head of household), remarried (mother and stepfather), remarried (father and stepmother), and remarried (both parents). He found that for children who were having difficulties in stepfamilies, it was not easy to determine if the difficulties were lingering from problems with the divorce (family conflict, loss of a parent, etc.) or were actually the result of the new family formation. Ultimately, Burchinal (1964) concluded that remarriage and stepfamilies can be either a positive or a negative experience for children. Figure 13.1 lists Internet resources for getting help and support in the areas of divorce and step-parenting.

Cherlin (1978) refers to remarriage as an *incomplete institution* because roles are not well defined among members in these blended family configurations. In addition, Cherlin argues that the then high rate of divorce among the remarried, a rate that has been declining, pointed to its instability and impermanence. He contends that people were less satisfied in their second marriages than in their first. Subsequent to that writing, he and Furstenberg reconsidered some of their earlier thinking on remarriage and stepfamilies. Based on research available for review, Cherlin and Furstenberg (1994) conclude that it takes years for people to adjust to remarriages and stepfamily life. They also note that remarriages are at

---

Figure 13.1

Internet Connections for Help and Support with Divorce and Stepparenting

The following websites might be helpful regarding divorce, remarriage, and stepfamilies. Some of these sites provide interactive advice; others provide guidelines regarding legal issues; and still others give direct access to articles and books, or make it possible for you to order materials online.

www.stepfam.org/
Stepfamily Association of America, 650 J Street, Suite 205, Lincoln, NE 86508

www.selfgrowth.com/stepf.html
This is the site for Self-Improvement Online. Lots of links are given.

www.positivesteps.com/
Solutions to Establishing Positive Stepfamilies. Positive Steps, 2605 Loftsmoor Lane, Plano, TX, 75025

www.stepfamily.net
Stepfamily Network (nonprofit)

www.secondwivesclub.com/
This site provides interactive problem solving and many suggested resources.

www.divorcesource.com/index.html
The Divorce Source. Legal information is provided for each state of the United States as well as other selected countries. Family law links and suggested readings are given.

greater risk for divorce than first marriages. In addition, though recognizing the economic advantage a stepparent can bring to a family system, the researchers also conclude that on other measures, children in remarriages are no better or worse off than children in one-parent families.

Cherlin's incomplete institution thesis has been challenged. Grizzle (1996) argues that there are problems with comparing divorce rates of first-marrieds and remarrieds. It is possible that some people in their first marriages might be miserable but unwilling or unable to go through with a divorce. Thus, there is no "sound evidence" (Grizzle 1996: 195) that stepfamilies are incomplete or dysfunctional.

There are, of course, both stresses and successes of remarried couples and their families. Just as these families face some constraints, they also are offered some unique opportunities. For instance, stepfamilies must work through their own definitions of what it means to be a family. Some, for instance, may opt to view themselves as not *really* a stepfamily. Others might consciously pursue "ordinary" life or patiently wait for all the children to be launched. Of course, it is quite possible that the adults and children will all come to this family system with different views on appropriate childrearing. Additionally, the adults might experience differences of opinions regarding former spouses. One thing that might help remarried couples is "their ability to reformulate their concepts of marriage and family to fit the remarried couple and family" (Keshet, 1998: 309). The stepfamily can be an exciting place of learning and relearning; it does not have to be a collection of strangers waiting for time to displace them from each other.

What can confidently be said about stepfamilies and remarriage in the United States? Children's adjustment in stepfamilies is contingent on an array of factors, such as the child's age at time of the remarriage, circumstances surrounding the loss of a parent, effectiveness of parent-child communication, predictability in household routines, and flexibility in parent-child interactions (Henry and Lovelace 1995; Bernstein 1997). Further, it may be that the arrival of a stepfather can be particularly helpful in easing some of the financial strains typical of single-mother households (Cherlin and Furstenberg 1994). Marital adjustment in remarriages also appears contingent on an array of factors. Most of these factors are the same as for first-marrieds: overall well-being, self-confidence, health, and stress (Coleman and Ganong 1990).

Summary

Divorce, the legal dissolution of marriage, is a worldwide phenomenon. Given the tendency of researchers to focus on divorce and its correlates in Western societies, particularly the United States, information about divorce in non-Western nations and cross-cultural comparisons of divorce rates and patterns is of more recent vintage.

One of the earlier theses regarding divorce rates and modernization predicted that, as with the United States, as other nations industrialized, they also would see increases in divorce rates. However, this has not always been the case, especially in Southeast Asia. It appears that many factors actually influence a nation's divorce rate, such as larger cultural norms that either accept or discourage divorce, the emphasis placed on family and kinship rather than the marital relationship itself, government policies, the status of women, women's labor force participation, and wives' relative dependency on husbands' incomes. Even these factors, however, have slightly different influences, depending on the country's cultural norms and current political climate.

In any country that holds the view that divorce is problematic, then it does, in fact, become a social problem. In nations such as the United States, as in China, divorce is seen by some as a sign of social disintegration. In the United States, divorce critics tend to want to repeal divorce laws in an effort to get people to maintain their moral commitment to permanent marriage. In China, the government takes exception to divorce for different reasons. Yet, Chinese leaders, too, are trying to make divorce more difficult to get. In Indonesia, a formerly high-divorce country, popular opinion to the effect that divorce is uncouth appears to be curtailing divorce rates, along with the increasing educational attainment of women.

In Ghana, efforts are being refined to ensure equitable settlements for women and adequate care of children after divorce. The kin support system is assisting divorced adults and their children financially and otherwise, while at the same time resorbing the adults back into their systems. When this is not adequate, the government has a mechanism for supplementing women's wages to ensure children's care.

In the United States, divorce rates have declined and are expected to stay at this lower level or drop even lower. However, public displeasure with divorce continues. Efforts to rescind the no-fault provisions and to make divorce tougher to secure continue.

Divorce in the United States tends to bring with it myriad personal and social woes. American children and women tend to disproportionately suffer financially long after a divorce has been finalized. This is also true for women and children in other countries. Noncustodial fathers tend to taper off and then cease visitation and support of their children. In some cases, aging fathers may have completely lost track of their children.

Remarriage and stepfamilies are relatively widely, yet inadequately, studied in the United States. Much of the limitations of the research are probably reflective of a problems-oriented view of stepfamilies. This is unfortunate, given that a relatively high proportion of American families are, in fact, stepfamilies.

It has been argued that remarriage and stepfamilies represent incomplete institutions. Perhaps Goode (1993: 345) has provided the soundest advice for regular citizens and researchers alike regarding this: "We should accept the fact that most developed nations can now be seen as high divorce rate systems, and we should *institutionalize* divorce—accept it as we do other institutions, and build adequate safeguards as well as social understandings and pressures to make it work reasonably well." This chapter has attempted to provide adequate understandings.

Readings for In-Depth Focus

Debate over the Economic Effects of Divorce

As you learned in Chapter 2 of this text, carefulness in research is expected in sociology. Although sociologists cannot be blamed for any use or misuse of their research, it is expected that all data will be verified before being reported and that any subsequent errors also will be made public.

In the landmark book titled *The Divorce Revolution*, Lenore J. Weitzman (1985) provided data comparing predivorce and postdivorce median incomes for couples married less than 10 years and for couples married 18 years or more. Her findings indicated that approximately one year after divorce, divorced men saw a 42 percent increase in their standard of living, whereas the standard of living for divorced women, on average, declined by 73 percent. Weitzman (1985: 339) concludes, "Divorce is a financial catastrophe for most women." She argues that the reasons for the decline in the divorced women's standard of living are due to many factors, including lack of child support and alimony awards, the fact that women tend to be awarded custody and upkeep of children even though women are paid less and cannot rely on payments from former husbands, and the fact that divorced women's financial outputs increases at the same time that the husbands' decreases (pp. 340–343). Weitzman concludes that no-fault divorce, rather than being the liberating divorce provision it was proposed to be, actually caused a serious gender gap between divorced men and women. Thus, she concludes that no-fault divorce results in the *feminization of poverty*.

As can be seen in the first article by Richard P. Peterson (1996a), Weitzman's book was an incredible source. It has been heavily used in court cases and has been cited numerous times in other scholarly articles, textbooks, and magazines. Weitzman herself has testified before Congress based on the findings of her study. But has a mistake been made?

As you read the reanalysis provided by Peterson, Weitzman's reply to Peterson, and Peterson's subsequent response to Weitzman, ask yourself, How significant is the replication of studies? Use the checklist provided in Chapter 2, "Evaluating Family Scholarship" (page 54) to decide whether Peterson and Weitzman have each adhered to standard, sound practices in family scholarship.

■ ■ ■

A Re-Evaluation of the Economic Consequences of Divorce

Richard R. Peterson

For several reasons, one book, Weitzman's *The Divorce Revolution* (1985), stands out among studies of the economic consequences of divorce. First, Weitzman reported that the decline in women's standard of living after divorce was much worse than was previously thought. Prior studies had reported an average decline for women of between 13 percent and 35 percent. Weitzman reported that the average standard of living for women who divorced in Los Angeles in 1977 declined by 73 percent after divorce, which is particularly striking when one considers that the *maximum* possible decline is 100 percent. Second, the gender gap in standards of living after divorce was much greater than previously thought. While the average decline for women was 73 percent, Weitzman reported that men's standard of living improved by 42 percent. Finally, she argued that these economic consequences of divorce are due to no-fault divorce and other reforms introduced in California in 1970. These reforms eliminated fault-based grounds for divorce, based alimony awards on financial need, required equal division of marital property, and included new procedures to reduce hostility and conflict. Because those supporting reform had claimed that no-fault divorces would place men and women on an equal footing, Weitzman's book has raised serious questions about no-fault legislation.

The Divorce Revolution received considerable attention in academic, legal, and popular publications. It was reviewed in at least 22 social science journals, 12 law reviews, and 10 national magazines and newspapers. The book received the American Sociological Association's 1986 Book Award for "Distinguished Contribution to Scholarship" (Weitzman 1986). From 1986 to 1993, it was cited in 348 social science articles (based on a search of the Social Science Citation Index) and in more than 250 law review articles (based on a search of legal periodicals indexed in Westlaw). *The Divorce Revolution* was also discussed widely in the popular press: It was cited over 85 times in newspapers and over 25 times in national magazines from 1985 to 1993. Re-

Direct correspondence to Richard R. Peterson, Social Science Research Council, 810 Seventh Avenue, New York, NY 10019 (peterson@ssrc.org). An earlier version of this paper was presented at the 1994 annual meeting of the American Sociological Association in Los Angeles. I thank Jo Dixon, Claire Fratello, Kathleen Gerson, Saul Hoffman, Robert Max Jackson, Herbert Jacob, the *ASR* Editor, Deputy Editor, and three *ASR* reviewers for their helpful comments on earlier drafts of this paper. Heather J. Naylor provided valuable research assistance. Anne Colby, Director of the Murray Research Center of Radcliffe College was instrumental in facilitating this project. Tonya Zucconi, Mimi Shields, and Cathy Maraist of the Murray Research Center generously provided assistance and advice in accessing the data. [Reviewers acknowledged by the author include Thomas J. Espenshade, Karen Holden, Lynn Smith-Lovin, and Annemette Sørensen. —ED.]

Richard R. Peterson, "A Re-Evaluation of the Economic Consequences of Divorce," *American Sociological Review*, 61 (June 1996), pp. 528–536. Used with permission of the American Sociological Association and the author.

markably, *The Divorce Revolution* has also been cited in at least 24 legal cases in state Appellate and Supreme courts (based on a search of legal cases indexed in Westlaw), and was cited once by the U.S. Supreme Court (Abraham 1989).

Much of the attention received by *The Divorce Revolution* focused on the contrast between the 73 percent *decline* in women's standard of living and the 42 percent *rise* in the standard of living of men. Most reviews reported this as a major finding, describing it as staggering, startling, or dramatic. A legal history of American women cited Weitzman's results and concluded ". . . it is difficult to exaggerate the economic problems created by no-fault reform of divorce" (Hoff 1991; also see Hewlett 1986). A review by Polikoff (1986) concluded ". . . the serious research in this book should form the basis for moving forward with much needed legal reforms" (p. 116). In fact, the findings on the economic consequences of divorce did affect subsequent divorce law reforms and debates about those reforms. For example, the California State Senate Task Force on Family Equity was formed in response to *The Divorce Revolution*, and some of its recommendations were enacted in 1987 and 1988 (Weitzman 1992).

The most cited statistic from *The Divorce Revolution is* the finding that women's average standard of living declines by 73 percent in the first year after divorce. While this finding continues to be cited, some scholars began to question it soon after the book was published (Thornton 1986; Furstenberg 1987; Sugarman 1990). Some raised questions about the sample, which consisted of 228 individuals who received a divorce in Los Angeles in 1977. Among the criticisms were assertions that the sample was too small (Furstenberg 1987; Abraham 1989), that the sample was not representative of Los Angeles because of the low response rate (42 percent) (Thornton 1986; Hoffman and Duncan 1988; Abraham 1989) and that California is not representative of the U.S. because few states have similar divorce legislation (Jacob 1988). Others noted that the findings were in-

consistent with results based on representative national samples (Thornton 1986; Peterson 1989; Morgan 1991). Analyses based on such samples found that women's standard of living declines between 13 percent and 35 percent in the first year after marital disruption (Nestel, Mercier, and Shaw 1983; Duncan and Hoffman 1985; David and Flory 1989; Peterson 1989; Stirling 1989; see Holden and Smock 1991 and Sørenson 1992 for reviews). Similarly, estimates based on national samples showed that men's standard of living increases by 11 to 13 percent after marital disruption (Duncan and Hoffman 1985; David and Flory 1989). These percentages are not nearly as large as those reported by Weitzman.

One of the most serious critiques of Weitzman's book was whether the 73 percent decline reported for women in Figure 3 (1985:338) is consistent with other data Weitzman presented. Using income data for subsets of the sample presented in other tables in the book, Hoffman and Duncan (1988) estimated that the decline in the standard of living for divorced women in the sample is about 33 percent. They concluded that if the data in the other tables were accurate, Weitzman's estimate of a 73 percent decline for women is probably in error. Faludi (1991) highlighted and defended Hoffman and Duncan's findings. However, considerably more attention has been given to the findings in *The Divorce Revolution* than to critiques of those findings.

In spite of numerous questions and critiques, many still accept Weitzman's estimates. The findings continue to be cited without question in some social science articles (e.g., Lonsdorf 1991; Seiling and Harris 1991; Butler and Weatherly 1992; Haffey and Cohen 1992), law review articles (e.g., Fineman 1986; Melli 1986; Woodhouse 1990; Allen 1992), and newspapers and magazines (e.g., Mansnerus 1995; Thurow 1995). Okin (1991) defends the findings, arguing that they "are far less surprising than is the fact that people have been so surprised by them" (p. 384). Critics of no-fault legislation cite the 73 percent decline reported for women as evidence that no-fault has had disastrous economic consequences for women and children (e.g., Hewlett 1986; Okin 1991; Parkman 1992).

▪ ▪ ▪

I reanalyze Weitzman's data and demonstrate that the results reported in *The Divorce Revolution* are in error. I also find that the erroneous results cannot be attributed to weaknesses of the sample or to errors in the dataset.

DATA

I analyze the dataset used by Weitzman (1985) in *The Divorce Revolution* The original sample was drawn from the court dockets of divorces recorded in Los Angeles County between May and July 1977. Interviews were conducted in 1977 and 1978 with respondents from 228 of these couples. Only one member of each couple was selected for interviewing. Respondents were selected to yield a final sample with equal numbers of men and women (114 each). Long-married couples and high-SES couples were oversampled and weights were used to correct for this oversampling.

The data I analyze are derived from the computer files and paper records of the original interviews as provided by Weitzman to the Murray Research Center at Radcliffe College. Two computer files are available: one is an SPSS system file and the other file contains the raw data. Weitzman (personal communication) and the staff of the Murray Research Center reported that each computer file contained inaccurately transcribed data, and that there were numerous inaccuracies in the data for the income variables. I compared data for selected variables from each computer file to the original paper records to determine which computer file most accurately duplicated the data in the paper records. I found that the raw data file contained fewer discrepancies than did the SPSS system file.[1] Because the raw data file was more accu-

rate, I used it to create a third data file, corrected using the information from the paper records.

To create this corrected file of raw data, I compared the raw data in the computer file to the responses from the paper records of the original interviews. Coding from the paper records focused on the approximately 100 variables needed to analyze the economic consequences of divorce. Whenever data in the computer file differed from information in the paper records, I corrected the data in the computer file.[2] Errors were found in one or more income variables for 27 cases. Except where otherwise noted, all analyses in this paper are based on the corrected raw data file I created.

MEASURES

Measures were created to replicate the original analysis as described in Weitzman (1985, chap. 10). However, because Weitzman did not explain how she handled a variety of measurement problems, I describe in detail the procedures I used to create the measures.

Like Weitzman, I use the *ratio of income to needs* as a measure of the standard of living. Respondents were asked to report their own and their spouse's income in the year before their separation, as well as their own and their ex-spouse's income at the time of the interview (i.e., within one year of the divorce). Weitzman's findings are based on three measures of the income/needs ratio for each divorced couple: one for the couple's household in the year before separation, one for the husband's post-divorce household, and one for the wife's post-divorce household. Although only one member of each couple was interviewed, each respondent was asked to report information about his or her ex-spouse as well as for him- or herself. Therefore data on husbands' post-divorce households are based on reports from the male respondents for 114 couples plus reports from the female respondents about their ex-husbands for the other 114 couples. Data for women's post-divorce households were similarly derived.

Also like Weitzman, I measure *changes in the standard of living* over the period between the year before the couple separated (stopped living together) and the year after a legal divorce was granted. Since the time between separation and divorce is longer for some couples than for others, the change in the income/needs ratio was measured over different lengths of time for different individuals. For most couples (81 percent), this time period was three years or less, and for virtually all couples (96 percent), the change was measured over a period of seven years or less.

Predivorce income is the sum of the incomes of the husband and the wife for the year prior to their separation. Those who were not working for pay and who reported no other sources of income were coded as having no income. Predivorce income was coded as missing for 33 cases who mistakenly reported income from a year *after* their year of separation. Because the year of separation varied, I adjusted predivorce income for inflation and converted to 1977 dollars.

Husband's post-divorce income is his income at the time of the interview after *subtracting* the annual amount of any awards for alimony and/or child support. The wife's post-divorce income includes her income at the time of the interview after *adding* the annual amount of any alimony and/or child support awards.[3] Weitzman used (and I use) the amount of *awards* rather than the amount of actual *payments* to estimate the effects of full compliance with court-ordered payments.

In Weitzman's study, questions on post-divorce income of husbands and wives did not ask about any income provided by a new spouse or by any other adults in the household. Because many respondents remarried or had live-in partners (31 percent of men and 14 percent of women), this income measure underestimated the income of some households. Although they were not asked, 26 respondents did include income from spouses or other adults in the household when reporting post-divorce income. These amounts were subtracted from the post-divorce income they reported, because this information was not available for all respondents in the sample.

When annual income data were missing, data on weekly, bimonthly, or monthly earnings were annualized and used to estimate annual income. Although I made every effort to identify an accurate measure of income from the data available in the questionnaire, predivorce and/or post-divorce income data remained missing for 66 men and 67 women. These cases are excluded from the analyses I report in this paper. Weitzman did not report how missing data were handled in her analysis of income/needs ratios.

The measure of economic need used by Weitzman is based on the Bureau of Labor Statistics' Lower Standard Budget for an urban family of four in 1977 (Weitzman 1985: 481–82). She adjusted for family size, age of the household head, age of the oldest child, and whether one or both spouses lived in the household. Making these adjustments with this dataset is problematic, however, due to inconsistencies in the type and quality of available data. Among those respondents for whom income data were available, age of the household head was missing for one male respondent. Since economic need could not be computed for this case, I excluded it from the analysis, increasing the total number of men with missing data to 67. The adjustments for family size and age of the oldest child are subject to error because some information on household composition was not available. For the predivorce household, no questions were asked about the presence of stepchildren or of adults other than the parents. The measure of predivorce need therefore assumes that the household includes only the married couple and their own children, if any. For the post-divorce household, data is available on the presence of a new spouse or cohabitor.[4] However, information about the number of stepchildren and other adults in the post-divorce household is available only for respondents' households (not for their ex-spouses' households). I use the procedure employed by Weitzman (1985)—I include all available information about household composition in calculating measures of post-divorce need.[5] However, as noted earlier, information on post-divorce *income* provided by new spouses, cohabitors, or other adults in the household was not available. In Weitzman's study, and in this paper, new spouses, cohabitors and other adults are included in the calculation of economic need, but are *not* included in the calculation of income.

RESULTS

Weitzman (1985) reports results on the change in the average income/needs ratio from the time of separation to one year after a legal divorce was granted (Weitzman 1985: 323). Although she does not specify whether the "average" she uses is the median or the mean, she describes her analysis (Weitzman 1985:337) as following the method used by Hoffman and Holmes (1976). As they report changes in the mean income/needs ratio, I present my results based on the mean.

Results based on the corrected raw data file using the measures of the income/needs ratio described above show that the effects of divorce are not nearly as large as those reported by Weitzman (1985) (see Table 1, Panel A). The mean income/needs ratio is 10 percent higher for men in the year after divorce than it was in the year before separation: for women the mean income/needs ratio was 27 percent lower.

These findings represent as exact a replication of the original analysis as is possible. They are based on data coded from the original interviews, the results are weighted, and the analysis replicates all the key methodological decisions described by Weitzman in *The Divorce Revolution*. The measures of post-divorce income exclude income of new spouses or new partners. New spouses or partners, however, are counted

TABLE 1   Changes in Income/Needs Ratio for Men and Women: Divorced Individuals Sample, Los Angeles, 1977–1978

Variable	Men	Women
PANEL A		
Income/Needs Ratio and Percent Change Based on Corrected Raw Data File		
Mean income/needs ratio in year prior to separation	4.42	4.58
Mean income/needs ratio in year after divorce	4.88	3.34
Percent change	+10%	−27%
Number of cases	161	161
PANEL B		
Percent Change Based on Uncorrected Raw Data File		
Percent change	+7%	−28%
Number of cases	155	157
PANEL C		
Percent Change Based on Uncorrected SPSS System File		
Percent change	+7%	−20%
Number of cases	135	140

Note: See text for a description of the three data files. Means and percentages are weighted; unweighted Ns are reported to reflect true sample size.

as members of the post-divorce household and therefore increase economic need. Post-divorce income measures assume full compliance with alimony and child support awards. Based on the findings reported here, it is clear that the results reported in *The Divorce Revolution* for the change in the average standard of living are in error. They could not have been derived from the data and methods described in the book.

The results presented here for both men and women are within the range of results reported from analyses of representative national samples. Thus, while the quality and representativeness of the Los Angeles sample are still open to question, the differences between Weitzman's results and those of other studies cannot be attributed to problems with the sample. The result for women reported here (–27 percent) is also reasonably close to the –33 percent estimated by Hoffman and Duncan (1988) who used the incomplete income tables presented in a Weitzman's book.

To explore the likelihood that the data could have produced Weitzman's reported results, I examined changes experienced by individuals in the sample. Approximately 10 percent of the weighted sample of women experienced a decline in their standard of living of 73 percent or more. While this suggests that a subgroup of women do experience the severe economic consequences Weitzman described, the small size of this group indicates that the *average* decline cannot be 73 percent.[6]

To determine whether Weitzman's findings on changes in standard of living were affected by her methodological decisions (which I have replicated here), I re-estimated the results under a variety of assumptions using the corrected raw data file (results not shown). Results for the median income/needs ratio differ only slightly from results based on the mean. Because respondents' reports of post-divorce data for their ex-spouses are likely to reflect some guessing and errors, I also examined results based solely on respondents' reports of their own income and household composition. Results based on respondents' self-reports show that the mean standard of living increased by 11 percent for men after divorce, and declined by 34 percent for women. Because adjusting post-divorce income to reflect alimony and child support *awards* may overstate the amount of income actually transferred, I adjusted the post-divorce income of men and women based on the reported amounts of alimony and child support *actually paid*. This analysis produces little change in the

results.[7] Since data on the income of new spouses and cohabitors were not available in the dataset, I also conducted an analysis to determine the consequences of excluding these household members from the estimation of economic need. If new spouses and cohabitors are not counted as contributing to post-divorce economic need, the mean standard of living for men increases by 20 percent after divorce, while the mean for women declines by 25 percent.

I also attempted to assess the effects of alternative ways of handling missing income data (results not shown). If cases with imputed estimates of annual income based on weekly, bimonthly, or monthly income data are removed, men's standard of living increases by 15 percent, while women's declines by 28 percent. To determine whether having income data for all cases in the dataset could substantially change the results, I made some radical assumptions. For men, I imputed $0 of income to all those for whom pre-divorce income was missing. For women, I imputed $0 of post-divorce income to all those for whom post-divorce income was missing. This approach maximizes the gender disparity in results. Under these extreme (and unrealistic) assumptions, men's standard of living increases by 23 percent, while women's declines by 34 percent. These results suggest that even having complete income data from all respondents would not produce substantially different results.

Taken together, all of these alternative analyses suggest that the findings I report are stable across different estimation methods. In other words, analyses based on a variety of different assumptions do not produce results substantially different from those I report in Table 1, Panel A.

As described above, examining the paper records from Weitzman's study revealed that both the raw data file and the SPSS system file contained inaccurately transcribed data. Since an analysis of one of these uncorrected data files may have produced the erroneous results reported in Weitzman (1985), I conducted analyses using each of the uncorrected data files. Estimates of changes in the standard of living based on the uncorrected raw data file (Table 1, Panel B) are similar to those based on the corrected raw data file (Table 1, Panel A). The mean standard of living increases by 7 percent for men after divorce, while the mean for women declines by 28 percent. Estimates based on an analysis of the SPSS system file, which contained more errors than the uncorrected raw data file, actually show a *smaller* decline for women (Table 1, Panel C). The mean standard of living increases by 7 percent for men after divorce, and declines by 20 percent for women. These analyses indicate that the data errors in the two computer files do *not* account for the incorrect results reported by Weitzman.

I tried to replicate Weitzman's analysis as closely as possible with the information she presented in her book. I also examined reasonable alternative approaches for analyzing the corrected data file, and I examined the two uncorrected data files. I have been unable to discover how Weitzman's results could have been obtained. The most likely explanation is that errors in her analysis of the data were responsible for producing her results,

CONCLUSION

I have used the same data analyzed in Weitzman's (1985) *The Divorce Revolution*, have replicated the procedures she reported as closely as possible, and have demonstrated that her reported results are in error. Weitzman's much-cited estimate of a 73 percent decline in women's standard of living after divorce is inaccurate and the estimate of a 42 percent increase for men is inaccurate as well. The figures based on the corrected data are –27 percent and +10 percent, respectively, for women and men.

Although I have shown that the economic consequences of divorce are not as severe as those described by Weitzman, this reanalysis is

not intended to minimize the significance of a 27 percent decline in women's standard of living after divorce. The gender gap in economic outcomes after divorce is a significant problem and must be addressed through legal reforms and public policy. However, as Weitzman acknowledges, others reported the gender gap in economic outcomes after divorce long before she did (Hoffman and Holmes 1976; Espenshade 1979). Yet others' estimates of the economic consequences of divorce did not receive much attention, while the inaccurately large estimates reported by Weitzman were widely publicized.

The estimates I report, as well as estimates from previous research, provide a more solid basis for considering policy remedies to address the serious economic problems women face after divorce. For example, the severe economic consequences of divorce described in *The Divorce Revolution* have been used to campaign against no-fault divorce in the United States (see Faludi 1991:19). The inaccurate findings have distorted the debate over no-fault legislation because some critics attributed differences between Weitzman's results, based on a California sample, and those of other studies to California's no-fault divorce laws. These critics argued that the economic consequences of divorce for women were much more severe in California than elsewhere in the United States because of California's no-fault divorce legislation. In fact, I have demonstrated that the findings reported by Weitzman were inaccurate. The corrected findings reported here do not support the argument that the economic consequences of divorce for women were more severe in California than elsewhere.

Clearly, Weitzman is not responsible for all the arguments made by those who cite her data—she did not argue in *The Divorce Revolution* that states should return to fault-based divorce laws. However, extreme findings are likely to be noticed and to be used to support extreme points of view. When extreme results are in error, they distort discussions of public policy and social issues (Cherlin 1990).

Social scientists must draw conclusions and develop new research projects based on reliable results from prior studies. Weitzman's findings have unnecessarily raised questions about the results of other studies and have diverted attention from more reliable estimates of the economic consequences of divorce. I hope the corrected results I report here resolve these questions and redirect our attention to more reliable data for developing policy recommendations.

ENDNOTES

1. In addition to errors in the income data, over 450 variables were incorrectly coded for 67 cases in the SPSS system file because they had been merged into the file using incorrect ID numbers.

2. Paper records were missing for 11 of the 228 cases. Data for these cases were drawn entirely from the computer file containing the raw data. This may introduce small errors in the analyses. Also, paper records for a section of the questionnaire concerning child support were missing for 40 of the 119 respondents who had children at the time of the divorce. These data were also derived from the computer file containing the raw data. While this procedure may cause some error, it is likely to be small—for the 69 cases where paper records on this section of the questionnaire are available, only 4 errors were found in the computer records.

3. Because 51 respondents (mostly women) reported their income *after* taking alimony and child support payments into account, the post-divorce income data for these respondents was corrected before making the adjustments described here.

4. For women in the sample who remarried or are cohabiting, data on the age of their spouse or partner is not available. In such cases, the woman's age was used as a proxy for age of household head.

5. When age of oldest child was missing (N = 18 for men, N = 17 for women), economic need was based on the typical level of need for a family of the same size and type.

6. Interestingly, about 9 percent of men also experienced a decline in standard of living of 73 percent or more after divorce. Weitzman did not address this finding.

7. That little change was observed can be explained by three factors: First, in many divorces, alimony or child support was not awarded. Second, when alimony and child support were awarded, many ex-husbands were paying the full amount of the award or more. Finally, when ex-husbands paid less than the amount of the award, the difference between the amount of the payment and the award was not usually large.

REFERENCES

Abraham, Jed H. 1989. "'The Divorce Revolution' Revisited: A Counter-Revolutionary Critique." *Northern Illinois Law Review* 9:251–98.

Allen, Monica. 1992. "Child-State Jurisdiction." *Family Law Quarterly* 26:293–318.

Butler, Sandra S. and Richard A. Weatherly. 1992. "Poor Women at Midlife and Categories of Neglect." *Social Work* 37:51–15.

Cherlin, Andrew. 1990. "The Strange Career of the 'Harvard-Yale Study.'" *Public Opinion Quarterly* 54:117–24.

David, Martin and Thomas Flory. 1989. "Changes in Marital Status and Short-Term Income Dynamics." Pp. 15–22 in *Individuals and Families in Transition*, edited by H. V. Beaton, D. A. Ganni, and D. T. Frankel. Washington, DC: U.S. Bureau of the Census.

Duncan, Greg and Saul Hoffman. 1985. "A Reconsideration of the Economic Consequences of Divorce." *Demography* 22:485–97.

Espenshade, Thomas J. 1979. "The Economic Consequences of Divorce." *Journal of Marriage and the Family* 41:615–25.

Faludi, Susan. 1991. *Backlash*. New York: Crown Publishers.

Fineman, Martha L. 1986. "Illusive Equality: On Weitzman's *Divorce Revolution*." *American Bar Foundation Research Journal* 1986:781–90.

Furstenberg, Frank F. 1987. "The Divorce Dilemma: After the Revolution." *Contemporary Sociology* 16:556–55.

Haffey, Martha and Phyllis Malkin Cohen. 1992. "Treatment Issues for Divorcing Women." *Families in Society* 73:142–48.

Hewlett, Sylvia. 1986. *A Lesser Life*. New York: William Morrow.

Hoff, Joan. 1991. *Law, Gender, and Injustice*. New York: New York University Press.

Hoffman, Saul and Greg Duncan. 1988. "What Are the Economic Consequences of Divorce?" *Demography* 25:641–45.

Hoffman, Saul and John Holmes. 1976. "Husbands, Wives, and Divorce." Pp. 23–75 in *Five Thousand American Families,* edited by G. Duncan and J. Morgan. Ann Arbor, MI: Institute for Social Research.

Holden, Karen C. and Pamela J. Smock. 1991. "The Economic Costs of Marital Dissolution." *Annual Review of Sociology* 17:51–75.

Jacob, Herbert. 1986. "Faulting No-Fault." *American Bar Foundation Research Journal* 1986:773–80.

———. 1985. *Silent Revolution.* Chicago, IL: University of Chicago Press.

Lonsdorf. Barbara J. 1991. "The Role of Coercion in Affecting Women's Inferior Outcomes in Divorce." *Journal of Divorce and Remarriage* 16:69–106.

Mansnerus, Laura. 1995. "The Divorce Backlash." *Working Woman* 20(February):41–45.

Melli, Marygold. 1986. "Constructing a Social Problem: The Post-Divorce Plight of Women and Children." *American Bar Foundation Research Journal* 1986:759–72.

Morgan, Leslie A. 1991. *After Marriage Ends.* Newbury Park, CA: Sage.

Nestel, Gilbert, Jacqueline Mercier, and Lois B. Shaw. 1983. "Economic Consequences of Midlife Change in Marital Status." Pp. 109–25 1 in *Unplanned Careers* edited by L. B. Shaw. Lexington, MA: Lexington Books.

Okin, Susan Molier. 1991. "Economic Equality after Divorce." *Dissent* 38:383–87.

Parkman, Allen M. 1992. *No-Fault Divorce.* San Francisco, CA: Westview.

Peterson, Richard R. 1989. *Women, Work, and Divorce.* Albany, NY: State University of New York Press.

Polikoff, Nancy D. 1986. Review of *The Divorce Revolution* by Lenore J. Weitzman. *American Bar Association Journal* 72:112–16.

Seiling, Sharon B. and Harriet Harris. 1991. "Child Support Awards: Links with Alimony and In-Kind Support." *Journal of Divorce and Remarriage* 16:121–35.

Sørenson, Annemette. 1992. "Estimating the Economic Consequences of Separation and Divorce: A Cautionary Tale from the United States." Pp. 263-82 in *Economic Consequences of Divorce: The International Perspective,* edited by L. J. Weitzman and M. MacLean. New York: Oxford University Press.

Stirling, Kate J. 1989. "Women Who Remain Divorced: The Long-Term Economic Consequences," *Social Science Quarterly* 70:549–61.

Sugarman, Stephen D. 1990. "Dividing Financial Interests on Divorce." Pp. 130–65 in *Divorce Reform at the Crossroads,* edited by S. D. Sugarman and H. H. Kay. New Haven, CT: Yale University Press.

Thornton, Arland. 1986. "The Fragile Family." *Family Planning Perspectives* 18:243–44.

Thurow, Lester. 1995. "Companies Merge; Families Break Up." *New York Times,* September 3, p. 11.

Weitzman, Lenore J. 1985. *The Divorce Revolution: The Unexpected Social and Economic Consequences for Women and Children in America.* New York: The Free Press.

———. 1986. "Bringing the Law Back In." *American Bar Foundation Research Journal* 1986:791–97,

———. 1992. "Alimony: Its Premature Demise and Recent Resurgence in the U.S." Pp. 247–62 in *Economic Consequences of Divorce: The International Perspective,* edited by L. J. Weitzman and M. MacLean. New York: Oxford University Press.

Woodhouse, Barbara B. 1990. "Towards a Revitalization of Family Law." *Texas Law Review* 69:245–90.

■ ■ ■

Women Still Suffer the Economic Consequences of Divorce More
What Weitzman Said Back to Peterson

Brenda J. Vander Mey[1]

Generally speaking, sociologists are socialized to expect that their research will receive critical appraisals from time to time. I would be the first to say that there aren't too many of us who welcome critical appraisal when it is more negative than positive. Nonetheless, we generally expect that our work, once out in the public, will be carefully reviewed by our colleagues. And, no doubt, it is sometimes hard to adequately convey one's response back to one's critics. Put simply, it can be very difficult at times. Undoubtedly, this becomes even more challenging when the work in question has been "out"—in circulation—for some time.

Thus, that Peterson would take a second look at Weitzman's data is in keeping with the self-correction of the science itself. And, of course, it is reasonable to expect that criticism of one's work may not be seen as all that welcome.

How does Weitzman respond to Peterson? Professor Weitzman recognizes that Professor Peterson was asking whether she had conducted her research in a responsible manner, and also whether her study met the rigor generally expected of studies such as this (Weitzman, 1996). This, of course, is not surprising given the fact that the Ethical Code for the American Sociological Association (http://www.asanet.org/ecoderev.htm) requires that sociologists be careful, thorough, and honest in their research.

Professor Weitzman begins her response by congratulating Professor Peterson for undertaking the seemingly Herculean task of reconstructing her data. She states that the greatest challenge here was the fact that the original data files had been lost. Apparently, she has been unable to find these files for some time. They might have been lost during relocations to several universities around the country. Each time she moved, new data programmers were assigned the task of maintaining and cleaning her data files. Thus, how clean the "master file" is is debatable. (Therefore, Peterson's analysis of her data would be debatable as well.) To compound the situation, different programmers apparently merged smaller subfiles, and these subfiles replaced the original clean master file (Weitzman: 1996: 462). According to Weitzman, she in good faith and conscience thought she was relying on clean data when she wrote her now famous book.

At this point in the article, in my view, Weitzman's explanation becomes a little confusing, since it is not made clear exactly what happened to the original files. Regardless, Professor Weitzman basically asserts that unbeknownst to her, others working on her data files either lost the original file and/or created dirty files from which she conducted her analysis.

In addition, she suggests that the high figure (73%) might be due to a weighting error that occurred during the analysis (p. 463). She also reminds Professor Peterson that the scholarly awards and numerous accolades accorded her book were not because of one paragraph or one single statistic in her book; rather, the attention and rewards were forthcoming because her book illustrated that the effects of divorce on women constitute a social problem. Furthermore, her book documented that the economic decline women experience after divorce has serious effects on the lives of children. To that end, then, the book was useful in that it was used to alter policy in California. According to Weitzman, this book was used successfully to pass 14 new laws in California. Implied here was that these 14 laws passed as a result of her work were directed toward abating gender-based discrimination in divorce settlements. Ultimately, she argues that extent of the gap aside, the fact that a gap exists between men and women when it comes to the economic effects of divorce is an issue worthy of considered and sustained attention (Weitzman 1996: 463).

I would encourage readers to secure their own copy of her article as it appeared in the *American Sociological Review*. A solid class exercise might be to see if I have adequately captured her major points in her rebuttal and explanation. Some of the essence of her article is reflected in Peterson's rejoinder to Weitzman's response. By careful reading of his rejoinder, it becomes apparent that Professor Peterson is not convinced by Weitzman's explanations. And, he remains concerned that laws and policies were influenced by faulty research.

ENDNOTE

1. Professor Weitzman refused to allow the reprinting of her article in this text. Several attempts were made to obtain her permission. Nearly ten months after the original request, which was followed up with repeat requests, Professor Weitzman offered a one-word response. That response was: "NO."

REFERENCES

American Sociological Society. ASA Code of Ethics, Approved by ASA Membership in Spring of 1997. Washington, DC: American Sociological Society. http://www.asanet.org/ecoderev.htm

Weitzman, Lenore J. "The Economic Consequences of Divorce are Still Unequal: Comment on Peterson." *American Sociological Review*, 61 (June 1996), 537–538. Author refused to allow the reprinting of this article.

■ ■ ■

Statistical Errors, Faulty Conclusions, Misguided Policy
Reply to Weitzman[1]

Richard R. Peterson

Lenore Weitzman (1996) and I agree that there is a significant gender gap in the economic consequences of divorce, that this gap results in financial hardship for many divorced women and their children, and that legal reforms and public policy must address this hardship. I made these points not only in the article published here, but also in my book (Peterson 1989), which examines in-depth the economic problems women face after divorce. I share the concerns of Weitzman and many other scholars who have addressed these problems, and I hope that no one reading our exchange will ignore these very important points of agreement between us.[2]

In this rejoinder to Weitzman, I develop three points. First, none of the issues she raises regarding the computer files or the sample weights change my conclusion that her estimates are inaccurate. Second, my results lead to different conclusions about the effect of no-fault divorce legislation on divorced women's standard of living. Finally, Weitzman's inaccurate estimates have seriously distorted policy discussions about no-fault divorce.

Weitzman (1996) now concedes that her estimates of changes in standard of living after divorce are incorrect. She claims that mistakes were made by computer experts, who botched the original analysis, did not properly check the data or analysis, incorrectly constructed the data files, and finally lost them. Her discussion of these problems may lead readers to conclude

that it is now impossible to use the data to draw any conclusions about the magnitude of changes in standard of living after divorce. This is not the case. Because I had access to the paper records from the original interviews, I was able to reproduce a "clean" data file. In doing so, I discovered all the problems she mentions, and I was able to resolve them satisfactorily.

The Murray Research Center archives include virtually all of the paper records of the original interviews. Note 2 in my paper (Peterson 1996:53–31) describes what was missing; these materials are missing because Weitzman did not archive them at the Center. Using these paper records, supplemented by information from the computer file of raw data, I created a corrected raw data file. I was able to clarify incomplete or inconsistent responses by examining the answers to related questions and the explanations that were sometimes written in the margins of the questionnaires. This corrected raw data file reconstructs the (lost) "cleaned" data file Weitzman refers to.

Weitzman's (1996) claim that the errors resulting from mismatched ID numbers cannot be corrected is inaccurate. As I explained in note 1 (Peterson 1996), I examined the paper records to determine which ID number was correct, and corrected the errors that had been created by mismatching files.

Weitzman's (1996) reference to "dirty data" in two computer files might suggest to some

Richard R. Peterson, "Statistical Errors, Faulty Conclusions, Misguided Policy: Reply to Weitzman," *American Sociological Review*, 61 (June 1996), pp. 539–540. Used with permission of the American Sociological Association and the author.

readers that the erroneous figures in her book were the result of analyzing these "dirty" data files. Yet I analyzed these two "uncorrected data files" and could not reproduce the erroneous results (Peterson 1996: 533, table 1, panels B and C).

Weitzman (1996) suggests that her erroneous findings may have resulted from a sample weighting error. I conducted unweighted analyses using the corrected raw data file to determine whether failure to apply weights could produce the erroneous figures. The unweighted results showed a 43 percent decline for women's standard of living and a 26 percent increase for men. While these results are larger than those based on weighted analyses, they are not nearly as large as those reported in *The Divorce Revolution* (Weitzman 1985). It is also unlikely that an incorrect application of the weights could have produced the 73 percent figure, since only 15 percent of the women in the unweighted sample experienced a decline as large as 73 percent. In summary, none of the problems or alternative explanations discussed in Weitzman's (1996) comment explains how the erroneous findings were arrived at.

Second, my results lead to different conclusions about the impact of no-fault divorce legislation on the gender gap in economic outcomes after divorce. In *The Divorce Revolution* Weitzman (1985) concluded that her findings on changes in men's and women's standards of living after divorce ". . . make it clear that, for all its aims at fairness, the current no-fault system of divorce is inflicting a high economic toll upon women and children" (p. 401). However, my re-analysis of Weitzman's data shows that the changes in standard of living after divorce in California were similar to those reported in other studies conducted both before and after Weitzman's. This suggests that no-fault legislation and related reforms did *not* increase the gender gap in economic outcomes. Rather, the gender gap remained as serious as it had been under the fault-based system. This significantly undermines the argument that specific features

of the no-fault legislation resulted in larger declines in women's standard of living after divorce than had been prevalent under the fault-based system.

This brings me to my final point—Weitzman's inaccurate estimates were widely circulated, and the conclusions drawn from them have seriously distorted policy discussions about no-fault divorce. Weitzman (1996) contends that her analysis of the law in action, not her erroneous statistics, were responsible for the attention *The Divorce Revolution* received. Certainly Weitzman's analysis of the legal system was reported as a major finding. However it is misleading for her "to put in perspective the 73/42 percent datum" by arguing, "It is one statistic in a 500-page book" (Weitzman 1996: 537). These figures are featured prominently on the book jacket, as well as in the introduction and the concluding chapter. Most reviews of her book cited the figures as a major finding, as *did Weitzman herself* in testimony at a Congressional hearing (Weitzman 1986), and the figures propelled *The Divorce Revolution* into the eyes of the public and policymakers.

Furthermore, even if Weitzman believed that these results were not a major finding, she must have been aware that they were receiving considerable publicity. Yet when she realized that there were problems with her figures, she did not publish or disseminate a warning that she could not replicate them.

Weitzman (1996) takes credit for what she and I agree are some beneficial policy changes resulting from *The Divorce Revolution*, and neither she nor I support a return to fault-based divorce. However, Weitzman's erroneous results have lent support to those seeking to restrict access to no-fault divorce (see Faludi 1996). Whether or not one agrees with those restrictions, and whether or not the incorrect figures influence the passage of new restrictions, policy arguments about no-fault legislation should not be clouded by the use of the erroneous figures reported in *The Divorce Revolution*. While social scientists cannot control how results are reported or used in policy debates, we need to take responsibility for correcting errors that may lead to faulty conclusions or to misguided policies. I hope that my article contributes to a clarification of the conclusions that can be drawn from Weitzman's data and to a redirection of the policy debate to address what Weitzman and I agree is an unfair and unjust gender gap in the economic consequences of divorce.

ENDNOTES

1. Direct correspondence to Richard R. Peterson, Social Science Research Council, 810 Seventh Ave., New York, NY 10019 (peterson@ssrc.org).

2. Weitzman's (1996) concluding sentence may lead readers to misinterpret how I view my results. She states, ". . . the post-divorce standards of living drop, as Peterson contends, an average of *only* about 30 percent for women, and rise *only* about 10 percent for men . . ." (p. 538, her italics). I never used the word "only" to characterize my findings (Peterson 1996), nor did I imply that such changes in the standard of living are insignificant.

REFERENCES

Faludi, Susan. 1996. "Statistically Challenged." *The Nation* 262 (No. 15):10.

Peterson, Richard R. 1989. *Women, Work and Divorce.* Albany: State University of New York Press.

———. 1996. "A Re-Evaluation of the Economic Consequences of Divorce." *American Sociological Review* 61: 528–36.

Weitzman, Lenore J. 1985. *The Divorce Revolution: The Unexpected Social and Economic Consequences for Women and Children in America.* New York: The Free Press.

———. 1986. "Divorce: The Impact on Children and Families." Testimony presented at a Hearing before the Committee on Children, Youth and Families of the U.S. House of Representatives, June 19.

———. 1996. "The Economic Consequences of Divorce are Still Unequal." *American Sociological Review* 61:537–38.

Critical Thinking Questions

1. What key scientific and ethical points does Peterson make subsequent to his reanalysis of Weitzman's data?

2. Do you agree with Peterson's reservations of Weitzman's sample? Why or why not?

3. Is Weitzman's "feminization of poverty thesis" still valid? Does Peterson's reanalysis still give some merit to the "feminization of poverty thesis"? What other evidence do both Peterson and Weitzman provide in support of it?

4. Based on evidence provided by Peterson, do you think it might be more appropriate to argue that divorce is related to the "childrenization of poverty"? Explain your decision.

5. How do you think other sociologists have responded to Peterson's reexamination of Weitzman's data? Explain why you think they have responded in this way.

14 Singlehood in Perspective

1 t may seem odd to find a chapter on being single in a marriage and family textbook. The word *family* conjures images of married couples with children, not single people. However, being single is the one marital status that *all people* hold at some point in their lifetimes. In addition to being single prior to marriage, individuals also can become single again following a divorce or after the death of a spouse, and some choose not to marry. The majority of students who attend college during the "traditional" ages of 18 to 21 are single. Thus, the lack of a chapter on singles would be a huge oversight.

If singlehood is such a common experience, why, for years, have "family sociologists . . . either ignored singles or relegated them to boring, out-of-date discussions of dating" (Cargan 1983: 547)? The answer is rooted partially in cultural norms. Until recently, singlehood for both men and women was socially defined as a "temporary period prior to or in-between marriages" (Cargan 1983: 547). The United States has long had a *coupled culture,* in which it is expected that adults will marry and have children (Cargan and Melko 1982; Schwartzberg, Berliner, and Jacob 1995). Singlehood was ignored in family sociology for so long because it was seen as simply a way station on the route to marriage. Those who never married were generally dismissed as deviant.

The Rise in Singlehood: A Sociological Analysis

Today, single people can no longer be regarded simply as those who have not yet had the good fortune of finding a mate. The unmarried are one of the fastest-growing segments of the American population (Keith 1986). From 1900 to 1960, there was a steady drop in the number of singles (Buunk and van Driel 1989; Cargan and Melko 1982), but after 1960, the trend and the number of singles began to rise dramatically. Between 1970 and 1994, the number of never-married adults almost doubled, from 21.4 million to 44.2 million (Peterson 1996). In only 10 years, from 1980 to 1990, the number of singles increased at a rate 2.5 times faster than overall population growth ("The Singles Scene" 1992). In 1998, approximately 43.6 percent of Americans over the age of 15, 91.3 million people, were single (U.S. Bureau of the Census 1999).

The dramatic increase in the number of single people in recent decades has brought singlehood to the forefront of family studies. Sociologists have sought to answer two overriding questions about singles: Why has the number of single people risen so dramatically in recent years? and What is it like living as a single adult in a culture that strongly encourages marriage?

Statistics are valuable for identifying social trends, but the real work of the sociologist is *explaining why the trends occur.* If you were asked to explain why the number of single people has risen significantly since the 1960s, what would you say? After some consideration, you probably would conclude that the increase of single people is the result of several interrelated social forces. These social forces can be broadly divided into three categories: economic factors, demographic factors, and cultural factors.

Economic Factors

Economic factors include property, wealth, income, occupation, and employment, which relate to other factors of social class, such as education. The increase in singles can be attributed partly to economic changes. The Industrial Revolution, for example, had a tremendous impact on the social structure and family life, as you saw in Chapter 1. Staples (1981) argues that the change from an agrarian to an industrialized economy ultimately contributed to growth in the number of singles. With industrialization, more people migrated to urban areas, the economic base of families was weakened, and the amount of leisure time available to individuals grew as the new middle class expanded. These factors contributed to an increase in both the acceptance and practice of remaining single. However, industrialization alone cannot account for the rise in the number of singles, because the number of unmarried individuals steadily declined through the first half of the twentieth century, after the country was fully industrialized. Therefore, other factors also must explain the increase of singles.

The **consumer demand model** has been used to describe other economic factors that explain the rise in the number of singles during the latter part of the twentieth century. The consumer demand model assumes that privacy is a valued commodity that individuals are willing to pay for when they have the economic resources. This model suggests that the rise in average income following World War II allowed people to purchase autonomy and privacy; more people could afford to live alone, which ultimately led to a rise in the number of single households (Pampel 1983; Santi 1990). However, immediately following World War II, when the economy was strongest, the number of singles declined (Santi 1990). Also, the economic recession of the 1970s did not precipitate a drop in the number of singles. Income alone, then, cannot account for the rise in the number of single households.

Demographic Factors

The dramatic growth in the number of young people eligible for marriage is one demographic factor that helps explain the growth in the single population. Children born in the post–World War II baby boom became young adults of marriageable age in the 1960s (Buunk and van Driel 1989). Additionally, baby boomers departed from their parents' pattern of marrying young and remained single longer by postponing marriage. The median age at first marriage for males hit at an all-time low of 22.5 years in 1956. That same year, the median age for marriage of females was 20.1. By 1998, the median age at first marriage was 26.7 for men and 25.0 for women (U.S. Bureau of the Census 1999; Peterson 1996).

Prior to World War II, young adults who were not married were expected to live at home with their parents. As more young people attended college and postponed marriage, this expectation changed. Instead of staying home, young people were expected to move out of the family home as soon as they completed their formal education, whether high school or college, and found steady employment. The tendency for young adults to establish an independent household led to an increase in singles because young people no longer needed a marriage certificate as a passport to independence (Goldscheider and Goldscheider 1987; "The Singles Scene" 1992).

Divorce and Widowhood

Many single people are divorced. The rapid rise in divorce rates, which grew from a rate of 2.2 per 1,000 in 1960 to a record high of 5.2 per 1,000 marriages in 1980, helps account for the growing singles population (U.S. Bureau of Census 1994). In 1997, 19.3 million adults were divorced and not remarried (Lugaila 1998). Additionally, divorced people are waiting longer to remarry, which increases the amount of time they live as singles (Cargan 1983). Rising divorce rates may contribute indirectly to a growth in the number of singles by prompting some individuals to postpone marriage for fear that it will end in divorce (Staples 1981). As people look around at the number of divorces among their families and friends, they may decide that if they are extremely cautious in selecting a mate and take plenty of time to get to know their potential partner, they may be able to avoid divorce.

Cultural Factors

Significant demographic shifts must be examined within a cultural context. The women's rights movement and the sexual revolution in the United States, for example, help explain the rapid growth in singlehood. The women's movement, which gained momentum in the 1960s, gave rise to many cultural changes that promoted growth in the single population. One of the primary messages of the movement was that women should strive for greater independence, both economically and emotionally. More and more people challenged the traditional assumption that from birth to death, a woman must be cared for and economically supported by a man. As a result, many women decided to postpone marriage until after they received their college degrees and established themselves in a career (Cherlin 1992b; Macklin 1987). Additionally, legislative changes sparked by the women's movement increased occupational opportunities for women. A woman who works hard to become successful in a satisfying career may hesitate to marry for fear of losing her freedom and independence.

More reliable contraception and increased sexual permissiveness also contributed significantly to the rise in the single population (Cherlin 1992b; Macklin 1987; "The Singles Scene" 1992). The birth control pill was approved for marketing by the Food and Drug Administration in 1960 and rapidly became the most commonly used form of contraception in the United States (The Boston Women's Health Book Collective 1998; Sapiro 1999). The Pill, which is close to 100 percent effective if taken properly, allowed couples to engage in intercourse with little fear of pregnancy. At the same time that the Pill became widely available, more young people were attending college and had the freedom to experiment with sexual activity. The result was what has been labeled *the sexual revolution*. Premarital sex became more socially acceptable, and individuals no longer felt compelled to marry to enjoy an active sex life.

As you learned previously, increased sexual permissiveness also led to an increase in cohabitation. Not only were young people having sex outside of marriage but they also began doing so openly by living together in intimate relationships without the commitment of marriage. Changing social norms allowed individuals to remain single, yet still have the companionship and sexual interaction that is a part of marriage.

As more people remained single, social acceptance of single life-styles grew, as did the opportunities for living alone (Stein 1985). Increases in the number of people living as singles, in turn, led to greater social acceptance of remaining single (Pampel 1983). Businesses were established that cater almost exclusively to singles, who account for 27 percent of all consumer spending units, and made it easier for them to enjoy active social lives (Shipp 1988). For example, as the singles population expanded, the construction of apartments and condominiums designed to be more affordable and practical for single people also expanded. The travel and tourism industry and a variety of voluntary associations also have successfully targeted singles.

Clearly, social changes removed many of the obstacles to remaining single. No longer was it taboo for unmarried individuals to have active sex lives, and with the Pill, sex could be enjoyed without fear of pregnancy. It became possible to live in a marriagelike relationship without the ceremony and commitment. Furthermore, the acceptance of the single life-style and the rapid growth of singles made living alone and meeting companions easier.

Singlehood and Socioeconomic Status

Socioeconomic status is one of the most important factors influencing the quality of life of single individuals. For example, across all age groups, single men earn more than single women, with the largest gap in earnings occurring between the ages of 45 to 54 (Shipp 1988). Younger singles, regardless of sex, tend to have the most discretionary income because fewer of them are helping to support children and they are not living on fixed incomes like many older singles are.

Older single women generally face the greatest financial struggles because they are likely to have earned less money throughout their working years. Therefore, they have less money saved and invested, and they collect less money in social security and retirement benefits than older men do. Furthermore, health care expenditures are much greater for older women, primarily because they pay higher rates for health insurance (Shipp 1988). Elderly single women often find it necessary to keep working beyond the traditional retirement age of 65. Their earnings, however, are likely to be meager. The average earnings of women over the age of 65 is only $22,869. Men who are the same age earn an average of $40,229 (U.S. Bureau of the Census 1996).

Access to economic resources not only allows one to live more comfortably and enjoy better health but it also influences one's ability to meet partners and have companionship. Many cruise lines and vacation resorts are designed specifically to allow single people to meet and socialize. Other services—such as personal advertisements, social introduction services, and electronic and telephone networks—have been developed to assist singles in meeting companions. However, only those who enjoy economic security can afford to utilize most of these services.

Singlehood and Gender

In addition to socioeconomic status, the cultural construction of gender norms makes the experience of being single quite different for women and men. Although negative labels often are attached to both male and female singles, the cultural images of single men have a positive counterpart, as well. A single man is called a *bachelor*, a term that conjures up the image of a carefree, handsome, virile man who has voluntarily remained single (Sapiro 1999). The term *confirmed bachelor* is sometimes used to emphasize the fact that this man could have married at any time but elected to remain single. A single woman, on the other hand, is a *spinster*—a lonely, old, unattractive, prudish woman who was never able to snag a husband (Sapiro 1999). The pejorative labels attached to single women reflect the importance placed on marriage for women. Historically, women had to marry and bear children to acquire social status and obtain financial security. Although times have somewhat changed, it is clear—even in the language we use— that marriage is considered more important for women than for men and that singleness is not a desired status for women.

The tremendous importance placed on marriage for women and the fear and dread associated with women becoming "spinsters" was both reflected and reinforced in a famous piece of social science research called the *Harvard-Yale study* (Cherlin 1992b; Faludi 1991). On February 13, 1986, a reporter named Lisa Marie Petersen was writing a Valentine's Day story for a Stamford, Connecticut, newspaper. As part of her story, she interviewed a few men at the Stamford Town Center mall who were shopping for flowers and candy. She then called the department of sociology at Yale University to get some filler information on marriage for the article.

The reporter was directed to sociologist Neil Bennett, who told her that he had been working with two other sociologists, Patricia Craig at Yale University and David Bloom at Harvard University, on a paper about the marriage chances of black women and white women with different levels of education. As part of the study, the researchers had run some preliminary projections of the probability of single women marrying. Bennett told the reporter that based on their calculations, college-educated women who were still single at age 30 had only a 20 percent chance of ever marrying. By age 35, these women had only a 5 percent chance of marrying, and by age 40, the probability of a college-educated single woman ever marrying dropped to 1.3 percent.

Using the figures Bennett provided, Peterson wrote a small feature article about Valentine's Day. An Associated Press reporter picked up these figures and they were printed in newspapers across the country. The statistics on the low probability of single, college-educated women ever marrying sparked a nationwide frenzy of interest. Suddenly, newspapers, magazines, and talk shows all contained discussions of the "problem" of educated single women being "unable" to marry. The June 2, 1986, issue of *Newsweek* featured a graph from the Harvard-Yale study on the front cover and described the chances of a 40-year-old, college-educated, white woman marrying as being so low that she was "more likely to be killed by a terrorist" (Cherlin 1992b). Faludi (1991: 9–10) describes the way the Harvard-Yale statistics were "absorbed by every outlet of mass culture." She writes:

> The statistics received front-page treatment in virtually every major newspaper and top billing on network news programs and talk shows. They wound up in sitcoms from "Designing Women" to "Kate and Allie"; in movies from Crossing Delancey to When Harry Met Sally to Fatal Attraction; in women's magazines from Mademoiselle to Cosmopolitan; in dozens of self-help manuals, dating-service mailings, night-class courses on relationships, and greeting cards. Even a transit advertising service, "The Street Fare Journal," plastered the study's findings on display racks in city buses around the nation, so single straphangers on their way to work could gaze upon a poster of a bereft lass in a bridal veil, posed next to a scorecard listing her miserable nuptial odds.

In short, the Harvard-Yale study sparked a panic that if women stayed in school and established themselves in a career, they would be forsaking marriage and a family.

Amidst the media flurry, demographer Jeanne Moorman of the U.S. Bureau of the Census quietly questioned the Harvard-Yale statistics. Using a slightly different statistical model and a more complete data set, she projected the probability that college-educated women would marry and got quite different results (see Table 14.1 on page 474). Moorman found that a college-educated woman who was single at age 30 had a 58 to 66 percent chance of marrying (a figure 3 times higher than that found in the Harvard-Yale study). At age 35, she had a 32 to 41 percent chance of marrying (7 times higher than the Harvard-Yale study); and at age 40, she had a 17 to 23 percent chance of marrying (23 times higher than the Harvard-Yale study). The data from the U.S. Bureau of the Census also suggested

Table 14.1 Comparison of Harvard-Yale and
Census Bureau Calculations of a College
Educated Woman's Chance of Marrying

Woman's Age	Harvard-Yale Statistics	Census Bureau Statistics
30	20.0%	58–66%
35	5.0%	32–41%
40	1.3%	17–23%

that single, college-educated women are more likely to marry than single women of the same age with only a high school diploma (Faludi 1991). These findings were never broadcast nationwide, however, because television and print media did not find them interesting. The U.S. Bureau of the Census statistics appeared only in a small article in the *Washington Times* (Cherlin 1992b).

Most sociologists today believe that data from the U.S. Bureau of the Census are more accurate than the projections from the Harvard-Yale study. After reviewing the procedures of Bennett and his colleagues, demographers have concluded that they based their mathematical model on an inaccurate marriage model. First, the Harvard-Yale researchers were working with the incorrect assumption that women, regardless of race or class, faced a "marriage squeeze" (i.e., that there were far more single women than marriageable single men of compatible ages). Second, Bennett, Craig, and Bloom's mathematical model did not take into consideration that college-educated women generally marry later than high school-educated women, which led to an underestimation of the chances of marriage for well-educated women (Cherlin 1992b; Faludi 1991).

The panic that followed the Harvard-Yale study demonstrates how gender norms are closely tied to the perception and experience of being single. It was automatically assumed that all single women someday hoped to marry and that they currently were living a lonely "spinster" existence. In reality, surveys of single women revealed a much different story. Many single women report being quite happy with their life-style. In a *Glamour* magazine survey, 90 percent of the never-married women interviewed said the reason they were not married was because "they haven't wanted to yet" (Faludi 1991: 15). Additionally, most never-married women were not lonely and living alone. Many single women were cohabiting with intimate partners (Faludi 1991).

The gender norms attached to the single experience become even more glaring if one considers a parallel hypothetical situation involving single men. What if the Harvard-Yale statistics regarding the low probability of marriage had been about college-educated men rather than women? Would the mass media have considered those findings newsworthy? Note how many social scientists were busy calculating college-educated women's chances of marrying without also investigating college-educated men's chances of marrying. Certainly the research questions social scientists investigate reveal just as much about social life as the data they generate.

Gender stereotypes clearly influence behavior. More men than women are never-married in all but the oldest age group (Shostak 1987). Sociologists argue that middle-age men are culturally defined as more attractive than middle-age women. Therefore, men feel comfortable remaining single, knowing that they will still be considered desirable dates, even to much younger women. It is socially acceptable for older men to date younger women, but the reverse is often regarded as inappropriate. Hence, single men have a large pool of eligible dates, ranging from women much younger than them to women their own age or older. Men are more likely to remain single because they do not bear children. Women, on the other hand, have considerably more social pressure to marry at least once during their childbearing years (Shostak 1987). All of these factors, rooted in our cultural notions of gender, help explain differences between men and women in the experience of singlehood.

In a classic demographic study, sociologist Jessie Bernard (1972) described a **marriage gradient** in which men tend to marry women who are slightly younger, less educated, and have lower occupational prestige than they do. Conversely, women tend to marry men who are slightly older and more educated and have more occupational prestige than themselves. Bernard points out that the marriage gradient reveals much about men and women who do not marry. Heterosexual men who remain single would be the bottom of the barrel; that is, they cannot find women with any lower education or status than themselves. Single women, on the other hand, would be the "cream of the crop," for there would be no men with superior education or status for them to marry.

Although Bernard makes these comments somewhat tongue-in-cheek, her observations are not far from the truth. Single men over age 30 tend to have lower educational levels and lower income. Single women over age 30 generally are well educated and earn substantial incomes, which suggests that although the authors of the Harvard-Yale study may have miscalculated the probability of educated women's chances of marrying, they were correct in asserting that as education levels increase, women are less likely to marry (Buunk and van Driel 1989).

The inverse relationship between education and marriage for women has been explained in several ways (Buunk and van Driel 1989; Bennett, Bloom, and Craig 1989). First, better educated women may remain single longer because they are independent and successful and do not want the traditional housewife role. Second, because they are economically self-sufficient, well-educated women do not feel compelled to marry for financial security. Third, acquiring higher education requires time, dedication, and economic investment that women may fear will be wasted if they become burdened with marital and parental responsibilities. Finally, men, who traditionally have been in control of relationships, may be intimidated or uncomfortable in relationships with independent, highly educated women.

Singlehood and Race and Ethnicity

Research on race and ethnicity and single life-styles has focused almost exclusively on comparisons between African Americans and whites. Statistics indicate that African Americans are less likely to marry than other races. In 1997, 13.9 percent of people who were 25 to 34 years old had never been married (Lugaila 1998). For blacks in the same age group, 54.2 percent had never been married (Lugaila 1998). Lack of economic opportunities for young black males may discourage marriage (Macklin 1987; Wilson 1996). An unbalanced sex ratio between black males and females further reveals why African Americans are more likely to remain single than other races. Black women face a so-called marriage squeeze because they outnumber black men in the prime marrying ages of 20 to 49. The sex imbalance is caused, in part, by birth ratios; fewer males than females are born within the African American population (O'Hare et al. 1997). Furthermore, black males have higher homicide, suicide, and incarceration rates between the ages of 20 and 25, traditionally the prime ages for first marriage (O'Hare et al. 1997; Wilson 1996). Also, black men intermarry with white women at three times the rate that black women marry white men, which further reduces black women's marriage opportunities (Doudna and McBride 1981; Staples 1981).

The combined impact of race, educational level, and gender on remaining single has generated much debate among scholars. In his study of college-educated, middle-class blacks between the ages of 25 and 45, Staples (1981) found that, like whites, black men with the lowest education and black females with the highest education were least likely to marry. Staples (1981) argues that middle-class black women want to marry black men with as least as much educa-

What economic, demographic, and cultural factors tend to be associated with single status in the United States? How do the perennial variables of gender, race and ethnicity, and socioeconomic status relate to being single?

tion as they have, but there are far fewer college-educated black men than women. Staples believes that the dearth of college-educated black men stems from a historical pattern that emerged in rural southern black families in which daughters, rather than sons, were sent to college. The reason for this was black men had several occupational choices, whereas black women were limited to becoming either domestic servants or teachers. Since a college degree is required to become a teacher, many families struggled and sacrificed to send daughters to college, a pattern that persists even today (Chapman 1988).

Other scholars believe that the probability of college-educated black women marrying is more complex than Staples acknowledges. Higginbotham (1981) found that college-educated black women from middle class families were more likely to marry than women from working-class backgrounds. Higginbotham argues that black women whose parents were middle class and college educated were expected to go to college and marry, whereas black women from working-class families were taught to put their college education ahead of all other goals, including marriage.

Still other researchers have found that the relationship between education and marriage is different for African American women than it is for white women. Bennett and colleagues (1989) argue that although increasing levels of education decrease the probability of marriage for white women, the opposite holds true for black women. They contend that "better-educated black women are more likely to ever marry than blacks who have not graduated from high school" (Bennett et al. 1989: 716).

Stereotypes and Problems Singles Encounter

What is life like for single adults in American culture? The answer to this question is complicated, because the experience of being single varies dramatically, depending on a variety of personal and social factors in addition to socioeconomic status, gender, and race and ethnicity. Many people do not realize that single adults are a heterogeneous population with a wide range of life-styles. Instead, many negative stereotypes of single adults have emerged in popular culture that can be quite detrimental.

Although remaining single longer, even permanently, has become increasingly common, statistics indicate that 94 percent of the American population marries at some point in their lives (Shostak 1987). In 1997, 55.9 percent of the adult population (109.2 million people) were married and living with their spouses (Lugaila 1998). Those who remain single, especially those not involved in a romantic relationship, are deviating from the cultural norm. Cargan and Melko (1982) use the phrase *being single on Noah's ark* to convey the awkwardness of being single in a coupled culture. Unfortunately, it seems to be a universal pattern that those who deviate from social norms are characterized by negative stereotypes. Singles are no exception.

Historically, Americans' attitudes toward single people have been negative (Buunk and van Driel 1989). In colonial times, singles were penalized with higher taxes to encourage marriage and reproduction. In the late 1950s, 80 percent of the adult population surveyed in the United States believed a woman must be "sick, neurotic, or immoral" to remain unmarried (Buunk and van Driel 1989: 25). By 1978, the proportion who agreed with that statement had dropped drastically, but still 25 percent of those surveyed believed that these characteristics describe single women. As Schwartzberg and colleagues (1995) discuss in the article at the end of this chapter, negative attitudes toward singles continue even as we move into the new millennium.

Today, there are dual, contradictory stereotypes of singles in American culture (Buunk and van Driel 1989; Stein 1976). On the one hand, singles are often characterized as carefree, uncommitted sexual moderns who enjoy fortune, friends, and good health. On the other hand, singles also are stereotyped as lonely, unattractive losers. As you have read, single men are more likely to be perceived as carefree, whereas single women are more often portrayed as homely and unfortunate.

Although both sets of stereotypes are prominent in our culture, research shows that neither is entirely accurate. A survey conducted by the National Opinion Research Center (NORC) further dispels both the carefree and unfortunate stereotypes of singles (Shostak 1987). Far from being untroubled, singles report that they face both interpersonal and institutional discrimination as well as concerns about unemployment and urban crime. Nevertheless, most singles do not find their lives miserable and boring. The majority of single respondents (55 percent) said that they found their lives generally exciting, 41 percent said their lives were routine, and only 4 percent perceived singlehood as dull (Shostak 1987).

Although social science research may prove stereotypes of singles inaccurate, the misperceptions persist in society and create problems for the unmarried (Schwartzberg et al. 1995). Employers may perceive single men as less responsible and reliable than married men, making it difficult for them to secure a job. Landlords may be reluctant to lease to singles, fearing they will have noisy parties. Obtaining credit and home mortgages may be particularly difficult for single women who do not have a husband's salary supporting them.

Diversity among Singles

Now that common misperceptions about single life-styles have been dispelled, consider how you might describe the so-called typical single adult. Like most people, you probably thought of a young adult who has never been married and is living on his or her own. Several decades ago, these characteristics would have described the "typical" single adult. Today, however, the single population is much more diverse. People are single for a variety of reasons—some by choice, others by circumstance. Although many single adults indeed live alone, some live with family or friends, and still others live in intimate cohabiting heterosexual or homosexual relationships. Furthermore, singles vary widely in age, from young adults to the elderly. Each of these factors—reasons for being single, living arrangements, and age—influences one's experience of being single.

Reasons for Being Single

The U.S. Bureau of the Census divides singles into four categories: never-married, widowed, separated, and divorced. In using this classification scheme, the U.S. Bureau of the Census acknowledges that people are single for different reasons. Some are single because they have never married, others have been married but are now single because of death, separation, or divorce. Yet, even the categories designated by the U.S. Bureau of the Census do not reveal much about individuals' reasons for being single. Some who have never married have had plenty of opportunities for marriage, but simply enjoy being single. Others classified as never-married are actively pursuing marriage and are distressed that they have not found a mate. And, as with divorce and separation, some may have sought to leave their marriages and are satisfied with their renewed single status, whereas others desperately wanted their marriages to succeed and wish they were not single.

Stein (1976, 1981) was the first to draw attention to the multitude of reasons people are single. He argues that some people are single voluntarily, whereas others are single involuntarily. Furthermore, some perceive their single status as temporary, whereas others perceive that they will remain single permanently. Using these two dimensions—voluntary versus involuntary and temporary versus stable—Stein created a typology of singlehood. Subsequently, Shostak (1987) labeled each type of single as either *ambivalent, wishful, resolved,* or *regretful.* The result is the typology presented in Table 14.2 on page 480.

Note that boundaries between the categories within the typology are sometimes difficult to determine. Consider the person who enters adulthood desiring marriage, but comes to accept a single status and decides to make the best of being single. Would this person be considered voluntarily or involuntarily single? Furthermore, the boundaries between categories often are quite fluid. Throughout the life cycle, individuals can move from one category to the next, such as the person who, after a divorce, is voluntarily resolved to be single, but several years later becomes lonely and begins searching for a mate, thus becoming wishful of marriage (Buunk and van Driel 1989).

Stein's typology does not consider one important, politically volatile reason why some people remain involuntarily single: They are legally prohibited from marrying. Today, homosexual marriages are not legally sanctioned in any of the 50 United States, although Hawaii is considering permitting gay marriages. Debate rages over whether homosexuals should be allowed to marry legally. A *Newsweek* poll found that 58 percent of those surveyed believe that gay marriages should not be legally sanctioned, whereas 33 percent said that same-sex marriages should be legally recognized (Kaplan and Klaidman 1996). Proponents argue that marriage is a basic human right guaranteed in the Declaration of Independence as part of the right to "life, liberty and the pursuit of happiness" (Sullivan 1996b). Furthermore, legalizing gay marriage would provide spousal benefits such as health insurance, pension plans, and inheritance rights, which advocates of gay marriages claim that long-term partners deserve (Stengel 1996). Some advocates argue that allowing gays to marry will ultimately provide greater social stability because marriage tends to "domesticate" or "tame" young men (Stengel 1996).

Table 14.2   **Typology of Singlehood**

Voluntary	Involuntary	
	Ambivalent	*Wishful*
Temporary	Young adults who have postponed marriage for education or career. Also includes those who have divorced by choice and those who are currently cohabiting but plan to marry someday. Individuals who are open to marriage, but do not consider marriage a priority.	Individuals who want and expect to marry. These individuals are actively seeking a mate. Individuals who consider marriage a priority and believe that they will eventually marry.
	Resolved	*Regretful*
Stable	Adults who have never married and did not plan to marry. Also includes those who are divorced and do not wish to remarry and those who are cohabiting with no intention of marriage. Priests and nuns who do not plan to marry for religious reasons are included in this category, as well. Individuals who prefer to be single.	Older divorced, widowed, and never-married individuals who wanted to marry or remarry but did not find a mate. Individuals who want to marry but are resigned to a permanent status of singlehood.

Sources: Adapted from *Single Life: Unmarried Adults in Social Context* by Peter J. Stein, 1981, New York: St. Martin's Press; and "Singlehood" by Arthur B. Shostak in *Handbook of Marriage and the Family* by Marvin B. Sussman and Suzanne K. Steinmetz (Eds.), 1987, New York: Plenum Press.

Opponents of permitting gay marriages often cite religious beliefs that homosexuality is a sin and should not be condoned or blessed by a covenant with God (Stengel 1996). Opponents also fear that gay marriages endanger societal morality by exposing children to "gay alternatives too early in life" (Stengel 1996: 53).

Much of the argument about permitting homosexual marriages centers on the definition of *marriage*. Opponents argue that marriage has evolved over thousands of years as a procreation union between a man and a woman, and same-sex marriages would jeopardize this socially beneficial institution (Stengel 1996). Conservative columnist William Bennett (1996) contends that if the definition of marriage is expanded to include gay unions, then soon the definition would be stretched even further to allow fathers to wed daughters or sisters to wed each other. Advocates of gay marriages respond that the social definition of marriage easily can (and should) be changed. They point out that throughout much of U.S. history, marriage was wrongly defined as a union between two people of the same race and that the definition was eventually changed; similarly, the definition of marriage could easily be changed to include people of the same sex (Sullivan 1996a). Advocates further argue that marriage is not solely for the purpose of procreation, because those who are elderly and those who are sterile or infertile are permitted to marry.

Sullivan (1996a), an outspoken advocate of gay marriages, suggests that the issue of gay unions should not be clouded by political rhetoric. He succinctly explains why he believes gay marriages should be permitted (Sullivan 1996a: 26):

> *People ask us why we want the right to marry, but the answer is obvious. It's the same reason anyone wants the right to marry. At some point in our lives, some of us are lucky enough to meet the person we truly love. And we want to commit to that person in front of our family and country for the rest of our lives.*

Stein's typology and the debate over legalizing homosexual marriages highlight the importance of understanding individuals' reasons for being single. Certainly, one's life satisfaction and experience living as a single person are influenced by whether one is voluntarily or involuntarily, temporarily or permanently, single. One of the first steps to take in determining what is life like for single adults is learning why they are single.

Living Arrangements

The majority of singles who are not cohabiting with intimate sexual partners live alone. In fact, the television portrayal of single adults on popular shows of the 1990s such as *Seinfeld* and *The Single Guy*, in which young singles are living on their own in an apartment in an urban area, are generally accurate (Adams 1981; Buunk and van Driel 1989). Urban areas often offer greater tolerance of diversity and a variety of social and employment opportunities as well as convenient housing and transportation for young singles. Older singles, however, tend to live in rural or suburban areas in single-family dwellings ("The Singles Scene" 1992).

What myths and stereotypes exist about singlehood? What reasons do singles give for being single? What are the living arrangements for singles, and how do age factors affect their life-styles?

Waite, Golscheider, and Witsberger (1986) found that living alone influences the attitudes of single individuals, especially young women. They discovered that young women who established independent households prior to marriage became less traditional, more accepting of employed mothers, and more career oriented as a result of living alone. The researchers concluded that living alone influences attitudes for several reasons. First, living away from home lessens parental control, allowing young adults to form their own attitudes. Second, young adults gain self-confidence by living alone, as they learn to maintain their own finances and household unassisted. Last, young adults who live alone have a wider range of experiences than those living at home.

Although most singles live alone, it is important to recognize that there are a variety of other living arrangements available. Many unmarried individuals live with family members, such as their children, parents, or siblings. Other singles live with same-sex roommates. Increasingly, singles are choosing to live platonically with a roommate of the opposite sex or to live communally with several other singles with whom they share expenses and household duties (Adams 1981; Buunk and van Driel 1989).

Age Factors

Singles can be divided into three distinct age categories: young singles (ages 18 to 28), middle-age or baby boomer singles (ages 29 to 45), and older singles (age 45 and above). Young singles make up about 29 percent of the singles population (DeWitt 1992). The vast majority of young singles (98 percent) have never been married, but over 90 percent report that they plan to marry sometime (De-

Witt 1992; Stein 1985). Clearly, younger singles are postponing marriage, but do not foresee themselves as permanently single. Most young singles would be classified as *ambivalent* in Stein's (1981) typology (Table 14.1).

The perception of singlehood seems to change as singles move into the middle-age classification. Between ages 28 to 32, often referred to in the literature as the *age 30 transition*, never-married singles often feel increased societal pressure to marry as well as personal confusion about whether they want to remain single (Schwartzberg et al. 1995; Stein 1985). At this age, many singles often have friends who are marrying and the unmarried may begin to feel lonely or left out. The age 30 transition is when many singles shift from being *ambivalent* to *wishful*.

Baby boomers comprise 37 percent of singles (DeWitt 1992). Two-thirds of middle-age singles have never married and most of the remaining third is divorced. DeWitt (1992: 44) characterizes middle-age singles as a group "dominated by single parents and by people whose busy careers make a social life difficult." Middle-age singles can fall into all four categories of Stein's (1981) typology.

Older singles are predominantly widowed women who married in their twenties (DeWitt 1992). Only about 5 percent of older singles have never married (Rubinstein 1987). Interestingly, the small group of never-married older singles report greater happiness than those of similar age who have been divorced or widowed (Ward 1981). Rubinstein (1987) found that elderly never-married singles, like all singles, are diverse. Never-married elderly singles differ in their reasons for being single; some would be classified in Stein's typology as *regretful*, whereas others are *resolved*. Additionally, elderly singles differ in their living arrangements; some have lived alone all of their lives, whereas others have lived with friends or relatives. Elderly never-married singles generally do not have children they can rely on for assistance, although they often have a close circle of friends that provide social and physical support when needed (Rubinstein 1987).

Age is one of the most important characteristics that determines what life is like for singles. Age certainly influences the two variables previously examined: reason for being single and living arrangements. Whether one is 25, 45, or 65 years old affects whether one perceives oneself as voluntarily or involuntarily and temporarily or permanently single. Likewise, age influences one's perceptions of living arrangements. Young singles are likely to enjoy the freedom and independence of living alone without loneliness; work can provide a friendship network as well as discretionary income to enjoy social activities. Elderly singles, on the other hand, may be less satisfied living alone. Poorer health and a fixed retirement income may limit independence; roommates can provide much needed physical assistance as well as companionship.

Summary

Until fairly recently, singles were not discussed in marriage and family textbooks. The rise in the number of singles—which resulted from economic, demographic, and cultural shifts—sparked scholars' interest in understanding what life is like for the growing minority of the unmarried. The experience of being single is shaped by the perennial variables of socioeconomic status, gender, and race. Those who are wealthier enjoy better health and have more opportunities to meet companions. Women who remain single are stigmatized as lonely, unattractive, spinsters, whereas single males often are perceived as handsome, carefree, and virile. As such, women encounter more pressure to marry—a pressure well-illustrated by the response to the Harvard-Yale study. African Americans are more likely to be single than other races because of limited economic opportunities and an unbalanced sex ratio. Singles encounter a number of negative stereotypes, including the mistaken belief that singles are either lonely social rejects or that they are promiscuous and irresponsible. In reality, singles differ on a number of dimensions, including reasons for being single, living arrangements, and age.

Readings for In-Depth Focus

The Realities and Perceptions of Singlehood

Most people consider the decision of whether to marry or remain single very personal and individual. Rarely do we stop to think about how social factors affect this most intimate choice. In the following reading, Natalie Schwartzberg, Kathy Berliner, and Demaris Jacob clearly outline how social factors since World War II have shaped the rate of singlehood as well as the perception and treatment of people who remain single. As you read the following article, pay special attention to the way social and historical forces shape individuals' decisions about marriage and singlehood. Put yourself in the place of a single person in each decade. How would you probably be treated? How would you feel about yourself?

■ ■ ■

The Couples Culture and the Single Adult

Natalie Schwartzberg
Kathy Berliner
Demaris Jacob

People living and working within a larger social system tend to evaluate themselves by the criteria of that system. By that standard, single people, living in a culture in which the majority of people are married, cannot help but evaluate their lives in relationship to the institution of marriage. As a result their definitions of self must always lack a quality that the larger system values. To understand the full scope of how this negative attribute affects people, it is important to examine the meaning that the dominant culture assigns to marriage.

THE 1950S: REALIZATION OF THE AMERICAN DREAM

Of all the influences on Americans in the 1950s, the needs of the expanding post-war economy had the most profound impact on people's lives. The immediate pressure for women to leave the workplace so that men returning from combat could regain their jobs translated into newsreels and movies of women doing their patriotic duty of rearing children and baking apple pies. Employment opportunities in an expanding economy enabled middle-class men with ambition to move up the professional ladder and blue-collar workers to find stable employment. Because of the "family wage system," in which men's salaries were supposed to support the entire family, the social structure of men working and women tending the home fires became an almost a universal ideal. This structure became a goal symbolizing upward mobility. In fact, men took pride in the fact that their wives did not have to work (Ehrenreich, 1983).

Although the society accepted this ideal wholeheartedly, it locked women and men into a somewhat unfortunate financial interdependency. Women were dependent on men to raise their standard of living, since even if they did work their wages would not support them. This, in fact, upped the ante for women to marry. Although men were also expected to marry, many were fearful of what was then experienced as lifetime responsibility, since the full burden of family finances weighed heavily on them (Ehrenreich, 1983).

Nevertheless, expectations to marry and fulfill oneself completely through this process were extremely high. Marriage was idealized, to say

the least. "Patriotism, prosperity, and parenthood reigned" (Lang, 1991). By 1957, in fact, 96% of Americans of marriageable age were married (Eisler, 1986). Americans in the 1950s were focused on marrying, having children and raising them. "The increase was most spectacular among college women; they were abandoning careers to bear four, five and six or more children," wrote historian William Manchester (1973, p. 22).

Education for women began to slide. Only 35% of college students were women, compared with 40% before World War II. Of those who did go to college during this period two-thirds dropped out, including our previous First Lady, Barbara Bush. Most dropped out to help their husbands in their careers or "headed off in search of greener husband hunting territories" (Lang, 1991, p. 34).

The value placed on marriage during the 1950s was completely new. At no time in the history of the United States had there been such an emphasis on finding all of life's satisfactions within the nuclear family (Coontz, 1992). Since this notion was supported in every area of public life, single people felt particularly out of the mainstream and acutely disadvantaged during this era. Television, the powerful infant of the 1950s, both picked up messages from the culture and profoundly influenced it as well. Situation comedies proliferated, glorifying white middle-class suburban life. *Leave it to Beaver, Ozzie and Harriet, Father Knows Best*—all reflected families who were happy in their "intactness" and in the upwardly mobile suburbs.

The messages to marry, to propagate, to acquire more possessions, and to advance one's social status were everpresent. Even the much adored and seemingly innocuous *I Love Lucy* show advanced this notion. Underlying the pranks and get-rich schemes were clear expectations that Lucy, Desi, and the Mertzes were couples who were on their way. *The Honeymooners* and *The Life of Riley* also depicted families who laughed and bantered but clearly aimed to raise their social class (Taylor, 1989). The middle-class wisdom of these shows implied that there was enough to go around in a society rooted in benign, happy, traditional family life.

Single people weren't the only group that the popular culture did not reflect. People of color and homosexuals were almost completely invisible. Despite the fact that 25% of American families were poor, these shows reflected only the "good life." The American economy needed the ever constant expectation for people to move into the middle class, with acquisition of the material goods that reflected this status. The message was both overt in advertisements for shiny new cars, homes, and appliances, and covert in television storylines implying that consumerism was good (Coontz, 1992).

The needs of the expanding economy were serviced by the proliferation and purchases of consumer goods. Nearly the entire increase in the gross national product in the mid 1950s, in fact, was due to increased spending on consumer durables and residential construction, mostly for nuclear families (May, 1988).

What emerged from this pressured push for marriage, family, and consumerism was a distinct focus on what was "normal." Supporting the correctness of traditional family life came the entrance of "experts" into American consciousness. Turning for advice to baby books, marriage manuals, and even psychoanalytic literature, Americans became consumers of "observed self consciousness" (Ehrenreich & English, 1978). The psychological material available to the public very much supported the notion of home and family as "developmental tasks." In 1953 psychologist R. J. Havinghurst conceptualized eight tasks of early adulthood. The list affected the consciousness of the nation, and as such was repeated for the next three decades in many different forms and by many different representatives of the culture. It included the following: (1) selecting a mate, (2) learning to live with a marriage partner, (3) starting a family, (4) rearing children, (5) managing a home, (6) getting started in an occupation, (7) taking on civic re-

sponsibilities, and (8) finding a congenial social group (Ehrenreich, 1983).

Marriage became proof of maturity, the only acceptable way to move into the adult world. Deviations in performing this transitional task became pathological, a term that made its way from psychoanalytic literature into the popular culture. Ehrenreich (1983) cites Dr. Paul Popenjoe, who appeared regularly in *The Ladies Home Journal*, where he blamed bachelorhood on "emotional immaturity and infantile fixations" and referred to unmarried women as biological inferiors and discards who do not offer good matrimonial prospects. Is it any wonder that in 1957, 80% of Americans polled said that people who chose not to marry were "sick, neurotic, and immoral" (Coontz, 1992).

The experts who defined the "correct way" to live very much supported the American dream. This dream locked the culture into such rigid notions of psychological correctness that it influenced Americans for decades to come. Images of proper living denied the actual diversity in America, particularly the significant amount of poverty in this country. The dream persisted despite the fact that many people were living in circumstances that excluded them from being part of it. At a time when ethnic and racial minorities were almost entirely excluded from the gains of the white middle class, for example, many people did not have a "household to manage."

Marriage, a family, and a home were definitely equated with normalcy. The fact that after the losses in World War II not everybody could have an available potential partner was never an issue for the popular mythology of the day.

Sexual mores in the 1950s were quite restrictive and were based on a double standard between women and men. Women, who were supposed to save themselves for marriage bore the responsibility to hold the sexual line, whereas it was considered natural for men to be sexually aggressive. These sexual mores were not only unequal but also quite confusing, and ultimately led to a profusion in early marriages (Coontz, 1992).

The conformity of American society in the 1950s clearly left very little room for those people who remained single. Not only did single people experience themselves as peripheral to the larger society, but they were also very much aware that they were labeled as deviants. This was particularly true for women. As Ehrenreich and English wrote about the typical single woman, "She might be brilliant, famous, visibly pleased with herself, successful in every way— but the judgment hung over her that she had failed as a woman" (1978, p. 287).

Interestingly enough, the conformity of "normal life" didn't suit everyone. The popularity of books like *The Man in the Grey Flannel Suit,* for example, reflected a growing discomfort with massive conformity. The 1957 cult film, *The Invasion of the Body Snatchers,* satirized the paranoid McCarthy era. Both works depicted people in the culture as automated creatures locked into a soulless life. The startling popularity of Elvis Presley's overt sexuality reflected some of the dissatisfaction with the restrictions of this era.

Despite the evidence of these dissatisfactions, as well as a sense of emptiness beneath the dream, the American mainstream persisted with this dream far into the turbulence of the next decade.

THE 1960S: WHAT THE REVOLUTION WAS ALL ABOUT AND HOW IT AFFECTED OUR NOTIONS OF FAMILY

The coming of age of the greatest number of young people in this century during the 1960s was felt with tremendous force throughout the United States. The convulsions this society experienced during this era were no doubt influenced by the millions of young people moving into adulthood at this time. Authors offered a myriad of explanations for the dismemberment

of the social structure, ranging from the permissiveness of the parents of the Dr. Spock generation to the revolutionary impact of books like *The Greening of America* (Michener, 1993). There is no question, however, that the 1960s saw the underpinnings of the basic values of American life become "unglued."

While young people were witnessing an adult world attempting to conform to somewhat rigid moralistic values of family life, they were also being barraged with information from the media that presented outright contradictions to these values. In the larger community, events were developing which, thanks to television, were exploding into the livingrooms of this country. Civil rights confrontations, previously written about in newspapers, were now being observed by people as they happened. The sight of African-American civil rights marchers being hosed and clubbed by law enforcement officials brought into question the legitimacy of authority for many young adults (Coontz, 1992).

Not only were the overt actions of the law enforcement officials open to question, but the underlying issues that were being confronted also exposed the hypocrisy of the status quo. The civil rights that were being demanded, in fact, were already supposed to be the law of the land!

In November of 1963 President John F. Kennedy was brutally murdered. Here was a President who not only appealed to the youth of the country by his appearance and demeanor but also involved them in building a new society. After seeing this terrible event repeated over and over on their television sets, people then witnessed the violent and unlawful death of the man who was accused of Kennedy's murder. Less than five years later, Martin Luther King, the humanist and proponent of nonviolent protest, was also murdered. The pain and confusion following these tragedies set the stage for a major societal upheaval in response to the expansion of an extremely unpopular war.

The American buildup in Vietnam, which started in the administration of President John Kennedy, continued and expanded throughout the decade of the 1960s. This war was different from World War II, since the issues were much more confusing to many people. When people actually witnessed the battles on their television sets, it was impossible to ignore the horrors of war. As the 1960s became the 1970s, this war, which exacted a high cost in American and Vietnamese lives, showed no sign of abating. It became, in fact, a symbol of misguided policy and outright betrayal by the government. Many soldiers who had enlisted with the idea of saving the world from Communism became painfully disillusioned (Tischler, 1989).

For the first time since World War II, significant numbers of citizens resisted the government's judgment and profoundly questioned its morality. The nation was deeply divided about this war, with older adults joining with young people in questioning the status quo. Conflicts between deeply patriotic people and those who nevertheless questioned the authority of the government changed the idea of the consumer society's moral correctness forever (Coontz, 1992).

The family had been the focus of the moral integrity of the nation in the fifties. With the ethical structure of the entire nation in question, the moral structure of the family also came under attack. The gender role structure that had been the basis for the traditional family of the 1950s began to loosen. Betty Friedan's landmark book, *The Feminine Mystique*, published in 1963, opened up minds to feminist thinking. Its huge popularity represented the fact that American women were ready for this change. Certainly many people—both men and women—were stifled and disillusioned by the marriages of the 1950s (Coontz, 1992).

During the sixties women entered the work force in significant numbers. Many families needed two wages to support the consumer lifestyles they had created. Increased awareness of the limits of women's positions in the 1950s marriages, along with growing financial power, opened the way to new feminist thought.

Schooled in the civil rights and anti-war movements, early feminists were ready to question the holy grail of the gender-based social structure. In consciousness-raising groups, books and magazine articles, women questioned the old facts of family life. "The immutable maternal instinct, the sanctity of 'vaginal orgasms' as representative of female emotional maturity, the child's need for exclusive mothering, the theory of female masochism, all the shibboleths of mid-century psychomedical theory, shriveled in the light of feminist thinking" (Ehrenreich & English, 1978, p. 315).

Whether or not women developed their thinking as feminists, the questioning of gender stereotypes affected the families of our nation in many powerful ways. Certainly complete acceptance of the status quo of family life was a thing of the past.

Equally significant to the feminist revolution, and in many ways interwoven with it was the sexual revolution. The growth of a significant counterculture who rebelled against what they saw as the hypocrisy of the older generation's values had a profound impact on the wider culture. Not only did this culture reject materialism, but in rejecting rigid moral values it also opened up possibilities for much more liberal sexual mores. The development and more widespread use of birth control methods made sexual activity outside of marriage more acceptable (Coontz, 1992).

Later in the decade, this openness affected the homosexual movement as well, as gay men and lesbians began to question the exclusive definition of sexual freedom in terms of heterosexuality. Societal repression of homosexual activity had severely affected the expression of sexuality in their community, since most of the time they could not be open. In 1969, riots occurred at the Stonewall bar in New York City's

Greenwich Village; this marked a turning point, with more gays and lesbians becoming defiantly activist (Silverstein, 1991). Gradually more rights were secured than ever before, although homosexuals continued to be marginalized in the larger society. Nevertheless, the successes of these efforts led to more pride and ultimately to increased openness in the gay community.

The many changes in gender relationships and sexual openness affected family life in somewhat contradictory ways. While these trends created more flexibility in family relationships, people were left struggling to sort out new roles.

■ ■ ■

Violence continued to envelop the nation, with the deaths of the leaders of the decade: Bobby Kennedy, Medgar Evers, and Malcolm X. With the continued escalation of the Vietnam War, and the devastation that was witnessed, a pervasive cynicism enveloped the nation. Everything that was previously associated with their parents' morality was seen as suspect by young people. The symbolism of many anti-war movement slogans, like "Make Love Not War," suggested that previous generations hypocritically concerned themselves with chastity as a moral issue but permitted violence. Many of the young acted out their disillusionment by dropping out of middle-class lives and becoming involved with open sex and drugs. This confrontation of the entire moral and social structure led people to seriously questioning the "holy grail" of family life. As a result, many young adults chose other options than marriage or else married later in life.

For the first time, people began spending a significant period of time on their own and away from their families. As a result, a sizable singles population developed (Coontz, 1992). This population, having few role models, developed its own unique value structure and its own set of mores. Somewhat more liberated than their counterparts in the 1950s, they nevertheless continued to experience alienation from the larger society.

A singles industry quickly developed in response to this alienation. It provided a proliferation of activities geared to the supposed tastes of this population. This industry provided both a guide to a lifestyle heretofore unknown (and certainly unheralded) and an image that was often distorted and difficult to emulate. The groundbreaking *Sex and the Single Girl* by Helen Gurley Brown (1962) was an early contribution to the development of an image that was both liberating and misleading. Most single girls as well as single boys of the 1960s were hard-pressed to imitate the sexual prowess of the images suggested.

Guidelines for men and women had previously been clear. The new expectations were confusing at best and, for those who remained single, almost nonexistent. The single people of the 1960s shared the uneasiness of the times. The old structure had been rejected, but there were no new rules to follow.

THE 1970S: AMERICA MOVES INTO HARD TIMES

The shifts in family structure that started in the 1960s continued and escalated throughout the next decade. Although there were many factors contributing to these changes, one significant precipitant was the deteriorating economic climate.

The country's move into a series of deep recessions brought unemployment for many, and for others severe drops in "real income." Coontz notes that "between 1929 and 1932, during the Great Depression, per capita income fell by 27%. Between 1973 and 1986, the median income of families headed by a person under 30 fell by almost the same amount" (1992, p. 261).

This financial devastation, obviously, played havoc with people's lives. Typically, it was felt most severely by people who could least afford it—people who had limited educational opportunities and limited prospects. The poverty rate for young married couples with children doubled between 1973 and 1988 (Coontz, 1992).

Economic instability placed additional pressures on families, increasing stressors on marriages and parenting. Even those people who managed to maintain their living standards felt more pressed for quality time with their families, since they had to focus more on work. Government cutbacks fell hard on the blue-collar occupations and urban regions, which particularly affected African-American communities (Zinn & Eitzen, 1987). Despite the perceptions of the rest of the world, clearly the era of middle-class aspirations for everyone in America was over.

It was no longer possible for most families to be supported by one wage earner. Although in the 1970s 78% of married women under age 45 said they believed it was better for men to earn the family living and women to be home-makers, the decline in the family's "real income" made two wage earners a necessity (Van Horn, 1988). Unprecedented numbers of mothers entered the labor force in the 1970s, bringing the growth rate of women in the labor force to 41% (Van Horn, 1988). Obviously, the numbers of working women in families had a tremendous impact on the structure of marriage and family life.

For African-Americans the changes had to do mainly with the increased stresses that financial hardships had on family life. Because of the labor practices where black workers often filled the jobs left by white workers, black workers lost their jobs when the economy dipped. As a result, this community suffered severe financial setbacks during this period. The long historical pattern of role sharing between husband and wife, however, served as a buffer and support against this harsh reality (Staples & Johnson, 1993).

In Caucasian families the family structure had been traditionally based on the man being the wage earner and the woman remaining at home rearing the children. When women moved into the economic marketplace, profound changes were experienced in the operations of family life. The changing responsibilities between husbands and wives placed pressure on marriages, since household chores were now added to marital systems with very little time to spare. With women now working outside of the home, many were still responsible for household tasks. More of these chores were shared by husbands, but rarely at a level commensurate with the number of hours women put in at work.

Although women inevitably wound up working what actually could be considered a double shift, the amount of selfhood they gained by employment outside of the home not only was experienced as a profound source of satisfaction but also promoted changes in the power relationships between husbands and wives (Hochschild & Machung, 1989). The feminist movement in this country was strengthened by these changes and provoked even further shifts in the way women and men operated together. In marriages this took the form of challenging long-term roles.

Jessie Bernard's 1982 book, *The Future of Marriage,* reflected the questions people were having about roles in marriages. Her research on marriage, for example, indicated that women and men experienced this institution very differently. Marriage was experienced so differently, in fact, that one could almost say that there were two separate marriages—"his" marriage and "hers" (Bernard, 1982). Bernard pointed out that, even though men might rail against marriage, on the whole they experienced it as a much more satisfying institution than did women. The women who were interviewed, for the most part, reported a lowering of life satisfactions in marriage. This was due to the differences between what they expected in the married state and what they actually experienced. They were generally not prepared to deal with the unacknowledged expectations to conform to their husband's demands, as well as the abrupt lowering of status between the courtship period and the married state.

Contrary to the messages from the larger society that marriage was the only viable state for women, single women fared much better in terms of mental and physical health than their married counterparts. Single men, on the other hand, fared much worse than married men on measures of mental and physical health.

Bernard's book supported the notion that the traditional family and gender structure was no longer meeting the needs of men and, particularly, women. As the economy increasingly required two working parents, it necessitated drastic alterations in family life.

While these societal shifts changed family structure, they also changed the expectations and behavior of single adults. Not only were single people questioning conventional interactions in dating behavior, but they were also looking beyond tradition to see what changed expectations meant for future marriages. While there were no wholesale transformations, people started challenging time-honored gender roles prescribing active and passive positions for men and women. Standards that were previously unquestioned were now uncertain. Who calls for a date? Who pays? What would a potential partner think if you broke the rules? While these questions certainly added more anxiety to dating, they also opened up possibilities for new behavior.

Economic pressures and changing role relationships certainly played havoc with families during the 1970s. The divorce rate practically doubled in this decade, profoundly affecting the forms and expectations of family life (Ehrenreich, 1983). Divorced people had few guideposts to follow and often functioned within complex logistical and legal requirements. While financial supports, child-care arrangements, and single-parent authority issues were of primary concern, these newly single adults needed to be with other singles and reentered the dating world.

Suddenly, a new group of single people entered the consciousness of the American culture. More previously married single people, many with children, became visible. Not only did these people have to balance all of the complications of single-parent families, but they also had to manage dating relationships. Even with organizations like Parents Without Partners, many found themselves too overwhelmed with responsibilities to negotiate in a singles world. For these single people and their families, there were no role models. Few people knew how to balance their own adult needs while also meeting the needs of their children. While remarrying seemed like a solution for many people, few were prepared for the problems this would introduce (McGoldrick & Carter, 1989).

Meanwhile, the problems in the economy resulted in delayed first marriages. When people did marry, most delayed having children, so that fewer children were born overall. In the 1970s women reproduced at a record low rate of 1.7 babies each (Lang, 1991). At the same time, the numbers of women achieving college degrees increased dramatically, enabling women to enter the work force on a different level from previous generations. There was an overall awareness that the economy had permanently changed and that women were now expected to participate in families as "breadwinner."

In 1978, I (NS) recall speaking to a colleague who was the father of a young woman. He remarked that he knew things were changing when he began to worry that his daughter may not have chosen the right occupation to make a living. In contrast, he recalled his father worrying that his daughter might not be able to marry and find somebody to take care of her. Many people shared my colleague's sense of change. There was a certain amount of anxiety present in the larger society, a sense that the simpler times were gone forever. The Watergate crisis and the subsequent resignation of the President of the United States added a sense of disillusionment to the frustrations involved with the downturn in the economy.

With less free time available, the American people turned to television for easy and inexpensive entertainment. Television not only reflected the anxieties and disillusionment of the times but had its own effects. In television narratives the concerns of the time were articulated and, in the particular ways of television, resolved. In contrast to the harmonious families of the 1950s and 1960s, domestic life of the 1970s comedies and dramas was in turmoil. Shows that depicted minority families and divorced families, as well families with more serious problems, entered the livingrooms of America. In the sitcoms of this era characters tended to represent social issues, and the arguments that took place reflected the tensions between tradition and modernity, between women and men, between generations, classes, and social groups (Taylor, 1989).

The anger that lay beneath the surface in past decades opened up as a result of the financial setbacks in this era, as well as the dismantling of many of the social controls. This was expressed in the comedies of this period, and in many ways had a cathartic effect. The immense popularity of the *All in the Family* and other shows centered on social issues spoke to the need for this kind of public airing of previously hidden topics (Taylor, 1989).

Equally relevant to this era were the shows portraying work families. The success of *The Mary Tyler Moore* show and *M*A*S*H* generated a series of shows with occupational settings. Essentially, what these shows accomplished was a shift in focus from the traditional family to a benign surrogate work family. Characters in these sitcoms were provided with the stability and nurturance in the workplace that was missing from the vision of "home" in the 1970s (Taylor, 1989).

Television depicted strong, competent women for the first time, illustrating the possibility of women surviving well on their own. It also gave the message that single people could be happy and were capable of forming surrogate families. These shows accurately picked up the mood of this era. Responding to people's need for new guidelines to follow, they illustrated ways one could survive without traditional home and family life.

Difficult as it was to live through this era, many positive changes seem to have occurred. Movements to expand the rights of previously disenfranchised groups were successful and many laws were enacted to pave the way for social equality. The rights of unmarried couples and gays and lesbians were expanded, reducing the state's power to define normalcy (Coontz, 1992).

Some of the changes that started in the 1960s moved to a different level. Sexual relationships outside of marriage were not seen as a revolution anymore, but became an accepted part of normal life. People no longer entered marriages primarily for the purpose of sexual gratification. At the same time, people who remained single were freer to satisfy these needs.

At the end of this era, the structure of marriage seemed to have been changed permanently. Many different family forms were considered normal, including a large and growing singles population. Single people were no longer hidden. They were now reflected in television and movies, and industries that catered to them were blossoming.

THE 1980S: THE BOOM YEARS

The economics of the 1980s divided the larger society along class lines, widening the gap between the "haves" and the "have-nots" to an unprecedented degree. After a recession in 1982, the country gradually moved into an economic recovery. This recovery, however, did not raise the living standards across the board. In fact, the government figures showing rising averages obscured the growing polarization of incomes. In 1987 income inequality was greater than at the height of the earlier recession. Opportunities for those in the poorer sectors of society decreased rapidly as half of the new jobs created in the

1980s paid a wage lower than the poverty figure for a family of four. (Mishel & Frankel, 1991). As economic and social safety nets unraveled, more people fell into the ranks of the poor; more over, 40% of the poor had incomes less than half the amount designated as poverty level by the federal government (Whitman, 1990).

The "haves," although financially successful, in many cases felt their level of achievement was precarious. Some were making money at young ages and living in tremendously inflated ways, while others were struggling with multiple jobs and pressured living situations.

The value of "making it" in American society is shared across races and classes. When so many struggling people witnessed others making enormous amounts of money in activities unrelated to providing any kind of goods or services, it affected the moral consciousness of the country. The reaction to Wall Street speculators, corporate raiders, HUD bandits, and S&L criminals was, unfortunately, that only "suckers" worked for low salaries. In fact, it was a fitting commentary on the times that Tom Wolfe's "morality play" book, *Bonfire of the Vanities,* became the smash hit of the 1980s.

Coontz (1992) commented that the cynicism this kind of economic climate engendered in people was acted out in the withdrawal of interest in community support. The developing family found itself trying to survive in a sea of pressures and cynicism—far from ideal for healthy functioning. At the same time, the country's political swing to the right brought with it exhortations to return to "traditional family values." Many of the country's ills were placed on "the decaying family."

Although attitudes had moved in a conservative direction, it didn't change the tide of divorce. The 1991 demographic statistics, reflecting family structural changes of the 1980s, indicated that one-fifth of white children, one-third of hispanic children, and one-half of black children were living in "mother only" homes

(Ahrons, 1994). Alternative family structures and alternative lifestyles were here to stay.

The gay and lesbian movement brought many inequities of the larger system into focus, and while the overall culture may have shifted to the right, some legal decisions were being made to protect these minorities (Adam, 1987).

Later in the decade, when the economy had taken a severe downturn, many middle- and lower-class families were affected, as jobs were cut back and people laid off. Economic tensions once again opened the way for blaming the deterioration of the family for the country's ills. The result of this mood was a backlash against any movement that was seen as "destroying" the American family. The backlash was directed against any number of so-called deviant populations: "selfish parents" who divorced rather than rear the children in a two-parent home, gays, singles, "militant African-Americans," and finally, women who embraced feminist values. These women were seen as fundamentally to blame for abandoning the ethic of care that was the backbone of American family life (Faludi, 1991).

The television world attempted to illustrate some of the issues of the period by portraying varieties of domestic life in the United States. Workplace shows were vastly different from before. *Cagney and Lacy, Thirty-something, L.A. Law,* and finally, *Hill Street Blues* all reflected the moral confusions of the day. Not only were there pulls between career and home life, but the job itself presented moral ambiguities not previously presented on television. Gone was the workplace as a benign substitute for a confusing family life.

The unprecedented success of *The Cosby Show,* which aired in 1984 and ran to the end of the decade and beyond, represented the national hunger for normalcy and structure. In the Cosbys, we have an example of a family surviving the political and economic times in great style. The Cosbys, in fact, represent a return to an intact family, but with some slight variance from 1950. Mother works in an equally prestigious job as father, but, of course, has all the time in the world for her husband and children. Parents return to an all-knowing position, and the world was right again for one half-hour on Thursday evenings (Taylor, 1989).

THE 1990S

The world of the 1990s was certainly not all right. This decade opened with bitter struggles being fought over abortion rights, minority rights, and governmental apportionment of money, with all sides claiming the moral high ground. The presidential election of 1992 embodied that struggle, with the battleground being over the values and problems of American families. Society again focused on family values rather than the deterioration of the economic underpinnings of these families.

Certainly the constant, open struggle over what is normal and what is abnormal in living situations in the 1990s is quite different from the decades immediately after World War II, when none but the most rigid picture of home and intact family life was considered proper. There was not even room for a difference of opinion in this arena, much less open warfare.

The large numbers of single people now living in this country are mostly centered in large urban areas. They are living at a time when families are no longer seen as idealized containers of civilization. The traditional family appears to be under question in all areas, particularly when the media portrays alternative types of families as viable options. In fact, tradition in general is being questioned.

The singles population, incorporating huge numbers of previously married people, is growing larger and much more visible. One would think that this would be the ideal time for single people to live. Nevertheless, single people continue to feel alienated from the larger society, and those who enter therapy in the 1990s still

feel acutely aware of their "differentness." Many still long for the safety, normalcy, and connectedness of married life. The reason for this apparent anomaly is important to understand.

Unfortunately, no matter how much the traditional foundations of our society have changed, there are substantial lags in the establishment of institutional structures that truly support a lifestyle deviant from mainstream culture. Also, despite appearances, the media has lagged in whole-heartedly endorsing a singles lifestyle. While a multitude of different family forms do proliferate, on television the underlying subtexts in these programs, as well as within the accompanying advertisements, support the 1990s version of venerated love and marriage.

Too many single people are still being portrayed as silly, as in the TV show *Seinfeld*, vulnerable, as in the movie *Single White Female*, or predatory, as in *Pacifc Heights*. Nowhere can single people, heterosexual or homosexual, observe role models who are thoughtful and well developed people.

Not only have there been inadequate role models for single people to observe in the media, but there has also been few role models within the main institutions that organize adult life in American culture. In fact, for the most part these institutions—*work, spirituality, and community*—are still organized around marriage and family. This is not immediately obvious, since when small changes are reported in the news it gives the overall impression that major changes are happening (Williams, 1994). As a result, single people wind up blaming themselves for not achieving a connected and meaningful life.

Most work systems, for example, are subtly organized around a premise of family life. Christmas parties, dinner dances, and corporate picnics are typically arranged with the wife or husband in mind. As people move up in work systems, the enormous responsibilities of executives are almost impossible to manage without a "spousal support staff" working behind the scenes to arrange for dinner parties, car pooling, and maintaining contacts with relatives.

The fact that women's salaries continue to be lower than men's across the nation keeps single women in the uncomfortable position of not quite being able to make it on their own. This fact continues to place women in the position of needing to marry to raise their standard of living.

Although they enjoy income possibilities that exceed those of women, men's work life may still be affected by their single status. In a survey of fifty major corporations in 1981, for example, 80% of the heads of responding companies stated that single executives tended to make snap judgments, and 25% said that singles were less stable than married people (Stein, 1981). Although these stereotypes continue to change as companies become less conservative, many singles still perceive themselves to be on the outside of informal work structures.

Since the work system is highly significant to single people as a source of livelihood and as a socialization network, potential problems in this area can become quite threatening to their well-being. When, as too often is the case, work systems are not sensitive to their needs, single people feel different, excluded and sometimes even exploited.

For example, as more companies are relying on a mobile work force, single people are seen as being more transient than their married counter-parts. Since friendship networks are the most important support systems single people have outside of work, they risk the disruption of their major emotional supports when asked to move alone to another city. When businesses are not sensitive to this issue, single people can easily experience themselves as dispensable.

The lack of sensitivity to the needs of single people can also be seen in church communities. Although more and more religious institutions, particularly in urban areas, are becoming aware of their single members, few are aware of what single people require to feel included.

Certainly, negative messages about sexuality outside of the institution of marriage target single people. A less apparent but equally important message, however, is that there is usually no clear path for the single person to follow as a member of the church community. When the rhythm of formal religious life is centered around marriage and birth, single people experience themselves on the outside of life's important events. The more single people feel that their needs are not reflected by the institutions in which they participate, the more they feel peripheral to society. People may not be immediately aware of how much this sense of marginality affects their well-being.

In this same light, the fact that the culture exalts family forms that are not accessible to single people trivializes the world in which they live. The most important adult emotional connections single people have are often with their friends. As Willa Cather wrote, "Only solitary people know the full joys of friendship. Others have their families, but to a solitary and an exile his friends are everything" (in Holland, 1992). The friendship networks single people develop are experienced as every bit as important as blood relatives, but are not treated this way by the institutions in which they participate.

This message is echoed by the families from which single people emerge. The friendship system is seen by most families as secondary—one which should be sacrificed if a blood relative is in need. Parents, emerging from the more rigid value structures of the 1950s and 1960s, continue to believe that their job has not been completed until their children are "safely married." Their children's ability to form loving and committed friendship systems is not enough evidence of their successful negotiation of the adult world. As a result, single adults get messages from all around that their lives are incomplete.

In one sense single people are no longer invisible, since their lives are now depicted in television and in movies. Advertisements show sexy singles meeting each other in exotic places, and companies are putting out food products that can be consumed by "one." At the same time the real needs of single people to be validated as complete people and to participate fully in the institutions of society are not being met. As long as they experience their lives as peripheral to the important "goings on" in the world, they will experience their state as painful—one which must be changed at any cost.

REFERENCES

Adam, B. D. (1987). *The rise of a gay and lesbian movement*. Boston: Twayne Publishers.

Ahrons, C. R. (1994). *The good divorce*. New York: Harper-Collins.

Bernard, J. (1982). *The future of marriage*. New Haven, CT: Yale University Press.

Brown, H. (1962). *Sex and the single girl*. New York: Simon & Schuster.

Coontz, S. (1992). *The way we never were*. New York: Basic Books.

Ehrenreich, B. (1983). *The hearts of men*. New York: Anchor Books.

Ehrenreich, B., & English, D. (1978). *For her own good*. New York: Doubleday.

Eisler, B. (1986). *Private lives*. New York: Franklin Watts.

Faludi, S. (1991). *Backlash*. New York: Crown.

Hochschild, A., & Machung, A. (1989). *The second shift: Working parents and the revolution at home*. New York: Viking.

Holland, B. (1992). *One's company*. New York: Ballantine.

Lang, S. (1991). *Women without children*. New York: Pharos.

Manchester, W. (1973). *The glory and the dream: A narrative history of America 1932–1972*. New York: Bantam.

May, E. (1988). *Homeward bound: American families in the cold war era*. New York: Basic Books.

McGoldrick, M., & Carter, B. (1989). Forming a remarried family. In B. Carter, M. McGoldrick (Eds.), *The changing family life cycle* (2nd ed., pp. 399–429). Boston: Allyn & Bacon.

Michener, J. (1993, January 11). After the war: The victories at home. *Newsweek, 2*, 26–27.

Mishel, L., & Frankel, D. (1991). *The state of working America*. Armonk, NY: M. F. Sharpe.

Silverstein, C. (1991). Psychotherapy and psychotherapists: A history. In C. Silverstein (Ed.), *Gays, lesbians, and their therapists* (pp. 1–14). New York: Norton.

Staples, R., & Johnson, L. B. (1993). *Black families at the crossroads: Challenges and prospects*. San Francisco: Jossey-Bass.

Stein, P. (1981). Understanding single adulthood. In P. Stein (Ed.), *Single life: Unmarried adults in social contexts* (pp. 9–20). New York: St. Martin's Press.

Taylor, E. (1989). *Prime time families*. Berkeley, CA: University of California Press.

Tischler, B. (1989). Voices of protest. In B. Tischler (Ed.), *Sights on the sixties* (pp. 197–209). New York: Penguin.

Van Horn, S. (1988). *Women, work, and fertility, 1900 to 1986*. New York: New York University Press.

Whitman, D. (1990, October 15). The rise of the hyper poor. *U.S. News and World Report*, 40–42.

Williams, L. (1994, May 29). Childless workers demand equality in the corporate world. *The New York Times*, pp. A1, A22.

Zinn, M., & Eitzen, S. (1987). *Diversity in American families*. New York: Harper & Row.

Critical Thinking Questions

1. Identify social factors that have influenced the perceptions of singlehood from the 1950s through the 1990s.

2. How has the economy affected the practicality of remaining single?

3. Discuss the media's portrayal of single people over the past four decades. Has the media portrayal changed significantly? What impact does the image of singles in the media have on the perception and treatment of single people in the culture?

4. How have changing gender norms affected the rates of singlehood?

References

Adams, Bert N. "Fifty Years of Family Research." *Journal of Marriage and the Family*, 50 (1988): 5–17.

Adams, Margaret. "Living Singly." In *Single Life: Unmarried Adults in Social Context*, edited by Peter J. Stein. New York: St. Martin's Press, 1981.

Ahlburg, Dennis A., and Carol J. DeVita. "New Realities of the American Family." *Population Bulletin*, 47 (August 1992).

Ahuvia, Aaron C., and Mara B. Adelman. "Formal Intermediaries in the Marriage Market: A Typology and Review." *Journal of Marriage and the Family*, 54 (1992): 452–463.

Aldous, Joan, Gail M. Mulligan, and Thoroddur Bjarnason. "Fathering over Time: What Makes the Difference?" *Journal of Marriage and the Family*, 60 (1998): 809–820.

Aldous, Joan, and Wilfried Dumon. "Family Policy in the 1980s: Controversy and Consensus." *Journal of Marriage and the Family*, 52 (1990): 1136–1151.

Allen, D. M., and K. J. Tarnowski. "Depressive Characteristics of Physically Abused Children." *Journal of Abnormal Child Psychology*, 17 (1989): 1–11.

Allgeier, Elizabeth R., and Michael W. Wiederman. "Love and Mate Selection in the 1990s." *Free Inquiry*, 11 (Summer 1991): 25–27.

Alwin, Duane F. "Trends in Parental Socialization Values: Detroit, 1959–1983." *American Journal of Sociology*, 90 (1984): 359–382.

Amato, Paul R., and Alan Booth. "The Consequences of Parental Divorce and Marital Unhappiness for Adult Well-Being." *Social Forces*, 69 (1991): 895–914.

Amato, Paul R., and Alan Booth. "Changes in Gender Role Attitudes and Perceived Marital Quality." *American Sociological Review*, 60 (1995): 58–66.

Amato, Paul R., and Bruce Keith. "Parental Divorce and Adult Well-Being: A Meta-Analysis." *Journal of Marriage and the Family*, 53 (1991a): 43–58.

Amato, Paul R., and Bruce Keith. "Parental Divorce and Adult Well-Being: A Meta-Analysis." *Psychological Bulletin*, 110 (1991b): 26–46.

Ambry, Margaret K. "Childless Dances." *American Demographics*, 14 (1992): 55.

Anderson, Karen. *Wartime Women: Sex Roles, Family Relations, and the Status of Women During World War II*. Westport, CT: Greenwood Press, 1981.

Anderson, Karen. *Changing Woman: A History of Racial Ethnic Women in Modern America*. New York: Oxford University Press, 1996.

Anyon, Jean. "Social Class and the Hidden Curriculum of Work." In *Transforming Urban Education*, edited by Joesph Kretovics and Edward J. Nussel. Boston: Allyn and Bacon, 1994.

Arditti, Joyce A. "Factors Related to Custody, Visitation, and Child Support for Divorced Fathers: An Exploratory Analysis." *Journal of Divorce and Remarriage*, 17 (1992): 23–42.

Arnett, Elsa C. "With More Multiple Births, Costs and Risks Multiply, Too." *San Jose Mercury News*. December 26, 1998. Available: <www7.mercurycenter.com:80/premium/national/docs/octuplets.26.html>.

Aronson, Elliot, Timothy D. Wilson, and Robin M. Akert. *Social Psychology* (3rd ed.). New York: Longman, 1999.

Aseno-Okyere, W., S. Y. Atsu, and I. S. Obeng. *Communal Property Resources in Ghana: Policies and Prospects*. Discussion Paper No. 27, University of Ghana. Legon, Ghana: Institute for Statistical, Social and Economic Research, 1993.

Assimeng, Max. *Social Structure in Ghana: A Study in Persistence and Change*. Accra-Tema, Ghana: Ghana Publishing, 1981.

Assimeng, Max. *Saints and Social Structure*. Accra-Tema, Ghana: Ghana Publishing, 1986.

Axinn, William G., and Arland Thornton. "The Relationship between Cohabitation and Divorce: Selectivity or Causal Influence?" *Demography*, 29 (1992): 357–374.

Babbie, Earl R. "The Essential Wisdom of Sociology." *Teaching Sociology*, 19 (1990): 526–530.

Baca Zinn, Maxine. "Family, Race, and Poverty in the Eighties." *Signs: Journal of Women in Culture and Society*, 14 (1989): 856–874.

Baca Zinn, Maxine. "Adaptation and Continuity in Mexican-Origin Families." In *Minority Families in the United States: A Multicultural Perspective*, edited by Ronald L. Taylor. Englewood Cliffs, NJ: Prentice-Hall, 1994.

Bachman, R., and L. E. Saltzman. *Violence against Women: Estimates from the Redesigned Survey*. Washington, DC: U.S. Department of Justice, Bureau of Justice Statistics, 1995.

Bachu, Amara. "Fertility." In *Current Population Reports, Special Studies Series*, P23–189. 1995. Available: <www.census.gov/population/pop–profile/p23–189.pdf>.

Backstrom, Charles H., and Gerald Hursh-César. *Survey Research* (2nd ed.). New York: John Wiley, 1981.

Badinter, Elisabeth. *Mother Love—Myth and Reality: Motherhood in Modern History*. New York: Macmillan, 1981.

Baher, Connie. "How to Avoid Communication Clashes." *HR Focus*, 71 (1994): 3.

Bailey, Beth L. *From Front Porch to Back Seat: Courtship in Twentieth-Century America.* Baltimore, MD: John Hopkins University Press, 1988.

Bailey, J. Michael, Steven Gaulin, Yvonne Agyei, and Brian A. Gladue. "Effects of Gender and Sexual Orientation on Evolutionary Relevant Aspects of Human Mating Psychology." *Journal of Personality and Social Psychology,* 66 (1994): 1081–1093.

Ball, Richard E. "Marital Status, Household Structure, and Life Satisfaction of Black Women." *Social Problems,* 30 (1983): 400–409.

Ball, Richard E. "Children and Marital Happiness of Black Americans." *Journal of Comparative Family Studies,* 24 (1993): 2203–2218.

Balswick, Jack, and Charles W. Peek. "The Inexpressive Male: A Tragedy of American Society." *The Family Coordinator,* 20 (1971): 363–368.

Bardis, Panos D. "Family Forms and Variations Historically Considered." In *Handbook of Marriage and the Family,* edited by Harold T. Christensen. Chicago: Rand McNally, 1964.

Barnes, Gordon E., Leonard Greenwood, and Reena Sommer. "Courtship Violence in a Canadian Sample of Male College Students. *Family Relations,* 40 (1991): 37–44.

Barnet, Ann B., and Richard J. Barnet. *The Youngest Minds: Parenting and Genes in the Development of Intellect and Emotion.* New York: Simon & Schuster, 1998.

Barnet, Rosalind, and Caryl Rivers. *She Works, He Works: How Two-Income Families Are Happy, Healthy, and Thriving.* Cambridge, MA: Harvard University Press, 1996.

Barnett, O. W., C. L. Miller-Perrin, and R. D. Perrin. *Family Violence across the Lifespan: An Introduction.* Thousand Oaks, CA: Sage, 1997.

Barnett, O. W., T. E. Martinez, and M. Keyson. "The Relationship between Violence, Social Support, and Self-Blame in Battered Women." *Journal of Interpersonal Violence,* 11 (1996): 221–233.

Basow, Susan A. *Gender: Stereotypes and Roles* (3rd ed.). Pacific Grove, CA: Brooks/Cole, 1992.

Baumann, Carol. "Examining Where We Were and Where We Are: Clinical Issues in Adoption 1985–1995." *Child & Adolescent Social Work Journal,* 14, no. 5 (1997): 313–334.

Baxter, Janeen. "Gender Equality and Participation in Housework: A Cross-National Perspective." *Journal of Comparative Family Studies,* 28 (1997): 220–247.

Beal, Carole R. *Boys and Girls: The Development of Gender Roles.* New York: McGraw-Hill, 1994.

Becerra, Rosine M. "The Mexican-American Family." In *Ethnic Families in America: Patterns and Variations* (pp. 153–171), edited by Charles H. Mindel, Robert W. Haberstein, and Roosevelt Wright, Jr. Upper Saddle River, NJ: Prentice-Hall, 1998.

Begley, Sharon. "Your Child's Brain." *Newsweek,* February 19, 1996, pp. 55–59, 61, 62.

Belsky, Jay. "Parental and Nonparental Child Care and Children's Socioemotional Development: A Decade in Review." *Journal of Marriage and the Family,* 52 (1990): 885–903.

Belsky, Jay, and J. Vondra. "Lessons from Child Abuse: The Determinants of Parenting." In *Child Maltreatment: Theory and Research on the Causes and Consequences of Child Abuse and Neglect,* edited by D. Cicchetti and V. Carlson. New York: Cambridge University Press, 1989.

Belsky, Jay, and Michael Rovine. "Patterns of Marital Change across the Transition to Parenthood: Pregnancy to Three Years Postpartum." *Journal of Marriage and the Family,* 52 (1990): 5–19.

Bem, Sandra L. "The Measurement of Psychological Androgyny." In *Readings in Social Psychology* (3rd ed.), edited by Wayne A. Lesko. Boston: Allyn and Bacon, 1997.

Benneh, George. "Family and Development in Ghana: An Overview." In *Family and Development in Ghana* (pp. 1–12), edited by Elizabeth Ardayfio-Schandorf. Accra-Tema, Ghana: Ghana Universities Press, 1994.

Bennett, Claudette, and Barbara Martin. "The Asian and Pacific Islander Population." *Current Population Reports, Special Studies Series,* P23–189. 1995. Available: <www.census.gov/population/pop–profile/p23–189 .pdf>.

Bennett, Claudette, and Kymberly Debarros. "The Asian and Pacific Islander Population in the United States: March 1996 (Update)." *Current Population Reports,* P20–503, October 1997.

Bennett, Neil G., David E. Bloom, and Patricia H. Craig. "The Divergence of Black and White Marriage Patterns." *American Journal of Sociology,* 95 (1989): 692–722.

Bennett, William. "Leave Marriage Alone." *Newsweek,* June 3, 1996, p. 27.

Berg, Barbara J. *The Crisis of the Working Mother: Resolving the Conflict between Family and Work.* New York: Summit Books, 1986.

Bergen, R. K. *Wife Rape: Understanding the Response of Survivors and Service Providers.* Thousand Oaks, CA: Sage, 1996.

Bernard, Jessie. *The Future of Marriage.* New York: Bantam, 1972.

Bernard, Jessie. "The Good Provider Role." In *Men's Lives,* edited by Michael S. Kimmel and Michael A. Messner. New York: Macmillan, 1989.

Bernstein, Anne C. "Stepfamilies from Siblings' Perspectives." *Marriage & Family Review,* 26 (1997): 153–177.

Berry, Ruth E., and Flora L. Williams. "Assessing the Relationship between Quality of Life and Marital and Income Satisfaction: A Path Analytic Approach." *Journal of Marriage and the Family,* 49 (1987): 107–116.

Bianchi, Suzanne M. "America's Children: Mixed Prospects." *Population Bulletin,* 45 (June 1990).

Bidwell, Lee. "Gender, Social Roles, and Emotion: A Qualitative Study." Ph.D. dissertation, University of Tennessee, 1992.

Bidwell, Lee, and P. White. "The Family Context of Marital Rape." *Journal of Family Violence,* 1 (1986): 277–287.

Bielby, W. T., and D. D. Bielby. "Family Ties: Balancing Commitments to Work and Family in Dual-Earner Households." *American Sociological Review,* 54 (1989): 776–789.

Biggs, S., C. Phillipson, and P. Kingston. *Elder Abuse in Perspective.* Bristol, PA: Open University Press, 1995.

"Big Picture—Marriage: The Art of Compromise." *American Demographics,* 29 (1998): 41.

Billingsley, Andrew. *Climbing Jacob's Ladder: The Enduring Legacy of African-American Families.* New York: Simon & Schuster, 1992.

Bird, Gloria W., Sandra M. Stith, and Joann Schladale. "Psychological Resources, Coping Strategies, and Negotiation Styles as Discriminators of Violence in Dating Relationships." *Family Relations,* 40 (1991): 45–50.

Blau, David M. "Labor Force Dynamics of Older Married Couples." *Journal of Labor Economics,* 16 (1998): 595–639.

Blood, Robert O., and Donald M. Wolfe. *Husbands and Wives: The Dynamics of Married Living.* Glencoe, IL: Free Press, 1960.

Bloom, David, and Adi Brender. "Labor and the Emerging World Economy." *Population Bulletin,* 48 (October 1993).

Blumer, Herbert. *Symbolic Interactionism: Perspective and Method.* Englewood Cliffs, NJ: Prentice-Hall, 1969.

Blumstein, Philip, and Pepper Schwartz. *American Couples: Money, Work, Sex.* New York: Pocket Books, 1983.

Borders, L. DiAnne, Lynda K. Black, and B. Kay Palsey. "Are Adopted Children and Their Parents at Greater Risk for Negative Outcomes?" *Family Relations,* 47 (1998): 237–241.

Boss, Pauline G., William J. Doherty, Ralph LaRossa, Walter R. Schumm, and Suzanne K. Steinmetz (Eds.). *Sourcebook of Family Theories and Methods: A Contextual Approach.* New York: Plenum Press, 1993.

Boston Women's Health Book Collective. *The New Our Bodies, Ourselves.* New York: Simon & Schuster, 1998.

Boudreau, Frances A., and Donald M. Peppard, Jr. "New Game in Town." *Connecticut College Magazine,* (1994): 26–29.

Bouvier, Leon F., and Carol J. Devita. "The Baby Boom—Entering Midlife." *Population Bulletin* 46 (November 1991).

Bower, Bruce. "Adapting to Adoption: Adopted Kids Generate Scientific Optimism and Clinical Cautions." *Science News,* 146 (August 13, 1994): 104–106.

Bowker, L. H. "Marital Rape: A Distinct Syndrome." *Social Casework: The Journal of Contemporary Social Work,* 64 (1983): 347–352.

Bowles, S., and H. Gintis. *Schooling in Capitalist America: Educational Reform and the Contradictions of Economic Life.* New York: Basic Books, 1976.

Bowser, Benjamin. "African-American Male Sexuality through the Early Life Course." In *Sexuality across the Life Course,* edited by Alice S. Rossi. Chicago: University of Chicago Press, 1994.

Boyd, Monica, and Doug Norris. "Leaving the Nest? The Impacts on Family Structure." *Canadian Social Trends,* 38 (1995): 14–17.

Brandth, Berit, and Elin Kvande. "Masculinity and Child Care: The Reconstruction of Fathering." *Sociological Review,* 46 (1998): 293–313.

Brannen, J., and P. Moss. "Fathers in Dual-Earner Households—Through Mother's Eyes." In *Reassessing Fatherhood,* edited by C. Lewis and M. O'Brien. Beverly Hills, CA: Sage, 1987.

Braver, Sanford L., and R. Curtis Bay. "Assessing and Compensating for Self-Selection Bias (Non-Representativeness) of the Family Research Sample." *Journal of Marriage and the Family,* 54 (1992): 925–939.

Brecher, Edward M. *Love, Sex, and Aging: A Consumers Union Report.* Boston: Little, Brown, 1984.

Briato, Rita, and Donna Anderson. "Singles and Aging: Implications for Needed Research." In *Single Life: Unmarried Adults in Social Context,* edited by Peter J. Stein. New York: St. Martin's Press, 1981.

Bridges, Judith S., and Anne Marie Orza. "Black and White Employed Mothers' Role Experiences. *Sex Roles,* 35 (1996): 377–385.

Brinkerhoff, David B., Lynn K. White, and Suzanne T. Ortega. *Essentials of Sociology* (4th ed.). Belmont, CA: Wadsworth, 1999.

Broderick, Carlfred B. "To Arrive Where We Started: The Field of Family Studies in the 1930s." *Journal of Marriage and the Family,* 50 (1988): 569–584.

Bronfenbrenner, Urie. "Socialization and Social Class through Time and Space." In *Readings in Social Psychology,* edited by E. E. Maccoby, T. M. Newcomb, and E. L. Hartley. New York: Holt, Rinehart and Winston, 1958.

Brown, Susan L., and Alan Booth. "Cohabitation versus Marriage: A Comparison of Relationship Quality." *Journal of Marriage and the Family,* 58 (1996): 668–678.

Browne, K., and M. Herbert. *Preventing Family Violence.* Chichester, England: John Wiley, 1997.

Browning, J., and D. Dutton. "Assessment of Wife Assault with the Conflict Tactics Scale: Using Couple Data to Quantify the Differential Reporting Effect." *Journal of Marriage and the Family,* 48 (1986): 375–379.

Bulcroft, Kris, and Margaret O'Connor. "The Importance of Dating Relationships on Quality of Life for Older Persons." *Family Relations*, 35 (1986): 397–401.

Bullough, Vern L., and Fang Fu Ruan. "Marriage, Divorce and Sexual Relations in Contemporary China." *Journal of Comparative Family Studies*, 25 (1994): 383–393.

Bumpass, Larry L., and James A. Sweet. "Differentials in Marital Instability: 1970." *American Sociological Review*, 37 (1972): 754–766.

Bumpass, Larry L., and James A. Sweet. "National Estimates of Cohabitation." *Demography*, 26 (1989): 615–625.

Bumpass, Larry L., James A. Sweet, and Andrew Cherlin. "The Role of Cohabitation in Declining Rates of Marriage." *Journal of Marriage and the Family*, 53 (1991): 913–927.

Bumpass, Larry L., R. Kelly Raley, and James A. Sweet. "The Changing Character of Stepfamilies: Implications of Cohabitation and Nonmarital Childbearing." *Demography*, 32 (1995): 425–436.

Burchinal, Lee G. "Characteristics of Adolescents from Unbroken, Broken, and Reconstituted Families." *Journal of Marriage and the Family*, 26 (1964): 44–51.

Bureau of Justice Statistics. *Criminal Victimization in the United States, 1991.* Washington, DC: U.S. Department of Justice, 1992 (NCJ No. 139563).

Burgess, Ernest W. "The Wise Choice of a Mate." In *Successful Marriage* (pp. 14–27), edited by Morris Fishbein and Ernest W. Burgess. Garden City, NY: Doubleday, 1947/1963.

Burgess, Ernest W., Harvey J. Locke, and Mary Margaret Thomas. *The Family, From Traditional to Companionship* (4th ed.). New York: Van Nostrand Reinhold, 1971.

Burgess, Ernest W., and Leonard S. Cottrell, Jr. *Predicting Success or Failure in Marriage.* New York: Prentice-Hall, 1939.

Burgess, R. L., and P. Draper. "The Explanation of Family Violence: The Role of Biological, Behavioral, and Cultural Selection." In *Family Violence*, edited by L. Ohlin and M. Tonry. Chicago: University of Chicago Press, 1989.

Burke, P. J., J. E. Stets, and M. A. Pirog-Good. "Gender Identity, Self-Esteem, and Physical and Sexual Abuse in Dating Relationships." *Social Psychology Quarterly*, 51 (1988): 272–285.

Burley, Kim A. "Family Variables as Mediators of the Relationship between Work-Family Conflict and Marital Adjustment among Dual-Career Men and Women." *Journal of Social Psychology*, 135 (1995): 483–497.

Burr, Wesley R., Geoffrey K. Leigh, Randall P. Day, and John Constantine. "Symbolic Interaction and the Family." In *Contemporary Theories about the Family* (Vol. 2), edited by W. R. Burr, R. Hill, F. I. Nye, and I. Reiss. New York: Free Press, 1979.

Buss, David M., and David P. Schmitt. "Sexual Strategies Theory: An Evolutionary Perspective on Human Mating." *Psychological Review*, 100, no. 2 (1993): 204–232.

"But Severe Poverty Afflicts a Quarter of the World." *UN Chronicle*, 34, no. 1 (1997): 33.

Buunk, Bram P., and Barry van Driel. *Variant Lifestyles and Relationships.* Newbury Park, CA: Sage, 1989.

Buzawa, E. S., and C. G. Buzawa. "The Scientific Evidence Is Not Conclusive: Arrest Is No Panacea." In *Current Controversies on Family Violence*, edited by R. J. Gelles and D. R. Loseke. Newbury Park, CA: Sage, 1993.

Buzawa, E. S., and C. G. Buzawa. *Domestic Violence: The Criminal Justice Response* (2nd ed.). Thousand Oaks, CA: Sage, 1996.

Bynum, Melissa K., and Mark W. Durm. "Children of Divorce and Its Effect on Their Self-Esteem." *Psychological Reports*, 79 (1996): 447–450.

Campbell, Donald J., Kathleen M. Campbell, and Daniel Kennard. "The Effects of Family Responsibility on the Work Commitment and Job Performance of Nonprofessional Women." *Journal of Occupational and Organizational Psychology*, 67 (1994): 283–296.

Cancian, Francesca M. *Love in America: Gender and Self-Development.* New York: Cambridge University Press, 1987.

Cancian, Maria, and Daniel R. Meyer. "Who Gets Custody?" *Demography*, 35 (1998): 147–157.

Caplan, Paula J., and Jeremy B. Caplan. *Thinking Critically about Research on Sex and Gender* (2nd ed.). New York: HarperCollins, 1999.

Cargan, Leonard. "Singles: An Examination of Two Stereotypes." In *Family in Transition* (4th ed.), edited by Arlene S. Skolnick and Jerome H. Skolnick. Boston: Little, Brown, 1983.

Cargan, Leonard, and Matthew Melko. *Singles: Myths and Realities.* Beverly Hills, CA: Sage, 1982.

Carlson, Allan. "The Family: Where Do We Go from Here?" *Society*, 32 (July–August, 1995): 63–71.

Carlson, Bonnie E. "Dating Violence: A Research Review and Comparison with Spouse Abuse." *Social Casework*, (1987): 16–23.

Carlson, Bonnie E. "Dating Violence: Student Beliefs about Consequences." *Journal of Interpersonal Violence*, 11 (1996): 3–18.

Carlson, Christopher. "The American Family in History." In *Perspectives on the Family: History, Class, and Feminism*, edited by Christopher Carlson. Belmont, CA: Wadsworth, 1990a.

Carlson, Christopher. "Three Perspectives on the Family." In *Perspectives on the Family: History, Class, and Feminism*, edited by Christopher Carlson. Belmont, CA: Wadsworth, 1990b.

Carr, Dara, and Ann Way (Eds.). *Women's Lives & Experiences: A Decade of Research Findings from the Demographic and Health Surveys Program.* Calverton, MD: Macro International DHS Program, 1994.

Casper, Lynn. "My Daddy Takes Care of Me! Fathers as Care Providers." *Current Population Reports*, P70–59 (September 1997).

Chadiha, Letha A., Joseph Veroff, and Douglas Leber. "Newlywed Narrative Themes: Meaning in the First Year of Marriage for African American and White Couples." *Journal of Comparative Family Studies*, 29 (1998): 115–130.

Chafe, William H. *The American Woman: Her Changing Social, Economic, and Political Roles 1920–1970*. London: Oxford University Press, 1972.

Chambers, Victoria J., John R. Christiansen, and Phillip R. Kunz. "Physiognomic Homogamy: A Test of Physical Similarity as a Factor in the Mate Selection Process." *Social Biology*, 30 (1983): 151–157.

Chandra, Anjani, and Elizabeth Hervey Stephen. "Impaired Fecundity in the United States: 1982–1995." *Family Planning Perspectives*, 30 (1998): 34–42.

Chapman, Audrey B. "Male-Female Relations: How the Past Affects the Present." In *Black Families* (2nd ed.), edited by Harriette Pipes McAdoo. Newbury Park, CA: Sage, 1988.

Charon, Joel M. *Symbolic Interactionism: An Introduction, An Interpretation, An Integration* (6th ed.). Upper Saddle River, NJ: Prentice-Hall, 1998.

Chen, Xiangming. "The One-Child Policy, Modernization and the Extended Chinese Family." *Journal of Marriage and the Family*, 47 (1985): 193–202.

Cherlin, Andrew J. "Remarriage as an Incomplete Institution." *American Journal of Sociology*, 84 (1978): 634–650.

Cherlin, Andrew J. *Marriage, Divorce, and Remarriage* (rev. ed.). Cambridge, MA: Harvard University Press, 1992a.

Cherlin, Andrew J. "The Strange Career of the 'Harvard-Yale Study.'" In *Family in Transition* (7th ed.), edited by Arlene S. Skolnick and Jerome H. Skolnick. New York: HarperCollins, 1992b.

Cherlin, Andrew J. "Marriage and Marital Dissolution among Black Americans." *Journal of Comparative Family Studies*, 29 (1998): 147–158.

Cherlin, Andrew J., and Frank F. Furstenberg, Jr. "Stepfamilies in the United States: A Reconsideration." *Annual Review of Sociology*, 20 (1994): 359–371.

Cherlin, Andrew J., Frank F. Furstenberg, Jr., P. Lindsay Chase-Lansdale, Kathleen E. Kiernan, Philip K. Robins, Donna Ruane Morrison, and Julien O. Teitler. "Longitudinal Studies on Effects of Divorce on Children in Great Britain and the United States." *Science*, 252 (1991): 1386–1389.

Cherlin, Andrew J., P. Lindsay Chase-Lansdale, and Christine McRae. "Effects of Parental Divorce on Mental Health throughout the Life Course." *American Sociological Review*, 63 (1998): 239–250.

Chittum, Samme. "Is It Worth the Risks?" *New York Post*. December 22, 1998. Available: <www.nypostonline.com: 80/122298/news/8669.html>.

Chomesky, Alice. "Multicultural Perspectives on Menopause and the Climacteric." *Affilia: Journal of Women and Social Work*, 13 (1998): 31–46.

Christopher, F. Scott, and Rodney M. Cate. "Premarital Sexual Involvement: A Developmental Investigation of Relational Correlates." *Adolescence*, 23 (Winter 1988): 793–803.

Clark, M. L., Joyce Beckett, Mabel Wells, and Delores Dungee-Anderson. "Courtship Violence among African American College Students." *Journal of Black Psychology*, 20 (1994): 264–281.

Clark, Roger, and Terry Clifford. "Towards a Resources and Stressors Model: The Psychological Adjustment of Adult Children of Divorce." *Journal of Divorce and Remarriage*, 25 (1996): 105–136.

Clarke, Sally Cunningham, and Barbara Foley Wilson. "The Relative Stability of Remarriage: A Cohort Approach Using Vital Statistics." *Family Relations*, 43 (1994): 305–310.

Colburn, Kenneth, Jr., Phylis Lan Lin, and Mary Candace Moore. "Gender and the Divorce Experience." *Journal of Divorce and Remarriage*, 17 (1992): 87–108.

Coleman, James William, and Donald R. Cressey. *Social Problems* (7th ed.). New York: Longman, 1999.

Coleman, Marilyn, and Lawrence H. Ganong. "Remarriage and Stepfamily Research in the 1980s: Increased Interest in an Old Family Form." *Journal of Marriage and the Family*, 52 (1990): 925–940.

Coleman, Richard, and Lee Rainwater. *Social Standing in America: New Dimensions of Class*. New York: Basic Books, 1978.

Coleman, V. E. *Violence between Lesbian Couples: A between Groups Comparison*. Unpublished doctoral dissertation, 1990. University Microfilms International, 9109022.

Collins, Randall. "Women and Men in the Class Culture." *Journal of Family Issues*, 9 (1988): 27–50.

Coltrane, Scott. *Family Man: Fatherhood, Housework, and Gender Equity*. New York: Oxford University Press, 1996.

Conly, Shanti R. "Sub-Saharan Africa at the Turning Point." *Humanist*, 58 (1998): 19–23.

Constable, Pamela. "Immigrants Discover a Formula for Prosperity." *Washington Post*, August 31, 1998, p. A11.

Constable, Pamela, and D'Vera Cohn. "Culture Clashes Put Immigrant Women on the Front Lines." *Washington Post*, September 1, 1998, p. A1.

Conte, J. "Child Sexual Abuse: Looking Backward and Forward." In *Family Sexual Abuse: Frontline Research and Evaluation*, edited by M. Q. Patton. Newbury Park, CA: Sage, 1991.

Conte, J. "Sexual Abuse of Children." In *Family Violence: Prevention and Treatment*, edited by R. L. Hamilton, T. P. Gullotta, G. R. Adams, E. H. Potter, and R. P. Weissberg. Newbury Park, CA: Sage, 1993.

Contraceptive Use. Alan Guttmacher Institute. June 3, 1997. Available: <agi–usa.org/pubs/fb_contraceptives1.html>.

Cooley, Charles Horton. *Human Nature and Social Order.* New York: Scribner's, 1902.

Cooley, Charles Horton. *Social Organization.* New York: Scribner's, 1909.

Cooney, Teresa, and Peter Uhlenberg. "The Role of Divorce in Men's Relations with Their Adult Children at Mid-Life." *Journal of Marriage and the Family,* 52 (1990): 677–688.

Coontz, Stephanie. *The Way We Never Were: American Families and the Nostalgia Trap.* New York: Basic Books, 1992.

Copeland, Anne P., and Kathleen M. White. *Studying Families.* Newbury Park, CA: Sage, 1991.

Corsaro, William A. *The Sociology of Childhood.* Thousand Oaks, CA: Sage, 1997.

Cortese, Anthony J. "Subcultural Differences in Human Sexuality: Race, Ethnicity, and Social Class." In *Human Sexuality: The Societal and Interpersonal Context,* edited by Kathleen McKinney and Susan Sprecher. Norwood, NJ: Ablex, 1989.

Costigan, Catherine L., Frank J. Floyd, Kristina S. M. Harter, and Joseph C. McClintock. "Family Process and Adaptation to Children with Mental Retardation: Disruption and Resilience in Family Problem-Solving Interactions." *Journal of Family Psychology,* 11 (1997): 515–529.

Cott, Nancy F. *The Bonds of Womanhood: "Women's Sphere" in New England, 1780–1835.* New Haven, CT: Yale University Press, 1977.

Cowan, Caroline P., and Phillip A. Cowan. *When Partners become Parents: The Big Life Change for Couples.* New York: Basic Books, 1992.

Creighton, Linda. "Kids Taking Care of Kids." *U.S. News & World Report,* December 20, 1993, pp. 26–33.

Dalaker, Joseph, and Mary Naifeh. "Poverty in the United States: 1997." *Current Population Reports,* P60–201. Washington, DC: Government Printing Office, 1998. Available: <www.census.gov/prod/3/98pubs/p60–201.pdf>.

DaVanzo, Julie, Allan M. Parnell, and William H. Foege. "Health Consequences of Contraceptive Use and Reproductive Patterns: Summary of a Report from the U.S. National Research Council." *Journal of the American Medical Association,* 265 (1991): 2692–2696.

David, Deborah S., and Robert Brannon (Eds.). *The Forty-Nine Percent Majority: The Male Sex Role.* Reading, MA: Addison-Wesley, 1976.

Davidson, T. *Conjugal Crime: Understanding and Changing the Wifebeating Problem.* New York: Hawthorn Books, 1978.

Davis, Simon. "Men as Success Objects and Women as Sex Objects: A Study of Personal Advertisements." *Sex Roles,* 23 (1990): 43–50.

Davis-Brown, Karen, Sonya Salamon, and Catherine A. Surra. "Economic and Social Factors in Mate Selection: An Ethnographic Analysis of an Agricultural Community." *Journal of Marriage and the Family,* 49 (1987): 41–55.

"Definition of AIDS, The." In *The Relationship between the Human Immunodeficiency Virus and the Acquired Immunodeficiency Syndrome.* March 11, 1997. Available: <www.mediaconsult.com/frames/aids/shareware1/aids/1.html>.

Degler, Carl N. *At Odds: Women and the Family in America from the Revolution to the Present.* New York: Oxford University Press, 1980.

de Kretser, D. M. "Male Infertility." *Lancet,* 349, no. 9054 (1997): 787–790.

Deloria, Vine, and Clifford M. Lytle. *American Indians, American Justice.* Austin: University of Texas Press, 1983.

del Pinal, Jorge. "The Hispanic Population." *Current Population Reports, Special Studies Series,* P23–189. 1995. Available: <www.census.gov/population/pop-profile/p23–189.pdf>.

Demos, John. "The American Family in Past Times." *American Scholar,* 43 (1974): 422–446.

Demos, John. "Images of the American Family, Then and Now." In *Changing Images of the Family,* edited by Virginia Tufte and Barbara Myerhoff. New Haven, CT: Yale University Press, 1979.

Demos, John. "The Changing Faces of Fatherhood: A New Exploration in American Family History." In *Father and Child: Developmental and Clinical Perspectives,* edited by C. Stanley, A. Gurwitt, and J. M. Ross. Boston: Little, Brown, 1982.

Derevensky, Jeffrey L., and Lisa Deschamps. "Young Adults from Divorced and Intact Families: Perceptions about Preferred Custodial Arrangements." *Journal of Divorce and Remarriage,* 27 (1997): 105–122.

De Vita, Carol J. "The United States at Mid-Decade." *Population Bulletin,* 50 (1996): 2–49.

DeWitt, Paula M. "All the Lonely People." *American Demographics,* 14 (1992): 44–46, 48.

DeWitt, Paula M. "In Pursuit of Pregnancy." *American Demographics,* 15 (1993): 48–53.

Diamond, David. "Custody vs. Culture." *USA Weekend,* October 13–15, 1995, pp. 4–6.

DiBeneditto, B., and C. K. Tittle. "Gender and Adult Roles: Role Commitment of Women and Men in a Job-Family Trade-Off Context." *Journal of Counseling Psychology,* 37 (1990): 41–48.

DiCanio, Margaret. *The Encyclopedia of Marriage, Divorce, and the Family.* New York: Facts on File, 1989.

Dilworth-Anderson, Peggye, and Harriette Pipes McAdoo. "The Study of Ethnic Minority Families: Implications for Practitioners and Policymakers." *Family Relations,* 37 (1988): 265–267.

Dilworth-Anderson, Peggye, Linda Burton, and Leanor Boulin Johnson. "Reframing Theories for Understanding Race, Ethnicity, and Families." In *Sourcebook of Family Theories and Methods: A Contextual Approach*, edited by P. G. Boss, W. J. Doherty, R. LaRossa, W. R. Schumm, and S. K. Steinmetz. New York: Plenum Press, 1993.

"Distribution of AIDS Cases." In *The Relationship netween the Human Immunodeficiency Virus and the Acquired Immunodeficiency Syndrome.* March 11, 1997. Available: <www.mediconsult.com/frames/aids/shareware/aids/27.html>.

Dobash, R. P., and R. E. Dobash. *Violence against Wives: A Case Against the Patriarchy.* New York: Free Press, 1979.

Dobash, R. P., and R. E. Dobash. "How Theoretical Definitions and Perspectives Affect Research and Policy." In *Family Violence: Research and Public Policy Issues*, edited by D. J. Besharov. Washington, DC: AEI Press, 1990.

Dodoo, F. Nii-Amoo. "Relative Spousal Status and Child Health in Sub-Sahara Africa: The Case of Ghana." *Sociological Quarterly*, 36 (1994): 507–519.

Dodoo, F. Nii-Amoo. "Men Matter: Additive and Interactive Gendered Preferences and Reproductive Behavior in Kenya." *Demography*, 35 (1998): 229–242.

Doherty, William J., Pauline G. Boss, Ralph LaRossa, Walter R. Schumm, and Suzanne K. Steinmetz. "Family Theories and Methods: A Contextual Approach." In *Sourcebook of Family Theories and Methods: A Contextual Approach*, edited by P. G. Boss, W. J. Doherty, R. LaRossa, W. R. Schumm, and S. K. Steinmetz. New York: Plenum Press, 1993.

Domestic Violence: Faces of Fear. PBS Video, New Jersey Network, 1996.

Dortch, Shannon. "Money and Marital Discord." *American Demographics*, 16 (1994): 11–13.

Doudna, Christine, and Fern McBride. "Where Are the Men for the Women at the Top?" In *Single Life: Unmarried Adults in Social Context*, edited by Peter J. Stein. New York: St. Martin's Press, 1981.

Dunford, F. W., D. Huizinga, and D. Elliott. *The Omaha Domestic Violence Police Experiment: Final Report to the National Institute of Justice and the City of Omaha.* Boulder, CO: Institute of Behavioral Science, 1989.

Dunn, Seth. "Can the North and South Get in Step?" *World Watch*, 11(1998): 19–27.

Duxbury, Linda, Christopher Higgins, and Catherine Lee. "Work-Family Conflict: A Comparison by Gender, Family Type, and Perceived Control." *Journal of Family Issues*, 15 (1994): 449–467.

Dworetzby, John P. *Introduction to Child Development* (4th ed.). St. Paul, MN: West, 1990.

Edelman, Marian Wright. *Families in Peril: An Agenda for Social Change.* Cambridge, MA: Harvard University Press, 1987.

Edelson, J. L. "Coordinated Community Responses." In *Woman Battering: Policy Response*, edited by M. Steinman. Cincinnati, OH: Anderson, 1991.

Edmonson, Brad, Judith Waldrop, Diane Crispell, and Linda Jacobsen. "Childless Couples." *American Demographics*, 15 (1993): 34–35.

Edwards, John N., and Alan Booth. "Sexuality, Marriage, and Well-Being: The Middle Years." In *Sexuality across the Life Course*, edited by Alice S. Rossi. Chicago: University of Chicago Press, 1994.

Egeland, B. "Breaking the Cycle of Abuse: Implications for Prediction and Intervention." In *Early Prediction and Prevention of Child Abuse*, edited by K. D. Browne, C. Davies, and P. Stratton. New York: John Wiley, 1988.

Egeland, B. "A History of Abuse Is a Major Risk Factor for Abusing the Next Generation." In *Current Controversies on Family Violence*, edited by R. J. Gelles and D. R. Loseke. Newbury Park, CA: Sage, 1993.

Eggebeen, David J., and Daniel T. Lichter. "Race, Family Structure, and Changing Poverty among American Children." *American Sociological Review* 56 (1991): 801–817.

Ekerdt, David J., and Barbara H. Vinick. "Marital Complaints in Husband-Working and Husband-Retired Couples." *Research on Aging*, 13 (1991): 364–382.

Elder, Glen H., Jr. "The Life Course as Developmental Theory." *Child Development*, 69 (1998): 1–12.

Elias, Marilyn. "Motherhood Can Work Well in Home or Job." *USA Today*, March 1, 1999, p. D1.

Elkin, Frederick, and Gerald Handel. *The Child & Society: The Process of Socialization* (5th ed.). New York: Random House, 1989.

Ellwood, David T. *Poor Support: Poverty in the American Family.* New York: Basic Books, 1988.

Endocrine Society, The. *Endocrinology and Male Infertility.* Available: <www.endo–society.org/pubaffai/factshee/maleinf.html>.

Engel, John W. "Marriage in the People's Republic of China: Analysis of a New Law." *Journal of Marriage and the Family*, 46 (1984): 955–961.

Engels, Frederick. *The Origin of the Family, Private Property, and the State.* Chicago: Charles H. Kerr, 1902.

"Environmental Toxins and Infertility." *Nutrition Health Review*, 76 (1996): 5.

Erickson, M. F., and B. Egeland. "Child Neglect." In *The APSAC Handbook on Child Maltreatment*, edited by J. Briere, L. Berliner, J. A. Julkley, C. Jenny, and T. Reid. Thousand Oaks, CA: Sage, 1996.

Erickson, Robert. "Social Class of Men, Women, and Families." *Sociology*, 18 (1984): 500–514.

Erlanger, H. S. "Social Class and Corporal Punishment in Childrearing: A Reassessment." *American Sociological Review* 39 (1974): 68–85.

Eshleman, J. Ross (Ed.). "Introduction." In *Perspectives in Marriage and the Family: Text and Readings.* Boston: Allyn and Bacon, 1969.

Eshleman, J. Ross. *The Family* (8th ed.). Boston: Allyn and Bacon, 1997.

Eslinger, Kenneth N., Alfred C. Clarke, and Russell R. Dynes. "The Principle of Least Interest, Dating Behavior, and Family Integration Settings." *Journal of Marriage and the Family*, 34 (1972): 269–272.

Espiritu, Yen Le. "The Refugees and the Refuge: Southeast Asians in the United States." In *The Minority Report: An Introduction to Racial, Ethnic, and Gender Relations* (3rd ed.), edited by Anthony Gary Dworkin and Rosalind J. Dworkin. Fort Worth, TX: Harcourt Brace, 1999.

Etaugh, Claire, and Marsha B. Liss. "Home, School, and Playroom: Training Grounds for Adult Gender Roles." *Sex Roles*, 26 (1992): 129–147.

"Fallacy: Intermarried Couples Have Exactly the Same Rights as Non-Intermarried Couples in Reform Congregations." February 4, 1999. Available: <www.landfield.com/faqs/judiams/FAQ/10–Reform/section–30.html>.

Faludi, Susan. *Backlash: The Undeclared War against American Women*. New York: Crown, 1991.

Farber, Bernard. *Family: Organization and Interaction*. San Francisco: Chandler, 1964.

Farr, K. A. "Fetal Abuse and the Criminalization of Behavior During Pregnancy." *Crime & Delinquency*, 41, no. 2 (1995): 235–245.

Farrington, Keith, and Ely Chertok. "Social Conflict Theories of the Family." In *Sourcebook of Family Theories and Methods: A Contextual Approach*, edited by P. G. Boss, W. J. Doherty, R. LaRossa, W. R. Schumm, and S. K. Steinmetz. New York: Plenum Press, 1993.

Feingold, Alan. "Gender Differences in Mate Selection Preferences: A Test of the Parental Investment Model." *Psychological Bulletin*, 112 (1992): 125–139.

Fendrich, M., M. E. Mackesy-Amiti, and J. Wislar. "Childhood Abuse and the Use of Inhalants: Differences by Degree of Use." *American Journal of Public Health*, 87 (1997): 765–769.

Ferguson, Susan J., and Carla Perry. "Rewriting Menopause: Challenging the Medical Paradigm to Reflect Women's Experiences." *Frontiers*, 19 (1998): 20–41.

Fertilitext: Infertility Treatment Information. Stadtlander Pharmacy. 1998. Available: <www.fertilitext.org/>.

Fertility, Family Planning, and Women's Health: Data Highlights. National Center for Health Statistics. May 1, 1997. Available: <www.cdc.gov/nchswww/product/pubd/series/sr23/pre–1/sr23_19.html>.

Fiagbey, Emmanuel D. K. "Literacy and Family Planning in Rural Ghana." *Journal of Adolescent & Adult Literacy*, 41 (1997): 308–310.

Field, Connie (Producer and Director). *The Life and Times of Rosie the Riveter*. Los Angeles: Direct Cinema, 1987.

Field, H., and L. Bienan. *Jurors and Rape: A Study in Psychology and Law*. Lexington, MA: D. C. Heath, 1980.

Finkelhor, D., and K. Pillemer. "Elder Abuse: Its Relation to Domestic Violence." In *Family Abuse and Its Consequences*, edited by G. Hotaling, D. Finkelhor, J. Kirkpatrick, and M. Straus. Newbury Park, CA: Sage, 1988.

Finkelhor, D., and K. Yllö. *License to Rape: Sexual Abuse of Wives*. New York: Holt, Rinehart and Winston, 1985.

Firmin-Sellers, K. "The Politics of Property Rights." *American Political Science Review*, 89 (1995): 867–882.

Flaks, David, Ilda Ficher, Franker Masterpasqua, and Gregory Joseph. "Lesbians Choosing Motherhood: A Comparative Study of Lesbian and Heterosexual Parents and Their Children." *Developmental Psychology*, 31 (1995): 105–144.

Flanzer, J. P. "Alcohol and Other Drugs Are Key Causal Agents of Violence." In *Current Controversies on Family Violence*, edited by R. J. Gelles and D. R. Loseke. Newbury Park, CA: Sage, 1993.

Flexner, Eleanor. *Century of Struggle: The Women's Rights Movement in the United States* (rev. ed.). Cambridge, MA: Belknap Press of Harvard University Press, 1975.

Folbre, Nancy. "The Unproductive Housewife: Her Evolution in Nineteenth-Century Economic Thought." *Signs: Journal of Women in Culture and Society*, 16 (1991): 463–484.

Folbre, Nancy, and Marjorie Abel. "Women's Work and Women's Households: Gender Bias in the U.S. Census." *Social Research*, 56 (1989): 545–569.

Follingstad, Diane R., Shannon Wright, Shirley Lloyd, and Jeri Sebastian. "Sex Differences in Motivations and Effects in Dating Violence." *Family Relations*, 40 (1991): 51–57.

Forehand, Rex, Michelle Wierson, Amanda McCombs Thomas, Robert Fauber, Lisa Armistead, Tracy Kempton, and Nicholas Long. "A Short-Term Longitudinal Examination of Young Adolescent Functioning Following Divorce: The Role of Family Factors." *Journal of Divorce and Remarriage*, 19 (1991): 97–111.

Fowler, Floyd J., Jr. *Survey Research Methods*. Beverly Hills: Sage, 1984.

Frank, Ellen, and Carol Anderson. "The Sexual Stages of Marriage." In *Marriage and Family in a Changing Society* (2nd ed.), edited by James M. Henslin. New York: Free Press, 1985.

Franklin, Clyde W. *Theoretical Perspectives in Social Psychology*. Boston: Little, Brown, 1982.

Franklin, John Hope. "A Historical Note on Black Families." In *Black Families* (2nd ed.), edited by Harriette Pipes McAdoo. Newbury Park, CA: Sage, 1988.

Franzwa, Gregg, and Charles Lockhart. "The Social Origins and Maintenance of Gender: Communication Styles, Personality Types and Grid-Group Therapy." *Sociological Perspectives*, 41 (1998): 185–208.

Freeston, Mark H., and Michael Plechaty. "Reconsideration of the Locke-Wallace Marital Adjustment Test: Is It Still Relevant for the 1990s?" *Psychological Reports*, 81 (1997): 419–434.

Friedrich, W. N., A. J. Enbender, and W. J. Luecke. "Cognitive and Behavioral Characteristics of Physically Abused Children." *Journal of Consulting and Clinical Psychology*, 51 (1983): 313–314.

Friedrich, W. N., and K. K. Wheeler. "The Abusing Parent Revisited: A Decade of Psychological Research." In *Child Abuse: A Multidisciplinary Survey* (Vol. 3), edited by B. Finkelman. New York: Garland, 1995.

Frieze, I. H. "Investigating the Causes and Consequences of Marital Rape." *Signs: Journal of Women in Culture and Society*, 8 (1983): 532–553.

Fujiwara, Lynn H., and Dana Y. Takagi. "Japanese Americans: Stories about Race in America." In *The Minority Report: An Introduction to Racial, Ethnic, and Gender Relations* (3rd ed.), edited by Anthony Gary Dworkin and Rosalind J. Dworkin. Fort Worth, TX: Harcourt Brace, 1999.

Furstenberg, Frank F., Jr. "Industrialization and the American Family: A Look Backward." *American Sociological Review*, 32 (1966): 326–337.

Furstenberg, Frank F., and Andrew Cherlin. *Divided Families: What Happens to Children when Parents Part?* Cambridge, MA: Harvard University Press, 1991.

Gage, M. Geraldine, and Donna Hendrickson Christensen. "Parental Role and the Transition to Parenthood." *Family Relations,*, 40 (1991): 332–337.

Gallagher, Stephanie. "The Many Roads to Adoption: To Choose One, Adoptive Parents Must Balance Time, Money and Emotional Risk." *Kiplinger's Personal Finance Magazine*, 52, no. 4 (1998): 50–52.

Gano-Phillips, Susan, and Frank D. Fincham. "Assessing Marriage via Telephone Interviews and Written Questionnaires: A Methodological Note." *Journal of Marriage and the Family*, 54 (1992): 630–635.

Ganong, Lawrence, and Marilyn Coleman. "Gender Differences in Expectations of Self and Future Partner." *Journal of Family Issues*, 13 (1992): 55–64.

Ganong, Lawrence, Marilyn Coleman, Annette Kusgen McDaniel, and Tim Killian. "Attitudes Regarding Obligations to Assist an Older Parent or Stepparent Following Later-Life Remarriage." *Journal of Marriage and the Family*, 60 (1998): 595–610.

Gans, Herbert J. *The Urban Villagers*. New York: Free Press, 1982.

Gans, Herbert J. "Deconstructing the Underclass: The Term's Danger as a Planning Concept." *Journal of the American Planning Association*, 56 (Summer 1990): 271.

Garbarino, J. "The Incidence and Prevalence of Child Maltreatment." In *Family Violence*, edited by L. Ohlin and M. Tonry. Chicago: University of Chicago Press, 1989.

Gardner, Saundra. "Exploring the Family Album: Social Class Differences in Images of Family Life." *Sociological Inquiry*, 61 (1991): 242–251.

Garrison, M. Betsy, Lydia B. Blalock, John J. Zarski, and Penny B. Merritt. "Delayed Parenthood: An Exploratory Study of Family Functioning." *Family Relations*, 46 (1997): 281–290.

Gatland, Laura. "Putting the Blame on No-Fault." *ABA Journal*, 83 (1997): 50–53.

Gatlin, Rochelle. *American Women since 1945*. Jackson: University Press of Mississippi, 1987.

Gecas, V. "The Influence of Social Class on Socialization." In *Contemporary Theories about the Family* (Vol. 1), edited by F. Ivan Nye and I. Reiss. New York: Free Press, 1979.

Gelles, R. J. "Child Abuse as Psychopathology: A Sociological Critique and Reformulation." *American Journal of Orthopsychiatry*, 43 (1973): 611–621.

Gelles, R. J. "An Exchange/Social Control Theory." In *The Dark Side of Families: Current Family Violence Research*, edited by D. Finkelhor, R. J. Gelles, G. T. Hotaling, and M. A. Straus. Beverly Hills, CA: Sage, 1983.

Gelles, R. J. "Alcohol and Other Drugs Are Associated with Violence—They Are Not Its Cause." In *Current Controversies on Family Violence*, edited by R. J. Gelles and D. R. Loseke. Newbury Park, CA: Sage, 1993.

Gelles, R. J., and C. P. Cornell. *Intimate Violence in Families* (2nd ed.). Newbury Park, CA: Sage, 1990.

Gelles, R. J., and M. A. Straus. "Is Violence toward Children Increasing?" *Journal of Interpersonal Violence*, 2 (1987): 212–222.

Gelles, R. J., and M. A. Straus. *Intimate Violence*. New York: Simon & Schuster, 1988.

Geronimus, Arline T. "Teenage Childbearing and Social and Reproductive Disadvantage: The Evolution of Complex Questions and the Demise of Simple Answers." *Family Relations*, 40 (1991): 463–471.

"Gets Worse for Who?" *The Middle East*, 238 (1994): 5.

"Ghana: The National Council on Women and Development." *Women's International Network News*, 22 (Autumn 1996): 60. (From National Council on Women and Development, Accra, Ghana).

Gibbs, J. *Sociological Theory Construction*. Hensdale, IL: Dryden Press, 1972.

Gilbert, Bonny. "Infertility and the ADA: Health Insurance Coverage for Infertility Treatment." *Defense Counsel Journal*, 63 (1996): 42–57.

Gilgun, J. F. "Resilience and the Intergenerational Transmission of Child Sexual Abuse." In *Family Sexual Abuse: Frontline Research and Evaluation*, edited by M. Q. Patton. Newbury Park, CA: Sage, 1991.

Glass, Jennifer L., and Sarah Beth Estes. "The Family Responsive Workplace." *Annual Review of Sociology*, 23 (1997): 289–313.

Glenn, Evelyn Nakano, and Stacey G. H. Yap. "Chinese American Families." In *Minority Families in the United States: A Multicultural Perspective*, edited by Ronald L. Taylor. Englewood Cliffs, NJ: Prentice-Hall, 1994.

Glenn, Norval D. "Psychological Well-Being in the Post-parental Stage: Some Evidence from National Surveys." *Journal of Marriage and the Family*, 37 (1975): 105–110.

Glenn, Norval D. "Interreligious Marriage in the United States: Patterns and Recent Trends." *Journal of Marriage and the Family*, 44 (1982): 555–567.

Glenn, Norval D. "Quantitative Research on Marital Quality in the 1980s: A Critical Review." *Journal of Marriage and the Family*, 52 (1990): 818–831.

Glenn, Norval D. "The Recent Trend in Marital Success in the United States." *Journal of Marriage and the Family*, 53 (1991): 261–270.

Glick, Paul C. "Fifty Years of Family Demography: A Record of Social Change." *Journal of Marriage and the Family*, 50 (1988): 861–873.

Glick, Paul C., and Graham B. Spanier. "Cohabitation in the United States." In *Single Life: Unmarried Adults in Social Context*, edited by Peter J. Stein. New York: St. Martin's Press, 1981.

Goldscheider, Calvin, and Frances Goldscheider. "Moving Out and Marriage: What Do Young Adults Expect?" *American Sociological Review*, 52 (1987): 278–285.

Goldson, E. "Children with Disabilities and Child Maltreatment." *Child Abuse & Neglect*, 22 (1998): 663–667.

Goldthorpe, John H. "Women and Class Analysis: In Defence of the Conventional View." *Sociology*, 17 (1983): 465–488.

Goliber, Thomas J. "Population and Reproductive Health in Sub-Saharan Africa." *Population Bulletin*, 52, no. 4 (1997) 1–44.

Golini, Antonio. "How Low Can Fertility Be? An Empirical Exploration." *Population and Development Review*, 24 (1998): 59–73.

Gomes-Schwartz, B, J. M. Horowitz, and A. P. Cardarelli. *Child Sexual Abuse: The Initial Effects*. Newbury Park, CA: Sage, 1990.

Gondolf, E. W., and R. A. Foster. "Pre-Program Attrition in Batterer Programs." *Journal of Family Violence*, 6 (1991): 337–349.

Goode, William J. *Women in Divorce* (originally published as *After Divorce*). New York: Free Press, 1956.

Goode, William J. "A Theory of Role Strain." *American Sociological Review*, 25 (1960): 483–496.

Goode, William J. *World Revolution and Family Patterns*. New York: Free Press, 1963.

Goode, William J. *The Family*. Englewood Cliffs, NJ: Prentice-Hall, 1964.

Goode, William J. "Why Men Resist." In *Men's Lives*, edited by Michael S. Kimmel and Michael A. Messner. New York: Macmillan, 1989.

Goode, William J. *World Changes in Divorce Patterns*. New Haven, CT: Yale University Press, 1993.

Goodwin, Robin. "Sex Differences among Partner Preferences: Are the Sexes Really Very Similar?" *Sex Roles*, 23 (1990): 501–512.

Gordon, M. *The American Family: Past, Present, and Future*. New York: Random House, 1978.

Gorney, B. "Domestic Violence and Chemical Dependency: Dual Problems, Dual Interventions." *Journal of Psychoactive Drugs*, 21 (1989): 229–238.

Gottman, John M., James Coan, Sybil Carrere, and Catherine Swanson. "Predicting Marital Happiness and Stability from Newlywed Interactions." *Journal of Marriage and the Family*, 60 (1998): 5–22.

Gould, Lois. "X: A Fabulous Child's Story." *Ms.*, 1 (December, 1972): 74–76, 105–106.

Graham, John W. "A Comment on 'Why Did Child Support Award Levels Decline from 1978 to 1985?' by Philip K. Robins." *Journal of Human Resources*, 30 (1995): 622–631.

Grayson, Deborah A. "Mediating Intimacy: Black Surrogate Mothers and the Law." *Critical Inquiry*, 24 (1998): 525–546.

Green, Donald. "Native Americans." In *The Minority Report: An Introduction to Racial, Ethnic, and Gender Relations* (3rd ed.), edited by Anthony Gary Dworkin and Rosalind J. Dworkin. Fort Worth, TX: Harcourt Brace, 1999.

Greenblat, Cathy Stein. "Sexuality in the Early Years of Marriage." In *Marriage and Family in a Changing Society* (2nd ed.), edited by James M. Henslin. New York: Free Press, 1985.

Greenstein, Theodore. "Marital Disruption and the Employment of Married Women." *Journal of Marriage and the Family*, 52 (1990): 657–676.

Greenstein, Theodore. "Gender Ideology, Marital Disruption, and the Employment of Married Women." *Journal of Marriage and the Family*, 57 (1995): 31–42.

Greenwald, Maurine Weiner. *Women, War, and Work: The Impact of World War I on Women Workers in the United States*. Westport, CT: Greenwood Press, 1980.

Griffin, M. K. "In 44 States, It's Legal to Rape Your Wife." *Student Lawyer*, 9 (1980): 20–23, 57–61.

Grizzle, Gary L. "Remarriage as an Incomplete Institution: Cherlin's (1978) Views and Why We Should Be Cautious about Accepting Them." *Journal of Divorce and Remarriage*, 26 (1996): 191–201.

Groth, A. N., and T. S. Gary. "Marital Rape." *Medical Aspects of Human Sexuality*, 15 (1981): 122–132.

Grunebaum, Henry. "The Relationship of Family Theory to Family Therapy." *Journal of Marital and Family Therapy*, 14 (1988): 1–14.

Gwanfogbe, Philomina N., Walter R. Schrum, Meredith Smith, and James L. Furrow. "Polygyny and Marital Life Satisfaction: An Exploratory Study from Rural Cameroon." *Journal of Comparative Family Studies*, 28 (1997): 55–71.

Hall, David R. "Marriage as a Pure Relationship: Exploring the Link between Premarital Cohabitation and Divorce in Canada." *Journal of Comparative Family Studies*, 27 (1996): 1–12.

Hall, David R., and John Z. Zhao. "Cohabitation and Divorce in Canada: Testing the Selectivity Hypothesis." *Journal of Marriage and the Family*, 57 (1995): 421–427.

Hansen-Shaevitz, M. H. *The Superwoman Syndrome.* New York: Warner, 1984.

Hanson, Sandra L. "The Economic Costs and Rewards of Two-Earner, Two-Parent Families." *Journal of Marriage and the Family*, 53 (1991): 622–634.

Hanson, Sandra L., Gretchen T. Cornwell, Gordon F. De-Jong, and C. Shannon Stokes. "Consequences of Involuntary Low Parity for Women's Perceptions of Homemaker and Work Roles: Findings From a 24-Year Longitudinal Study." *Sociology and Social Problems*, 68 (1984): 326–349.

Hanson, Thomas L., Irwin Garfinkel, Sara S. McLanahan, and Cynthia K. Miller. "Trends in Child Support Outcomes." *Demography*, 33 (1996): 483–496.

Hareven, Tamara K. "American Families in Transition: Historical Perspectives on Change." In *Family in Transition* (7th ed.), edited by Arlene S. Skolnick and Jerome H. Skolnick. New York: HarperCollins, 1992.

Harris, Lynn. "The Hidden World of Dating Violence." *Parade Magazine*, September 22, 1996, pp. 4–6.

Harris, Sarah B. "For Better or Worse: Spouse Abuse Grown Old." *Journal of Elder Abuse & Neglect*, 8 (1996): 1–34.

Hart, S. N., R. B. Germain, and M. R. Brassard. "The Challenge: To Better Understand and Combat Psychological Maltreatment of Children and Youth." In *Psychological Maltreatment of Children and Youth*, edited by M. R. Brassard, R. Germain, and S. N. Hart. New York: Pergamon Press, 1987.

Hatfield, Elaine, and Richard L. Rapson. *Love and Sex: Cross-Cultural Perspectives.* Boston: Allyn and Bacon, 1996.

Haviland, William A. *Anthropology* (7th ed.). Fort Worth, TX: Harcourt Brace, 1994.

Haws, Wendy Amstutz, and Brent Mallinckrodt. "Separation-Individuation from Family of Origin and Marital Adjustment of Recently Married Couples." *American Journal of Family Therapy*, 26 (1998): 293–306.

Hayden, Mary F., and Jon Goldman. "Families of Adults with Mental Retardation: Stress Levels and Need for Services." *Social Work*, 41 (1996): 657–667.

Hayghe, Howard V., and Suzanne Bianchi. "Married Mothers Work Patterns: The Job-Family Compromise." *Monthly Labor Review*, 117, no. 6 (1994): 24–30.

Hays, Sharon. *The Cultural Construction of Motherhood.* New Haven, CT: Yale University Press, 1996.

Heckert, D. Alex, Thomas C. Nowak, and Kay A. Snyder. "The Impact of Husbands' and Wives' Relative Earnings on Marital Disruption." *Journal of Marriage and the Family*, 60 (1998): 690–703.

Heiss, Jerold. "Social Roles." In *Social Psychology*, edited by Morris Rosenberg and Ralph Turner. New York: Basic Books, 1981.

Hendrix, Lewellyn, and Willie Pearson, Jr. "Spousal Interdependence, Female Power and Divorce: A Cross-Cultural Examination." *Journal of Comparative Family Studies*, 26 (1995): 217–232.

Henifin, Mary S. "New Reproductive Technologies: Equity and Access to Reproductive Health care." *Journal of Social Issues*, 49 (1993): 61–74.

Henry, Carolyn S., and Sandra G. Lovelace. "Family Resources and Adolescent Family Life Satisfaction in Remarried Family Households." *Journal of Family Issues*, 16 (1995): 765–786.

Henry, William. "Beyond the Melting Pot." *Time*, 135, no. 15 (1990): 28–31.

Henshaw, Stanley K., and Kathryn Kost. "Abortion Patients in 1994–1995: Characteristics and Contraceptive Use." *Family Planning Perspectives*, 28 (1996): 140–147.

Hewitt, John P. *Self and Society: A Symbolic Interactionist Social Psychology* (7th ed.). Boston: Allyn and Bacon, 1997.

Hien, Denise, and Nina M. Hien. "Women, Violence with Intimates, and Substance Abuse: Relevant Theory, Empirical Findings, and Recommendations for Further Research." *American Journal of Drug and Alcohol Abuse*, 24 (1998): 419–438.

Higginbotham, Elizabeth. "Is Marriage a Priority? Class Differences in Marital Options of Educated Black Women." *In Single Life: Unmarried Adults in Social Context*, edited by Peter J. Stein. New York: St. Martin's Press, 1981.

Higgins, Christopher, Linda Duxbury, and Catherine Lee. "Impact of Life-Cycle Stage and Gender on the Ability to Balance Work and Family Responsibilities." *Family Relations*, 43 (1994): 144–150.

Hill, Rubin. "Campus Values in Mate Selection." *Journal of Home Economics*, 37 (1945): 554–558.

Hiller, D. V., and J. Philliber. "Maximizing Confidence in Married Couple Samples." *Journal of Marriage and the Family*, 47 (1985): 729–732.

Hiller, Dana, and William Philliber. "Determinants of Social Class Identification of Dual-Earner Couples." *Journal of Marriage and the Family*, 48 (1986): 583–587.

Hirschel, J. D., I. W. Hutchinson, C. W. Dean, J. J. Kelley, and C. E. Pesackis. *Charlotte Spouse Assault Replication Project: Final Report* (Grant No 89IJ–CK–K004). Washington, DC: National Institute of Justice, 1991.

HIV Infection and AIDS. Public Health Service. March 11, 1997. Available: <www.mediconsult.com/frames/aids/shareware/hiv_aids/hivdefine.html>.

Hochschild, Arlie. *The Second Shift: Working Parents and the Revolution at Home.* New York: Viking, 1989.

Hoffman, Lois W. "Changes in Family Roles, Socialization, and Sex Differences." In *Childhood Socialization*, edited by Gerald Handel. New York: Aldine De Gruyter, 1988.

Hoffman, Lois Wladis, and Jean Denby Manis. "The Value of Children in the United States: A New Approach to the Study of Fertility." *Journal of Marriage and the Family*, 41 (1979): 583–596.

Hollingsworth, Leslie Doty. "Effect of Transracial Adoption on Children's Racial and Ethnic Identity and Self-Esteem: A Meta-Analytic Review." *Marriage & Family Review*, 25 (1997): 99–130.

Hollingsworth, Leslie Doty. "Promoting Same-Race Adoption for Children of Color." *Social Work*, 43 (1998): 104–116.

Holman, Linda J. "Working Effectively with Hispanic Immigrant Families." *Phi Delta Kappan*, 78 (April 1997): 647.

Homans, George C. "Social Behavior as Exchange." *American Journal of Sociology*, 63 (1958): 597–606.

Hope, Toni Gerber. "The Ultimate Fertility Guide," *Redbook*, November 1998, p. 146.

Hornby, Garry, and Tracey Ashworth. "Grandparents' Support for Families Who Have Children with Disabilities." *Journal of Child and Family Studies*, 3 (1994): 403–412.

Howard, Judy. "The Influence of Children's Development Dysfunctions on Marital Quality and Interaction." In *Child Influences on Marital and Family Interaction* (pp. 275–298), edited by Richard M. Lerner and Graham B. Spanier New York: Academic Press, 1978.

Howard, Michael C., and Janet Dunaif-Hattis. *Anthropology: Understanding Human Adaptation*. New York: HarperCollins,1992.

Howell, Susan H., Pedro R. Portes, and Joseph H. Brown. "Gender and Age Differences in Child Adjustment to Parental Separation." *Journal of Divorce and Remarriage*, 27 (1997): 141–158.

Huang, K., and L. Uba. "Premarital Sexual Behavior among Chinese College Students in the United States." *Archives of Sexual Behavior*, 21, no. 3 (1992): 227–240.

Hunsley, John, Celine Pinsent, Monique Lefebvre, Susan James-Tanner, and Diana Vito. "Construct Validity of the Short Forms of the Dyadic Adjustment Scale." *Family Relations*, 44 (1995): 231–237.

Huston, J., and R. Burgess (Eds.). "Social Exchange in Developing Relationships: An Overview." In *Social Exchange in Developing Relationships*. New York: Academic Press, 1979.

Huttman, Elizabeth. "A Research Note on Dreams and Aspirations of Black Families." *Journal of Contemporary Family Studies*, 22, no. 2 (Summer 1991): 147–158.

Idle, Tracey, Eileen Wood, and Serge Desmarais. "Gender Role Socialization in Toy Play Situations: Mothers and Fathers with Their Sons and Daughters." *Sex Roles*, 28 (1993): 679–691.

Ingall, Marjorie. "S-E-X in the U.S.A.: Wake Us When It's Over." *Ms.*, 5 (January/February 1995): 93.

Ishii-Kuntz, Masako. "International Relationships among Chinese, Japanese, and Korean Americans." *Family Relations*, 46 (1997): 23–32.

Island, D., and P. Letellier. *Men Who Beat the Men Who Love Them*. New York: Harrington Park Press, 1991.

Ivy, Diana K., and Phil Backlund. *Exploring GenderSpeak: Personal Effectiveness in Gender Communications*. New York: McGraw-Hill, 1994.

Jacobson, N. *When Men Batter*. New York: Simon & Schuster, 1998.

Jasinski, Jana L., Nancy L. Asdigian, and Glenda Kaufman Kantor. "Ethnic Adaptations to Occupational Strain: Work-Related Stress, Drinking, and Wife Assault among Anglo and Hispanic Husbands." *Journal of Interpersonal Violence*, 12 (December 1997): 814.

Jedlicka, Davor. "Automated Go-Betweens: Mate Selection of Tomorrow?" *Family Relations*, 30 (1981): 373–376.

Jezl, David R., Christian E. Molidor, and Tracy L. Wright. "Physical, Sexual and Psychological Abuse in High School Dating Relationships: Prevalence Rates and Self-Esteem Issues." *Child and Adolescent Social Work Journal*, 13 (1996): 69–87.

Johnson, Elizabeth M., and Ted L. Huston. "The Perils of Love, or Why Wives Adapt to Husbands during the Transition to Parenthood." *Journal of Marriage and the Family*, 60 (1998): 195–204.

Jones, Gavin. "Modernization and Divorce: Contrasting Trends in Islamic Southeast Asia and the West." *Population and Development Review*, 23 (1997): 95–104.

Jones, Russell A. *Research Methods in the Social and Behavioral Sciences*. Sunderland, MA: Sinauer Associates, 1985.

Jost, Kenneth, and Marilyn Robinson. "Divorce and Children." *CQ Researcher*, 1 (1991): 351–363.

Jowell, Roger. "How Comparative Is Comparative Research?" *American Behavioral Scientist*, 42 (1998): 168–177.

Judge, Sharol Lesar. "Parental Coping Strategies and Strengths in Families of Young Children with Disabilities." *Family Relations*, 47 (1998): 263–268.

Julian, Teresa W., Patrick W. McKenny, and Kevin Arnold. "Psychosocial Predictors of Stress Associated with Male Midlife." *Sex Roles*, 22 (1990): 707–722.

Kahn, Joan R., and Kathryn A. London. "Premarital Sex and Risk of Divorce." *Journal of Marriage and the Family*, 53 (1991): 845–855.

Kalick, S. Michael, and Thomas E. Hamilton. "The Matching Hypothesis Re-Examined." *Journal of Personality and Social Psychology*, 51 (1986): 673–682.

Kalish, Susan. "Minorities Still Less Likely to Own Homes." *Population Today*, 22, no. 12 (1994): 3.

Kalmijn, Matthijs. "Shifting Boundaries: Trends in Religious and Educational Homogamy." *American Sociological Review*, 56 (1991a): 786–800.

Kalmijn, Matthijs. "Status Homogamy in the United States." *American Journal of Sociology*, 97 (1991b): 496–523.

Kalmuss, Debra. "Adoption and Black Teenagers: The Viability of a Pregnancy Resolution Strategy." *Journal of Marriage and the Family*, 54 (1992): 485–495.

Kamo, Yoshinori, and Ellen L. Cohen. "Division of Household Work between Partners: A Comparison of Black and White Couples." *Journal of Comparative Family Studies*, 29 (1998): 131–142.

Kannae, Lawrence, and Brian F. Pendleton. "Socioeconomic Status and Use of Family Planning among Ghanaian Government Workers." *Social Biology*, 45 (1989): 113–133.

Kaplan, David A., and Daniel Klaidman. "A Battle, Not the War." *Newsweek*, June 3, 1996, pp. 24–30.

Katchadourian, Hernant A. *Fundamentals of Human Sexuality* (4th ed.). New York: Holt, Rinehart and Winston, 1985.

Kaufman, J., and D. Cicchetti. "The Effects of Maltreatment on School-Aged Children's Socio-Emotional Development: Assessments in a Day-Camp Setting." *Developmental Psychology*, 25 (1989): 516–524.

Kaufman, J., and E. Zigler. "Do Abused Children become Abusive Parents?" *American Journal of Orthopsychiatry*, 57 (1987): 186–192.

Kaufman, J., and E. Zigler. "The Intergenerational Transmission of Abuse Is Overstated." In *Current Controversies on Family Violence*, edited by R. J. Gelles and D. R. Loseke. Newbury Park, CA: Sage, 1993.

Keith, Pat M. "Isolation of the Unmarried in Later Life." *Family Relations*, 35 (1986): 389–395.

Kelleher, K., M. Chaffen, and J. Hollenberg. "Do Abused Children Become Abusive Parents?" *American Journal of Orthopsychiatry*, 57 (1987): 186–192.

Kelleher, K., M. Chaffen, and J. Hollenberg. "Alcohol and Drug Disorders among Physically Abusive and Neglectful Parents in a Community-Based Sample." *American Journal of Public Health*, 84 (1994): 1586–1590.

Kelly, E. E., and L. Warshafsky. *Partner Abuse in Gay Male and Lesbian Couples.* Paper presented at the Third National Violence Research Conference, Durham, NC, 1987.

Kemp, A. *Abuse in the Family: An Introduction.* Pacific Grove, CA: Brooks/Cole, 1998.

Kempton, Tracy, Lisa Armistead, Michelle Wierson, and Rex Forehand. "Presence of a Sibling as a Potential Buffer Following Parental Divorce: An Examination of Young Adolescents." *Journal of Clinical Child Psychology*, 2 (1991): 434–438.

Kenkel, William F. *The Family in Perspective* (3rd ed.). Pacific Palisades, CA: Goodyear, 1973.

Kenrick, Douglas T., Gary E. Groth, Melanie R. Trost, and Edward K. Sadalla. "Integrating Evolutionary and Social Exchange Perspectives on Relationships: Effects of Gender, Self-Appraisal, and Involvement Level on Mate Selection Criteria." *Journal of Personality and Social Psychology*, 64 (1993): 951–969.

Kerlinger, Fred N. *Foundations of Behavioral Research* (2nd ed.). New York: Holt, Rinehart and Winston, 1973.

Keshet, Jamie K. "The Remarried Couple: Stresses and Successes." In *Public and Private Families: A Reader* (pp. 297–310), edited by Andrew J. Cherlin. Boston: McGraw-Hill, 1998.

Kilmartin, Christopher T. *The Masculine Self.* New York: Macmillan, 1994.

Kimball, M. M. "Television and Sex Role Attitudes." In *The Impact of Television: A Natural Experiment in Three Communities*, edited by T. M. Williams. Orlando, FL: Academic Press, 1986.

King, Donna, and Carol E. MacKinnon. "Making Difficult Choices Easier: A Review of Research on Day Care and Children's Development." *Family Relations*, 37 (1988): 392–398.

Kinnunen, Ulla, and Saija Mauno. "Antecedents and Outcomes of Work-Family Conflict among Employed Women and Men in Finland. *Human Relations*, 51 (1998): 157–177.

Kirk, Dudley, and Bernard Pillet. "Fertility Levels, Trends, and Differentials in Sub-Saharan Africa in the 1980s and 1990s." *Studies in Family Planning*, 29 (1998): 1–22.

Kitamura, Toshinori, Mitsuka Aoki, Masako Fujino, Chiaka Ura, Mayumi Watanabe, Kyoko Watanabe, and Shigeki Fujihara. "Sex Differences in Marital and Social Adjustment." *Journal of Social Psychology*, 138 (1998): 26–32.

Kitson, Gay C., and Leslie A. Morgan. "The Multiple Consequences of Divorce: A Decade Review." *Journal of Marriage and the Family*, 52 (1990): 913–924.

Klaus, P., and M. Rand. *Special Report: Family Violence.* Washington, DC: U.S. Department of Justice, Bureau of Justice Statistics, 1992.

Klein, F. "Violence against Women." In *The Women's Annual 1982–1983*, edited by B. Haber. Boston: G. K. Hall, 1983.

Kleine, Doug. "Who Will Feed China?" *Journal of Soil and Water Conservation*, 52 (1997): 398.

Kluwer, Esther S., Jose A. M. Heesink, and Evert van de Vliert. "Marital Conflict about the Division of Household Labor and Paid Work." *Journal of Marriage and the Family*, 58 (1996): 958–969.

Kluwin, Thomas N., and Martha Gonter Gaustad. "The Role of Adaptability and Communication in Fostering Cohesion in Families with Deaf Adolescents. *American Annals of the Deaf*, 139 (1994): 329–335.

Knox, David, and Kenneth Wilson. "Dating Behaviors of University Students." *Family Relations,* 30 (1981): 255–258.

Knudsen, D. D. *Child Maltreatment: Emerging Perspectives.* Dix Hills, NY: General Hall, 1992.

Koblinsky, Sally A., and Christine M. Todd. "Teaching Self-Care Skills to Latchkey Children: A Review of Research." *Family Relations,* 38 (1989): 431–435.

Koerin, Beverly B. "Women as Homemakers: How Social Workers Can Help." *Social Casework,* 66 (1985): 98–105.

Kohn, Melvin L. "The Effects of Social Class on Parental Values and Practices." In *Perspectives on the Family: History, Class, and Feminism,* edited by Christopher Carlson. Belmont, CA: Wadsworth, 1990.

Kolko, D. J. "Child Physical Abuse." In *The APSAC Handbook on Child Maltreatment,* edited by J. Briere, L. Berliner, J. A. Julkley, C. Jenny, and T. Reid. Thousand Oaks, CA: Sage, 1996.

Kolko, J. R., E. H. Blakely, and D. Engleman. "Children Who Witness Domestic Violence: A Review of Empirical Literature." *Journal of Interpersonal Violence,* 11 (1996): 281–293.

Komarovsky, Mirra. *Blue-Collar Marriage.* New York: Vintage Books, 1967.

Korn, Sam J., Stella Chess, and Paulina Fernandez. "The Impacts of Children's Physical Handicaps on Marital and Quality and Family Interaction." In *Child Influences on Marital and Family Interaction* (pp. 299–326), edited by Richard M. Lerner and Graham B. Spanier. New York: Academic Press, 1978.

Kornblum, William, and Joseph Julian. *Social Problems* (9th ed.). Upper Saddle River, NJ: Prentice-Hall, 1998.

Kotlowitz, Alex. *There Are No Children Here: The Story of Two Boys Growing Up in the Other America.* New York: Doubleday, 1991.

Kozol, Jonathan. *Savage Inequalities: Children in America's Schools.* New York: Crown, 1991.

Krajewski, Sandra S., Mary Fran Rybarik, Margaret F. Dosch, and Gary D. Gilmore. "Results of a Curriculum Intervention with Seventh Graders Regarding Violence in Relationships." *Journal of Family Violence,* 11 (1996): 93–112.

Krishman, Satya P., Judith C. Hilbert, Dawn Van Leeuwen, and Raiza Kolia. "Documenting Domestic Violence among Ethnically Diverse Populations: Results from a Preliminary Study." *Family Community Health,* 20 (1997): 32–38.

Krishnan, Vijaya. "Premarital Cohabitation and Marital Disruption." *Journal of Divorce & Remarriage,* 28 (1998): 157–169.

Kronsberg, Sandra, Karen Schmaling, and Beverly I. Fagot. "Risk in a Parent's Eyes: Effects of Gender and Parenting Experience." *Sex Roles,* 13 (1985): 329–341.

Kruger, Arnold. "The Midlife Transition: Crisis or Chimera?" *Psychological Reports,* 75 (1994): 1299–1305.

Ku, Leighton, Freya L. Sonenstein, and Joseph H. Pleck. "Neighborhood, Family, and Work: Influences on the Premarital Behaviors of Adolescent Males." *Social Forces,* 73 (1993): 479–503.

Kuhn, Thomas S. *The Structure of Scientific Revolutions.* Chicago: University of Chicago Press, 1962.

Kulczychi, Andrzej, Malcolm Potts, and Allan Rosenfield. "Abortion and Fertility Regulations." *Lancet,* 347 (1996): 1663–1668.

Kurdek, Lawrence A. "Predictors of Increases in Marital Distress in Newlywed Couples: A 3-Year Prospective Longitudinal Study." *Developmental Psychology,* 27 (1991): 627–636.

Kurdek, Lawrence A. "The Allocation of Household Labor in Gay, Lesbian and Heterosexual Married Couples." *Journal of Social Issues,* 49 (1993): 127–139.

Kurdek, Lawrence A. "Relationship Outcomes and Their Predictors: Longitudinal Evidence from Heterosexual Married, Gay Cohabiting, and Lesbian Cohabiting Couples." *Journal of Marriage and the Family,* 60 (1998): 553–568.

La Gaipa, J. J. "Interpersonal Attraction and Social Exchange. In *Theory and Practice in Interpersonal Attraction,* edited by Steve Duck. New York: Academic Press, 1977.

Lambert, Susan J. "Processes Linking Work and Family: A Critical Review and Research Agenda." *Human Relations,* 43 (1990): 239–257.

Landale, Nancy S., and Katherine Fennelly. "Informal Unions among Mainland Puerto Ricans: Cohabitation or an Alternative to Legal Marriage?" *Journal of Marriage and the Family,* 54 (1992): 269–280.

Landes, A., J. Quiram, and N. R. Jacobs. *Child Abuse: Betraying a Trust.* Wylie, TX: Information Plus, 1995.

Landis-Kleine, Cathy, Linda A. Foley, Loretta Nall, Patricia Padgett, Leslie Walters-Palmer. "Attitudes toward Marriage and Divorce Held by Young Adults." *Journal of Divorce and Remarriage,* 23 (1995): 63–70.

Landry, Bart. *The New Black Middle Class.* Berkeley: University of California Press, 1987.

Langhinrichsen-Rohling, Jennifer, and Colleen Dostal. "Retrospective Reports of Family-of-Origin Divorce and Abuse and College Student's Pre-Parenthood Cognitions." *Journal of Family Violence,* 11 (1996): 331–346.

Langman, Lauren, "Social Stratification." In *Handbook of Marriage and the Family,* edited by Marvin B. Sussman and Suzanne K. Steinmetz. New York: Plenum Press, 1987.

LaRossa, Ralph. "Fatherhood and Social Change." *Family Relations,* 37 (1988): 451–457.

LaRossa, Ralph. *The Modernization of Fatherhood: A Social and Political History.* Chicago: University of Chicago Press, 1997.

LaRossa, Ralph, and Donald C. Reitzes. "Symbolic Interactionism and Family Studies." In *Sourcebook of Family Theories and Methods: A Contextual Approach,* edited by P. G. Boss, W. J. Doherty, R. LaRossa, W. R. Schumm, and S. K. Steinmetz. New York: Plenum Press, 1993.

Larson, Jan. "Cohabitation Is a Premarital Step." *American Demographics,* 13 (November 1991): 20–21.

Larson, Richard F., Mervin F. White, and Marc L. Petrowsky. *Introduction to Sociology: Order and Change in Society* (6th ed.). Dubuque, IA: Kendall/Hunt, 1998.

Lasch, Christopher. *Haven in a Heartless World: The Family Besieged.* New York Basic Books, 1977.

Lauer, Robert. *Social Problems and the Quality of Life* (7th ed.). Boston: WCB McGraw-Hill, 1998.

Laumann, Edward O., John H. Gagnon, Robert T. Michael, and Stuart Michaels. *The Social Organization of Sexuality: Sexual Practices in the United States.* Chicago: University of Chicago Press, 1994.

Lavee, Yoav, and David C. Dollahite. "The Linkage between Theory and Research in Family Science." *Journal of Marriage and the Family,* 53 (1991): 361–373.

Lawson, Erma Jean, and Aaron Thompson. "Black Men Make Sense of Marital Distress and Divorce." *Family Relations,* 44 (1995): 211–218.

Lear, Dana. *Sex and Sexuality: Risk and Relationships in the Age of AIDS.* Thousand Oaks, CA: Sage, 1997.

Leavy, Walter. "Sex in Black America: Reality and Myth." *Ebony,* 48 (August 1993): 126–130.

Lee, Gary R. "The Utility of Cross-Cultural Data: Potentials and Limitations for Family Sociology." *Journal of Family Issues,* 5 (1984): 519–541.

Lee, Gary R. "Comparative Perspectives." In *Handbook of Marriage and the Family* (pp. 59–80), edited by Marvin B. Sussman and Suzanne K. Steinmetz. New York: Plenum Press, 1987.

Lee, Gary R., Chuck W. Peek, and Raymond T. Coward. "Race Differences in Filial Responsibility Expectations among Older Parents." *Journal of Marriage and the Family,* 60 (1998a): 404–412.

Lee, Gary R., Marion C. Willetts, and Karen Seccombe. "Widowhood and Depression: Gender Differences." *Research on Aging,* 20 (1998b): 611–630.

Lee, Gary R., Jeffrey W. Dwyer, and Raymond T. Coward. "Gender Differences in Parent Care: Demographic Factors and Same-Gender Preferences." *Journal of Gerontology,* 48 (1993): 59–68.

Lee, Sharon M. "Asian Americans: Diverse and Growing." *Population Bulletin,* 53, no. 2 (June 1998): 2–39.

Lee, Sharon M., and Marilyn Fernandez. "Trends in Asian American Racial/Ethnic Intermarriage: A Comparison of 1980 and 1990 Census Data." *Sociological Perspectives,* 41, no 2 (Summer 1998): 323–333.

Lein, Laura. "Male Participation in Home Life: Impact of Social Supports and Breadwinner Responsibility on the Allocation of Tasks." *The Family Coordinator,* 28 (1979): 489–495.

Leiulfsrud, Hakon, and Alison Woodward. "Women at Class-Crossroads: Repudiating Conventional Theories of Family Class." *Sociology,* 21 (1987): 393–412.

LeMasters, E. E. "Parenthood as Crisis." *Journal of Marriage and Family Living,* 19 (1957): 325–355.

LeMasters, E. E. *Blue-Collar Aristocrats: Life-Styles at a Working-Class Tavern.* Madison: University of Wisconsin Press, 1975.

LeMasters, E. E., and John DeFrain. *Parents in Contemporary America: A Sympathetic View* (5th ed.). Belmont, CA: Wadsworth, 1989.

Leslie, Gerald R. *The Family in Social Context* (5th ed.). New York: Oxford University Press, 1982.

Lever, Janet. "Sex Differences in the Complexity of Children's Play and Games." In *Childhood Socialization,* edited by Gerald Handel. New York: Aldine De Gruyter, 1988.

Levine, Robert V. "Is Love a Luxury?" *American Demographics,* 15 (February 1993): 27–29.

Lewis, Oscar. "The Culture of Poverty." *Scientific American,* 215, no. 4 (1966): 19–25.

Lewis, Robert A. "Emotional Intimacy among Men." *Journal of Social Issues,* 34 (1978): 108–121.

Lewis, Robert A., and Graham B. Spanier. "Theorizing about the Quality and Stability of Marriage." In *Contemporary Theories about the Family: Research-Based Theories* (Vol. 1, pp. 268–294), edited by Wesley R. Burr, Reuben Hill, F. Ivan Nye, and Ira L. Reiss. New York: Free Press, 1979.

Liberty, M., D. Hughey, and R. Scaglion. "Rural and Urban Omaha Indian Fertility." *Human Biology,* 48 (1976): 59–71.

Lichter, Daniel L., Robert N. Anderson, and Mark D. Hayward. "Marriage Markets and Marital Choice." *Journal of Family Issues,* 16 (1995): 412–431.

Lichter, Daniel T., and Nancy S. Landale. "Parental Work, Family Structure, and Poverty Among Latino Children." *Journal of Marriage and the Family,* 57 (May 1995): 346–354.

Lie, G-Y, R. Schilit, R. Bush, M. Montagne, and L. Reyes. "Lesbians in Currently Aggressive Relationships: How Frequently Do They Report Aggressive Past Relationships?" *Violence and Victims,* 6 (1991), 121–135.

Lillard, Lee A., Michael J. Briend, and Linda J. Waite. "Premarital Cohabitation and Subsequent Marital Dissolution: A Matter of Self-Selection?" *Demography,* 32 (1995): 437–457.

Lin, Jan. "Chinese Americans: From Exclusion to Prosperity?" In *The Minority Report: An Introduction to Racial, Ethnic, and Gender Relations* (3rd ed.), edited by Anthony Gary Dworkin and Rosalind J. Dworkin. Fort Worth, TX: Harcourt Brace, 1999.

Litwak, Eugene. "Occupational Mobility and Extended Family Cohesion." *American Sociological Review*, 25 (1960): 9–20.

Lloyd, Sally. "The Darkside of Courtship: Violence and Sexual Exploitation." *Family Relations*, 40 (1991): 14–20.

Locke, Harvey J., and Karl M. Wallace. "Short Marital-Adjustment and Prediction Tests: Their Reliability and Validity." *Marriage and Family Living*, 21 (1959): 251–254.

Loftus, E. "The Reality of Repressed Memories." *American Psychologist*, 48 (1993): 518–537.

Loomis, Laura, and Nancy S. Landale. "Nonmarital Cohabitation and Childbearing among Black and White American Women." *Journal of Marriage and the Family*, 56 (1994): 949–962.

Lovin, Vickie. *The Evaluation of Infertility*. 1997. Available: <www.leggs.com/articles/9701/infertility.H/html>.

Lugaila, Terry A. "Marital Status and Living Arrangements: March 1997 (Update)." *Current Population Reports*, P20–506, June 1998.

Luker, Kristin. "Dubious Conceptions: The Controversy over Teen Pregnancy." In *Families in Transition* (8th ed.), edited by Arlene S. Skolnick and Jerome H. Skolnick. New York: HarperCollins, 1994.

Lundberg-Love, P., and R. Geffner. "Date Rape: Prevalence, Risk Factors, and a Proposed Model. In *Violence in Dating Relationships: Emerging Social Issues*, edited by M. A. Pirog-Good and J. E. Stets. New York: Praeger, 1989.

Lykken, David T., and Auke Tellegen. "Is Human Mating Adentitious or the Result of Lawful Choice: A Twin Study of Mate Selection." *Journal of Personality and Social Psychology*, 65 (1993): 56–68.

Lynd, Robert S., and Helen M. Lynd. *Middletown*. New York: Harcourt, Brace, 1929.

Maccorquodale, Patricia. "Gender and Sexual Behavior." In *Human Sexuality: The Societal and Interpersonal Context*, edited by Kathleen McKinney and Susan Sprecher. Norwood, NJ: Ablex, 1989.

MacGaffey, Wyatt. "Husbands and Wives." *Transition*, 6 (1996): 122–130.

Macionis, John J. *Sociology* (7th ed.). Upper Saddle River, NJ: Prentice-Hall, 1999.

Mackey, Richard A., and Bernard A. O'Brien. "Marital Conflict Management: Gender and Ethnic Differences." *Social Work*, 43 (1998): 128–141.

MacKinnon, Carole E., and Donna King. "Day Care: A Review of Literature, Implications for Policy, and Critique of Resources." *Family Relations*, 37 (1988): 229–236.

Macklin, Eleanor. "Cohabiting College Students." In *Single Life: Unmarried Adults in Social Context*, edited by Peter J. Stein. New York: St. Martin's Press, 1981.

Macklin, Eleanor. "Nontraditional Family Forms." In *Handbook of Marriage and the Family*, edited by Marvin B. Sussman and Suzanne K. Steinmetz. New York: Plenum Press, 1987.

Madden, R. G. "State Actions to Control Fetal Abuse: Ramifications for Child Welfare Practice." *Child Welfare*, 72 (1993): 129–140.

Main, M., and R. Goldwyn. "Predicting Rejection of Her Infant from Mother's Representation of Her Own Experience: Implications for the Abused-Abusing Intergenerational Cycle." *Child Abuse & Neglect*, 3 (1984): 203–217.

Mainemer, Henry, Lorraine C. Gillman, and Elinor W. Ames. "Parenting Stress in Families Adoption Children from Romanian Orphanages." *Journal of Family Issues*, 19 (1998): 164–180.

Makepeace, J. M. "Gender Differences in Courtship Violence Victimization." *Family Relations*, 35 (1986): 383–388.

Makepeace, J. M. "Dating, Living Together, and Courtship Violence." In *Violence in Dating Relationships: Emerging Social Issues*, edited by Maureen A. Priog-Good and Jan E. Stets. New York: Praeger, 1989.

Makepeace, J. M. "Courtship Violence as Process: A Developmental Theory." In *Violence between Intimate Partners: Patterns, Causes, and Effects*, edited by A. P. Cardarelli. Boston: Allyn and Bacon, 1997.

Mannes, Marc. "Factors and Events Leadings to the Passage of the Indian Child Welfare Act." *Child Welfare*, 74 (1995): 264–282.

Manning, Wendy D., and Nancy S. Landale. "Racial and Ethnic Differences in the Role of Cohabitation in Premarital Childbearing." *Journal of Marriage and the Family*, 58 (1996): 63–77.

Manning, Wendy, and Pamela Smock. "Why Marry? Race and the Transition to Marriage Among Cohabitors." *Demography*, 32 (1995): 509–520.

Mantsios, Gregory. "Class in America: Myths and Realities." In *Race, Class, and Gender in the United States: An Integrated Study* (3rd ed.), edited by Paula S. Rothenberg. New York: St. Martin's Press, 1995.

Mare, Robert D. "Five Decades of Educational Assortive Mating." *American Sociological Review*, 56 (1991): 15–32.

Marks, S. R. "Multiple Roles and Role Strain: Some Notes on Human Energy, Time and Commitment." *American Sociological Review*, 42 (1977): 921–936.

Marshall, Ray, and Beth Paulin. "Employment and Earnings of Women: Historical Perspective." In *Working Women: Past, Present, Future*, edited by Karen Shallcross Koziara, Michael H. Moskow, and Lucretia Dewey Tanner. Washington, DC: Bureau of National Affairs, 1987.

Martin, John D., Garland E. Blair, Robert Nevels, and Joyce H. Fitzpatrick. "A Study of the Relationship of Styles of Loving and Marital Happiness." *Psychological Reports*, 66 (1990): 123–128.

Masnick, George, and Mary Jo Bane. *The Nation's Families: 1960–1990*. Cambridge, MA: Joint Center for Urban Studies of MIT and Harvard University, 1980.

Mason, Mary Ann, and Jane Mauldon. "The New Stepfamily Requires a New Public Policy." *Journal of Social Issues*, 52 (1996): 11–27.

Masters, William H, Virginia E. Johnson, and Robert C. Kolodny. *Human Sexuality* (5th ed.). New York: HarperCollins, 1995.

Mathes, Eugene W., and Cheryl L. Moore. "Reik's Complementarity Theory of Romantic Choice." *Journal of Social Psychology*, 125 (1985): 321–327.

Mattessich, Paul, and Reuben Hill. "Life Cycle and Family Developments." In *Handbook of Marriage and the Family* (pp. 437–469), edited by Marvin B. Sussman and Suzanne K. Steinmetz. New York: Plenum Press, 1987.

Mattson, Mark T. *Atlas of the 1990 Census*. New York: Macmillan, 1992.

Mayseless, Ofra. "Adult Attachment Patterns and Courtship Violence." *Family Relations*, 40 (1991): 21–28.

McAdoo, Harriette Pipes. "Factors Related to Stability in Upwardly Mobile Black Families." *Journal of Marriage and the Family*, 40 (1978): 761–778.

McBride Murry, Velma, and James Ponzetti, Jr. "American Indian Female Adolescents' Sexual Behavior: A Test of the Life-Course Experience Theory." *Family and Consumer Sciences Research*, 26 (September 1997): 75.

McCabe, Kristen M. "Sex Differences in the Long-Term Effects of Divorce on Children: Depression and Heterosexual Relationship Difficulties in the Young Adult Years." *Journal of Divorce and Remarriage*, 27 (1997): 123–135.

McCullough, Marie. "Experts Leery of Such Large Multiple Births." *Philadelphia Inquirer*. December 22, 1998. Available: <www.phillynews.com:80/inquirer/98/Dec/22/natoinal/MED22.htm>.

McDonald, Gerald W. "Structural Exchange and Marital Interaction." *Journal of Marriage and the Family*, 43 (1981): 825–839.

McFalls, Joseph A. Jr. "Population: A Lively Introduction." *Population Bulletin*, 53, 3 (1998): 3–48.

McGregor, P. P. L., and V. K. Borooah. "Is Low Spending or Low Income a Better Indicator of Whether of Not a Household Is Poor? Some Results from the 1985 Family Expenditure Survey." *Journal of Social Policy*, 21 (1992): 53–69.

McLennan, John Ferguson. *Primitive Marriage: An Inquiry into the Origin of the Form of Capture in Marriage Ceremonies*. London: Bernard Quaritch, 1865.

Mead, George Herbert. *Mind, Self, & Society from the Standpoint of a Social Behaviorist*, edited by Charles W. Morris. Chicago: University of Chicago Press, 1934/1962.

Mead, Margaret. *Sex and Temperament in Three Primitive Societies*. New York: Morrow, 1935/1963.

Meadow-Orlans, Kathryn P. "Sources of Stress for Mothers and Fathers of Deaf and Hard of Hearing Infants." *American Annals of the Deaf*, 4 (1995): 352–357.

Menaghan, E. G., and T. L. Parcel. "Parental Employment and Family Life: Research in the 1980s." *Journal of Marriage and the Family*, 52 (1990): 1079–1098.

Mendenhall, Tai J., Harold D. Grotevant, and Ruth G. McRoy. "Adoptive Couples: Communication and Changes Made in Openness Levels." *Family Relations*, 45 (1996): 223–229.

Mensa-Bonsu, Henrietta J. A. N. "The Maintenance of Children Decree—Some Implications for Child Welfare and Development." In *Family and Development in Ghana* (pp. 111–122), edited by Elizabeth Ardayfio-Schandorf. Accra, Ghana: Ghana Universities Press, 1994.

Merton, Robert K. *Social Theory and Social Structure*. New York: Free Press, 1968.

Metts, Sandra, and William R. Cupach. "The Role of Communication in Human Sexuality." In *Human Sexuality: The Societal and Interpersonal Context*, edited by Kathleen McKinney and Susan Sprecher. Norwood, NJ: Ablex, 1989.

Michael, Robert T., John H. Gagnon, Edward O. Laumann, and Gena Kolata. *Sex in America: A Definitive Survey*. Boston: Little, Brown, 1994.

Miller, B., B. Robbins, and D. Thomas. "On Methods of Studying Marriages and Families." *Journal of Marriage and the Family*, 44 (1982): 851–873.

Miller, Susan L., and Sally S. Simpson. "Courtship Violence and Social Control: Does Gender Matter?" *Law and Society Review*, 25 (1991): 335–365.

Mills, Jon K., Jennifer Daly, Amy Longmore, and Gina Kilbride. "A Note on Family Acceptance Involving Interracial Friendships and Romantic Relationships." *The Journal of Psychology*, 129 (1995): 349–351.

Milner, J. S., and C. Chilamkurti. "Physical Child Abuse Perpetrator Characteristics: A Review of the Literature." In *Child Abuse: A Multidisciplinary Survey* (Vol. 3), edited by B. Finkelman. New York: Garland, 1995.

Mindel, Charles H., and Robert W. Habenstein (Eds.). "Family Life Styles of America's Ethnic Minorities: An Introduction." In *Ethnic Families in America: Patterns and Variations*. New York: Elsevier, 1976.

Mirandé, Alfredo. "Chicano Families." In *Marriage and Family in a Changing Society* (2nd ed.), edited by James M. Henslin. New York: Free Press, 1985.

Mitchell, Barbara A., and Ellen M. Gee. "'Boomerang Kids' and Middle Class Parental Marital Satisfaction." *Family Relations*, 45 (1996): 442–448.

Mitchell, Jennifer D. "Before the Next Doubling." *World Watch,* 11 (1998): 21–28.

Moen, Phyllis, and Donna Dempster-McClain. "Employed Parents: Role Strain, Work Time, and Preferences for Working Less." *Journal of Marriage and the Family,* 49 (1987): 579–590.

Money, J., and A. Ehrhardt. *Man and Woman, Boy and Girl.* Baltimore, MD: Johns Hopkins University Press, 1972.

Money, J., and P. Tucker. *Sexual Signatures: On Being a Man or a Woman.* Boston, MA: Little, Brown, 1975.

Moore, A. M. "Intimate Violence: Does Socioeconomic Status Matter?" In *Violence Between Intimate Partners: Patterns, Causes, and Effects,* edited by A. P. Cardarelli. Boston: Allyn and Bacon, 1997.

Moore, Dahlia. "Role Conflict: Not Only for Women? A Comparative Analysis of 5 Nations." *International Journal of Comparative Sociology,* 36 (1995): 17–35.

Morgan, Lewis Henry. "Letters on the Iroquois." *The American Review,* 5 (1847): 177–190.

Morgan, Lewis Henry. *Ancient Society: Or, Researches in the Lines of Human Progress from Savagery through Barbarism to Civilization.* New York: Henry Holt, 1877.

Morgan, M. "Television and Adolescents' Sex Role Stereotypes: A Longitudinal Study." *Journal of Personality and Social Psychology,* 43 (1982): 947–955.

Motavalli, Jim. "Contents under Pressure." *E,* 7 (1996): 28–36.

Mullan, Bob. *The Mating Trade.* London: Routledge & Kegen Paul, 1984.

Murdock, George Peter. *Social Structure.* New York: Macmillan, 1949.

Murdock, George Peter. *World Ethnographic Atlas.* Pittsburgh: University of Pittsburgh Press, 1957.

Murdock, George Peter. "World Ethnographic Sample." *American Anthropologist,* 59 (1959): 664–687.

Murphy, Bianca Cody. "Difference and Diversity: Gay and Lesbian Couples." In *A Queer World: The Center for Lesbian Gay Studies Reader* (pp. 345–357), edited by Martin Duberman. New York: New York University Press, 1997.

Murrin, John. *Liberty, Equality, Power: A History of the American People.* New York: Harcourt Brace, 1997.

Myths and Facts about Domestic Violence. 1997. Available: <www.famvi.com/dv_facts.htm www.famvi.com/dv_facts.htm>.

Naifeh, Mary. "Trap Door? Revolving Door? Or Both?" *Current Population Reports,* P70-63 (July 1998).

National Child Abuse Coalition. "Facts about Child Abuse." May 20, 1998. Available: <www.casanet.org/library/abuse/costs_ab.html>.

National Coalition against Domestic Violence. 1997. Available: <www.healthtouch.com/level1/leaflets/ncadv/ncadv004.htm>.

National Domestic Violence Fact Sheet and Statistics. National Domestic Violence Hotline. 1998. Available: <www.inetport.com/~ndvh/~ndvh2.html>.

National Research Council. *Understanding Child Abuse and Neglect.* Washington, DC: National Academy Press, 1993.

National Victim Center. *Rape in America: A Report to the Nation.* Charlotte, SC: Author, 1992.

Nazzar, Alex, Phillip B. Adongo, Fred N. Binka, James F. Phillips, and Cornelius Debprur. "Developing a Culturally Appropriate Family Planning Program for the Navrongo Experiment." *Studies in Family Planning,* 26 (1995): 307–334.

"New Survey Shows Attitudes More Open toward Interracial Relationships." *Jet,* 88 (October 2, 1995): 22.

Nickman, Steven L. "Challenges of Adoption." *Harvard Mental Health Letter,* 12, no. 7 (1996): 5–7.

Nimkoff, M. F., and William F. Ogburn. *The Family.* Boston: Houghton Mifflin, 1934.

1998 HHS Poverty Guidelines, The. *Federal Register,* 63, no. 36 (February 24, 1998): 9235–9238. Available: <www.aspe.os.dhhs.gov/poverty/98poverty.htm>.

Nock, Steven L. "Divorce." In *Encyclopedia of Sociology* (Vol. 1, pp. 505–513), edited by Edgar F. Borgatta and Marie L. Borgatta. New York: MacMillan, 1992.

Nordenberg, Tamar. "Overcoming Infertility." *FDA Consumer,* 31 (1997): 18–21.

Norment, Lynn. "Black Men/White Women." *Ebony,* 50 (November 1994): 44–50.

Novello, A. "From the Surgeon General, U.S. Public Health Service, A Medical Response to Domestic Violence." *Journal of the American Medical Association,* 267 (June 17, 1992): 3132.

Nukunya, G. K. *Tradition and Change in Ghana: An Introduction to Sociology.* Accra, Ghana: Ghana Universities Press, 1992.

Nye, F. Ivan. "Fifty Years of Family Research, 1937–1987." *Journal of Marriage and the Family,* 50 (1988): 305–316.

Nyinah, Stella. "Cultural Practices in Ghana." *World Health,* 50 (1997): 22–23.

O'Brien, M. J. "Taking Sibling Abuse Seriously." In *Family Sexual Abuse: Frontline Research and Evaluation,* edited by M. Q. Patton. Newbury Park, CA: Sage, 1991.

O'Hare, William P. "America's Minorities—The Demographics of Diversity." *Population Bulletin,* 47, no. 4 (1992).

O'Hare, William P., and Brenda Curry-White. "Is There a Rural Underclass?" *Population Today,* 20, no. 3 (1992): 6–8.

O'Hare, William P., Kevin M. Pollard, Taynia L. Mann, and Mary M. Kent. "African Americans in the 1990s." *Population Bulletin,* 46, no. 1 (1991).

O'Hare, William P., Kevin M. Pollard, Taynia L. Mann, and Mary M. Kent. "African-Americans in the 1990s." In *Family in Transition* (9th ed.), edited by Arlene S. Skolnick and Jerome H. Skolnick. New York: Longman, 1997.

O'Leary, K. D. "Through a Psychological Lens: Personlity Traits, Personality Disorders, and Levels of Violence." In *Current Controversies on Family Violence*, edited by R. J. Gelles and D. R. Loseke. Newbury Park, CA: Sage, 1993.

Oates, Gary L. "Self-Esteem Enhancement through Fertility? Socioeconomic Prospects, Gender and Mutual Influence." *American Sociological Review*, 62 (1997): 965–973.

Oggins, Jean, Joseph Veroff, and Douglas Leber. "Perceptions of Marital Interaction among Black and White Newlyweds." *Journal of Personality and Social Psychology*, 65 (1993): 484–511.

Oheneba-Sakyi, Yaw, and Tim B. Heaton. "Effects of Socio-Demographic Variables on Birth Intervals in Ghana." *Journal of Comparative Family Studies*, 24 (1993): 113–135.

Olds, D., C. Henderson, and H. Kitzman. "Does Pre-Natal and Infancy Nurse Home Visitation Have Enduring Effects on the Qualities of Parental Care Giving and Child Health at 25 to 50 Months of Life?" *Pediatrics*, 93 (1994): 89–98.

Olds, D., C. Henderson, R. Chamberlin, and R. Tatelbaum. "Preventing Child Abuse and Neglect: Randomized Trial of Nurse Home Visiting." *Pediatrics*, 78 (1986): 65–78.

Oliver, Mary Beth, and Constantine Sedikides. "Effects of Sexual Permissiveness on Desirability of Partner as a Function of Low and High Commitment to a Relationship." *Social Psychology Quarterly*, 55 (1992): 321–323.

Olson, David H., and John DeFrain. *Marriage and the Family: Diversity and Strengths* (2nd ed.). Mountain View, CA: Mayfield, 1997.

Oppenheimer, Valerie Kincade. *The Female Labor Force in the United States*. Berkeley, CA: Population Monograph Series, 1970.

Oppenheimer, Valerie Kincade. "Structural Sources of Economic Pressure for Wives to Work: An Analytical Framework." In *Framing the Family*, edited by Burt N. Adams and John L. Campbell. Prospect Heights, IL: Waveland Press, 1984.

Orenstein, Peggy. *School Girls: Young Women, Self-Esteem, and the Confidence Gap*. New York: Anchor Books, 1994.

Oropesa, R. S. "Normative Beliefs about Marriage and Cohabitation: A Comparison of Non-Latino Whites, Mexican Americans, and Puerto Ricans." *Journal of Marriage and the Family*, 58 (1996): 49–62.

Ortiz, Vilma. "The Diversity of Latino Families." In *Understanding Latino Families: Scholarship, Policy, and Practice*. Thousand Oaks, CA: Sage, 1995.

Osborn, Albert F. "Assessing the Socio-Economic Status of Families." *Sociology*, 21 (1987): 429–448.

Osmond, Marie Withers. "Radical-Critical Theories." In *Handbook of Marriage and the Family*, edited by Marvin B. Sussman and Suzanne K. Steinmetz. New York: Plenum Press, 1987.

Oyserman, Daphna, and Izumi Sakamoto. "Being Asian American: Identity, Cultural Constructs, and Stereotype Perception." *Journal of Applied Behavioral Science*, 33 (December 1997): 435–453.

Padilla, Mary Lou, and Garry L. Landreth. "Latchkey Children: A Review of the Literature." *Child Welfare*, 68 (1989): 445–454.

Pagani, Linda, Bernard Boulerice, Richard E. Tremblay, and Frank Vitaro. "Behavioural Development in Children of Divorce and Remarriage." *Journal of Divorce and Remarriage*, 38 (1997): 769–781.

Pagelow, M. D. *Family Violence*. New York: Praeger, 1984.

Paisano, Edna L. "The American Indian, Eskimo, and Aleut Population." *Current Population Reports, Special Studies Series*, P23–189. 1995. Available: <www.census.gov/population/pop–profile/p23–189.pdf>.

Palumbo, B. "Marriage, Land, and Kinship in a Nzema Village." *Ethnology*, 31 (1992): 233–258.

Pampel, Fred C. "Changes in the Propensity to Live Alone: Evidence from Consecutive Cross-Sectional Surveys, 1960–1976." *Demography*, 20 (1983): 433–447.

Panafrican News Agency. "Ghana Laments High Rate of Maternal Deaths." October 15, 1997. Available: <www.africanews.org/pan/science/19971015/feat4.html>.

Panuccio, T. "Rural Women in Ghana: Their Workloads, Access and Organizations." In *Development: Rhetoric versus Reality* (pp. 85–129), edited by W. P. Lineberry. Boulder, CO: Westview Press, 1989.

Pappas, Leslie. "China's New Family Values." *Newsweek*, August 24, 1998, p. 36.

Parks, Cheryl. "Lesbian Parenthood: A Review of the Literature." *American Journal of Orthopsychiatry*, 68 (1998): 376–389.

Parsons, Talcott. *Social Structure and Personality*. New York: Free Press, 1964.

Parsons, Talcott, and Robert F. Bales. *Family Socialization and Interaction Process*. Glencoe, IL: Free Press, 1955.

Peak, K., and F. S. Del Papa. "Criminal Justice Enters the Womb: Enforcing the 'Right' to be Born Drug-Free." *Journal of Criminal Justice*, 21 (1993): 245–263.

Pearson, Veronica, and Tim W. L. Chan. "The Relationship between Parenting Stress and Social Support in Mothers of Children with Learning Disabilities." *Social Science & Medicine*, 32 (1993): 267–274.

Pérez, Lisandro. "Cuban Families in the United States." In *Minority Families in the United States: A Multicultural Perspective*, edited by Ronald L. Taylor. Englewood Cliffs, NJ: Prentice-Hall 1994.

Perry-Jenkins, Maureen, and Karen Folk. "Class, Couples, and Conflict: Effects of the Division of Labor on Assessments of Marriage in Dual-Earner Families." *Journal of Marriage and the Family*, 56 (1994): 165–180.

Peterson, Karen S. "Single Life Gaining on Couplehood." *USA Today*, March 13, 1996, p. 1D.

Peterson, Richard R. *Women, Work and Divorce*. Albany: State University of New York Press, 1989.

Peterson, Richard R. "A Re-Evaluation of the Economic Consequences of Divorce." *American Sociological Review*, 61 (1996a): 528–536.

Peterson, Richard R. "Statistical Errors, Faulty Conclusions, Misguided Policy: Reply to Weitzman." *American Sociological Review*, 61 (1996b): 539–540.

Phillips, Donald F. "Reproductive Medicine Experts Till an Increasingly Fertile Field." *Journal of the American Medical Association*, 280 (December 9, 1998): 1893.

Phillips, L. R. "Theoretical Explanations of Elder Abuse: Competing Hypotheses and Unresolved Issues." In *Elder Abuse: Conflict in the Family*, edited by K. A. Pillemer and R. S. Wolf. Dover, MA: Auburn House, 1986.

Piccinino, Linda J., and William D. Mosher. "Trends in Contraceptive Use in the United States: 1982–1995." *Family Planning Perspectives*, 30 (1998): 4–12.

Pillemer, K. "The Dangers of Dependency: New Findings on Domestic Violence against the Elderly." *Social Problems*, 33 (1985): 146–158.

Pillemer, K. "The Abused Offspring Are Dependent: Abuse Is Caused by the Deviance and Dependence of Abusive Caregivers." In *Current Controversies on Family Violence*, edited by R. J. Gelles and D. R. Loseke. Newbury Park, CA: Sage, 1993.

Pillemer, K., and Finkelhor, D. "Prevalence of Elder Abuse: A Random Sample Survey. *Gerontologist*, 28 (1988): 51–57.

Piotrkowski, C. S., R. N. Rapoport, and R. Rapoport. "Families and Work." In *Handbook of Marriage and the Family*, edited by M. B. Sussman and S. K. Steinmetz. New York: Plenum Press, 1987.

Pitts, Jesse R. "The Structural-Functional Approach." In *Handbook of Marriage and the Family*, edited by Harold T. Christensen. Chicago: Rand McNally, 1964.

Pleck, E., J. H. Pleck, M. Grossman, and P. B. Bart. "The Battered Data Syndrome: A Comment on Steinmetz' Article." *Victimology*, 2 (1978): 680–684.

Pleck, Joseph H. "The Male Sex Role: Definitions, Problems, and Sources of Change." *Journal of Social Issues*, 32, no. 3 (1976): 155–164.

Pleck, Joseph H. *Working Wives/Working Husbands*. Beverly Hills, CA: Sage, 1985.

Pleck, Joseph H. "The Contemporary Man." In *Men's Lives*, edited by Michael S. Kimmel and Michael A. Messner. New York: Macmillan, 1989.

Plotkin, Mark. *Tales of a Shaman's Apprentice*. New York: Penguin Books, 1993.

Plunkett, Scott W., Marla G. Sanchez, Carolyn S. Henry, and Linda C. Robinson. "The Double ABCX Model and Children's Post-Divorce Adaptation." *Journal of Divorce and Remarriage*, 27 (1997): 17–50.

Pollock, Alann D., Ann H. Die, and Richard G. Marriott. "Relationship of Communication Style to Egalitarian Role Expectations." *The Journal of Social Psychology*, 130 (1990): 19–24.

Pollock, Linda. *Forgotten Children*. New York: Cambridge University Press, 1983.

"Population 2050: 9.4 billion." *UN Chronicle*, 34, no. 3 (1997): 72.

Powers, Mary G. (Ed.). "Measures of Socioeconomic Status: An Introduction." In *Measures of Socioeconomic Status: Current Issues*. Boulder, CO: Westview Press, 1982.

"Pregnancy and Childbearing among U.S. Teens." In *Planned Parenthood Fact Sheet*. June 3, 1997. Available: <www.ppfa.org/ppfa/teen_ pregnancy_sheet.html>.

Prevention. Public Health Service. March 11, 1997. Available: <www.mediaconsult.com/frames/aids/shareware/hiv_aids/prevent.html>.

Price, John A. "North American Indian Families." In *Ethnic Families in America: Patterns and Variations*, edited by Charles H. Mindel and Robert W. Habenstein. New York: Elsevier, 1976.

"Quantifying the Epidemic." In *The Relationship between the Human Immunodeficiency Virus and the Acquired Immunodeficiency Syndrome*. March 11, 1997. Available: <www.mediconsult.com/frames/aids/shareware/aid/3html>.

Queen, Stuart A., Robert W. Habenstein, and Jill S. Quadagno. *The Family in Various Cultures* (5th ed.). New York: HarperCollins, 1985.

Quinn, M. J., and S. K. Tomita. *Elder Abuse and Neglect* (2nd ed.). New York: Springer, 1997.

Rabinowitz, Fredric E., and Sam V. Cochran. *Man Alive: A Primery of Men's Issues*. Pacific Grove, CA: Brooke/Cole, 1994.

Raloff, Janet. "The Human Numbers Crunch: The Next Half-Century Promises Unprecedented Challenges." *Science News*, 149 (1996): 396–397.

Rank, Mark R., and Craig W. LeCroy. "Toward a Multiple Perspective in Family Theory and Practice: The Case of Social Exchange Theory, Symbolic Interactionism and Conflict Theory." *Family Relations*, 32 (1983): 441–448.

Rapoport, Rhona, Robert N. Rapoport, and Ziona Strelitz. *Fathers, Mothers, and Society*. New York: Vintage Books, 1980.

Rapp, Gail S., and Sally A. Lloyd. "The Role of 'Home as Haven' Ideology in Child Care Use." *Family Relations,* 38 (1989): 426–430.

Rapp, Rayna. "Family and Class in Contemporary America: Notes Toward an Understanding of Ideology." In *Rethinking the Family: Some Feminist Questions,* edited by Barrie Thorne and Marilyn Yalom. New York: Longman, 1982.

"Reform's Position on . . . Mixed (Interfaith) Marriages." February 4, 1999. Available: <www.landfield.com/faqs/judaism/FAQ/10–Reform/section–21.html>.

Reiss, Ira L. *Family Systems in America* (3rd ed.). New York: Holt, Rinehart and Winston, 1980.

Renzetti, C. M. "Violence and Abuse among Same-Sex Couples." In *Violence between Intimate Partners: Patterns, Causes, and Effects,* edited by A. P. Cardarelli. Boston: Allyn and Bacon, 1997.

Renzetti, C. M. *Violent Betrayal: Partner Abuse in Lesbian Relationships.* Newbury Park, CA: Sage, 1992.

Reuters. "Risks from Pill Wear Off." January 7, 1999. Available: <www.abcnews.go.com/sections/lving/DailyNews/contraceptives990107.html>.

Revisions to the Standards for the Classification of Federal Data on Race and Ethnicity. Office of Management and Budget. October 12, 1998. Available: <www.whitehouse.gov/WH/EOP/OMB/html/fedreg?Ombdir15.html>.

Reynolds, Larry T. *Interactionism: Exposition and Critique* (3rd ed.). Dix Hills, NY: General Hall, 1993.

Rice, E. Philip. *Intimate Relationships, Marriages, and Families.* Mountain View, CA: Mayfield, 1990.

Richardson, D., and J. L. Campbell. "The Effect of Alcohol on Attributions of Blame for Rape." *Personality and Social Psychology Bulletin,* 8 (1982): 468–476.

Richardson, Laurel. *The New Other Woman: Contemporary Single Women in Affairs with Married Men.* New York: Free Press, 1985.

Richmond-Abbott, Marie. *Masculine & Feminine: Gender Roles Over the Life Cycle* (2nd ed.). New York: McGraw-Hill, 1992.

Riggs, David S., and Daniel O'Leary. "A Theoretical Model of Courtship Aggression." In *Violence in Dating Relationships: Emerging Social Issues,* edited by Maureen A. Priog-Good and Jan E. Stets. New York: Praeger, 1989.

Riley, Nancy E. "Gender, Power and Population Change." *Population Bulletin,* 52, no. 1 (1997): 1–48.

Rist, Ray C. *The Urban School: A Factory for Failure.* Cambridge, MA: MIT Press, 1973.

Robertson, Gary. "Coed Dorms Now Accepted Part of Campus Life." *Richmond Times-Dispatch,* September 8, 1996, pp. B3–B4.

Robinson, Ira, Bill Ganza, Stuart Katz, and Edward Robinson. "Twenty Years of the Sexual Revolution, 1965–1985: An Update." *Journal of Marriage and the Family,* 53 (1991): 216–220.

Robinson, John P., and Melissa A. Milkie. "Back to the Basics: Trends in and Role Determinants of Women's Attitudes toward Housework.." *Journal of Marriage and the Family,* 60 (1998): 205–218.

Roche, John P., and Thomas W. Ramsbey. "Premarital Sexuality: A Five-Year Follow-Up Study of Attitudes and Behavior by Dating Stage." *Adolescence,* 28 (Spring 1993): 67–80.

Rodriguez, Nestor P., and Jacqueline Hagan. "Central Americans in the United States." In *The Minority Report: An Introduction to Racial, Ethnic, and Gender Relations* (3rd ed.), edited by Anthony Gary Dworkin and Rosalind J. Dworkin. Fort Worth, TX: Harcourt Brace, 1999.

Rogers, Stacy J., and Lynn K. White. "Satisfaction with Parenting: The Role of Marital Happiness, Family Structure, and Parents' Gender." *Journal of Marriage and the Family,* 60 (1998): 293–308.

Rogers, Stacy J., and Paul R. Amato. "Is Marital Quality Declining? The Evidence from Two Generations." *Social Forces,* 75 (1997): 1089–1100.

Rohypnol. Drug Enforcement Administration, U.S. Department of Justice. May 21, 1998. Available: <www.usdoj.gov/dea/pubs/rohypnol/rohypnol.htm>.

Rollins, Boyd C., and Harold Feldman. "Marital Satisfaction over the Life Cycle." *Journal of Marriage and the Family,* 32 (1970): 20–28.

Rollins, Boyd C., and Richard Galligan. "The Developing Child and Marital Satisfaction of Parents." *In Child Influences on Marital and Family Interaction: A Life-Span Perspective* (pp. 71–105), edited by Richard M. Lerner and Graham B. Spanier. New York: Academic Press, 1978.

Root, Maria P. "Multiracial Asians: Models of Ethnic Identity." *Amerasia Journal,* 23 (1997): 29–41.

Rosen, Ellen Israel. *Better Choices: Blue-Collar Women In and Out of Work.* Chicago: University of Chicago Press, 1987.

Rosenberg, D. A. "Web of Deceit: A Literature Review of Munchausen Syndrome by Proxy." *Child Abuse & Neglect,* 11 (1987): 547–563.

Rosenblatt, Paul C., and Cynthia Meyer. "Imagined Interactions and the Family." *Family Relations,* 35 (1986): 319–324.

Rosenfeld, Alvin A., Daniel J. Pilowsky, Paul Fine, Marilyn Thorpe, Edith Fein, Mark D. Simms, Neal Halfon, Martin Irwin, Jose Alfaro, Ronald Saletsky, and Steven Nickman. "Foster Care: An Update." *Journal of the American Academy of Child and Adolescent Psychiatry,* 36 (1997): 448–457.

Rotundo, E. Anthony. "American Fatherhood: A Historical Perspective." *American Behavioral Scientist,* 29, no. 1 (1985): 7–25.

Roy, M. "A Current Survey of 150 Cases." In *Battered Women: A Psychosociological Study of Domestic Violence*, edited by M. Roy. New York: Van Nostrand Reinhold, 1977

Rubin, Lillian B. *Worlds of Pain: Life in the Working Class Family*. New York: Basic Books, 1976/1992.

Rubin, Lillian B. *Erotic Wars: What Happened to the Sexual Revolution?* New York: Farrar, Straus and Giroux, 1990.

Rubin, Lillian B. "The Culture of Adolescent Sexuality." In *Families in Transition* (8th ed.), edited by Arlene S. Skolnick and Jerome H. Skolnick. New York: Harper-Collins, 1994.

Rubin, Lillian B. *Families on the Fault Line*. New York: HarperPerennial, 1995.

Rubinstein, Robert L. "Never Married Elderly as a Social Type: Re-evaluating Some Images." *Gerontologist*, 27 (1987): 108–113.

Russell, D. E. H. *Rape in Marriage*. New York: Macmillan, 1982.

Ryan, John, Michael Hughes, and James Hawdon. "Marital Status, General-Life Satisfaction and the Welfare State: A Cross-National Comparison." *International Journal of Comparative Sociology*, 39 (1998): 224–236.

Sadovsky, Robert. "Oral Contraceptive Use and Risk of Cardiovascular Disease." *American Family Physician*, 58 (1998): 561–562.

Saenz, Rogelio. "Mexican Americans." In *The Minority Report: An Introduction to Racial, Ethnic, and Gender Relations* (3rd ed.), edited by Anthony Gary Dworkin and Rosalind J. Dworkin. Fort Worth, TX: Harcourt Brace, 1999.

Sanchez, Laura, and Elizabeth Thomson. "Becoming Mothers and Fathers: Parenthood, Gender and the Division of Labor." *Gender & Society*, 11 (1997): 747–772.

Sandelowski, Margarete. "Separate, but Less Equal: Fetal Ultrasonography and the Transformation of Expectant Motherhood/Fatherhood." *Gender & Society*, 8 (1994): 230–245.

Santi, Lawrence. "Household Headship among Unmarried Persons in the United States, 1970–1985." *Demography*, 27 (1990): 219–232.

Sapiro, Virginia. *Women in American Society: An Introduction to Women's Studies* (4th ed.). Mountain View, CA: Mayfield, 1999.

Sarpong, Peter. *Ghana in Retrospect: Some Aspects of Ghanaian Culture*. Accra-Tema, Ghana: Ghana Publishing, 1974.

Saunders, D. *Who Hits First and Who Hurts Most? Evidence for the Greater Victimization of Women in Intimate Relationships*. Paper presented at the Annual Meeting of the American Society of Criminology, Reno, NV, November 1989.

Saunders, D. "Husbands Who Assault: Multiple Profiles Requiring Multiple Responses." In *Legal Responses to Wife Assault*, edited by N. Z. Hilton. Newbury Park, CA: Sage, 1993.

Sawyer, Jack. "On Male Liberation." *Liberation*, 15 (1970): 32–33.

Scanzoni, John. *Sexual Bargaining* (2nd ed.). Chicago: University of Chicago Press, 1982.

Scanzoni, John, and William Marsiglio. "New Action Theory and Contemporary Families." *Journal of Family Issues*, 14 (1993): 105–132.

Schaefer, C. "Defining Verbal Abuse of Children: A Survey." *Psychological Reports*, 80 (1997): 626.

Schafer, Robert B., and Pat Keith. "Matching by Weight in Married Couples: A Life Cycle Perspective." *Journal of Social Psychology*, 130 (1990): 657–664.

Schemo, D. J. "Husband and Wife Arrested in Beating of Their 6-Week-Old Son." *New York Times*, August 16, 1992.

Schimmerling, Thomas E. "The No-Fault Debate: Is Blame Better?" *Trial*, 33 (1997): 33–36.

Schoen, Robert. "First Unions and the Stability of First Marriages." *Journal of Marriage and the Family*, 54 (1992): 281–284.

Schrof, Joannie M., and Betsy Wagner. "Sex in America." *U.S. News and World Report*, 117, no. 15 (October 17, 1994): 74–81.

Schwartz, J. "After School." *American Demographics*, 9 (June 1987): 60–61.

Schwartzberg, Natalie, Kathy Berliner, and Demaris Jacob. *Single in a Married World: A Life Cycle Framework for Working with the Unmarried Adult*. New York: W. W. Norton, 1995.

Seccombe, Karen. "So You Think I Drive a Cadillac?" *Welfare Recipients' Perspectives on the System and Its Reform*. Boston: Allyn and Bacon, 1999.

"Second Report on the People's Republic of China On: Implementation of the Nairobi Forward-Looking Strategies for the Advancement of Women, The." *Women's International Network News*, 21 (Autumn 1995): 65–66. (From All-China Women's Federation, 15 Jianguomennei St., Beijing, China.)

Sedlack, A. J., and D. D. Broadhurst. *Executive Summary of the Third National Incidence Study of Child Abuse and Neglect*. May 21, 1998. Available: <www.casanet.org/library/abuse/stabuse.htm>.

Seff, Monica A. "Cohabitation and the Law." *Marriage and Family Review*, 21, no. 3–4 (1995): 141–168.

Segalen, Martine. "The Industrial Revolution: from Proletariat to Bourgeoisie." In *A History of the Family*, edited by André Burguiére, Christiane Klapisch-Zuber, Martine Segalen, Françoise Zonabend. Cambridge, MA: Harvard University Press, 1996.

Seltzer, Judith A. "Consequences of Marital Dissolution for Children." *Annual Review of Sociology*, 20 (1994): 235–266.

Seltzer, Judith A. "Father by Law: Effects of Joint Legal Custody on Nonresident Fathers' Involvement with Children." *Demography*, 35 (1998): 135–146.

Seltzer, Judith A., Nora Cate Schaeffer, and Hong-Wen Charng. "Family Ties after Divorce: The Relationship between Visiting and Paying Child Support." *Journal of Marriage and the Family*, 51 (1989): 1013–1032.

Serovich, Julianne M., Sharon J. Price, Steven F. Chapman, and David W. Wright. "Attachment between Former Spouses: Impact on Co-Parental Communication and Parental Involvement." *Journal of Divorce and Remarriage*, 17 (1992): 109–119.

Settersen, Richard A., Jr. "A Time to Leave Home and a Time Never to Return? Age Constraints on the Living Arrangements of Young Adults." *Social Forces*, 76 (1998): 1373–1400.

"Sexual and Contraceptive Behavior among U.S. Teens." In *Planned Parenthood Fact Sheet*. June 3, 1997. Available: <www.ppfa.org/ppfa/teensex.html>.

Shapiro, Laura. "Guns and Dolls." *Newsweek*, May 28, 1990, pp. 56–62, 65.

Sharma, Anu R., Matthew K. McGue, and Peter L. Benson. "The Psychological Adjustment of United Stated Adopted Adolescents and Their Nonadopted Siblings." *Child Development*, 69 (1998): 791–802.

Shelton, Beth Anne. "Variations in Divorce Rates by Community Size: A Test of the Social Integration Explanation." *Journal of Marriage and the Family*, 49 (1987): 827–832.

Sherman, L. W., and R. Berk. "The Specific Deterrent Effects of Arrest for Domestic Assault." *American Sociological Review*, 49 (1984): 261–272.

Shipp, Stephanie. "How Singles Spend." *American Demographics*, 10 (April 1988): 22–27.

Shon, Steven P., and Davis Y. Ja. "Asian Families." In *Families in Transition* (7th ed.), edited by Arlene S. Skolnick and Jerome H. Skolnick. New York: HarperCollins, 1992.

Shostak, Arthur B. "Singlehood." In *Handbook of Marriage and the Family*, edited by Marvin B. Sussman and Suzanne K. Steinmetz. New York: Plenum Press, 1987.

Siegel, Deborah H. "Open Adoption of Infants: Adoptive Parents' Perceptions of Advantages and Disadvantages." *Social Work*, 38 (1993): 15–23.

Silverstein, Merrill, and Jeffrey D. Long. "Trajectories of Grandparents' Perceived Solidarity with Adult Grandchildren: A Growth Curve Analysis over 23 Years." *Journal of Marriage and the Family*, 69 (1998): 912–923.

Simon, Rita J. "Transracial Adoptions: In the Children's Best Interests." *Black Issues in Higher Education*, 12, no. 5 (1995): 36–37.

Simon, Rita J. "Adoption and the Race Factor: How Important Is It?" *Sociological Inquiry*, 68 (1998): 274–279.

Simon, Rita J., and Howard Altstein. *Transracial Adoptees and Their Families: A Study of Identity and Commitment.* New York: Praeger, 1987.

Simpson, Ida Harper, David Stark, and Robert A. Jackson. "Class Identification Processes of Married Working Men and Women." *American Sociological Review*, 53 (1988): 284–293.

"Singles Scene, The." *American Demographics Desk Reference*, 14, Supplement (July1992): 18–23.

Skidmore, W. *Theoretical Thinking in Sociology.* Cambridge: Cambridge University Press, 1979.

Skolnick, Arlene. *Embattled Paradise: The American Family in an Age of Uncertainty.* New York: Basic Books, 1991.

Small, Meredith F. *What's Love Got to Do with It? The Evolution of Human Mating.* New York: Doubleday, 1995.

Smith, Deborah B., and Phyllis Moen. "Spousal Influence on Retirement: His, Her, and Their Perceptions." *Journal of Marriage and the Family*, 69 (1998): 734–744.

Smith, Ralph E. *Women in the Labor Force in 1990.* Washington, DC: Urban Institute, 1979.

Smith, Susan Livingston, and Jeanne A. Howard. "The Impact of Previous Sexual Abuse on Children's Adjustment in Adoptive Placements." *Social Work*, 39 (1994): 491–501.

Smith, Tom W. "Attitudes toward Sexual Permissiveness: Trends, Correlates, and Behavioral Connections." In *Sexuality across the Life Course*, edited by Alice S. Rossi. Chicago: University of Chicago Press, 1994.

Sobol, Michael P., Sharon Delaney, and Brian M. Earn. "Adoptees' Portrayals of the Development of Family Structure." *Journal of Youth and Adolescence*, 23 (1994): 385–401.

Sorenson, Susan B., Dawn M. Upchurch, and Haikang Shen. "Violence and Injury in Marital Arguments: Risk Patterns and Gender Differences." *American Journal of Public Health*, 86 (1996): 35–40.

South, Scott. "Sociodemographic Differentials in Mate Selection Preferences." *Journal of Marriage and the Family*, 53 (1991): 928–940.

Spanier, Graham B. "Measuring Dyadic Adjustment: New Scales for Assessing the Quality of Marriage and Similar Dyads." *Journal of Marriage and the Family*, 38 (1976): 15–29.

Spanier, Graham B., and Paul C. Glick. "Mate Selection Differentials between Whites and Blacks in the United States." *Social Forces*, 58 (1980): 707–725.

Spickard, Paul R. "What Must I Be? Asian Americans and the Question of Multiethnic Identity." *Amerasia Journal*, 23 (Winter 1997): 43–60.

Sprague, Heather E., and Jennifer M. Kinney. "The Effects of Interparental Divorce and Conflict on College Students' Romantic Relationships." *Journal of Divorce and Remarriage*, 27 (1997): 85–104.

Sprecher, Susan, and Kathleen McKinney. *Sexuality.* Newbury Park, CA: Sage, 1993.

Sprecher, Susan, Kathleen McKinney, and Terri L. Orbuch. "Has the Double Standard Disappeared? An Experimental Test." *Social Psychology Quarterly*, 50 (1987): 24–31.

Sprecher, Susan, Kathleen McKinney, and Terri L. Orbuch. "The Effect of Current Sexual Behavior on Friendship, Dating, and Marriage Desirability." *Journal of Sex Research*, 28 (1991): 387–408.

Sprey, Jetse. "Conflict Theory and the Study of Marriage and the Family." In *Contemporary Theories about the Family* (Vol. 2), edited by W. R. Burr, R. Hill, F. I. Nye, and I. Reiss. New York: Free Press, 1979.

Stack, Steven, and J. Ross Eshelman. "Marital Status and Happiness: A 17-Nation Study." *Journal of Marriage and the Family*, 60 (1998): 527–536.

Staples, Robert. "Black Singles in America." In *Single Life: Unmarried Adults in Social Context*, edited by Peter J. Stein. New York: St. Martin's Press, 1981.

Staples, Robert. "The Emerging Majority: Resources for Nonwhite Families in the United States." *Family Relations*, 37 (1988): 348–354.

Staples, Robert, and Alfrdo Mirandé. "Racial and Cultural Variations among American Families." *Journal of Marriage and the Family*, 42 (1980): 887–903.

Staples, Robert, and Alfredo Mirandé. "Racial and Cultural Variations among American Families: A Decennial Review of the Literature on Minority Families." In *Family in Transition* (4th ed.), edited by Arlene S. Skolnick and Jerome H. Skolnick. Boston: Little, Brown, 1983.

Staples, Robert, and Leanor Boulin Johnson. *Black Families at the Crossroads: Challenges and Prospects.* San Francisco: Jossey-Bass, 1993.

"Status of Women in Ghana, The." *Women's International Network News*, 18 (Summer 1992): 50–51.

Stein, Catherine H., Virginia A. Wemmerus, Marcia Ward, Michelle E. Gaines, Andrew L. Freeburg, and Thomas C. Jewell. "'Because They're My Parents': An Intergenerational Study of Felt Obligation and Parental Care-Giving." *Journal of Marriage and the Family*, 60 (1998): 611–622.

Stein, Peter J. *Single.* Englewood Cliffs, NJ: Prentice-Hall, 1976.

Stein, Peter J. "The Voluntary Singles." In *Marriage and Family in a Changing Society* (2nd ed.), edited by James M. Henslin. New York: Free Press, 1985.

Stein, Peter J. (Ed.). "Understanding Single Adulthood." In *Single Life: Unmarried Adults in Social Context*, edited by Peter J. Stein. New York: St. Martin's Press, 1981.

Steinmetz, S. K. "Wife Beating, Husband Beating—A Comparison of the Use of Physical Violence between Spouses to Resolve Marital Fights." In *Battered Women*, edited by M. Roy. New York: Van Nostrand Reinhold, 1977.

Steinmetz, S. K. "The Battered Husband Syndrome." *Victimology*, 2 (1978): 499–509.

Steinmetz, S. K. "Women and Violence: Victims and Perpetrators." *American Journal of Psychotherapy*, 34 (1980): 334–350.

Steinmetz, S. K. *Duty Bound: Elder Abuse and Family Care.* Newbury Park, CA: Sage, 1988.

Steinmetz, S. K. "The Abused Elderly Are Dependent: Abuse Is Caused by the Perception of Stress Associated with Providing Care." In *Current Controversies on Family Violence*, edited by R. J. Gelles and D. R. Loseke. Newbury Park, CA: Sage, 1993.

Stengel, Richard. "For Better or for Worse." *Time*, June 3, 1996, pp. 52–53.

Stephens, Linda S. "Will Johnny See Daddy This Week? An Empirical Test of Three Theoretical Perspectives on Postdivorce Contact." *Journal of Family Issues*, 17 (1996): 466–494.

Stephens, William N. *The Family in Cross-Cultural Perspective.* Lanham, MD: University Press of America, 1963.

Sterk-Elifson, Claire. "Sexuality among African-American Women." In *Sexuality across the Life Course*, edited by Alice S. Rossi. Chicago: University of Chicago Press, 1994.

Sternbach, Harvey. "Age-Associated Testosterone Decline in Men: Clinical Issues for Psychiatry." *American Journal of Psychiatry*, 155 (1998): 1310–1318.

Stets, Jan E., and Debra A. Henderson. "Contextual Factors Surrounding Conflict Resolution while Dating: Results from a National Study." *Family Relations*, 40 (1991): 29–36.

Straus, M. A. "A Sociological Perspective on the Causes of Family Violence." In *Violence and the Family*, edited by M. R. Green. Boulder, CO: Westview, 1980.

Straus, M. A. "Physical Assaults by Wives: A Major Social Problem." In *Current Controversies on Family Violence*, edited by R. J. Gelles and D. R. Loseke. Newbury Park, CA: Sage, 1993.

Straus, M. A. "State to State Differences in Social Inequality and Social Bonds in Relation to Assaults on Wives in the United States." *Journal of Comparative Family Studies*, 25 (1994): 7–24.

Straus, M. A., and R. J. Gelles. "Societal Change and Change in Family Violence from 1975 to 1985 as Revealed by Two National Surveys." *Journal of Marriage and the Family*, 48 (1986): 465–479.

Straus, M. A., and R. J. Gelles. *Physical Violence in American Families.* New Brunswick, NJ: Transaction Books, 1990.

Straus, M. A., R. J. Gelles, and S. K. Steinmetz. *Behind Closed Doors: Violence in the American Family.* New York: Anchor, 1981.

Straus, M. A., S. L. Hamby, S. Boney-McCoy, and D. B. Sugarman. *The Revised Conflict Tactics Scales (CTS2): Development and Preliminary Psychometric Data.* Durham, NH: Family Violence Research Laboratory, 1995.

Strong, Bryan, and Christine DeVault. *The Marriage and Family Experience* (5th ed.). St. Paul, MN: West, 1992.

Stryker, Sheldon. "The Interactional and Situational Approaches." In *Handbook of Marriage and the Family*, edited by Harold T. Christensen. Chicago: Rand McNally, 1964.

Sugarman, David B., and Gerald T. Hotaling. "Dating Violence: Prevalence, Context, and Risk Markers." In *Violence in Dating Relationships: Emerging Social Issues*, edited by Maureen A. Priog-Good and Jan E. Stets. New York: Praeger, 1989.

Suitor, J. Jill. "Marital Quality and Satisfaction with the Division of Household Labor across the Family Life Cycle." *Journal of Marriage and the Family*, 53 (1991): 221–230.

Suitor, J. Jill, and Karl Pillemer. "Family CareGiving and Marital Satisfaction: Findings from a 1-Year Panel Study of Women Caring for Parents with Dementia." *Journal of Marriage and the Family*, 56 (1994): 681–690.

Sullivan, Andrew. "Let Gays Marry." *Newsweek*, June 3, 1996a, p. 26.

Sullivan, Andrew. "Liberation." *New Republic*, May 6, 1996b, p. 6.

Sullivan, Maureen. "Rozzie and Harriett? Gender and Family Patterns of Lesbian Couples." *Gender & Society*, 10 (1996): 747–767.

Surra, Catherine. "Research and Theory on Mate Selection and Premarital Relationships in the 1980s." *Journal of Marriage and the Family*, 52 (1990): 844–865.

Suzuki, Bob H. "Asian-American Families." In *Marriage and Family in a Changing Society* (2nd ed.), edited by James M. Henslin. New York: Free Press, 1985.

Sweet, James A. *Women in the Labor Force*. New York: Seminar Press, 1973.

Swisher, Raymond R., Glen H. Elder, Jr., Frederick O. Lorenz, and Rand D. Conger. "The Long Arm of the Farm: How an Occupation Structures Exposure and Vulnerability to Stressors across the Role Domain." *Journal of Health and Social Behavior*, 39 (1998): 72–89.

Syers, M., and J. L. Edleson. "The Combined Effects of Coordinated Criminal Justice Intervention in Woman Abuse. *Journal of Interpersonal Violence*, 7 (1992): 490–502.

Szinovacz, Maximiliane E. "Using Couple Data as a Methodological Tool: The Case of Marital Violence." *Journal of Marriage and the Family*, 45 (1983): 633–644.

Takyi, Baffour K., and Yaw Oheneba-Sakyi. "Customs, Practices, Family Life, and Marriage in Contemporary Ghana, West Africa." *Family Perspectives*, 28 (1994): 257–281.

Takyi, Baffour K., and Yaw Oheneba-Sakyi. "Gender Differentials in Family Size among Ghanaian Couples." *Journal of African and Asian Studies*, 32 (1997): 296–306.

Tatara, T. *Elder Abuse: Questions and Answer—An Information Guide for Professionals and Concerned Citizens*. Washington, DC: National Center on Elder Abuse, 1996.

Taylor, Robert Joseph, Bogart R. Leashore, and Susan Toliver. "An Assessment of the Provider Role as Perceived by Black Males." *Family Relations*, 37 (1988): 426–431.

Taylor, Robert Joseph, Linda M. Chatters, and Vickie M. Mays. "Parents, Children, Siblings, In-Laws, and Non-Kin as Sources of Emergency Assistance to Black Americans." *Family Relations*, 37 (1988): 298–304.

Taylor, Robert Joseph, Linda M. Chatters, M . Belinda Tucker, and Edith Lewis. "Developments in Research on Black Families: A Decade Review." *Journal of Marriage and the Family*, 52 (1990): 993–1014.

Teachman, Jay D., Karen A. Polonko, and John Scanzoni. "Demography of the Family." In *Handbook of Marriage and the Family*, edited by M. B. Sussman and S. K. Steinmetz. New York: Plenum Press, 1987.

Teen Sex & Pregnancy. Alan Guttmacher Institute. June 3, 1997. Available: <www.206. 215.210.5/pubs/fb_ teensex1.html>.

Teichner, Gordon, and Rosanne Farnden-Lyster. "Recently Married Couples' Length of Relationship, Marital Communication, Relational Style, and Marital Satisfaction." *Psychological Reports*, 80 (1997): 490.

Theodorson, George A., and Achilles G. Theodorson. *A Modern Dictionary of Sociology*. New York: Barnes & Noble, 1969.

Thibaut, John W., and Harold H. Kelley. *The Social Psychology of Groups*. New York: Wiley, 1959.

Thibodeau, Patrick. "Deadbeat Tracking Systems Lag." *ComputerWorld*, February 6, 1998, pp. 41–42.

"Third World: Feast or Famine? Food Security in the New Millennium." *Race and Class*, 38 (1997): 63–71.

Thomas, Darwin L., and Jean Edmondson Wilcox. "The Rise of Family Theory: A Historical and Critical Analysis." In *Handbook of Marriage and the Family*, edited by Marvin B. Sussman and Suzanne K. Steinmetz. New York: Plenum Press, 1987.

Thomas, W. I., and Dorothy Swaine Thomas. *The Child in America: Behavior Problems and Programs*. New York: Knopf, 1928.

Thompson, Edward H., Jr. "The Maleness of Violence in Dating Relationships: An Appraisal of Stereotypes." *Sex Roles*, 24 (1991): 261–278.

Thompson, L., and A. J. Walker. "Gender in Families: Women and Men in Marriage, Work, and Parenthood." *Journal of Marriage and the Family*, 51 (1989): 845–871.

Thomson, Elizabeth, and Ugo Colella. "Cohabitation and Marital Stability: Quality or Commitment?" *Journal of Marriage and the Family*, 54 (1992): 259–267.

Thornton, Arland. "Cohabitation and Marriage in the 1980s." *Demography*, 25 (1988): 497–508.

Thornton, Arland. "Changing Attitudes Toward Family Issues in the United States." *Journal of Marriage and the Family*, 51 (1989): 873–893.

Thornton, Arland, and Deborah Freedman. "Changes in the Sex Role Attitudes of Women, 1962–1977: Evidence From a Panel Study." *American Sociological Review*, 44 (1979): 831–842.

Torrecilha, Ramon S., Lionel Cantu, and Quan Nguyen. "Puerto Ricans in the United States." In *The Minority Report: An Introduction to Racial, Ethnic, and Gender Relations* (3rd ed.), edited by Anthony Gary Dworkin and Rosalind J. Dworkin. Fort Worth, TX: Harcourt Brace, 1999.

Tower, C. C. *Understanding Child Abuse and Neglect* (2nd ed.). Boston: Allyn and Bacon, 1993.

Townsend, Aloen L., and Melissa M. Franks. "Quality of Relationship between Elderly Spouses: Influence on Spouse Caregivers' Subjective Effectiveness." *Family Relations*, 46 (1997): 33–39.

Townsend, John Marshall, and Lawrence Roberts. "Gender Differences in Mate Preference among Law Students: Divergence and Convergence Criteria." *Journal of Psychology*, 127 (1993): 507–528.

Transmission. Public Health Service. March 31, 1997. Available: <www.mediaconsult. com/frames/aids/shareware/hiv_aids/trans.html>.

Trantham, Patricia. "The Infertile Couple." *American Family Physician*, 54 (September 1, 1996): 1001–1010.

Treboux, Dominique A., and Busch-Rossnagel, Nancy. "Sexual Behavior, Sexual Attitudes, and Contraceptive Use, Age Differences in Adolescents." In *Encyclopedia of Adolescence* (Vol. 2), edited by R. M. Lerner, A. C. Petersen, and J. Brooks Gunn. New York: Garland, 1991.

Troost, Jan. "Family Structure and Relationships: The Dyadic Approach." *Journal of Comparative Family Studies*, 27 (1996): 395–408.

Trute, Barry. "Gender Differences in the Psychological Adjustments of Parents of Young, Developmentally Disabled Children." *Journal of Child Psychology and Psychiatry and Allied Disciplines*, 36 (1995): 36–42.

Tsui, Ming. "Changes in Chinese Urban Family Structure." *Journal of Marriage and the Family*, 51 (1989): 737–747.

Tudge, C. "Relative Danger." *Natural History*, 106 (1997): 28–31.

Turner, Jonathan H. *The Structure of Sociological Theory*. Homewood, IL: Dorsey Press, 1974.

United Nations. *Report on the World Social Situation 1997*. United Nations Publication Sales No. E.97.IV.1. New York: Author, 1997.

United Nations International Children's Emergency Fund (UNICEF). "The Progress of Nations 1996, Women: League Table of Maternal Death." Available: <www. unicef.org/pon96/leag1wom.html>.

"United Nations World Population Projections to 2150." *Population and Development Review*, 24 (1998): 183–189.

U.S. Bureau of the Census. *Historical Statistics of the United States, Colonial Times to 1970, Bicentennial Edition, Part 1*. Washington, DC: Government Printing Office, 1975.

U.S. Bureau of the Census. *Statistical Abstract of the United States: 1994* (114th ed.). Washington, DC: Government Printing Office, 1994.

U.S. Bureau of the Census. "Population Profile of the United States: 1995." *Current Population Reports, Special Studies Series*, P23–189. 1995. Available: <www. census.gov/population/pop–profile/p23–189.pdf>.

U.S. Bureau of the Census. *Statistical Abstract of the United States: 1996* (116th ed.). Washington, DC: Government Printing Office, 1996.

U.S. Bureau of the Census. *Statistical Abstract of the United States: 1998* (118th ed.). Washington, DC: Government Printing Office, 1998a.

U.S. Bureau of the Census. "Who's Minding Our Preschoolers? Fall 1994 (Update)." *Current Population Reports*, P70–62. January 14, 1998b. Available: <www.census. gov/population/socdemo/child/p70–62/tab02.txt>.

U.S. Bureau of the Census. "1990 Census of Population, Housing, Public Use Microdata Samples." June 10, 1998c. Available: <www.census.gov/population/socdemo/race/interractab2.txt>.

U.S. Bureau of the Census. "Table 1. Race of Wife by Race of Husband: 1960, 1970, 1980, 1991, and 1992." June 10, 1998d. Available: <www.census.gov/population/socdemo/race/interractab1.txt>.

U.S. Bureau of the Census. "Census Facts for Native American Month." October 12, 1998e. Available: <www. census.gov/Press–Release/fs97–11.html>.

U.S. Bureau of the Census. "Findings on Questions of Race and Hispanic Origin Tested in the 1996 National Content Survey." October 12, 1998f. Available: <www.census.gov/population/www/socdemo/96natcontentsurvey.html>.

U.S. Bureau of the Census. "Income 1997." December 15, 1998g. Available: <www.census.gov/hhes/income/income97/in97dis.html>.

U.S. Bureau of the Census. "Money Income in the United States: 1997 (with Separate Data on Valuation of Noncash Benefits)." *Current Population Reports*, P60–200. Washington, DC: Government Printing Office, 1998h. Available: <www.census.gov/hhes/income/income97/inc97hi.html>.

U.S. Bureau of the Census. "Marital Status and Living Arrangements: March 1998 (Update)." *Current Population Reports*, Series P20–514. January 1999. Available: <www.census.gov/population/socdemo/ms–la/tabms–1.txt>.

U.S. Department of Justice. "Women Usually Victimized by Offenders They Know." August 16, 1995. Available: <www.famvi.com/deptjust.htm>.

U.S. Department of Justice, Federal Bureau of Investigation [FBI]. *Crime in the United States, 1991.* Washington, DC: Government Printing Office, 1992.

Utech, M. R. *Violence, Abuse, and Neglect: The American Home.* Dix Hills, NY: General Hall, 1994.

Vander Mey, B. J. "Incest." In *Encyclopedia of Sociology* (Vol. 2, pp. 885–890), edited by Edgar F. Borgatta and Marie L. Borgatta. New York: Macmillan, 1992.

Vander Mey, B. J. "Establishing Gender Sensitive IPM: A Cowpea Programme in Ghana." In *Women and IPM: Issues, Practices, and Strategies,* edited by E. Van de Fliert and J. Proost. Amsterdam, The Netherlands: The Royal Tropical Institute; and London: Intermediate Technologies, 1999.

Vander Mey, B. J., Joyce Haleegoah, J. E. Hawdon, and A. Langyintuo. *Integrated Pest Management as Participatory, Sustainable Development: An Example from Ghana, West Africa.* Paper presented at the Annual Meetings of the Southern Sociological Society, Atlanta, GA, April 1998.

Vander Mey, B. J., and R. L. Neff. *Incest as Child Abuse: Research and Applications.* New York: Praeger, 1986.

Vanneman, Reene, and Lynn Weber Cannon. *The American Perception of Class.* Philadelphia: Temple University Press, 1987.

Vannoy, Dana. "Social Differentiation, Contemporary Marriages, and Human Development." *Journal of Family Issues,* 12 (1991): 251–267.

Vega, William A. "Hispanic Families in the 1980s: A Decade of Research." *Journal of Marriage and the Family,* 52 (1990): 1015–1024.

Vera, Herman, Donna H. Berardo, and Felix M. Berardo. "Age Heterogamy in Marriage." *Journal of Marriage and the Family,* 47 (1985): 553–565.

Vest, David. "Prime-Time Pilots: A Content Analysis of Changes in Gender Representation." *Journal of Broadcasting and Electronic Media,* 36 (1992): 25–43.

Vobejda, Barbara. "Research Group Confirms Decrease in Births to Teens." *Washington Post,* October 29, 1996, p. A3.

Voyandoff, Patricia. "Economic Distress and Family Relations: A Review of the Eighties." *Journal of Marriage and the Family,* 52 (1990): 1099–1115.

Voydanoff, Patricia, Brenda W. Donnelly, and Mark A. Fine. "Economic Distress, Social Integration and Family Satisfaction." *Journal of Family Issues,* 9 (1988): 545–564.

Wagner, Marsden, and Patricia A. St. Clair. "Are In-Vitro Fertilization and Embryo Transfer of Benefit to All?" *Lancet,* 2, no. 8670 (1989): 1027–1031.

Waite, Linda. "Does Marriage Matter?" *Demography,* 32 (1995): 483–507.

Waite, Linda, Francis Kobrin Goldscheider, and Christina Witsberger. "Nonfamily Living and the Erosion of Traditional Family Orientation among Young Adults." *American Sociological Review,* 51 (1986): 541–554.

Waldrop, Judith. "Living in Sin." *American Demographics,* 12 (April 1990): 12–13.

Walker, L. E. *The Battered Woman.* New York: Harper & Row, 1979.

Wallace, H. *Family Violence: Legal, Medical, and Social Perspectives.* Boston: Allyn and Bacon, 1996.

Wallace, Pamela M., and Ian H. Gotlib. "Marital Adjustment during the Transition to Parenthood: Stability and Predictors of Change." *Journal of Marriage and the Family,* 51 (1990): 21–29.

Wallerstein, Judith S. "Children of Divorce: The Psychological Tasks of the Child." *American Journal of Orthopsychiatry,* 53 (1983): 230–243.

Wallerstein, Judith S., and Sandra Blakeslee. *Second Chances, Men, Women and Children a Decade After Divorce.* New York: Ticknor & Fields, 1989.

Walters, Lynda H., Joe F. Pittman, Jr., and J. Elizabeth Norrell. "Development of a Quantitative Measure of a Family from Self-Reports of Family Members." *Journal of Family Issues,* 5 (1984): 497–514.

Ward, Russell A. "The Never-Married in Later Life." In *The Single Life: Unmarried Adults in Social Context,* edited by Peter J. Stein. New York: St. Martin's Press, 1981.

Ward, Sally K., Kathy Chapman, Ellen Cohn, Susan White, and Kirk Williams. "Acquaintance Rape and the College Social Scene." *Family Relations,* 40 (1991): 65–71.

Warner, W. Lloyd, J. O. Low, Paul S. Lunt, and Leo Snole. *Yankee City.* New Haven, CT: Yale University Press, 1963.

Warshaw, Robin. *I Never Called It Rape.* New York: Harper & Row, 1988.

Watson, John B., and Rosemary Rayner. "Conditioned Emotional Reactions." *Journal of Experimental Psychology,* 3 (1920): 1–14.

Webster, Pamela S., Terri L. Orbuch, and James S. House. "Effects of Childhood Family Background on Adult Marital Quality and Perceived Stability." *American Journal of Sociology,* 101 (1995): 404–432.

Weekly Compilation of Presidential Documents. "Proclamation 7145—National Adoption Month, 1998." Available: <www.web4/searchbank.com/infotrac/session/461/167/3484533w5/111!xrn_1>.

Weinberg, Daniel H. "Income and Poverty 1997." September 24, 1998. Available: <www.census.gov/hhes/income/income97/prs98asc.html>.

Weiner, Lynn Y. *From Working Girl to Working Mother: The Female Labor Force in the United States, 1820–1980.* Chapel Hill: University of North Carolina Press, 1985.

Weis, J. G. "Family Violence Research Methodology and Design." In *Family Violence,* edited by L. Ohlin and M. Tonry. Chicago: University of Chicago Press, 1989.

Weitzman, Lenore J. *The Divorce Revolution: The Unexpected Social and Economic Consequences for Women and Children in America.* New York: Free Press, 1985.

Weitzman, Lenore J. "The Economic Consequences of Divorce Are Still Unequal: Comment on Peterson." *American Sociological Review*, 61 (1996): 537–538.

Welter, Barbara. "The Cult of True Womanhood: 1820–1860." *American Quarterly*, 18 (1966): 151–174.

Westhoff, Charles F. "International Population Policy." *Society*, 32 (1995): 11–15.

White, James M. "Not the Sum of its Parts." *Journal of Family Issues*, 5 (1984): 515–518.

White, Lynn K. "Determinants of Divorce: A Review of Research in the Eighties." *Journal of Marriage and the Family*, 52 (1990): 904–912.

White, Lynn K., and Alan Booth. "Divorce over the Life Course: The Role of Marital Happiness." *Journal of Family Issues*, 12 (1991): 5–21.

Whitman, David. "Was It Good for Us?" *U.S. News and World Report*, 122, no. 19 (May 19, 1997): 56–64.

"Why People Choose to Date Outside Their Race." *Jet*, 81 (February 3, 1992): 12–14, 16.

Whyte, Martin King. *Dating, Mating, and Marriage*. New York: Aldine de Gruyter, 1990.

Wilhelm, Brenda. "Changes in Cohabitation across Cohorts: The Influence of Political Activism." *Social Forces*, 77 (1998): 289–314.

Wilkie, Jane Riblett, Myra Marx Feree, and Kathryn Strother Ratcliff. "Gender and Fairness: Marital Satisfaction in Two-Earner Couples." *Journal of Marriage and the Family*, 60 (1998): 577–594.

Wilkinson, Doris. "Ethnicity." In *Handbook of Marriage and the Family*, edited by Marvin B. Sussman and Suzanne K. Steinmetz. New York: Plenum Press, 1987.

Williams, Robert M, Jr. *American Society: A Sociological Interpretation*. New York: Knopf, 1952.

Williamson, John B., David A. Karp, John R. Dalphin, and Paul S. Gray. *The Research Craft: An Introduction to Social Science Research Methods* (2nd ed.). Boston: Little, Brown, 1982.

Willie, Charles Vert. *A New Look at Black Families* (4th ed.). Dix Hills, NY: General Hall, 1991.

Wilson, John. *Social Theory*. Englewood Cliffs, NJ: Prentice-Hall, 1983.

Wilson, M. N., A. J. Baglioni, and D. Downing. "Analyzing Factors Influencing Readmission to a Battered Women's Shelter." *Journal of Family Violence*, 4 (1989): 275–284.

Wilson, Stephan M., and Nilufer P. Medora. "Gender Comparisons of College Students' Attitudes toward Sexual Behavior." *Adolescence*, 25 (1990): 615–627.

Wilson, William Julius. *The Truly Disadvantaged: The Inner City, The Underclass, and Public Policy*. Chicago: University of Chicago Press, 1987.

Wilson, William Julius. *When Work Disappears: The World of the New Urban Poor*. New York: Vintage Books, 1996.

Wiltfang, Gregory, and Mark Scarbecz. "Social Class and Adolescents' Self-Esteem: Another Look." *Social Psychology Quarterly*, 53 (1990): 174–183.

Winch, Robert F. *The Modern Family* (rev. ed.). New York: Holt, Rinehart and Winston, 1963.

Winton, Chester A. *Frameworks for Studying Families*. Guilford, CT: Dushkin, 1995.

Wolf, Naomi. *The Beauty Myth: How Images of Beauty Are Used against Women*. New York: Anchor Books, 1991.

Wolfe, David B. "The Psychological Center of Gravity." *American Demographics*, 20 (1998): 16–19.

World Health Organization (WHO). "Maternal Mortality Figures Substantially Underestimated, New Study Says." Press release. February 5, 1996. Available: <www.who.int/inf-pr-1996/pr96-07.html>.

"World Population Data Sheet: Maternal Mortality." *WIN News*, 23 (Summer 1997): 21.

Wrobel, Gretchen Miller, Susan Ayers-Lopez, Harold D. Grotevant, Ruth G. McKay, and Meredith Friedrick. "Openness in Adoption and the Level of Child Participation." *Child Development*, 67 (1996): 2358–2374.

Wu, Zheng. "The Stability of Cohabitation Relationships: The Role of Children." *Journal of Marriage and the Family*, 58 (1995): 231–236.

Wurtele, S. K., and C. L. Miller-Perrin. *Preventing Child Sexual Abuse: Sharing the Responsibility*. Lincoln: University of Nebraska Press, 1992.

Yellowbird, Michael, and C. Matthew Snipp. "American Indian Families." In *Minority Families in the United States: A Multicultural Perspective*, edited by Ronald L. Taylor. Englewood Cliffs, NJ: Prentice-Hall, 1994.

Ylló, K. A. "Through a Feminist Lens: Gender, Power, and Violence." In *Current Controversies on Family Violence*, edited by R. J. Gelles and D. R. Loseke. Newbury Park, CA: Sage, 1993.

Yogev, Sara, and Jeanne Brett. "Perceptions of the Division of Housework and Child Care and Marital Satisfaction." *Journal of Marriage and the Family*, 47 (1985): 609–618.

Zambrana, Ruth E., and Claudia Dorrington. "Economic and Social Vulnerability of Latino Children and Families by Subgroup: Implications for Child Welfare." *Child Welfare*, 77 (1998): 5–27.

Zerbe Enns, C., C. L. McNeilly, J. M. Corkery, and M. S. Gilbert. "The Debate about Delayed Memories of Child Sexual Abuse: Feminist Perspective." *Counseling Psychologist*, 23 (1995): 181–279.

Zimbardo, Phillip. *Psychology and Life* (10th ed.). Glenview, IL: Scott, Foresman, 1979.

Name Index

Subject Index

Photo Credits

Part I: p. 1 (top right), Bill Strode/Woodfin Camp & Associates; p. 1 (bottom), John Jackson/The Image Works; p. 3, Black Box/Index Stock Imagery; p. 13, Corbis/Bettmann; p. 21, Lambert/Archive Photos; p. 37, Joel Gordon; p. 51, Elizabeth Crews/Stock, Boston; p. 61, Elizabeth Crews/The Image Works; p. 69, Tibor Fischl/Index Stock Imagery; p. 78, Hazel Hankin/Stock, Boston; p. 87, John Nordell/The Image Works; p. 89, Margaret Shostak/Anthro Photo; p. 94, Lionel Delevingne/Stock, Boston; p. 99, Adam Tanner/The Image Works.

Part II: p. 109 (top right), Joel Gordon; p. 109 (lower right), Spencer Grant/Index Stock Imagery; p. 109 (lower left), Anna Kaufman Moon/Stock, Boston; p. 111, Lawrence Migdale/Stock, Boston; p. 121, James Carroll/Stock, Boston; p. 133, Joel Gordon; p. 149, Eric Johnston/Associated Press, *Lodi News Sentinel;* p. 162, Joan Clifford/Index Stock Imagery; p. 170, Lionel Delevingne/Stock, Boston; p. 189, Arnold Zann/Black Star; p. 197, Corbis/Bettmann; p. 204, Bob Daemmrich/Stock, Boston.

Part III: p. 225 (top), S. Rubin/The Image Works; p. 225 (bottom), Mimi Forsyth/Monkmeyer; p. 227, Kaluzny/Thatcher/Tony Stone Images; p. 236, John Eastcott/Yva Momatiuk/The Image Works; p. 243, Richard Shock/Liaison Agency; p. 265, Susan Orisuo-Oristaglio/Liaison Agency; p. 274, David Young Wolff/Tony Stone Images; p. 281, Reuters/Mark Leong/Archive Photos; p. 297, Will Hart; p. 313, Sports File/Index Stock Imagery; p. 319, Dana Schuerholz/Impact Visuals; p. 341, Nancy Richmond/The Image Works; p. 349, Bill Mares/Monkmeyer; p. 356, David J. Sams/Stock, Boston; p. 373, Grant LeDuc/Monkmeyer; p. 379, I. T. Stock International/Index Stock Imagery; p. 404, Nubar Alexanian/Corbis; p. 423, Anna Kaufman Moon/Stock, Boston; p. 435, Will Hart; p. 446, M. Schwarz/The Image Works; p. 467, Bob Daemmrich/Stock, Boston; p. 476, Frank Siteman/Index Stock Imagery; p. 482, Myrleen Cate/Index Stock Imagery.